CHINA

BUSINESS

**World Trade Press
Country Business Guides**

CHINA Business
HONG KONG Business
JAPAN Business
KOREA Business
MEXICO Business
SINGAPORE Business
TAIWAN Business

CHINA
BUSINESS

The Portable Encyclopedia
For Doing Business With China

Christine A. Genzberger   Edward G. Hinkelman
David E. Horovitz   William T. LeGro
Jonathan W. Libbey   Charles Smithson Mills
James L. Nolan   Stacey S. Padrick
Karla C. Shippey, J.D.   Kelly X. Wang
Chansonette Buck Wedemeyer   Alexandra Woznick

Auerbach International • Arthur Andersen & Co.
Baker & McKenzie • China Business Review
CIGNA Property and Casualty • Ernst & Young
Far Eastern Economic Review • Foreign Trade
Reed Publishing (USA) Inc.

Series Editor: Edward G. Hinkelman

WORLD
TRADE
PRESS ®

Resources for International Trade

1505 Fifth Avenue
San Rafael, California 94901
USA

Published by World Trade Press
1505 Fifth Avenue
San Rafael, CA 94901
USA

Cover and book design: Brad Greene
Illustrations: Eli Africa
Color Maps: Gracie Artemis
B&W maps: David Baker
Desktop Publishing: Kelly R. Krill and Gail R. Weisman
Charts and Graphs: David Baker and Kelly R. Krill
Publication Review: Aanel Victoria

Library of Congress Cataloging-in-Publication Data
China business : the portable encyclopedia for doing business with
    China / Christine Genzberger . . . [et al.].
       p. cm. – (World Trade Press country business guides)
    Includes bibliographical references and index.
    ISBN 0-9631864-3-4 : $24.95
     1. China—Economic conditions—1976- 2. China—Economic
policy—1976- 3. Investments, Foreign—Government policy—China.
4. International business enterprises—China. I. Genzberger,
Christine. II. Series.
HC427.92.C4636 1994   93-45977
330.951–dc20   CIP

ACKNOWLEDGMENTS

Contributions of hundreds of trade and reference experts have made possible the extensive coverage of this book.

We are indebted to numerous international business consultants, reference librarians, travel advisors, consulate, embassy, and trade mission officers, bank officers, attorneys, global shippers and insurers, and multinational investment brokers who answered our incessant inquiries and volunteered facts, figures, and expert opinions.

A special note of gratitude is due to our friends at the U.S. Department of Commerce, to those at the Singapore Trade Development Board, and to Hand Lu, Deputy Representative of the U.S. Office, China Chamber of International Commerce, Washington D.C.

We relied heavily on the reference librarians and resources available at the Marin County Civic Center Library, Marin County Law Library, San Rafael Public Library, San Francisco Public Library, University of California at Berkeley libraries, and U.S. Department of Commerce Library in San Francisco.

Thank you to attorneys Robert T. Yahng and Anne M. Kelleher, with Baker & McKenzie, San Francisco, and John Lo and Frankie Leung, with Lewis, D'Amato, Brisbois & Bisgaard, San Francisco, who spent precious time in assisting us with the law section. We extend our sincere appreciation to Barry Tarnef, with CIGNA Property and Casualty Co., who graciously supplied information on world ports.

We also acknowledge the valuable contributions of Philip B. Auerbach of Auerbach International, San Francisco, for translations; Yuan Maozi, Professor of English, Yantai Education College, Yantai, China, for translation and research services; all the patient folks at Desktop Publishing of Larkspur, California; and Yu Hua, Leslie Endicott, and Susan August for reviewing, proofing, and correcting down to the smallest details.

Special thanks to Elizabeth Karolczak for establishing the World Trade Press Intern Program, and to the Monterey Institute of International Studies for its assistance.

To Jerry and Kathleen Fletcher, we express our deep appreciation for their immeasurable support during this project.

Very special thanks to Mela Hinkelman whose patience, understanding, generosity, and support made this project possible.

DISCLAIMER

We have diligently tried to ensure the accuracy of all of the information in this publication and to present as comprehensive a reference work as space would permit. In determining the contents, we were guided by many experts in the field, extensive hours of research, and our own experience. We did have to make choices in coverage, however, because the inclusion of everything one could ever want to know about international trade would be impossible. The fluidity and fast pace of today's business world makes the task of keeping data current and accurate an extremely difficult one. This publication is intended to give you the information that you need in order to discover the information that is most useful for your particular business. As you contact the resources within this book, you will no doubt learn of new and exciting business opportunities and of additional international trading requirements that have arisen even within the short time since we published this edition. If errors are found, we will strive to correct them in preparing future editions. The publishers take no responsibility for inaccurate or incomplete information that may have been submitted to them in the course of research for this publication. The facts published indicate the result of those inquiries and no warranty as to their accuracy is given.

Contents

Chapter 1	Introduction	1
Chapter 2	Economy	3
Chapter 3	Current Issues	21
Chapter 4	Opportunities	31
Chapter 5	Foreign Investment	43
Chapter 6	Foreign Trade	53
Chapter 7	Import Policy & Procedures	61
Chapter 8	Export Policy & Procedures	67
Chapter 9	Industry Reviews	71
Chapter 10	Trade Fairs	95
Chapter 11	Business Travel	137
Chapter 12	Business Culture	155
Chapter 13	Demographics	171
Chapter 14	Marketing	175
Chapter 15	Business Entities & Formation	207
Chapter 16	Labor	225
Chapter 17	Business Law	235
Chapter 18	Financial Institutions	285
Chapter 19	Currency & Foreign Exchange	309
Chapter 20	International Payments	315
Chapter 21	Corporate Taxation	329
Chapter 22	Personal Taxation	335
Chapter 23	Ports & Airports	339
Chapter 24	Business Dictionary	343
Chapter 25	Important Addresses	359
	Index	403

Introduction

With nearly 1.2 billion people, the People's Republic of China (PRC) is the world's largest country and the world's fastest-growing economy. A sprawling inward-looking nation three-quarters of whose population is still directly involved in agriculture, China is struggling to overcome its traditional isolation from the rest of the world, an isolation that deepened during the years following the success of its Communist revolution in 1949.

Since its opening to the outside world in 1978 China has begun building a modern, internationally oriented industrial economy based on imports of technology and export-oriented production. China's economy grew at a startling average rate of 22.7 percent per year between 1978 and 1992. The world's eleventh largest trading economy, China saw its trade grow at an annual rate of 16 percent between 1978 and 1992.

China is an intriguing market and one well worth investigating from a number of perspectives. For buyers China can provide a wide range of quality goods at highly competitive prices. It is a major producer of textiles, apparel, and footwear; foodstuffs; a wide range of machinery; metals and metal products; chemicals; raw materials; toys, games, and sporting goods; and handicrafts, among many other items. Its businesses can handle orders ranging from the smallest to the largest.

From the seller's standpoint China needs a wide range of agricultural and industrial raw materials, intermediate components, and specialty items to feed its rapidly expanding industries. Both the upgrading of its industry and its large public-sector development projects require materials, capital goods, and service inputs. And the still-small but rising demand from China's hundreds of millions of potential consumers offers the opportunity to place goods in the country's nascent consumer markets.

For manufacturers China has a pool of semi-skilled to highly skilled labor in the areas already noted as well as in many others. In addition to its low-cost and rapidly improving industrial plant,

China is building a variety of specialized production facilities. The PRC's growing infrastructure and capabilities offer a competitively priced base to satisfy a variety of outsourcing needs.

For investors China is in the process of opening up additional areas of its economy that had previously been off-limits to foreigners, including some areas of its growing domestic markets and service and financial sectors. It particularly encourages foreign participation in its high-technology industries.

China is so large and has so many needs that concentrating its activities to further meaningful development that can be sustained within the limits of its existing social and economic structure, even as that structure changes, is difficult. China is in the process of refocusing its economy on market-driven production, giving up its reliance on centrally dictated outputs. The virtually unending nature of its needs and the adaptability of its small- and medium-sized businesses, especially in the growing private sector, argue that China will successfully make the transition to a new economy. This process will be long and hard, offering a host of opportunities for foreign business people to provide the necessary expertise and inputs.

China's political face is changing, albeit gradually, and it has a growing core of forward-looking technocrats committed to economic reform. The overall pace and level of change is expected to accelerate over the near term as China moves along the learning curve, making it an even more complex and challenging—as well as compelling—place to do business.

CHINA Business was designed by business people experienced in international markets to give you an overview of how things actually work and what current conditions are in China. It will give you the head start you need as a buyer, seller, manufacturer, or investor to be able to evaluate and operate in Chinese markets. Further, it tells you where to go to get more specific information in greater depth.

The first chapter discusses the main elements of the country's **Economy**, including its development, present situation, and the forces determining its future prospects. **Current Issues** explains the top concerns affecting the country and its next stage of development. The **Opportunities** chapter presents 11 major areas of interest to importers and 10 additional hot prospects and 14 major areas for exporters plus 12 more hot opportunities. The chapter also clarifies the nature of the government procurement process that will drive China's development plans. **Foreign Investment** details policies, incentives, regulations, procedures, and restrictions, with particular reference to China's focus on energy, transportation, industrial development, and high technology.

Although still heavily dependent on agriculture, the Chinese economy has many thriving low- and medium-technology operations, a growing number of pockets of high-tech, and a nascent services sector. The **Foreign Trade**, **Import Policy & Procedures**, and **Export Policy & Procedures** chapters delineate the nature of China's trade: what and with whom it trades, trade policy, and the practical information, including nuts-and-bolts procedural requirements, necessary to trade with it. The **Industry Reviews** chapter outlines China's 11 most prominent industries and their competitive position from the standpoint of a business person interested in taking advantage of these industries' strengths or in exploiting their competitive weaknesses. **Trade Fairs** provides a comprehensive listing of trade fairs in China, complete with contact information, and spells out the best ways to maximize the benefits offered by these chances to see and be seen.

Business Travel offers practical information on how to travel to China, including travel requirements, resources, internal travel, local customs, and ambiance, as well as comparative information on accommodations and dining in Beijing, Guangzhou, and Shanghai, the main business markets in China. **Business Culture** provides a user-friendly primer on local business style, mind-set, negotiating practices, and numerous other tips designed to improve your effectiveness, avoid inadvertent gaffes, and generally smooth the way in doing business with the Chinese. **Demographics** presents the basic statistical data needed to assess the Chinese market, while **Marketing** outlines resources, approaches, and specific markets in the country, including five ways to build a good business relationship, seven rules for selling your product, a checklist for choosing a local distributor or agent, and five ways to help a local agent. Discussions of 14 major sectoral growth areas and a section on China's Special Economic Zones and major cities follow.

Business Entities & Formation discusses recognized business entities and registration procedures for setting up operations in China. **Labor** assembles information on the availability, capabilities, and costs of labor in China, as well as terms of employment and business-labor relations. **Business Law** interprets the structure of the Chinese legal system, giving a digest of substantive points of commercial law prepared from Martindale-Hubbell with additional material from the international law firm of Baker & McKenzie. **Financial Institutions** outlines the workings of the financial system, including banking and financial markets, and the availability of financing and services needed by foreign businesses. **Currency & Foreign Exchange** explains the workings of China's complex foreign exchange system. **International Payments** is an illustrated step-by-step guide to using documentary collections and letters of credit in trade with China. Ernst and Young's **Corporate Taxation** and **Personal Taxation** provide the information on tax rates, provisions, and status of foreign operations and individuals needed to evaluate a venture in the country.

Ports and Airports, prepared with the help of CIGNA Property and Casualty Company, gives current information on how to physically access the country. The **Business Dictionary**, a unique resource prepared especially for this volume in conjunction with Auerbach International, consists of over 425 entries focusing specifically on Chinese business and idiomatic usage to provide the business person with the basic means for conducting business in China. More than 850 **Important Addresses** include contact information for Chinese government agencies and international and foreign official representatives; local and international business associations; trade and industry associations; financial, professional, and service firms; transportation and shipping agencies; media outlets; and sources of additional information to enable businesspeople to locate the offices and the help they need to operate in China. Full-color, detailed, up-to-date **Maps** aid the business traveler in getting around the major business venues in China. The volume is cross-referenced and fully indexed to provide ease of access to the specific information needed by busy businesspeople.

CHINA Business gives you the information you need both to evaluate the prospect of doing business in China and to actually begin doing it. It is your invitation to this fascinating society and market. Welcome.

Economy

Although China has a history extending back 5,000 years, it remained essentially isolated from the rest of the world until 150 years ago, and it began to enter the modern economic world only in the past 15 years. With 9.575 million square km (3.696 square miles) of territory, China is the third largest country in the world, ranking after Russia and Canada and ahead of the United States. At an estimated 1.2 billion, China is the most populous nation in the world and home to over one-fifth of the world's people. Overall population density was more than 120 inhabitants per square km (313 per square mile) in 1991. However 90 percent of the population lives in 15 percent of China's total land area. (The outback autonomous regions of Tibet, Xinjiang, and Inner Mongolia account for half of China's territory but support less than 5 percent of its population.) Most people live in the fertile river valleys where agriculture first developed, or along China's 18,000 km (11,250 mile) coastline.

About 60 percent of China's total land area is mountainous, and two-thirds is arid. Some 14 percent is forested, 31 percent consists of grasslands, and 10 percent is cultivated; the remaining 45 percent represents deserts, urban areas, and open water. Only 26 percent of China's population lives in urban areas; the remaining 74 percent is rural. As recently as 1949, 89 percent of China's population was rural. More than 92 percent of the populace are ethnic Chinese, although China recognizes 56 minority nationalities. There are more than 91 million minority people, most of whom live in frontier areas.

The country is rich in natural resources. However, exploiting them and moving the resulting products to where they are needed within its vast territory pose problems that have kept China from capitalizing on its natural wealth. Traditionally agricultural and inward-looking, China only recently began to look outside itself to the rest of the world for help in exploiting its opportunities and profiting from them.

HISTORY OF THE ECONOMY

The Chinese date their beginnings to the legendary Xia dynasty, circa 2200 BC. The nation was unified for the first time during the Qin dynasty in 221 BC. The resulting *Middle Kingdom*—the center of the earth—was occupied by the relatively homogeneous Han Chinese ethnic group. China experienced periods during which it was unified and during which it fragmented into autonomous regional units, but from early on its culture was distinctly Chinese.

China developed in relative isolation from the rest of the world. It did carry on external trade over the silk road which linked it with the Middle East and Europe during the Tang dynasty (AD 618-907). China was also invaded by outsiders, such as the Mongols and the Manchus, who conquered the country. However, these conquerors were ultimately absorbed by the Chinese.

This pattern continued until the 1840s when the British forcibly opened up the country to foreign trade during the First Opium War (1839-1842). They and other Western nations and later Japan forced China to grant territorial and other concessions. The humiliated Chinese were overwhelmed by the modern military and industrial technology and the new commercial and social concepts that the foreign "barbarians" brought with them, and they spent the next 70 years trying to maintain their old isolationist ways against strong external pressures. The last Chinese dynasty, the bankrupt Q'ing, was overthrown in 1911.

Entering the Modern Era

Sun Yatsen, whose aim was to modernize China, established the Chinese Republic and the Kuomintang (KMT) Party in 1912. Sun was unable to unify the country, and for much of the first half of the 20th century, a fragmented China was ruled over by competing warlords. It was in this unsettled context that the Chinese Communist Party was founded in 1921. Eventually, the struggles that had wracked China boiled down to a fight between the Communists and the KMT. In 1934, the KMT routed the Communists, forcing them to flee to the hinterlands in an event referred to as the Long March.

The Japanese, who seized Manchuria in 1931, started the Sino-Japanese War in 1937, which led to a three-way fight in which the KMT, the Communists, and the Japanese all battled for control, without any of the parties being able to gain the upper hand, although the KMT and the Communists did join in an uneasy alliance against the Japanese.

After Japan's defeat in 1945, which was due to outside events rather than to the effectiveness of Chinese resistance, the Communists and the KMT returned to their open civil war. This ended in 1949 when two million KMT supporters fled to Taiwan from the mainland and established a government-in-exile there. In October 1949 Mao Zedong, the head of the People's Liberation Army and leader of the Chinese Communist Party, proclaimed the Communist People's Republic of China (PRC).

The Communist Experiment

The Chinese immediately set about countering the effects of centuries of economic mismanagement and 40 years of armed conflict. By 1952, despite having participated in the Korean War (1950-1953), they had brought industrial production back to pre-war levels, gotten inflation under control, and instituted land and political reform.

In 1953 the Communists inaugurated the first of their series of Five-Year Plans. Following the Soviet model of central planning, the Chinese regime focused on the development of basic heavy industry and the collectivization of agricultural production. By decade's end, the Chinese began to back off from

their early commitment to heavy industry and concentrate instead on their agricultural sector, the importance of which every subsequent Five-Year Plan has been forced to acknowledge.

The Chinese broke with the Soviets in 1960. Relations between the two nations, which share a long northern border were tense and hostile for almost 30 years. In 1966, Mao instituted the Cultural Revolution, a violent back-to-basics movement that set China's society and economy back until Mao's death brought it to a close in 1976. The old-guard radicals, referred to by opponents as the Gang of Four, were deposed by the more moderate faction following Mao's demise.

In 1971 China was recognized by the United Nations, and it began to open relationships with non-Communist countries, most importantly the United States. This was a sign that not only was China coming out of its old isolationist shell even before beginning to adjust ideologically and economically to new realities, but also that it was achieving legitimacy in the international community. Deng Xiaoping, a pragmatist, led the way for economic reform by promulgating the Four Modernizations—of agriculture, industry, science and technology, and national defense—in 1978. He initiated the Open Door policy in 1979, by which China began looking to the outside for help in developing its economy.

The Turnaround

In 1992 the Fourteenth National Congress of the People's Communist Party of China, the official ruling body, came down squarely on the side of a so-called *socialist market* economy, that is one in which the means of production are owned by the state but managed according to free market principles. How-

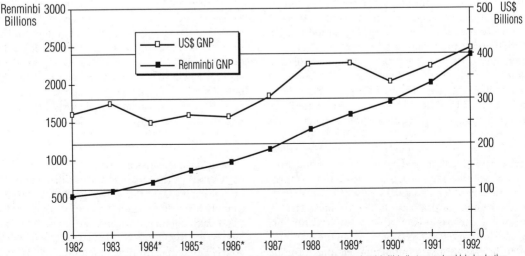

China's Gross National Product (GNP)

Note: Historical GNP data is from official sources. Data in Renminbi were converted to dollars using year end rates. Asterisks(*) indicate years in which devaluation of the Renminbi was at least 15 percent, accounting for some of the discrepancies between Renminbi and Dollar figures. Source: Beijing Review Press

ever, China has so far refused to allow political or social reforms that would loosen the authoritarian grip of party leadership.

Attempts to link social and political openness with economic openness took the form of massive popular protests in April 1989. After a period of vacillation, the party hierarchy imposed martial law, eventually calling in the army to crush the so-called democracy protesters in June 1989. The international outcry and withdrawal of support from China, coupled with a badly overheated economy, triggered a recession, and China spent most of the next three years trying to undo the damage and find a workable way of keeping economic development on track while avoiding confrontation over ideology.

SIZE OF THE ECONOMY

Despite having the world's largest population, China's undeveloped economy was only a tenth the size of Japan's as recently as 1992, and it was only twice as large as that of Taiwan, which is much smaller. China, whose gross national product (GNP) is only 28 percent larger than that of South Korea, barely beat out that country for the position of fourth largest exporter in Asia.

The National Basis

China's gross domestic product (GDP) was US$411.6 billion in 1992, up from US$372.1 billion in 1991, a 12.8 percent rise on an inflation adjusted basis. Some 50 percent of the growth came from the private sector, which in 1990 accounted for fewer than 5 percent of the enterprises in China.

China's GDP was only US$25 billion in 1978, the baseline year for the new economic reforms. China's economy has grown at an average inflation-adjusted rate of 8.9 percent annually. China's eighth Five-Year Plan for the years 1991 through 1995 called initially for an annual growth rate of 5 to 6 percent, but the figure has been corrected upward to 8 to 9 percent to bring it closer to reality. By mid-1993, the government was officially predicting an overall 13 percent growth rate for the year, which seemed low given the fact that the economy had expanded at an annualized rate of 13.9 percent during the first six months. By June the economy had overheated to such an extent that officials instituted austerity measures to cut off credit and brake the headlong growth. However, GDP should reach US$475 billion for all of 1993, more than 15 percent in unadjusted terms.

The Individual Basis

China's 1992 per capita income was US$353, up 19 percent in nominal terms from 1991. Mid-year estimates suggest that 1993 per capita income will equal US$387, a 10 percent rise. However, these figures are skewed by the use of China's official exchange rate which has been maintained at unrealistically high levels, meaning that the rise in actual purchasing power is less. China's per capita GDP places it ahead of the poorer African nations, on a par with India, and behind most Latin American nations. Government statistics show that in 1992 urban Chinese consumption of meat was up 60 percent from 1978, egg consumption was up 160 percent, and seafood consumption was up 17 percent. Per capita living space was up by 240 percent. In June 1993 78 percent of urban households had color television sets, 85 percent had washing machines, and 55 percent had refrigerators.

Average 1991 per capita income was US$255. In urban areas, it was US$319, up 8.8 percent, while in rural areas it rose by only 5.9 percent, to US$144. Urban incomes have grown nearly two-and-a-half times since 1987 in real terms, but rural incomes have remained essentially the same. The growing discrepancy between rural and urban incomes and standards of living is a growing concern for China, which not only is ideologically bound to equalize incomes but also is concerned about social unrest among the three-quarters of its population that grow the food.

CONTEXT OF THE ECONOMY

Although China has been one of the world's great cultures for centuries, its economy was a disaster under the corrupt Q'ing rulers for at least 100 years prior to the Communist takeover almost 45 years ago. Despite many setbacks and inefficiencies, China's government has at the very least improved the lot of the average inhabitant to the extent that starvation is no longer a real and frequent threat for large segments of the population. Although the PRC is generally classed as one of the world's most authoritarian regimes, it has provided internal order, external peace and sovereignty, and material improvements for the vast bulk of the population. In China's emerging socialist market economy, there is public ownership on virtually all levels, state guidance on the macro level, and, at least in theory, market allocation of resources on the micro level.

The State-Run Economy

China's state-focused economy is not really all that different from those in many other authoritarian Asian countries which have pursued planned economic models since the late 1940s. However, China, which started with the Soviet model, has carried it further than any of its neighbors. While other authoritarian economies have utilized state-run enterprises to a greater or lesser extent—for example, in both nominally capitalist Taiwan and Communist China, state-run large enterprises account for about one-third of GDP—China has forestalled the development of the privately owned firms which have provided the impetus for economic growth throughout Asia. And while state enterprises in other Asian nations may be fat and inefficient, those nations have a much larger, more dynamic private sector that can afford to support the public sector, at least during a period of transition. In China, the massive state sector overshadows the small private sector.

In 1992 the state sector accounted for 55 percent of China's industrial production, and it employed 106 million workers, 73 percent of all urban workers. There were about 75,000 large- and medium-sized state-sector firms in 1992. State enterprises absorbed US$7.8 billion in direct subsidies during the same year, when the national budget deficit was US$4.1 billion. In 1993 the government was expected to pour US$9 billion in loans into state-run enterprises in an attempt to buy labor peace. According to official estimates, one-third of China's state-run enterprises are losing money, and the real figure is probably substantially higher, perhaps closer to 40 percent, 50 percent in some regions and sectors. In northeastern Liaoning Province, where much plant dates from before World War II, the official figure was 43 percent in mid-1993.

The Chinese state sector is considered overstaffed by at least 10 to 30 percent with some enterprises supporting two to three times the number of workers that they actually need. The general inefficiency of the state sector is compounded by the need to find make-work jobs for excess workers. Quality control is poor, plants are outdated, maintenance is deferred indefinitely, and the goods produced are often uncompetitive or unmarketable. Some companies still hold excess inventories of unsold and unsalable goods, such as Mao jackets, dating back several years. Moreover, state enterprises provide expensive and comprehensive cradle-to-grave social services and guaranteed employment—the so-called iron rice bowl (that is, unbreakable) for their workers.

The government has been loath to enter the modern era by allowing these state enterprises to fail, partially for ideological reasons and partially because it fears the social unrest that would ensue if large numbers of workers lost their jobs. Workers have rioted when plants were closed. With unemployment and underemployment at record levels, the government is extremely reluctant to pull the plug on moribund state enterprises. Nevertheless, there were 346 declared bankruptcies, including 104 state-run enterprises, during the first 10 months of 1992, leaving 1.4 million urban workers unemployed. In the past these workers would have been transferred to other comparable work. Now they are being offered lesser service jobs or given a severance package and left on their own. China has experimented with privatization of state enterprises in a very limited way. These experiments have remained small-scale and tentative, and until China lifts restrictions on independent operations such experiments are expected to remain minor.

In 1993 the government also announced a campaign to streamline its bloated bureaucracy, calling for all official departments to cut staff by 25 percent. This is expected to result in the eventual loss of 2 million jobs and greater confusion, dislocation, and inefficiency.

An additional aspect of the negative impact of China's state-run enterprises is that in the absence of independent capital markets, the government makes funding allocations and it traditionally has channeled virtually all internal investment funds to the public sector. In China, crowding out has been literal: the austerity program imposed in June 1993 meant that firms had to close down because working capital was not available.

The Growing Private Sector

The bright spot in this tale of woe is the unprecedented success of China's private sector. The Chinese claim that, while 90 percent of the total economy was subject to direct state planning in 1980, only 12 percent of the total was directly planned by 1992. While this number overstates the situation, because it includes the shift from collectivized agriculture to a system under which farmers become nominal independent contractors to the state, it still indicates that economic rationalization has made great strides. In 1992 there were nearly 140,000 private enterprises operating in China. Whereas much of the state-run heavy industrial sector is in trouble, China's small- and medium-sized light industrial sector is, if not state-of-the-art, generally relatively efficient. Low labor costs and economies of scale keep the cost of its products down, although it has problems with supply, maintenance, and distribution.

Even more dynamic are the numerous small service-oriented businesses that are springing up in China. The motto of these entrepreneurs is *xia hai*—plunging into the sea—an indication of the new focus on risk taking in China today.

In fact, it seems that almost everybody is getting into the act. For example, the People's Liberation Army (PLA) has become active in developing private businesses. It is heavily involved in cosmetics, jewelry, and food manufacture, processing, and retailing. It also has a hand in the manufacture of refrigerators and cars. On the service front, it has invested heavily in bars and the luxury Palace Hotel in Beijing, which it runs with a Filipino joint venture partner. The PLA's business endeavors historically were directed to arms sales, but the breakup of the Soviet Union has meant that lower-priced, higher-quality arms are coming onto the market, forcing the PLA to focus elsewhere.

The Numbers Game

All this entrepreneurial activity is coming off a low initial base. China's economy is a numbers game: Even if growth is double-digit, it will still take China decades to transform its economy. The dynamic private sector is only the wagging tail on a very large and slow-moving dog. Some 74 percent of the population is still rural and predominately agricultural, agriculture still makes up the core of its economy, and state-run enterprises still dominate the nonagricultural sector. And there is still a large expertise gap. China has much to learn if it wants to become competitive in global markets.

One unavoidable aspect of the numbers is population. Annual population growth was 1.2 percent in 1992, an improvement over the 1.7 percent growth rate experienced as recently as 1987. But it still means that 14 million people were added to the population that year.

Despite the phenomenal climb in its industrial and economic indices, China remains an agricultural society, and its agriculture is suffering. Income for farmworkers is less than half what it is for urban workers, and production has stagnated, partly as a result of the fact that the government has kept a lid on the prices paid to producers for agricultural commodities since 1990. Agricultural products must be sold to government buyers at low official prices under a production contract. Producers are allowed to sell only their excess production above the elevated official contract quotas on the more lucrative free market.

Moreover, government banks have paid farmers with scrip off and on since 1989. These IOUs have been either unredeemable or heavily discounted. Meanwhile, cash costs of fertilizer and farm equipment have doubled since 1990, and consumer prices have jumped as well, so farmers are facing a cash flow problem that in some regions has led to riots. Although the government has said that it will stop issuing scrip, redeem existing scrip, and allocate US$6.6 billion for rural infrastructure projects and small business seed money, there have as yet been few tangible results. The government's short-term focus on salvaging state industry and placating urban workers has kept it from honoring past promises of rural development funds. Millions of peasants are leaving the countryside and crowding into the cities in hopes of finding better jobs.

The Individual Component

Although other authoritarian Asian governments have kept citizens on a relatively short leash when it comes to political activity, China has attempted to sever all links between economic liberalization on the one hand and political and social liberalization on the other. Observers doubt that the next generation of Chinese party leaders will be able to maintain control while advancing modernization, and ultimately modernization is expected to win out.

However, even with these pressures, the Chinese Communist Party, which runs virtually everything in China, has continued to grow. Applications for membership were up 20 percent in 1992, and the party accepted 2 million new members, bringing its total membership to 52 million. There is little concern now for ideology and orthodoxy. Rather, most people see the party as a way of getting on the inside track to opportunities not available to the general public.

Tensions within the body politic are increasing. Regionalism and centrifugal decentralization are speeding up, as are ethnic tensions among several minority groups. Although crime is still minor by Western standards, it is rising, along with violence and disorder, which are anathema to the government as well as to most Chinese. There is a certain Wild West flavor to China at present, as the Chinese try to come to terms with their new situation.

THE UNDERGROUND ECONOMY

In the past, state control of China's economy left little room for maneuvering outside of official channels. Traditionally, a worker effectively was tied to his *dan wei* or work unit for life. Ironically, the disruptions associated with the Cultural Revolution helped to open up new, nontraditional opportunities as displaced people had to find places for themselves outside the system. In recent years, increasing numbers of people have been finding independent options. Now, such careers are not only officially allowed but even praised, although the official standing of a great deal of this activity remains unclear and marginal.

Corruption

The concept of *guanxi* or connections is very strong in China. Although *guanxi* has traditionally been less crass and direct than the blatant culture of bribery that is common elsewhere in Asia, part of China's modernization includes increasingly prevalent and matter-of-fact demands for material considerations. *Guanxi* generally refers to favors given and favors owed as well as to relationships that may or may not involve direct material compensation, but without which activity will be blocked.

The Chinese have long resented privilege, and many consider much of the ruling party hierarchy to be new mandarins who have simply appropriated the perks which used to go to the pre-revolutionary

China
Inflation: 1982-1992

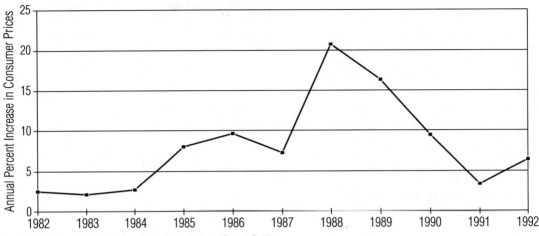

Note: 1993 inflation is running almost 20%. Sources: Beijing Review, Handbook of Economic Statistics

authorities. The result is that many Chinese presume corruption to be widespread. All too often, this presumption seems justified, especially in the current unsettled environment.

Corruption is especially prevalent in the more affluent South, notably in Guangdong Province, where there are special opportunities for making money. Fiscal malfeasance is apparently common, with officials using inside information to manipulate incipient Chinese stock exchanges and make insider profits on business deals. At the end of 1991 there were 117 economic development zones in China. By the end of 1992 there were 8,700, only 30 of which had been approved by the central authorities and only 2 percent of which were active. The rest had been set up by local bigwigs primarily as vehicles for real estate speculation. In August 1993 the central government closed 1,000 of these, arguing primarily that the projects were of dubious value and that they had misappropriated land that should have been allocated to agricultural production.

At least some of the rapidly growing numbers of rural refugees are the result of effective bankruptcies due to heavy and unofficial taxes and fees levied by local authorities.

Officials and company employees have also been involved in financial speculation using public or company funds, building up paper profits that can turn into real losses, which then get charged to the entities they represent. For example, the authorities created a government bond market in 1991, which collapsed in 1992 because of rampant speculation by inept traders playing with other people's money. Subsequent bond issues have been directly placed or sold abroad while authorities try to set up better controls on future trading. The lines between public and private are increasingly blurred as public firms masquerade as private and vice versa to take advantage of tax breaks and other incentives.

In a country where it is difficult to keep substantial assets private, there is a strong incentive to convert everything into cash or luxury goods that can be moved, used, concealed, or bartered. Hong Kong is a major destination for flight capital, and sources there estimate that as much as US$28 billion has flowed out of China. Even some public entities in China are moving their funds outside the country, buying Hong Kong real estate as a hedge against domestic risk. Conversely, some Chinese are beginning to bring in hard currency to make their fortunes funding speculative investments and lending at usurious rates in the cash-starved Chinese economy.

Although official corruption by government functionaries and businesspersons receives the most attention, the market for underground goods and services continues to grow, and smuggling (primarily of luxury goods and automobiles), drug trafficking, and prostitution are beginning to thrive. The police, who are overworked and underpaid, are readily drawn into the underground system, because they can supplement their income and avoid trouble by going along.

Not that there are no penalties for antisocial behavior. More than 21,000 cases of fraud, smuggling, and counterfeiting were concluded with convictions in the first half of 1993, and the government renewed its crackdown on speculation, graft, and corruption in June 1993. In August 1993 it announced the arrest of 100 financial officials at all levels in Sichuan Province. The government also charged a vice minister of China's State Science and Technology Commission with fraud. The official is accused of participating in

China
Consumer Price Index (CPI)

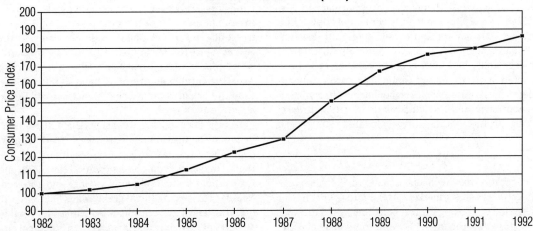

Note: 1993 nationwide inflation averaged 14.5%. Inflation was approximately 20% in the 35 largest metropolitan areas. Sources: Beijing Review, Handbook of Economic Statistics

a speculative bond scheme that defrauded 200,000 investors of US$175 million. By mid-1993 the number of graft cases involving sums greater than RMB 1 million had more than doubled from the comparable period during the previous year to nearly 100. Courts have handed down harsh sentences, including the death penalty, for graft, bribery, and embezzlement.

The Permeable Legal Barrier

One reason for China's apparent lawlessness is its approach to law. China has voluminous regulations, but enforcement and interpretation are arbitrary and depend on the point that authorities are trying to make at any given time. (Refer to "Business Law" chapter.) China has traditionally regulated its affairs by central decree and local official discretion, not by the statutes and precedents that characterize Western jurisprudence. Regulations are either vague or overly specific, and often contradictory. China still lacks solid business, commercial, and securities law, not to mention accounting standards, which in much of the rest of the world have the force of law. Civil law is rudimentary, and criminal law is draconian and arbitrary. Lawyers are also government employees rather than independent advocates, although the government has stated that it intends to reform the system and allow greater autonomy for attorneys and the judiciary.

Decentralization

One consequence of the new decentralization is that, local officials are ignoring central policy. Provincial governments were allowed to approve foreign investments of up to US$30 million as well as to set fees and taxes, and negotiate their fiscal contribution to the central government. For example, Guangdong Province got 80 percent of its budget from Beijing in 1980. In 1992 it received only 2 percent from the central government and contributed US$1 billion to central coffers. Beijing asked for more and Guangdong successfully resisted. The central government promulgated a reform measure in January 1994 that would set formal requirements for provincial contributions and limits on provincial autonomy. Provincial authorities are resisting these controls on their newfound freedom of operation and revenue streams.

While local officials have more room to respond to local conditions, the door has been opened to potential abuses. In early 1993 Sichuan officials were operating an unofficial stock exchange that drew daily crowds of 30,000, who paid a fee of about US$0.50 to trade unlisted shares in 50 local companies. Central authorities have so far authorized only two formal stock exchanges, in more highly developed and controlled Shenzhen and Shanghai, which list a total of only 98 shares, most of them local. The activity responds to local demands, but without the safeguards that the central go-slow approach has established in the national exchanges. Observers also suspect that the revenues derived from the operation are finding their way into private pockets rather than into official accounts.

According to a Chinese saying, the mountains are high and the emperor is far away. Much can be interpreted or even ignored at the local level. The conflicting Chinese desires for order and for freedom from control amounting to anarchy are feeding the confusion during this period of major change.

Intellectual Property

In 1992 China signed an agreement with the United States regarding intellectual property issues.

The US and many of China's other trading partners, are concerned about protection of software, recordings, agricultural chemicals, and pharmaceuticals. China agreed to upgrade its treatment of copyrights, patents, trademarks, and trade secrets to international standards. It also agreed to step up enforcement, which had been lax. The agreement led the United States to remove China from its special-concerns list, although enforcement seems to remain a low priority, and US-China relations remain touchy over this issue flaring up again in late 1993.

INFLATION

Inflation has been a headache for China since it began to open its markets in the late 1970s. In the absence of a strong central bank that could manage the growth of the money supply, there has been virtually no control over the Chinese economy. Periodic crackdowns, which take the form of austerity programs, have been used to choke off credit and bring growth back to manageable levels. The most recent was instituted between June and November 1993. However, as the private economy grows and the general economy becomes increasingly market oriented, the negative side effects of the crackdown technique are becoming more pronounced, most noticeably in the inability of firms to obtain necessary capital.

By the end of 1992 the Chinese government had lifted most price controls, and it was allowing the market to set prices for 80 percent of China's industrial and farm products. The result was a run-up in consumer prices. In August 1993 the government froze prices on subsidized goods and services for the remainder of the year, with shortages being noted almost immediately. By October 1993 the government was backing off from its austerity program because it had been only marginally successful in controlling inflation and was having dire effects in closing off funds needed to keep the economy going. Some observers worry that the premature end to the campaign would allow inflation to regain the upper hand.

Inflation averaged 20 percent in urban areas throughout the 1980s, falling, at least officially, to between 3 and 5 percent during the early 1990s. A recession slowed the rate of growth in 1990 and 1991, but official inflation figures reported a rise of 6.4 percent in 1992. In July 1993, inflation in urban areas was estimated at between 15 and 25 percent with a tendency toward the higher figure. At the end of 1993 the government announced that inflation for the year was 20 percent in the 35 largest urban areas, while nationwide inflation was 14.5 percent. Rural inflation was pegged at 13 percent.

Inflation has generally been assumed to be a less important factor in the rural areas than in the cities, because the cash economy is less prevalent in rural areas. However, the new market focus is drawing funds away from the countryside, and newly freed prices for consumer needs are rising as the prices paid for agricultural products stagnate, which places added pressure on the rural economy. Also, the rural standard of living is so much lower than the urban standard that any effect will be exaggerated.

As 1994 began there were signs that inflation was beginning to heat up again, rising to nearly 24 percent in urban areas. This was at least partially due to new taxes, including a value-added tax (VAT), and luxury tax on such items as alcohol and tobacco. Reports of rises in official grain prices led to hoarding, shortages, and overnight price rises for food of 40 percent in Beijing and 20 percent in Shanghai and Guangzhou. In January 1994 the alarmed government slapped price controls on 27 major commodities and threatening to crack down on hoarders and profiteers.

The Money Supply

Because there is no effective central authority to manage such things, statistics about the Chinese money supply are at best educated guesses. The currency in circulation is estimated to have grown by 46 percent during the first quarter of 1993 alone. In 1992 state banks lent US$61 billion, and other sources are estimated to have contributed an additional US$35 billion. Unofficial, off-the-books activity has also served to speed the growth of the money supply. Speculation and the imbalance between supply and demand have kept the money supply and inflation growing at alarming rates that are unlikely to slow in the near future.

LABOR

China has a labor force of about 650 million, about 55 percent of the population. Of this total, about 485 million are located in rural areas, while the remaining 165 million are located in urban areas. According to the 1990 census, 60 percent of the work force is agricultural, 22 percent works in industry, and the service sector employs the remaining 18 percent. Among urban workers roughly 75 million are industrial workers in state enterprises, while the remaining 75 million members of the officially acknowledged urban work force are civil servants, members of the military, or employed in recognized service industries. In 1992 China counted 8.4 million people—1.3 percent of the total work force—as self-employed or working in the private sector, helping to account for the discrepancy between the official urban total and the actual, more inclusive figure. During 1992 7.4 million new workers entered the work force, according to official statistics. The official unemployment figure was 2.3 percent in 1992, down slightly from previous years.

Unofficially, things look somewhat different. Some estimates argue that agriculture employs closer to 75 percent of the total. If the true figure is closer to the higher one, then the figures for unemployment or unofficial employment must be adjusted upward. The discrepancy of 95 million between the official and unofficial figures for population employed in agriculture can be at least partially accounted for by underemployment or seasonal employment in rural manufacturing and service sectors.

The unemployment rate ignores those outside the official system as well as the category "youth waiting for employment," who numbered 6 million in 1990. In that year, the state placed only half of the 12 million new job seekers, leaving the other 6 million without work—in labor limbo but not officially counted as unemployed.

Underemployment is a still greater problem. Even officials now acknowledge that rural underemployment is around 100 million and that it is likely to rise to 200 million by the end of the decade. At least 30 million and perhaps as many as 100 million people have migrated to towns and cities in search of work. Many urban workers hold several jobs. For example, in Beijing and Guangzhou, some 30 percent of all workers are estimated to hold an unofficial second job, while in Shanghai and Chongqing, the figure reaches 40 percent.

Although some of these moonlighters are trying to make ends meet, many, especially in the cities where more opportunities exist for such scams, have bribed the work unit executive committee to keep them on the payroll so they can receive benefits while they pursue more lucrative work in the emerging private sector. Most private work pays considerably better than state work, although it carries few of the traditional benefits, such as housing, which, in view of the shortages, may be difficult to acquire at any price without work unit affiliation.

Wage Rates

Workers in state enterprises are paid according to a flat set scale. The highest-grade industrial worker makes only three times more than the lowest-grade worker. The range is more liberal for technicians and bureaucrats, where the highest salary is as much as 15 times the lowest. Although deductions can leave workers with as little as 15 percent of their total compensation as disposable income, the deductions take care of virtually all their expenses, including subsidized housing, utilities, health care, pensions, and various other benefits. Because food and clothing are the only major expenses that must be paid out of pocket (and many enterprises provide some meals as well) and all adults usually work, actual disposable income can be remarkably high. However, the absence of a regular free market in many of commodities means that one may forfeit access to essential goods and services if one tries to make one's way outside the work unit, although this situation is changing.

Given these facts and the multiplicity of local conditions in China, wage figures are almost meaningless. Official figures for 1992 calculate the nationwide average weekly wage at US$4.90. In urban areas, the average weekly industrial wage was US$6.43. In rural areas, the average weekly agricultural wage was US$2.76.

Structure of the Chinese Economy - 1990

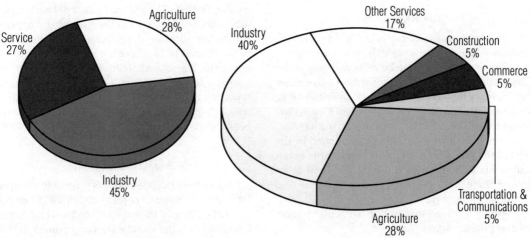

Note: Figures are rounded to the nearest percentage point. Source: Singapore Trade Connection

These figures are misleading, because they account for only 30 to 50 percent of actual total compensation, which usually includes benefits as well as subsidies and bonuses. Undoubtedly there are rural areas where the average wage is zero because these zones are effectively outside the cash economy. In contrast, in Shenzhen City in wide open Guangdong Province, the average weekly wage is estimated at US$48, almost ten times the national average and in several large urban areas average wages rise about US$1,000 on a yearly basis. Even at this level, Chinese labor costs far less than labor in such former low-wage countries as South Korea—US$295 per week—and Taiwan—US$245—not to mention Japan where the average weekly wage has soared to US$705.

Employment Reforms

Under industrial reforms instituted in 1985 workers may be paid relative to the profit of their enterprise as well as to their individual productivity. In principle, reform allows employers to dismiss employees, although dismissal is still uncommon and remains a touchy issue. The introduction of labor contracts brought the idea of limited-term employment. However, it remains to be seen whether employers will in fact be allowed to terminate workers at the end of their contracts.

These reforms are designed to replace the traditional employment system which guaranteed the worker a job and a salary no matter how poorly he or the company did. This situation left little room for incentives that could be used to encourage productivity, and it did not encourage people to take on responsibility.

In late 1992 the government announced an experimental plan to convent 100 medium- and large-sized state firms into limited liability companies, allowing them, among other things, to reduce personnel to profitable levels.

The Workweek

The standard workweek is currently 45 hours, down from the 48 hour workweek of just a few years ago. There are no vacation benefits and only seven paid holidays per year. It is impossible to give a useful figure for the average workweek given the range of situations that are encountered in China. The farmer works around the clock during the harvest, but may have little or nothing to do much of the rest of the year. The urban worker may or may not put in his 45 hours with the state and hold down two or three other part-time jobs on the side. And although the average worker may put in long hours, the work performed may not be particularly arduous or productive.

Unions

Although no individual worker is required to belong to a union, every firm must belong to the All China Federation of Trade Unions (ACFTU). This organization, which is controlled by the government, sees its role as one of increasing production not of representing the worker. Outside independent unions are outlawed, and although they do exist, they are still in their infancy, and they operate underground. Workers technically have the right to strike, although stoppages are not condoned. Slowdowns, sabotage, and physical confrontations are more common than actual strikes. During a seven month period in 1992, Liaoning Province reported 276 incidents in which workers attacked supervisors to show their displeasure over labor-management issues. Recently labor unrest has arisen among workers employed in some foreign enterprises with workers asserting that some employers have failed to follow official procedures and shortchanged them in the process.

SECTORS OF THE ECONOMY

China is still primarily an agricultural economy. In 1990 the agricultural sector employed between 60 and 70 percent of China's work force, but it produced only 28.4 percent of the nation's income. Industry contributed 44.3 percent of the national income and employed 22 percent of the work force, while the service sector generated 27.3 percent of income and employed 18 percent of workers. China's gross industrial and agricultural production reached US$789 billion in 1992, while domestic retail sales were at an all-time high of US$189 billion, and savings hit US$211.4 billion.

Despite the fact that several indicators reached all-time highs in 1992 and the balance of trade was favorable by US$4.4 billion, China saw its international reserves fall by 8 percent to US$41.4 billion in September 1993, down from US$45 billion at the beginning of 1993. The official budget deficit for 1992 was only US$4.1 billion, but the government appears to have been drawing down funds at an alarming rate in its scramble to shore up shaky areas of the economy. The unavailability of hard currency will continue to hamper China's development for some time, and the problem will only get worse as China tries to juggle its scarce resources to keep domestic peace while modernizing its economy.

AGRICULTURE

Agriculture has been China's economic mainstay for millennia. Some 40 percent of China's 280 million acres of cultivated land are irrigated, second only to India. China is the world's largest producer of rice, millet, tobacco, barley, and sweet potatoes, and it is either second or third in the production of wheat, soybeans, cotton, tea, raw silk, and oilseeds. Other significant crops include peanuts, sugar beets, sugarcane, and a variety of fruits and vegetables. Moreover, China ranks first in the world in the production of meat, seafood, and eggs. Grain crops account for roughly 80 percent of China's cultivated land. The country exports rice, but it must import wheat as well as other foodstuffs. Even when China produces enough agricultural products to meet its domestic needs, transport, storage, and other logistical problems have prevented it from attaining self-sufficiency.

In 1990 the agricultural sector contributed 28.4 percent of China's GNP. Production was up 6.4 percent in 1992 and more than double the figure recorded for 1978. Although production of many major products is up sharply since 1978, with rice up by 45 percent, cotton by 108 percent, oilseeds by 215 percent, and meat by 242 percent, much of the advance results from increased state funding and price supports, and it is somewhat overstated when viewed from the perspective of constant prices and real economic contribution. The small size of the average acreage worked and the average size of the family contract farm unit inhibits the use of efficient large-scale mechanized methods. And although China counted more than 19 million rural township and village enterprises employing more than 100 million workers and producing more than US$283.7 billion, US$20 billion of that in foreign exchange, in 1992, rural productivity and underemployment remain thorny problems for China's economy.

MANUFACTURING AND INDUSTRY

The manufacturing and industrial sector, which includes mining, utilities, and construction, accounted for 44.3 percent of China's GNP in 1990, while employing 22 percent of its work force. Gross industrial output was up by 26.7 percent in 1992, and since 1987 it has increased annually by an average of 13.2 percent. China's leaders look to manufacturing to work the miracles that it has achieved elsewhere in Asia. The country has 2.2 million industrial enterprises, of which 100,000 are private, covering the full range of industries. However, the majority of these enterprises are underdeveloped, outdated, and inefficient.

China is the world's largest producer of coal, cement, cotton yarns, cloth, silk, clothing, knitwear, bicycles, and washing machines. It is also a world leader in the production of steel (it ranks fourth), synthetic fibers, wool fabric, nonferrous metals, oil (fifth in the world, ahead of Mexico), and electric power (fourth in the world). But much of its production is of poor quality and more expensive than it should be because of poor plant, bad work habits, and transport problems.

Heavy Industry

Heavy industry provides the starkest example of China's industrial woes. China's steel output has grown by 152 percent since 1978. More important, the industry can produce 1,400 varieties of product to 20,000 specifications, up from 100 varieties and 400 specifications in the 1950s. However, only 60 percent of China's output currently meets international standards. China has cut back on its development of the steel industry because its products have not been competitive in the international market and domestic demand cannot justify the expense of a major upgrade.

In 1992 China exported 20 million tons of coal. However, coal, which supplies 75 percent of China's power, is polluting, often of low grade, and difficult to transport to the localities where it is needed. Moreover, artificially low official pricing has fore-

China's Foreign Trade

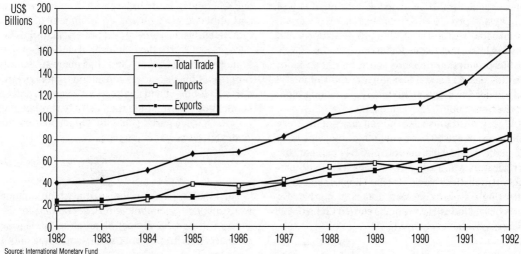

Source: International Monetary Fund

China's Leading Exports By Commodity - 1991

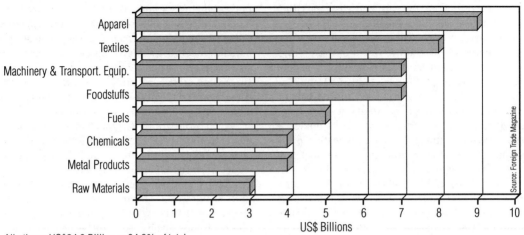

Source: Foreign Trade Magazine

US$ Billions

All others: US$24.9 Billion or 34.6% of total
Total 1991 Exports: US$71.9 Billion

stalled investment to upgrade mining operations. Overall, the coal industry lost US$2 billion in 1992. China's mining industry has become a major exporter of tungsten, tin, mercury, antimony, and such rare metals as vanadium, germanium, gallium, and polycrystalline silicon, but these products still play a minor economic role.

China is the world's fifth-largest shipbuilder, and it continues to push and expand its range of maritime products. Construction, which contributed 4.8 percent of GNP in 1990, is another significant industry. Like shipbuilding, it depends on cheap unskilled and semi-skilled labor. Although the primary market is domestic, China has bid on and won overseas construction projects worth US$25.5 billion since 1979. In 1993 China received the contract to upgrade Romania's international airport.

Medium and Light Industry

Medium and light industry presents a more encouraging picture. Here investment in plant is less critical, and private enterprise has made the greatest inroads. Textiles are China's main exports and they are important to the domestic economy as well. Textile production depends more on cheap labor than it does on capital investment, and China still has a major advantage in this area. For example, cloth production is up 67.7 percent since 1978.

Light industry also depends on many of the same conditions. Since 1978 production of bicycles is up 371 percent, television sets are up 5,347 percent, and refrigerators are up 16,864 percent. However, production in all these categories has slipped since 1991, reflecting a slow-to-develop domestic market. Exports of light industrial products earned China US$26 billion in foreign exchange in 1992.

High-Technology

Technology-oriented industries are burgeoning in China, with electronics accounting for 30 percent of industrial output. In contrast to other Asian countries, China has not attempted to set itself up as a high-technology center, and its developing high-tech sector is directed primarily toward domestic growth.

However, China has a surprising edge in several narrow areas of technology, such as electronics, computer components, biotechnology, superconductivity, and aerospace, where it offers satellite launch services based on simple, low-cost, reliable technology. China's high-tech exports increased by 40 percent in 1992 to US$3.9 billion.

The nation's scientists have had remarkable success in using gene-splicing techniques to produce a hepatitis B vaccine, high-yield rice strains, virus-resistant tomatoes and potatoes, and genetically engineered tobacco. Chinese research on superconductivity places it among the world's leaders in this field, and China also leads in lasers and optics research and applications with the development of crystal growth and laser surgery technology. Materials science, especially the development of carbon isotopes, is another area in which China has made substantial progress. China's leaders are encouraging research and development and applications research and are supporting focused high-tech activity through support for science parks. (Refer to "Opportunities" and "Industry Reviews" chapters.)

SERVICES

In 1990 China's service sector, which includes transport and communications, accounted for 27.3 percent of its GNP, almost as much as the agricultural sector (28.4 percent), while employing only 18

China's Leading Imports By Commodity - 1991

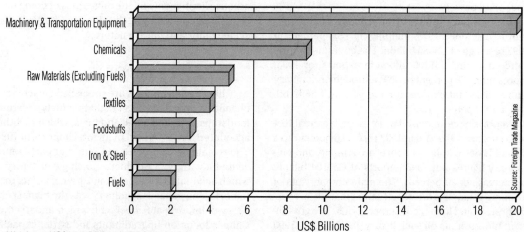

All others: US$17.8 Billion or 27.9% of total
Total 1991 Imports: US$63.8 Billion

percent of the work force. It is expected that this sector will grow in the future from its current relatively low and unsophisticated base. In contrast to other Asian economies, which are at least nominally making a bid to become financial and service sector centers, China continues to focus on its core needs of improving agriculture and upgrading industry.

In fact, the service sector figures only tangentially in the government's plans and priorities, and discussion of service development to date has been limited to the promotion of tourism, domestic distribution of consumer goods, and improvement of managerial skills. Even in such areas as communications and financial services, the emphasis is on infrastructure rather than on service delivery. And often services are either part of vertically integrated large enterprises or, more likely, afterthoughts and dumping grounds for expendable workers who are still on the work unit's books. No real jobs? We can always start a restaurant!

Financial Services

China's financial services sector is rudimentary. The absence of a freely convertible currency and the shortage of foreign exchange has done as much to hamper the development of a financial system as ideological barriers. Official banks are still state organs, and foreign banks can do little more than provide tourist-oriented consumer services and facilitate trade. There is effectively no legal private lending market, although semi-official swap markets exist where those with hard currency can make their best deal for domestic currency. These swap markets were beginning to be recognized as setting a shadow exchange rate for the unconvertible renminbi, providing businesses with liquidity and capital. The government has indicated that it intends

to make the renminbi convertible in 1994, eliminating its two-tier exchange system as part of its plan to liberalize currency activity. However, observers question the government's resolve to loosen the reins as far as adopting full convertiblity.

Such markets are fueled by China's estimated US$160-plus billion savings and especially by speculative hard currency brought in legally or otherwise from abroad. Individuals' hard currency deposits in the Bank of China rose by 28 percent to more than US$8 billion during the first seven months of 1993. Much of this money will be put out in speculative lending.

China opened two official stock exchanges in Shanghai and Shenzhen in 1990 and 1991. Uncontrolled, unofficial exchanges have sprung up elsewhere. The two official markets trade shares in local companies that had a combined market value of US$18.3 billion as of the end of 1992, about on a par with exchanges in Indonesia and the Philippines, but smaller than Turkey's emerging bourse. In comparison, Hong Kong's exchange had a market value of US$167 billion in mid-1993. (Refer to "Financial Institutions" chapter.)

TRADE

In 1992 China was eleventh among the world's trading nations, up from fifteenth place in 1991 and seventeenth place in 1982. In 1992 China reported total trade of US$165.6 billion, 24.4 percent above the US$133.1 billion reported in 1991. Total trade was US$129.5 billion during the first nine months of 1993. Preliminary figures for 1993 put total trade at US$196 billion, up 18.4 percent. In 1960 China's total trade was only US$1.1 billion, but it had grown to US$20.6 billion in 1978 for an average annual increase of 17.5

percent. Between 1978 and 1992 trade grew eight-fold, or 16 percent a year.

Exports have grown by an average of 16.7 percent a year since 1978, jumping by 18.2 percent in 1992 to a high of US$85 billion. The government predicted a record US$100 billion in exports for 1993, representing 20 percent of GNP, although preliminary figures list total exports for the year at US$92 billion, an 8.2 percent rise.

Imports have increased by an average annual 15.4 percent since 1978, and in 1992 rose 23.6 percent to a high of US$80.6 billion. Imports are surging, and preliminary figures put 1993 imports at US$104 billion, an increase of 29 percent. The main components of the jump in imports are construction materials, especially steel, and luxury consumer goods. The government placed limits on such luxury goods in July 1993 in an attempt to slow the growth of its trade deficit.

Balance of Trade

China's balance of trade was negative until 1990, when the dollar value of its exports passed the value of its imports, fueled largely by devaluation of the renminbi. China had a trade surplus of US$8.7 billion in 1990, 7.6 percent of total trade. This figure has dropped since, registering US$4.4 billion (2.7 percent of total trade) in 1992. Preliminary figures for 1993 show a whopping deficit of US$12 billion, 6 percent of total trade, and potentially enough to scare officials into import curbs.

EXPORTS

China's main exports are apparel and textiles, foodstuffs, machinery and transportation equipment, fuels, metal products, chemicals, and non-fuel raw materials, which together account for 65.4 percent of its total exports. The export economy is highly diversified, and China lists 35 different product categories as major exports. The largest product category, textiles and apparel, accounted for only 23.6 percent of its exports in 1991, while the next six largest categories accounted for an additional 41.8 percent. More than 60 percent of China's exports represent categories that individually contribute less than 2.5 percent to the total. China has shifted its export focus from raw materials and semi-processed items, which made up 53.5 percent of its exports in 1978 but only 20.1 percent of exports in 1991, to higher value-added finished products. Such products accounted for 79.9 percent of China's exports in 1991, up from less than half in 1978.

China has benefited from the surging costs in other Asian economies. Even in high-wage zones, such as Guangdong, its labor costs are one fifth of current wages in such countries as Taiwan and South Korea. This fact plus the government's policy of cur-

rency devaluation, has made China an export powerhouse limited only by the difficulties of doing business there created by such things as China's lack of skilled labor and infrastructure.

IMPORTS

China's main imports are specialized machinery, chemicals, raw materials (excluding fuels), textiles, foodstuffs, iron and steel, and fuels, which together accounted for 72 percent of its total imports in 1991. The remaining 28 percent of China's imports represented a variety of products, no single category of which accounted for more than 2 percent of its total imports. Specialized machinery was the highest category of imports at 9.4 percent, which underscores China's focus on upgrading its industrial capacity. The other leading categories reflect China's reliance on semi-processed materials to fuel its industry and on inputs that support its agriculture, such as fertilizers, and make up for its insufficiencies, such as grains, mostly wheat.

TRADING PARTNERS

China maintains trading relations with 221 countries, and currently it is trying to increase its trade with many smaller nations. China's three largest trading partners take two-thirds of its exports and four countries provide two-thirds of its imports. Hong Kong and Macao take 44.7 percent of China's exports and provide 27.4 percent of its imports. These numbers are deceptive, because very few of these products either originate in or remain in Hong Kong (Macao is unimportant), which serves as the main access point for business between China and the outside world.

At 14.3 percent, Japan has been the next largest consumer of Chinese exports, and it provides 15.7 percent of China's imports. In fact, Japan passed Hong Kong as China's main trading partner during the first nine months of 1993, providing 22 percent of China's imports and taking 16 percent of its exports. It remains to be seen whether this situation will prevail over time.

The United States takes 8.6 percent of China's exports and provides 12.5 percent of its imports. Although Taiwan prohibits direct trade between the two countries, it matches the United States in imports by providing 12.5 percent, and a significant percentage of China's exports to Hong Kong are destined ultimately for Taiwan. Germany and the former Soviet Union are other major trading partners while Singapore and South Korea each take around 3 percent of China's exports.

China's next six largest trading partners after Hong Kong take 34.6 percent of its exports, leaving

20.8 percent of exports to be distributed to the remainder of the world. China's top six trade partners account for all but 23.7 percent of its imports. China maintains foreign trading subsidiaries in 120 foreign countries.

FOREIGN PARTICIPATION IN THE ECONOMY

For centuries, China excluded foreigners. However, the Chinese have realized that they need outside inputs and expertise to upgrade their economy, and they are struggling with their traditional xenophobia to make their economy more open to outsiders. They also are realizing that such contacts will require the development of long-term equal relationships rather than the one-sided, hit-and-run deals they tried to negotiate in the 1970s and early 1980s.

The Role of Foreign Investment in the Economy

In 1992 direct foreign investment in China surpassed foreign capital received from all other sources combined, including loans, aid, and trade, for the first time. In that year, direct foreign investment topped US$11 billion, 150 percent above the level in 1991. Some 48,858 foreign invested enterprises received official approval, 3.7 times the number in 1991 and more than the cumulative number registered between 1979 and 1991. By the end of 1992 China had received a cumulative total of US$38.18 billion in direct foreign investment and approved 84,771 investment deals. Direct foreign investments, including joint ventures, cooperative enterprises and wholly foreign-owned firms, are known collectively as *sanzi qiye*. In 1992 such foreign invested firms accounted for 9 percent of production and total trade of US$43.75 billion—26.4 percent of China's total trade—and they produced and sold 20 percent of China's total exports.

During 1993 signed direct foreign investment contracts were expected to top US$100 billion in total value, with about US$20 billion of that actually being received. During the first nine months of the year, some 62,789 investments were approved, nearly one-third more than in all of 1992.

Sources of Foreign Investment

Some 80 percent of the cumulative direct foreign investment in China has come from overseas Chinese. In China, who you know is important, and ancestral connections go a long way toward gaining local cooperation. As China's economy develops, the importance of such connections should diminish. However, currently they are important, and it is the overseas Chinese who have driven the private economy.

As of the end of 1992 Hong Kong investors had brought in US$10 billion, starting 25,000 factories in Guangdong alone, while the Taiwanese made an estimated 6,000 investments worth a total of US$4 billion. Many of the Hong Kong investments may represent fronts for Taiwanese who cannot legally invest directly in China. Ethnic Chinese investors from Singapore, Malaysia, Indonesia, and Thailand also are becoming active in China. The Japanese are the largest group of non-Chinese Asian investors, with US$5.5 billion in cumulative investment in China, US$2.2 billion of it in 1992 alone. United States-based investors have projects totalling US$8 billion.

The Where of Investment

Following China's adoption of the Open Door policy in 1978, the country began slowly opening to foreigners. Its first concern was to isolate foreigners and the damage that they might do and to attract the attention of overseas Chinese who might be interested in investing in their ancestral home areas. In 1980 Special Economic Zones (SEZs) were established in Shenzhen, Zhuhai, and Shantou in Guangdong Province, close to Hong Kong, and in Xiamen and Hainan, also on the southeast coast. Foreign contamination was considered to be already well advanced in these areas.

In 1984 14 additional Coastal Cities were opened, mostly in the northeast. In 1985 the government opened the Pearl River Delta, the Yangtze River Delta, Fujian Province in the south, and Shandong and Liaoning Provinces in the northeast. In the early 1990s new economic zones with ambitious plans for new infrastructure were designated in Yangpu in Hainan Province and Pudong, across from Shanghai. Another 28 cities and eight regions along the Yangtze have been opened up since then, as have 13 Free Trade Areas and various additional quasi-official zones, for a nationwide total of 8,700 in 1992. The central government has closed some 1,000 of these, but most of the ones closed represented unofficial and dormant speculative local ventures rather than real investment opportunities.

The Special Economic Zones, the most prominent of which is Shenzhen, offer incentives to foreign business that include favorable tax rates, reduced tariffs, ease of entry and exit for personnel, and a relatively free hand in managerial practices. The goal has been to attract foreign investment, gain access to technology, monitor and serve an apprenticeship in world market activity, expand exports, increase foreign exchange earnings, and train personnel. Between 1980 and 1992 Shenzhen increased annual output by an average of 45.4 percent, annual industrial output by 61.6 percent, and annual export value by 63.7 percent. In 1992 total trade from the five Special Economic Zones was US$24.3 billion, which represented 14.7 percent of China's total trade.

In 1992 total trade in the 14 open Coastal Cities was worth US$29.2 billion, up 24.3 percent from 1991. The 13 designated Free Trade Areas are still in the process of getting up and running, but by the end of 1992, according to official sources, 1,000 firms with capital of US$2 billion, half of which represented foreign investment funds, had set up for business operations in these areas.

Restrictions on Investment

China is still protectionist, and it prohibits foreigners from setting up businesses that compete directly with local manufactures either in domestic or export markets. These include consumer appliances, such as television sets, refrigerators, washing machines, radios, cassette players, air conditioners, motorcycles, and light trucks. Import licenses are required for such items as sugar, tobacco, wool, timber and wood pulp, steel, and computers. The Ministry of Foreign Trade and Economic Cooperation (MOFTEC) publishes annual lists of items restricted for import. The list varies depending on current policy and needs.

Quotas are established for allowed investments, and the quotas for specific types of investments can run out before the end of the year. As part of its bid to join the General Agreement on Trade and Tariffs (GATT), China eliminated export subsidies in 1991. In 1992 the government abolished regulatory tariffs and reduced tariffs on a total of 3,596 import categories for an overall reduction in tariffs of 7.3 percent. The authorities have announced that a further reduction of 8.8 percent on 2,900 items will go into effect in 1994.

The Changing Climate

In late 1992 China eased rules that had barred foreign investors from producing for the domestic market and opened some aspects of communications, power generation, and port construction to foreign participation. However, China has announced a proposed change in its tax code that would hike personal taxes for foreign personnel and gradually phase out the tax edge that foreigners currently have over domestic operations by lowering the rate that domestic firms pay to equal that paid by foreign firms. A new value-added tax (VAT) will also affect foreigners. China has also announced that it plans to require that foreign personnel operating in China be more "friendly" to Chinese interests, which some observers see as an attempt to exert greater control over foreigners.

GOVERNMENT ECONOMIC DEVELOPMENT STRATEGY

Since the beginning of Communist rule, China's leaders have used a series of Five-Year Plans to direct the development of the economy. In the 1950s the plans focused on developing heavy industry, then the development of agriculture and light industry. As reality set in, priorities were realigned to place agriculture first, ahead of light and heavy industry. As China prepared to enter the global economy in the late 1970s, the emphasis shifted to internal consumption, while economic stabilization came to the fore in the early 1980s. After the recession of the late 1980s and early 1990s, China's government shifted to a more focused strategy designed to improve its infrastructure and modernize its economy.

China's blueprint since 1979 has called for reform in state functions, aimed at increasing the market component in economic management and planning, pricing, banking, wage setting, and social programs. Policymakers seem to have envisioned evolutionary change as the leading means of accomplishing these goals, whereby the Chinese people could slowly absorb knowledge of modern techniques while avoiding contamination by the foreigners who purveyed the necessary knowledge. As a practical matter, upgrading the Chinese economy would require China to gain substantial amounts of foreign exchange, which it could accomplish only by playing the foreigners' game. China's efforts have been handicapped by its lack of managerial experience and expertise, inefficient production, and poor quality control.

China advertised for investment as a way of gaining needed technology and foreign exchange. It began to promote tourism primarily to gain foreign exchange but also to familiarize the world community with China. The first efforts to bring the country forward into the 1990s foundered on an inadequate and crumbling infrastructure.

China currently is focused on actualizing its energy potential and transmitting its power resources to where they are needed. The country is building nuclear power plants and upgrading its hydropower and fossil fuel power-generating capability and its transmission grid.

Second on its list is a major upgrade of China's telecommunications and data processing capabilities. China needs computerized data switching capability and computerization in general, but it must first deal with more fundamental problems such as the fact that much of the populace lacks access to telephones. For example, China has one telephone for every 76.9 people. In contrast, Hong Kong has one for every 1.6 people.

Transportation remains a problem for a country the size of China. Resources and food cannot be utilized if they cannot be moved where they are needed.

Improved roads are a part of China's plan, but rail links and port improvements are the primary focus of current plans. And more efficient food production, processing, and distribution are always a concern of planners.

In contrast to other Asian countries, which have tried to make up for lost time all at once, China has largely remained at the low-tech end of the spectrum, recognizing that changing its massive economy will require a lengthy ground up overhaul, not a quick fix tune-up.

The specifics of the eighth Five-Year Plan (1991-1995) put the highest priority on the development of China's energy sector. Energy production is to grow by 3 percent annually. The second goal is to maintain growth. The measures set for this element require increasing GNP to resolve shortages of goods and generate the income needed to purchase them. The revised target growth rate is an annual 8 to 9 percent, one calculated to be strong enough to ensure an adequate rate of progress without causing the economy to overheat. Keeping inflation under control is an important subsidiary element of this goal. Preliminary figures for 1993 suggest that growth approached an overheated 13 percent while inflation hit 14.5 percent, neither of which is satisfactory, especially over the long-term.

The plan identifies four means for managing the economy: a consumer focus, a free market economy; managerial independence—including responsibility for profits and losses and power to hire and fire, and decentralized control. The plan calls for the development of 23 major projects and investment in US$200 billion in infrastructure by the year 2000. This means an annual US$70 to $80 billion in supporting imports. These reforms are to be completed by the year 2000.

It remains to be seen whether the government will have the will needed to allocate the resources necessary to achieve its long-term goals. In the past, it has used those scarce resources to shore up the status quo. Even more important, the government will have to keep its hands off if the reforms are to have a chance of succeeding. This has proved impossible for it to do in the past.

POLITICAL OUTLOOK FOR THE ECONOMY

China faces an increasingly unstable future. Its huge population continues to grow, as do the regional disparities in the effects of growth. The open, more accessible coastal areas are attracting investment, and incomes are disproportionately high, while the rural hinterlands are both missing out on the benefits of growth and suffering from its pernicious side effects. The old socialist models are acknowledged to be bank-

rupt, but no clear new model has been developed. Unrest is growing among those whom the old system can no longer support, especially among ethnic minorities on the fringes of the economy, and anarchy among adherents of the new profit ethic is rising.

Deng Xiaoping, the patriarch of the pragmatists, relied on his stature to push through economic reforms, but he no longer holds any significant post in the government and is fading as a major force. His likely successors seem to lack his vision and strength of command.

China has traditionally used force to maintain control. The country's Asian neighbors are uneasy over the continuing buildup of China's military forces. The military budget was up 12.5 percent in 1992, and US intelligence sources place actual expenditures at more than double the official figure. China maintains more than 3 million troops under arms, and it is in the process of upgrading its naval and air arms and becoming a medium-tech military power. The country has recently increased its pressure on neighbors over territorial and resource disputes. China is scheduled to regain sovereignty over Hong Kong in 1997 and over Macao in 1999 and has taken a more belligerent stance regarding the degree of autonomy it is ready to accord to these special districts. The question of Taiwan continues to be a thorny one, with both entities claiming to be the true China. Informal relations already exist between China and Taiwan, but it is likely that the official status quo will be maintained for the foreseeable future as the two economies grow closer together despite their continuing ideological and political differences.

China continues to bristle at outside criticisms of its human rights policies, which it, and much of Asia, considers to constitute interference in domestic affairs. Nevertheless, the authorities have wavered somewhat, although usually with specific pragmatic goals in mind. China released political prisoners as a gesture of goodwill as part of its bid to host the Olympics in the year 2000. When it lost its bid to Sydney, Australia, it instituted a renewed crackdown on dissidents. However, it has subsequently offered to allow International Red Cross inspection of some prisons. Basically, China remains ambivalent, trying to decide how much domestic freedom is too much while remaining somewhat unclear on the concept of human rights as understood in the West.

If China's leadership is to remain in charge of the country in the future, it will have to forego certain traditional prerogatives. One area in which observers suggest action is urgently needed is law. Throughout its history, China has depended on governing by executive fiat. As that means becomes increasingly unproductive, the only way for China's leaders to retain control may be to shift to a strong centrally directed and carefully administered code of laws, as many other modern nations have already done.

There are signs that the Chinese leadership is looking in this direction, albeit grudgingly, as the next step in the ongoing modernization of China. In 1992 China allowed foreign law firms to set up in the country. As of mid-1993 44 had done so, with license approval waiting for an additional 100 firms. Although foreign law firms are currently restricted to consulting for and representing foreign companies, their presence represents a foot in the door to begin the development of a legal code.

The rapidly increasing foreign business presence is considered important in educating the Chinese to contemporary world business practices and standards. Greater exposure is bound to have its effect on China's closed society, although overall change will be slow.

CHINA'S INTERNATIONAL ROLE

Since China began to open up in the 1970s, it has joined a variety of international organizations. It became a member of the United Nations in 1971, holds a permanent seat on the Security Council, and is a member of most major UN agencies. China also established diplomatic relations with major Western nations during the 1970s and 1980s. Currently it has diplomatic ties with 155 nations. China has applied for membership in the General Agreement on Tariffs and Trade (GATT), and it is active in other world forums. Its political role as a focus for nonaligned nations has faded somewhat, but it is taking a more active economic role in regional forums, such as Asia Pacific Economic Cooperation (APEC).

Current Issues

LEADERSHIP STRUGGLES WITHIN CHINA

Throughout its history China has been subject to political turmoil and a variety of power struggles. Even after the Communist victory in 1949, China's leaders have frequently been promoted, demoted, destroyed, rehabilitated, and generally at each others' throats. Deng Xiaoping, China's current effective leader, has been removed from power and rehabilitated no less than three times during his political career. China's tumultuous political history continues to repeat itself even today.

One Party, Two Factions

During the Tiananmen Square protests in 1989, fierce political infighting occurred behind the closed doors of the Politburo. While hard-liner Li Peng refused to talk at all with the students, reform-minded Zhao Ziyang went out to speak with them in the Square, yet Zhao finally had to acknowledge that he had come "too late." Two weeks later Zhao was gone and troops stormed the square. It was evident to the world that the hard-liners had won the ideological fight, reasserting China's traditional means of dealing with dissent

Li Peng, China's Moscow-trained staunchly conservative prime minister, wanted to see conservatives firmly in charge of not only China's politics but also of its economy. He fought moves toward free-market policy reforms and has continued to stand behind the idea of state owned-and-operated enterprises directed by central planning. While reformers spoke of development and economic growth for China, conservatives spoke of "spiritual pollution" and "bourgeois liberalization." In their view, no economic benefits were worth the dangers of ideological dilution and the undermining of state power, especially when they were the ones administering that power.

After the immediate crisis had blown over and foreign investors were again clamoring to resume contacts and investment in China, Deng Xiaoping once again surfaced to preach the gospel of economic reform. Although he had readily acquiesced to the crackdown on the protesters, fearing anarchy and the loss of state control more than the loss of the economic advances he had championed, Deng resumed the lead role in dismantling state controls over the economy once the situation cooled off. Deng's resolve led to increased internal bickering within the party between supporters of economic reform and the traditionally oriented hard-liners. By 1991 this conflict had outgrown the confines of closed party conclaves, and spilled over into the public pages of the *People's Daily,* China's national newspaper.

In early 1992 Deng made his now famous trip to Guangdong and the Special Economic Zones. Although he had relinquished his official position, Deng's endorsement of the economic reforms in the southeast demonstrated that he was still the one calling the shots. During his trip, Deng made reference to the "capitalist measures" that were needed to move China forward. A decade earlier, a leader, no matter how firmly entrenched, would have risked being purged for merely voicing such ideas, much less openly advocating them. After Deng bestowed his blessing upon the business culture in the southeast, internal reformers and foreign observers breathed a sigh of relief. China could expect to resume its journey on the road to economic reform.

At this point, it seems the reform-minded pragmatists are in control. Whereas the 1992 National People's Congress meeting saw Li Peng speak scathingly about reformers, in 1993 he and other conservatives appeared to be promenading alongside the reformers. No demurrers were heard after Deng's call for growth of 8 to 9 percent—growth that could only be achieved by continued adherence to reform policies—and Li Peng even talked about cutting the civil service, the bastion of the party faithful, by 25 percent. Perhaps, Li was appeased by the vote of the national congress confirming him as Prime Minister for five more years. By the 1993 party congress Li had been even more firmly co-opted, adding his voice to Deng's in stating that "slow growth is not socialism."

When the Big Guy Goes

Although Deng has officially stepped down, he will rule until he dies—continuing in Chinese dynastic tradition. Politically the leadership appears relatively stable at this time. However, many both inside China and abroad nervously await impending power struggles after the octogenarian and ailing Deng dies. Deng has expended great effort to put in place a team of like-minded technocrats who will ensure a smooth transition of power and proceed with his economic reforms while allowing the party to remain in full political control.

Despite having been the force behind economic reform, Deng has shown no interest in furthering political reform. Although substantial government authority was intentionally passed to the Provinces during the late 1980s, the government has recently been attempting to recentralize many of the functions that it had delegated. Due to heightened paranoia over the weakening of party control and to growing outside political influence, Deng has recently led efforts to once again merge leadership roles and vest the party's power in the hands of stronger central government leaders. A case in point is the decision ratified by the National People's Congress to designate Jiang Ze Min as President, General Secretary of the Chinese Communist Party, and Chairman of the Central Military Committee—three primary leadership roles. The National People's Congress also elected a younger and better educated group of leaders to form the new cabinet. The congress intended these measures to provide for stability and establish a mechanism for the transition to power after Deng dies.

Who's On First? Speculation inevitably turns to who will assume leadership after Deng. There is no obvious candidate. The list of names is short, and most potential candidates could be disqualified from assuming the mandate of heaven on a number of grounds. The younger technocrats lack the stature and seasoning to assume leadership in a society that values age and experience. Jiang Ze Min, despite his assumption of the unified title of president, general secretary, and commander in chief, is not generally considered to possess the ideas, skills, and charisma needed to become a forceful primary leader. Despite his position as prime minister, Li Peng's hard-line views are out of favor and at variance with China's apparent future direction, limiting his potential for a greater leadership role.

One name mentioned for future leadership is Zhu Rongji, currently Vice-Premier and head of the People's Bank of China (PBOC), the central bank. Zhu is a former mayor of Shanghai, a politician skilled at handling both insiders and foreigners, and a highly educated and experienced technocrat with impeccable progressive credentials. Zhu was called in to administer the austerity program in summer 1993, a job that many observers considered to be the kiss of death. His disappearance from the public eye during fall 1993 led to speculation that he had fallen from favor. However, he reemerged at the time of the 1993 National Party Congress to have his financial reforms certified by the congress. Despite his credentials and manifest skills, Zhu is not universally beloved. His progressive views have not endeared him to the old guard, and his attempts to slow economic growth to a more manageable level have led him to be rebuked by no less a personage than Deng himself. He is also considered to be somewhat abrasive, and his strong-armed tactics in recentralizing financial power—taking it away from the provincial and municipal authorities who had begun to savor their newfound fiscal independence—could leave him with an inadequate support base outside the narrow confines of the technocracy.

Chinese sources suggested in January 1994 that Zhu was set to resign from the PBOC as early as March. Such rumors have been circulating for some time, although it is still uncertain whether this will occur and what it will mean if it does.

But Can They Maintain Control After Deng Dies? Some observers argue that all Deng's efforts could go for naught should he die before his successors are firmly in control. Others point out that the Chinese people have tasted too much meat to be satisfied with cabbage and rice again. Many consider that it is only a matter of time before the liberalization, already under way in the economic sector, expands into the social and political sectors as well. With Western goods more accessible than ever before and living standards increasing at a faster pace than had previously been imaginable, many speculate that the Chinese people—and, increasingly, their leaders—will develop amnesia in matters of ideology. After wearing blue jeans and Western fashions, why risk having to return to Mao jackets over orthodoxy?

This is exactly Deng's strategy. It is not only "the capitalist running dogs" who are getting fat from the profits of reform, but also party members. In fact, the Communist Party has experienced a surge in applications for membership from people motivated not by ideology but by the hope of getting on the inside track to fame and, more importantly, fortune. With so many people reaping the benefits of economic reforms, Deng hopes to keep the lid on dissent—from the grumbling of increasingly out-of-favor hard-liners as well as dissidents calling for increased participation. As long as the economy is sailing before brisk capitalistic winds, Deng is hoping no one will rock the boat.

MARKET REFORMS IN CHINA

From Mao to Markets

In the late 1970s the doors to China, tightly closed since the triumph of the Communist revolution in 1949, began to creak open following the death of Mao Zedong. Slowly relations with the West were reestablished and economic ties developed and strengthened. With the political rehabilitation of Deng Xiaoping and the conviction among China's leaders of their need to modernize the country's flailing and isolated economy, China began a fast paced journey toward economic reform and development.

Between 1979 and 1989 China's national output grew at a real average annual rate of 9.5 percent, compared with growth rates of between 2 and 4 percent in the western world. In 1986 rampant inflation set in, particularly in the rapidly developing coastal regions. By 1988 inflation was running as high as 80 percent in some locations for months at a time, threatening to sabotage the market experiment.

A Detour on the Road to Reform

The government responded by imposing a national austerity program in 1988, but by then it was already too late. Escalating inflation, unemployment, crime, corruption, and social disintegration couldn't be stopped by the government's abrupt credit squeeze, which wreaked added hardship on the populace, triggering growing popular discontent. This unrest ebbed and flowed, reaching a flashpoint in May 1989 when thousands took to the streets. Although the western press characterized the countrywide wave of incidents as democracy protests,

they were, at least at the beginning, primarily concerned with economic reform and its attendant dislocations. After weeks of unrest and uncertainty, the government finally decided to view the protests as representing agitation for democracy and thus a threat to state order and sovereignty. On June 4, 1989, the government crushed the movement and punished sympathetic leaders as a lesson to all.

By fall 1989 the government was strictly enforcing its severe austerity program in an effort to further consolidate its hold on power, cutting off its economic nose to spite its political face. Political administration, which had been at least partially decentralized, was recentralized, reversing many of the tentative steps taken toward reform during the previous five years. Once again central planners were given control over production targets, supplies, and exports, while the new-found autonomy of rural collectives and new private enterprises contracted. As a result, millions of small enterprises went bankrupt.

These hardships did not sway the leadership whose primary concern lay in strengthening its own hold on power and reinforcing wounded ideological orthodoxy. Relations with foreign governments worsened, and any comments regarding the Tiananmen debacle were viewed as attempts by foreigners to undermine China's embattled authorities. In a show of disapproval, foreign governments, particularly the United States, postponed new investment and loans, froze existing aid projects, halted official contacts, and discouraged tourism.

China continued its austerity program in 1990, closing the tap by raising interest rates and imposing credit controls. The austerity program did suc-

'There is chaos everywhere, the stockmarket situation is excellent.'

ceed in curtailing inflation—it dropped from an official high of 20.7 percent in 1988 to 3.4 percent in 1991—yet it also drastically affected other areas of the economy, particularly industrial growth which fell sharply. The economy was salvaged only by a steep devaluation of the renminbi, making exports more competitive and encouraging international traders to venture back despite home government disapproval.

Life after Austerity

Faced with ailing—and in many instances terminal—state enterprises and a crippled rural economy, China was forced to make changes. In the early 1980's state enterprises had accounted for 80 percent of China's industrial output. By 1992 the figure had fallen to 55 percent and was declining fast. Moreover, as of 1991 total output of state industries grew only 8 percent while that of private enterprises grew by 24 percent. Seeing the manifest growth in the Special Economic Zones—the only successful sector of the economy—Deng Xiaoping recognized the need to embark once again on the road of reform. Deng, one of the more adamant repressors of the 1989 protests, again pushed for moves toward a "socialist" market oriented society. In the early part of 1991 he made his newsworthy tour of the booming southern coastal regions, touting them as the official models for China's future economic growth.

Although Deng received sharp attacks and accusations from the more conservative element in China's leadership, in time most of the conservatives grudgingly climbed on board the reform band wagon. Today, many in the Communist Party still pay lip-service to the "good old days" of central planning, but in actuality, they appear to be enjoying the benefits of capitalist ways. Although retaining much of the old rhetoric, the government has adopted a pragmatic approach that allows the state to be concerned with macroeconomic policy and big national projects, such as infrastructure development, while letting the market lead the economy on the micro level.

Not Without Problems

Inflation Although the reforms have been steaming ahead, the economy has not been immune to side-effects and growing pains. Of most recent concern is inflation, raising the question: How fast should the economy be allowed to grow? With inflation rates in 1993 at 20 percent in China's cities and with an unhealthy gap between official and free market exchange rates, many observers fear a financial meltdown of the overheated economy.

Lack of Replacement Mechanisms The primary problem has been not so much that the reforms themselves were flawed but that the government did not to establish the framework of new tools and in-

stitutions necessary to support reform. For instance, there is still no effective financial sector to take over the task of allocating funds; enterprises are strangling for lack of financial support at the same time that overall domestic credit is expanding at astronomical rates, putting pressure on the stability of China's economy. The technocratic progressives, led by central bank governor Zhu Rongji, fear that the overheated economy could implode and have argued that banks need to exercise more caution in extending credit, particularly to state firms notorious for running losses.

Wayward Local Officials Although authorities in Beijing might have a good idea of what needs to be done (or so they think), their power over the economy is slipping through their fingers as the provincial and municipal governments develop greater autonomy. Banks and local offices of state agencies are much more likely to follow the lead of local officials who have co-opted them in many cases. In fact, in 1992 banks extended twice as many loans as Beijing had authorized, largely at the behest of local officials.

The central government originally had instituted a degree of decentralization of economic decision making, to cut red tape and enable local officials to be more responsive in the cause of helping the economy. However, many local officials have been using their newfound power to their own advantage and in the service of parochial interests. Some have used scarce funds to subsidize inefficient operations to protect local jobs. Moreover, the local authorities have not always exercised good judgment in the projects they have espoused, nor have they implemented national monetary and fiscal policies.

Problems with Infrastructure As industry develops and moves inland, the inadequacy of China's infrastructure becomes ever more apparent. Particularly needed is infrastructure connecting financial and management centers on the coast, such as Shanghai and Guangzhou, with the burgeoning production areas in the interior. Yet, as construction of infrastructure and housing has surged throughout China, prices of labor and of certain materials have skyrocketed—in some places rising at double-digit rates on a monthly basis—short-circuiting growth.

Unemployment With the push for more competitive industries, workers who once could fritter their day away reading magazines and going out for a smoke are finding their jobs in jeopardy. China has one of the longest nominal work weeks in the world, but worker productivity is embarrassingly low. Most enterprises simply have too many bodies on the payroll. Unemployment most likely will be the most painful side effect of economic change during the 1990s. The "iron rice bowl" which guaranteed employment for life is melting in the furnace of economic reform.

Future of Reform

The Pessimists Outside of China, pessimists point to the smoke coming from China's overheating economic engine, the pending death of Deng Xiaoping, and the inevitable party power struggles expected to ensue following that event as warning signs of the major blowout about to occur in China. This fear is even stronger in the minds of   China's leaders who remember 1989 all too well when rampant inflation and political corruption contributed greatly to the unrest and protests in Tiananmen Square that very nearly got out of hand.

At least during the protests in 1989 the government was able to convince the peasants in the countryside (who make up three-quarters of the population) that the stir was largely over a few hooligans in Tiananmen Square and had nothing to do with them. That trick may not work twice. During 1993 peasant workers from rural areas rioted because of high prices and corruption among local officials and party members. The peasantry has been hardest hit by inflation because their paltry rural incomes have not kept pace with rising urban incomes and rising prices. Peasants are becoming increasingly discontent with escalating prices for fertilizer, equipment, and consumer goods which are unmatched by the prices they receive for their output. Millions have gravitated to urban areas seeking work and have ended up either underemployed or worse, unemployed and crowded together in train stations, in the streets, or on the outskirts of towns. The government conservatively predicts that by the year 2000 more than 200 million peasants will be underemployed. This, pessimists point out, is a sure sign of coming crises.

The Optimists Although they certainly acknowledge that problems exist, the optimists prefer to focus on China's incomparable potential as a market, its stunning growth—China's gross national product (GNP) grew 12.8 percent in real terms in 1992 and was expected to top 13 percent in 1993—and its productive capacity in terms of labor and natural resources. They are delighted to welcome China into global economic partnership. China, already the world's eleventh largest trader, is expected to grow to become the top trader and manufacturer not only in Asia but in the world.

Although acknowledging valid concerns about the side effects of moving too quickly toward a market economy, the optimists point to the undeniable successes of the private sector in contrast to the record of the moribund state sector. In 1991 while the private sector racked up record profits, state sector losses reached an estimated US$5.7 billion on top of US$22 billion in unpaid taxes and uncounted arrears in interest and principal repayments on state loans.

Moreover, the optimists argue, foreign investors are not only benefiting from the new economic boom, they are also benefiting from decentralization. Rather than being limited by the dictates of Beijing on setting up a joint venture—such as where and with which Chinese firm—foreign firms now have the opportunity to cut their best deal in a number of different locations.

Walking the Tightrope

In 1993 the National People's Congress *officially* approved Deng's free market policies. The struggle has been won (at least for the time being) and a "socialist market economy" will replace central planning. However, Deng's plan calls for China to scrap central planning while keeping central party politics. Chinese authorities argue that it is necessary to build a strong new market economy separate from any consideration of social or political liberalization. They point to the crisis in Russia as evidence of what happens when both economic and political reforms are attempted simultaneously.

Many wonder if this will work. China's leaders continue to walk the tightrope between the discredited but familiar command economy and the seductive free market one, hovering precariously above the canyon of rampant inflation and social upheaval.

MORE FREEDOMS, MORE PRODUCTS, MORE PROBLEMS

Millions of Chinese are cashing in on China's rapid economic development, in many cases moving from rags to riches, or at least from utilitarian cotton to glad rags. Economic development has led to greater access not only to products, but also to different ideas, values, and lifestyles. It has also led to increased problems for the socialist government. An estimated 100 million people have been displaced to date, mostly in rural areas. Many of these have descended on China's already overburdened cities, resulting in great disruption.

The New Materialist Classes

Although most citizens in China are reaping the benefits of moves toward modernization, the younger generation (ages fourteen to twenty-eight) have clearly been influenced the most by economic openness. Having had all thoughts of political reform quashed in Tiananmen Square, these young Chinese have lost faith in the government and are disillusioned with anything of a political nature. They are now focusing exclusively on the economic sphere and its rewards. With more goods available and increasing per capita income, spending on nonessentials such as luxury items and entertainment has risen markedly. The younger Chinese in particular, letting go of community and filial piety, are latching onto individualism and Western trends, not only in

...FOUR MORE YEARS!

...HE MEANS ONLY FOUR MORE YEARS!

HONGKONG '97

fashion, cosmetics and compact disks, but in values concerning marriage, attitudes toward parents, and social relationships in general. Many of those who sang songs of praise to Chairman Mao and the party as young children, are now singing either rock ballads or outright paeans to materialism.

Many of the older generation, worn by years of living in China's harsh and unpredictable political environment, have also taken the opportunity provided by the reforms to go into private business. In doing so, many are seeking to detach themselves from the web of repressive political controls in China. The older generation, although perhaps more cautious in its buying patterns, is finally releasing its pent-up consumer demand. These older Chinese can now wash their clothes in a washing machine using any of a number of brands of sweet smelling detergent, grab a cold soft drink from the refrigerator, and pick up a cellular telephone to chat with their children. Even more important to the Chinese, they can demonstrate their prosperity by showing to neighbors the foreign goods and brand name products they can afford to buy.

One anomaly of the new China is the role played by the participants of the Cultural Revolution in building its economy. At the end of the Cultural Revolution in the late 1970s the majority of Chinese were able to fade back into their former roles. However, there was a significant group of both victims and Red Guards who were unable to do so even after more moderate political order was restored—the victims due to lost time and opportunity and certain Red Guards due to their extremeness no longer in line with the ruling order. These two disparate, marginalized groups produced many of the earliest entrepreneurs as China began its economic reorganization, setting the parameters of its initial free market operations.

Does Money Grow on Trees?

With wages notoriously low when compared with average earnings elsewhere in the world, how can the Chinese have so much money to spend on costly luxury items and trendy fashions? The nationwide average income in China was officially $353 a year in 1992, somewhat higher in the cities and much lower in the countryside. However, by adding income from moonlighting jobs in private business and blackmarket activities, more accurate estimates place real incomes at as much as $1,000 to $2,500. But what can that buy? A lot considering that the work unit subsidizes housing, education, health care, transportation, retirement, and some meals. Although nominal wages are low, all adults in the household usually work and are paid bonuses and allowances. Take home pay represents most of gross pay and is disposable income. With state subsidies paying for the necessities of life, the Chinese worker goes home with a nearly full pocket to pay for nonessential items.... Hello Reebok, Avon, and Coca Cola.

The bad news is that the oft extolled 1.2 billion person Chinese domestic market for consumer goods is still largely a mirage, even with the higher than anticipated incomes noted. In the first place, the government does its best to keep consumer goods to a minimum, especially foreign consumer goods. In the second place, three-quarters of the population is still rural, living in areas where there is minimal participation in the cash economy and where China's minimal transportation and distribution system has yet to allow the penetration of substantial consumer goods of any stripe. And even in the more consumer oriented and relatively affluent cities, the bulk of Chinese consumption of foreign consumer goods is still on the basis of novelty: The worker who tries a McDonald's hamburger once, has a Coca-Cola every couple of weeks, or buys a pair of foreign-made stylish pants (with pleats and a logo) that last a long, long time.

At the other end of the spectrum is the large scale conspicuous consumption of the few successful elites, the *caiye* or cash gods, as the Chinese call their new millionaires, and the *yapishi* or up and coming yuppies. Such big spenders scorn geegaws such as the Mao chopsticks, tote bags, and good luck charms peddled at the tomb of *ta lao renjia*, or "the old guy," as Mao is known. They are after bigger items: foreign cars, race horses, and status symbols such as exotic purebred dogs (illicitly imported French poodles can sell for more than US$25,000). In 1993 there were more than 1 million private cars registered in China; in 1978 there were none.

The Good, The Bad, and The Ugly

As the officials open the doors to China, they have been unable to simultaneously welcome the positive while filtering out the negative influences that are flowing across its borders. As private enterprises, dynamic and helpful to China's economic growth, pop up everywhere, other socially destabilizing forms of business are rearing their ugly heads: prostitution, drug-trafficking, and smuggling. Corruption and crime are also on the rise. In 1993 total crime grew at an official 6.2 percent rate. Although the overall rate has held more or less steady since 1982, serious crime is rising at a 23 percent annual rate. Authorities more than doubled the arrest of gang members and organized criminals, detaining a reported 780,000 in 1993. And China's younger generation of materialists was found to be responsible for over 70 percent of all robberies in 1992. With so many enticing Western goods from which to choose, many juveniles turn to crime to obtain them.

Such *liumang* or rip-and-run petty street thugs, even the ones who hold up trains, are mere nuisances compared to the criminal rings that steal luxury cars in Hong Kong and float them to Guangzhou. Illicit imports of stolen foreign cars are officially estimated to have reached 100,000 in 1993, while 90,000 bicycles were reported stolen in Shanghai alone.

Another increasingly popular status symbol is a *bangjia* or helper mate, apparently often kept in China by ethnic Chinese business people from Hong Kong and Taiwan as well as by local magnates. Such mistresses are closely followed by—and often precede, in bragging order—female bodyguards, some of whom are trained by the Public Security Bureau (the secret police) as a for-profit sideline venture.

A more open society and the flight of rural refugees to the cities has also led to an explosion of prostitution. Known as *yeji* or wild chickens, prostitutes haunt many public places. Some luxury Beijing hotels have installed cameras in their elevators in an attempt to prevent assignations in these venues. In summer 1992 a reported 250,000 people involved in prostitution were arrested.

Hong Kong authorities reported that acts of corruption increased by 44 percent in 1993, the vast majority attributed to Hong Kong based individuals who bribe Chinese officials to further their own business interests. A survey found that 70 percent of Hong Kong companies admitted to routinely giving "gifts" to Chinese officials.

The chagrined Chinese government has finally acknowledged that not only do such activities take place but that they could not take place without official collusion. China's *Guangming Daily* reported in early 1994 that security agencies found that most criminals are linked to 10 or more Chinese officials who they rely on for protection. And authorities recently uncovered theft or malfeasance involving some US$95 million by a reported 300,000 individual bureaucrats and officials in Anhui Province, one of the most backward, most isolated, and least wealthy Provinces in China. It is common knowledge that in many locations officials regularly solicit bribes before they will provide services.

The government is also concerned that the surge of materialism has resulted in a corresponding demise of appropriate political consciousness among its people. As the Chinese have begun to worship at the shrine of the free market, political consciousness has gone out the window. Thoroughly modern Chinese have no time to worry about ideology. These new materialists are far too busy trying to make money. This news, as troubling as it is for the government, holds promise for the foreign investor salivating over the proverbial one billion-plus Chinese market.

MOST FAVORED NATION TRADING STATUS AND THE PEOPLE'S REPUBLIC OF CHINA

The Issue

Most Favored Nation (MFN) status refers to a category of nondiscriminatory trading relationship between the United States and the majority of nations in the world. A nation granted MFN status can trade with the United States with few restrictions, enjoying relatively low duties on its products. As the title implies, this status indicates a favorable trading relationship, although MFN status has really become the norm and any lesser status is viewed as being punitive in nature.

Until five years ago, the annual renewal of China's MFN status occurred without much controversy or even much notice. All that changed with Beijing's crackdown on domestic protesters in June, 1989. The United States reacted by halting aid programs, ban-

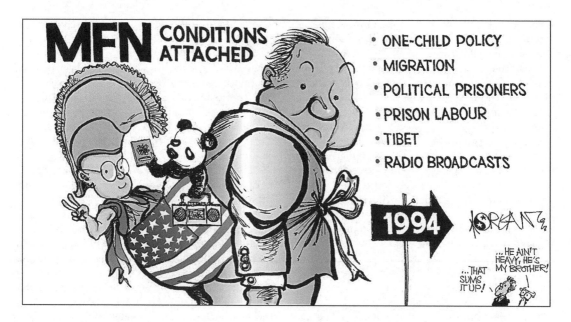

ning visits by US officials, and announcing a reassessment of its commercial relationships with China designed to link future activity to improvements in China's human rights record. Now China must put up with much finger-pointing as Congress debates the renewal of its MFN status each June.

The Perspectives

The Human Rights Argument Those against renewing China's MFN status have argued that, as much of the world saw on its television screens in June 1989, the Chinese government clearly abuses and suppresses the individual rights of its people. Reports of torture, arrests, imprisonment, and executions have been voluminously documented by human rights groups such as Amnesty International and Asia Watch. How, they ask, can the United States continue to bestow the economic rewards of MFN status on China while at the same time claiming to promote democracy and freedom throughout the world? Human rights advocates claim that the withholding of MFN status would serve as an excellent political lever to improve human rights and advance the political pluralization of China. They believe it is the duty of the US government to use its power to stand up against abuses. With this in mind, numerous members of the US congress, spearheaded by Representative Nancy Pelosi of California, have participated in the drafting of legislation that would make China's MFN status subject to its meeting strict conditions. If all requirements, including the release of political prisoners, greater political participation by the populace at large, and restrictions on the development of nuclear technology and deployment of missiles, are not met, China would be in jeopardy of losing its MFN status. Moreover, some argue that China's growing

US$13 billion trade surplus with the United States, resulting largely from closed Chinese markets, provides an additional reason to refuse to renew its MFN status, at least until China more fully opens its own markets to the United States.

The Free Trade Argument Others in government and business see little value in attaching a long list of conditions onto MFN status. They have argued that refusal to renew China's MFN status would further harm millions of Chinese people. In particular, the very regions that are in the forefront of China's economic development, as well as the entrepreneurs and progressive technocrats leading that reform, would be the ones to suffer most from such an action. Without MFN status, tariffs on imports coming into the United States from China would soar from an average rate of roughly 8 percent to around 40 percent according to some estimates. Ensuing lost business could result in the bankruptcy of as many as one-third of the enterprises in southern China. Revocation of MFN status would also have dire effects on Hong Kong's economy and on many importers in the United States, causing sharp hikes in prices paid by consumers for Chinese products sold in the US. For example, tariffs on toys imported from China could jump from around 7 percent to as much as 70 percent. In recent years China has become the primary supplier of such products to the US market; major price and supplier instability would profoundly impact this and other markets.

Moreover, China might well respond to such action by again turning inward and clamping down on the newly opened lines of communication with the outside world, severely limiting any future positive influence that the US government or business might exert. Some proponents of free trade argue that MFN status is strictly an economic tool and should not be loaded down with extraneous political baggage. The most effective way to encourage greater and lasting political reform, they claim, is to first help pave the way by promoting economic reform.

The Official Chinese Perspective The Chinese government has responded to threats to its MFN status by accusing the United States of seeking to apply foreign standards of justice and morality to nonwestern nation-states. Officials strongly resist what they see as self-righteous US attempts to tell China what should and should not be done and meddling in China's internal affairs. The Chinese government has threatened to retaliate, particularly in the trade sphere, should the United States continue to attempt to intervene in areas of China's national sovereignty.

At the same time, individual Chinese entrepreneurs see continued business strength as the only hope for influencing change in their country, and see such advances as dependent on continued MFN status.

Trends

During the 1992 US presidential campaign, candidate Bill Clinton stated that if elected he would, in contrast to previous administrations, push to attach more requirements to China's MFN status. And when MFN status was renewed in 1993, President Clinton signed an executive order making future renewals contingent on improvements in China's human rights conduct. However, Clinton has since softened his position, leaning toward renewing China's MFN status on existing terms or even crafting some special permanent MFN status arrangement, largely for pragmatic reasons.

The problem is further complicated by a range of subsidiary trade issues such as concerns about intellectual property, quota violations, use of forced prison labor, and unauthorized military sales. The United States contends that despite having agreed to abide by international conventions regarding the protection of intellectual property, China has failed to live up to its end of the agreement. For instance, US trade negotiators charge that China has licensed 26 factories that annually produce some 54 million compact discs consisting of pirated material.

At the beginning of 1994 the United States also threatened to slash China's quotas for apparel—one of its most important exports—by 25 to 35 percent depending on the product category, charging that China had systematically shipped such goods to US markets amounting to 140 percent of its allotted quotas. This was accomplished by transshipping the goods to third countries and passing them off as having originated in those countries rather than in China. Chinese authorities did not directly deny the allegations, but argued that any such violations were the responsibility of individual independent enter-

prises over which the authorities had no effective control or responsibility. After much posturing, China and the US reached an accord whereby China would more closely monitor exports from its factories and the US would keep the current quota levels in place while the two negotiated a renewal of the specific quota agreement.

In fall 1993 the United States also charged China with shipping restricted US-derived technology having military applications to a third party in violation of international and bilateral agreements. And allegations of the use of prisoners to produce export goods in violation of US policy continue to be a roadblock to good relations.

Although the US has been a very important trading partner for China, China is also becoming increasingly important to the US. For geopolitical reasons involving security (China is a major nuclear power and manufacturer and exporter of nuclear missiles and other arms) and politics (China wields increasing influence in Asia and the world and has played an important role in international affairs, such as in the crises involving Iraq and Cambodia), as well as economics, it is in the interest of the US to maintain good relations with China. However, it is also difficult for the United States to stand idly by as China acts in ways that seem to violate negotiated agreements and the US's sense of what constitutes appropriate behavior. In some cases, US authorities have resorted to brinkmanship, arguing that such tactics have been necessary to get China's serious attention. In others, the US seems to have misjudged the Chinese response to its complaints.

By the same token, it is easy to see control-oriented China's frustration over its inability to exercise effective control over certain of the activities of its nationals and national entities. Given China's size and variety and the magnitude of change that it has experienced in recent years, it is difficult to see how it could exercise such control.

By strict definition, China is well within its rights in arguing that its internal policies, standards, and activities are its own affair, with outside attempts to modify conduct or even comment on it unfavorably representing interference. However, China has been remarkably thin-skinned in its ability to take such criticism. Its defensive, ethnocentric reaction is conditioned by its perception of itself as the central polity on earth. And these cultural differences have been legitimately reinforced by the nature of its contact with outsiders, which includes the Opium Wars from the 1830s to 1860, the Boxer Rebellion in the 1890s, the Pacific War (1937-1945), and its demonization by the West during much of the 1950s and 1960s, all instances in which China was worsted by foreigners.

China dodged the US's bullet in 1993, and since renewal of MFN status business appears to be con-

tinuing as usual. Few US companies have argued for
more stringent conditions for China and even fewer
have pulled out to protest human rights abuses, the
exception being Levi Straus which canceled Chinese
apparel contracts. On the other hand, Boeing, which
is relying on large orders from Chinese airlines to
keep its US plants humming, has been quietly but
actively lobbying for maintenance of the status quo.

China has been recently showing signs that it is
getting the message and is trying to behave in a more
conciliatory fashion by making some legitimate attempts to deal with US substantive concerns. Nevertheless, the 1994 review of China's MFN status is
expected to be more contentious and complicated,
with US domestic political considerations clouding
the issue as much as Chinese sensitivity to imposi-
tions on its sovereignty.

Opportunities

OPPORTUNITIES FOR IMPORTING FROM CHINA

China's exports have steadily diversified since the mid-1980s, when clothing, petroleum (crude oil), and textiles accounted for more than half of exports. Exports of light manufactured goods have grown most rapidly, with the greatest export increases registered in toys and games, electronics and machinery, footwear, and leather travel goods.

This diversification in exports reflects China's competitive strength, which has been bolstered in recent years by the relocation of large numbers of export-oriented processing and assembly plants from Hong Kong and Taiwan to the Chinese mainland. Today, reexports constitute over 70 percent of China's exports, and the growth rate of the reexport market is likely to continue to outpace that of the domestic export market. The following section describes both exports and reexports as areas of opportunity for importing from China.

APPAREL

China is one of the world's top exporters of clothing and textiles, and garments and textiles together represent over 25 percent of China's total exports. As of mid-1993, approximately half of China's textile and garment exports were subject to textile quotas under international or bilateral agreements.

Employing more than 8 million workers, the industry has expanded with the relocation of many manufacturers from Hong Kong to Shenzhen in Guangdong Province. According to the Ministry of Textiles, China hopes to reach production levels of US$49 billion by 1995 and US$62.5 billion by the year 2000. Currently, China's largest export apparel markets are Hong Kong, Japan, Europe, and the United States.

In the past, exports of textiles have outpaced those of garments, but sources within the industry project that by 1995 garments will represent 65 percent of all textile exports. A central theme in China's apparel industry is the need to upgrade quality as well as production capability, especially if China is to remain competitive in the international market. Manufacturers also face the challenge of retaining their domestic market share once foreign competition is fully permitted.

The materials for clothing and fashion accessories—for example, blouses, pants, jackets, belts, hats, gloves, scarves, neckties, and travel bags—are often imported from Hong Kong or Taiwan, assembled in China, and then reexported.

Some of the HOT items:

- blouses
- briefcases, suitcases, and travel bags
- coats and jackets
- down products
- fur products
- gloves
- knitwear
- scarves
- silk piece goods
- sportswear
- sweaters
- woolen piece goods

OPPORTUNITIES
TABLE OF CONTENTS

Opportunities for Importing from China 31

Opportunities for Exporting to China 35

Opportunities for Growth 39

Public Procurement Opportunities 41

Public Procurement Process 42

TEXTILES

China's textile industries—spinning, weaving, and knitting—have sought to expand and diversify product development. During the early 1990s, exports grew at annual rates of 10 to 30 percent. Knitted and cotton cloth, cotton yarn, and pure woolen fabrics have had the highest growth. In addition, according to the China Resources Silk Corporation, China's exports of silk materials account for 90 percent of the world total.

Export-oriented factories are now being constructed to provide the capacity for manufacturing finished products. While natural fibers such as silk, cotton, wool, and ramie continue to be important to China's textile industry, synthetic fibers promise to be even more important to the future of the industry.

Some of the HOT items:
- cotton
- fur products
- linen fabrics
- silk
- synthetic fibers
- textile yarns and fabrics
- wool

FOOTWEAR

Shoe manufacturing remains a labor-intensive industry in many Asian countries. In recent years, the footwear industry has been facing labor shortages and escalating costs. To solve these problems, Hong Kong manufacturers, in particular, have relocated their plants to nearby Guangdong and Fujian Provinces. This development has helped promote industrial upgrading as well as the limited manufacture of name-brand products.

Some of the HOT items:
- athletic shoes
- canvas and rubber shoes
- leather sandals
- plastic shoes
- slippers

MACHINERY AND ELECTRONIC PRODUCTS

Because China views the export of machinery and electronic products as fundamental to its foreign trade, government policies favor exports of these items. Average annual increases in export earnings from machinery and electronic products now exceed 40 percent. Processing and assembly operations, cooperation from original equipment manufacturers, and compensation and border trade also play a major role in overall trade promotion.

As demand in the international market increases, China's exports of basic machinery products continue to grow. Reasonable prices, application of more advanced technology, and compatibility with foreign product standards enhance the competitiveness of Chinese products. The machinery industries in the cities of Xuzhou, Luoyang, Xian, Baoji, and Lanzhou within the Longhai-Lanxin economic zone account for half of the total machinery industry in China. Beijing, Shanghai, and Tianjin are also leading production centers.

In addition to basic machinery parts such as bearings, tightening parts, and chains, machinery exports include cutting and measuring tools, forging and casting, motors, meters and instruments, machine tools and equipment. The top two household machinery products are bicycles and sewing machines.

Some of the HOT items:
- aeronautics parts
- automobile parts
- bearings
- bicycles and parts
- electric motors
- hydraulic parts and systems
- machine tools
- meters and instruments
- plant equipment
- sewing machines
- tightening parts and chains

TIMEPIECES

China has traditionally produced and exported mechanical watches. More recently, LCD and electronic watches and clocks of various types and sizes have entered the export market. Other export items include cases, metal bands, and movements.

Some of the HOT items:
- clocks
- metal wristbands
- stainless steel watch casings
- watches (quartz and LCD)

ELECTRONICS AND ELECTRONIC COMPONENTS

As a result of domestic research, transfers of technology, and the relocation of assembly operations to China, China's electronics industry is advancing rapidly. Reexports are growing at a more rapid rate than domestic electronic exports. Guangdong, Beijing, Shanghai, and Jiangsu are the main production centers.

Passive components are China's primary export. These include capacitors, diodes, relays, resistors, transformers, and transistors. Consumer electronic products include televisions, radios, electronic games, telephones, and videotapes.

Some of the HOT items:
- capacitors
- diodes
- electric fans
- household electrical appliances
- liquid crystal displays (LCDs)
- radios
- tape recorders
- transistors, resistors, and switches
- TVs, parts and components
- videotapes

METALS, MINERALS, AND BY-PRODUCTS

China is a major exporter of tungsten, tin, mercury, and antimony. The country has deposits of most metals and commercial deposits of almost 130 types of minerals. The world's largest reserves of titanium, phosphate, molybdenum, and tungsten, and a dozen other minerals are in China.

China has recently become an important producer and exporter of vanadium, titanium, germanium, gallium, and polycrystalline silicon. These rare metals are essential to aerospace, electronics, and other high-technology industries.

Metal products, hardware, and building supplies are also available throughout China. Leading products include fasteners (screws, nuts, bolts, and washers) as well as hinges, pipes, and light bulbs. Building materials include cement, glass, stone products, and ceramics.

Some of the HOT items:
- alloys
- antimony
- brass products
- ceramic products
- coal
- fasteners
- iron and steel products
- nonferrous metals and products
- pipes
- rare metals
- tin
- tungsten

TOYS

Beyond its domestic production, China's toy industry serves as a major processor and assembler for Hong Kong manufacturers. The bulk of the industry's exports consists of plush and stuffed toys

and dolls. Exports of electronic toys and games are also rising.

Some of the HOT items:
- dolls
- electronic toys and games
- inflatables
- plush toys

RUBBER AND PLASTIC PRODUCTS

Both rubber and plastic are transformed into a wide range of products made in China. As a result, China's rubber and plastics industries are closely tied to developments in the petrochemical, automotive, and light industry sectors. As export diversification and technical upgrading continue, both rubber and plastic will have increasingly widespread uses.

Rubber products have been one of China's traditional, albeit slow-growth, export items. In light of international demand for rubber goods, foreign cooperation is being extended, with the aim of doubling China's current export volume by 1995. Export items include tires, rubber-soled shoes, hoses, belts, air mattresses, and carbon black.

China is also a leading producer and exporter of a diverse range of plastic products, including fashion accessories, handicrafts, electronics, and houseware goods.

Some of the HOT items:
- air mattresses
- automotive parts
- carbon black
- emulsion products
- houseware products
- plastic cases
- plastic woven bags
- primary plastics
- rubber hose
- sporting goods
- tires
- tubing

ARTS AND HANDICRAFTS

Arts and handicrafts have a long and established history in China. Taking advantage of abundant labor, low wages, and improvements in manufacturing techniques, China's arts and crafts industry produces a wide range of items.

Some of the HOT items:
- art tapestries
- artificial flowers
- bamboo and cane products

- baskets
- carved jewelry
- ceramics
- Christmas decorations
- cloisonné
- embroidered articles
- enamel products
- furniture
- glassware
- jade jewelry
- lacquer products
- porcelain
- pottery
- rugs and carpets
- screens
- semi-precious jewelry
- tablecloths
- woven products

AGRICULTURE AND ANIMAL BY-PRODUCTS

China is one of the world's largest agricultural producers. Although much of its output is sold on the domestic market, foodstuffs and animal by-products are also exported.

Some of the HOT items:

- brushes and bristles
- canned fruits and vegetables
- confectionery products
- down products
- dried fruits
- fur-skin products
- leather travel goods
- leather working gloves
- rice, maize, and soybeans
- spices, oils, and seasonings
- wine and spirits

TEN EXTRA PROSPECTS FOR IMPORTING FROM CHINA

- automobiles
- building materials and supplies
- chemicals
- health and hygiene products
- information and communication products
- medical instruments and apparatus
- musical instruments
- optical products
- paper products
- pharmaceuticals and medicines

OPPORTUNITIES FOR EXPORTING TO CHINA

A wide variety of foreign name-brand products are familiar to Chinese consumers. Items in demand include designer clothes, cellular telephones, and automobiles. Such is the case despite China's traditional trade policy of discouraging the importation of foreign goods as a way of enhancing self-sufficiency and conserving foreign exchange. Demand is also particularly strong for high-technology goods and services computer software, hardware and peripherals, medical instrumentation, and industrial manufacturing equipment. As China's economy becomes increasingly decentralized, foreign exporters will undoubtedly consider the Chinese market to be strategically important. Selling in this market may be more challenging, but the opportunities are greater. The industries described here offer some of the best prospects for foreign companies exporting to China.

COMPUTERS AND PERIPHERALS

The computerization of both the private and public sectors in China is in the early stages. As of 1993 there were approximately 400,000 personal computers for China's 1.1 billion people. Despite great pent-up demand for workstations, network systems, printers, and peripherals, stringent import licensing requirements have limited imports of computers and peripherals. On a positive note, the Chinese government recently reduced the import duties on computers, along with other high-tech products.

Some of the HOT items:
- dot-matrix printers
- laser printers
- network systems
- 386 and 486 computers
- workstations

PRINTED CIRCUIT BOARD EQUIPMENT

Demand for printed circuit board (PCB) equipment is strong in joint and wholly foreign-owned ventures and in China's large state enterprises. Because several emerging industries require high volumes of quality PCBs, many observers believe that growing demand will offer numerous opportunities to foreign exporters. Desired products include computer-aided design and manufacturing (CAD/CAM) workstations, optical analysis instruments, and equipment for manufacturing PCBs.

The largest source of potential growth in the market is foreign invested electronics firms, mostly in Fujian, Shanghai, and Guangdong. Many of these firms would like to acquire PCB equipment and technology. The booming domestic market for finished electronic goods is another source of growth for this industry.

Some of the HOT items:
- CAD and CAM workstations
- cleaning machines
- digital control drilling machines
- optical analysis instruments
- soldering systems
- surface mount technology (SMT) equipment
- testing machines

COMPUTER SOFTWARE

Although China is developing its own PC software, over two-thirds of all software in the country is imported. Much of the imported software consists of illegal copies of foreign products. Most of the foreign software is modified to accommodate Chinese characters (hanzified). While Singapore and Hong Kong are moving toward adopting the standard of internal coding used in China, Taiwanese systems are still incompatible.

Because much of China's PC software is copied, it is difficult to place a value on the potential market. But with the recent introduction of regulations to protect intellectual property, it is estimated that the Chinese computer software market will expand at an annual average rate of 20 percent between 1993 and 1995. Operating systems, business software, CAD, CAM, and CAE software, and computer languages are in high demand.

Some of the HOT items:
- CAD, CAM, and CAE software
- Chinese input systems
- computer languages
- database management software
- desktop publishing systems
- operating systems software
- spreadsheet software
- word processing software

PHARMACEUTICALS

Due to inadequate domestic supply, China will continue to import pharmaceutical products used to treat life-threatening diseases. Although China has significantly increased its production of antibiotics during the past five years, antibiotics produced abroad are considered to be superior in quality.

Total imports of pharmaceutical products reached US$319 million in 1992, of which foreign prescription medicines accounted for US$128 million. Chinese doctors are familiar with many foreign drugs and, as living standards rise, Chinese patients are becoming increasingly receptive to them.

Foreign invested enterprises in China are beginning to manufacture some pharmaceutical products, which should decrease China's reliance on imports in line with the country's trade policy.

Some of the HOT items:
- analgesic drugs and preparations
- bulk preparations for manufacture of antibiotics
- cancer drugs
- cardiovascular drugs
- drugs and inhalants to treat respiratory diseases

MEDICAL EQUIPMENT

The medical equipment market in China was US$1.1 billion in 1992 and is expected to expand by 8 percent annually through 1995. Imports of medical equipment are expected to grow by 8 to 10 percent a year. Imports of X-ray apparatus, ultrasound scanners, and other electrodiagnostic devices show the strongest potential for growth.

In China, US medical equipment is in the highest demand, followed by equipment from Germany and Japan. South Korea and Taiwan are also aggressively marketing their products, but these countries are generally regarded as lower-end suppliers. To capitalize on export opportunities, foreign suppliers should monitor the medical research programs of the World Bank and other multilateral agencies.

Some of the HOT items:
- blood sugar meters
- blood testing instruments
- carbon-dioxide incubators
- computerized axial tomography (CAT) scanners
- cystoscopes
- diagnostic equipment for detecting cancer
- digital thermometers
- electrocardiograph (EKG) machines
- kidney dialysis machines
- microtomes
- monitors for blood oxygen, body temperature, and other functions
- pregnancy test kits
- ultrasonic diagnostic instruments
- X-ray machines

LABORATORY INSTRUMENTS

China's modernization efforts have led to a growing demand for advanced laboratory instruments. The majority of these instruments are imported, due to the lack of technology and skilled labor. As China's

scientific institutions continue to demand state-of-the-art equipment, numerous opportunities will emerge for foreign suppliers. The best prospects include automatic temperature control instruments, measuring and process control instruments, and advanced analytical instruments.

Some of the HOT items:
- advanced instruments for forensic science
- auto-analytical apparatus
- microplate readers
- sterilization systems
- supercool refrigerators (-60° to -85°C)
- temperature control instruments

PRINTING EQUIPMENT

China's current Five-Year Plan (1991-1995) calls for expenditures of US$60 million to import advanced printing technology and equipment. The desired high-efficiency products include color scanners, computerized typesetting equipment, offset printing presses, and binding machines. Although most provincial newspapers adopted computer typesetting in 1990, several smaller newspapers have yet to acquire this technology.

China's import substitution policy still poses barriers to would-be foreign suppliers of printing equipment for the emerging private sector. However, foreign exports to state enterprises appear to face fewer restrictions. The most common method of exporting printing equipment is in combination with transfers of technology or through cooperative assembly arrangements, rather than direct sales.

Some of the HOT items:
- binding machines
- color scanners
- computer typesetters
- phototypesetting equipment
- platemaking equipment
- platen presses
- post-print equipment
- printing presses
- rotary offset presses

FOOD PROCESSING AND PACKAGING MACHINERY

China processes and packages only 5 to 10 percent of its food output. Strengthening and modernizing the food processing and packaging industry have been key goals of economic development and industrial planning. China is now engaged in serious efforts to boost its export of processed and packaged foods, which will in turn boost its demand for food processing and packaging machinery. Activities that make use of such machinery include meat processing and dairy production; the preparation of soups, baby foods, and frozen foods; and beer brewing.

Some of the HOT items:
- alternative packaging materials
- bottling technology
- breakable parts (e.g., ring belts)
- bundlers
- composite cans
- electric heating components
- plastic packaging materials
- sealing for automatic components
- sealing machines for plastic bags
- shaping, filling, and sealing machines
- electric-resistant can-welding equipment

TEXTILE EQUIPMENT

Imported equipment and technology will play a pivotal role as China's textile industry modernizes to compete in the international market. Under China's current Five-Year Plan, the East China region alone will invest a total of US$1.14 billion to restructure its textile industry.

US$260 million on imported equipment and technology, $US420 million on plant and infrastructure construction, and $US460 million on domestic equipment.

The principal opportunities for foreign exporters lie in equipment for cotton spinning, weaving, dyeing, and finishing as well as equipment for wool processing and garment production.

Some of the HOT items:
cotton spinning
- combined line of blowing and carding machines
- components of ring-spinning frames
- roving frames

weaving and preparing
- projectile and rapier looms
- signing machines
- warping machines
- water and air-jet looms

dyeing and finishing
- comprehensive shrinking machines
- duplex printing machines
- flat and rotary screen printing machines
- mercerizing ranges
- schreinering machines

wool processing
- advanced flat knitting machines
- wool spinning machines

knitting and garment production
- circular knitting machines
- computerized cutting machines
- hosiery, steaming, and ironing machines

OIL AND GAS FIELD MACHINERY

The recent opening of the East China Sea to foreign exploration and production will provide foreign companies with good opportunities to export oil and gas field machinery to China. Recent discoveries in the Tarima Basin and other offshore areas are also expected to create a need for additional production equipment and pipeline facilities. Given China's emphasis on energy development, imports of oil and gas field machinery are likely to increase by 10 percent annually for the next few years.

Some of the HOT items:
- geophysical instruments
- offshore production equipment and services
- onshore equipment and services
- pipeline equipment and facilities
- secondary recovery equipment

TELECOMMUNICATIONS EQUIPMENT

China's telecommunications market is expected to reach US$20 billion by the end of the decade. Telecommunications equipment is in particularly strong demand. In 1992 China spent US$7 billion in 1993 on direct purchases and joint development of advanced wireless systems, fiber optics and digital transmission systems, terminals, switching systems, and intelligent network systems. It should be noted, however, that China does not permit foreigners to participate in the joint management of telecommunications companies.

Some of the HOT items:
- cellular (wireless) equipment
- earth satellite stations
- facsimile machines
- intelligent networks
- PBX and digital switches
- transmission equipment

AIRCRAFT, AVIONICS, AND SUPPORT EQUIPMENT

In its effort to modernize, China is looking to upgrade its aircraft and build new airport facilities. To achieve these goals, China has loosened import controls on aircraft and avionics equipment. The market for aircraft and avionics equipment is projected to grow at an annual rate of 20 to 25 percent over the next few years.

Some of the HOT items:
- aircraft parts
- automatic ground systems
- baggage and cargo handling equipment

- communications equipment
- navigational aids
- passenger bridges
- passenger jet aircraft
- radio and radar equipment
- wide-body jet aircraft

INDUSTRIAL PROCESS CONTROL

Under the current Five-Year Plan, the Chinese government has given high priority to the development of high-tech equipment and processes, which will require better standards of industrial control. Opportunities for foreign exporters exist in the areas of power plant instrumentation, chemical process controls, and numerically controlled machinery. Imports of industrial process control equipment are expected to increase by at least 8 percent a year through 1995.

Some of the HOT items:

- gas analyzers
- multimeters
- oscilloscopes
- potentiometers
- power plant instrumentation
- spectroscopic analyzers

CONSTRUCTION EQUIPMENT AND BUILDING SUPPLIES

China's heavy emphasis on infrastructure construction, especially in the energy and transportation industries, has heightened the demand for large high-tech construction equipment. The current boom in residential and commercial building construction is also likely to result in increased opportunities for foreign suppliers. Demand for building products such as hardware, lumber, and specialty cements is also growing. The markets for construction equipment and building supplies are expected to grow by an average of 8 to 10 percent through 1995.

Some of the HOT items:

- building hardware and fixtures
- dump trucks
- large earth-moving equipment
- road-paving equipment
- specialty cements
- wood products

TWELVE EXTRA PROSPECTS FOR EXPORTING TO CHINA

- agricultural chemicals
- apparel
- architectural, construction, and engineering services
- chemical production machinery
- construction equipment
- dental equipment
- electronic components
- electronic production and test equipment
- industrial process controls
- plastic materials and resins
- pollution control equipment
- port and shipbuilding equipment

OPPORTUNITIES FOR GROWTH

MANUFACTURING

Thousands of farsighted foreign companies have invested in such local operations in China, as a means of low-cost sourcing or as a way to obtain an entree in the domestic market. Recent reforms promise to make such investment easier in the future. Nearly half of foreign investment projects in China involve manufacturing, with the majority of these in electronics. In some industries, including aircraft and locomotives, foreign companies have set up joint ventures to produce products or components for export in order to meet Chinese countertrade requirements. High-tech products, capital goods, and industrial materials will continue to find markets within China, particularly in the targeted areas of energy, telecommunications, electronics, and transportation.

OIL EXPLORATION AND PETROCHEMICALS

There are signs that government restrictions on foreign participation in the development of inland oil reserves may soon be relaxed. This easing is expected to lead to a marked expansion of foreign involvement in China's oil industry. New technology could increase the recovery rate in existing oil fields, and foreign cooperation is being sought in 10 provinces and in one autonomous region.

Soaring economic growth and strong regional demand will continue to spur expansion in China's burgeoning petrochemical industry. China's major petrochemical company, China National Petrochemical Corporation (SINOPEC), has plans to begin eight large-scale projects between 1993 and 1995. Several other huge foreign invested projects are planned in Huizhou (in Guangdong Province), in Shanghai, and in Liaoning Province. State-owned Tianjin Petrochemical Corporation is building three refineries, three ethylene crackers, and many other facilities.

Faced with mature markets and sluggish economies at home, foreign companies are eager to participate in the development of Asia's growing chemical market. Royal Dutch, Britain's ICI, Union Carbide Corporation, and TEC of Japan are among the major foreign companies involved in petrochemical projects in China. Other promising growth areas lie in providing petrochemical equipment, technical design, and engineering services for the construction of oil and gas pipelines.

CABLE TELEVISION

China's cable TV industry is developing according to an executive order of the State Council. All systems are operated by local governments or affiliated agencies. Private operation of networks is not allowed.

Conditions seem ripe for rapid growth in the cable television industry. Regulators, contractors, and operators are all working together to increase the size of the network as quickly as possible. Programming far superior to regular Chinese television is readily available through satellite systems, primarily Star TV, based in Hong Kong. And because Chinese customers are required to pay in advance for cable hookup, the fledgling cable television industry has sizable cash reserves for investment.

Total imports of hardware in the cable TV industry were estimated at US$100 million in 1993 and are expected to double in 1994. This demand is felt throughout China, but is especially strong along the eastern coast. Sources indicate that the Ministry of Radio, Film, and Television envisions connecting all agricultural villages into a nationwide network.

The best markets are for foreign companies that manufacture compressors, converters, combiners, modulators, optical transmitters and receivers, cables, amplifiers, extenders, and distributors.

REAL ESTATE

China hopes to attract more foreign investment in its real estate market. Land development is now one of the hottest areas for foreign investment. News reports appear daily in Hong Kong about new land deals in various parts of China.

Many cities offer special incentives for real estate projects. According to press reports, projects from Tianjin to Fujian are in the works, with additional ones expected in Beijing, Hangzhou, and Shenyang. A widely publicized example was the decision by a consortium of Hong Kong and Chinese companies to proceed with long-standing plans to purchase the rights to develop a 30-square-km (12-square-mile) tract of land in the Yangpu area of Hainan island. Government sources have commented that the development projects in Hainan's Yangpu and Shanghai's Pudong typify the sort of deals that China hopes to conclude.

SERVICES

Expansion of services is the focus of intense interest in China. Government officials view an efficient service industry as valuable in transforming the centrally planned economy into a market-driven one. Liberalization in the service sector will create many new opportunities for foreign firms. At the present time foreign competition in services is highly regulated. Detailed regulations for each industry are determined by the relevant ministry, and provincial and local officials are responsible for enforcing them. In the past two years the government has begun to ease controls in such areas as banking and accounting. The government also has authorized a limited number of joint ventures in service activities. Continued liberalization will present a number of opportunities for foreign service providers in many industries:

Investment Banking

Many foreign investment banks provide services to China's rapidly growing market through Hong Kong subsidiaries. Chinese firms are now using these services to register on stock exchanges in Hong Kong and other areas. Foreign companies are also assisting Chinese firms on the domestic stock exchanges in Shanghai and Shenzhen. And foreign companies are involved in innovative fee-based deals with individual provinces and large commercial groups. This type of activity is likely to increase in the wake of the national securities law enacted in 1993.

Accounting

Most of the major international accounting firms have a presence in China. Many serve the rapidly expanding base of foreign invested firms. They are also forming joint ventures with local companies that hope to tap into international capital markets. The introduction of new accounting laws should also increase the opportunities for foreign accounting services.

Legal Services

In 1992 a dozen foreign law firms were licensed to operate in Beijing, Guangzhou, and Shanghai. Foreign lawyers are not allowed to appear in Chinese courts, but they are permitted to represent foreign clients in China; they may also represent Chinese companies abroad. The liberalization of legal services increased the number of private Chinese law firms, which are referred to as cooperative law offices.

Advertising

Many foreign advertising agencies with a presence in China serve foreign clients. However, most agencies feel that the key to longer-term profitability rests in representing Chinese clients selling to the domestic market. Agencies now have access to nearly all marketing tools used in the West, including radio, television, print, and billboard advertising.

Consulting and Engineering Services

Foreign consulting and engineering firms have received a considerable amount of business as a result of aid programs sponsored by multilateral development banks and foreign countries. Net foreign exchange earners—petroleum exploration services, aviation maintenance services, and hotels and restaurants—have concluded joint venture agreements with foreign consulting and engineering companies. In addition, foreign firms in China commonly purchase consulting services from other foreign firms.

Shipping

China is seeking foreign investment in its air freight and cargo shipping industries. Under an agreement between the US Federal Maritime Commission and Chinese authorities, Sealand and APL have been allowed to enter the cargo handling business. Firms from other countries have been allowed to assist the US companies and Chinese authorities in port management and warehousing. In the air freight business, some foreign firms have been allowed to enter into joint ventures with Chinese enterprises.

Retail

Fueled by rapid increases in consumer spending, the retail industry is booming. Consumer goods such as cellular telephones and private automobiles are in high demand, especially among the more affluent consumers in southern China.

Many foreign manufacturers of consumer goods have established profitable ventures in Guangdong Province. Japan-based Yaohan has announced that it will open at least 1,000 supermarkets in China by the year 2000. Hong Kong-based firms such as China Fortune, Wing On, Asia Commercial, Welcome, and Watsons have also announced plans to expand their activities in this market. Lippo, based in Indonesia, also has access to prime commercial real estate in Beijing. Another large retail project involving the Thai-invested Chia Tai group comprises a department store, a shopping mall, and other retail outlets.

Franchising

A number of foreign franchises, including McDonald's, Kentucky Fried Chicken, Pizza Hut, and Dairy Queen, have established joint venture operations in China. Taiwanese and Japanese fast-food franchises are also represented, and other foreign franchises have plans to enter the market.

Hotels and Restaurants

Foreign hotel and restaurant operators have been active in China's large cities. The tremendous economic growth occurring throughout most of China now presents them with opportunities to establish themselves in secondary cities. If political stability and economic growth continue, these industries are likely to enjoy rapid expansion.

PUBLIC PROCUREMENT OPPORTUNITIES

Recent reforms in China have decentralized government decision making to some extent, but public procurement in such priority areas as energy and transportation is still largely determined by central government officials in Beijing. Nonetheless, promising opportunities exist for foreign suppliers of technology and equipment needed for the exploration of China's natural resources and the development of the country's infrastructure. Public projects financed through multilateral loans and grants present further possibilities for foreign contractors.

In accordance with the latest Five-Year Plan, China is now channeling state investment and foreign funds into the development of four key sectors:

- agriculture and water conservation
- energy and raw materials exploration
- transportation and telecommunications
- electronics

Many of China's most critical industries have been targeted for technological upgrading. New factories and other facilities will be constructed, and essential equipment and technology will be imported. Areas of opportunity include:

- Energy-saving techniques and equipment in such industries as steel, nonferrous metals, and building materials.
- Technical upgrading of equipment used in the electronics, communications, light manufacturing, textile, packaging, medical, and chemical industries.

Among the top prospects for foreign suppliers:

- Aircraft and parts for wide-body jets, medium-sized passenger jets (100 to 200 passengers).
- Agricultural and industrial chemicals, chemical production machinery, and urea.
- Machinery for oil and gas drilling and refining as well as pipeline equipment and facilities.
- Computers and peripherals workstations, personal computers, printers, and networking products.
- Mining and construction equipment.

For further information regarding public procurement opportunities, contact your nearest Chinese embassy or consulate, or the trade promotion section of your own country's embassy in China. Another alternative is to address your inquiries directly to one of the major foreign trade corporations (FTCs) under the Ministry of Foreign Trade and Economic Cooperation (MOFTEC) on the following list. For addresses and telephone numbers of embassies, consulates, and FTCs, refer to the "Important Addresses" chapter.

Major Foreign Trade Corporations Under MOFTEC

- China National Aerotechnology Import and Export Corporation
- China National Automobile Import and Export Corporation
- China National Automotive Industry Import and Export Corporation
- China National Arts and Crafts Import and Export Corporation (ARTCHINA)
- China National Building Materials and Equipment Import and Export Corporation
- China National Cereals, Oils, and Foodstuffs Import and Export Corporation (CEROILFOOD)
- China National Chemicals Import and Export Corporation (SINOCHEM)
- China National Coal Import and Export Corporation
- China National Electronics Import and Export Corporation
- China National Export Bases Development Corporation
- China National Import and Export Packaging Corporation (CHINAPACK)
- China National Light Industrial Products Import and Export Corporation (INDUSTRY)
- China National Machinery Import and Export Corporation (MACHIMPEX)
- China National Medicine and Health Products Import and Export Corporation (MEHECO)
- China National Metals and Minerals Import and Export Corporation (MINMETALS)
- China National Native Produce and Animal By-Products Import and Export Corporation (CHINATUHSU)
- China National Nonferrous Metals Import and Export Corporation
- China National Packaging Import and Export Corporation
- China National Precision Machinery Import and Export Corporation
- China National Pulp and Paper Import and Export Corporation
- China National Silk Import and Export Corporation (CHINASILK)
- China National Technical Import and Export Corporation (TECHIMPORT)
- China National Technical Machinery Import and Export Corporation
- China National Textiles Import and Export Corporation (CHINATEX)

PUBLIC PROCUREMENT PROCESS

The approval process required to participate in government-sponsored infrastructure projects typically involves six stages, and every project must receive explicit official consent at several points along the way. While the uniformity of the process provides some predictability, local political rivalries and disagreements between local and central government officials can cause delays or other problems.

The six stages in the approval process for infrastructure projects are:

- conceptual proposal
- preliminary approval
- preliminary design
- establishment of the plan
- feasibility study
- final approval

Foreign companies should seek to participate in the approval process at the earliest stage. Contacts established at each stage can prove useful when formal bidding begins.

CONCEPTUAL PROPOSAL

The project managers, who are officials of either a central ministry or a provincial government, circulate a conceptual proposal (*xiangmu jianyi shu*). The proposal identifies the nature of the particular project (for example, transportation, communications, power supply, water management, or land development). It also discusses in general terms the estimated schedule for construction, the resources needed, the cost, and the project financing.

PRELIMINARY APPROVAL

The conceptual proposal is submitted to a zone planning committee at the national, provincial, or municipal level. The preliminary approval signifies the government's initial endorsement of the project. Depending on government priorities, the planning committee will often designate various combinations of funds, limits on borrowing foreign exchange, and preferential rights to the use of land or other resources.

PRELIMINARY DESIGN

Next, the project managers draft a preliminary design (*chubu sheji*) in cooperation with one of several state architectural design institutes. The preliminary design often details the equipment to be used.

ESTABLISHMENT OF THE PLAN

If the preliminary design is approved, the project must be formally established (*lixiang*) within the context of the government's long-term economic development plans.

FEASIBILITY STUDY

Project managers now initiate a feasibility study (*kexingxing yanjiu*), in which engineers estimate the labor and material requirements, and economists and financiers calculate costs and explore capital sources. The study entails extensive consultation with both domestic and foreign suppliers and investors. Companies also submit prequalification documents (*zige pingshen*), which function essentially as preliminary bids or informal contracts.

FINAL APPROVAL

After the planning committee reviews the final feasibility report and the final design plans, the entire project may receive final approval (*zuihou pizhun*). The project managers then proceed with formal bidding (*zhengshi zhaobiao*) and contracting.

REGULATORY ENVIRONMENT

Projects valued over RMB 150 million require approval by the national State Planning Commission or the State Council. Provincial authorities may handle projects valued below this amount. The Special Economic Zones (SEZs) and some large cities make independent planning decisions and need only notify the provincial government of their choices. For example, Shenzhen, a Special Economic Zone, and Guangzhou, an autonomous municipality, have status equal to that of Guangdong Province in matters of economic planning. Guangzhou's special Economic and Technological Development Zone (ETDZ) also enjoys extensive autonomy under the direction of its own mayor.

To retain control of larger projects, provinces and autonomous cities sometimes divide a project into phases, each valued at less than RMB 150 million. Local governments have also been known to deliberately underestimate the cost of construction—a dodge that requires the local authorities to have the necessary funds at hand. Capital-rich areas can survive such hedging; in less prosperous regions, projects may lose funding, leaving contractors and suppliers unpaid.

Foreign Investment

INVESTMENT CLIMATE AND TRENDS

A complex and often conflicting system of administrative controls regulates access by foreign investors to China's market. Among the major hurdles that investors face are a multiplicity of seemingly arbitrary rules and regulations, the limited availability of foreign exchange, inadequate protection for intellectual property, barriers to market access and production controls, treatment that is unequal when compared with that of domestic companies, and the lack of an adequate mechanism for resolving disputes. Even so, a total of 48,858 ventures involving direct foreign investment were approved in 1992—3.7 times the number approved in the preceding year and more than all the investments approved between 1979 and 1991. Signed investment contracts represented US$83 billion during the first nine months of 1993 and were expected to hit US$100 billion by year-end. A total of perhaps US$20 billion was actually invested. This dramatic increase in foreign investment indicates just how attractive China's economy has become, despite the many difficulties that investors face. But China has announced its intention to improve the investment climate through a series sweeping reforms. If the changes that have been announced are successful, China can expect to become a magnet for foreign investment.

Regulations Lack Transparency In general China's trade and investment system lacks transparency. Rules and regulations are not readily accessible, they are often applied inconsistently, and they can vary by region. Both foreign nationals and many Chinese officials themselves lack a solid understanding of China's regulations. Moreover, although Article 15 of the 1986 State Council Provisions to Encourage Foreign Investment clearly states that foreign invested enterprises (FIEs) are to have autonomy in the management of their operations, the managers of FIEs often complain of administrative interference in their business operations. (FIEs can be either partially foreign-owned enterprises, such as joint ventures, or wholly foreign-owned enterprises.)

In response to these problems, the Chinese government pledged in mid-1992 to increase transparency in matters affecting foreign investment and FIE operations. The predecessor of the current Ministry of Foreign Trade and Economic Cooperation (MOFTEC), which is responsible for regulating foreign activity, announced that it would publish all laws and regulations affecting foreign trade, including those promulgated in the past 10 years. The MOFTEC has also stated its intention to publish clear guidelines on the scope of authority and the duties of various government agencies with respect to FIEs. Foreign governments have consistently urged China to adhere to a policy of enforcing only published laws and regulations. Although China has made some progress in this regard, the request itself poses problems for a country that has long operated on the basis of arbitrary decree as well as jealously guarding its prerogatives.

Foreign Exchange Regulations China's central government exerts such strict control over the allocation of foreign exchange that acquisition of sufficient foreign exchange is itself a significant nontariff barrier to doing business in China. The PRC's regulations for FIEs require that profits be remitted, imported components or raw materials be purchased, and foreign personnel be compensated in foreign currency rather than in China's domestic currency, renminbi (RMB). If an FIE is in short supply of foreign currency (usually because it is not exporting its products), it will find these transactions hard to conduct.

FIEs producing for China's domestic market often cite the fact that Chinese currency is not convertible as a serious problem in the conduct of business. For example, there are only a limited number of ways in which an FIE can obtain sufficient foreign exchange to repatriate its profits. The Chinese government strongly encourages exporting as a primary means of earning foreign exchange. Other methods include selling goods in the domestic economy for foreign exchange, which is unrealistic, because few customers in China have access to hard currency, and the use of foreign exchange swap centers.

The swap centers were established in the 1980s to enable firms with foreign ownership or extensive international operations to obtain badly needed foreign exchange. The firms were allowed to swap renminbi with enterprises (such as hotels) that had a surplus of foreign exchange. Subsequently, swap centers opened to domestic firms as well. Several dozen centers now operate throughout the country. Some swap centers, such as the one in Shanghai, have admitted brokers to help create a more liquid market. Exchange rates are routinely reported in the press.

Even with the recent proliferation of swap centers, the reports from FIEs in their dealings with swap centers are mixed. In theory, foreign exchange is permitted to flow from one swap center to another to equalize supply and demand, but in practice local authorities often block the flow of foreign exchange from centers in their jurisdiction. Some centers refuse to sell foreign exchange to companies outside their own area.

Of course, one solution to the exchange problem would be to float the renminbi and make it convertible. But for reasons of short-term stability, China's monetary authorities have been unwilling to take this step. However, before long, the widening gap between the official rate and the swap center rate could have made the renminbi all but worthless. In Guangzhou Province, the renminbi's swap market rate rose from RMB 5.88 per US$1 in January 1992 to RMB 7.69 per US$1 in December of same year. Midway through 1993, the swap rate was approximately RMB 10.00 per US$1, while the official rate was RMB 5.7. The discrepancy is the result of increased demand for foreign exchange as the volume of imports and foreign investment rises. In response to problems such as these, the Chinese government announced a reorganization of its currency system to take effect in January 1994. This would allow a managed float and a unification of the official exchange rate with the de facto swap market exchange rate, resulting in an effective devaluation of approximately 50 percent. This is expected to pave the way to greater convertibility.

Intellectual Property Protection Lack of adequate protection for intellectual property is another significant disincentive to investment in China. FIEs have complained of insufficient patent protection, which has inhibited the transfer of advanced chemical and pharmaceutical technologies, and lack of software protection, which has curtailed investment and technology licensing by computer companies and other manufacturers whose business centers on software.

China also lacks a framework for determining when intellectual property rights have been violated and how such violations should be handled. Local authorities have been known to protect an enterprise in their own regions if an enterprise from another region files a complaint.

In early 1994 the Chinese agreed to exercise greater regulatory supervision of such issues as copyright violation at the behest of the United States. It remains to be seen whether the situation will improve materially.

Market Access Many foreign investors with advanced technology are interested in joining forces with productive enterprises in China to sell products in the domestic market. But even if these investors become participants in joint ventures or establish independent operations of their own, and are able to meet their foreign exchange requirements, they often face barriers to market access because the prevailing system is designed to acquire and hoard foreign exchange while reserving domestic markets.

Production controls set by government authorities, such as import license requirements for imported components; annual approval of production volumes; and limited access to critical raw materials usually make investment in large, capital-intensive projects unfeasible. Extensive capital investments can be justified only by economies of scale, low production costs, and large sales volumes. Under current conditions, investments of this nature will strike most as too risky.

Differential Treatment of FIEs and State Enterprises Recent proposals by Chinese officials call for giving state enterprises the same beneficial treatment that most FIEs receive. This treatment includes autonomy in management and personnel issues as well as low tax rates in line with those accorded to FIEs. While such benefits would undoubtedly help to revitalize China's domestic industry, state enterprises already receive preferential treatment that is not available to FIEs and could have the affect of making China less attractive to foreign investors.

State enterprises have priority in applications for loans and in the purchase of raw materials, which are available in limited quantities at low, fixed prices. Even when raw materials and other supplies originate in China, FIEs are sometimes required to pay in foreign currency. Otherwise, they must import their materials, for which they need hard currency.

Dispute Resolution For many companies, the highly personalized nature of conducting business in China, the absence of a strong contractual and legal tradition, and the limited number of suppliers and customers can make arbitration or other legal remedies impractical when disputes arise. Even when a foreign investor has a strong case, he or she often decides against arbitration out of fear that it would permanently alienate critical business associates. Investors must learn to cope with China's underdeveloped legal system in which contracts are often unenforceable. Often legal disputes are settled on a case-by-case basis, without regard for prior rulings. However, leading government officials, especially Vice Premier Zhu Rongji, have signaled their intention to overhaul China's legal system to bring it more in line with the practice in modern, developed nations.

Reforms Follow Increased Investment Despite numerous formal and informal barriers to foreign investment, the pace of international economic activity in China is intensifying. As if in response, the government recently embarked on a monumental liberalization program. In October 1992 the government of China announced its intention to switch from a centrally planned economy to one that is more decentralized and determined by market forces.

Leading the way to reform is Vice Premier Zhu Rongji, China's most influential policy planner. Zhu aims to reform China's institutions, so that officials of the central government will act less like micro managers and more like long-range policy planners. Reforms will target five key areas: banking, investment, the legal system, taxation, and privatization of state enterprises. Provincial and local officials will be responsible for the enforcement of regulations. Officials in existing Special Economic Zones and Free Trade Areas will have greater administrative autonomy.

But, like other large bureaucracies, China's government seems to be better at reacting to events than at guiding them. Economic activity (much of it international) has increased dramatically along China's coastal regions, especially in the southeastern provinces closest to Hong Kong and Taiwan, largely without official acknowledgment or adjustment.

Another positive development is the emergence of alternative importing and distribution channels. The giant Ministry of Materials and Equipment (see address below) which in the past was responsible for the allocatation of industrial products and raw materials accounting for a third of China's GNP, no longer plays such a dominant role. Instead, thousands of trading companies have formed since the early 1980s to import products and raw materials. As recently as 1986 more than 900 products and raw materials were subject to allocation and price controls. By 1992 the MOFTEC had cut that number to fewer than 80. Trading companies no longer need licenses to import most commodities, and they are largely free to buy and sell commodities at prices determined by the market. This development has opened a vast new distribution network directly to foreign suppliers.

Ministry of Materials and Equipment
25 Yuetanbei Jie, Xicheng Qu
Beijing 100834, China
Tel: [86] (1) 8021247, 8391108 Fax: [86] (1) 8391148
Tlx: 2001SSWUZIJCN

Overall, FIEs have significantly more managerial autonomy than do most Chinese enterprises. Chinese enterprises do enjoy certain advantages because they are patronized by local or national government officials, to whom they report. However, it is significant that the vast majority of Chinese state enterprises are anxious to form joint ventures, an indication that they see an opportunity for increased freedom in decision-making, not to mention potentially higher profit margins.

As old mechanisms of regulation and central planning are relaxed or dismantled, there is frequently no established system to take their place. Determining just who is in charge is becoming increasingly difficult. But while investing in China can be more confusing than it is elsewhere, the rewards can also be greater for those willing to take a risk.

LEADING INVESTORS

Many joint ventures or wholly foreign-owned firms operate manufacturing and assembly facilities that play a major role in China's growing foreign trade. Enterprises with foreign ownership were responsible for trade worth US$43.75 billion in 1992, an increase of 51 percent over the preceding year. This figure amounts to one-quarter of China's total volume of trade and one-fifth of the country's exports in 1992. By the end of 1992 China had approved a cumulative total of 84,771 FIEs. In that year along US$57.5 billion in direct foreign investment was contracted and US$11.6 billion was actually invested.

The vast majority (an estimated 80 percent) of direct foreign investments have been made by overseas Chinese, most of whom operate export-oriented firms in Hong Kong, Taiwan, and other countries, including the United States, in which there are significant concentrations of entrepreneurs of Chinese extraction. Hong Kong is the leading investor in China, with total cumulative investment amounting to US$10 billion at the end of 1992. The United States is the second largest official investor in China, with approximately US$8 billion by the end of 1992. Japan is now third, with investments of US$5.5 billion by the end of 1992, US$2.2 billion of which flowed into China in that year alone. Taiwan is the fourth largest investor, with US$4 billion. (Officially, Taiwan and China do not maintain trade relations. However, many Taiwanese operate out of Hong Kong, using Hong Kong front companies to conduct trade with the mainland.)

While past investments involved the exploitation of natural resources (mainly petroleum and coal) and property development (principally hotels catering to foreign visitors), most new investment has been in manufacturing ventures. Investments in high-tech industries and manufacturing firms geared to exports are encouraged. Conversely, investment in industries that produce low-tech consumer goods faces a mixed reception by Chinese officials. Much of the service sector remains highly restricted, but the situation appears to be changing.

INVESTMENT AND TRADE POLICY

Until the early 1980s, China had no stated policy on foreign investment and trade. Before that time, China's central government ministries and state-run enterprises exerted virtual monopoly control over the country's foreign trade. The little foreign investment that entered the country was permitted only for highly specific purposes: to acquire a new technology, ensure an adequate supply of capital and raw materials for domestic industries, and promote exports.

During the last decade, China has become increasingly open to foreign trade and investment, and interest in China as an investment destination has correspondingly grown, becoming especially pronounced in the early 1990s. The first areas in which investment was encouraged or tolerated included oil drilling and refining, coal mining, and property development, such as the building of hotels and resorts catering to foreign visitors. A surge of investment in labor-intensive manufacturing and assembly industries, such as textiles, apparel, footwear, and toys, followed.

While investment in labor-intensive industries is still common, China is more interested in developing such capital-intensive industries as telecommunications equipment and automobile manufacturing. But despite China's ongoing process of trade liberalization, the complex system of administrative controls and regulations affecting foreign investment and trade still reflects the time when the country was largely closed to the rest of the world. However, it is encouraging that China has recently signaled its intentions to carry out sweeping reforms in all sectors of business, trade, and investment.

Joint Ventures Establishment of a joint venture is the most common form of foreign investment in China. According to the Joint Venture Law of 1979, a foreign investor is limited to a maximum 25 percent of the total capital invested in a joint venture. But, as is often the case, the law has not kept pace with actual conditions. There are now many foreign investors with more than a 25 percent share in joint ventures, and the number of wholly foreign-owned enterprises is also increasing. The most common methods of investment take the form of cash, equipment, and introduction of new technologies, in such industries as telecommunications, transportation,

petroleum, coal, nonferrous metals, real estate, hotels, and restaurants.

In most cases, the Chinese partner in a joint venture handles dealings with government officials. There are five main steps in the establishment of a joint venture. First, submit a letter of application to the MOFTEC or its designate. Second, all parties concerned in the venture conduct a joint feasibility study and prepare a joint venture agreement. Next, three copies of the joint venture agreement and three copies in the foreign language are submitted to the MOFTEC, together with a contract signed by the parties. Fourth, prepare a list of the directors appointed by the parties to the venture identifying its chairman and vice chairman and each of the board members. Last, obtain a certificate of ratification from the local affiliate of the State Industry and Commerce Administration.

All joint ventures must be approved by the local government affiliate of the MOFTEC after the agreement is finalized. Within one month of gaining the MOFTEC's approval, the representatives of the joint venture must register with the local branch office of the State Administration for Industry and Commerce (SAIC). This agency reviews the joint venture and issues a business license.

Ministry of Foreign Trade & Economic Cooperation (MOFTEC)
2 Dongchangan Jie, Dongcheng Qu
Beijing 100731, PRC
Tel: [86] (1) 5198714, 5198322, 5198804
Fax: [86] (1) 5129568, 5198904 Tlx: 22168

State Administration for Industry and Commerce
8 Sanlihe Dong Lu, Xicheng Qu
Beijing 100833, PRC
Tel: [86] (1) 8031133, 8013300
Fax: [86] (1) 4914783, 8013394

Wholly Foreign-Owned Enterprises While China prefers that foreign investors form joint ventures, wholly foreign-owned ventures are becoming increasingly numerous. In the 1980s enterprises with 100 percent foreign ownership were allowed to set up operations only in Special Economic Zones. (*See* Investment Incentives.) But enactment of the Law on Enterprises Operated Exclusively with Foreign Capital makes it possible to set up a venture of this type in most parts of China. However, the law still requires such a venture to be export oriented and to employ advanced equipment and technology.

Chinese Trading Corporations When China began opening to foreign trade and investment at the beginning of the 1980s, the Chinese government established a limited number of trading corporations through which all imported and exported goods were channeled. The number of Chinese entities currently allowed to engage directly in foreign trade has mushroomed to nearly 8,000 by some counts.

Some of the most important trading corporations under the jurisdiction of the MOFTEC include the China National Textiles Import and Export Corporation (ChinaTex); China National Cereals, Oils, and Foodstuffs Import and Export Corporation (COFCO); China National Chemicals Import and Export Corporation (SinoChem); China National Machinery Import and Export Corporation (CMC); China National Light Industrial Products Import and Export Corporation (ChinaLight); China National Metals and Minerals Import and Export Corporation (MinMetals); China National Electronics Import and Export Corporation (CEIEC); China North Industries Corporation (Norinco); and China National Technical Import and Export Corporation (ChinaTech). (Refer to "Important Addresses" chapter for complete addresses.)

With the official announcement in October 1992 that China would begin to replace much of its central planning apparatus for market-oriented mechanisms, some 900 manufacturing companies have been granted authority to import and export products directly. The companies span several industries, including machinery, electronics, metallurgy, petrochemicals, light industry, and textiles. Whereas in the past only a few FIEs were granted direct trading rights, several hundred FIEs now have them.

In March 1993 more than 100 science and technology institutes were granted business licenses to conduct their own importing and exporting. This move is expected to benefit the development and promotion of advanced technologies, which currently account for less than 10 percent of China's total exports. It also creates an opportunity for foreign investors in various high-tech fields to pursue joint ventures with Chinese firms and research institutes.

New legislation is now under way that, if approved, could make trading rights available to thousands of enterprises, including FIEs. Eligible firms would include enterprises that have exported more than US$4 million per year for two consecutive years, enterprises that manufacture mechanical or electrical products with exports of more than US$175,000 per year for two consecutive years, high-tech enterprises with exports of more than US$175,000 for two consecutive years, and research oriented organizations with exports of more than US$500,000 per year for two consecutive years.

Eligible firms would apply to the MOFTEC in addition to the appropriate industrial ministry (machine building, electronics, and so forth) and to:

State Economic and Trade Commission
25 Yuetan North Street
Beijing 100834
Tel: [86] (1) 8392227 Fax: [86] (1) 8392222

As with so many of the other developments in China in recent years, observers are quick to point out that the gradual dispersion and decentralization of trading rights has been less a case of enlightened leadership than a matter of pressure from entrepreneurs, whose activity effectively presents the central government's with a fait accompli.

Export and Import Licensing In an effort to exercise strict control over all commodities that are either exported from or imported into China, the central government requires all trade to be channeled through licensed trading companies. The MOFTEC is responsible for issuing import and export licenses as well as general business licenses to trading companies. Foreign investors should make certain that a given Chinese trading company does in fact have a license to trade in a specific commodity, as there have been numerous cases in which officials at ports of entry or exit discover fake licenses and reject passage of a shipment. To make matters worse, local and provincial governments sometimes impose restrictions of their own on importing and exporting.

Generally, exporting is much easier than importing, given China's preference for export promotion. Originally 234 categories of commodities required their own export licenses or were subject to quota controls. In January 1993 the Chinese government cut the list by more than 50 percent to 138 categories. Commodities still requiring export licenses include corn, soybeans, tea, coal, crude oil, and refined oil.

Import licensing is a fairly complicated affair, as it is one of China's principal means of controlling imports. The Chinese government requires trading companies to have import licenses for commodities ranging from consumer goods to production equipment and raw materials. Additional restrictions, including quotas and outright bans on such products as computer hardware, televisions, and such building materials as aluminum doors and pane glass windows, are imposed on imported goods. However, late in 1992 the Chinese government committed itself to easing restrictions on at least two-thirds of all imported goods within two to three years.

Early in 1993 the Chinese government agreed to allow FIEs that manufacture export-oriented or high-tech products to import office equipment and some materials directly. These imports are also now exempt from import duties.

Compensation Trade China's enterprises often use a form of trade known as compensation trade. In exchange for advanced equipment and technology brought in by a foreign investor, the Chinese enterprise makes installment payments in finished products. In principal, the Chinese enterprises employ the imported equipment or technology to manufacture the products used as payment. Other products may be substituted if both parties have reached a prior agreement and if the MOFTEC gives its approval.

Service Barriers China's market has been all but closed to most foreign service industries, including banking, insurance, law, accounting, shipping, and provision of after-sales service. Foreign lawyers, accountants, bankers, and insurance agents must largely limit their activities to servicing foreign firms, and even then they must operate under the pretext of providing liaison between the firms and domestic service providers.

However, recent reforms have opened some service industries to foreign investment. Tourism-related services are relatively open. Negotiations between the United States and China concluded in 1991 permit American shipping companies to establish joint ventures in China and solicit cargo directly. China has opened the market to airlines by allowing two US carriers to add flights between the two countries. Retailing is also opening to foreign investment, as are banking and insurance. Over time, these and other major service industries are expected to open to foreign investment, but when and to what degree depend on the success of the reform efforts currently under way.

INVESTMENT INCENTIVES

China offers foreign investors a number of incentives. Many take the form of tax breaks and exemptions, reduced tariff rates, ease of entry and exit for foreign businesspeople, and relative autonomy in the management of overall business operations. To take advantage of such incentives, an investor must usually become a partner in a joint venture or establish his own operations in one of the designated commercial zones. However, these conditions are becoming less relevant as China continues to liberalize its economy.

Special Economic Zones Beginning in 1980 the Chinese government established five Special Economic Zones in Shenzhen, Zhuhai, and Shantou in Guangdong Province; on the entire island Province of Hainan; and in Xiamen in Fujian Province. In 1984 the government opened the following 14 additional cities to foreign investment (from north to south): Qinhuangdao, Dalian, Tianjin, Yantai, Qingdao, Lianyungang, Nantong, Shanghai, Ningbo, Wenzhou, Fuzhou, Guangzhou, Beihai, and Zhanjiang. Special economic zones are relatively independent administrative units that are largely free from central government control. As a result, they are able to adapt relatively quickly to changing economic conditions.

The 19 special zones are meant to serve a variety of purposes: attract foreign investment, import advanced technology, keep current with trends in international markets, expand export trade, increase foreign exchange earnings, and provide a training ground for scientific and technical personnel. In 1992 the total value of imports to and exports from the original five Special Economic Zones amounted to US$24.3 billion and accounted for 14.7 percent of the total value of China's trade.

Special economic zones offer foreign investors a variety of incentives:

- Manufacturing companies in Special Economic Zones pay an enterprise tax of just 15 percent, and they may be exempt from paying any tax after 10 years of continuous operation.

- Foreign investors in the zones do not have to pay income tax on the portion of their profits that they remit abroad.

- Foreign firms or individuals without operations in China who collect share dividends, interest, rents, royalty fees, or other income originating from such zones have their income tax reduced to 10 percent.

- All enterprises within such zones are exempt from consolidated industrial and commercial taxes on building materials, production equipment, raw materials, parts and components, transportation vehicles, and office equipment imported for their own use.

- With the exception of some export products restricted by the state, all export products manufactured by enterprises in the economic zones are exempt from export customs duties.

- Foreign investors as well as foreign staff and technicians are exempt from customs duties on household goods and personal vehicles imported for their own use within reason.

- Export-oriented enterprises and enterprises employing advanced technologies in the zones are given the same priority treatment in the supply of water, power, and transportation and communication services that domestic, state-run enterprises enjoy.

New Development Zones The Pudong New Development Zone is a 350 square km (135 square miles) area located on the eastern bank of the Huangpu River opposite Shanghai. The zone is designed to turn Pudong into a shipping and receiving center for the economic activity of the cities further up the Yangtze River. The Pudong Zone should also help promote Shanghai as an international finance and trade center. (Shanghai is currently home to China's largest stock market.) In addition to offering most of the preferential treatment granted enterprises in the Special Economic Zones, the Pudong Zone allows foreign businesspeople to open such establishments as financial institutions, department stores, supermarkets, and other service enterprises.

The Yangpu Development Zone, which covers a 30 square km (11.5 square miles) area in the north-

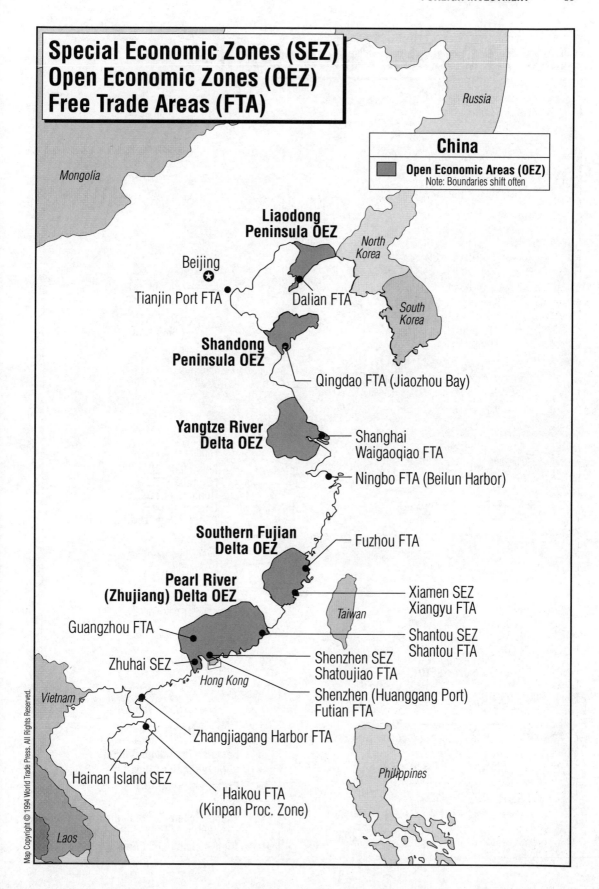

Special Economic Zones (SEZ)
Open Economic Zones (OEZ)
Free Trade Areas (FTA)

Russia

Mongolia

China

Open Economic Areas (OEZ)
Note: Boundaries shift often

Liaodong Peninsula OEZ

North Korea

Beijing

Tianjin Port FTA — Dalian FTA

South Korea

Shandong Peninsula OEZ

Qingdao FTA (Jiaozhou Bay)

Yangtze River Delta OEZ

Shanghai Waigaoqiao FTA

Ningbo FTA (Beilun Harbor)

Southern Fujian Delta OEZ — Fuzhou FTA

Pearl River (Zhujiang) Delta OEZ

Xiamen SEZ
Xiangyu FTA

Taiwan

Guangzhou FTA

Shantou SEZ
Shantou FTA

Zhuhai SEZ

Shenzhen SEZ
Shatoujiao FTA

Hong Kong

Shenzhen (Huanggang Port)
Futian FTA

Vietnam

Zhangjiagang Harbor FTA

Philippines

Hainan Island SEZ

Haikou FTA
(Kinpan Proc. Zone)

Laos

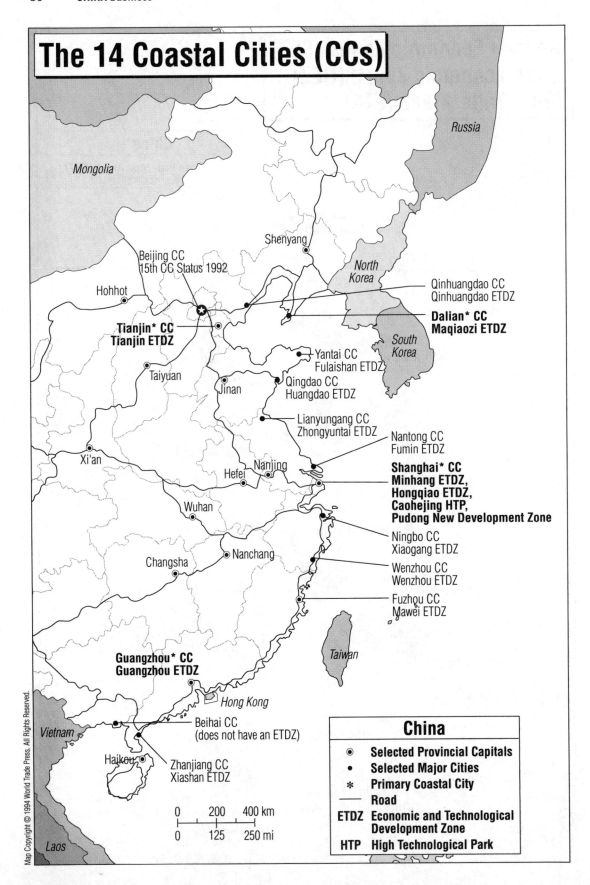

The 14 Coastal Cities (CCs)

Russia

Mongolia

Shenyang

North Korea

Beijing CC
15th CC Status 1992

Hohhot

Qinhuangdao CC
Qinhuangdao ETDZ

Tianjin* CC
Tianjin ETDZ

Dalian* CC
Maqiaozi ETDZ

South Korea

Taiyuan

Yantai CC
Fulaishan ETDZ

Jinan

Qingdao CC
Huangdao ETDZ

Lianyungang CC
Zhongyuntai ETDZ

Nantong CC
Fumin ETDZ

Xi'an

Nanjing

Hefei

Shanghai* CC
Minhang ETDZ,
Hongqiao ETDZ,
Caohejing HTP,
Pudong New Development Zone

Wuhan

Ningbo CC
Xiaogang ETDZ

Nanchang

Wenzhou CC
Wenzhou ETDZ

Changsha

Fuzhou CC
Mawei ETDZ

Taiwan

Guangzhou* CC
Guangzhou ETDZ

Hong Kong

Beihai CC
(does not have an ETDZ)

Vietnam

Haikou

Zhanjiang CC
Xiashan ETDZ

China	
⊙	**Selected Provincial Capitals**
•	**Selected Major Cities**
✳	**Primary Coastal City**
—	**Road**
ETDZ	**Economic and Technological Development Zone**
HTP	**High Technological Park**

0   200   400 km
0   125   250 mi

Laos

west of Hainan Island (China's southernmost territory), is intended to become an important center for international freight transport. It has a deepwater harbor, and it is close to international shipping lanes. The Hainan provincial government began development of the zone in mid-1993, and is committed to offering large parcels of land to investors along with comprehensive incentive packages. Economic policies in the Yangpu Zone are expected to resemble those of free ports in other countries.

Free Trade Areas Between 1990 and 1992 China established 13 Free Trade Areas ranging in size from 5 square km (2 square miles) to 0.2 square km (.08 square miles). These areas are designed specifically for export processing, and the tariffs and customs duties imposed on goods processed there are minimal. Enterprises operating in these areas have extensive autonomy with respect to management of operations, importing, and exporting. Nearly 1,000 enterprises had entered the Free Trade Areas, investing US$2 billion by the end of 1992, half of the amount coming from foreign investors. The Free Trade Areas are located near China's major coastal cities and extend the entire length of the country's coast.

Free Trade Areas have been established in Waiguoqiao (Shanghai), Tianjin, Dalian, Shatoujiao and Futian (Shenzhen), Guangzhou, Zhangjiagang, Haikou, Qingdao, Ningbo, Fuzhou, Xiangu (Xiamen), and Shantou. (Refer to "Marketing" chapter for greater detail on China's special zones.)

CHINA'S IMPORT PAYMENT PRACTICES

The provision of loans and credit in China is largely dominated by the state-owned banks. Some Chinese trust and investment corporations also provide project financing. Specialized and comprehensive banks are organized under China's central bank. One of the specialized banks, the Bank of China (BOC), is China's main foreign exchange bank. In the past, the BOC had sole authority to issue letters of credit (L/Cs). But in recent years, all the other specialized banks, and a number of other financial institutions, such as the Industrial and Commercial Bank of China (ICBC), have also been granted authority to issue L/Cs. Imports into China often require import licenses and approval to spend foreign exchange. However, if the BOC or another state-owned bank issues an L/C, the foreign seller can usually be assured that the importer has obtained the necessary approvals.

For most L/Cs, the foreign exporter receives payment from the Chinese bank only after it has obtained the export documents. Obtaining the documents usually requires that the foreign exporter wait 10 to 20 days before collecting payment for goods delivered. Typically, an exporter arranges for all export documents to be shipped to the BOC and then waits for the BOC and the importer to review the documents before being paid.

Even with these terms of payment, L/Cs remain the preferred payment mechanism for exports to China, since they follow standardized practice. Although China is not a member of the International Chamber of Commerce, PRC banks generally treat L/Cs as subject to its Uniform Customs and Practices. In addition, Chinese banks usually require cash or some other form of collateral from the importer.

Letters of guarantee (L/Gs) from Chinese banks to back up importer obligations are also fairly common. They are considered much weaker than L/Cs for several reasons: First, the terms of L/Gs vary considerably and often include ambiguous references to underlying contract terms or penalties and deductions. Second, L/Gs are not usually governed by the International Chamber of Commerce Uniform Customs and Practices or other international guidelines. Third, L/Gs are understood to be secondary obligations of the issuer under Chinese law. Lastly, Chinese banks do not always require collateral from importers for L/Gs. Nevertheless, L/Gs are commonly offered for transactions involving payment extending over one year or more and by importers who do not wish to encumber their cash or credit lines by issuing L/Cs.

Open account terms are also used for shipments to China, usually by companies with long-standing relationships with Chinese entities. Both Western and Chinese banks lack power to enforce prompt payment to importers for open account transactions.

Another Chinese payment practice affects large sales of equipment and technology to China. For such sales, Chinese buyers typically make a 10 to 25 percent down payment, then pay 70 to 75 percent on delivery and the remainder on installation. However, at the time of the initial down payment, Chinese buyers often require a standby letter of credit from the seller's bank guaranteeing that the down payment will be returned if sales terms are not met. A problem arises when a foreign exporter does not have a credit line sufficient to issue the required standby L/C. However, this special provision does not usually apply to sales of commodities or to sales of simple goods.

LOANS AND CREDIT AVAILABILITY

Other important lenders for foreign investors in China are the World Bank, the Asian Development Bank, and the Overseas Economic Cooperation Fund (Japan's economic assistance program). These organizations all require international competitive bidding. Foreign investors have won important contracts on projects financed by these donors.

Chinese buyers also look to tied soft loans and mixed credits to help finance their purchases. Here, US exporters often find themselves at a serious disadvantage with exporters from Europe and Canada, who are sometimes able to use attractive loan packages offered by their own governments. However, under the terms of an agreement which became effective in October 1992 among the members of the Organization for Economic Cooperation and Development (OECD), such loans will be offered only for projects that are not considered to be commercially viable, such as the construction of major roads or bridges.

USEFUL ADDRESSES

In addition to the organizations listed here, individuals and firms should contact other government agencies with special jurisdiction, embassies, banks and financial service centers, local consultants, lawyers, and resident foreign businesses for assistance and information (Refer to "Important Addresses" chapter for a more complete listing.)

People's Bank of China
32 Chengfang Street
Beijing 100800
Tel: [86] (1) 6016491, 6016722 Fax: [86] (1) 6016724

Bank of China
Bank of China Building
410 Fuchengmen Nei Dajie
Beijing 100818, PRC
Tel: [86] (1) 6016688 Fax: [86] (1) 6016869
Tlx: 22254

China International Trust and Investment
Corporation
19 Jian Guo Men Wai Dajie
Beijing 100004, PRC
Tel: [86] (1) 5002255, 5122233
Fax: [86] (1) 5001535, 5004851 Tlx: 22305

China Investment Bank
B-11 Fuxing Lu
Beijing 100859, PRC
Tel: [86] (1) 8015900 Fax: [86] (1) 8016088
Tlx: 22537

Industrial and Commercial Bank
13 Cuiwei Lu, Haidian Qu
Beijing 10036, PRC
Tel: [86] (1) 8217273 Fax: [86] (1) 8217920
Tlx: 22770

Foreign Trade

The People's Republic of China (PRC) has the largest population in the world, the third-largest territory, and some of the world's largest reserves of many key natural resources. For much of its history China has been inwardly focused, doing its best not merely to maintain self-sufficiency and limit trade with the rest of the world but to essentially deny the existence of that world. All that has changed since the PRC instituted its open-door policy in 1978 in an attempt to bring its economy into the 20th century. Since then international trade has grown by leaps and bounds, surging more than 700 percent between 1978 and 1992 for an average annual growth rate of 16 percent in nominal terms. China was the eleventh-largest trading economy in the world in 1992, up from fifteenth in 1991, and seventeenth in 1982.

China's trade is highly controlled and highly focused, designed primarily to acquire and conserve as much foreign exchange as possible, while securing the maximum in critical capital goods and technology at a minimum cost. Chinese traders have been known to buy high and sell low in order to fulfill the goal of getting foreign exchange. However, foreign traders should not expect to be able to take advantage of such manipulations. The Chinese are extremely tough negotiators, and they usually focus—often with a great deal of success—on getting the most for the least. The alleviation of production shortages and bottlenecks is a secondary aim of Chinese trade, with the provision of consumer and other nonessential goods falling a distant and heavily discouraged third. Nevertheless, as China's window on the rest of the world and its primary means of modernizing its economy, trade is extremely dynamic and fraught with possibilities.

SIZE OF CHINA'S TRADE

In 1992 total trade was US$165.6 billion, representing 40 percent of China's gross national product (GNP). By comparison, trade represents about 15.2 percent of Japan's economy, 17.5 percent of that of the United States, 54 percent of South Korea's, 76.9 percent of Taiwan's, and 246 percent of Hong Kong's economy. The Chinese figure indicates both how important trade is to China as well as how massive the rest of China's economy is in comparison with the domestic economies of neighboring Korea, Taiwan, and Hong Kong.

Although trade is becoming important throughout China, nowhere is it more important than in the southeast, particularly in Guangdong Province. In 1992 Guangdong's total trade was US$29.6 billion. This figure is considered to understate Guangdong's trade by perhaps one-third, because it ignores direct foreign invested enterprise transfers and the province's booming illicit trade. Nevertheless, the official figure represents almost 18 percent of China's total trade as well as about 22 percent of all exports and 13 percent of all imports. At current growth rates, 31.8 percent for exports and 25 percent for imports in 1992, Guangdong could account for half of all of China's trade by the year 2010.

EXPORTS AND IMPORTS

In 1991 China's leading export, apparel, accounted for 12.5 percent of total exports. This was followed by textiles (an additional 11.1 percent), foodstuffs (9.7 percent), machinery and transportation equipment (9.7 percent), fuels (7 percent), metal products (5.6 percent), chemicals (5.6 percent), and raw materials excluding fuels (4.2 percent). Together these eight categories accounted for 65.4 percent, or two-thirds, of all exports. In the same year machinery and transportation equipment led imports with a 31.3 percent share, followed by chemicals (14.1 percent), raw materials excluding fuels (7.8 percent), textiles (6.3 percent), foodstuffs (4.7 percent), iron and steel (4.7 percent), and fuels (3.1 percent). Together these categories represented 72 percent of imports, with remaining categories each accounting for less than 3 percent of the total.

During the first six months of 1993 total trade

Leading Importers from China (in US$ millions, 1992 monthly average)

Hong Kong

Clothing	$645
Machinery, incl. electric	610
Textile yarn, cloth & manufactures	386
Toys	203
Travel goods	139

United States

Clothing	$461
Machinery, incl. electric	344
Toys	329
Footwear	299
Travel goods	97

Japan

Clothing	$317
Petroleum products	148
Textile, yarn, cloth & manufactures	81
Fruit & vegetables	69
Machinery, incl. electric	63

Germany

Clothing	$183
Machinery, incl. electric	87
Toys	37
Travel goods	32
Footwear	31

Source: Foreign Trade Magazine

Leading Exporters to China (in US$ millions, 1992 monthly average)

Hong Kong

Machinery, incl. electric	$604
Textile yarn, cloth & manufactures	465
Plastic materials	188
Scientific instruments	112
Transport equipment	63

Japan

Machinery, incl. electric	$360
Iron & steel	117
Transport equipment	62
Textile yarn, cloth & manufactures	57
Chemical elements & compounds	33

United States

Transport equipment	$153
Machinery, incl. electric	125
Fertilizers, manufactured	54
Cereals & preparations	28
Scientific instruments	27

Germany

Machinery, incl. electric	$137
Transport equipment	65
Iron & steel	18
Chemical elements & compounds	9
Scientific instruments	9

Source: Foreign Trade Magazine

was US$77.8 billion, up 13.4 percent from the same period a year earlier. However, exports were up an anemic 4.4 percent to US$37.2 billion, while imports surged 23.2 percent to US$40.7 billion. Preliminary full-year figures for 1993 show total trade of US$196 billion, up 18.4 percent. However, exports were up only 8.2 percent to US$92 billion, while imports surged to US$104 billion, a rise of 29 percent. The rise in imports is nearly double the 15.4 percent annual rise imports posted between 1978 and 1992. The stall in export growth is cause for concern, given the fact that exports, which are necessary to fund imports, grew at an annual average rate of 16.7 percent from 1978 through 1992 double 1993's rate.

During the first half of 1993 China increased its imports of construction materials, especially steel, oil, textile machinery, automobiles, metalworking machinery, aircraft, and videotapes as well as other "luxury" consumer goods. It reduced its demand for outside sugar, rubber, lumber, pulp and paper, cotton, synthetic fabrics, and fertilizers—which bodes ill for growth because many of those items represent raw materials needed to fuel fixture productions.

China also increased its exports of machinery, electronics products, apparel, footwear, plastics, toys, and certain agricultural commodities such as sugar and tea. However, export growth was not enough to balance growth in imports.

Not only has China's trade been growing in volume, but it has also been growing in the general sophistication of its products. In 1978 finished goods represented 46.5 percent of Chinese exports, with the remainder representing primarily agricultural commodities and raw materials. By 1992 higher-value-added finished goods had risen to 79.9 percent of exports, with a corresponding drop in exports of low-value bulk commodities. Since 1978 capital goods have consistently accounted for around 80 percent of all imports by design.

China is in an uncomfortable position in that it needs to maintain a high level of imports to avoid strangling its economic growth. Although some technocrats want to rein in the rate of growth, top leadership has insisted that the economy remain on the fast track. But China must also increase its exports to be able to afford the necessary imports, and officials have called for exports to reach US$100 billion in 1994, a jump of around 17.5 percent. China's jerry-rigged production system could easily be derailed by even a relatively slight misstep in this balancing act. Indeed, some observers argue that China's mid-1993 austerity program, designed to keep the economy from overheating, short-circuited production and resulted in the drop in products available for export (however, others maintain that domestic market inefficiencies are more to blame for the lack of exports).

An example of this complex balancing act is found in China's oil industry and trading situation. China is the world's fifth-largest oil producer and has been a substantial exporter of crude petroleum. It expects to export 140 million barrels mostly of crude oil in 1993, down from 150 million barrels in 1992, reducing the foreign exchange contribution from the industry. At the same time, it expects to import 110 million barrels, mostly of more costly refined petroleum products, up from 90 million barrels in 1992. The growth in China's economy is such that it is consuming more of its production domestically, with demand expected to equal production as early as next year and surpass it thereafter. Not only will China have to forego foreign exchange from export sales of crude, but it will also have to spend precious foreign exchange on increased imports of higher-cost refined fuels, while at the same time investing in new

production, transport, and refining capacity just to keep up with demand.

SOLVING EXPORT PROBLEMS

China's plans to promote its exports face several hurdles. The main one is China's inconvertible and artificially valued currency. At the end of 1993 the Chinese announced that the renminbi would be valued through a managed float beginning in January 1994, thus bringing its value more into line with that of other world currencies (and resulting in an effective devaluation of about 50 percent). Although China has also stated that it will allow limited convertibility sometime in 1994, foreign exchange restrictions and scarcity should continue to be a problem for the economy in general and for trade in particular.

Because of the roadblocks to traditional buying and selling represented by China's lack of an open trading system and the foreign exchange to operate one, Chinese and foreign traders have developed elaborate and evolving systems to get around these difficulties. These arrangements include various forms of countertrade, compensation trade, and processing and assembly agreements.

COUNTERTRADE AND OTHER ARRANGEMENTS

Countertrade allows payments to be made in goods and services rather than in cash but requires offsetting purchases (that is, there is no purchase without an equivalent sale). Variations include counterpurchase, in which the sales and purchases are separate but linked by a contractual understanding; co-production, in which one party—usually the foreigner—provides management expertise or other

Hong Kong's Re-exports to China* (in US$ millions)			
Commodity	**1992**	**1991**	**% change**
Textile yarns, fabrics & related products	$5,526	$4,582	20%
Telecommunications parts & equipment	997	773	28
Textile & leather machinery	739	442	67
Thermionic, cold cathode & photocathode valves; transistors & semiconductors	634	555	14
Leather	633	444	42
Polymers of styrene	582	500	16
Oil	575	459	25
Paper & paperboard	566	425	33
Automobiles	540	190	183

* Goods sent to China through Hong Kong by third countries   *Source: Foreign Trade Magazine*

China's Exports by Commodity
(in $US billions)

Commodity	1991	1990	% change
Garments	$9	$7	29%
Textiles	8	7	14
Food & live animals	7	7	0
Machinery & transport equipment	7	6	17
Mineral fuels & oil	5	5	0
Metal products	4	3	33
Chemicals	4	4	0
Crude materials, except fuels	3	4	- 25
Others	25	20	25
Total, including Others	$72	$62	16%

Source: Foreign Trade Magazine (note: rounded to nearest billion)

critical inputs needed to produce goods which are then shared; barter, which is a direct swap and usually conducted in commodities on a government-to-government basis; switch, in which goods received in payment are consigned to a third party for other goods or for sale for cash proceeds; and evidence accounts, a sort of running tab in which sales and purchases by the parties are expected to balance out over a specified period at agreed-upon levels.

Compensation trade involves the delivery of goods, usually capital goods, that are used to produce items, a portion of which are assigned to the original seller of the equipment as payment. Processing and assembly agreements involve the renting of a Chinese factory by a foreign entity to produce goods to specification. The foreigner supplies the specifications and may or may not supply materials, while the Chinese usually supply the facility, power, and labor. The foreigner pays the costs and a processing fee, resulting in a savings based on lower labor and overhead costs, and takes the manufactured products. Many operations in southeast China function on this basis, serving foreign entities based in Hong Kong.

Although these types of arrangements avoid the problem of hard cash, they have been used relatively little because of difficulties in arriving at mutually agreeable valuations and conditions for what each party gives and receives. The government has not encouraged the wider development of such deals because it does not want to lose out on foreign exchange from outright sales. Nor has it been willing to give up to foreigners desirable goods that are in demand, especially if it will subsequently have to compete with those foreigners in either domestic or international markets. Given these limitations, relatively few foreigners have been able to negotiate deals that satisfy their needs or provide the necessary profit margins. As both parties develop more expertise, such arrangements can be expected to become more common and more mutually acceptable.

OPENING OF TRADE

Trade has been an official monopoly that could only be conducted through Chinese foreign trade corporations (FTCs). More than 35 of these organizations exist, each responsible for a specific product line and industry. Traditionally, Chinese producers were not allowed to deal directly with foreigners, and all trade was negotiated through the FTCs. This practice allowed the FTCs to develop fairly high levels of expertise, exercise monopoly power, and serve government policy goals. Beginning in the early 1980s major producers and other entities were allowed to cut their own deals directly without reference to the FTCs, which were put in direct competition with the factories themselves. This situation led to loss of face by FTC personnel, anarchy, and an outflow of foreign exchange, so that the system was recentralized. However, since 1987 more and more entities have been allowed to trade directly; currently more than 8,000 entities are authorized to deal directly with foreigners.

These include all FIEs, nearly 6,000 FTCs and their subsidiaries, nearly 840 large- and medium-sized enterprises, 100 scientific institutes, and 300 specialized FTCs operating directly under the MOFTEC. There are also plans to form new product area specialized enterprise groups which would function somewhat like cooperative marketing units.

Although many entities are authorized to deal directly in foreign trade, the degree to which they actually do so varies widely. Many of the larger enterprises have become fairly aggressive, opening overseas trading offices, while most smaller entities have so far continued to rely on existing FTCs.

In an effort to boost exports and corporate development, officials, especially in Guangdong, have been trying to convert certain large export-producing companies into independent, vertically integrated trading companies that would handle virtually all aspects of operations from importing inputs to producing goods to cutting export deals. Eventually, these entities could be expected to serve as intermediaries for other operations and to provide some financing, functioning somewhat as Japanese trading companies do.

EXPORT AND IMPORT CONTROLS

Export licenses are required, primarily for commodities rather than for finished goods, and some exports are subject to quotas. Chinese quotas, mainly on food exports to Hong Kong, are designed primarily as price-regulating measures. Others, such as those for textiles, are set by foreign governments. Central plan quotas determine what projects can be undertaken internally: no imports of outside items and no production of items for export can be undertaken unless the operations are found to be within economic plan guidelines and have received specific authorization. Once the authorized amount of plan items has been produced, new projects will be disallowed.

China still strictly controls its imports, although, as part of its attempts to join the General Agreement on Tariffs and Trade (GATT), it has begun lowering some of its more outrageous duties on industrial and some consumer goods. At the end of 1993 China temporarily reduced its import duties to offset the jump in prices caused by the devaluation as well as to comply with GATT prescriptions. However, observ-

ers expect that although nominal tariffs will fall, additional levies will continue to control imports by keeping the cost of many items—such as cars, which are subject to duties of 150 percent under the new system—at prohibitive levels.

TRADE REGULATION AND PROMOTION

Chinese contract law as it applies to trade is poorly developed, and many foreign businesspeople consider contracts to be unenforceable. In addition, separate rules for domestic and foreign contracting parties exist. Contracts involving foreign parties are subject to official review and authorization and can be abrogated at any time on the grounds of incompatibility with official policy, an extremely broad and discretionary criterion. However, in most cases actual practice is more accommodating, and most parties are interested in making the deal work once they understand what the needs of the other party are.

China's trade is regulated by the Ministry of Foreign Trade and Economic Cooperation (MOFTEC). Formerly known as the Ministry of Foreign Economic Relations and Trade (MOFERT), it is the ultimate authority responsible for trade, although it has usually delegated most day-to-day operations to either its local branches or the FTCs. Under the new system, MOFTEC is even less directly involved except at the policy level.

China has two official agencies designed specifically to promote trade in particular and business in general, although neither is involved in substantive business activities. The China Council for the Promotion of International Trade (CCPIT), founded in 1952, is mainly involved in organizing trade fairs and international exhibits and conferences. The All China Federation of Industry and Commerce (ACFIC) was

China's Imports by Commodity (in US$ billions)			
Commodity	**1991**	**1990**	**% change**
Machinery & transport equipment	$20	$17	18%
Chemicals	9	7	29
Crude materials, except fuel	5	4	25
Textiles	4	3	33
Food & live animals	3	3	0
Iron & steel	3	3	0
Mineral fuels & oil	2	1	100
Other	19	16	19
Total, including Others	$64	$53	21%

Source: Foreign Trade Magazine (note: rounded to nearest billion)

China's Leading Trade Partners

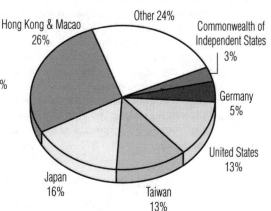

Exports - 1991

Other 21%
Commonwealth Of Independent States 3%
Hong Kong 44%
Singapore 3%
South Korea 3%
Germany 3%
United States 9%
Japan 14%

Total 1991 Exports: US$ 71.9 Billion

Source: Singapore Trade Connection
note: figures rounded to nearest whole percent

Imports - 1991

Hong Kong & Macao 26%
Other 24%
Commonwealth of Independent States 3%
Germany 5%
United States 13%
Japan 16%
Taiwan 13%

Total 1991 Imports: US$ 63.8 Billion

formed in 1953 and acts essentially as a chamber of commerce. It advises on policy and disseminates information on business practices.

LIMITS TO TRADE

China's trade-related infrastructure—transport, storage, distribution, and other systems—is woefully inadequate. This problem, as much as official restrictions, has limited the effective expansion of trade, keeping it within a few coastal areas. However, as those areas become overcrowded and trade develops, more activity can be expected in the vast hinterlands.

Even more limiting than geography and facilities is the lack of expertise. There are not enough experienced and qualified personnel to go around. As with virtually everything else in China, the trade system is in flux, and the participants are to a greater or lesser extent making things up as they go along. This practice adds a considerable element of uncertainty and greater inefficiency as many Chinese previously unfamiliar with foreigners, trade norms and procedures, or the negotiating process try to come up to speed. Moreover, the increasing number of Chinese entities eligible to deal directly with foreigners means that they are not only learning the ropes of such dealings, but also how to compete appropriately with each other for business. In many respects, the situation can only be described as anarchic.

BALANCE OF TRADE

China expects to register its first trade deficit in four years in 1993, at a time when its economy is experiencing difficulties, exacerbated by a growth rate of 13 percent. With few exceptions, China's insatiable needs and relatively primitive industry have led it to import more than it exported since it began to open up in 1978. Following the austerity crackdown in 1989 and the devaluation of the renminbi in 1990, China was able to book trade surpluses in 1990, 1991, and 1992.

The austerity crackdown in mid-1993 set back production, although it did little to interrupt imports that were already in the pipeline. Even though production was reportedly booming by year-end, China's export engine still has a lot of catching up to do. The January 1994 devaluation should help Chinese export competitiveness; however, the country may not be in a position to record a surplus for some time in the future.

INTERNATIONAL RESERVE POSITION

At the end of September 1993 China's international reserves stood at US$41.4 billion, down about 8 percent from the peak of US$45 billion registered at year-end 1992. China is trying to formalize its financial system to attract private savings, much of it held in hard currencies either as cash at home or in bank accounts abroad, into the formal sector in an effort to tap such reserves to shore up its burdened economy. China's international credit rating is not among the highest, and, as its economy suffers sharp swings, the government has had to raid hard currency reserves to support imports and to underwrite budget deficits at home. It has few means of replenishing such foreign currency reserves.

TRADE PARTNERS

Hong Kong has long been China's primary trading partner, taking 44.7 percent of its exports and providing 27.4 percent of its imports in 1991. In 1992 exports to Hong Kong dropped slightly to 44 percent, while imports from the colony fell to 25 percent, an indication of China's expanding international economy. China earns somewhere between 30 and 40 percent of its foreign exchange through Hong Kong, which serves as its entrepôt. Very few of the goods moving between China and the colony either originate or stay in Hong Kong.

Japan is China's next-largest trading partner. In 1991 Japan took 14.3 percent of China's exports and provided 15.7 percent of its imports. In 1992 exports to Japan fell to 14 percent of the total, while imports from Japan rose to 17 percent. China's third largest trading partner is the United States. In 1991 the United States took 8.6 percent of Chinese exports and sold China 12.6 percent of its imports. In 1992 the United States stepped up its purchases to take 10 percent of exports, while dropping its sales to 11 percent of imports.

In 1991 these top three trading partners accounted for 67.6 percent of all of China's exports, while providing 55.7 percent of all of its imports. In 1992 exports to the big three rose slightly to 68 percent, while imports from them fell somewhat to 53 percent.

Among second-tier trading partners, Germany took 3.3 percent of exports in 1991, followed by South Korea with 3 percent, Singapore (2.8 percent), and the former Soviet Union (2.5 percent). The remaining 20 percent plus of exports went to countries that each took less than 2.5 percent of China's total exports.

Taiwan was credited as the source of 12.5 percent of China's imports in 1991, an amount roughly equal to that of the United States, although Taiwan considers trade with the PRC illegal. Much of the Taiwanese trade with China is disguised through Hong Kong intermediaries. China trade is estimated to account for around 10 percent of Taiwan's total trade, and Taiwan is China's fourth-largest trading partner.

Following Taiwan on the import side is Germany with 4.8 percent of imports and the former Soviet Union with 3.3 percent. The remaining 23.6 percent of 1991 imports came from countries that each sold less than 3.3 percent of the total to China.

China's goal is to diversify its trade. It has particularly targeted the former Soviet Union, Southeast Asia, the Middle East, and Africa. To this end it maintains trade and diplomatic relations with more than

Hong Kong–Chinese Reexports			
(in US$ billions)			
	1992	**1991**	**% change**
reexports from China	$52.2	$40.6	28%
reexports to China	$27.4	$19.7	39%
Source: Foreign Trade Magazine			

221 countries and has overseas trade subsidiaries in 120 countries and trade missions in more than 200. China joined the United Nations in 1971. It holds a permanent seat on the Security Council and is a member of most UN agencies. China reapplied for membership in GATT in 1992 and has been working to adjust its tariffs and trade policies in order to meet GATT eligibility requirements. China has backed off somewhat from its earlier strident role among the developing nations, although it is moving to strengthen its position among Asian nations. In particular, it has become active in such regional economic and trade organizations as the Asia Pacific Economic Cooperation group.

EXTERNAL RELATIONS AFFECTING TRADE

Relations with Hong Kong, or rather with Great Britain, Hong Kong's master until 1997, have turned frosty. China has threatened to nullify contracts negotiated under the British, which could have a negative effect on foreign business funneled through Hong Kong, although there is as yet no indication that trade is being affected.

China and the United States have also had brittle relations over human rights issues, the transfer to third parties of restricted US technology, especially military technology, Chinese shipments of goods through third countries to avoid quotas, inadequate protection for intellectual property, and trade barriers that have resulted in a large trade surplus with the United States. The United States has threatened to revoke China's Most Favored Nation (MFN) status over these contretemps. Although China has downplayed the importance of such a move, it clearly would damage China's still-fragile trading economy and devastate Hong Kong. At the end of 1993 China announced that it would drop a range of import restrictions. However, it simultaneously announced a new set of restrictive rules governing imports of such items as machinery, equipment, and electronics.

In early 1994 the United States announced that it was lowering China's quotas for apparel by as much as 35 percent for some products because of alleged shipments through third countries. China immediately threatened retaliatory limits on US products. Some observers suggest that the move was an attempt to force China to stop dragging its feet on new quota negotiations and that the penalties were likely to be reversed. China ultimately agreed to some restraints on third party shipments and intellectual property safeguards, while still protesting its innocence and need to protect its sovereignty. At the same time there were indications that the United States might deny China MFN status over human rights concerns, a move that could raise duties on Chinese goods from around 8 percent to 40 percent and would be a severe setback to China's growing trade economy.

Import Policy & Procedures

INTRODUCTION

In October 1992, China agreed to reform significant parts of its import regime. Among the reforms are a substantial reduction of import tariffs on virtually all commodities, the elimination of import licensing requirements on most categories of goods, and an end to multiple, overlapping nontariff barriers used to limit imports. These reforms are to become effective December 31, 1993, but in all likelihood they will be phased in over time. Thus, importing into China is likely to continue being a complicated affair, although the reforms promise foreign suppliers much greater access to China's market.

Other changes are also improving the prospects for foreign exporters and for firms in China that wish to import. Whereas in the past only a limited number of approved foreign trade corporations were allowed to import goods and services, now thousands of factories and companies have substantial freedom to decide what they will purchase from abroad. However, most enterprises must still obtain permission to import from the government or foreign trade companies, and then they must work through a Chinese intermediary, such as an approved foreign trade corporation or other tendering company. (In the future, foreign suppliers will be able to deal directly with China-based enterprises, without an intermediary.) Many enterprises have been newly authorized to handle foreign trade, and foreign exporters should be careful to check the credibility of their Chinese intermediary.

The following chapter discusses China's import policy and procedures. This information is useful for people who want to sell goods and services to China, for those who establish manufacturing facilities or other operations in China, and for foreign investors. (Refer to "Marketing" chapter for information on selling in China.)

REGULATORY AUTHORITY

The Ministry of Foreign Trade and Economic Cooperation (MOFTEC) in Beijing (formerly known as the Ministry of Foreign Economic Relations and Trade, or MOFERT) formulates and implements the PRC's foreign trade policy. The trend is toward greater decentralization of foreign trade, with industrial ministries and local and provincial enterprises establishing import and export corporations authorized to conduct technical and commercial transactions with foreign firms. Some factories are allowed direct contact with foreign firms; they have authority to negotiate sales contracts directly and are responsible for their own profits and losses. Nevertheless, most foreign trade is carried out by MOFTEC-approved national foreign trade corporations (FTCs). MOFTEC also develops an annual import plan that determines what may and may not be imported, and it issues the required import and export licenses. The State Planning Commission, the State Council's Machinery and Electronics Coordination Office, and the State Economic and Trade Commission also administer certain nontariff barriers at central and provincial levels. However, only about 20 percent of total imports are now specifically planned. These primarily involve raw materials, such as cotton, grain, fertilizer, timber, and iron ore.

Foreign firms are no longer limited to making initial contact only with the appropriate FTC, industrial ministry, or the China Council for the Promotion of International Trade (CCPIT). Each province and municipality has a separate foreign trade system, with a foreign trade bureau, FTCs, and investment and trust corporations. Within certain limits, firms wishing to do business in a specific province may contact the local FTC, which coordinates and oversees local branches of national foreign trade organizations. FTC head offices in Beijing can provide information on other trading entities in various provinces and municipalities. As of the beginning of 1993 there were approximately 6,000 FTCs, 850 large- and medium-sized enterprises, and 100 scientific institutes authorized to engage directly in foreign trade. In addition, all foreign invested enterprises (FIEs) are authorized to trade. Large domestic enterprises are more adventurous in trading, and many maintain overseas trade offices. Smaller entities tend to go through established FTCs.

In general, all enterprises that are not registered FTCs need MOFTEC-authorized approval from the local foreign trade bureau as well as a license from the local bureau for industry and commerce to engage in foreign trade. Foreign export firms should clarify for themselves the nature and extent of a Chinese entity's authority before pursuing a contract. Most provincial and local trade organizations can contract for commodities not under central government control and those for which government pricing and quantity guidelines have been established. Even so, such authorization is subject to change. Moreover, contracts for large quantities may need approval from Beijing, even when the local organization has authorization to negotiate. Contracts for many government-controlled commodities—including cotton, petroleum products and crude oil, silk, and coal—must be authorized by central government representatives.

A few if the major FTCs and agencies are listed below. For more complete list, refer to the "Important Addresses" chapter.

Ministry of Foreign Trade and Economic
Cooperation (MOFTEC)
2 Dongchangan Jie, Dongcheng Qu
Beijing 100731, PRC
Tel: [86] (1) 5198114, 5198322 Fax: [86] (1) 5129568
Tlx: 22168

Beijing Foreign Trade Corporation
Building 12, Yong An Dong Li, Jian Guo Men Wai
Beijing 100022, PRC
Tel: [86] (1) 5001315, 5958210 Fax: [86] (1) 5001668
Tlx: 210064

State Economic and Trade Commission
25 Yuetan North Street
Beijing 100834, PRC
Tel: [86] (1) 8392227 Fax: [86] (1) 8392222

Customs General Administration
Building East
6 Jian Guo Men Wai Dajie
Beijing 100730, PRC
Tel: [86] (1) 5194414 Fax: [86] (1) 5126020, 5194004

IMPORT POLICY AND PROCEDURES

Import Approval

Imports are regulated through a complex approval process. For controlled products, permission from both local and central government authorities is generally required. Grain, sugar, steel, fertilizers, oil, timber, polyester fibers, tobacco, cotton, and pesticides may be imported only with central government approval. Wool, wood pulp, plywood, hard and corrugated paper, chemicals, scrap ships, and television tubes are also tightly controlled. As many as 15 clearances from various ministries or bureaus may be required, depending upon the locality.

Customs Classification

On January 1, 1992, China adopted the Harmonized System for customs classification and statistics.

Import Licenses

Foreign exporters must obtain approval from various Chinese government agencies and from MOFTEC. In principle, MOFTEC automatically issues licenses for controlled goods that have been approved for import by all other relevant agencies; in practice, however, MOFTEC can deny a license. In many cases, the ministry that oversees the domestic manufacture of a product is involved in the import approval process, and a parent ministry has an interest in protecting the products that sustain its budget and that provide domestic employment.

Fifty-three product categories require import licenses, including various consumer goods, raw materials, and production equipment. Together, the products account for about 50 percent of China's trade. Certain combinations of controls and licenses effectively ban the importation of some types of products. In 1992, China committed to dismantling almost 90 percent of its nontariff import restrictions over a five-year period. The elimination of the first set of import licensing requirements, effective December 31, 1993, applies to:

- agrochemicals
- apparel
- auto parts
- autos
- beer, wine, and other alcoholic beverages
- chemicals
- computers
- electrical appliances
- film and instant print film
- instant cameras
- machinery products
- medical equipment
- mineral waters
- pharmaceuticals
- photocopiers
- steel
- telecommunications
- wood products

Tariffs

China charges two levels of tariffs: minimum if the shipment's country of origin is one with which China has a trade agreement extending mutually beneficial tariff status, and general if it is not. Official tariff rates on many goods are prohibitively high, ranging from 3 percent on imports China wishes to encourage, to 250 percent on imports considered threatening to domestic manufacturing. In mid-1993 sample tariffs included 150 percent on cigarettes; 120 percent on beer and cosmetics, 100 percent on record and cassette players, refrigerators, color television sets, and video games; 90 percent on jewelry; 20 percent on coffee and telephones; 15 percent on chocolates and 12 percent on facsimile machines. Duties on automobiles could approach 250 percent.

Certain products are eligible for exemption from official rates, at the discretion of local customs officers. Thus different duty rates are often assessed on identical products entering at different ports. Among the products exempt from customs duties are raw materials imported for further processing, provided the finished products are exported within a specific period. Most imports by joint ventures are also exempt from customs duties. Actual customs charges are often the result of negotiation between businesspeople and Chinese customs officers. A separate system of tariffs is levied on goods exclusively imported into Tibet for use there.

Tariff Reductions

China has effected the following tariff reductions in the past few years:

- January, 1991: Duties were reduced to 5 percent on 40 commodities used by both agricultural and industrial sectors, including chemical fertilizers, farming chemicals, and some raw materials.
- January 1, 1992: Tariffs on 225 products were reduced from an average rate of 45 percent to 30 percent.
- December, 1992: Duties were lowered by an average of 7.3 percent on 3,371 items.
- Effective December 31, 1993, reductions of 8.8 percent are planned for 2,900 items, including categories of the following:
  - articles of iron and steel
  - cosmetic and toiletry preparations
  - edible fruits and nuts
  - electrical machinery and parts
  - games
  - machinery and mechanical appliances
  - miscellaneous chemical products
  - perfumery
  - photographic and cinematographic goods
  - vegetable oils

Taxes Applicable to Imports

In addition to tariffs, industrial and commercial taxes and value-added taxes are charged on imports. These taxes add substantially to the official tariff rate.

Although these taxes are charged on both imports and domestic products, they are not applied uniformly and are often open to negotiation. Other taxes include:

- Port tax, up to RMB 4 (about US$0.50) per ton of cargo or RMB 50 (about US$5.75) per international container on all imports (and exports) using the country's 26 main ports; and
- Enterprise income tax, 10 percent of gross income on foreign offices profiting from consulting, liaison, and market research services.

Duty and Tax Exemptions

Some items are eligible for duty reduction or exemption either because of international trade agreements or as a result of special regulations. Eligible items include:

- raw materials imported for further processing (also exempt from commercial tax);
- most imports and exports by joint ventures;
- goods damaged or lost before release from customs;
- advertising material not commercially valuable;
- trade samples not commercially valuable;
- materials by foreign governments or international organizations; and
- articles of a quantity or value below the fixed dutiable limit.

Goods Stored in Bonded Warehouses

Imported goods stored in bonded warehouses may remain in bond for one year with duties suspended. A one-year extension may be approved, after which time the goods must be reexported or licensed for import, and import duties paid.

Valuation

Chinese customs officials generally assesses duty on the basis of a shipment's cost, insurance, and freight (CIF) value, taking all pre-clearance charges into consideration, including the normal wholesale price in the country of origin, freight, packing charges, insurance, export duties, and commissions. If customs officials cannot ascertain the normal wholesale price in the exporting country, they calculate duty based on the current average domestic wholesale price minus importation fees and business expenses. Customs officials also determine dutiable value for special transactions.

Appeals of Duty Assessment

Persons dissatisfied with a customs decision may appeal in writing within 30 days after the Duty Memorandum is issued. Customs reconsiders the case and either modifies the original ruling or forwards the appeal and its comments to the Customs General

Administration for a decision. At each level the appeals process takes up to 15 days. If the Customs General Administration ruling is unacceptable to the duty payer, legal action may be taken at the People's Court within 15 days after receipt of the decision.

Customs Clearance

Except for imports under bond, customs clearance and payment of duty must be accomplished within three months of importation. Imports for which these procedures are not followed are subject to forfeiture.

Temporary Imports

Goods imported on a temporary basis with customs approval must either be reexported or moved within the territory within six months of importation. Extensions may be granted.

Countertrade

Barter and countertrade practices are governed by internal regulations that are not available outside of the official domain. Most countertrade arrangements are conducted under government-to-government agreements that involve balanced trade exchanges (barter trade). Arrangements involving buybacks (direct compensation trade) or counterpurchases (indirect compensation transactions), in which the values of imports and exports are not necessarily equal, are restricted to trade with capitalist countries.

China is particularly interested in buybacks because they provide for transfers of foreign machinery and technology, and guarantee export markets. Counterpurchases are viewed primarily as a means to allow small and medium-size enterprises to upgrade technology without the use of foreign exchange. However, MOFTEC strictly controls the type of goods that may be used for payment in counterpurchase arrangements; products that could be exported for hard currency do not qualify for counterpurchase.

China's foreign trade corporations are required to engage in barter and countertrade. Enterprises are given an annual quota of goods to export in this manner that they would otherwise be unable to sell.

MOFTEC approves all barter and countertrade transactions on a case-by-case basis. Transactions with Western firms are handled by MOFTEC's Import/Export Department.

Samples and Advertising Materials

Independent advertising is not permitted in China. Exporters wishing to send samples to China must obtain advance permission from the relevant FTC. The following types of samples enter duty free as long as they are valued at under RMB 500 (about US$60), or are supplied free of charge, exchanged, or imported by a Chinese FTC licensed for that product:

- advertising samples
- samples for analysis and testing
- samples exchanged under an intergovernmental scientific and technological cooperation agreement.

An import license may be required for samples whose value exceeds the specified limit.

Commodity Inspection

China requires that most import and export commodities be inspected. Noncommercial imports and exports, such as aid materials, gifts, and samples, are exempt from inspection. The State Administration of Import and Export Commodity Inspection (SAIECI) is the primary government agency responsible for overseeing commodity inspections. SAIECI has established relationships with foreign notary organizations, including the American International Group, and it recognizes inspections of commodities conducted by these bodies. Applicable standards are those specified in the contract of sale for quality, weight, quantity, packing, sampling, and inspection methods. If these are not defined in the contract, standards that are no less China's own national standards apply.

The China National Import and Export Commodities Inspection Corporation (CIECIC) and its provincial branches are authorized to conduct most inspections. CIECIC acts as an independent notary, issuing legal documentation for customs, account settlement, dispute resolution, certificates of origin and value, and for letter of credit purposes. CIECIC also inspects all shipments of listed commodities; certifies the condition of cargoes during warehousing, transportation, loading, and discharge; and assesses loss from fire, pilferage, or theft.

Foreign inspection services are not allowed to operate in China, but foreign businesses can commission the services of CIECIC. To apply for an inspection by CIECIC, a business must state its requirements in a letter or telegram to CIECIC, and submit copies of the contract, letter of credit, invoice, bill of lading, packing list, and inspection standards.

State Administration of Import and
Export Commodity Inspection (SAIECI)
12 Jian Guo Men Wai Dajie
Beijing 100022, PRC
Tel: [86] (1) 5003344, 5001830 Fax: [86] (1) 5002387

China National Import and Export Commodities
Inspection Corporation (CIECIC)
12 Jian Guo Men Wai Dajie
Beijing 100022, PRC
Tel: [86] (1) 5004626, 5003344
Fax: [86] (1) 5004625 Tlx: 210076

Contractual Specification of Inspection

Due to recent liberalization, some commodities do not require inspection but, to date, there is no published list of such commodities. If a foreign exporter requests an inspection for a shipment that does not require inspection and an inspection certificate, either SAIEC or CIECIC may be specified in the contract. Most international standards may be specified; when no standard is requested, China's national standards pertain.

Methods of Settlement

Residents are not allowed to pay for imports with local currency. The Bank of China (BOC) provides foreign exchange for imports on the basis of import licenses and approval by the State Administration of Exchange Control (SAEC), a unit of the People's Bank of China.

Technology Imports

Contracts for transfer of technology such as patents and industrial property rights, formulas, designs, quality control, and technical services may not exceed a 10-year term without special permission, and may not prohibit China's use of the technology after the contract's expiration.

Shipping Marks

The contract generally specifies any special information to be placed by the shipper on each package, crate, or box. Exporters should always request specific requirements from the importer.

Marking and Labeling of Retail Packages

The usual requirements for the labeling of retail packages include weight, dimensions, contract number, port of destination, and specific handling instructions. Cigarettes must be labeled "Sold exclusively by the China National Tobacco Corp."

Electric Current

The electric current used in China is AC, 50 cycle, 220/380 volts, 1, 3 phases, 2, 4 wires. Plugs are normally two roundpin or three oblique flat blades with ground; hotel rooms usually have one connection for a two-pin round continental-type plug.

Shipping Restrictions

China does its own shipping through three national corporations:

- The China Ocean Shipping Company (COSCO) books shipping space, cargo transshipment, and cargo and passenger services, and operates China's flag vessels and controls Chinese ships operating under foreign flags.
- The China National Foreign Trade Transportation Corporation (SINOTRANS) arranges customs clearance for import and export cargoes, handles domestic transportation of Chinese imports and exports, acts as an authorized agent for clearing and delivering goods in transit through Chinese ports, and arranges for insurance and initiates claims for cargo owners.
- The China National Chartering Corporation (known as *Zhongzu* or SINOCHART) cooperates with the China National Foreign Trade Transportation Corporation, chartering foreign vessels and booking shipping space for Chinese import and export cargoes.

China Ocean Shipping Company (COSCO)
6 Donchangan Jie
Beijing 100740, PRC
Tel: [86] (1) 5121188, 5121702 Fax: [86] (1) 5122408
Tlx: 22264 CPCPK CN

China National Foreign Trade Transportation Corporation (SINOTRANS)
Import Building
Erligou, Xijiao
Beijing 100044, PRC
Tel: [86] (1) 8328709 Fax: [86] (1) 8311070 Tlx: 22153

China National Chartering Corporation (SINOCHART)
21 Xisanhuan Bei Lu
Beijing 100081, PRC
Tel: [86] (1) 8415313/4 Fax: [86] (1) 84153212 Tlx: 222508 CHART CN

DOCUMENTATION

Most state trading entities use standard contract forms to which they rigidly adhere. All relevant material, such as price data, required packing and shipping marks, required shipping documentation, technical specifications, payment terms, and inspection and insurance arrangements, is attached to and becomes port of the contract. Independent entities may be more flexible in negotiating non-standard contracts. However, there are minimum legal standards, and various authorities can overrule contractual provisions that do not follow "policy."

Commercial contracts with Chinese import enterprises always stipulate the documentary requirements specific to that transaction. These requirements must be followed to the letter. There should be no discrepancies between goods shipped and those described in a contract. Even seemingly insignificant changes must be cleared with the importing enterprise. Packing instructions in contracts and accompanying documents must also be followed to the letter.

Stipulations for documentation generally include:
- accepted language(s)
- any certification or legalization necessary
- any regulations that must be met by the goods shipped under that specific contract
- any special certificates required
- documents required
- number of copies of each document
- what each document must contain.

Packing, marking, and labeling requirements are also specified in the contract.

Consular and Customs Invoices

There are no requirements governing the content or form of consular and customs invoices.

Commercial Invoice

A commercial invoice must precisely conform to the requirements of the import contract, but there is no standard format. The goods must be clearly, concisely, and thoroughly described, including costs. The invoice must concur with the importer's instructions and requirements of contract, and it must bear the certifying signature of a responsible official or authorized agent of the exporting firm. In some cases the invoice must be certified by a chamber of commerce or legalized by a Chinese official.

Pro Forma Invoice

A pro forma invoice may be required during the negotiation of an import contract. The importing organization generally indicates whether it is required.

Bill of Lading

There are no special requirements regarding the form of a bill of lading, but all marks and case numbers appearing on the packages in the shipment must appear on it. Grouping of marks or numbers on shipments of mixed commodities is not permitted. For air shipments, air waybills replace bills of lading. Bills of lading and air waybills must conform strictly to the conditions and terms of the buyer's letter of credit.

Packing List

A packing list showing the weight and contents of each package is required with each shipment.

Certificate of Origin

If a contract calls for a certificate of origin, the standard form available in stationery stores should be used. The certificate should be issued in duplicate and agree with the other documents. It must be signed by a responsible member of the exporting firm. In some cases, certificates of origin must be certified by a chamber of commerce or legalized by Chinese officials.

Insurance Certificates

The state-owned People's Insurance Company of China (PICC) insures China's foreign trade. Chinese FTCs generally buy goods on an FOB (free on board) basis, taking on insurance and freight charges.

People's Insurance Company of China (PICC)
410 Fuchengmen Nie Dajie
Beijing, PRC
Tel: [86] (1) 6016688 Fax: [86] (1) 6011869
Tlx: 22532

SPECIAL ECONOMIC ZONES (SEZS)

SEZs have been established in Shantou, Shenzhen, Xiamen, Zhuhai, and on Hainan Island, as well as in 14 economic and technological development areas, where foreigners, and Chinese from overseas, Hong Kong, and Macao may invest in and open factories. Imports by and for the use of these enterprises enter duty-free and exempt from commercial and industrial taxes, and entry and exit procedures are simplified. (Refer to "Marketing," "Economy," and "Foreign Investment" chapters for detailed discussions of SEZs and other investment zones.) Exempted imports include:

- raw materials;
- equipment;
- machinery, parts and components;
- means of transportation; and
- other means of production.

Imports brought into the Waigaoqiao bonded zone that are not sold domestically are free from all duties and taxes.

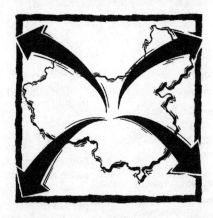

Export Policy & Procedures

INTRODUCTION

In the late 1980s and early 1990s, China ushered in a series of reforms intended to liberalize the export process. Among these reforms are measures that allow Chinese managers greater freedom to run their enterprises and to establish direct contact with foreign buyers. Despite this new freedom and despite the fact that planning authorities no longer set specific export plans, most exports are still channeled through approved foreign trade corporations or other officially sanctioned entities. Foreign importers now have direct access to a greater choice of China-based suppliers. But while most enterprises are largely free to earn their own profits, there is less certainty that the state will rescue them in the event they incur a loss as was the case in the past. Therefore, foreign importers must make certain they select a supplier that will be able to deliver once a contract is negotiated.

Exporting from China is generally somewhat easier than importing into the country. Although the government claims to have suspended direct financial subsidies to export manufacturers early in 1991, it still employs a mixture of indirect export subsidies, including the provision of low-priced energy, raw materials, and labor. Moreover, state enterprises and trading companies typically receive loans at preferential rates, and often the loans are not repaid. Foreign firms in China that produce for export are also generally eligible for similar preferential treatment.

The following chapter discusses China's export policy and procedures. This information is useful for people who want to purchase products from China, for those who establish manufacturing facilities or other operations in China, and for foreign investors.

REGULATORY AUTHORITY

The Ministry of Foreign Trade and Economic Cooperation (MOFTEC) in Beijing (formerly known as the Ministry of Foreign Economic Relations and Trade, or MOFERT) formulates and implements the PRC's foreign trade policy. MOFTEC develops the annual export plan that determines what may and may not be exported, and issues required export licenses. Though trade is no longer monopolized by MOFTEC, that body still authorizes, oversees, controls, and monitors exporting corporations and enterprises. Each province and municipality has a separate foreign trade system, with a foreign trade bureau, foreign trade corporations (FTCs), and investment and trust corporations operating in most localities. Within certain limits, firms wishing to do business in a specific province may contact the local FTC, which coordinates and oversees local branches of national foreign trade organizations. FTC head offices in Beijing can provide further information on other trading entities in various provinces and municipalities.

Other government agencies responsible for aspects of foreign trade include the State Economic and Trade Commission and the Customs General Administration. A few of the important contacts are:

Ministry of Foreign Trade and Economic Cooperation (MOFTEC)
2 Dongchangan Jie, Dongcheng Qu
Beijing 100731, PRC
Tel: [86] (1) 5198114, 5198322 Fax: [86] (1) 5129568
Tlx: 22168

Beijing Foreign Trade Corporation
Building 12, Yong An Dong Li, Jian Guo Men Wai
Beijing 100022, PRC
Tel: [86] (1) 5001315, 5958210 Fax: [86] (1) 5001668
Tlx: 210064

State Economic and Trade Commission
25 Yuetan North Street
Beijing 100834, PRC
Tel: [86] (1) 8392227 Fax: [86] (1) 8392222

Customs General Administration
Building East
6 Jian Guo Men Wai Dajie
Beijing 100730, PRC
Tel: [86] (1) 5194414 Fax: [86] (1) 5126020, 5194004

EXPORT POLICY

Export Authorization

All foreign trade corporations (FTCs) and factories owned by the state require MOFTEC authorization to export. Three levels of FTCs, as well as factories meeting stringent criteria, are authorized to negotiate export contracts directly with foreign buyers. Authorized entities have complete autonomy for most straightforward transactions involving consumer products. FTCs act as a warehouse provider and/or liaison between factory and buyer, placing the order or supplying the contract with merchandise from their warehouse. FTCs often buy products from the factory and then negotiate price, delivery, and other elements of the sale. Transactions involving strategic commodities, government-controlled commodities, extremely large quantities, or merchandise subject to quota usually require additional approvals either from MOFTEC or the State Economic and Trade Commission. Approvals to export are limited to prescribed commodities for each FTC.

Not only must the Chinese supplier be authorized to export the goods under negotiation, but each export shipment must be licensed. Failure to observe this requirement can cause lengthy delays in shipping and, in a worst-case scenario, the voiding of the contract and forfeiture of any moneys paid. The foreign buyer should always examine the exporting enterprise's business registration and approvals and licenses pertinent to the commodity before beginning negotiations. Inquiries should be addressed to MOFTEC.

MOFTEC-Approved National Foreign Trade Corporations

Each of the MOFTEC-approved national FTCs operates as an autonomous trading organization handling a specified group of commodities. Most have provincial branch offices, and some have overseas branches. These FTCs are responsible for their own profits and losses; they make their own business decisions and plans, negotiate and sign contracts, obtain the goods from the manufacturers, and so on. Ministries other than MOFTEC and some larger industrial organizations have established autonomous foreign trade corporations for commodities under their jurisdiction. Some of these FTCs are as large as the MOFTEC-approved FTCs and have branches in the provinces. Most are rigidly limited to specific products handled by the parent organization.

Provincial Foreign Trade Corporations

FTCs set up by provincial and regional authorities to deal in regional products also operate autonomously, some with branches outside their province or region. Cooperative trading agreements between provinces enable foreign buyers to obtain goods from all over China without traveling beyond the major trading areas.

Factories

Some factories are authorized to sell to foreign buyers directly. A small percentage of large-scale factories having consistently exported US$3 million in products per year, and having proven exporting expertise and experience, can export directly to foreign buyers without going through FTCs. These factories are fully autonomous and are responsible for all aspects of their production and foreign trade processes. Factories with less experience and smaller export volume are not authorized to conduct their own foreign trade. They may hire FTCs to serve as authorized agents, paying the FTC a commission and retaining responsibility for profit and loss. Other factories are less autonomous and must obtain MOFTEC approval for contracts to sell a specified quantity of goods annually to official FTCs, who then negotiate with foreign buyers.

EXPORT PROCEDURES

Pre-Negotiation Preparation

Because not all entities in China are authorized to export, or to export all types of products, and because export methods depend on the enterprise's level of autonomy, foreigners wishing to buy from China must make thorough inquiries regarding a supplier's authorization to fulfill an order. It is essential to verify an enterprise's authorization to conduct foreign trade and to sell the specific types of goods before a contract is negotiated. As a preliminary, a foreign buyer should examine the supplier's government-issued business license—a namecard (business card) is not sufficient. A buyer's inquiries should then focus on the exact product and quantity specifications. All technical documents should be accurately translated into Chinese.

Information about a supplier's authorization can also be requested from:

MOFTEC Foreign Trade Department
2 Dongchangan Jie, Dongcheng Qu
Beijing 100731, PRC
Tel: [86] (1) 5197420, 5198328 Tlx: 22168

Export Licenses

The State Council publishes a list of controlled commodities that require export licenses. MOFTEC's Foreign Trade Department in Beijing or its provincial affiliates issue export licenses. Each license is valid only for a specified shipment and quantity. No export license is required for unlisted goods that are purchased from an approved exporting entity, or for samples or advertising material exported by an approved exporter. Generally, export licenses are not required for manufactured goods, but they are necessary for many raw materials that are especially price-sensitive in world markets or in short supply in China. Export licenses are also required for certain commodities destined for Hong Kong or Macao.

Quotas

Export documents for nontextile goods subject to quota by trade arrangement with the importing country must include an export quota license. If the quota commodity is a textile, a certificate of origin (available from branches of the Commodity Inspection Bureau and the China Council for the Promotion of International Trade) must be submitted.

Customs Approval

Special customs approval is required for:

- exports to be used in PRC-sponsored exhibitions but that will also be for sale while abroad;
- exports under countertrade or loan agreements; and
- Chinese goods exported by foreign bodies or diplomatic missions.

Penalties

Each export shipment must conform exactly to the details on the license, including the descriptions, specifications, quantity, unit prices, total value of goods; the names of the exporting and importing companies, trading method, port of loading, and so on. If the license for a shipment has expired, application for extension must be submitted to the original issuing authority. Any violation of the Chinese export licensing system is an offense. It is an offense to forge, alter, transfer, or give false information regarding export licenses. All the required documents must accompany the export shipment through customs, or the goods will not be released for shipment. Noncompliance with licensing and other documentary requirements can result in the forfeiture of the goods, and even criminal prosecution.

Commodity Inspection

China requires that most import and export commodities be inspected. Noncommercial imports and exports, such as aid materials, gifts, and samples, are exempt from inspection. The State Administration of Import and Export Commodity Inspection (SAIECI) is the main government agency that is responsible for overseeing commodity inspections. Applicable standards are those specified in the contract of sale for quality, weight, quantity, packing, sampling, and inspection methods. If these are not defined in the contract, standards that are no less

than China's own national standards apply.

The China National Import and Export Commodities Inspection Corporation (CIECIC) and its provincial branches are authorized to conduct most inspections. CIECIC acts as an independent notary, issuing legal documentation for customs, account settlement, dispute resolution, certificates of origin and value, and for letter of credit purposes. CIECIC also inspects all shipments of listed commodities; certifies the condition of cargoes during warehousing, transportation, loading, and discharge; and assesses loss from fire, pilferage, or theft.

Foreign inspection services are not allowed to operate in China, but foreign businesses can commission the services of CIECIC. To apply for an inspection by CIECIC, a business must state its requirements in a letter or telegram to CIECIC, and submit copies of the contract, letter of credit, invoice, bill of lading, packing list, and inspection standards.

State Administration of Import and Export Commodity Inspection (SAIECI)
12 Jian Guo Men Wai Dajie
Beijing 100022, PRC
Tel: [86] (1) 5003344 Fax: [86] (1) 5002387

China National Import and Export Commodities Inspection Corporation (CEICIC)
12 Jian Guo Men Wai Dajie
Beijing 100022, PRC
Tel: [86] (1) 5004626, 5003344
Fax: [86] (1) 5004625 Tlx: 210076

Contractual Specification of Inspection

Due to recent liberalization, some commodities do not require inspection but, to date, there is no published list of such commodities. If a foreign importer requests an inspection for a shipment that does not require inspection and an inspection certificate, either SAIEC or CIECIC may be specified in the contract. Most international standards may be specified, but when no standard is requested, China's national standards pertain. A fee is charged to the overseas buyer, to cover the costs of inspection.

Countertrade

Barter and countertrade practices are governed by internal regulations unavailable to non-government officials. Most countertrade arrangements are conducted under government-to-government agreements that involve balanced trade exchanges (barter trade). Arrangements involving buybacks (direct compensation trade) or counterpurchases (indirect compensation transactions), in which the values of imports and exports are not necessarily equal, are restricted to trade with capitalist countries.

China is particularly interested in buybacks because they provide for transfers of foreign machinery and technology, and guarantee export markets.

Counterpurchases are viewed primarily as a means to allow small and medium-size enterprises to upgrade technology without the use of foreign exchange. However, MOFTEC strictly controls the type of goods that may be used for payment in counterpurchase arrangements; products that could be exported for hard currency do not qualify for counterpurchase.

Many enterprises in China are required to engage in barter and countertrade. They are given an annual quota of goods to export in this manner that they would otherwise be unable to sell.

MOFTEC approves all barter and countertrade transactions on a case-by-case basis. Transactions with Western firms are handled by MOFTEC's Import/Export Department.

Methods of Settlement

For small shipments, Chinese exporters normally prefer CIF (cost, insurance, and freight). CF (cost and freight) terms are acceptable, but FOB (free on board) terms are seldom accepted. Exporters usually expect payment at sight by confirmed and irrevocable letter of credit. Documents against acceptance (D/A) or documents against payment (D/P) are accepted on rare occasions for creditworthy buyers who have a good long-term relationship with the supplier. China follows international practices and conventions for letters of credit.

DOCUMENTATION

Unless otherwise specified in the letter of credit or contract, several types of documentary requirements can be incorporated into the invoice, such as packing lists, weight and measurement lists, and certificates of origin when required. Signatures on Chinese documents are usually stamped, not original. The China Council for Promotion of International Trade (CCPIT) is the only body authorized to certify or authenticate an export document. Foreign-consulate certification is not acceptable.

China Council for the Promotion of International Trade (CCPIT)
1 Fu Xing Men Wai Dajie
Beijing 100860, PRC
Tel: [86] (1) 8013344, 8013866 Fax: [86] (1) 8011370
Tlx: 22315 CCPIT CN

Bill of Lading

The bill of lading (or, for air shipments, the air waybill) constitutes the document of title to the merchandise. It must conform strictly with the terms in the letter of credit. For shipments under cost, insurance, and freight (CIF), cost, freight/carriage and insurance paid (CIP), or other related methods, the supplier contracts and pays for the freight. However,

many buyers prefer to arrange for the shipment themselves in cooperation with a local freight forwarder, consolidator, or shipping line. In this case, payment is made under such terms as free alongside ship (FAS), free on board (FOB), free on board airport (FOA), or other related methods. Buyers should make certain that the shipping agent is aware of the correct terms and how the freight charges will be paid. This information will help the carrier prepare the bill of lading in accordance with the conditions of the letter of credit, purchase contract, and other documents.

The bill of lading lists the port of departure, port of discharge, name of the carrying vessel, and date of issue. The date of issue is very important because it indicates whether goods have been shipped within the time period required in the letter of credit. Suppliers must submit all required documents on time to receive payment under the terms of the credit.

Bills of lading can be either negotiable or nonnegotiable. A negotiable bill of lading is made to the order of the shipper, who makes a blank endorsement on the back, or it is endorsed to the order of the bank that issues the letter of credit. A nonnegotiable bill of lading is consigned to a specific party (to the buyer or buyer's representative) and endorsement by the shipper is not required. In this case, the consignee must produce the original bill of lading in order to take delivery.

SPECIAL ECONOMIC ZONES (SEZS)

SEZs in Shenzhen, Zhuhai, Shantou, Xiamen, and on Hainan Island benefit joint ventures and wholly-owned foreign businesses. There are also Economic and Technological Development Zones (ETDZs) in most Coastal Cities. (Refer to "Marketing," "Economy," and "Foreign Investment" chapters for detailed discussions of SEZs, ETDZs, and other investment zones.) Incentives vary from zone to zone, but they generally involve:

- duty-free entry of imported machinery and equipment, raw materials, and other items used in manufacturing within the zone;
- tax holidays;
- tax advantages;
- land-use advantages;
- preferential cost of Chinese raw materials, machinery, and equipment;
- export tax exemptions.

Industry Reviews

This chapter describes the status of and trends in major Chinese industries. It also lists key contacts for finding sources of supply, developing sales leads and conducting economic research. We have grouped industries into 11 categories, which are listed below. Some smaller sectors of commerce are not detailed here, while others may overlap into more than one area. If your business even remotely fits into a category don't hesitate to contact several of the organizations listed; they should be able to assist you further in gathering the information you need. We have included industry-specific contacts only. General trade organizations, which may also be very helpful, particularly if your business is in an industry not covered here, are listed in "Important Address."

Each section has two segments: an industry summary and a list of useful contacts. The summary gives an overview of the range of products available in a certain industry and that industry's ability to compete in worldwide markets. The contacts listed are government agencies, trade associations, publica-

tions, and trade fairs which can provide information specific to the industry. An entire volume could likely be devoted to each area, but such in-depth coverage is beyond the scope of this book. Our intent is to give you a basis for your own research.

All addresses and telephone numbers given are located in the People's Republic of China, unless otherwise noted. The telephone country code for the PRC is [86]; other telephone country codes are shown in square brackets where appropriate. Telephone city codes, if needed, appear in parentheses.

We highly recommend that you peruse the chapters on Trade Fairs and Important Addresses, where you will find additional resources including a variety of trade promotion organizations, chambers of commerce, business services, and media.

ELECTRONIC CONSUMER AND COMPONENT PRODUCTS

Most Chinese electronics manufacturers concentrate on domestic markets, and exports account for less than 20 percent of total output.

Every Chinese ministry operates its own factories and produces electronic items suited to its own needs; although most have outdated equipment and limited funds for upgrades. However, small nongovernment businesses are manufacturing an increasing share of China's electronic products. These manufacturers are concentrated in Guangdong, Beijing, Shanghai, and Jiangsu, and there are major manufacturers in every province and region except Tibet. Some Chinese electronics firms are joint ventures or have technology transfer agreements with foreign companies.

Electronic products made in China include finished consumer goods and electronic components. Of exported items, most are produced on order for major electronics companies in Japan, the United States, and Europe.

Consumer Electronic Goods Major exports of consumer electronic goods include televisions, ra-

INDUSTRY REVIEWS TABLE OF CONTENTS

Electronic Consumer and
   Component Products 71
Food and Beverages 74
Footwear 77
Handicrafts, Jewelry, Timepieces,
   Luggage, and Fashion Accessories 78
Housewares, Household Appliances,
   and Stationery Products 80
Chemicals, Minerals, and Materials 81
Industrial Machinery 84
Medical Products 87
Textiles and Apparel 89
Tools 92
Toys, Sporting Goods, and Recreational
   Equipment 93

dios, radio cassette recorders, audio equipment, tape recorders, speakers, video cassette recorders, and videotapes. This sector of China's electronics industry is growing slowly but steadily.

Electronic Components Basic electronic components produced in China include display and electronic tubes, such as cathode ray tubes (CRTs) and liquid crystal displays (LCDs); semiconductors, such as integrated circuits (ICs), memory devices, and logical elements; and passive components, including capacitors and printed circuit boards.

Of Chinese-made electronic components, passive components are the most significant exports. Companies produce such passive components as resistors, transistors, capacitors, varacitors, connectors, rectifiers, transformers, potentiometers, and printed circuit boards (PCBs). Approximately 400 PCB manufacturing facilities operate in China, most of them small firms or producers of low-end products. PCBs constitute a substantial amount of the passive component output. At least 70 percent of Chinese-made PCBs are used in consumer products (televisions, tape recorders, and radios), while the rest are incorporated into computers and telecommunications switches. Chinese electronics firms manufacture a wide variety of PCBs, including single-sided, double-sided, multilayered, and flexible boards. About 30 percent of the PCBs are exported.

Competitive Situation

China's electronics firms face several difficulties in becoming more competitive in global markets. Most of these firms operate as joint ventures and under technology transfer arrangements. As a result,

expansion of production and advances in technology have slowed since 1989, when several joint venture companies left China in the wake of political unrest. In addition, domestic demand for consumer electronics, a once promising market, has slowed because of government austerity policies. Chinese electronics firms also encounter recurring problems in acquiring high-quality raw materials and imported components at reasonable cost. The soaring cost of technology upgrades may limit the ability of Chinese state enterprises to expand production.

Nevertheless, China plans manufacture more electronic components locally and to export higher-quality electronic products. Firms that produce PCBs are diversifying their product lines to include high-standard single-sided PCBs used in industrial equipment and flexible PCBs for cameras and other consumer goods. These firms have also increased production of the PCBs that are in high domestic demand, such as double-sided and multilayered PCBs for consumer electronic goods and telecommunication projects. The major Chinese PCB producers have automated their production lines, and many are shifting production to surface mount technology.

Government Agencies

China Patent Agency (HK) Ltd.
16th Fl., China Resources Building
25 Harbour Road
Wanchai, Hong Kong
Tel: [852] 8317199 Tlx: 73277 CIREC HX

Ministry of Communications
10 Fuxing Lu, Haidian Qu
Beijing 100845
Tel: (1) 8642371, 3265544 Tlx: 22462

Restructuring Government Ministries and Renaming of MOFERT
China's central economic bureaucracy has been restructured.

In its March 1993 session, the National People's Congress of the PRC adopted in principle a plan to reform the State Council and its ministries by the end of 1993. Seven ministries are to be dissolved or divided and renamed. These include: the Ministry of Energy Resources, the Ministry of Machine-Building and Electronics Industry, the Ministry of Aeronautics and Astronautics Industry, the Ministry of Light Industry, the Ministry of Textile Industry, the Ministry of Commerce, and the Ministry of Materials and Equipment.

Under the plan, six new ministries are to be created: the State Economic and Trade Commission, the Ministry of Power

Industry, the Ministry of Coal Industry, the Ministry of Machine-Building Industry, the Ministry of Electronics Industry, and the Ministry of Internal Trade. The Ministry of Aeronautics and Astronautics Industry is to be divided into two specialized semi-autonomous corporations, provisionally named the China National Aviation Industry Corporation (CNAIC) and the China National Space Industry Corporation. The China National Aero-Technology Import and Export Corporation will report to CNAIC.

In addition, the Ministry of Foreign Economic Relations and Trade ("MOFERT") was renamed the Ministry of Foreign Trade and Economic Cooperation.

Reprinted from Asia Pacific Legal Developments Bulletin, vol. 8, no. 3, Baker & McKenzie, Sept. 1993, with permission of the author, John V. Grobowski, Hong Kong, and the law firm of Baker & McKenzie, Hong Kong.

Ministry of Electronics Industry
27 Wanshou Road
Beijing 100846
Tel: (1) 8282233 Fax: (1) 8221838

State Science and Technology Commission
54 Sanlihe Road
Beijing 100862
Tel: (1) 8012594 Fax: (1) 8012594

Foreign Trade Corporations

China Electronics Corporation (CEC)
27 Wan Shou Lu
Beijing 100846
Tel: (1) 8212233
Fax: (1) 8212801, 8221835, 8213745
Tlx: 22383 MEI CN

China National Electric Wire & Cable Export
Corporation
Langjianyuan Jianguomen Wai
Beijing 100026
Tel: (1) 5021163, 5002998 Fax: (1) 582714
Tlx: 22614 CCC CN

China National Electronics Import and Export
Corporation
23A Fuxing Lu, P.O.Box 140
Beijing 100036
Tel: (1) 8219532, 8022711 Fax: (1) 8223907, 8212352
Tlx: 222716 CEIEC CN

China United Electric Export Corporation
A16 Da Hongmen Road West, Yong Wai
Beijing 100075
Tel: (1) 7214614, 7214624 Fax: (1) 7214619

Trade Organizations

China Chamber of Commerce for Import and
Export of Machinery and Electronics
127 Xuan Wu Men Wai Dajie
Beijing 100031
Tel: (1) 6015627

China Electrical Material Association
20 Fucheng Lu
Beijing 100036
Tel: (1) 8314685 Fax: (1) 8011242

Chinese Society for Electrical Engineering
1 Baiguang Lu, Ertiao
Beijing 100761
Tel: (1) 3273322 Tlx: 22466 MWREP CN

Directories/Publications

Asian Electricity
(11 per year)
Reed Business Publishing Ltd.
5001 Beach Road, #06-12 Golden Mile Complex
Singapore 0719
Tel: [65] 2913188 Fax: [65] 2913180

Asian Electronics Engineer
(Monthly)
Trade Media Ltd.
29 Wong Chuck Hang Road
Hong Kong
Tel: [852] 5554777 Fax: [852] 8700816

Asian Sources: Electronic Components
(Monthly)
Asian Sources Media Group
22nd Fl., Vita Tower
29 Wong Chuk Hang Road
Wong Chuk Hang, Hong Kong
Tel: [852] 5554777 Fax: [852] 8730488

China's Electronics & Electrical Products
(Annual)
China Phone Book Company
Citicorp Centre, 24th Fl.
18 Whitfield Road
Hong Kong
Tel: [852] 8328300 Fax: [852] 5031526

Electronic Business Asia
(Monthly)
Cahners Publishing Company
275 Washington St.
Newton, MA 02158, USA
Tel: [1] (617) 964-3030 Fax: [1] (617) 558-4506

Trade Fairs

Refer to the Trade Fair chapter for complete listings, including contact information, dates, and venues. Trade fairs with particular relevance to this industry include the following, which are listed in that chapter under the headings given below:

Comprehensive
- International Expo on Patent, High Technology & New Products
- International Science & Technology Fair
- International Science, Peace & Health Care Exhibition

Electronic & Electric Equipment
- CABLEWIRE SHANGHAI (International Exhibition on Cable & Wire Manufacturing)
- CHINA MECTT (International Machinery, Factory Automation, Electronics Technology Exhibition for China)
- China (Shenzhen) International Household Electric Appliances Exhibition
- China High Tech
- China International Electronics Fair (CEE)
- China International Electronics Trade Fair
- CONSUMTRONICS SHANGHAI (International Exhibition on Consumer Electronics and Household Appliances)
- Electronic Toys & Games
- Guangzhou Electronics and Components Expo
- Guangzhou Office Automation, Telcom and Electronics Expo
- International Electronics Exhibition
- International Exhibition on Consumer Electronics and Household Appliances
- International Laser & Opto-Electronic Product Exhibition
- International Machinery & Electronic Technology (CHINA METE)

- International PC Board Making and Electro-Chemicals Exhibition
- International Telecommunications / Computer Electronics Exhibition and Conference
- International Trade Fair for Electronics and Electrical Equipment (Electronics China)
- Internepcon / Semiconductor
- National Fair on the Achievements of China's Sparking Program—New and Hi-Tech Products
- Semiconductor China

For other trade fairs that may be of interest, we recommend that you also consult the headings Computer & Information Industries; Construction & Housing; and Environmental & Energy Industries.

FOOD AND BEVERAGES

The food industry is one of China's largest commercial sectors. The industry is primarily commodity-oriented, and only about 5 to 10 percent of its total food output is processed. Even so, processed food production accounts for over 10 percent of China's total industrial output. The major export markets are Southeast Asia and Japan, with smaller amounts going to Europe and the United States.

China's food industry is characterized by many small and mid-sized factories, with few major food processing facilities. The government bureaucracy that oversees food processing is remarkably complex, involving many organizations that have overlapping responsibilities. Major products include alcoholic and nonalcoholic drinks, canned foods, dairy products, edible oils, frozen foods, prepared foods, sugar and syrup, and food additives and spices.

Beverages China's beverage processing companies export fruit drinks, soft drinks, tea, wine, and beer. Fruits widely used in China's juice and soft drink industry include passion fruit, mangos, pineapples, olives, lemons, lohans, kiwi, and Chinese apricots. Canned fruit juices and drinks are exported mainly to Japan, Hong Kong, and Southeast Asia. In general, bottling technology in Chinese plants is not up to world standards, although it is considered adequate for most domestic needs.

Beer is one of the country's most significant beverage exports, and China ranks among the world's top five beer producers. Major export markets for Chinese beer are Vietnam, Laos, and Cambodia. Certain provisions in China's complex price structure favor this industry, allowing it to retain control of its export earnings and to invest in upgrading facilities. As a result, China's breweries have fairly advanced technology and equipment, and they are undertaking large-scale expansion of their facilities. However, domestic grain shortages are frequent. Heavily dependent on Australian barley imports, Chinese breweries are now diversifying to other supply sources.

Dairy Products Dairy products are in high demand in China's domestic markets, and shortages are frequent. Chinese-produced dairy products include fresh, powdered, and reconstituted milk, ice cream, and yogurt. Prices for milk and yogurt are controlled, so companies cannot pass on increased packaging expenses to consumers. Areas of particular growth in China's dairy industry include Inner Mongolia, Zhejiang, Liaoning, Jilin, and Heilongjiang. Exports are minimal.

Canned Foods Canned foods are among China's most important light industrial export products. About 170 canneries throughout the country produce food for export; 70 percent of these are in coastal cities.

Canned fruits and vegetables are the country's most important processed food export, and China is a top world exporter of canned mushrooms. Other important canned vegetable exports are asparagus, bamboo shoots, broad beans, water chestnuts, tomatoes, tomato ketchup, and green soy beans. China is a major producer of pineapples, oranges, tangerines, lemons, kumquats, lichees, longans, mangos, kiwi, olives, passion fruit, lohans, Chinese apricots, bananas, and watermelons. Sliced canned pineapples are China's most significant fruit export, and almost all lichees and longans produced are exported as canned or dried fruit. China's canneries also produce a large variety of dried fruits and vegetables. Provinces particularly noted for production of canned and dried vegetables and fruits include Sichuan, Hubei, and Guangxi.

China also exports canned pork, beef, poultry, and aquatic products. Canned meats have become an important food export, primarily to markets in Asia, with smaller amounts going to European customers. Meat processing plants are located throughout China, with major concentrations in the cities of Shanghai, Tianjin, and Dalian, and in the provinces of Sichuan, Jiangsu, and Zhejiang. Major meat-producing provinces include Hunan, Hubei, Henan, Hebei, and Shandong. China's northeast provinces are expanding their cattle industry and are exploring exports of meat products to Russia. Some Chinese meat processors are considering diversifying into processed meats for pet foods, with the intention of moving into European and US markets. Exports of pork are increasing as Chinese authorities are urging a shift in domestic consumption away from pork to beef and mutton.

Food Additives, Spices, and Starch A variety of food additives and spices are made in China, including enzymes and fermentation agents, such as yeasts. Major Chinese exports include soy sauce, salt, and wild herbs used in Chinese medicines. China's salt industry produces sea, lake, rock, and well salt in centers along the coast and in Sichuan, Hubei, Hunan,

Jiangxi, Xinjiang, and Inner Mongolia. Another important export is Chinese cassava root, a source of high-quality food starch, which is used in a variety of food products and has textile and other minor industrial applications. Guangxi Province produces almost half of China's exported cassava starch.

Frozen Foods China's frozen food industry is export-oriented, and it has surged in recent years to meet increasing worldwide demand. Products include frozen vegetables, fruits, prawns, dumplings, and specialty foods. Most of China's frozen foods are exported to Japan, Hong Kong, and Southeast Asia, although a significant amount of frozen prawns are shipped to the United States. Many of the frozen food plants are centered along the seacoast in Fujian, Guangdong, Zhejiang, and Shanghai.

Prepared Foods Domestic demand for prepared food sector has traditionally been weak. However, as living standards rise in China, local demand for prepared foods is growing, and China's small prepared food sector is expanding production. Prepared foods include soups, instant noodles, and baby food. Anticipating increasing market demand, many Chinese firms are diversifying their product lines.

Sugar and Syrup China's sugar mills produce refined sugar, high-fructose syrup, and various candies and confectioneries. Sugar is an essential ingredient for China's canned food industry, but domestic sugar production is constrained by a shortage of sugar cane and sugar beets. As a result, exports are minimal, and China imports much of its refined sugar.

Competitive Situation

China processes only 5 to 10 percent of its food output. Chinese food producers have been hindered by political uncertainty and instability, lack of advanced technology, inability to finance expansion of production facilities, and shortages of packaging and processing materials, including pulp, paper, high-grade plastics, and galvanized iron. Except for a few industries, such as beer and dairy products, food processing technology in China is below world standards. Upgrading the food processing industry will require the import of advanced technology and equipment, but the central government has not allocated much foreign exchange to this sector. Moreover, some food processors cannot obtain reliable supplies of raw foodstuffs because farmers prefer to sell to the more profitable fresh markets. High domestic demand is also causing prices to soar for locally produced agricultural products such as fruit, vegetables, and meat.

Nevertheless, China's food processing industry has a competitive edge over other countries that export food products. Labor costs are relatively low, and domestic agricultural resources, except in a few areas, are abundant. High competition among Chinese food producers has kept export prices stable. The government views modernizing the food industry as a key goal, and therefore serious efforts are under way to upgrade facilities and to increase exports of processed and packaged foods, especially exports of processed meat, dairy products, prepared soups, baby foods, sugar, frozen foods, and beer. Development of food industries in inland provinces is seen as a means to enhance rural economies throughout China. Food producers in China are also being encouraged to enter into joint ventures and technology transfer arrangements with foreign companies, particularly in Taiwan and Hong Kong.

For now, however, China's food exports are restricted because many countries have highly regulated standards for food imports. For example, China's processed, chilled, and frozen meat cannot be exported to the United States because they are not approved by the US Food and Drug Administration. In Japan, customers demand prime cuts of pork and beef and specialty chicken parts, products superior to those processed in China. To diversify into other export markets, China's food producers are importing specialized food processing machinery that meets foreign requirements.

Government Agencies

China National Light Industry Council
B22 Fuwaidajie
Beijing 100833
Tel: (1) 8396338 Fax: (1) 8396351

Ministry of Agriculture
11 Nonzhanguan Nanli, Hepinli
Beijing 100026
Tel: (1) 5003366, 5004606 Fax: (1) 5002448
Department of State Farms & Land Reclamation
Tel: (1) 5001285

Ministry of Public Health
44 Houhaibeiyan, Xicheng Qu
Beijing 100725
Tel: (1) 4033387 Fax: (1) 4014338 Tlx: 22193

Foreign Trade Corporations

Beijing General Corporation of Agriculture, Industry, and Commerce (BGCAIC)
9 Bei Huan Dong Lu, De Sheng Men Wai
Beijing
Tel: (1) 2014499 x347, x322, x30l
Fax: (1) 2010030 Tlx: 222620 GWTS CN

China Beverage and Foodstuffs Import and Export Company
11th Fl., Jingxin Building
2A Dongsanhuanbei Lu
Beijing 100027
Tel: (1) 4660838 Fax: (1) 4660632
Tlx: 210479 BEFCO CN

China Feeding Stuffs Import and Export
Corporation (TUHSU)
82 Donganmen Dajie
Beijing 100747
Tel: (1) 5125193, 5129116 Fax: (1) 5124736
Tlx: 210203 CHFS CN

China Flavor & Fragrances Import and Export
Corporation (TUHSU)
82 Donganmen Dajie
Beijing 100747
Tel: (1) 5124319, 5124606 Fax: (1) 5121626
Tlx: 22893 TUHSU CN

China Food Industry and Techniques
Development Corporation (CFITDC)
No. 3, Hong Tong Xiang
Dong Zong-bu Hutong, Dongdon
Beijing
Tel: (1) 548710, 5122435

China Grain and Oil Import Company
9th Fl., Jingxin Building
2A Dongsanhuanbei Lu
Beijing 100027
Tel: (1) 4660645 Fax: (1) 4660678
Tlx: 210315 GRAIN CN

China Guangxi Native Produce
Import and Export Corporation
Qixing Road
Nanning, Guangxi Province
Tel: (771) 20828 Fax: (771) 20914
Tlx: 48153 PRONG CN

China Livestock & Poultry Associated Company
82 Donganmen Dajie
Beijing 100747
Tel: (1) 5124006 Tlx: 22281 CEROF CN

China National Animal Breeding Stock Import and
Export Corporation (CABS)
10 Yangyi Hutong Jia, Dongcheng Qu
Beijing 100005
Tel: (1) 5131107 Fax: (1) 5128694 Tlx: 210101

China National Cereals, Oils and Foodstuffs
Import and Export Corporation (CEROILFOOD)
6-11th Fl., Jingxin Building
2A Dongsanhuanbei Lu
Beijing 100027
Tel: (1) 4660854, 4660686 Fax: (1) 4660636
Tlx: 210237, 210239 CEROF CN

China National Corporation for Development of
Agricultural Produce & Native Products
45 Fuxingmen Nei Street
Beijing 100801
Tel: (1) 651833, 668581 Tlx: 222212 CFSMC CN

China National Native Produce and Animal By-
Products Import and Export Corporation
82 Donganmen Dajie
Beijing 100747
Tel: (1) 5124304, 553808, 5124370
Fax: (1) 5121626 Tlx: 22469 TUHSU CN

China National Packaging Corporation
31 Dongchangan Street
Beijing 100005
Tel: (1) 5138837 Fax: (1) 5124128
Tlx: 22234 CNPC CN

China National Packaging Import and Export
Corporation
28 Donghouxiang, Andingmenwai
Beijing 100731
Tel: (1) 4214058, 4211747 Fax: (1) 4212124 Tlx:
22490 CPACK CN

China National Seed Corporation
31 Min Feng Hu Tong, Xidan
Beijing 100032
Tel: (1) 652592, 651179 Fax: (1) 6012808
Tlx: 22598

China National Tobacco Corporation
1 Hufang Lu
Beijing
Tel: (1) 3015330 Fax: (1) 652171 Tlx: 222366

China Processed Food Import and Export
Company
6-11th Fl., Jingxin Building
2A Dongsanhuanbei Lu
Beijing 100027
Tel: (1) 4660641 Tlx: 210478 PROPD CN

China Sugar and Sundries Import and Export
Company
9th Fl., Jingxin Building
2A Dongsanhuanbei Lu
Beijing 100027
Tel: (1) 4660681 Fax: (1) 4660642
Tlx: 210058 COFCD CN

China Superfood Import and Export Corporation
(TUHSU)
82 Donganmen Dajie
Beijing 100747
Tel: (1) 5124716 Fax: (1) 5124716
Tlx: 22892 TUHSU CN

China Tea Import and Export Corporation (TUHSU)
82 Donganmen Dajie
Beijing 100747
Tel: (1) 5124192, 5124785 Fax: (1) 5124775
Tlx: 22898 TUHSU CN

China Tobacco Import and Export Corporation
A2 Hou Niu Rou Wan Lane
Beijing 100031
Tel: (1) 655492 Fax: (1) 652171
Tlx: 222366 CNTC CN

Shanghai Native Produce and Animal By-Products
Import and Export Corporation
23, Zhong Shan Road, E-1
Shanghai
Tel: (21) 3215630 Fax: (21) 3291883
Tlx: 33065 ANIBY CN

Zhejiang Native Produce & Animal By-Products
Import and Export Corporation
102 Feng Qi Road
Hangzhou, Zhejiang
Fax: (1) (571) 552310 Tlx: 35013, 351054 TUHSU CN

Trade Organizations

China Dairy Cattle Association
56 Zhuanta Lane, Xisi
Beijing 100810
Tel: (1) 6018095　Fax: (1) 6024845

China National Food Industry Association
5 Taipingqiao, Dongli
Guanganmenwai
Beijing 100055
Tel: (1) 3062244　Tlx: 222983 CNFIA CN

China Society of Fisheries
31 Minfeng Lane, Xidan
Beijing 100032
Tel: (1) 6020794　Fax: (1) 6012808

Chinese Association of Agricultural Science
Society
11 Nongzhanguan Lanli
Beijing 100026
Tel: (1) 5003366　Tlx: 22233 MAGR CN

Chinese Fisheries Association
11 Nongzhanguan Nanli
Beijing 100026
Tel: (1) 5003366　Fax: (1) 5002448

Chinese Society of Agricultural Economics
30 Baishiqiao Lu, Xijiao
Beijing 100081
Tel: (1) 8314433

Directories/Publications

Agricultural Knowledge (Nongye Zhishi)
(Monthly; Chinese)
7 Shimuyuan Dongjie
Jinan, Shandong Province
Tel: (531) 42238

Asia Pacific Food Industry Business Report
(Monthly)
Asia Pacific Food Industry Publications
24 Peck Sea St., #03-00 Nehsons Building
Singapore 0207
Tel: [65] 2223422　Fax: [65] 2225587

Asia Pacific Food Industry
(Monthly)
Asia Pacific Food Industry Publications
24 Peck Sea St., #03-00 Nehsons Building
Singapore 0207
Tel: [65] 2223422　Fax: [65] 2225587

Beijing Agriculture
(Monthly; Chinese)
Beijing Shi Nongye Ju
19 Bai Sanhuan Dong Lu, Dewai
Beijing 100029
Tel: (1) 2012244

China Agribusiness Report
(Biweekly)
Asia Letter Group
GPO Box 10874
Hong Kong
Tel: [852] 5262950　Fax: [852] 5267131
Tlx: 4X61166 HKNW
US subscriptions: PO Box 92619
Los Angeles CA 90009, USA

Trade Fairs

Refer to the Trade Fair chapter for complete listings, including contact information, dates, and venues. Trade fairs with particular relevance to this industry include the following, which are listed in that chapter under the headings given below:

Agriculture & Forestry
• Agro Expo China
• Chinese Down Products Export Fair
Food, Beverages & Food Processing
• DRINKTECH SHANGHAI
• International Beverage Technology & Machinery Exhibition
• INTERFOOD SHANGHAI
• International Food & Food Processing Machinery Exhibition
• Shenzhen International Food & Food Processing Machinery Trade Fair

FOOTWEAR

China's production and exports of footwear are growing dramatically, particularly exports of athletic shoes. Footwear constitutes a significant portion of the output from China's light industry sector and over 15 percent of that sector's exports. Major export markets are Japan and the United States.

Much of the domestic shoe production is on an original equipment manufacturing (OEM) basis. Shoe manufacturers are located throughout China, with major concentrations in Jiangxi, Guangdong, Shanghai, Sichuan, Hainan, Harbin, Henan, Shenzhen, and Xian.

Products A wide array of footwear is exported from China, including leather sandals; slippers; textile, rubber, leather, and plastic shoes; and moccasins. Men's, women's, and children's shoes are produced in all price ranges.

Competitive Situation

Many of China's footwear factories are small to midsized operations that are unable to finance needed expansions of facilities. As a result, these firms have difficulty competing in international markets. The larger producers, however, are upgrading their technology, with particular emphasis on athletic shoes.

Government Agencies

China National Light Industry Council
22-B Fuwai Dajie
Beijing 100833
Tel: (1) 8396338　Fax: (1) 8396351

China National Textile Council
12 Dongchanan Jie
Beijing 100742
Tel: (1) 5129303　Fax: (1) 5136020

Foreign Trade Corporations

China Fur & Leather Import and Export
Corporation (TUHSU)
Taiwan Hotel, Office Building
Beijing 100006
Tel: (1) 5132362/3 Fax: (1) 5132358
Tlx: 210654 TUHSU CN

China Light Footwear and Headgear Import
and Export Corporation
82 Donganmen Dajie
Beijing 100747
Tel: (1) 5124354 Fax: (1) 5124354
Tlx: 22282 LIGHT CN

China Light Stationery & Sporting Goods Import
and Export Corporation
82 Donganmen Dajie
Beijing 100747
Tel: (1) 5123703 Fax: (1) 5123703 Tlx: 210031
LIGHT CN

Trade Organizations

All-China Sports Federation
9 Tiyuguan Lu
Beijing 100763
Tel: (1) 7016669 Fax: (1) 7015858

Shanghai Rubber Industry Trade Council
107 Fuzhou Lu
Shanghai 200002
Tel: (21) 3214029

Directories/Publications

Asia Pacific Leather Directory
(Annual)
Asia Pacific Leather Yearbook
(Annual)
Asia Pacific Directories Ltd.
6th Fl., Wah Hen Commercial Center
381 Hennessy Road
Hong Kong
Tel: [852] 8936377 Fax: [852] 8935752

China Plastics and Rubber Journal
(Quarterly; Chinese)
Adsale Publishing Co.
PO Box 20032, Hennessy Road
Hong Kong
Tel: [852] 8920511 Fax: [852] 8384119

Trade Fairs

Refer to the Trade Fair chapter for complete listings, including contact information, dates, and venues. Trade fairs with particular relevance to this industry include the following, which are listed in that
chapter under the heading given below:

Leather Goods & Footwear
- CHINA LEATHER (International Leather &
  Footwear Processing Machinery & Leather
  Goods Exhibition)
- China Textiles, Garments, Shoes & Hats Fair
- International Exhibition on Leather Industry &
  Shoemaking

- International Footwear Industry Trade Fair
- International Garment & Shoe Industry
  Exhibition
- International Leather Products & Machinery
  Fair
- International Shoe and Leather Exhibition
- International Shoes and Shoe-Making Machin-
  ery & Technology Fair
- LEATHER (International Leather Trade Fair)
- Tianjin Leather & Shoes

For other trade fairs that may be of interest, we
recommend that you also consult the headings Hobbies & Recreation; and Textiles & Apparel.

HANDICRAFTS, JEWELRY, TIMEPIECES, LUGGAGE, AND FASHION ACCESSORIES

China's exports of jewelry, timepieces, handicrafts, luggage, and fashion accessories hold nearly
a 40 percent share of international markets. These
products also account for more than 35 percent of
exports from China's light industry sector. Exports
are shipped to over 150 countries and regions, with
major markets in Japan, Hong Kong, Southeast Asia,
the United States, and Europe.

Most of the firms are small to mid-size, and many
are collectively owned or jointly operated with other
trades and enterprises.

Products China's handicraft industry produces a
broad variety of goods: items made of metal, wood,
feathers, shells, bark, cloth, paper, pottery, porcelain,
leather, bamboo, rattan, and palm fiber. Jewelry made
in China includes pearl and gemstone settings in precious and semi-precious metals, as well as costume
jewelry. China's timepiece industry produces a wide
variety of items, including alarm clocks, radio alarm
clocks, wall clocks, and multifunctional digital, quartz,
and analog watches. Many types of materials, including leather, synthetic leather, pigskin, and textiles, are
used in manufacturing handbags, wallets, suitcases,
and other luggage. Of fashion accessories, the most
significant exports are umbrellas, parasols, and silk
scarves and other accessories.

Competitive Situation

Enterprises that make handicrafts, jewelry, timepieces, luggage, and fashion accessories in China
remain competitive in global markets because of low
labor costs, an ability to adapt product lines to diverse and changing market demands, and readily
available raw materials from domestic sources. In
general, the larger-scale enterprises have technologically advanced equipment and comparatively high
productivity. Although these manufacturers are still
relatively labor-intensive and primarily produce
small inexpensive items, they are profitable because

they can produce a large quantity of goods for a fairly low capital investment.

China's larger handicraft companies have concentrated on automating production lines, and most processes are at least semi-mechanized. By combining traditional processes with modern scientific and technological advances, these companies have improved their product quality and design. Nevertheless, many handicraft processes, such as engraving, embroidery, and drawnwork, still involve substantial manual labor. To improve profitability and product quality, many small collectives have been converted into large enterprises that allow for better management of raw material usage and diversification of product lines.

Government Agency

China National Light Industry Council
B22 Fuwaidajie
Beijing 100833
Tel: (1) 8396338 Fax: (1) 8396351

Foreign Trade Corporations

China Culture & Art Articles Import and Export Corporation
A24 Xiaoshiqiao Lane, Xicheng Qu
Beijing
Tel: (1) 4014613, 5126906 Fax: (1) 4014613

China Feather Products Import and Export Corporation (TUHSU)
82 Donganmen Dajie
Beijing 100747
Tel: (1) 5124741 Fax: (1) 5121626
Tlx: 22897 TUHSU CN

China Gifts Import and Export Corporation
Jingxin Building
2A Dongsanhuanbei Lu
Beijing 100027
Tel: (1) 4661842 Fax: (1) 4661825

China Light Suitcases, Bags & Safety Products Import and Export Corporation
82 Donganmen Dajie
Beijing 100747
Tel: (1) 5123703 Fax: (1) 5123703
Tlx: 210031 LIGHT CN

China National Arts & Crafts Import and Export Corporation
Jing Xin Building
2A Dong San Huan Bei Lu
Beijing 100027
Tel: (1) 4663366 Fax: (1) 4661821

China National Pearl, Diamond Gems & Jewelry Import and Export Corporation
14th Fl., Jingxin Building
2A Dongsanhuanbei Lu
Beijing 100027
Tel: (1) 4661645 Fax: (1) 4661641
Tlx: 22155 CNART CN

China Sundries & Flowers Import and Export Corporation (TUHSU)
82 Donganmen Dajie
Beijing 100747
Tel: (1) 5132381 Fax: (1) 5132380
Tlx: 210653 TUHSU CN

Chinatex Accessories Import and Export Corporation
82 Donganmen Jie
Beijing 100747
Tel: (1) 5124507, 5123048 Fax: (1) 556172
Tlx: 210026 CNTEX CN

Minmetals Precious & Rare Minerals Import and Export Corporation
Erligou, Xijiao
Beijing 100044
Tel: (1) 8317733 x4167, 8315344
Fax: (1) 8315079 Tlx: 22190 MIMET CN

Shanghai Arts & Crafts Import and Export Corporation
16, Zhong Shan Road, E. 1
Shanghai 200002
Tel: (21) 3212100 Fax: (21) 3291871
Tlx: 33053 ARTEX CN

Trade Organization

Chinese Ceramic Society
Baiwanzhuang
Beijing 100831
Tel: (1) 8311144 Fax: (1) 8311497

Directories/Publications

Asian Sources: Gifts & Home Products
Asian Sources: Timepieces
(All publications are monthly)
Asian Sources Media Group
22nd Fl., Vita Tower
29 Wong Chuk Hang Road
Wong Chuk Hang, Hong Kong
Tel: [852] 5554777 Fax: [852] 8730488

Fashion Accessories
(Monthly)
Asian Sources Media Group
22nd Fl., Vita Tower
29 Wong Chuk Hang Road
Wong Chuk Hang, Hong Kong
Tel: [852] 5554777 Fax: [852] 8730488

Jewellery News Asia
(Monthly)
Jewellery News Asia Ltd.
Rm. 601-603, Guardian House
32 Oi Kwan Road
Wanchai, Hong Kong
Tel: [852] 8322011 Fax: [852] 8329208

World Jewelogue
(Annual)
Headway International Publications Co.
907 Great Eagle Center
23 Harbour Road
Hong Kong
Tel: [852] 8275121 Fax: [852] 8277064

Trade Fairs

Refer to the Trade Fair chapter for complete listings, including contact information, dates, and venues. Trade fairs with particular relevance to this industry include the following, which are listed in that chapter under the heading given below:

Gifts, Jewelry & Stationery
- Beijing International Fair of Fine Daily Novelties
- China International Gifts & Housewares Expo
- Consumer Goods, Gifts & Housewares Exhibition China
- International Jewelry & Timepieces Trade Fair
- International Toys & Gifts Exhibition
- International Watch & Clock Making Machinery & Technology Exhibition for China (CHINA TIME)
- International Watches, Clocks and Jewelry Exhibition
- Tianjin International Trade Fair for Arts & Crafts (CHINA ARTS & CRAFTS)

For other trade fairs that may be of interest, we recommend that you also consult the headings Furniture & Housewares; Health & Safety; Leather Goods & Footwear; and Textiles & Apparel.

HOUSEWARES, HOUSEHOLD APPLIANCES, AND STATIONERY PRODUCTS

Housewares, household appliances, and stationery products account for over 10 percent of exports from China's light industry sector. A large array of goods is produced for daily home and office use in both domestic and foreign markets. Chinese-made household and stationery products are shipped to over 100 countries and regions. Major production centers are in Shanghai, Guangdong, Guizhou, Harbin, Shenzhen, Tianjin, and Xian.

Products Household items made in China include light bulbs, flashlights, matches, buttons, thimbles, feeding bottle nipples, hair pins, needles, rolling pins, knives, scissors, locks, pots, bowls, and kitchen utensils. Houseware manufacturers offer enamelware, ceramic place settings, and glassware. Chinese-made household appliances include electric fans, irons, fluorescent and other lamps, vacuum cleaners, microwaves, sewing machines, air conditioners, washing machines, and refrigerators. Stationery products range from artists materials to office supplies, including computer, tissue, wrapping, embossed, stencil, typing, and writing paper; typewriters and ribbons; staplers and punches; photograph and stamp albums; diaries; pens, pencils, erasers, and pencil sharpeners; oil paints, glues, drafting boards and instruments, chalks, crayons, clay, inks, and watercolors.

Competitive Situation

China's household and stationery product manufacturers often fail to meet domestic market demand because of outdated equipment, crowded factories, low worker productivity, and limited funding for production expansion and technological upgrades. To increase production and exports, manufacturers have installed automatic and semi-automatic production lines. Product quality is being enhanced through application of more advanced technologies in electronics, microwaves, and lasers. In addition, many firms have instituted quality control systems. New products, patterns, and packaging designs are constantly being developed, and firms are shifting to production of high-grade products to follow changes in consumer demands. Major household good producers are undertaking new marketing strategies, including promotion of their own brand names, establishment of direct retail sales outlets, and active participation in trade fairs and exhibitions.

Government Agency

China National Light Industry Council
B22 Fuwaidajie
Beijing 100833
Tel: (1) 8396338 Fax: (1) 8396351

Foreign Trade Corporations

China Furniture Import and Export Corporation
Jingxin Building
2A Dongsanhuanbei Lu
Beijing 100027
Tel: (1) 4661848 Fax: (1) 4661851

China Light Housewares Import and Export Corporation
82 Donganmen Dajie
Beijing 100747
Tel: (1) 5124349 Fax: (1) 5124349
Tlx: 210035 LIGHT CN

China Light Stationery & Sporting Goods Import and Export Corporation
82 Donganmen Dajie
Beijing 100747
Tel: (1) 5124354 Fax: (1) 5124339
Tlx: 210034 LIGHT CN

Trade Organizations

Chinese Ceramic Society
Baiwanzhuang
Beijing 100831
Tel: (1) 8311144 Fax: (1) 8311497

China Technical Association of Paper Industry
12 Guanghua Lu
Beijing 100020
Tel: (1) 5002880 Tlx: 222717 LIMDI CN

Publication

Asian Sources: Gifts & Home Products
(Monthly)
Asian Sources Media Group
22nd Fl., Vita Tower
29 Wong Chuk Hang Road
Wong Chuk Hang, Hong Kong
Tel: [852] 5554777 Fax: [852] 8730488

Trade Fairs

Refer to the Trade Fair chapter for complete listings, including contact information, dates, and venues. Trade fairs with particular relevance to this industry include the following, which are listed in that chapter under the headings given below:

Construction & Housing
- International Lighting Fixtures & Illuminators Fair
- International Refrigeration, Heating, Ventilation And Air-Conditioning Exhibition
- South China International Exhibition on Construction, Building Services and Interior Decoration

Furniture & Housewares
- China (Shenzhen) International Household Electric Appliances Exhibition
- China Home & Office Style
- China International Gifts & Housewares Expo
- Construction & Interior Decoration
- Consumer Goods, Gifts & Housewares Exhibition China
- CONSUMTRONICS SHANGHAI (International Exhibition on Consumer Electronics and Household Appliances)
- Ideal Home
- Ideal Office (International Exhibition on Consumer Electronics and Household Appliances)
- International Household Electrical Appliances Exhibition
- National Exhibition of 2000 Household Consuming Pattern
- Woodworking & Furniture Fair China

Gifts, Jewelry & Stationery
- Beijing International Fair of Fine Daily Novelties
- International Toys & Gifts Exhibition
- Tianjin International Trade Fair for Arts & Crafts (CHINA ARTS & CRAFTS)

For other trade fairs that may be of interest, we recommend that you also consult the headings Computer & Information Industries; Electronic & Electric Equipment; Multimedia & Audiovisual Equipment; and Packaging, Printing & Paper.

CHEMICALS, MINERALS, AND MATERIALS

China is a major supplier of industrial chemicals and minerals in worldwide markets. Chemicals and minerals, particularly petrochemicals and coal, are among China's top five exports. China ranks third in the world in oil and coal production.

Coal China is estimated to have about 80,000 mines owned by provinces, counties, towns, and individuals, in addition to its state-owned coal mines. Vast reserves of coal exist throughout Inner Mongolia and Xinjiang. Domestic demand for coal is extremely high; nearly three-quarters of the nation's energy comes from coal. China's major export markets for coal are in Japan, Taiwan, and other Asian countries.

Because state-owned coal mines cannot meet domestic demand, private and semiprivate mining operations are expanding. Low production from Chinese coal mines is a result of several factors: artificially low coal prices under government control, underdeveloped transportation systems, weakening demand in international markets, and outmoded mining machinery. Markets for China's coal are expected to increase with the completion of new industrial projects in China, Taiwan, and other developing Asian countries. In addition, the government is investing funds to expand open-cast operations and to replace worn-out coal mining equipment.

Nonferrous Metals China's mining companies produce 10 major nonferrous metals: copper, aluminum, lead, zinc, nickel, tin, antimony, mercury, magnesium, and titanium. Production of these metals has gradually increased each year, aided by the development of large zinc, lead, copper, silver, and molybdenum mines in Inner Mongolia. China has risen to become one of the world's five top producers of lead, most of which is exported to the United States.

Petrochemicals China's largest oil-producing regions are in Shanghai and the provinces of Jiangsu, Zhejiang, and Anhui. East China produces about 27 percent of the country's total petrochemical output and an even larger share of related products. In addition to crude oil, China's petrochemical companies produce oil-related products: chemical fibers, pesticides, and fertilizers; plastics and resins; rubber tires and other items for automobiles, trucks, agricultural machinery, and mining equipment; gasoline, diesel oil, jet fuel, kerosene, and other fuels; lubricating oils for vehicles and ships; acids and alkalis; roofing and building asphalt; and paraffin and other waxes.

The production capacity of China's oil producers meets international standards for basic petrochemical products, but products are limited in variety and are of variable quality. However, China's petrochemical industry is growing rapidly, and Chinese oil companies are investing heavily in technical renovations of existing facilities and construction of new ones, such as catalytic splitting, acrylonitrite, and synthetic resin plants. China's oil companies are acquiring licenses for foreign technology and negotiating joint ventures to increase production of high value-added products.

Steel and Iron Ore China is among the world's top five iron ore and steel producers. Rolled steel is a significant export. Major centers of steel production are in Anshan, Taiyuan, Beijing, Urumqi, Wuhan, Shanghai, Tianjin, Baotou, Chengdu, and Panzhihua.

Competitive Situation

China's mining firms are undertaking substantial expansion projects, some as joint ventures with Japanese companies, to increase production of copper, lead, zinc, titanium, lithium salt, aluminum, and rare metals. Coal producers are expanding into the related field of methane recovery, particularly in regions where consumer demand is high for heating and cooking gas. To meet the increasing domestic market demand for high-tech mining equipment, some Chinese firms are developing and producing machinery through joint ventures with Japanese firms.

Government Agencies

Ministry of Chemical Industry
Building #16, Blk 7, Hepingli St.
Beijing 100013
Tel: (1) 4217764 Fax: (1) 4217764, 4215982

Ministry of Chemical Industry
Foreign Affairs Dept.
3rd Fl., Second Building, Building 16
Hepingli Qiqu, Dongcheng Qu
Beijing 100013
General Affairs & Liaison Div.
Tel: (1) 4217764 Fax: (1) 4225383/4
Economic Coop. Division Tel: (1) 4216025

Ministry of Coal Industry
21 Heping Beijie
Beijing 100713
Tel: (1) 4221864 Fax: (1) 4215610

Ministry of Forestry
18 Hepinglidong Jie, Dongchang Qu
Beijing
Tel: (1) 463061 Tlx: 22237

Ministry of Geology and Mineral Resources
64 Funei Dajie
Beijing
Tel: (1) 6018170, 6024522
Fax: (1) 6017791, 6024523 Tlx: 22531

Ministry of Metallurgical Industry
46 Dongsixi Dajie
Beijing 100071
Tel: (1) 5133322, 5131921 Fax: (1) 5130074

Ministry of Power Industry
137 Fuyou Street
Beijing 100031
Tel: (1) 6054131 Fax: (1) 6011370

State Bureau of Building Materials Industry
Baiwanzhuang
Beijing
Tel: (1) 8311144

Foreign Trade Corporations

Baoshan Iron and Steel Complex Corporation (Group)
2 Mundangjiang Lu
Shanghai
Tel: (21) 646944 Tlx: 33901

China Ceramics & General Trading Enterprise
Jingxin Building
2A Dongsanhuanbei Lu
Beijing 100027
Tel: (1) 4661648 Fax: (1) 4661651

China Metallurgical Import and Export Corporation (CMIEC)
46 Dongsi Xidajie
Beijing 100711
Tel: (1) 5133322 x 1123 Fax: (1) 5133792
Tlx: 22461 MIEC CN

China National Building Materials & Equipment Import and Export Corporation
Bai Wan Zhuang
Beijing 100831
Tel: (1) 8992420, 8311144 Fax: (1) 8023083
Tlx: 222940 CBMIE CN

China National Chemical Construction Corporation
16-7 Heipingli
Beijing
Tel: (1) 4213697 Fax: (1) 4515982 Tlx: 22492

China National Chemicals Import and Export Corporation (SINOCHEM)
Erligou, Xijiao
Beijing 100044
Tel: (1) 8311106, 8316023, 8423225
Fax: (1) 8423221
Tlx: 222732 CHEMI CN

China National Coal Import and Export Corporation (CNCIEC)
8 Xiaguangli, Chaoyang Qu
Beijing 100016
Tel: (1) 4678866, 4677032 Fax: (1) 4677038, 4664863
Tlx: 211273

China National Coal Mine Corporation
21 Bei Jie, Heipingli
Beijing
Tel: (1) 4217766 Tlx: 2102877

China National Geological Technology Development Import and Export Corporation
16 Dewai Street, Xicheng
Beijing 100011
Tel: (1) 2020087 Fax: (1) 6011321
Tlx: 22279 CGIEC CN

China National Metals and Minerals Import and Export Corporation
Building 15, Block 4
Anhuali, Chaoyang Qu
Beijing 100101
Tel: (1) 4916666 Fax: (1) 4917031, 4917652

China National Metals Products Import and Export
Corporation
8 Chedaogou, Haidian Qu
Beijing
Tel: (1) 8021201, 8316312 Fax: (1) 8316312
Tlx: 222864 MIMET CN

China National Minerals Import and Export
Corporation (Minmetals)
8 Chedaogou, Haidian Qu
Beijing
Tel: (1) 8021275, 8021324 Fax: (1) 8315079
Tlx: 22773 MIMET CN

China National Non-ferrous Metals Import and
Export Corporation (CNIEC]
12B Fuxing Lu
Beijing 100814
Tel: (1) 8514477 x1207 Fax: (1) 8515368
Tlx: 22086 CNIEC CN

China National Non-ferrous Metals Industry
Corporation
9 Xizhang Xiang
Beijing
Tel: (1) 657031 Tlx: 22086

China National Offshore Oil Corporation
International Liaison Dept.
23rd Fl., Jin Xin Building
Jia 2, Dong San Huan Bei Lu
Chaoyang Qu
Beijing 100027
Tel: (1) 4663697 Fax: (1) 4662994, 4669007

China National Oil Development Corporation
Liupukang
Beijing
Tel: (1) 444313 Tlx: 22312

China National Petro-Chemical Corporation
(SINOPEC)
24 Xiaoguan Jie, Andingmenwai
Beijing 100013
Tel: (1) 4216731 Fax: (1) 4216972 Tlx: 22655

China National Petroleum and Natural Gas
Corporation
Liu Pu Kang
Beijing 100724
Tel: (1) 2015544 , 2016107 Fax: (1) 4212347,
2018039 Tlx: 22312 CCPRC CN

China Petro-Chemical International Company
Jia 6, Dong Huixin Lu, Chaoyang Qu
Beijing 100092
Tel: (1) 4216402, 4227744 Fax: (1) 4216972
Tlx: 22655 CPCCI CN

Chinatex Raw Materials Import and Export
Corporation
2nd Fl., 33 Dongdan Santiao
Beijing
Tel: (1) 5129866 Fax: (1) 5123389
Tlx: 210025 CNTEX CN

Minmetals (Minerals Import and Export
Corporation) International Enterprises
Development Company
Erligou, Xijiao
Beijing 100044
Tel: (1) 8315344, 8317733 x4167
Fax: (1) 8315079 Tlx: 22190 MIMET CN

Minmetals International Non-ferrous Metals
Trading Company
8 Chedaogou, Haidian Qu
Beijing
Tel: (1) 8021327, 8021278 Fax: (1) 8315079
Tlx: 22773 MIMET CN

Minmetals Precious & Rare Minerals Import and
Export Corporation
Erligou, Xijiao
Beijing 100044
Tel: (1) 8317733 x4167, 8315344
Fax: (1) 8315079 Tlx: 22190 MIMET CN

Sinochem International Chemicals Company Ltd.
Yulong Hotel
40 Fucheng Road
Beijing 100044
Tel: (1) 8415588 Fax: (1) 8413120
Tlx: 222895 CHEMI CN

Sinochem International Petroleum Company Ltd.
Yulong Hotel
40 Fucheng Road
Beijing 100044
Tel: (1) 8316020, 8311151 Tlx: 22553 CHEMI CN

Sinochem Plastics Company Ltd.
Yulong Hotel
40 Fucheng Road
Beijing 100044
Tel: (1) 8413123 Fax: (1) 8413122
Tlx: 222898 CHEMI CN

Trade Organizations

Chemical Industry and Engineering
Society of China
20 Xueyuan Lu
Beijing 100083
Tel: (1) 2015805 Fax: (1) 2017108

China Association for Coal and Machinery Industry
21 Bei Jie, Hepingli
Beijing 100713
Tel: (1) 4217766 Fax: (1) 4214010

Chinese Ceramic Society
Baiwanzhuang
Beijing 100831
Tel: (1) 8311144 Fax: (1) 8311497

Chinese Chemical Society
Zhongguangcun
Beijing 100080
Tel: (1) 2568157 Fax: (1) 2568157

Chinese Society for Metals
46 Dongsi Xi Dajie
Beijing 100761
Tel: (1) 5133322 Fax: (1) 5124122

Directories/Publications

Asian Oil & Gas
(Monthly)
Intercontinental Marketing Corp.
P.O. Box 5056
Tokyo 100-31
Fax: [81] (3) 3667-9646

Asian Plastic News
(Quarterly)
Reed Asian Publishing Pte. Ltd.
5001 Beach Road
#06-12 Golden Mile Complex
Singapore 0719
Tel: [65] 2913188 Fax: [65] 2913180

China Coal Industry Yearbook
(Annual)
Economic Information & Agency
342 Hennessy Road, 10th Fl.
Hong Kong
Tel: [852] 5738217 Fax: [852] 8388304
Tlx: 60647 EICC HX

China's Chemicals and Petrochemicals Directory
(Annual)
China Phone Book Company
Citicorp Centre, 24th Fl.
18 Whitfield Road
Hong Kong
Tel: [852] 8328300 Fax: [852] 5031526

China Plastics and Rubber Journal
(Quarterly; Chinese)
Adsale Publishing Co.
PO Box 20032, Hennessy Road
Hong Kong
Tel: [852] 8920511 Fax: [852] 8384119

Trade Fairs

Refer to the Trade Fair chapter for complete listings, including contact information, dates, and venues. Trade fairs with particular relevance to this industry include the following, which are listed in that chapter under the headings given below:

Environmental & Energy Industries
- CHINA OIL, GAS EXPO
- CHEMICAL & PETROCHEMICAL EXPO/CHINA
- International Meteorological Equipment & Technology Exhibition
- International Trade Fair for Energy Industry & Energy Supply (ENERGY CHINA)

Industrial Materials & Chemicals
- CHINAPLAS (International Exhibition on Plastics and Rubber Engineering)
- International Ceramics Industry Exhibition
- International Chemical Fiber Industry Economic & Technical Cooperation Fair
- International Chemical Industry Trade Fair (ICIF)
- International Exhibition on Chemical Engineering & Specialty Chemicals (CHEM)
- International Exhibition on Chemical Engineer-
ing and Specialty Chemicals
- International Exhibition on Chemical Industry and Material
- International Exhibition on Surface Treatment Technology (CHINA SURFACE TREATMENT)
- International Plastic Industry Exhibition
- International Surface Finishing & Coatings Exhibition (SF CHINA)

Metal & Metal Finishing
- CABLEWIRE SHANGHAI (International Exhibition on Cable & Wire Manufacturing)
- Metal Expo
- Metallurgical Industry Expo/China - Ferrous & Nonferrous Metals Industries
- SHANGHAI METAL EXPO

Petroleum, Gas & Mining
- Gas & LPG
- International Exhibition on Gas Industry
- International Exhibition on the Gas Industry (CHINA GAS)
- Mining China
- Oil Expo China
- PETRO & CHEM CHINA
- Tianjin International Petroleum & Chemical Industrial Show

For other trade fairs that may be of interest, we recommend that you also consult the headings Agriculture & Forestry; Construction & Housing; and Packaging, Printing & Paper.

INDUSTRIAL MACHINERY

China's exports of industrial machinery are minimal, but gradually increasing. Primary markets for Chinese-made industrial machinery include Hong Kong, India, Germany, and Southeast Asia.

Most of China's industrial machinery manufacturers produce low-end equipment for domestic markets. Exports of industrial machinery are generally limited to four sectors: printed circuit board manufacturing equipment, food processing and packaging equipment, forging equipment, and printing presses and other printing machinery.

Printed Circuit Board (PCB) Manufacturing Equipment With dramatic growth in domestic and international market demand for printed circuit boards (PCBs), several Chinese electronics firms are developing PCB-making equipment for sale locally and abroad, primarily in Southeast Asia. Products include automated production lines, etching equipment, digitally controlled drilling machines, and exposure and other machines for double-sided PCB manufacturing. China's major PCB equipment manufacturers are located in the provinces of Shanxi, Hebei, Jiangsu, and Sichuan.

Fewer than 50 Chinese firms are producing this equipment, and most of their products are low-end and low-tech. As a result, exports are minimal and domestic demands are largely met by imports. Some Chinese firms have entered into joint ventures, primarily with Japanese and Hong Kong companies, to produce more technologically advanced machinery, such as radial inserts for television PCB assembly and surface mount technology equipment.

Food Processing and Packaging Machinery At least 350 companies are developing and producing food processing and packaging machinery in China. Products include plastic and paper packing equipment, canning equipment, label-printing equipment, and fruit and vegetable processing machinery. Some of this machinery for example, bottling, capping, and filling equipment is technologically adequate for domestic needs, but it fails to meet hygienic and appearance standards for exported food products. Moreover, production of this equipment meets at most only half of domestic demand. For these reasons, less than 10 percent of Chinese-made food processing and packaging machines is exported.

Despite high local demand for food processing and packaging machinery, China's manufacturers do not have adequate foreign exchange earnings to invest in upgrading their factories. Substantial shortages of raw materials used in food packaging pulp, paper, high-grade plastics, galvanized iron have forced China's food packagers to develop alternative packaging materials, such as a nontoxic polyvinyl chloride film to wrap candy and cigarettes, and packaging paper made from straw pulp. China's machinery manufacturers are developing machines that use these new materials. A number of firms have also entered into joint ventures with companies from Switzerland, Italy, Spain, Germany, and Japan.

Forging Equipment Approximately 130 Chinese enterprises produce foundry and forging equipment. Much of this equipment is sold domestically, to meet high demands from China's metallurgical industry, which is undergoing a substantial modernization. Most Chinese forging equipment is made by specialty forging facilities, which produce steam and pneumatic free-forging hammer and hydraulic presses and steam and pneumatic die-forging equipment.

To upgrade forging equipment, manufacturers are developing energy-saving and nonoxidation furnaces. They are also fabricating more mechanized systems, particularly for coal-fired furnace processes and free-forging hammers and hydraulic presses.

Printing Equipment Printing equipment is manufactured by about 260 collective and state-owned enterprises, about a quarter of which produce 80 percent of this industry's annual output. Production of technologically advanced printing equipment (phototypesetting units, color scanners, and computer typesetters) is limited to only a few factories that are specially designated by the government as industry leaders. Most smaller factories produce traditional platemaking equipment, lead typesetting equipment, platen press printing machinery, and simple post-print equipment for folding, cutting, and binding. Chinese-made printing presses include primary rotary offset presses and primary sheet-fed offset presses. Of these products, the most significant exports are post-printing equipment, primarily shipped to Hong Kong, Sri Lanka, Singapore, India, and Malaysia. Other major export markets are in Thailand, Russia, and Poland.

China's printing equipment manufacturers are unable to satisfy domestic demand, nearly half of which is met by imports. Few manufacturers have the resources needed to expand production or upgrade the technology of their products. Those that have sufficient resources are impeded by government policies that favor the factories designated as industry leaders. A few of the latter are producing and exporting printing equipment through joint ventures, particularly with German firms.

Government Agencies

Ministry of Machine-Building Industry
46 San Litte, Xicheng Qu
Beijing 100823
Tel: (1) 3294966 Fax: (1) 8013867

Ministry of Metallurgical Industry
46 Dongsixi Dajie
Beijing 100071
Tel: (1) 5133322, 5131921 Fax: 5130074

Press and Publishing Administration
85 Dongsi South Avenue
Beijing 100703
Tel: (1) 5127806 Fax: (1) 5127875

Foreign Trade Corporations

China National Agricultural Machinery Import and Export Corporation
Tel: (1) 8012416 Fax: (1) 8012871
Tlx: 22467 AMPRC CN

China National General Machinery Engineering Corporation
2A Taiping Street, Xuanwu Qu
Beijing 100050
Tel: (1) 3017636 Fax: (1) 335720
Tlx: 222233 CMEBJ CN

China National Machinery & Equipment Import and Export Corporation
16 Fu Xing Men Wai Jie
Beijing 100045
Tel: (1) 3268157, 3268202
Fax: (1) 3261865, 3268203 Tlx: 22186

China National Machinery Import and Export Corporation (MACHIMEX)
Erligou, Xijiao, P.O. Box 49
Beijing 100044
Tel: (1) 8317733 x5160, 8944944, 8494851
Fax: (1) 8314136/7, 8314143 Tlx: 22242, 22328

China National Textile Machinery and Technology Import and Export Corporation
75 Chaoyang Mennei Street
Beijing 100010
Tel: (1) 4011870, 4015691 Fax: (1) 4012139
Tlx: 211252 CTMTC CN

China National Transport Machinery Import and Export Corporation
Import Building, Erligou
P.O. Box 49
Beijing 100044
Tel: (1) 8317799 x4400/1/3, 8314128
Fax: (1) 8314136, 8021321 Tlx: 22882

China Textile Machine Technology Import and Export Corporation
15 Pujiang Road
Pujiang Hotel, Rm. 315
Shanghai 200080
Tel: (21) 3254564 Fax: (21) 3207354

Shanghai Machinery & Equipment Import and Export Corporation
400 Xikang Road
Shanghai 200040
Tel: (21) 2552540 Fax: (21) 3269616
Tlx: 33028 SCMEC CN

Trade Organizations

China Chamber of Commerce for Import and Export of Machinery and Electronics
127 Xuan Wu Men Wai Dajie
Beijing 100031
Tel: (1) 6015627

China Forging Industry Association
277 Wangfujing Dajie
Beijing 100740
Tel: (1) 5126679 Fax: (1) 5126675

Chinese Society of Agricultural Machinery
1 Beishatan
Deshengmenwai
Beijing 100083
Tel: (1) 2017131 Fax: (1) 2017326

Directories/Publications

Asiamac Journal: The Machine-Building and Metal Working Journal for the Asia Pacific Region
(Quarterly; English, Chinese)
Adsale Publishing Company
21st Fl., Tung Wai Commercial Building
109-111 Gloucester Road
Hong Kong
Tel: [852] 8920511 Fax: [852] 8384119, 8345014
Tlx: 63109 ADSAP HX

Asian Printing Directory
(Annual)
Travel & Trade Publishing (Asia)
16th Fl., Capitol Centre
5-19 Jardines Bazaar
Causeway Bay, Hong Kong
Tel: [852] 8903067 Fax: [852] 8952378

Oil & Gas News
(Weekly)
Al Hilal Publishing (FE) Ltd.
50 Jalan Sultan, #20-06, Jalan Sultan Centre
Singapore 0719
Tel: [65] 2939233 Fax: [65] 2970862

Petroleum News, Asia's Energy Journal
(Monthly)
Petroleum News Southeast Asia Ltd.
6th Fl., 146 Prince Edward Road West
Kowloon, Hong Kong
Tel: [852] 3805294 Fax: [852] 3970959

Trade Fairs

Refer to the Trade Fair chapter for complete listings, including contact information, dates, and venues. Trade fairs with particular relevance to this industry include the following, which are listed in that chapter under the headings given below:

Agriculture & Forestry
- International Exhibition on Preservation Technology and Processing Equipment for Grain and Meat
- International Exhibition on Technology and Equipment for Grain and Meat Processing and Storage
- International Grain & Oil Storage Equipment Exhibition
- International Meat Processing & Packaging Machinery Exhibition

Food, Beverages & Food Processing
- International Beverage Technology & Machinery Exhibition
- International Agricultural Machinery, Agrotechnology and Food Processing Exhibition
- International Food & Food Processing Machinery Exhibition
- International Food Processing & Packaging Machinery Exhibition
- International Food Processing Machinery & Packaging
- Shenzhen International Food & Food Processing Machinery Trade Fair

Machines & Instruments
- AHME (Asia Machinery/Hardware Exhibition)
- BOILER SHANGHAI
- CHINA INSTRUMENT (International Exhibition on Instrumentation & Technology)
- CHINA MECTT (International Machinery, Factory Automation, Electronics Technology Exhibition for China)
- CHINA WRITE (International Exhibition of Equipment & Technology for Production of Writing/Marking Instruments)
- China International Form Fabricating Fair (3F)
- China Machine Tools Show

- China StoneTech
- DETECHNIQUE CHINA (International Exhibition on Techniques of Machine Monitoring Fault Diagnosis & Maintenance)
- Engine China
- IBDMEX (International Exhibition on Building Decorative Material & Production Equipment Industry)
- INTERAD (International Exhibition on Advertising Technology)
- International Bearing Industry Exhibition (BEARING)
- International Boiler & Pressure Vessel Manufacturing & Welding Exhibition
- International Exhibition on Instruments, Public Security Equipment and Technology
- International Exhibition on Stone Processing and Woodworking Machinery
- International Heat Treatment Technology Exhibition
- International Machine Tool Show (CIMT)
- International Machinery & Electronic Technology (CHINA METE)
- International Machinery & Industrial Supplies Fair
- International Machinery & Materials Exhibition (ChinaMex Beijing)
- International Machinery & Materials Exhibition for China
- International Machinery and Equipment Exhibition (MACHINEX)
- International Meteorological Equipment & Technology Exhibition
- International Musical Instruments and Manufacturing Exposition (MUSIC CHINA)
- International Refractory Industrial Exhibition (REFRACTORY CHINA)
- International Timber & Stone Processing Machinery Exhibition
- International Woodworking Machinery and Technology Exhibition
- MACHIMPEX
- Shanghai International Light Industries Exhibition (SILIE)
- South China International Machinery Exhibition for Light Industries (LIMAC SOUTH CHINA)

Metal & Metal Finishing
- DIE & MOLD
- DIE & MOLD CHINA
- International Exhibition on Die & Mold Technology & Equipment
- International Boiler & Pressure Vessel Manufacturing & Welding Exhibition
- International Exhibition on Foundry, Forging and Heat Treatment (Foundry Shanghai)
- International Foundry, Forging, Furnace & Metallurgical Equipment Exhibition

Packaging, Printing & Paper
- FOODPACK CHINA
- INTERFOOD SHANGHAI (International Exhibition for Food Processing & Packaging Equipment
- International Exhibition on Papermaking Industry (PAPER OF CHINA)
- International Packaging & Printing Machinery and Materials Exhibition for China (PACK PRINT CHINA)
- International Printing Technology Exhibition (CHINA PRINT)
- Print Expo

For other trade fairs that may be of interest, we recommend that you also consult the headings Aerospace & Oceanic; Computer & Information Industries; Construction & Housing; Electronic & Electric Equipment; Environmental & Energy Industries; Leather Goods & Footwear; Petroleum, Gas & Mining; and Textiles & Apparel.

MEDICAL PRODUCTS

China's pharmaceutical industry is growing dramatically, and domestic demand for Western drugs is increasing. Exports of Chinese pharmaceutical products have risen gradually each year. Over 100 countries purchase China's medical products, with major export markets in Brazil, France, Germany, and the United States.

Of the more than 2,000 factories producing medicines in China, fewer than 50 are major firms. The larger drug manufacturers export from 30 to 60 percent of their total production.

Products Exports of pharmaceuticals include traditional Chinese medicines, Western medicines, surgical dressings, bulk preparations, final preparations, vaccines, and blood products.

Chinese herbs and medicines are produced throughout the country, with major centers in the provinces of Jiangsu, Fujian, Gansu, Shaanxi, Xian, and Shanxi. Export markets for traditional Chinese medicines are increasing slowly as foreign consumers begin to accept and experiment with these products.

Shanghai Municipality and the provinces of Heilongjiang, Gansu, Shandong, Liaoning, Hebei, and Guangdong are major centers for the production of Western drugs, mostly antibiotics and basic medicines for the treatment of acute or endemic diseases. Exports of Western drugs include penicillin, benzylpenicillin sodium, streptomycin sulphate, erythromycin, neomycin, mytomycin, lincomycin hydrochloride, oxacillin, piperacillin, cephalothin, oxytetracycline base, cephamamdole nafate, and cephaperazone. Others include adriamycin for cancer treatment, a wide array of vitamins, and increasing amounts of chemical, semi-finished, and bulk preparations.

Competitive Situation

Domestic production of pharmaceuticals does not entirely meet domestic demand. Chinese drug manufacturers do not have the technology needed to produce new and advanced drugs, and funds assigned to R&D have been minimal. Some estimates place Chinese production technology more than 10 years behind that of developed countries. Bulk preparations, needed to make antibiotics, are largely imported.

To encourage export growth in the pharmaceutical industry, the government has committed substantial funds to the construction of new pharmaceutical manufacturing facilities and to the technological renovation of existing ones. The State Science and Technology Commission has formed a drug R&D group to coordinate development of new products, such as cephalosporin and tetracyclines, and to encourage manufacturers to move beyond the copying of foreign drugs.

In an effort to become more competitive worldwide, China's major drug manufacturers are expanding production capacity and implementing quality control standards. A few firms have installed computerized production lines and have adopted the international Good Manufacturing Practices (GMP) standards. To accelerate technology upgrades, several Chinese drug firms are negotiating technology transfer arrangements and joint ventures with foreign companies, and the government has targeted new drug administration methods controlled release medicines, skin patches, nasal sprays, and inhalation preparations for foreign investment. At least 20 arrangements are under way with companies from England, Japan, Belgium, Sweden, Switzerland, and the United States to produce advanced medicines for the treatment of asthma, bronchitis, allergies, parasitic infestations, rheumatoid arthritis, cardiovascular hypertension and angina pectoris disorders, dermatological diseases, and hepatitis.

Government Agencies

Ministry of Agriculture
11 Nonzhanguan Nanli, Hepinli
Beijing 100026
Tel: (1) 5003366, 5004606 Fax: (1) 5002448

Ministry of Public Health
44 Houhaibeiyan, Xicheng Qu
Beijing 100725
Tel: (1) 4033387 Fax: (1) 4014338 Tlx: 22193

State Science & Technology Commission
54 Sanlihe Road
Beijing 100862
Tel: (1) 8012594 Fax: (1) 8012594

Foreign Trade Corporations

China National Medical Equipment & Supplies Import and Export Corporation
44 Houhai Beiyan
Beijing 100725
Tel: (1) 4012327 Fax: (1) 4012327
Tlx: 22193 MINIH CN

China National Medicine Corporation
38A, Beilishi Lu, Xizhimen
Beijing 100810
Tel: (1) 8318311

China National Medicine and Health Products Import and Export Corporation
L Suite, Huiyuan Apartments
8 Anding Menwai
Beijing 100101
Tel: (1) 4992632/4, 4917482
Fax: (1) 4917462, 4917476

China National Pharmaceutical Foreign Trade Corporation
38A, Beilishi Lu, Xizhimenwai
Beijing 100810
Tel: (1) 8316571/2, 8313344 Fax: (1) 8316571
Tlx: 22659 SPAC CN

The Oriental Scientific Instruments Import and Export Corporation
52 Sanlihe Road, Xicheng Qu
Beijing
Tel: (1) 8012342 Fax: (1) 8012412
Tlx: 20063 ASCHI CN

Trade Organizations

China Association of Traditional Chinese Medicine and Pharmacy
4A Yiunghua Lu
Hepingli Dong Jie
Beijing 100029
Tel: (1) 4218311/6

China Chamber of Commerce Medicines and Health Products Importers and Exporters
12 Jian Guo Men Wai Dajie, 12th Fl.
Beijing 100022
Tel: (1) 5001542, 5003344 Fax: (1) 5001150

Chinese Medical Association
42 Dongsi Xidajie
Beijing
Tel: (1) 5133311

Chinese Medical Society
42 Dongsi Xi Dajie
Beijing 100710
Tel: (1) 5127946 Fax: (1) 5123754

Chinese Pharmaceutical Association
38A Beilishi Lu
Beijing 100810
Tel: (1) 8316576

Directories/Publications

Abstracts of Chinese Medicines
(Quarterly)
Chinese University Hong Kong
Chinese Medical Materials Research Center
Shatin, New Territories, Hong Kong

Asian Hospital
(Quarterly)
Techni-Press Asia Ltd.
PO Box 20494
Hennessy Road
Hong Kong
Tel: [852] 5278682 Fax: [852] 5278399

Asian Medical News
(Bimonthly)
MediMedia Pacific Ltd.
Unit 1216, Seaview Estate
2-8 Watson Road
North Point, Hong Kong
Tel: [852] 5700708 Fax: [852] 5705076

Asia-Pacific Dental News
(Quarterly)
Adrienne Yo Publishing Ltd.
4th Fl., Vogue Building
67 Wyndham Street
Central, Hong Kong
Tel: [852] 5253133 Fax: [852] 8106512

China Pharmaceutical and Medical Instruments
(Chinese)
State Pharmaceutical Administration of China
Export Dept. of CNPIEC
PO Box 88, Chaonei St.
Beijing 100704
Fax: (1) 4015664

Far East Health
(10 per year)
Update-Siebert Publications
Reed Asian Publishing Pte
5001 Beach Road
#06-12 Golden Mile Complex
Singapore 0719
Tel: [65] 2913188 Fax: [65] 2913180

Medicine Digest Asia
(Monthly)
Rm. 1903, Tung Sun Commercial Centre
194-200 Lockhart Road
Wanchai, Hong Kong
Tel: [852] 8939303 Fax: [852] 8912591

Trade Fairs

Refer to the Trade Fair chapter for complete listings, including contact information, dates, and venues. Trade fairs with particular relevance to this industry include the following, which are listed in that chapter under the heading given below:

Medicine & Pharmaceuticals
- China International Exhibition of the Equipment and Technology for the Pharmaceutical Industry (CHINA PHARMACY)
- China International Medical Equipment &

Facilities Exhibition (SINOMED)
- Hospital Equipment Expo
- Hubei International Medical, Scientific & Educational Equipment Exhibition
- INTERMED CHINA (International Trade Fair on Medical & Pharmaceutical Equipment)
- International Exposition on Biotechnology and Life Science
- International Medical & Hospital Instruments and Equipment Exhibition (MEDICAL CHINA)
- International Medical Equipment Exhibition (WUHAN INTERMED)
- International Medical Exhibition (INTERMED KUNMING)
- International Medical Instruments, Health Care Equipment and Pharmaceuticals Exhibition (MEDEX)
- International Medicines & Health Products Exhibition
- International Meeting on Chemical Engineering and Biotechnology in the Far East (Achemasia)
- Shaanxi International Medical Exhibition (SHAANXI INTERMED)
- SHANGHAI MEDICAL EXPO
- Shanghai International Exhibition on Medical Equipment

For other trade fairs that may be of interest, we recommend that you also consult the headings Health & Safety; and Tools: Precision & Measuring.

TEXTILES AND APPAREL

Textiles and garments are among China's top three exports, generating about 25 percent of the country's foreign exchange. Major export markets for Chinese textiles and garments are in Hong Kong, Taiwan, South Korea, Japan, Europe, and the United States.

At least 24,500 textile factories in China produce such items as fabrics, yarns, threads, ribbons, garments, linens, and floor coverings of wool, cotton, silk, and synthetic fibers. Textile enterprises range in size from small, individually owned businesses of a few dozen workers to large state-owned factories that employ several thousand. Many garment makers are foreign-funded. Approximately half of China's textiles are produced in East China, with major centers in Shanghai and the provinces of Jiangsu, Zhejiang, and Anhui.

Fabrics Cotton textile factories constitute China's largest fabric-producing sector, followed by makers of silk and wool fabrics. China's textile factories supply most of the world's silk, and silk weavers have diversified their product lines to include such popular items as blended silk, cross-woven, and jacquard-woven fabrics. Cotton and cotton-blend fabrics made in China include broad-width cloth, high-count and densely woven cloth, high-density downproof fabric, and denim. The wool industry produces lightweight and soft fabrics, particularly cashmere, gabardine, and angora blends. Other significant exports are synthetic fiber fabrics and ramie fabrics, most commonly used in garments, furnishings, and various industrial applications.

Apparel Factories that produce apparel account for at least 40 percent of China's total textile production, and projections suggest that figure may reach 65 percent by 1995. International and domestic markets for apparel made of synthetic fibers are growing, and such apparel accounts for over half of all China's clothing sales. Major apparel exports are overcoats, women's shirts, men's suits, and children's wear. Products include jackets, pajamas, robes, overalls, denim jeans, army uniforms, ski and sport outfits, infant bibs, and hats.

Competitive Situation

Profits in China's textile industry have fallen in recent years because of decreasing efficiency in production, obsolete equipment, overproduction, shortages of domestic raw materials, rising cotton costs, and reduced international market demands due to the worldwide recession. Labor-intensive products, which are China's primary textile exports, are inconsistent in quality, and low worker productivity is offsetting China's otherwise competitive labor costs. Much of the textile machinery used by Chinese firms is over 30 years old, and at least 70 percent of the manufacturing equipment needs replacement or upgrading. China's indirect textile and garment trading system has also inhibited the quick transmission of market trends to local garment makers. To retain a competitive edge in global markets, Chinese firms are importing modern textile manufacturing equipment and acquiring technology licensing agreements in all industry sectors, including cotton and wool weaving, yarn spinning, garment assembly, and synthetic fiber production. Most firms are focusing on improvements in production efficiency and on the manufacture of higher-value goods, rather than increases in production capacity. In the spinning sector, for example, companies are replacing outdated spindles and looms with high-speed automated spinning and weaving equipment. Quality control systems are being implemented, with emphasis on five problems: yarn faults, filling bars, shading, skew weft, and shrinkage.

China's textile enterprises are also renovating mills, constructing new mills, diversifying product lines, and expanding production facilities for raw materials, particularly synthetic fibers. Firms are now producing cationic dyable polyester, high-tenacity modulus vinyl, and high-absorbency polyester. Also under development are fibers with special characteristics, such as materials that are flame-retardant, pilling-resistant, and static-free. New technologies being introduced into China's cotton, silk, and wool factories include improved dyes, flat and rotary screen printing, and various treatments for shrinkproofing, resin and chintz finishing, and embossing.

Government Agency

China National Textile Council
12 Dongchanan Jie
Beijing 100742
Tel: (1) 5129303 Fax: (1) 5136020

Foreign Trade Corporations

Beijing Knitwear Import and Export Corporation
2 Bei Jie, Xiao Huang Zhuang, He Ping L1, Chao Yang Qu
Beijing
Tel: (1) 4221610 Fax: (1) 4221896
Tlx: 210425, 210426 PKNIT CN

China Carpet Import and Export Corporation (TUHSU)
82 Donganmen Jie
Beijing 100747
Tel: (1) 5132392, 5124183 Fax: (1) 5124592
Tlx: 22896 TUHSU CN

China Fur & Leather Import and Export Corporation (TUHSU)
Taiwan Hotel, Office Building
Beijing 100006
Tel: (1) 5132362/3 Fax: (1) 5132358
Tlx: 210654 TUHSU CN

China National Silk Import and Export Corporation
105 Beiheyan Street, Dongcheng Qu
Beijing 100006
Tel: (1) 5125125, 5128336, 5123338
Fax: (1) 5126838, 5124746 Tlx: 210594

China National Silk Materials & Fabrics Import and Export Corporation
105 Beiheyan Street, Dongcheng Qu
Beijing 100006
Tel: (1) 5128331 Fax: (1) 5128353
Tlx: 210594 CSMIC CN

China National Textiles Import and Export Corporation
82 Donganmen Dajie
Beijing 100747
Tel: (1) 5123844, 5135533 Fax: (1) 5124711
Tlx: 22280 CNTEX CN

China Silk Garments Import and Export Corporation
105 Beiheyan Street, Dongcheng Qu
Beijing 100006
Tel: (1) 5138198 Fax: (1) 5136839
Tlx: 210596 CSGEC CN

China Silk Materials Import Corporation
105 Beiheyan Street, Dongcheng Qu
Beijing 100006
Tel: (1) 5125123 Fax: (1) 5136840
Tlx: 210081 CSMIC CN

Chinatex Yarns & Fabrics Import
and Export Corporation
82 Donganmen Dajie
Beijing 100747
Tel: (1) 5124718 Fax: (1) 5124713
Tlx: 210023 CNTEX CN

Chinatex Cotton Import and Export Corporation
3rd Fl., 33 Dongdan Santiao
Beijing
Tel: (1) 5124009 Fax: (1) 5124010/2 Tlx: 211278

Chinatex Garments Import and Export Corporation
82 Donganmen Dajie
Beijing 100747
Tel: (1) 5124728 Fax: (1) 5124768
Tlx: 22450 CNTEX CN

Chinatex Knitwear Manufactured Goods
Import and Export Corporation
82 Donganmen Dajie
Beijing 100747
Tel: (1) 5124388, 5124604 Fax: (1) 5124743
Tlx: 210024 CNTEX CN

Guangxi Textiles Import and Export Corporation
33A Tian Tao Road
Nanning, Guangxi 530022
Tel: (771) 27693, 29319, 23315, 23174
Fax: (771) 29023 Tlx: 48106 GXTEX CN

Jilin Provincial Textiles Import and Export
Corporation
A2, Pu Qing Road
Changchun 130061
Tel: (431) 860916/9 Fax: (431) 860611
Tlx: 83025 JCTIE CN

Shanghai Garments Import and Export
Corporation
1040 North Suzhou Road
Shanghai
Tel: (21) 3251000 Fax: (21) 3255148, 3248349
Tlx: 33036, 33056 GAREX CN

Shenyang Textiles Import and Export Corporation
No. 19, South Sanjing St., Shenhe Qu
Shenyang
Tel: (24) 21993, 28356, 23066, 727478
Fax: (24) 21993 Tlx: 8040-17 TIECS CN

Tianjin Textiles Import and Export Corporation
68, Dali Street
Tianjin
Fax: (31) 7843 Tlx: 23151 TJTEX CN

Zhejiang Garments Import and Export Corporation
No. 146A Nanshan Road
Hangzhou
Tel: (571) 771424 Fax: (571) 771761
Tlx: 351060, 351061 GMTHZ CN

Trade Organizations

China Textile Engineering Society
Inside Textile Dept. Institute
Yingjiafen, Dongjiao
Beijing 100025
Tel: (1) 5016537 Fax: (1) 5004780

China Chamber of Commerce
for Import and Export of Textiles
33A Dongdansantiao
Beijing 100005
Tel: (1) 5122029 Tlx: 211143 FANYN CN

Shanghai Cotton Spinning and Weaving Association
Rm. 306, 24 Zhongshan
Dong Yi Lu
Shanghai 200020
Tel: (21) 3214066

Directories/Publications

Asia Pacific Leather Directory
(Annual)
Asia Pacific Leather Yearbook
(Annual)
Asia Pacific Directories Ltd.
6th Fl., Wah Hen Commercial Center
381 Hennessy Road
Hong Kong
Tel: [852] 8936377 Fax: [852] 8935752

ATA Journal: Journal for Asia on Textile & Apparel
(Bimonthly)
Adsale Publishing Company
Tung Wai Commercial Building, 21st Fl.
109-111 Gloucester Road
Wanchai, Hong Kong
Tel: [852] 8920511 Fax: [852] 8384119

Beijing Textile (Beijing Fangzhi)
(Chinese)
Gongcheng Xuehui
2 Shilipu, Chaoyangmennwai
Beijing 100025
Tel: (1) 5004477 Fax: (1) 5004271

China Textile
(Bimonthly)
Adsale Publishing Co.
PO Box 20032, Hennessy Road
Hong Kong
Tel: [852] 8920511 Fax: [852] 8384119

Textile Asia Index
(Annual)
Business Press Ltd.
30-32 d'Aguilar Street
Tak Yan Commercial Building, 11th Fl.
GPO 185
Central Hong Kong
Tel: [852] 5247441 Tlx: 60275 TEXIA HX

Textile Asia: The Asian Textile and Apparel
Monthly
(Monthly)
Business Press Ltd.
11th Fl., California Tower
30-32 d'Aguilar Street
Central, Hong Kong
Tel: [852] 5247467 Fax: [852] 8106966

Trade Fairs

Refer to the Trade Fair chapter for complete listings, including contact information, dates, and venues. Trade fairs with particular relevance to this industry include the following, which are listed in that chapter under the headings given below:

Leather Goods & Footwear
- CHINA LEATHER (International Leather & Footwear Processing Machinery & Leather Goods Exhibition)
- China Textiles, Garments, Shoes & Hats Fair
- International Exhibition on Leather Industry & Shoemaking
- International Garment & Shoe Industry Exhibition
- International Leather Products & Machinery Fair
- International Shoe and Leather Exhibition
- International Shoes and Shoe-Making Machinery & Technology Fair
- LEATHER (International Leather Trade Fair)
- Tianjin International Trade Fair for Leather and Footwear Machinery and Equipment (CHINA LIGHT)
- Tianjin Leather & Shoes

Textiles & Apparel
- China Fashion Design Show
- China International Garments/Accessories Fair
- China Textiles, Garments, Shoes & Hats Fair
- Dalian International Fashion Festival
- International Exhibition on Garment and Textile Machinery
- International Fashion & Accessories Fair
- International Fashion Fair
- International Garment & Shoe Industry Exhibition
- SHANGHAI TEX (Multinational Exhibition on Textile Industry)
- TIANJINTEX (Tianjin International Textile/Garment Industrial Fair)

For other trade fairs that may be of interest, we recommend that you also consult the headings Furniture & Housewares; Hobbies & Recreation; Industrial Materials & Chemicals; and Machines & Instruments.

TOOLS

China's manufacturers of hand machine tools produce primarily low-end products, of which only about 17 percent are exported. Exports of machine tools, which are shipped mainly to Japan and the United States, have increased slightly each year.

The bulk of China's machine tools is for metalworking applications, such as metal cutting and forming. Most Chinese-made machine tools are of relatively simple technology; only 1.5 percent are numerically controlled (NC) products. Major machine tool making centers are located in Shanghai and in the province of Liaoning.

Competitive Situation

After declining in 1990, production of machine tools in China is gradually increasing. However, the industry is beset by inadequate technology and quality control standards. Many Chinese-produced tools are not as carefully engineered or manufactured as those made in advanced industrialized countries, and stockpiles of unmarketable Chinese machine tools continue to mount. Machine tool imports into China are high, with local manufacturers able to meet only about 60 percent of domestic demand. Domestic demand is rapidly increasing as the energy, transportation, agricultural, communication, and metallurgical industries continue to modernize.

The government is providing incentives to improve China's competitive position in world machine tool markets and to capture more of the growing domestic market. Emphasis is on upgrading technology, expanding product lines, improving standardization and quality, and restructuring factory management. China's machine tool makers are actively seeking foreign investors for joint ventures, technology transfers, and training and consulting services. Such arrangements are under way with Swiss, German, and US machine tool companies to produce exportable products, including computer numerically controlled (CNC) equipment.

Government Agency

Ministry of Machine-Building Industry
46 San Li He, Xicheng Qu
Beijing 100823
Tel: (1) 3294966 Fax: (1) 8013867

Foreign Trade Corporations

China Educational Instrument & Equipment Corporation
35 Damucang Hutong Xidan
Beijing 100816
Tel: (1) 652305 Tlx: 22014 SEDC CN

China National Instruments Import and Export Corporation (CNIIEC, Instrimpex)
Erligou, Xijiao
PO Box 1818
Beijing 100044
Tel: (1) 8317733, 8312921, 8495191 Fax: (1) 8315925, 8318380 Tlx: 22304 CIIEC CN

China National Instruments Import and Export Corporation, Technical Service Company
B7 Baishiquiao Road, Haidian Qu
Beijing
Tel: (1) 8327397, 8312166 Fax: (1) 8312166
Tlx: 222491 IMSTC CN

China National Machine Tool Corporation (CNMTC)
19 Fang Jia Xiaoxiang, An Nei
Beijing 100007
Tel: (1) 4033767, 4011682 Fax: (1) 4015657
Tlx: 210088 CNMTC CN

The Oriental Scientific Instruments Import and
Export Corporation
52 Sanlihe Road, Xicheng Qu
Beijing
Tel: (1) 8012342 Fax: (1) 8012412
Tlx: 20063 ASCHI CN

Trade Organizations

China Machine Tool and Tool Builders' Association
(CMTBA)
26 South Yue Tan Street
Beijing 100825
Tel: (1) 868261 x2668 Fax: (1) 8013472

Chinese Society of Measurement
PO Box 1413
Beijing 100013
Tel: (1) 4218704/9 Tlx: 210209 SBN CN

Shanghai Instrument Society
225 Longjiang Lu
Shanghai 200082
Tel: (21) 5417350

Directories/Publications

Asian Sources: Hardware
(Monthly)
Asian Sources Media Group
22nd Fl., Vita Tower
29 Wong Chuk Hang Road
Wong Chuk Hang, Hong Kong
Tel: [852] 5554777 Fax: [852] 8730488

China's Instruments & Meters
(Annual)
China Phone Book Company
Citicorp Centre, 24th Fl.
18 Whitfield Road
Hong Kong
Tel: [852] 8328300 Fax: [852] 5031526

Trade Fairs

Refer to the Trade Fair chapter for complete listings, including contact information, dates, and venues. Trade fairs with particular relevance to this industry include the following, which are listed in that
chapter under the heading given below:

Tools: Precision & Measuring
- AHME (Asia Machinery/Hardware Exhibition)
- China International Optics Exhibition
- China Machine Tools Show
- China National Machine Tool Industry Fair
- Hubei International Medical, Scientific &
  Educational Equipment Exhibition
- International Exhibition on Environmental
  Engineering & Measuring Instruments (EEMI)
- International Exhibition on Modern Machine
  Tools
- International Machine Tool Show (CIMT)
- International Optical Industry Exhibition for
  China (CHINA OPTICS)
- International Trade Fair for Laboratory

Equipment & Scientific Instruments (LAB
CHINA)
- Shanghai International Light Industries
  Exhibition (SILIE)

For other trade fairs that may be of interest, we
recommend that you also consult the headings Construction & Housing; Electronic & Electric Equipment; Machines & Instruments; and Metal & Metal
Finishing.

TOYS, SPORTING GOODS, AND RECREATIONAL EQUIPMENT

China's manufacturers of toys, sporting goods,
and recreational equipment are part of the country's
light industry sector. Shanghai, Guangdong, and
Jiangsu are China's main centers for the production
and export of sporting goods, recreational equipment, and toys.

Toys China's toy makers produce and assemble
toys of all kinds, including stuffed animals, dolls and
figurines, games, educational toys, electronic toys,
hand puppets, tricycles, radio-controlled toys,
masks, inflatable items, and kites. These toys are
made from a variety of materials, including bamboo,
ceramics, cloth, wood, plastic, rubber, and metal.

**Sporting Goods and Recreational Equip-
ment** Bicycles, bicycle parts, and accessories have
become major export items for Chinese sporting
goods firms. Nearly every Chinese province has a
bicycle manufacturer. Other export items are balls
for table tennis, football, tennis, and squash; rack-
ets for badminton and tennis; exercise equipment,
including barbells, weights, exercise bicycles, and
gymnasium equipment; ice and roller skates; and
camping and mountaineering gear, including tents,
sleeping bags, backpacks, and hunting knives.

Competitive Situation

China's toy, sporting goods, and recreational
equipment manufacturers have largely saturated the
domestic market, and are shifting to export markets
to sell overstocked items. To increase exports of toys
and sporting goods, firms are developing high-quality products that meet international standards and
trends. Quality control systems have been instituted,
and enterprises are intensifying their efforts to monitor and adapt to worldwide consumer demands.
China's sporting goods manufacturers are concentrating on producing equipment with modern designs, high durability, and multiple functions. Efforts
to expand exports have been undertaken by Chinese
agencies, which have permitted enterprises in various localities to export products on their own.

Government Agency

China National Light Industry Council
B22 Fuwaidajie
Beijing 100833
Tel: (1) 8396338 Fax: (1) 8396351

Foreign Trade Corporations

China Gifts Import and Export Corporation
Jingxin Building
2A Dongsanhuanbei Lu
Beijing 100027
Tel: (1) 4661842 Fax: (1) 4661825

China Light General Merchandise Import and
Export Corporation
82 Donganmen Dajie
Beijing 100747
Tel: (1) 5126840 Fax: (1) 5123708
Tlx: 210033 LIGHT CN

China Light Stationery & Sporting Goods Import
and Export Corporation
82 Donganmen Dajie
Beijing 100747
Tel: (1) 5124354 Fax: (1) 5124339
Tlx: 210034 LIGHT CN

China Plaited Products Import and Export
Corporation
Jingxin Building
2A Dongsanhuanbei Lu
Beijing 100027
Tel: (1) 4661838 Fax: (1) 4661841

Chinatex Oriental Trading Corporation
82 Donganmen Dajie
Beijing 100747
Tel: (1) 5124389, 5124067 Fax: (1) 5124738
Tlx: 4960 BEIJING

Sinochem Plastics Company Ltd.
Yulong Hotel
40 Fucheng Road
Beijing 100044
Tel: (1) 8413123 Fax: (1) 8413122
Tlx: 222898 CHEMI CN

Trade Organizations

All-China Sports Federation
9 Tiyuguan Lu
Beijing 100763
Tel: (1) 7016669 Fax: (1) 7015858

Chinese Association Light Industry of Science and
Technology
Inside Light Industry Dept.
22B Fuwai Dajie
Beijing
Tel: (1) 2015921

Shanghai Rubber Industry Trade Council
107 Fuzhou Lu
Shanghai 200002
Tel: (21) 3214029

Directories/Publications

Asian Manufacturing
Far East Trade Press Ltd.
2nd Fl., Kai Tak Commercial Building
317 Des Voeux Road
Central, Hong Kong
Tel: [852] 5453028 Fax: [852] 5446979

Asian Plastic News
(Quarterly)
Reed Asian Publishing Pte. Ltd.
5001 Beach Road
#06-12 Golden Mile Complex
Singapore 0719
Tel: [65] 2913188 Fax: [65] 2913180

Asian Sources: Gifts & Home Products
(Monthly)
Asian Sources Media Group
22nd Fl., Vita Tower
29 Wong Chuk Hang Road
Wong Chuk Hang, Hong Kong
Tel: [852] 5554777 Fax: [852] 8730488

China Plastics and Rubber Journal
(Quarterly; Chinese)
Adsale Publishing Co.
PO Box 20032, Hennessy Road
Hong Kong
Tel: [852] 8920511 Fax: [852] 8384119

Trade Fairs

Refer to the Trade Fair chapter for complete listings, including contact information, dates, and venues. Trade fairs with particular relevance to this industry include the following, which are listed in that chapter under the heading given below:

Hobbies & Recreation
- Electronic Toys & Games
- International Educational Materials Exhibition (CHINADIDAC)
- International Musical Instruments and Manufacturing Exposition (MUSIC CHINA)
- International Sporting Goods Exhibition (Intersport)
- International Sports Facilities Exhibition
- International Toys & Gifts Exhibition
- Shenzhen International Sporting Goods Exhibition
- TOYS
- International Toys Expo

For other trade fairs that may be of interest, we recommend that you also consult the headings Computer & Information Industries; Electronic & Electric Equipment; and Gifts, Jewelry & Stationery.

Trade Fairs

China hosts a wide range of trade fairs and expositions that should interest anyone who seeks to do business in this dynamic and expanding economy. Whether you want to buy Chinese goods or exhibit your own goods and services for sale to the Chinese market, you will almost undoubtedly find several trade fairs to suit your purposes.

The listing of trade fairs in this section is designed to acquaint you with the scope, size, frequency, and length of the events held in China and to give you contact information for the organizers. While every effort has been made to ensure that this information is correct and complete as of press time, the scheduling of such events is in constant flux. Announced exhibitions can be canceled; dates and venues are often shifted. If you are interested in attending or exhibiting at a show listed here, we urge you to contact the organizer well in advance to confirm the venue and dates and to ascertain whether it is appropriate for you. (See Tips for Attending a Trade Fair, following this introduction, for further suggestions on selecting, attending, and exhibiting at trade fairs.) The information in this volume will give a significant head start to anyone who has considered participating in a trade fair as an exhibitor or attendee.

In order to make access to this information as easy as possible, fairs have been grouped alphabetically by product category and within product category, alphabetically by name. Product categories, with cross references, are given in a table of contents following this introduction. Note that the first and last headings listed are out of alphabetical order. Trade fairs listed under *Comprehensive* do not focus on a single type of product but instead show a broad range of goods that may be from one geographic area or centered around a particular theme. The final category, *Others*, is a miscellaneous listing of fairs that do not fit easily into one of the other categories. When appropriate, fairs have been listed in more than one category. The breadth of products on display at a given fair means that you may want to investigate categories that are not immediately

obvious. Many exhibits include the machinery, tools, and raw materials used to produce the products associated with the central theme of a fair; anyone interested in such items should consider a wide range of the listings.

The list gives the names and dates of both recent and upcoming events, together with site and contact information. Many shows take place on a regular basis. Annual or biennial schedules are common. When we were able to confirm the frequency of a show through independent sources, it has been indicated. Many others on the list may also be regular events. Some are one-time events. Because specifics on frequency are sometimes difficult to come by and because schedules for many 1994 and 1995 shows were not available at press time, we have given both recent and future dates. It is quite possible that a fair listed for 1992 or 1993 will be held again in 1994 or 1995, so it would be worthwhile getting in touch with the contact listed for *any* show that looks interesting. Even if we were not able to confirm the frequency, you can infer a likely time cycle if several dates are given for a fair.

As you gather further information on fairs that appeal to you, do not be surprised if the names are slightly different from those listed here. Some large trade fairs include several smaller exhibits, some use short names or acronyms, and Chinese names can be translated in a variety of ways. Dates and venues, of course, are always subject to change.

For further information The number of trade fairs in China has increased dramatically in recent years. Unfortunately, there is no one organization to contact for comprehensive listings, and the information presented here has been gathered from a range of sources.

If you are seeking up-to-date information on a wide variety of trade fairs in China, one of the best places to start is the Hong Kong Trade Development Council (HKTDC). The Council publishes "Businessmen's Calendar : Trade Exhibitions & Conferences in China and Other Asian Countries" twice a year, in January and July. For upcoming shows, the calendar provides name, dates, site information, and contact details for organizers. Branch offices outside Hong Kong may carry copies of this publication, but it is likely that you will need to purchase it directly from the main office. The Trade Development Council also maintains an on-line trade information system called TDC-link. Contact the main office in Hong Kong or a HKTDC office in your country for more information.

Hong Kong Trade Development Council
38/F., Office Tower
Convention Plaza, 1 Harbour Road
Wanchai, Hong Kong
Tel: [852] 5844333 Fax: [852] 8240249
Tlx: 73595 CONHK HX

Another source of information on Chinese trade fairs is the Exhibition Department of the China Council for the Promotion of International Trade (CCPIT). However, you may find that organizations outside China will be able to provide the information more quickly.

Exhibition Department
China Council for the Promotion of International Trade (CCPIT)
1, Fuxingmenwai Street
Beijing 100860, PRC
Tel: [86] (1) 8012867, 8013344, 8011320
Fax: [86] (1) 8011370 Tlx: 210482 CCFNA CN

Other valuable sources of information include the commercial sections of Chinese diplomatic missions and Chinese chambers of commerce, and the embassies and consulates of your own country located in China. Professional and trade organizations in China involved in your area of interest, particularly the import-export corporations, may be worth contacting. (Refer to "Important Addresses" chapter for Chinese embassies and consulates, Chinese chambers of commerce, diplomatic missions located in China, and trade organizations.)

Beijing, Shanghai, and Guangdong Province are the major sites for international trade fairs. Many of the country's important exhibitions are held at the China International Exhibition Center in Beijing. The Shanghai International Trade Information and Exhibition Co. organizes a large number of the events in Shanghai, while the Guangdong International Trade and Exhibition Corp. is involved with trade fairs in Guangdong Province, including the cities of Guangzhou, Shenzhen, and Zhuhai.

China International Exhibition Center
6 East Beisanhuan Road
Chaoyang District
Beijing 100028, PRC
Tel: [86] (1) 4678309, 4671751 Fax: [86] (1) 4676811
Tlx: 210214

Shanghai International Trade
Information & Exhibition Co.
817-837 Dong Da Ming Road
Shanghai 200082, PRC
Tel: [86] (21) 5463810 Fax: [86] (21) 5455124
Tlx: 33046 SITIE CN

Guangdong International Trade & Exhibition Corp.
33 Jichang Lu, Sanyuanli
Guangzhou 510400, PRC
Tel: [86] (20) 6678331 Fax: [86] (20) 6678602
Tlx: 44476 GTE CN

Those interested in purchasing Chinese goods should consider attending the specialized Chinese export fairs that are held outside China, particularly in Singapore, where there were eight of such events in 1993, and in Hong Kong, which hosted 10 in 1993. For a calendar of Singapore trade fairs, see *Doing Business in Singapore* (World Trade Press, San Rafael, California), or contact the Singapore Trade Development Board main office or one of its 25 offices worldwide. For a calendar of Hong Kong fairs, see *Doing Business in Hong Kong* (World Trade Press, San Rafael, California) or contact the Hong Kong Trade Development Council at the address listed above or at one of its offices in your country. Since 1980, China has been promoting major trade exhibitions in the United States and Western Europe. Contact the commercial section of the Chinese diplomatic mission nearest you for schedules. (Refer to "Important Addresses" chapter for Chinese embassies and consulates.)

Singapore Trade Development Board
1 Maritime Square #10-40 (Lobby D)
World Trade Centre, Telok Blangah Rd.
Singapore 0409
Tel: [65] 2719388 Fax: [65] 2740770, 2782518
Tlx: RS 28617 TRADEV

While far from comprehensive, the annual directory *Trade Shows Worldwide* (Gale Research Inc., Detroit, Michigan) may be able to provide further information on some trade fairs in China, and it is worth seeking out at your local business library.

The Chinese Export Commodities Fair

The twice-yearly Chinese Export Commodities Fair, formerly known as the Canton Trade Fair, has been running since 1957. While China now has a large number of trade fairs throughout China that attract foreigners, the Chinese Export Commodities Fair was virtually the only place up until 1979 where foreign buyers could meet Chinese sellers face to face. The fair has lost some of its stature, and it is shorter now than it was in years past, but it remains an important exhibition, particularly for those interested in light industrial products and arts and crafts.

Now held for two weeks each in April and October, the fair is devoted almost exclusively to the promotion of Chinese export commodities, and little import business is done. Exhibitions are spread out over 130,000 square meters, but fortunately a comprehensive guide is available, which is a valuable resource in and of itself. The event is held at the China Foreign Trade Centre, 117 Liu Hua Road, Guangzhou, and it is organized by the China Foreign Trade Centre Group. Chinese end users, foreign trade corporation executives, and key officials are on hand, and negotiating rooms and tables are available for meetings.

You will need an invitation in order to attend the fair. You can obtain one in any of several ways. Apply through the Foreign Liaison Department of the China Foreign Trade Centre Group in Guangzhou, a Chinese foreign trade corporation that you are dealing with, the China Chamber of International Commerce, or directly to the commercial office of your nearest Chinese diplomatic mission. US visitors may also apply to the San Francisco office of the US China Travel Service. Allow a minimum of three to four months to obtain the invitation, secure a visa, and make travel and hotel arrangements. Once in Guangzhou, you will need a visitor card to gain admission to the fair. You obtain the card by submitting your invitation, passport, and photos and paying a small fee at the Trade Fair Reception office in the Dong Fang Hotel, which is directly across the street from the Trade Fair complex. You may be able to procure an invitation on the spot in the same office, but it is advisable to get one before arriving in Guangzhou.

Transport to Guangzhou from other mainland Chinese cities and from Hong Kong is hectic during this time, hotels are often booked solid, and transportation within Guangzhou itself can be difficult, so preparation is particularly important if you plan to attend this fair. (Refer to "Business Travel" chapter for details.)

China Chamber of International Commerce
1 Fuxingmenwai Street
Beijing 100860, PRC
Tel: [86] (1) 8012867, 8013344, 8011320
Fax: [86] (1) 8011370
Tlx: 210482 CCFNA CN

China Foreign Trade Center Group
117 Liu Hua Road
Guangzhou, PRC
Tel: [86] (20) 6678000
Fax: [86] (20) 3335880
Tlx: 44465 FAIR CN

US China Travel Service
212 Sutter Street, 2nd Floor
San Francisco, CA 94108, USA
Tel: [1] (415) 398-6627
Fax: [1] (415) 398-6669

TRADE FAIRS
TABLE OF CONTENTS

Comprehensive .... p. 102
Trade fairs exhibiting a wide range of goods

Aerospace & Oceanic .... p. 104

Agriculture & Forestry .... p. 105
See also: Food, Beverages & Food Processing

Automobiles, Automotive Parts & Transportation .... p. 106

Computer & Information Industries .... p. 107
Includes communications
See also: Electronic & Electric Equipment, Multimedia
& Audiovisual Equipment

Construction & Housing... p. 109
See also: Furniture & Housewares

Electronic & Electric Equipment .... p. 110
See also: Computer & Information Industries, Multimedia
& Audiovisual Equipment

Environmental & Energy Industries .... p. 112
See also: Petroleum, Gas & Mining

Food, Beverages & Food Processing .... p. 114
See also: Agriculture & Forestry

Furniture & Housewares .... p. 115
See also: Construction & Housing

Gifts, Jewelry & Stationery .... p. 116
Includes art, crafts, timepieces
See also: Hobbies & Recreation

Health & Safety .... p. 117
Includes security
See also: Medicine & Pharmaceuticals

Hobbies & Recreation .... p. 118
Includes books, education, sporting goods, toys

Industrial Materials & Chemicals .... p. 119
See also: Metal & Metal Finishing; Petroleum, Gas & Mining

Leather Goods & Footwear .... p. 121
See also: Textiles & Apparel

Machines & Instruments .... p. 122
See also: Tools: Precision & Measuring; other categories which
may include exhibitions with machines specific to those industries

Medicine & Pharmaceuticals .... p. 126
See also: Health & Safety

TRADE FAIRS
TABLE OF CONTENTS

Metal & Metal Finishing .... p. 128

    See also: Industrial Materials & Chemicals

Multimedia & Audiovisual Equipment .... p. 130

    See also: Computer & Information Industries, Electronic

    & Electric Equipment

Packaging, Printing & Paper .... p. 130

    Includes handling and storage

Petroleum, Gas & Mining .... p. 132

    See also: Industrial Materials & Chemicals, Environmental

    & Energy Industries

Textiles & Apparel .... p. 133

    See also: Leather Goods & Footwear

Tools: Precision & Measuring .... p. 134

    See also: Machines & Instruments; other categories which

    may include exhibitions with tools specific to those industries

Others .... p. 136

    Miscellaneous trade fairs

Tips for Attending a Trade Fair

Overseas trade fairs can be extremely effective for making face-to-face contacts and sales or purchases, identifying suppliers, checking out the competitors, and finding out how business really works in the host country. However, the cost of attending such fairs can be high. To maximize the return on your investment of time and money, you should be very clear about your goals for the trip and xgive yourself plenty of time for advance research and preparation. You should also make sure that you are aware of the limitations of trade fairs. The products on display probably do not represent the full range of goods available on the market. In fact, some of the latest product designs may still be under wraps. And while trade fairs give you an opportunity to make face-to-face contact with many people, both exhibitors and buyers are rushed, which makes meaningful discussions and negotiations difficult. These drawbacks can easily be minimized if you have sufficient preparation and background information. Allow at least three months for preparation—more if you also need to identify the fair that you will attend. Under ideal circumstances, you should begin laying the groundwork nine to 12 months in advance.

Tips for Attending a Trade Fair (cont'd)

Selecting an appropriate trade fair

Consult the listings of trade fairs here to find some that interest you. Note the suggestions for finding the most current calendars of upcoming fairs. Once you have identified some fairs, contact their organizers for literature, including show prospectus, attendee list, and exhibitor list. Ask plenty of questions. Do not neglect trade organizations in the host country, independent show-auditing firms, and recent attendees. Find out whether there are "must attend" fairs for your particular product group. Fairs that concentrate on other but related commodities might also be a good match. Be aware that there may be preferred seasons for trade in certain products. Your research needs to consider a number of points.

Audience • Who is the intended audience? Is the fair open to the public or only to trade professionals? Are the exhibitors primarily foreigners looking for local buyers or locals looking for foreign buyers? Many trade fairs are heavily weighted to one or the other. Decide whether you are looking for an exposition of general merchandise produced in one region, a commodity-specific trade show, or both.

Statistics • How many people attended the fair the last time it was held? What were the demographics? What volume of business was done? How many exhibitors were there? How big is the exhibition space? What was the ratio of foreign to domestic attendees and exhibitors?

Specifics • Who are the major exhibitors? Are particular publications or organizations associated with the fair? On what categories of products does the fair focus? Are there any special programs, and do they require additional fees? Does the fair have particular themes that change each time? How long has the fair been in existence? How often is it held? Is it always in the same location, or does it move each time? How much does it cost to attend? To rent space?

Before you go

- If you have not already spoken with someone who attended the fair in the past, make sure to seek someone out for advice, tips, and general information.
- Make your reservations and travel arrangements well in advance, and figure out how you are going to get around once you get there. Even if the fair takes place in a large city, do not assume that getting around will be easy during a major trade fair. If the site is a small city or less-developed area, the transportation and accommodation systems are likely to be saturated even sooner than they can be in metropolitan areas.
- Will you need an interpreter for face-to-face business negotiations? A translation service to handle documents? Try to line up providers well in advance of your need for their services.
- Do you need hospitality suites and/or conference rooms? Reserve them as soon as you can.
- Contact people you'd like to meet before you go. Organize your appointments around the fair.
- Familiarize yourself with the show hours, locations (if exhibits and events are staged at several different venues), and schedule of events. Then prioritize.

While you are there

- Wear businesslike clothes that are comfortable.
- Immediately after each contact, write down as much information as you can. Do not depend on remembering it .

After the fair

- Within a week after the conclusion of the fair, write letters to new contacts and follow up on requests for literature. If you have press releases and questionnaires, send them out quickly as well.
- Write a report evaluating the experience while it is still fresh in your mind. Even if you don't have to prepare a formal report, spend some time organizing your thoughts on paper for future reference and to quantify the results. Did you meet your goals? Why or why not? What would you do differently? What unforeseen costs arose?
- With your new contacts and your experience in mind, start preparing for your next trade fair.

If you are selling

- Set specific goals for sales leads, developing product awareness, selling and positioning current customers, and gathering industry information; for example, number of contacts made, orders written, leads converted into sales, visitors at presentations, brochures or samples distributed, customers entertained, seminars attended. You can also set goals for total revenue from sales, cost-to-return benefit ratio, amount of media coverage, and amount of competitor information obtained.

- Review your exhibitor kit, paying particular attention to show hours and regulations, payment policies, shipping instructions and dates, telephone installation, security, fire regulations, union regulations, and extra-cost services. Is there a show theme that you can tie into?

- Gear your advertising and product demonstrations to the audience. Should you stress certain aspects of your product line? Will you need brochures and banners in different languages? Even if you do not need to translate the materials currently in use into another language, do you need to re-write them for a different culture? Consider advertising in publications that will be distributed at the fair.

- Plan the display in your booth carefully; you will have only a few seconds to grab the viewer's attention. Secure a location in a high-traffic area—for example, near a door, restroom, refreshment area, or major exhibitor. Use banner copy that is brief and effective. Focus on the product and its benefits. Place promotional materials and giveaways near the back wall so that people have to enter your area, but make sure that they do not feel trapped. If you plan to use videotapes or other multimedia, make sure that you have enough space. Such presentations are often better suited to hospitality suites, because lights are bright and noise levels high in exhibition halls.

- Do not forget about the details. Order office supplies and printed materials that you will need for the booth. If you ordered a telephone line, bring your own telephone or arrange to rent one. Have all your paperwork—order forms, business cards, exhibitor kit and contract, copies of advance orders and checks, travel documents, and so on—in order and at hand. Draw up a schedule for staffing the booth.

- Plan and rehearse your sales pitch in advance, preferably in a space similar to the size of your booth.

- Do not sit, eat, drink, or smoke while you are in the booth.

- If you plan to return to the next show, reserve space while you're still at the fair.

- Familiarize yourself with import regulations for products that you wish to exhibit at the fair.

If you are buying

- Set specific goals for supplier leads and for gathering industry information; for example, number of contacts made, leads converted to purchases, seminars and presentations attended, booths visited. Other goals might be cost-to-return benefit ratio, amount of competitor information gathered, and percentage of projected purchases actually made.

- List all the products that you seek to purchase, their specifications, and the number of units you plan to purchase of each.

- Know the retail and wholesale market prices for the goods in your home country and in the country where you will be buying. List the highest price you can afford to pay for each item and still get a worthwhile return.

- List the established and probable suppliers for each of the products or product lines that you plan to import. Include their addresses and telephone numbers and your source for the information. Contact suppliers before you go to confirm who will attend and to make appointments.

- Familiarize yourself with customs regulations on the products that you seek to purchase and import into your own country or elsewhere. Be sure to include any products that you might be interested in.

Trade Fair	Site	Contact

COMPREHENSIVE Trade fairs exhibiting a wide range of goods

Trade Fair	Site	Contact
5th Asia-Pacific International Trade Fair (ASPAT '94) Jun. 7-13, 1994	Beijing China International Exhibition Center	China International Exhibition Center 6 East Beisanhuan Road Chaoyang District Beijing 100028 Tel: (1) 4678309, 4664433 Fax: (1) 4676811 Tlx: 210214 International Trade & Tourism Division UN-ESCAP The United Nations Building Rajdamnern Avenue Bangkok 10200 Thailand Tel: [66] (2) 2829161, 2829200, 2829381/9 Fax: [66] (2) 2829602, 2801749 Tlx: 82392 , 82315
Beijing International Fair (BIF) Every 2 years Last held: Apr. 2-8, 1993	Beijing China International Exhibition Center	China International Exhibition Center 6 East Beisanhuan Road Chaoyang District Beijing 100028 Tel: (1) 4678309, 4664433 Fax: (1) 4676811 Tlx: 210214
Coastal & Border Cities Trade Fair Last held: Mar. 2-7, 1993	Shenzhen	Shenzhen International Exhibition Center Shang Bu North Road Shenzhen Tel: (755) 2263838 Fax: (755) 2263753 Tlx: 420268
China International Industry Fair Last held: Oct. 22-27, 1992	Shanghai International Exhibition Center	Hong Kong Expositions 1102 Yardley Commercial Bldg. 1-6 Connaught Road West Hong Kong Tel: [852] 8542313 Fax: [852] 8150073 Tlx: 75388
China's Awarded Products in the Last Decade Last held: Aug. 19-23, 1993	Shenzhen	Coastal International Exhibition Co. 3808 China Resources Building 26 Harbour Road Hong Kong Tel: [852] 8276766 Fax: [852] 8275224 Tlx: 80295 Contact: Brenda Yau
Chinese Export Commodities Fair Twice a year (Apr./Oct.) 1993 dates: Apr. 15-29; Oct. 15-29	Guangzhou China Foreign Trade Center	China Foreign Trade Center Group 117 Liu Hua Road Guangzhou Tel: (20) 6678000 Fax: (20) 3335880 Tlx: 44465
Consumer China Last held: Jun. 8-13, 1993	Guangzhou Foreign Trade Center	Business & Industrial Trade Fairs 18/F., First Pacific Bank 51 Gloucester Road Hong Kong Tel: [852] 8652633 Fax: [852] 8661770 Tlx: 64882
Consumer Goods, Gifts & Housewares Exhibition China Last held: May 22-26, 1993	Shenzhen International Exhibition Center	Shenzhen International Exhibition Center Shang Bu North Road Shenzhen Tel: (755) 2263838 Fax: (755) 2263753 Tlx: 420268
Hong Kong-Shenzhen Industrial Trade Fair Last held: May 11-15, 1993	Shenzhen International Exhibition Center	Coastal International Exhibition Co. 3808 China Resources Building 26 Harbour Road Hong Kong Tel: [852] 8276766 Fax: [852] 8275224 Tlx: 80295 Contact: Brenda Yau
International Consumer Goods Fair Last held: Oct. 4-7, 1993	Shenzhen	Shenzhen International Exhibition Center Shang Bu North Road Shenzhen Tel: (755) 2263838 Fax: (755) 2263753 Tlx: 420268

Trade Fair	Site	Contact
International Cooperation Project Exhibition (CHINA PROJECT) Last held: Nov. 10-14, 1992	Tianjin Exhibition Center	CCPIT, Tianjin Sub-Council International Trade Bldg. 84 Jianshe Road, Heping District Tianjin Tel: (22) 301367 Fax: (22) 301344 Tlx: 23261
International Exhibition and Co-talks on Small & Medium Enterprises, New Products & Technology Last held: Nov. 17-23, 1992	Tianjin World Economy Trade & Exhibition Center	C&S Enterprise Co. Flat C2, 2/F. 82 Lai Chi Kwok Road Kowloon Hong Kong Tel: [852] 399192 Fax: [852] 3990197
International Exhibition on Quality Products & Goods for the Aged Last held: Nov. 1-6, 1993	Beijing China International Exhibition Center	China International Exhibition Center 6 East Beisanhuan Road Chaoyang District Beijing 100028 Tel: (1) 4678309, 4664433 Fax: (1) 4676811 Tlx: 210214
International Expo on Patent, High Technology & New Products Last held: Dec. 14-18, 1993	Guangzhou International Exhibition Center	Guangdong International Trade & Exhibition Corp. 33 Jichang Lu, Sanyuanli Guangzhou 510400 Tel: (20) 6678331 x1135 Fax: (20) 6678602 Tlx: 44476 Contact: Ms. Tang Ruiling CCPIT Guangdong Sub-Council 305 Dong Feng Zhong Lu Guangzhou, Guangdong Tel: (20) 33332756 Tlx: 44203 Organized with: China Patent Technology Dev. Co.
International Famous Brand Trade Fair Sep. 1-5, 1994	Beijing China International Exhibition Center	China International Exhibition Center 6 East Beisanhuan Road Chaoyang District Beijing 100028 Tel: (1) 4678309, 4664433 Fax: (1) 4676811 Tlx: 210214
International Modern Technology Trade Fair (ITF SOUTH CHINA) Last held: Sep. 8-13, 1992	Shenzhen International Exhibition Center	Shenzhen International Exhibition Center Shang Bu North Road Shenzhen Tel: (755) 2263838 Fax: (755) 2263753 Tlx: 420268
International Science & Technology Fair Last held: Oct.-Nov., 1993	Beijing China International Exhibition Center	China International Exhibition Center 6 East Beisanhuan Road Chaoyang District Beijing 100028 Tel: (1) 4678309, 4664433 Fax: (1) 4676811 Tlx: 210214
International Science, Peace & Health Care Exhibition Last held: Nov. 9-15, 1993	Zhuhai	Zhuhai International Trade & Exhibition (Group), Zhuhai Tel: (756) 332656 x 6002 Fax: (756) 333440
International Showcase Last held: Jan. 5-9, 1993	Guangzhou	Business & Industrial Trade Fairs 18/F., First Pacific Bank 51 Gloucester Road Hong Kong Tel: [852] 8652633 Fax: [852] 8661770 Tlx: 64882

Note: Country codes for telephone and fax numbers are not displayed unless they are *outside* of China. All country codes have square brackets around them, while city codes have parentheses. The country code for China is [86].

Trade Fair	Site	Contact
Joint Venture Products Exhibition Last held: Jan. 11-15, 1993	Shenzhen International Exhibition Center	Hong Kong Trade Development Council 36-39th Floor, Office Tower Convention Plaza 1 Harbour Road Hong Kong Tel: [852] 5844333 Fax: [852] 8240249 Tlx: 73595
Lady & Child Sep. 26-29, 1994	Shenzhen	Glahe International Inc. 1700 K Street N.W. Washington, D.C. 20006, USA Tel: [1] (202) 659-4557 Fax: [1] (202) 457-0776 Tlx: ITT 440322
MODERN LIFE International Consumer Goods Exhibition Last held: Sep. 24-28, 1993	Shanghai	Shanghai Int'l Trade Information & Exhibition Co. 817-837 Dong Da Ming Road Shanghai Tel: (21) 5463810 Fax: (21) 5455124 Tlx: 33046 Contact: Mr. Xu Zhiguo
Mother and Infant Expo Last held: Oct. 23-27, 1993	Shanghai	Glahe International Inc. 1700 K Street N.W. Washington, D.C. 20006, USA Tel: [1] (202) 659-4557 Fax: [1] (202) 457-0776 Tlx: ITT 440322
National Fair on Products & Technology of Enterprises with Taiwan Investments Last held: May 19-25, 1993	Beijing China International Exhibition Center	China International Exhibition Center 6 East Beisanhuan Road Chaoyang District Beijing 100028 Tel: (1) 4678309, 4664433 Fax: (1) 4676811 Tlx: 210214
WORLD BESTBRAND Last held: Jun. 5-10, 1993	Shanghai	Shanghai Int'l Trade Information & Exhibition Co. 817-837 Dong Da Ming Road Shanghai Tel: (21) 5463810 Fax: (21) 5455124 Tlx: 33046 Contact: Mr. Xu Zhiguo

AEROSPACE & OCEANIC

Trade Fair	Site	Contact
Aviation Expo Every 2 years Last held: Oct. 12-16, 1993	Beijing China International Exhibition Center	China Promotion Ltd. Rm. 2801, Tun Wai Commercial Bldg. 109 Gloucester Road Hong Kong Tel: [852] 5117427 Fax: [852] 5119692 Tlx: 76270 China International Exhibition Center 6 East Beisanhuan Road Chaoyang District Beijing 100028 Tel: (1) 4678309, 4664433 Fax: (1) 4676811 Tlx: 210214
China Aviation Last held: Dec. 5-11, 1992	Shanghai International Exhibition Center	Shanghai Int'l Trade Information & Exhibition Co. 817-837 Dong Da Ming Road Shanghai Tel: (21) 5463810 Fax: (21) 5455124 Tlx: 33046
International Marine & Naval Exhibition Nov. 8-11, 1994	Beijing China International Exhibition Center	China International Exhibition Center 6 East Beisanhuan Road Chaoyang District Beijing 100028 Tel: (1) 4678309, 4664433 Fax: (1) 4676811 Tlx: 210214

Trade Fair	Site	Contact
International Port Equipment Exhibition Last held: Dec. 1-5, 1993	Guangzhou International Exhibition Center	Guangdong International Trade & Exhibition Corp. 33 Jichang Lu, Sanyuanli Guangzhou 510400 Tel: (20) 6678331 x1135 Fax: (20) 6678602 Tlx: 44476 Contact: Ms. Tang Ruiling CCPIT Guangdong Sub-Council 305 Dong Feng Zhong Lu Guangzhou, Guangdong Tel: (20) 33332756 Tlx: 44203
MARINTEC China Every 2 years Dec. 7-10, 1993 Dec., 1995	Shanghai	Cahners Exhibitions (HK) 2808 Office Tower, Convention Plaza 1 Harbour Road Hong Kong Tel: [852] 8240330 Fax: [852] 8204026 Tlx: 62270 Organized with: Shanghai Society of Naval Architecture & Marine Engineering
South China & Hong Kong Airport and Aviation Nov. 22-26, 1994	Guangzhou	Glahe International Inc. 1700 K Street N.W. Washington, D.C. 20006, USA Tel: [1] (202) 659-4557 Fax: [1] (202) 457-0776 Tlx: ITT 440322

AGRICULTURE & FORESTRY
See also Food, Beverages & Food Processing

Trade Fair	Site	Contact
AGRO EXPO CHINA Every 2 years Apr., 1994	Beijing National Agricultural Exhibition Center	E.J. Krause & Associates 7315 Wisconsin Ave., Ste. 420 E. Bethesda, MD 20814 USA Tel: [1] (301) 986-7800 Fax: [1] (301) 986-4538 Tlx: 4944944 EJKEXPO
Chinese Down Products Export Fair Last held: Jan. 6-12, 1993	Shanghai International Trade Center	China National Native Produce and Animal By - Products Import Export Corporation 82 Donganmen Jie Beijing 100747 Tel: (1) 554124 Fax: (1) 5721626 Tlx: 22283
International Agricultural Machinery, Agrotechnology and Food Processing Exhibition Last held: Oct. 8-12, 1992	Guangzhou International Exhibition Center	Guangdong International Trade & Exhibition Corp. 33 Jichang Lu, Sanyuanli Guangzhou 510400 Tel: (20) 6678331 x1135 Fax: (20) 6678602 Tlx: 44476
International Exhibition on Preservation Technology and Processing Equipment for Grain and Meat Last held: Nov. 25-29, 1993	Beijing China International Exhibition Center	Coastal International Exhibition Co. 3808 China Resources Building 26 Harbour Road Hong Kong Tel: [852] 8276766 Fax: [852] 8275224 Tlx: 80295 Contact: Brenda Yau
International Exhibition on Technology and Equipment for Grain and Meat Processing and Storage Last held: Oct. 19-24, 1993	Tianjin	Tianjin World Economy Trade & Exhibition Center 30 Youyi Lu, Hexi Qu Tianjin 300061 Tel: (22) 342222 Fax: (22) 349855

Note: Country codes for telephone and fax numbers are not displayed unless they are *outside* of China. All country codes have square brackets around them, while city codes have parentheses. The country code for China is [86].

Trade Fair	Site	Contact
International Grain & Oil Storage Equipment Exhibition Last held: Nov. 2-5, 1993	Shenzhen	Shenzhen International Exhibition Center Shang Bu North Road Shenzhen Tel: (755) 2263838 Fax: (755) 2263753 Tlx: 420268
International Meat Processing & Packaging Machinery Exhibition Last held: Nov. 2-5, 1993	Shenzhen	Shenzhen International Exhibition Center Shang Bu North Road Shenzhen Tel: (755) 2263838 Fax: (755) 2263753 Tlx: 420268
International Timber & Stone Processing Machinery Exhibition Last held: Nov. 12-16, 1993	Shenzhen	Shenzhen International Exhibition Center Shang Bu North Road Shenzhen Tel: (755) 2263838 Fax: (755) 2263753 Tlx: 420268

AUTOMOBILES, AUTOMOTIVE PARTS & TRANSPORTATION

Trade Fair	Site	Contact
AUTO CHINA International Automobile and Manufacturing Technology Exhibition Annual, alternates between Beijing & Shanghai Jun. 22-27, 1993 Jun. 23-28, 1994	Shanghai International Exhibition Center (1993) Beijing China International Exhibition Center (1994)	For Beijing or Shanghai show: Adsale Exhibition Services 14/F., Devon House Taikoo Place 979 King's Road Quarry Bay, Hong Kong Tel: [852] 5110511 Fax: [852] 5165204 For Shanghai show only: Shanghai Int'l Trade Information & Exhibition Co. 817-837 Dong Da Ming Road Shanghai Tel: (21) 5463810 Fax: (21) 5455124 Tlx: 33046 Contact: Mr. Xu Zhiguo
China International Automotive Spare Parts, Accessories and Maintenance Equipment Exhibition Last held: Sep. 19-23, 1992	Shanghai Exhibition Center	Worldwide Conventions & Expositions 508 Silver Cord, Tower I 30 Canton Road Hong Kong Tel: [852] 3757721 Fax: 3750686 Tlx: 44874 WWXPO HX
China Motor International Auto Industry Exhibition Last held: Sep. 21-25, 1993	Shenzhen International Exhibition Center	Business & Industrial Trade Fairs 18/F., First Pacific Bank 51 Gloucester Road Hong Kong Tel: [852] 8652633 Fax: [852] 8661770 Tlx: 64882
International Motorcycle Exhibition Last held: Dec. 14-18, 1993	Guangzhou	Guangdong International Trade & Exhibition Corp. 33 Jichang Lu, Sanyuanli Guangzhou 510400 Tel: (20) 6678331 x1135 Fax: (20) 6678602 Tlx: 44476
Shenzhen International Automobile Technology Exhibition (AUTOTECH) Last held: Oct. 30-Nov. 3, 1993	Shenzhen International Exhibition Center	Shenzhen International Exhibition Center Shang Bu North Road Shenzhen Tel: (755) 2263838 Fax: (755) 2263753 Tlx: 420268
Subway & Urban Transport Jun. 18-22, 1994	Shanghai	Glahe International Inc. 1700 K Street N.W. Washington, D.C. 20006, USA Tel: [1] (202) 659-4557 Fax: [1] (202) 457-0776 Tlx: ITT 440322

Trade Fair	Site	Contact
Tianjin International Cycle Technology and Equipment Exhibition (CHINA B&M) Nov. 10-14, 1992 Last held: Sep. 15-20, 1993	Tianjin World Economy Trade & Exhibition Center	Tianjin World Economy Trade & Exhibition Center No. 30, You Yi Road Hexi District Tianjin Tel: (22) 318343 Fax: (22) 318341 Tlx: 234074
TRANSPORT International Exhibition on Transportation Every 2 years Last held: Sep. 1-6, 1993	Beijing China International Exhibition Center	Coastal International Exhibition Co. 3808 China Resources Building 26 Harbour Road Hong Kong Tel: [852] 8276766 Fax: [852] 8275224 Tlx: 80295 Contact: Brenda Yau

COMPUTER & INFORMATION INDUSTRIES Includes communications
See also Electronic & Electric Equipment, Multimedia & Audiovisual Equipment

Trade Fair	Site	Contact
China High Tech Last held: Jun. 25-29, 1993	Tianjin	SHK International Services Ltd. 6/F., China Harbour Bldg. 370-374 King's Road Hong Kong Tel: [852] 8077633 Fax: [852] 5705903
China's International Exhibition on the Computer and its Applications (CompuChina) Every 2 years Sep. 1-5, 1994	Beijing China International Exhibition Center	China International Exhibition Center 6 East Beisanhuan Road Chaoyang District Beijing 100028 Tel: (1) 4678309, 4664433 Fax: (1) 4676811 Tlx: 210214
Computer Expo Sep. 26-29, 1994	Shenzhen	Glahe International Inc. 1700 K Street N.W. Washington, D.C. 20006, USA Tel: [1] (202) 659-4557 Fax: [1] (202) 457-0776 Tlx: ITT 440322
Guangzhou Office Automation, Telcom and Electronics Expo Last held: Dec. 8-12, 1992	Guangzhou International Exhibition Center	China Promotion Rm. 2801, Tun Wai Commercial Bldg. 109 Gloucester Road Hong Kong Tel: [852] 5117427, 5117427 Fax: [852] 5119692 Tlx: 76270
Ideal Home May 11-15, 1994	Shanghai	Glahe International Inc. 1700 K Street N.W. Washington, D.C. 20006, USA Tel: [1] (202) 659-4557 Fax: [1] (202) 457-0776 Tlx: ITT 440322
Ideal Office May 11-15, 1994	Shanghai	Glahe International Inc. 1700 K Street N.W. Washington, D.C. 20006, USA Tel: [1] (202) 659-4557 Fax: [1] (202) 457-0776 Tlx: ITT 440322
International Telecommunication Equipment and Technology Fair Last held: Jun. 22-25, 1993	Guangzhou	Guangdong International Trade & Exhibition Corp. 33 Jichang Lu, Sanyuanli Guangzhou 510400 Tel: (20) 6678331 x1135 Fax: (20) 6678602 Tlx: 44476

Note: Country codes for telephone and fax numbers are not displayed unless they are *outside* of China. All country codes have square brackets around them, while city codes have parentheses. The country code for China is [86].

Trade Fair	Site	Contact
International Telecommunications / Computer Electronics Exhibition and Conference Last held: Oct. 30-Nov. 5, 1992	Beijing China International Exhibition Center	China International Exhibition Center 6 East Beisanhuan Road Chaoyang District Beijing 100028 Tel: (1) 4678309, 4664433 Fax: (1) 4676811 Tlx: 210214
International Telecommunications & Computer Show Last held: Jul. 2-7, 1993	Shanghai International Exhibition Center	Shanghai Int'l Trade Information & Exhibition Co. 817-837 Dong Da Ming Road Shanghai Tel: (21) 5463810 Fax: (21) 5455124 Tlx: 33046
International Automatic Identification and Bar Code Technology and Equipment Exhibition for China (AUTO-ID CHINA) Last held: Sep. 8-12, 1992	Shanghai Center	Business & Industrial Trade Fairs 18/F., First Pacific Bank 51 Gloucester Road Hong Kong Tel: [852] 8652633 Fax: [852] 8661770 Tlx: 64882
International Computer Last held: Dec. 1-12, 1992	Shanghai Center	China National Computer Association 47 Nancheng Road Shanghai Tel: (21) 3726055 Fax: (21) 3721566
International Computer Expo Last held: Sep. 3-7, 1993	Beijing China International Exhibition Center	China International Exhibition Center 6 East Beisanhuan Road Chaoyang District Beijing 100028 Tel: (1) 4678309, 4664433 Fax: (1) 4676811 Tlx: 210214
International Exhibition on Technology and Equipment for Banking and Finance Services (BANKING CHINA) Last held: Dec. 7-12, 1993	Beijing China International Exhibition Center	Adsale Exhibition Services 14/F., Devon House Taikoo Place 979 King's Road Quarry Bay, Hong Kong Tel: [852] 5110511 Fax: [852] 5165204
National Fair on the Achievements of China's Sparking Program: New and Hi-Tech Products Last held: Aug. 18-25, 1993	Beijing China International Exhibition Center	China International Exhibition Center 6 East Beisanhuan Road Chaoyang District Beijing 100028 Tel: (1) 4678309, 4664433 Fax: (1) 4676811 Tlx: 210214
P.T. Expo Comm China Every 2 years Oct. 25-30, 1994	Beijing China International Exhibition Center	China International Exhibition Center 6 East Beisanhuan Road Chaoyang District Beijing 100028 Tel: (1) 4678309, 4664433 Fax: (1) 4676811 Tlx: 210214
Scan-tech Apr. 12-18, 1994	Beijing China International Exhibition Center	China International Exhibition Center 6 East Beisanhuan Road Chaoyang District Beijing 100028 Tel: (1) 4678309, 4664433 Fax: (1) 4676811 Tlx: 210214
SINTECH Last held: Nov. 3-7, 1992	Shanghai Exhibition Center	Shanghai Int'l Trade Information & Exhibition Co. 817-837 Dong Da Ming Road Shanghai Tel: (21) 5463810 Fax: (21) 5455124 Tlx: 33046
TELECOM CHINA Last held: Oct. 5-9, 1993	Tianjin	CCPIT, Tianjin Sub-Council International Trade Bldg. 84 Jianshe Road, Heping District Tianjin Tel: (22) 301367 Fax: (22) 301344 Tlx: 23261

Trade Fair	Site	Contact

CONSTRUCTION & HOUSING
See also Furniture & Housewares

Trade Fair	Site	Contact
Building Materials Fair (CIBAC) Last held: Dec. 2-5, 1993	Shenzhen	Shenzhen International Exhibition Center Shang Bu North Road Shenzhen Tel: (755) 2263838 Fax: (755) 2263753 Tlx: 420268
China International Building & Construction Expo (ChinaBex) Every 2 years Last held: Oct. 13-17, 1993	Beijing China International Exhibition Center	China International Exhibition Center 6 East Beisanhuan Road Chaoyang District Beijing 100028 Tel: (1) 4678309, 4664433 Fax: (1) 4676811 Tlx: 210214
China International Building, Construction & Hotel Expo Last held: Dec. 1-4, 1992	Shenzhen International Exhibition Center	China Promotion Rm. 2801, Tun Wai Commercial Bldg. 109 Gloucester Road Hong Kong Tel: [852] 5117427, 5117427 Fax: [852] 5119692 Tlx: 76270
Construction & Interior Decoration May 11-15, 1994	Shanghai	Glahe International Inc. 1700 K Street N.W. Washington, D.C. 20006, USA Tel: [1] (202) 659-4557 Fax: [1] (202) 457-0776 Tlx: ITT 440322
Construction China Nov. 27-Dec. 1, 1994	Beijing China International Exhibition Center	China International Exhibition Center 6 East Beisanhuan Road Chaoyang District Beijing 100028 Tel: (1) 4678309, 4664433 Fax: (1) 4676811 Tlx: 210214
INTER BUILDING SHANGHAI International Urban Building & Construction Exhibition Last held: Oct. 8-12, 1993	Shanghai	Shanghai Int'l Trade Information & Exhibition Co. 817-837 Dong Da Ming Road Shanghai Tel: (21) 5463810 Fax: (21) 5455124 Tlx: 33046 Contact: Mr. Xu Zhiguo
International Building & Construction Exhibition (CHINA CONSTRUCT) Last held: Oct. 8-12, 1992	Shanghai Exhibition Center	Oriental Wesley Promotions China Harbour Building, 6/F. 370 King's Road Hong Kong Tel: [852] 8077633 Fax: [852] 5705903 Tlx: 89587 SHKIS HX
International City Construction Exhibition Last held: Sep. 3-8, 1993	Beijing China International Exhibition Center	China International Exhibition Center 6 East Beisanhuan Road Chaoyang District Beijing 100028 Tel: (1) 4678309, 4664433 Fax: (1) 4676811 Tlx: 210214
International Lighting Fixtures & Illuminators Fair Last held: Dec. 2-5, 1993	Shenzhen	Shenzhen International Exhibition Center Shang Bu North Road Shenzhen Tel: (755) 2263838 Fax: (755) 2263753 Tlx: 420268

Note: Country codes for telephone and fax numbers are not displayed unless they are *outside* of China. All country codes have square brackets around them, while city codes have parentheses. The country code for China is [86].

Trade Fair	Site	Contact
International Refrigeration, Heating, Ventilation and Air-Conditioning Exhibition Every 2 years 1995 (Dates to be announced)	Beijing	Beijing International Exhibition Center Room 415, 4/F. 2nd Central Building Hualong Street, Nanhey Beijing 100006 Tel: (1) 5125185 Fax: (1) 5125183
South China International Exhibition on Construction, Building Services and Interior Decoration BUILDING SOUTH CHINA Last held: Mar. 4-8, 1993	Guangzhou China Foreign Trade Center	Adsale Exhibition Services 14/F., Devon House Taikoo Place 979 King's Road Quarry Bay, Hong Kong Tel: [852] 5110511 Fax: [852] 5165204 China Foreign Trade Center Group 117 Liu Hua Road Guangzhou Tel: (20) 6678000 Fax: (20) 3335880 Tlx: 44465
Tianjin International Exhibition for Construction Equipment and Materials (CHINA CONSTRUCT) Last held: Oct. 26-29, 1993	Tianjin World Economy Trade & Exhibition Center	Tianjin World Economy Trade & Exhibition Center No. 30, You Yi Road Hexi District Tianjin Tel: (22) 318343 Fax: (22) 318341 Tlx: 234074 Glahe International Inc. 1700 K Street N.W. Washington, D.C. 20006, USA Tel: [1] (202) 659-4557 Fax: [1] (202) 457-0776 Tlx: ITT 440322

ELECTRONIC & ELECTRIC EQUIPMENT

See also Computer & Information Industries, Multimedia & Audiovisual Equipment

Trade Fair	Site	Contact
CABLEWIRE SHANGHAI International Exhibition on Cable & Wire Manufacturing Last held: Jun. 24-28, 1993	Shanghai	Shanghai Int'l Trade Information & Exhibition Co. 817-837 Dong Da Ming Road Shanghai Tel: (21) 5463810 Fax: (21) 5455124 Tlx: 33046 Contact: Mr. Xu Zhiguo
CHINA MECTT International Machinery, Factory Automation, Electronics Technology Exhibition for China Last held: Nov. 2-6, 1993	Shanghai	Shanghai Int'l Trade Information & Exhibition Co. 817-837 Dong Da Ming Road Shanghai Tel: (21) 5463810 Fax: (21) 5455124 Tlx: 33046 Contact: Mr. Xu Zhiguo
China (Shenzhen) International Household Electric Appliances Exhibition Last held: Oct. 5-8, 1993	Shenzhen International Exhibition Center	Shenzhen International Exhibition Center Shang Bu North Road Shenzhen Tel: (755) 2263838 Fax: (755) 2263753 Tlx: 420268
China High Tech Last held: Jun. 25-29, 1993	Tianjin	SHK International Services Ltd. 6/F., China Harbour Bldg. 370-374 King's Road Hong Kong Tel: [852] 8077633 Fax: [852] 5705903
China International Electronics Fair (CEE) Last held: Oct. 12-16, 1992	Tianjin	CCPIT, Tianjin Sub-Council International Trade Bldg. 84 Jianshe Road, Heping District Tianjin Tel: (22) 301367 Fax: (22) 301344 Tlx: 23261

Trade Fair	Site	Contact
China International Electronics Trade Fair Every 2 years Last held: Sep. 21-26, 1993	Beijing China International Exhibition Center	China International Exhibition Center 6 East Beisanhuan Road Chaoyang District Beijing 100028 Tel: (1) 4678309, 4664433 Fax: (1) 4676811 Tlx: 210214
CONSUMTRONICS SHANGHAI International Exhibition on Consumer Electronics and Household Appliances Last held: Dec. 17-20, 1993	Shanghai Exhibition Center	Shanghai Int'l Trade Information & Exhibition Co. 817-837 Dong Da Ming Road Shanghai Tel: (21) 5463810 Fax: (21) 5455124 Tlx: 33046 Contact: Mr. Xu Zhiguo Adsale Exhibition Services 14/F., Devon House Taikoo Place 979 King's Road Quarry Bay, Hong Kong Tel: [852] 5110511 Fax: [852] 5165204
Electronic Toys & Games Sep. 26-29, 1994	Shenzhen	Glahe International Inc. 1700 K Street N.W. Washington, D.C. 20006, USA Tel: [1] (202) 659-4557 Fax: [1] (202) 457-0776 Tlx: ITT 440322
Guangzhou Electronics and Components Expo Last held: Nov. 23-27, 1993	Guangzhou International Exhibition Center	China Promotion Rm. 2801, Tun Wai Commercial Bldg. 109 Gloucester Road Hong Kong Tel: [852] 5117427, 5117427 Fax: [852] 5119692 Tlx: 76270
Guangzhou Office Automation, Telcom and Electronics Expo Last held: Nov. 23-27, 1993	Guangzhou International Exhibition Center	China Promotion Rm. 2801, Tun Wai Commercial Bldg. 109 Gloucester Road Hong Kong Tel: [852] 5117427 Fax: [852] 5119692 Tlx: 76270
International Electronics Exhibition Last held: May 15-19, 1993	Guangzhou	Guangdong International Trade & Exhibition Corp. 33 Jichang Lu, Sanyuanli Guangzhou 510400 Tel: (20) 6678331 x1135 Fax: (20) 6678602 Tlx: 44476
International Exhibition on Consumer Electronics and Household Appliances Last held: Nov. 18-21, 1993	Guangzhou China Foreign Trade Center	Adsale Exhibition Services 14/F., Devon House Taikoo Place 979 King's Road Quarry Bay, Hong Kong Tel: [852] 5110511 Fax: [852] 5165204
International Laser & Opto-Electronic Product Exhibition Every 2 years Nov. 8-13, 1994	Beijing China International Exhibition Center	CIEC Exhibition Co. (HK) 21/F., China Resources Bldg. 26 Harbour Road Hong Kong Tel: [852] 8275078 Fax: [852] 8275535 Tlx: 81529 CIFC HX
International Machinery & Electronic Technology (CHINA METE) Last held: Sep. 21-26, 1992	Tianjin Exhibition Center	CCPIT, Tianjin Sub-Council International Trade Bldg. 84 Jianshe Road, Heping District Tianjin Tel: (22) 301367 Fax: (22) 301344 Tlx: 23261

Note: Country codes for telephone and fax numbers are not displayed unless they are *outside* of China. All country codes have square brackets around them, while city codes have parentheses. The country code for China is [86].

Trade Fair	Site	Contact
International PC Board Making and Electro-Chemicals Exhibition Every 2 years. Alternates between Beijing and Shanghai Apr. 17-21, 1993 1995 (Dates to be announced)	Beijing China International Exhibition Center (1993) Shanghai (1995)	Sinostar International 802 Wing On Investment Building 343-349 Nathan Road Kowloon, Hong Kong Tel: [852] 7107878 Fax: [852] 7808713 Tlx: 46070 SILHX
International Telecommunications / Computer Electronics Exhibition and Conference Last held: Oct. 30-Nov. 5, 1992	Beijing China International Exhibition Center	China International Exhibition Center 6 East Beisanhuan Road Chaoyang District Beijing 100028 Tel: (1) 4678309, 4664433 Fax: (1) 4676811 Tlx: 210214
International Trade Fair for Electronics and Electrical Equipment (Electronics China) Sep. 13-17, 1993 Sep. 26-29, 1994	Shenzhen International Exhibition Center	Shenzhen International Exhibition Center Shang Bu North Road Shenzhen Tel: (755) 2263838 Fax: (755) 2263753 Tlx: 420268 Glahe International Inc. 1700 K Street N.W. Washington, D.C. 20006, USA Tel: [1] (202) 659-4557 Fax: [1] (202) 457-0776 Tlx: ITT 440322
INTERNEPCON / SEMICONDUCTOR May 11-15, 1993 Apr. 26-29, 1994	Shanghai Exhibition Center (1993) Beijing China International Exhibition Center (1994)	For Shanghai or Beijing show: Cahners Exhibition (HK) 2808 Office Tower, Convention Plaza 1 Harbour Road Hong Kong Tel: [852] 8240330 Fax: [852] 8204026 Tlx: 62270 For Beijing show only: China International Exhibition Center 6 East Beisanhuan Road Chaoyang District Beijing 100028 Tel: (1) 4678309, 4664433 Fax: (1) 4676811 Tlx: 210214
National Fair on the Achievements of China's Sparking Program – New and Hi-Tech Products Last held: Aug. 18-25, 1993	Beijing China International Exhibition Center	China International Exhibition Center 6 East Beisanhuan Road Chaoyang District Beijing 100028 Tel: (1) 4678309, 4664433 Fax: (1) 4676811 Tlx: 210214
Semiconductor China Last held: May 25-28, 1993	Shanghai	Shanghai Int'l Trade Information & Exhibition Co. 817-837 Dong Da Ming Road Shanghai Tel: (21) 5463810 Fax: (21) 5455124 Tlx: 33046 Contact: Mr. Xu Zhiguo

ENVIRONMENTAL & ENERGY INDUSTRIES
See also Petroleum, Gas & Mining

CHINA OIL, GAS EXPO CHEMICAL & PETROCHEMICAL EXPO/CHINA Last held: Dec. 6-9, 1993	Shanghai	Shanghai Int'l Trade Information & Exhibition Co. 817-837 Dong Da Ming Road Shanghai Tel: (21) 5463810 Fax: (21) 5455124 Tlx: 33046 Contact: Mr. Xu Zhiguo

Trade Fair	Site	Contact
Environment Asia Last held: Oct. 6-9, 1993	Shanghai	Glahe International Inc. 1700 K Street N.W. Washington, D.C. 20006, USA Tel: [1] (202) 659-4557 Fax: [1] (202) 457-0776 Tlx: ITT 440322
EP (Energy & Power) China Every 2 years Oct. 24-29, 1994	Beijing China International Exhibition Center	China International Exhibition Center 6 East Beisanhuan Road Chaoyang District Beijing 100028 Tel: (1) 4678309, 4664433 Fax: (1) 4676811 Tlx: 210214
Guangzhou Electricity Expo Dec. 1-5, 1993 Dec. 2-6, 1994	Guangzhou International Exhibition Center	Guangdong International Trade & Exhibition Corp. 33 Jichang Lu, Sanyuanli Guangzhou 510400 Tel: (20) 6678331 x1135 Fax: (20) 6678602 Tlx: 44476 Contact: Ms. Tang Ruiling China Promotion Rm. 2801, Tun Wai Commercial Bldg. 109 Gloucester Road Hong Kong Tel: [852] 5117427 Fax: [852] 5119692 Tlx: 76270
International Electric Power Technology & Equipment Fair Last held: Jul. 22-26, 1993	Guangzhou	Guangdong International Trade & Exhibition Corp. 33 Jichang Lu, Sanyuanli Guangzhou 510400 Tel: (20) 6678331 x1135 Fax: (20) 6678602 Tlx: 44476
International Exhibition on Environmental Engineering & Measuring Instruments (EEMI) Last held: Sep. 22-26, 1992	Shenzhen International Exhibition Center	Coastal International Exhibition Co. 3808 China Resources Building 26 Harbour Road Hong Kong Tel: [852] 8276766 Fax: [852] 8275224 Tlx: 80295
International Exhibition on Sewage & Refuse Treatment Jun. 22-27, 1994	Beijing China International Exhibition Center	China International Exhibition Center 6 East Beisanhuan Road Chaoyang District Beijing 100028 Tel: (1) 4678309, 4664433 Fax: (1) 4676811 Tlx: 210214
International Meteorological Equipment & Technology Exhibition Last held: Oct. 5-9, 1993	Guangzhou International Exhibition Center	Guangdong International Trade & Exhibition Corp. 33 Jichang Lu, Sanyuanli Guangzhou 510400 Tel: (20) 6678331 x1135 Fax: (20) 6678602 Tlx: 44476 Contact: Ms. Tang Ruiling CCPIT Guangdong Sub-Council 305 Dong Feng Zhong Lu Guangzhou, Guangdong Tel: (20) 33332756 Tlx: 44203 Organized with: Guangdong Meteorology Bureau
International Trade Fair for Energy Industry & Energy Supply (ENERGY CHINA) Last held: Jul. 2-6, 1992	Tianjin World Economy Trade & Exhibition Center	Tianjin World Economy Trade & Exhibition Center No. 30, You Yi Road Hexi District Tianjin Tel: (22) 318343 Fax: (22) 318341 Tlx: 234074

Note: Country codes for telephone and fax numbers are not displayed unless they are *outside* of China. All country codes have square brackets around them, while city codes have parentheses. The country code for China is [86].

Trade Fair	Site	Contact
International Trade Fair for Environmental Protection Industry (ENVIRONMENT CHINA) Nov. 10-14, 1992 Last held: Sep. 22-26, 1993	Shenzhen International Exhibition Center	Shenzhen International Exhibition Center Shang Bu North Road Shenzhen Tel: (755) 2263838 Fax: (755) 2263753 Tlx: 420268
International Waste Regeneration Technology & Equipment Exhibition Last held: Nov. 3-6, 1993	Shenzhen	Shenzhen International Exhibition Center Shang Bu North Road Shenzhen Tel: (755) 2263838 Fax: (755) 2263753 Tlx: 420268
International Water Industry Exhibition (IWIE) Jul. 12-17, 1994	Beijing China International Exhibition Center	China International Exhibition Center 6 East Beisanhuan Road Chaoyang District Beijing 100028 Tel: (1) 4678309, 4664433 Fax: (1) 4676811 Tlx: 210214
Large-scale Hydro Power Station Equipment and Construction Expo (Special for Three Gorge Project) Last held: Jun. 18-23, 1993	Beijing China International Exhibition Center	Coastal International Exhibition Co. 3808 China Resources Building 26 Harbour Road Hong Kong Tel: [852] 8276766 Fax: [852] 8275224 Tlx: 80295 Contact: Brenda Yau

FOOD, BEVERAGES & FOOD PROCESSING
See also Agriculture & Forestry

Trade Fair	Site	Contact
DRINKTECH SHANGHAI International Beverage Technology & Machinery Exhibition Last held: Jun. 10-14, 1993	Shanghai	Shanghai Int'l Trade Information & Exhibition Co. 817-837 Dong Da Ming Road Shanghai Tel: (21) 5463810 Fax: (21) 5455124 Tlx: 33046 Contact: Mr. Xu Zhiguo
FOODPACK CHINA Apr. 26-30, 1994	Beijing China International Exhibition Center	China International Exhibition Center 6 East Beisanhuan Road Chaoyang District Beijing 100028 Tel: (1) 4678309, 4664433 Fax: (1) 4676811 Tlx: 210214
INTERFOOD SHANGHAI International Exhibition for Food Processing & Packaging Equipment Every 2 years Oct. 14-19, 1994	Shanghai Exhibition Center	Shanghai Int'l Trade Information & Exhibition Co. 817-837 Dong Da Ming Road Shanghai Tel: (21) 5463810 Fax: (21) 5455124 Tlx: 33046 Contact: Mr. Xu Zhiguo China National Food Industry Association Dept. of International Relations 5 Taipingqiao, Dongli Beijing 100055 Tel: (1) 3062244 x206 Tlx: 222983 CNFIA CN
International Agricultural Machinery, Agrotechnology and Food Processing Exhibition Last held: Sep. 22-26, 1992	Guangzhou International Exhibition Center	Guangdong International Trade & Exhibition Corp. 33 Jichang Lu, Sanyuanli Guangzhou 510400 Tel: (20) 6678331 x1135 Fax: (20) 6678602 Tlx: 44476
International Food & Food Processing Machinery Exhibition Last held: Nov. 22-Dec. 3, 1993	Zhuhai	Zhuhai International Trade & Exhibition (Group), Zhuhai Tel: (756) 332656 x 6002 Fax: (756) 333440

Trade Fair	Site	Contact
International Food Processing & Packaging Machinery Exhibition Every 2 years Last held: Nov. 2-7, 1993	Beijing China International Exhibition Center	China International Exhibition Center 6 East Beisanhuan Road Chaoyang District Beijing 100028 Tel: (1) 4678309, 4664433 Fax: (1) 4676811 Tlx: 210214
International Food Processing Machinery & Packaging Last held: May 14-18, 1993	Guangzhou	CCPIT Guangdong Sub-Council 305 Dong Feng Zhong Lu Guangzhou, Guangdong Tel: (20) 3332756 Tlx: 44203
Shenzhen International Food & Food Processing Machinery Trade Fair Last held: Nov. 22-26, 1993	Shenzhen	Shenzhen International Exhibition Center Shang Bu North Road Shenzhen Tel: (755) 2263838 Fax: (755) 2263753 Tlx: 420268

FURNITURE & HOUSEWARES
See also Construction & Housing

Trade Fair	Site	Contact
China (Shenzhen) International Household Electric Appliances Exhibition Last held: Oct. 5-8, 1993	Shenzhen International Exhibition Center	Shenzhen International Exhibition Center Shang Bu North Road Shenzhen Tel: (755) 2263838 Fax: (755) 2263753 Tlx: 420268
China Home & Office Style Last held: Aug. 26-30, 1993	Tianjin	CCPIT, Tianjin Sub-Council International Trade Bldg. 84 Jianshe Road, Heping District Tianjin Tel: (22) 301367 Fax: (22) 301344 Tlx: 23261
China International Gifts & Housewares Expo Last held: Dec. 1-5, 1993	Guangzhou International Exhibition Center	Guangdong International Trade & Exhibition Corp. 33 Jichang Lu, Sanyuanli Guangzhou 510400 Tel: (20) 6678331 x1135 Fax: (20) 6678602 Tlx: 44476 Contact: Ms. Tang Ruiling Organized with: Together Expo Ltd.
Construction & Interior Decoration May 11-15, 1994	Shanghai	Glahe International Inc. 1700 K Street N.W. Washington, D.C. 20006, USA Tel: [1] (202) 659-4557 Fax: [1] (202) 457-0776 Tlx: ITT 440322
Consumer Goods, Gifts & Housewares Exhibition China Last held: May 22-26, 1993	Shenzhen International Exhibition Center	Shenzhen International Exhibition Center Shang Bu North Road Shenzhen Tel: (755) 2263838 Fax: (755) 2263753 Tlx: 420268
CONSUMTRONICS SHANGHAI International Exhibition on Consumer Electronics and Household Appliances Last held: Dec. 17-20, 1993	Shanghai Exhibition Center	Shanghai Int'l Trade Information & Exhibition Co. 817-837 Dong Da Ming Road Shanghai Tel: (21) 5463810 Fax: (21) 5455124 Tlx: 33046 Contact: Mr. Xu Zhiguo Adsale Exhibition Services 14/F., Devon House Taikoo Place 979 King's Road Quarry Bay, Hong Kong Tel: [852] 5110511 Fax: [852] 5165204

Note: Country codes for telephone and fax numbers are not displayed unless they are *outside* of China. All country codes have square brackets around them, while city codes have parentheses. The country code for China is [86].

Trade Fair	Site	Contact
Ideal Home May 11-15, 1994	Shanghai	Glahe International Inc. 1700 K Street N.W. Washington, D.C. 20006, USA Tel: [1] (202) 659-4557 Fax: [1] (202) 457-0776 Tlx: ITT 440322
Ideal Office May 11-15, 1994	Shanghai	Glahe International Inc. 1700 K Street N.W. Washington, D.C. 20006, USA Tel: [1] (202) 659-4557 Fax: [1] (202) 457-0776 Tlx: ITT 440322
International Exhibition on Consumer Electronics and Household Appliances Last held: Nov. 18-21, 1993	Guangzhou China Foreign Trade Center	Adsale Exhibition Services 14/F., Devon House Taikoo Place 979 King's Road Quarry Bay, Hong Kong Tel: [852] 5110511 Fax: [852] 5165204
International Household Electrical Appliances Exhibition Last held: Aug. 26-30, 1993	Guangzhou	Guangdong International Trade & Exhibition Corp. 33 Jichang Lu, Sanyuanli Guangzhou 510400 Tel: (20) 6678331 x1135 Fax: (20) 6678602 Tlx: 44476
National Exhibition of 2000 Household Consuming Pattern Last held: Jun. 18-26, 1993	Beijing China International Exhibition Center	China International Exhibition Center 6 East Beisanhuan Road Chaoyang District Beijing 100028 Tel: (1) 4678309, 4664433 Fax: (1) 4676811 Tlx: 210214
Woodworking & Furniture Fair China Every 2 years Mar. 1-5, 1994	Beijing China International Exhibition Center	Adsale Exhibition Services 14/F., Devon House Taikoo Place 979 King's Road Quarry Bay, Hong Kong Tel: [852] 5110511 Fax: [852] 5165204

GIFTS, JEWELRY & STATIONERY Includes art, crafts, timepieces
See also Hobbies & Recreation

Trade Fair	Site	Contact
Beijing International Fair of Fine Daily Novelties Last held: Jun. 23-28, 1993	Beijing China World Trade Center	China World Trade Center (CWTC) 1 Jian Guo Men Wai Dajie Beijing 100004 Tel: (1) 5053853, 5052288 x 8445 Fax: (1) 5051002, 5021769 China Arts/Crafts Corp. 2/F., Jingxin Center South Beijing 100027 Tel (1) 4661643 Fax: (1) 4661821 Contact: Yang/Maozhong
China International Gifts & Housewares Expo Last held: Dec. 1-5, 1993	Guangzhou International Exhibition Center	Guangdong International Trade & Exhibition Corp. 33 Jichang Lu, Sanyuanli Guangzhou 510400 Tel: (20) 6678331 x1135 Fax: (20) 6678602 Tlx: 44476 Contact: Ms. Tang Ruiling Organized with: Together Expo Ltd.
Consumer Goods, Gifts & Housewares Exhibition China Last held: May 22-26, 1993	Shenzhen International Exhibition Center	Shenzhen International Exhibition Center Shang Bu North Road Shenzhen Tel: (755) 2263838 Fax: (755) 2263753 Tlx: 420268

Trade Fair	Site	Contact
International Jewelry & Timepieces Trade Fair Apr. 12-17, 1994	Beijing China International Exhibition Center	China International Exhibition Center 6 East Beisanhuan Road Chaoyang District Beijing 100028 Tel: (1) 4678309, 4664433 Fax: (1) 4676811 Tlx: 210214
International Toys & Gifts Exhibition Last held: Oct. 13-16, 1993	Shenzhen	Shenzhen International Exhibition Center Shang Bu North Road Shenzhen Tel: (755) 2263838 Fax: (755) 2263753 Tlx: 420268
International Watch & Clock Making Machinery & Technology Exhibition for China (CHINA TIME) Last held: Aug. 28-Sep. 1, 1992	Shanghai International Exhibition Center	Business & Industrial Trade Fairs 18/F., First Pacific Bank 51 Gloucester Road Hong Kong Tel: [852] 8652633 Fax: [852] 8661770 Tlx: 64882
International Watches, Clocks and Jewelry Exhibition Last held: May 20-24, 1993	Shenzhen International Exhibition Center	Shenzhen International Exhibition Center Shang Bu North Road Shenzhen Tel: (755) 2263838 Fax: (755) 2263753 Tlx: 420268
Tianjin International Trade Fair for Arts & Crafts (CHINA ARTS & CRAFTS) Last held: Dec. 15-19, 1992	Tianjin World Economy Trade & Exhibition Center	Tianjin World Economy Trade & Exhibition Center No. 30, You Yi Road Hexi District Tianjin Tel: (22) 318343 Fax: (22) 318341 Tlx: 234074

HEALTH & SAFETY Includes security
See also Medicine & Pharmaceuticals

Trade Fair	Site	Contact
Cosmetics, Hair & Beauty Jun. 18-22, 1994	Shanghai	Glahe International Inc. 1700 K Street N.W. Washington, D.C. 20006, USA Tel: [1] (202) 659-4557 Fax: [1] (202) 457-0776 Tlx: ITT 440322
International Beauty & Health Care Products Exhibition Last held: Sep. 16-22, 1993	Zhuhai	Zhuhai International Trade & Exhibition (Group), Zhuhai Tel: (756) 332656 x 6002 Fax: (756) 333440
International Cosmetics, Hair & Beauty Products Exhibition May 20-24, 1993 Sep. 26-29, 1994	Shenzhen	Shenzhen International Exhibition Center Shang Bu North Road Shenzhen Tel: (755) 2263838 Fax: (755) 2263753 Tlx: 420268 Glahe International Inc. 1700 K Street N.W. Washington, D.C. 20006, USA Tel: [1] (202) 659-4557 Fax: [1] (202) 457-0776 Tlx: ITT 440322
International Exhibition for Police, Civil Security and Fire Protection Equipment (CHINA SECURE) Jun. 19-23, 1994	Beijing Exhibition Center	Sinostar International 802 Wing On Investment Building 343-349 Nathan Road Kowloon, Hong Kong Tel: [852] 7107878 Fax: [852] 7808713 Tlx: 46070 SILHX

Note: Country codes for telephone and fax numbers are not displayed unless they are *outside* of China. All country codes have square brackets around them, while city codes have parentheses. The country code for China is [86].

Trade Fair	Site	Contact
International Science, Peace & Health Care Exhibition Last held: Nov. 9-15, 1993	Zhuhai	Zhuhai International Trade & Exhibition (Group), Zhuhai Tel: (756) 332656 x 6002 Fax: (756) 333440
International Security Equipment Exhibition Last held: Oct. 6-15, 1992	Shanghai Exhibition Center	Shanghai Science & Technology Exchange Center 370 Huashan Lu Shanghai Tel: (21) 4333576 Fax: (21) 2513801
Safety & Prevention Every 3 years Nov. 9-14, 1994	Beijing China International Exhibition Center	China International Exhibition Center 6 East Beisanhuan Road Chaoyang District Beijing 100028 Tel: (1) 4678309, 4664433 Fax: (1) 4676811 Tlx: 210214

HOBBIES & RECREATION   Includes books, education, sporting goods, toys

Trade Fair	Site	Contact
China International Book Fair Aug. 27-Sep. 8, 1994	Beijing China International Exhibition Center	China International Exhibition Center 6 East Beisanhuan Road Chaoyang District Beijing 100028 Tel: (1) 4678309, 4664433 Fax: (1) 4676811 Tlx: 210214
Electronic Toys & Games Sep. 26-29, 1994	Shenzhen	Glahe International Inc. 1700 K Street N.W. Washington, D.C. 20006, USA Tel: [1] (202) 659-4557 Fax: [1] (202) 457-0776 Tlx: ITT 440322
International Educational Materials Exhibition (CHINADIDAC) Every 2 years Nov. 10-15, 1994	Beijing China International Exhibition Center	CIEC Exhibition Co. (HK) 21/F., China Resources Bldg. 26 Harbour Road Hong Kong Tel: [852] 8275078 Fax: [852] 8275535 Tlx: 81529 CIFC HX
International Musical Instruments and Manufacturing Exposition (MUSIC CHINA) Last held: Sep. 19-23, 1992	Guangzhou International Exhibition Center	Guangdong International Trade & Exhibition Corp. 33 Jichang Lu, Sanyuanli Guangzhou 510400 Tel: (20) 6678331 x1135 Fax: (20) 6678602 Tlx: 44476
International Sporting Goods Exhibition (Intersport) Every 2 years May 20-25, 1994	Beijing China International Exhibition Center	China International Exhibition Center 6 East Beisanhuan Road Chaoyang District Beijing 100028 Tel: (1) 4678309, 4664433 Fax: (1) 4676811 Tlx: 210214
International Sports Facilities Exhibition Jun. 24-29, 1994	Beijing China International Exhibition Center	CIEC Exhibition Co. (HK) 21/F., China Resources Bldg. 26 Harbour Road Hong Kong Tel: [852] 8275078 Fax: [852] 8275535 Tlx: 81529 CIFC HX
International Toys & Gifts Exhibition Last held: Oct. 13-16, 1993	Shenzhen	Shenzhen International Exhibition Center Shang Bu North Road Shenzhen Tel: (755) 2263838 Fax: (755) 2263753 Tlx: 420268

Trade Fair	Site	Contact
Shenzhen International Sporting Goods Exhibition Last held: Apr. 26-29, 1993	Shenzhen International Exhibition Center	Shenzhen International Exhibition Center Shang Bu North Road Shenzhen Tel: (755) 2263838 Fax: (755) 2263753 Tlx: 420268
TOYS International Toys Expo Jun. 1-6, 1993 May 21-26, 1994	Beijing China International Exhibition Center	Coastal International Exhibition Co. 3808 China Resources Building 26 Harbour Road Hong Kong Tel: [852] 8276766 Fax: [852] 8275224 Tlx: 80295 Contact: Brenda Yau

INDUSTRIAL MATERIALS & CHEMICALS
See also Metal & Metal Finishing; Petroleum, Gas & Mining

CHINAPLAS International Exhibition on Plastics and Rubber Engineering Annual, alternates between Beijing and Shanghai May 20-24, 1993 Sep. 16-20, 1994	Shanghai (1993) Beijing China International Exhibition Center (1994)	Shanghai Int'l Trade Information & Exhibition Co. 817-837 Dong Da Ming Road Shanghai Tel: (21) 5463810 Fax: (21) 5455124 Tlx: 33046 Contact: Mr. Xu Zhiguo China International Exhibition Center 6 East Beisanhuan Road Chaoyang District Beijing 100028 Tel: (1) 4678309, 4664433 Fax: (1) 4676811 Tlx: 210214
International Ceramics Industry Exhibition Last held: Jun. 8-12, 1993	Guangzhou International Exhibition Center	Guangdong International Trade & Exhibition Corp. 33 Jichang Lu, Sanyuanli Guangzhou 510400 Tel: (20) 6678331 x1135 Fax: (20) 6678602 Tlx: 44476 CCPIT Guangdong Sub-Council 305 Dong Feng Zhong Lu Guangzhou, Guangdong Tel: (20) 3332756 Tlx: 44203 Organized with: State Building Materials Bureau
International Chemical Fiber Industry Economic & Technical Cooperation Fair Last held: May 11-15, 1993	Beijing	China Promotion Rm. 2801, Tun Wai Commercial Bldg. 109 Gloucester Road Hong Kong Tel: [852] 5117427 Fax: [852] 5119692 Tlx: 76270
International Chemical Industry Trade Fair (ICIF) Every 2 years Sep. 15-20, 1994	Beijing China International Exhibition Center	China International Exhibition Center 6 East Beisanhuan Road Chaoyang District Beijing 100028 Tel: (1) 4678309, 4664433 Fax: (1) 4676811 Tlx: 210214 International Exchange Center of the Ministry of Chemical Industry Tel: (1) 4226622 x 3212 Fax: (1) 4214052 Contact: Mr. Zhou Jianguo
International Exhibition on Chemical Engineering & Specialty Chemicals (CHEM) Last held: Dec. 8-12, 1992	Guangzhou International Exhibition Center	Coastal International Exhibition Co. 3808 China Resources Building 26 Harbour Road Hong Kong Tel: [852] 8276766 Fax: [852] 8275224 Tlx: 80295

Note: Country codes for telephone and fax numbers are not displayed unless they are *outside* of China. All country codes have square brackets around them, while city codes have parentheses. The country code for China is [86].

Trade Fair	Site	Contact
International Exhibition on Chemical Engineering and Specialty Chemicals Last held: Sep. 10-14, 1993	Tianjin	Coastal International Exhibition Co. 3808 China Resources Building 26 Harbour Road Hong Kong Tel: [852] 8276766 Fax: [852] 8275224 Tlx: 80295 Contact: Brenda Yau Tianjin World Economy Trade & Exhibition Center 30 Youyi Lu, Hexi Qu Tianjin 300061 Tel: (22) 342222 Fax: (22) 349855
International Exhibition on Chemical Industry and Material Last held: Jun. 23-27, 1992	Guangzhou International Exhibition Center	Guangdong International Trade & Exhibition Corp. 33 Jichang Lu, Sanyuanli Guangzhou 510400 Tel: (20) 6678331 x1135 Fax: (20) 6678602 Tlx: 44476
International Exhibition on Surface Treatment Technology (CHINA SURFACE TREATMENT) Last held: Sep. 22-26, 1992	Tianjin	CCPIT, Tianjin Sub-Council International Trade Bldg. 84 Jianshe Road, Heping District Tianjin Tel: (22) 301367 Fax: (22) 301344 Tlx: 23261
International Machinery & Materials Exhibition (ChinaMex Beijing) Nov., 1994	Beijing China International Exhibition Center	China International Exhibition Center 6 East Beisanhuan Road Chaoyang District Beijing 100028 Tel: (1) 4678309, 4664433 Fax: (1) 4676811 Tlx: 210214
International Machinery & Materials Exhibition for China Last held: Mar. 6-10, 1993	Guangzhou International Exhibition Center	Guangdong International Trade & Exhibition Corp. 33 Jichang Lu, Sanyuanli Guangzhou 510400 Tel: (20) 6678331 x1135 Fax: (20) 6678602 Tlx: 44476 Contact: Ms. Tang Ruiling Business & Industrial Trade Fairs 18/F., First Pacific Bank 51 Gloucester Road Hong Kong Tel: [852] 8652633 Fax: [852] 8661770 Tlx: 64882
International Plastic Industry Exhibition Last held: Mar. 6-10, 1993	Guangzhou International Exhibition Center	Guangdong International Trade & Exhibition Corp. 33 Jichang Lu, Sanyuanli Guangzhou 510400 Tel: (20) 6678331 x1135 Fax: (20) 6678602 Tlx: 44476 Contact: Ms. Tang Ruiling Business & Industrial Trade Fairs 18/F., First Pacific Bank 51 Gloucester Road Hong Kong Tel: [852] 8652633 Fax: [852] 8661770 Tlx: 64882
International Surface Finishing & Coatings Exhibition (SF CHINA) Every 2 years, alternates between Beijing and Shanghai Apr. 17-21, 1993 1995 (Dates to be announced)	Beijing China International Exhibition Center (1993) Shanghai (1995)	Sinostar International 802 Wing On Investment Building 343-349 Nathan Road Kowloon, Hong Kong Tel: [852] 7107878 Fax: [852] 7808713 Tlx: 46070 SILHX

Trade Fair	Site	Contact

LEATHER GOODS & FOOTWEAR
See also Textiles & Apparel

Trade Fair	Site	Contact
CHINA LEATHER International Leather & Footwear Processing Machinery & Leather Goods Exhibition Every 2 years Oct. 28-Nov. 2, 1994	Shanghai International Exhibition Center	Shanghai Int'l Trade Information & Exhibition Co. 817-837 Dong Da Ming Road Shanghai Tel: (21) 5463810 Fax: (21) 5455124 Tlx: 33046 Contact: Mr. Mr. Xu Zhiguo Organized with: China Leather Industry Association
China Textiles, Garments, Shoes & Hats Fair Last held: Mar. 24-28, 1993	Shenzhen International Exhibition Center	Shenzhen International Exhibition Center Shang Bu North Road Shenzhen Tel: (755) 2263838 Fax: (755) 2263753 Tlx: 420268
International Exhibition on Leather Industry & Shoemaking Every 2 years Last held: Oct. 14-19, 1993	Beijing China International Exhibition Center	Adsale Exhibition Services 14/F., Devon House Taikoo Place 979 King's Road Quarry Bay, Hong Kong Tel: [852] 5110511 Fax: [852] 5165204
International Footwear Industry Trade Fair May 6-11, 1994	Beijing China International Exhibition Center	China International Exhibition Center 6 East Beisanhuan Road Chaoyang District Beijing 100028 Tel: (1) 4678309, 4664433 Fax: (1) 4676811 Tlx: 210214
International Garment & Shoe Industry Exhibition Last held: Sep. 1-5, 1992	Tianjin Exhibition Center	CCPIT, Tianjin Sub-Council International Trade Bldg. 84 Jianshe Road, Heping District Tianjin Tel: (22) 301367 Fax: (22) 301344 Tlx: 23261
International Leather Products & Machinery Fair Last held: Jun. 1-4, 1993	Guangzhou	Guangdong International Trade & Exhibition Corp. 33 Jichang Lu, Sanyuanli Guangzhou 510400 Tel: (20) 6678331 x1135 Fax: (20) 6678602 Tlx: 44476
International Shoe and Leather Exhibition Last held: May 14-18, 1993	Guangzhou International Exhibition Center	Guangdong International Trade & Exhibition Corp. 33 Jichang Lu, Sanyuanli Guangzhou 510400 Tel: (20) 6678331 x1135 Fax: (20) 6678602 Tlx: 44476 Contact: Ms. Tang Ruiling Top Repute Co. Ltd. 186-192 Connaught Road West Hong Kong Tel: [852] 5477071 Fax: [852] 5495927
International Shoes and Shoe-Making Machinery & Technology Fair Last held: May 5-9, 1993	Shenzhen International Exhibition Center	Shenzhen International Exhibition Center Shang Bu North Road Shenzhen Tel: (755) 2263838 Fax: (755) 2263753 Tlx: 420268
Jiangsu International Leather Processing Machinery and Technology Exhibition (LEATHER TEQ NANJING) Last held: Jun. 29-Jul. 4, 1992	Nanjing Jiangsu Exhibition Hall	Goodwill Trading and Exhibition Promotion Co. 1801 Cameron Commercial Center 458-468 Hennessy Road Hong Kong Tel: [852] 8934338 Fax: [852] 8343137 Tlx: 62759 GTEX HX

Note: Country codes for telephone and fax numbers are not displayed unless they are *outside* of China. All country codes have square brackets around them, while city codes have parentheses. The country code for China is [86].

Trade Fair	Site	Contact
LEATHER **International Leather Trade Fair** Last held: Nov. 11-15, 1993	Shenzhen International Exhibition Center	Coastal International Exhibition Co. 3808 China Resources Building 26 Harbour Road Hong Kong Tel: [852] 8276766 Fax: [852] 8275224 Tlx: 80295 Contact: Brenda Yau Shenzhen International Exhibition Center Shang Bu North Road Shenzhen Tel: (755) 2263838 Fax: (755) 2263753 Tlx: 420268
Tianjin International Trade Fair for Leather and Footwear Machinery and Equipment (CHINA LIGHT) Last held: Oct. 13-17, 1992	Tianjin World Economy Trade & Exhibition Center	Tianjin World Economy Trade & Exhibition Center No. 30, You Yi Road Hexi District Tianjin Tel: (22) 318343 Fax: (22) 318341 Tlx: 234074
Tianjin Leather & Shoes Last held: Jul. 7-10, 1993	Tianjin	CCPIT, Tianjin Sub-Council International Trade Bldg. 84 Jianshe Road, Heping District Tianjin Tel: (22) 301367 Fax: (22) 301344 Tlx: 23261

MACHINES & INSTRUMENTS
See also Tools: Precision & Measuring; other categories which may include exhibitions with machines specific to those industries

AHME Asia Machinery/Hardware Exhibition Last held: Nov. 1-5, 1993	Tianjin	CCPIT, Tianjin Sub-Council International Trade Bldg. 84 Jianshe Road, Heping District Tianjin Tel: (22) 301367 Fax: (22) 301344 Tlx: 23261
BOILER SHANGHAI Last held: Jun. 24-28, 1993	Shanghai	Shanghai Int'l Trade Information & Exhibition Co. 817-837 Dong Da Ming Road Shanghai Tel: (21) 5463810 Fax: (21) 5455124 Tlx: 33046 Contact: Mr. Xu Zhiguo
CHINA INSTRUMENT International Exhibition on Instrumentation & Technology Last held: Sep. 17-21, 1993	Shanghai	Shanghai Int'l Trade Information & Exhibition Co. 817-837 Dong Da Ming Road Shanghai Tel: (21) 5463810 Fax: (21) 5455124 Tlx: 33046 Contact: Mr. Xu Zhiguo SHK International Services Ltd. 6/F., China Harbour Bldg. 370-374 King's Road Hong Kong Tel: [852] 8077633 Fax: [852] 5705903
CHINA MECTT International Machinery, Factory Automation, Electronics Technology Exhibition for China Last held: Nov. 2-6, 1993	Shanghai	Shanghai Int'l Trade Information & Exhibition Co. 817-837 Dong Da Ming Road Shanghai Tel: (21) 5463810 Fax: (21) 5455124 Tlx: 33046 Contact: Mr. Xu Zhiguo
CHINA WRITE International Exhibition of Equipment & Technology for Production of Writing/Marking Instruments Last held: Oct. 19-23, 1993	Shanghai	Shanghai Int'l Trade Information & Exhibition Co. 817-837 Dong Da Ming Road Shanghai Tel: (21) 5463810 Fax: (21) 5455124 Tlx: 33046 Contact: Mr. Xu Zhiguo

Trade Fair	Site	Contact
China International Form Fabricating Fair (3F) Jun., 1994	Beijing China International Exhibition Center	China International Exhibition Center 6 East Beisanhuan Road Chaoyang District Beijing 100028 Tel: (1) 4678309, 4664433 Fax: (1) 4676811 Tlx: 210214
China Machine Tools Show Last held: Jul. 17-24, 1992	Beijing China International Exhibition Center	China International Exhibition Center 6 East Beisanhuan Road Chaoyang District Beijing 100028 Tel: (1) 4678309, 4664433 Fax: (1) 4676811 Tlx: 210214
China StoneTech Every 2 years Apr., 1994	Beijing China International Exhibition Center	China International Exhibition Center 6 East Beisanhuan Road Chaoyang District Beijing 100028 Tel: (1) 4678309, 4664433 Fax: (1) 4676811 Tlx: 210214
DETECHNIQUE CHINA International Exhibition on Techniques of Machine Monitoring Fault Diagnosis & Maintenance Last held: Oct. 26-30, 1993	Tianjin	CCPIT, Tianjin Sub-Council International Trade Bldg. 84 Jianshe Road, Heping District Tianjin Tel: (22) 301367 Fax: (22) 301344 Tlx: 23261
Engine China Mar. 8-13, 1994	Beijing China International Exhibition Center	China International Exhibition Center 6 East Beisanhuan Road Chaoyang District Beijing 100028 Tel: (1) 4678309, 4664433 Fax: (1) 4676811 Tlx: 210214
IBDMEX International Exhibition on Building Decorative Material & Production Equipment Industry Last held: Nov. 23-27, 1993	Beijing China International Exhibition Center	Coastal International Exhibition Co. 3808 China Resources Building 26 Harbour Road Hong Kong Tel: [852] 8276766 Fax: [852] 8275224 Tlx: 80295 Contact: Brenda Yau
INTERAD International Exhibition on Advertising Technology Last held: May 26-30, 1993	Shanghai	Shanghai Int'l Trade Information & Exhibition Co. 817-837 Dong Da Ming Road Shanghai Tel: (21) 5463810 Fax: (21) 5455124 Tlx: 33046 Contact: Mr. Xu Zhiguo
International Bearing Industry Exhibition (BEARING) Last held: Nov. 24-28, 1992	Guangzhou International Exhibition Center	Guangdong International Trade & Exhibition Corp. 33 Jichang Lu, Sanyuanli Guangzhou 510400 Tel: (20) 6678331 x1135 Fax: (20) 6678602 Tlx: 44476
International Boiler & Pressure Vessel Manufacturing & Welding Exhibition Every 2 years Last held: Oct. 27-31, 1993	Beijing China International Exhibition Center	China International Exhibition Center 6 East Beisanhuan Road Chaoyang District Beijing 100028 Tel: (1) 4678309, 4664433 Fax: (1) 4676811 Tlx: 210214

Note: Country codes for telephone and fax numbers are not displayed unless they are *outside* of China. All country codes have square brackets around them, while city codes have parentheses. The country code for China is [86].

Trade Fair	Site	Contact
International Exhibition on Instruments, Public Security Equipment and Technology Last held: Jun. 9-13, 1992	Guangzhou International Exhibition Center	Guangdong International Trade & Exhibition Corp. 33 Jichang Lu, Sanyuanli Guangzhou 510400 Tel: (20) 6678331 x1135 Fax: (20) 6678602 Tlx: 44476
International Exhibition on Stone Processing and Woodworking Machinery Last held: Nov. 12-16, 1993	Shenzhen	Coastal International Exhibition Co. 3808 China Resources Building 26 Harbour Road Hong Kong Tel: [852] 8276766 Fax: [852] 8275224 Tlx: 80295 Contact: Brenda Yau
International Heat Treatment Technology Exhibition Last held: Sep. 21-25, 1993	Guangzhou International Exhibition Center	Guangdong International Trade & Exhibition Corp. 33 Jichang Lu, Sanyuanli Guangzhou 510400 Tel: (20) 6678331 x1135 Fax: (20) 6678602 Tlx: 44476 Contact: Ms. Tang Ruiling CCPIT Guangdong Sub-Council 305 Dong Feng Zhong Lu Guangzhou, Guangdong Tel: (20) 3332756 Tlx: 44203 Organized with: China Assn. of Surface Engineering
International Machine Tool Show (CIMT) Every 2 years Last held: May 5-11, 1993	Beijing China International Exhibition Center	China Machine Tool Builders Association (CMTBA) 26 South Yue Tan Street Beijing 100825 Tel: (1) 868261 X 2668 Fax: (1) 8013472 Contact: Mr. Li Xingbin, Director International Cooperation Department CIMT Preparatory Office Fax: (1) 8032517
International Machinery & Electronic Technology (CHINA METE) Last held: Sep. 21-26, 1992	Tianjin Exhibition Center	CCPIT, Tianjin Sub-Council International Trade Bldg. 84 Jianshe Road, Heping District Tianjin Tel: (22) 301367 Fax: (22) 301344 Tlx: 23261
International Machinery & Industrial Supplies Fair Last held: Oct. 21-25, 1993	Shenzhen International Exhibition Center	Shenzhen International Exhibition Center Shang Bu North Road Shenzhen Tel: (755) 2263838 Fax: (755) 2263753 Tlx: 420268
International Machinery & Materials Exhibition (ChinaMex Beijing) Nov., 1994	Beijing China International Exhibition Center	China International Exhibition Center 6 East Beisanhuan Road Chaoyang District Beijing 100028 Tel: (1) 4678309, 4664433 Fax: (1) 4676811 Tlx: 210214
International Machinery & Materials Exhibition for China Last held: Mar. 6-10, 1993	Guangzhou International Exhibition Center	Guangdong International Trade & Exhibition Corp. 33 Jichang Lu, Sanyuanli Guangzhou 510400 Tel: (20) 6678331 x1135 Fax: (20) 6678602 Tlx: 44476 Contact: Ms. Tang Ruiling Business & Industrial Trade Fairs 18/F., First Pacific Bank 51 Gloucester Road Hong Kong Tel: [852] 8652633 Fax: [852] 8661770 Tlx: 64882

Trade Fair	Site	Contact
International Machinery and Equipment Exhibition (MACHINEX) Last held: Aug. 18-22, 1992	Kunming Yuman Exhibition Hall	Goodwill Trading and Exhibition Promotion Co. 1801 Cameron Commercial Center 458-468 Hennessy Road Hong Kong Tel: [852] 8934338 Fax: [852] 8343137 Tlx: 62759
International Meteorological Equipment & Technology Exhibition Last held: Oct. 5-9, 1993	Guangzhou International Exhibition Center	Guangdong International Trade & Exhibition Corp. 33 Jichang Lu, Sanyuanli Guangzhou 510400 Tel: (20) 6678331 x1135 Fax: (20) 6678602 Tlx: 44476 Contact: Ms. Tang Ruiling CCPIT Guangdong Sub-Council 305 Dong Feng Zhong Lu Guangzhou, Guangdong Tel: (20) 3332756 Tlx: 44203 Organized with: Guangdong Meteorology Bureau
International Musical Instruments and Manufacturing Exposition (MUSIC CHINA) Last held: Sep. 19-23, 1992	Guangzhou International Exhibition Center	Guangdong International Trade & Exhibition Corp. 33 Jichang Lu, Sanyuanli Guangzhou 510400 Tel: (20) 6678331 x1135 Fax: (20) 6678602 Tlx: 44476
International Refractory Industrial Exhibition (REFRACTORY CHINA) Last held: Oct. 8-12, 1992	Guangzhou International Exhibition Center	Guangdong International Trade & Exhibition Corp. 33 Jichang Lu, Sanyuanli Guangzhou 510400 Tel: (20) 6678331 x1135 Fax: (20) 6678602 Tlx: 44476
International Security Equipment Exhibition Last held: Oct. 6-15, 1992	Shanghai Exhibition Center	Shanghai Science & Technology Exchange Center 370 Huashan Lu Shanghai Tel: (21) 4333576 Fax: (21) 2513801
International Timber & Stone Processing Machinery Exhibition Last held: Nov. 12-16, 1993	Shenzhen	Shenzhen International Exhibition Center Shang Bu North Road Shenzhen Tel: (755) 2263838 Fax: (755) 2263753 Tlx: 420268
International Woodworking Machinery and Technology Exhibition Last held: Nov. 2-6, 1993	Tianjin	SHK International Services Ltd. 6/F., China Harbour Bldg. 370-374 King's Road Hong Kong Tel: [852] 8077633 Fax: [852] 5705903
MACHIMPEX Apr. 26-30, 1994	Beijing China International Exhibition Center	China International Exhibition Center 6 East Beisanhuan Road Chaoyang District Beijing 100028 Tel: (1) 4678309, 4664433 Fax: (1) 4676811 Tlx: 210214
Shanghai International Light Industries Exhibition (SILIE) Last held: Sep. 17-22, 1992	Shanghai International Exhibition Center	Shanghai Int'l Trade Information & Exhibition Co. 817-837 Dong Da Ming Road Shanghai Tel: (21) 5463810 Fax: (21) 5455124 Tlx: 33046

Note: Country codes for telephone and fax numbers are not displayed unless they are *outside* of China. All country codes have square brackets around them, while city codes have parentheses. The country code for China is [86].

Trade Fair	Site	Contact
South China International Machinery Exhibition for Light Industries (LIMAC SOUTH CHINA) Annual Last held: Nov. 16-20, 1993	Guangzhou China Foreign Trade Center	Adsale Exhibition Services 14/F., Devon House Taikoo Place 979 King's Road Quarry Bay, Hong Kong Tel: [852] 5110511 Fax: [852] 5165204 China Foreign Trade Center Group 117 Liu Hua Road Guangzhou Tel: (20) 6678000 Fax: (20) 3335880 Tlx: 44465
WELDING SHANGHAI Every 2 years Last held: Jun. 24-28, 1993	Shanghai	Shanghai Int'l Trade Information & Exhibition Co. 817-837 Dong Da Ming Road Shanghai Tel: (21) 5463810 Fax: (21) 5455124 Tlx: 33046 Contact: Mr. Xu Zhiguo

MEDICINE & PHARMACEUTICALS
See also Health & Safety

Trade Fair	Site	Contact
China International Exhibition of the Equipment and Technology for the Pharmaceutical Industry (CHINA PHARMACY) Last held: Oct. 15-19, 1993	Shanghai Exhibition Center	Shanghai Int'l Trade Information & Exhibition Co. 817-837 Dong Da Ming Road Shanghai Tel: (21) 5463810 Fax: (21) 5455124 Tlx: 33046 Contact: Mr. Xu Zhiguo
China International Medical Equipment & Facilities Exhibition (SINOMED) Last held: Jun. 18-22, 1992	Beijing Exhibition Center	Worldwide Conventions & Expositions 508 Silver Cord, Tower I 30 Canton Road Hong Kong Tel: [852] 3757721 Fax: 3750686 Tlx: 44874
Hospital Equipment Expo Oct. 23-27, 1993 Jun. 18-22, 1994	Shanghai	Glahe International Inc. 1700 K Street N.W. Washington, D.C. 20006, USA Tel: [1] (202) 659-4557 Fax: [1] (202) 457-0776 Tlx: ITT 440322
Hubei International Medical, Scientific & Educational Equipment Exhibition Last held: Sep. 1-5, 1992	Wuhan Hubei International Exhibition Center	Copro International Services Rm. 805, Harvest Building 33 Wing Kut Street Hong Kong Tel: [852] 5419196 Fax: [852] 5457639 Tlx: 80577
INTERMED CHINA International Trade Fair on Medical & Pharmaceutical Equipment Jun. 10-15, 1992 Last held: Sep. 1-5, 1993	Tianjin World Economy Trade & Exhibition Center	CCPIT, Tianjin Sub-Council International Trade Bldg. 84 Jianshe Road, Heping District Tianjin Tel: (22) 301367 Fax: (22) 301344 Tlx: 23261 Tianjin World Economy Trade & Exhibition Center 30 Youyi Lu, Hexi Qu Tianjin 300061 Tel: (22) 342222 Fax: (22) 349855
International Exposition on Biotechnology and Life Science Every 2 years 1994 (Dates to be announced)	Beijing	Commedia-CICS 22/F., Sing Pao Bldg. 101 King's Rd. North Point, Hong Kong Tel: [852] 5716029 Fax: [852] 8070219 Tlx: 62489 CANDID

Trade Fair	Site	Contact
International Medical & Hospital Instruments and Equipment Exhibition (MEDICAL CHINA) Alternates between Beijing and Shanghai Jun. 3-8, 1992 Last held: Jun. 2-8, 1993	Beijing China International Exhibition Center (1993)	Bejing contact: CIEC Exhibition Co. (HK) 21/F., China Resources Bldg. 26 Harbour Road Hong Kong Tel: [852] 8275078 Fax: [852] 8275535 Tlx: 81529 CIFC HX
	Shanghai Exhibition Center (1992)	Shanghai contact: Top Repute Co. Ltd. 186-192 Connaught Road West Hong Kong Tel: [852] 5477071 Fax: [852] 5495927
International Medical Equipment Exhibition (WUHAN INTERMED) Last held: Nov. 11-15, 1992	Wuhan Exhibition Hall	Goodwill Trading and Exhibition Promotion Co. 1801 Cameron Commercial Center 458-468 Hennessy Road Hong Kong Tel: [852] 8934338 Fax: [852] 8343137 Tlx: 62759
International Medical Exhibition (INTERMED KUNMING) Last held: Aug. 18-22, 1992	Kunming Yunnan Exhibition Hall	Goodwill Trading and Exhibition Promotion Co. 1801 Cameron Commercial Center 458-468 Hennessy Road Hong Kong Tel: [852] 8934338 Fax: [852] 8343137 Tlx: 62759
International Medical Instruments, Health Care Equipment and Pharmaceuticals Exhibition (MEDEX) Last held: May 3-7, 1993	Guangzhou International Exhibition Center	Guangdong International Trade & Exhibition Corp. 33 Jichang Lu, Sanyuanli Guangzhou 510400 Tel: (20) 6678331 x1135 Fax: (20) 6678602 Tlx: 44476 Contact: Ms. Tang Ruiling China Promotion Rm. 2801, Tun Wai Commercial Bldg. 109 Gloucester Road Hong Kong Tel: [852] 5117427 Fax: [852] 5119692 Tlx: 76270
International Medicines & Health Products Exhibition Last held: Aug. 17-19, 1993	Beijing	China Chamber of Commerce of Medicines and Health Products Importers/Exporters 12 Jianguomenwai Dajie 12/F Beijing 100022 Tel: (1) 5001542, 5003344 Fax. (1) 5001150 Tlx: 7455
International Meeting on Chemical Engineering and Biotechnology in the Far East (Achemasia) Every 3 years 1995 (Dates to be announced)	Beijing China International Exhibition Center	Dechema Theodor-Heuss-Allee 25 Postfach 970146 D-6000 Frankfurt am Main 97, Germany Tel: [49] (69) 7564336 Fax: [49] (69) 7564201 Tlx: 412 490 DCHA D
Shaanxi International Medical Exhibition (SHAANXI INTERMED) Last held: Jul. 21-25, 1992	Xian Shaanxi Industrial Exhibition Hall	Goodwill Trading and Exhibition Promotion Co. 1801 Cameron Commercial Center 458-468 Hennessy Road Hong Kong Tel: [852] 8934338 Fax: [852] 8343137 Tlx: 62759 GTEX HX
SHANGHAI MEDICAL EXPO **Shanghai International Exhibition on Medical Equipment** Every 2 years Last held: Oct. 28-Nov. 1, 1993	Shanghai	Shanghai Int'l Trade Information & Exhibition Co. 817-837 Dong Da Ming Road Shanghai Tel: (21) 5463810 Fax: (21) 5455124 Tlx: 33046 Contact: Mr. Xu Zhiguo

Note: Country codes for telephone and fax numbers are not displayed unless they are *outside* of China. All country codes have square brackets around them, while city codes have parentheses. The country code for China is [86].

Trade Fair	Site	Contact

METAL & METAL FINISHING
See also Industrial Materials & Chemicals

Trade Fair	Site	Contact
Beijing – ESSEN Welding Sep. 2-6, 1994	Beijing China International Exhibition Center	China International Exhibition Center 6 East Beisanhuan Road Chaoyang District Beijing 100028 Tel: (1) 4678309, 4664433 Fax: (1) 4676811 Tlx: 210214
CABLEWIRE SHANGHAI International Exhibition on Cable & Wire Manufacturing Last held: Jun. 24-28, 1993	Shanghai	Shanghai Int'l Trade Information & Exhibition Co. 817-837 Dong Da Ming Road Shanghai Tel: (21) 5463810 Fax: (21) 5455124 Tlx: 33046 Contact: Mr. Xu Zhiguo
DIE & MOLD Apr. 26-30, 1994	Beijing China International Exhibition Center	China International Exhibition Center 6 East Beisanhuan Road Chaoyang District Beijing 100028 Tel: (1) 4678309, 4664433 Fax: (1) 4676811 Tlx: 210214
DIE & MOLD CHINA International Exhibition on Die & Mold Technology & Equipment May 11-16, 1994	Shanghai International Exhibition Center	Shanghai Int'l Trade Information & Exhibition Co. 817-837 Dong Da Ming Road Shanghai Tel: (21) 5463810 Fax: (21) 5455124 Tlx: 33046 Contact: Mr. Xu Zhiguo Organized with: China Die & Mold Industry Association
International Boiler & Pressure Vessel Manufacturing & Welding Exhibition Every 2 years Last held: Oct. 27-31, 1993	Beijing China International Exhibition Center	China International Exhibition Center 6 East Beisanhuan Road Chaoyang District Beijing 100028 Tel: (1) 4678309, 4664433 Fax: (1) 4676811 Tlx: 210214
International Exhibition on Foundry, Forging and Heat Treatment (Foundry Shanghai) Every 2 years Last held: May 11-15, 1993	Shanghai International Exhibition Center	Adsale Exhibition Services 14/F., Devon House Taikoo Place 979 King's Road Quarry Bay, Hong Kong Tel: [852] 5110511 Fax: [852] 5165204
International Exhibition on Surface Treatment Technology (CHINA SURFACE TREATMENT) Last held: Sep. 22-26, 1992	Tianjin	CCPIT, Tianjin Sub-Council International Trade Bldg. 84 Jianshe Road, Heping District Tianjin Tel: (22) 301367 Fax: (22) 301344 Tlx: 23261
International Foundry, Forging, Furnace & Metallurgical Equipment Exhibition Last held: Sep. 4-9, 1992	Beijing China International Exhibition Center	China International Exhibition Center 6 East Beisanhuan Road Chaoyang District Beijing 100028 Tel: (1) 4678309, 4664433 Fax: (1) 4676811 Tlx: 210214

Trade Fair	Site	Contact
International Surface Engineering Exhibition Last held: Sep. 21-25, 1993	Guangzhou International Exhibition Center	Guangdong International Trade & Exhibition Corp. 33 Jichang Lu, Sanyuanli Guangzhou 510400 Tel: (20) 6678331 x1135 Fax: (20) 6678602 Tlx: 44476 Contact: Ms. Tang Ruiling CCPIT Guangdong Sub-Council 305 Dong Feng Zhong Lu Guangzhou, Guangdong Tel: (20) 3332756 Tlx: 44203 Organized with: China Assn. of Surface Engineering
International Surface Finishing & Coatings Exhibition (SF CHINA) Every 2 years, alternates between Beijing and Shanghai Apr. 17-21, 1993 1995 (Dates to be announced)	Beijing China International Exhibition Center (1993) Shanghai (1995)	Sinostar International 802 Wing On Investment Building 343-349 Nathan Road Kowloon, Hong Kong Tel: [852] 7107878 Fax: [852] 7808713 Tlx: 46070 SILHX
International Welding & Soldering Equipment Exhibition Last held: Sep. 8-12, 1992	Guangzhou International Exhibition Center	Guangdong International Trade & Exhibition Corp. 33 Jichang Lu, Sanyuanli Guangzhou 510400 Tel: (20) 6678331 x1135 Fax: (20) 6678602 Tlx: 44476
Metal Expo Apr., 1995	Beijing	Glahe International Inc. 1700 K Street N.W. Washington, D.C. 20006, USA Tel: [1] (202) 659-4557 Fax: [1] (202) 457-0776 Tlx: ITT 440322
Metallurgical Industry Expo/China - Ferrous & Nonferrous Metals Industries Last held: Sep. 22-27, 1992	Beijing World Trade Center	China Promotion Rm. 2801, Tun Wai Commercial Bldg. 109 Gloucester Road Hong Kong Tel: [852] 5117427 Fax: [852] 5119692 Tlx: 76270
SHANGHAI METAL EXPO Last held: Dec. 6-9, 1993	Shanghai	Shanghai Int'l Trade Information & Exhibition Co. 817-837 Dong Da Ming Road Shanghai Tel: (21) 5463810 Fax: (21) 5455124 Tlx: 33046 Contact: Mr. Xu Zhiguo Glahe International Inc. 1700 K Street N.W. Washington, D.C. 20006, USA Tel: [1] (202) 659-4557 Fax: [1] (202) 457-0776 Tlx: ITT 440322
SURFACE CHINA International Exhibition on Surface Treatment, Heat & Welding Last held: Nov. 16-20, 1993	Tianjin	CCPIT, Tianjin Sub-Council International Trade Bldg. 84 Jianshe Road, Heping District Tianjin Tel: (22) 301367 Fax: (22) 301344 Tlx: 23261
WELDING SHANGHAI Every 2 years Jun. 24-28, 1993	Shanghai	Shanghai Int'l Trade Information & Exhibition Co. 817-837 Dong Da Ming Road Shanghai Tel: (21) 5463810 Fax: (21) 5455124 Tlx: 33046 Contact: Mr. Xu Zhiguo

Note: Country codes for telephone and fax numbers are not displayed unless they are *outside* of China. All country codes have square brackets around them, while city codes have parentheses. The country code for China is [86].

Trade Fair	Site	Contact

MULTIMEDIA & AUDIOVISUAL EQUIPMENT
See also Computer & Information Industries, Electronic & Electric Equipment

Trade Fair	Site	Contact
Beijing International Radio and TV Broadcasting Equipment Exhibition (BIRTV) Every 2 years Last held: Sep. 3-7, 1993	Beijing World Trade Center	Business & Industrial Trade Fairs 18/F., First Pacific Bank 51 Gloucester Road Hong Kong Tel: [852] 8652633 Fax: [852] 8661770 Tlx: 64882
International Audio - Visual, Broadcasting and Theater Technology and Equipment Exhibition for China (AV BROADCAST CHINA) Every 2 years Oct. 24-29, 1994	Beijing China International Exhibition Center	Business & Industrial Trade Fairs 18/F., First Pacific Bank 51 Gloucester Road Hong Kong Tel: [852] 8652633 Fax: [852] 8661770 Tlx: 64882
International Consumer AV Exhibition for China (AV CHINA) Last held: Jun. 8-13, 1993	Guangzhou Foreign Trade Center	Business & Industrial Trade Fairs 18/F., First Pacific Bank 51 Gloucester Road Hong Kong Tel: [852] 8652633 Fax: [852] 8661770 Tlx: 64882
International Exhibition of Equipment and Technology for Professional Sound, Light & Music (CHINA SOUND, LIGHT & MUSIC) Last held: May 7-12, 1993	Beijing Exhibition Center	Beijing International Exhibition Center Room 415, 4/F., 2nd Central Building Hualong Street, Nanhey Beijing 100006 Tel: (1) 5125185 Fax: (1) 5125183
International Trade Fair for Professional Audio, Video, Film & Lighting Equipment (AUDIO, VIDEO & FILM CHINA) Last held: May 19-23, 1993	Shenzhen International Exhibition Center	Shenzhen International Exhibition Center Shang Bu North Road Shenzhen Tel: (755) 2263838 Fax: (755) 2263753 Tlx: 420268

PACKAGING, PRINTING & PAPER Includes handling and storage

Trade Fair	Site	Contact
China International Packaging Technology Exhibition (CIP) Every 2 years Nov. 11-16, 1994	Beijing China International Exhibition Center	CIEC Exhibition Co. (HK) 21/F., China Resources Bldg. 26 Harbour Road Hong Kong Tel: [852] 8275078 Fax: [852] 8275535 Tlx: 81529
China Paper & China Forest Every 2 years Last held: Nov. 2-6, 1993	Beijing China International Exhibition Center	China International Exhibition Center 6 East Beisanhuan Road Chaoyang District Beijing 100028 Tel: (1) 4678309, 4664433 Fax: (1) 4676811 Tlx: 210214
FOODPACK CHINA Apr. 26-30, 1994	Beijing China International Exhibition Center	China International Exhibition Center 6 East Beisanhuan Road Chaoyang District Beijing 100028 Tel: (1) 4678309, 4664433 Fax: (1) 4676811 Tlx: 210214

Trade Fair	Site	Contact
INTERFOOD SHANGHAI International Exhibition for Food Processing & Packaging Equipment Every 2 years Oct. 14-19, 1994	Shanghai Exhibition Center	Shanghai Int'l Trade Information & Exhibition Co. 817-837 Dong Da Ming Road Shanghai Tel: (21) 5463810 Fax: (21) 5455124 Tlx: 33046 Contact: Mr. Xu Zhiguo China National Food Industry Association Dept. of International Relations 5 Taipingqiao, Dongli Beijing 100055 Tel: (1) 3062244 x206 Tlx: 222983 CNFIA CN
International Exhibition on Papermaking Industry (PAPER OF CHINA) Last held: Oct. 27-31, 1992	Tianjin Exhibition Center	CCPIT, Tianjin Sub-Council International Trade Bldg. 84 Jianshe Road, Heping District Tianjin Tel: (22) 301367 Fax: (22) 301344 Tlx: 23261
International Food Processing & Packaging Machinery Exhibition Every 2 years Last held: Nov. 2-7, 1993	Beijing China International Exhibition Center	China International Exhibition Center 6 East Beisanhuan Road Chaoyang District Beijing 100028 Tel: (1) 4678309, 4664433 Fax: (1) 4676811 Tlx: 210214
International Grain & Oil Storage Equipment Exhibition Last held: Nov. 2-5, 1993	Shenzhen	Shenzhen International Exhibition Center Shang Bu North Road Shenzhen Tel: (755) 2263838 Fax: (755) 2263753 Tlx: 420268
International Material Handling & Storage Equipment Exhibition Every 2 years Last held: Nov. 19-24, 1993	Beijing China International Exhibition Center	China International Exhibition Center 6 East Beisanhuan Road Chaoyang District Beijing 100028 Tel: (1) 4678309, 4664433 Fax: (1) 4676811 Tlx: 210214
International Meat Processing & Packaging Machinery Exhibition Last held: Nov. 2-5, 1993	Shenzhen	Shenzhen International Exhibition Center Shang Bu North Road Shenzhen Tel: (755) 2263838 Fax: (755) 2263753 Tlx: 420268
International Packaging & Printing Machinery and Materials Exhibition for China (PACK PRINT CHINA) Last held: Apr. 16-21, 1993	Shanghai	Business & Industrial Trade Fairs 18/F., First Pacific Bank 51 Gloucester Road Hong Kong Tel: [852] 8652633 Fax: [852] 8661770 Tlx: 64882
International Packaging Exhibition Last held: Sep. 4-14, 1992	Shanghai Center	Shanghai Science & Technology Exchange Center 370 Huashan Lu Shanghai Tel: (21) 4333576 Fax: (21) 2513801
International Packaging, Printing & Paper Exhibition (PPP CHINA) Last held: Sep. 1-5, 1992	Tianjin World Economy Trade & Exhibition Center	Tianjin World Economy Trade & Exhibition Center No. 30, You Yi Road Hexi District Tianjin Tel: (22) 318343 Fax: (22) 318341 Tlx: 234074

Note: Country codes for telephone and fax numbers are not displayed unless they are *outside* of China. All country codes have square brackets around them, while city codes have parentheses. The country code for China is [86].

Trade Fair	Site	Contact
International Printing Technology Exhibition (CHINA PRINT) Every 4 years Last held: Jun. 3-9, 1992	Beijing China International Exhibition Center	CIEC Exhibition Co. (HK) 21/F., China Resources Bldg. 26 Harbour Road Hong Kong Tel: [852] 8275078 Fax: [852] 8275535 Tlx: 81529 CIFC HX
Print Expo Every 4 years May 16-21, 1994	Beijing China International Exhibition Center	China International Exhibition Center 6 East Beisanhuan Road Chaoyang District Beijing 100028 Tel: (1) 4678309, 4664433 Fax: (1) 4676811 Tlx: 210214

PETROLEUM, GAS & MINING
See also Environmental & Energy Industries, Industrial Materials & Chemicals

Trade Fair	Site	Contact
CHINA OIL, GAS EXPO CHEMICAL & PETROCHEMICAL EXPO/CHINA Last held: Dec. 6-9, 1993	Shanghai	Shanghai Int'l Trade Information & Exhibition Co. 817-837 Dong Da Ming Road Shanghai Tel: (21) 5463810 Fax: (21) 5455124 Tlx: 33046 Contact: Mr. Xu Zhiguo
Gas & LPG Last held: Nov. 12-16, 1992	Shanghai International Exhibition Center	Shanghai Int'l Trade Information & Exhibition Co. 817-837 Dong Da Ming Road Shanghai Tel: (21) 5463810 Fax: (21) 5455124 Tlx: 33046
International Exhibition on Gas Industry Jun. 22-27, 1994	Beijing China International Exhibition Center	China International Exhibition Center 6 East Beisanhuan Road Chaoyang District Beijing 100028 Tel: (1) 4678309, 4664433 Fax: (1) 4676811 Tlx: 210214
International Exhibition on the Gas Industry (CHINA GAS) Last held: Oct. 20-24, 1992	Tianjin Exhibition Center	CCPIT, Tianjin Sub-Council International Trade Bldg. 84 Jianshe Road, Heping District Tianjin Tel: (22) 301367 Fax: (22) 301344 Tlx: 23261
Mining China Every 2 years Nov. 27-Dec. 1, 1994	Beijing China International Exhibition Center	Adsale Exhibition Services 14/F., Devon House Taikoo Place 979 King's Road Quarry Bay, Hong Kong Tel: [852] 5110511 Fax: [852] 5165204
Oil Expo China Last held: Mar. 10-15, 1993	Beijing China International Exhibition Center	China International Exhibition Center 6 East Beisanhuan Road Chaoyang District Beijing 100028 Tel: (1) 4678309, 4664433 Fax: (1) 4676811 Tlx: 210214
PETRO & CHEM CHINA Tianjin International Petroleum & Chemical Industrial Show Last held: Oct. 28-Nov. 1, 1993	Tianjin	CCPIT, Tianjin Sub-Council International Trade Bldg. 84 Jianshe Road, Heping District Tianjin Tel: (22) 301367 Fax: (22) 301344 Tlx: 23261

Trade Fair	Site	Contact

TEXTILES & APPAREL
See also Leather Goods & Footwear

Trade Fair	Site	Contact
China Fashion Design Show Nov. 20-24, 1992 Last held: Nov. 20-24, 1993	Shenzhen International Exhibition Center	Shenzhen International Exhibition Center Shang Bu North Road Shenzhen Tel: (755) 2263838 Fax: (755) 2263753 Tlx: 420268
China International Garment Machinery Exhibition Every 2 years Last held: Nov. 18-22, 1993	Beijing China International Exhibition Center	China International Exhibition Center 6 East Beisanhuan Road Chaoyang District Beijing 100028 Tel: (1) 4678309, 4664433 Fax: (1) 4676811 Tlx: 210214
China International Garments/Accessories Fair Last held: May 14-19, 1993	Beijing	Ministry of the Textile Industry No. 12 Chang'an St. (E) Dongcheng District Beijing 100742 Tel: (1) 5126633, 5129545 Fax: (1) 5136020
China Textiles, Garments, Shoes & Hats Fair Last held: Mar. 24-28, 1993	Shenzhen International Exhibition Center	Shenzhen International Exhibition Center Shang Bu North Road Shenzhen Tel: (755) 2263838 Fax: (755) 2263753 Tlx: 420268
Dalian International Fashion Festival Last held: Sep. 18-23, 1992	Dalian International Exhibition Center	Organizing Comm. of Dalian International. Fashion Festival 1 Stalin Square Dalian Tel: (411) 331831 Fax: (411) 337872
International Exhibition on Garment and Textile Machinery Last held: Oct. 12-16, 1993	Tianjin	Coastal International Exhibition Co. 3808 China Resources Building 26 Harbour Road Hong Kong Tel: [852] 8276766 Fax: [852] 8275224 Tlx: 80295 Contact: Brenda Yau Tianjin World Economy Trade & Exhibition Center 30 Youyi Lu, Hexi Qu Tianjin 300061 Tel: (22) 342222 Fax: (22) 349855
International Fashion & Accessories Fair Last held: Sep. 6-9, 1993	Shenzhen	Shenzhen International Exhibition Center Shang Bu North Road Shenzhen Tel: (755) 2263838 Fax: (755) 2263753 Tlx: 420268
International Fashion Fair Last held: Sep. 7-13, 1993	Guangzhou	Guangdong International Trade & Exhibition Corp. 33 Jichang Lu, Sanyuanli Guangzhou 510400 Tel: (20) 6678331 x1135 Fax: (20) 6678602 Tlx: 44476
International Garment & Shoe Industry Exhibition Last held: Sep. 1-5, 1992	Tianjin Exhibition Center	CCPIT, Tianjin Sub-Council International Trade Bldg. 84 Jianshe Road, Heping District Tianjin Tel: (22) 301367 Fax: (22) 301344 Tlx: 23261

Note: Country codes for telephone and fax numbers are not displayed unless they are *outside* of China. All country codes have square brackets around them, while city codes have parentheses. The country code for China is [86].

Trade Fair	Site	Contact
International Textile Machinery Exhibition Last held: Nov. 9-13, 1993	Guangzhou International Exhibition Center	Guangdong International Trade & Exhibition Corp. 33 Jichang Lu, Sanyuanli Guangzhou 510400 Tel: (20) 6678331 x1135 Fax: (20) 6678602 Tlx: 44476 Contact: Ms. Tang Ruiling CCPIT Guangdong Sub-Council 305 Dong Feng Zhong Lu Guangzhou, Guangdong Tel: (20) 3332756 Tlx: 44203 Guangdong Textile Industry Corporation
International Textile Machinery Exhibition (CITME) Every 2 years Oct. 6-12, 1994	Beijing China International Exhibition Center	Hong Kong Expositions Ltd. 1102 Yardley Commercial Bldg. 1-6 Connaught Road West Hong Kong Tel: [852] 8542313 Fax: [852] 8150073 Tlx: 75388
SHANGHAI TEX Multinational Exhibition on Textile Industry Every 2 years Last held: Jun. 18-23, 1993	Shanghai International Exhibition Center	Shanghai Int'l Trade Information & Exhibition Co. 817-837 Dong Da Ming Road Shanghai Tel: (21) 5463810 Fax: (21) 5455124 Tlx: 33046 Contact: Mr. Xu Zhiguo Adsale Exhibition Services 14/F., Devon House Taikoo Place 979 King's Road Quarry Bay, Hong Kong Tel: [852] 5110511 Fax: [852] 5165204 Organized with: Shanghai Textile Industry Bureau
Shanghai International Clothing Machinery Exhibition Last held: Jun. 12-17, 1993	Shanghai Exhibition Center	Adsale Exhibition Services 14/F., Devon House Taikoo Place 979 King's Road Quarry Bay, Hong Kong Tel: [852] 5110511 Fax: [852] 5165204
TIANJINTEX Tianjin International Textile/Garment Industrial Fair Last held: Oct. 15-20, 1993	Tianjin	CCPIT, Tianjin Sub-Council International Trade Bldg. 84 Jianshe Road, Heping District Tianjin Tel: (22) 301367 Fax: (22) 301344 Tlx: 23261

TOOLS: PRECISION & MEASURING

See also Machines & Instruments; other categories which may include exhibitions with tools specific to those industries

Trade Fair	Site	Contact
AHME Asia Machinery/Hardware Exhibition Last held: Nov. 1-5, 1993	Tianjin	CCPIT, Tianjin Sub-Council International Trade Bldg. 84 Jianshe Road, Heping District Tianjin Tel: (22) 301367 Fax: (22) 301344 Tlx: 23261
China International Optics Exhibition Every 2 years Last held: Oct. 8-12, 1993	Beijing China International Exhibition Center	China International Exhibition Center 6 East Beisanhuan Road Chaoyang District Beijing 100028 Tel: (1) 4678309, 4664433 Fax: (1) 4676811 Tlx: 210214

Trade Fair	Site	Contact
China Machine Tools Show Last held: Jul. 17-24, 1992	Beijing China International Exhibition Center	China International Exhibition Center 6 East Beisanhuan Road Chaoyang District Beijing 100028 Tel: (1) 4678309, 4664433 Fax: (1) 4676811 Tlx: 210214
China National Machine Tool Industry Fair Mar. 25-Apr. 1, 1994	Beijing China International Exhibition Center	China International Exhibition Center 6 East Beisanhuan Road Chaoyang District Beijing 100028 Tel: (1) 4678309, 4664433 Fax: (1) 4676811 Tlx: 210214
Hubei International Medical, Scientific & Educational Equipment Exhibition Last held: Sep. 1-5, 1992	Wuhan Hubei International Exhibition Center	Copro International Services Rm. 805, Harvest Building 33 Wing Kut Street Hong Kong Tel: [852] 5419196 Fax: [852] 5457639 Tlx: 80577
International Exhibition on Environmental Engineering & Measuring Instruments (EEMI) Last held: Sep. 22-26, 1992	Shenzhen International Exhibition Center	Coastal International Exhibition Co. 3808 China Resources Building 26 Harbour Road Hong Kong Tel: [852] 8276766 Fax: [852] 8275224 Tlx: 80295
International Exhibition on Modern Machine Tools Last held: Nov. 24-28, 1993	Guangzhou International Exhibition Center	Coastal International Exhibition Co. 3808 China Resources Building 26 Harbour Road Hong Kong Tel: [852] 8276766 Fax: [852] 8275224 Tlx: 80295 Contact: Brenda Yau
International Machine Tool Show (CIMT) Every 2 years Last held: May 5-11, 1993	Beijing China International Exhibition Center	China Machine Tool Builders Association (CMTBA) 26 South Yue Tan Street Beijing 100825 Tel: (1) 868261 x2668 Fax: (1) 8013472 Contact: Mr. Li Xingbin, Director International Cooperation Department CIMT Preparatory Office Fax: (1) 8032517
International Optical Industry Exhibition for China (CHINA OPTICS) Last held: Aug. 28-Sep. 1, 1992	Shanghai International Exhibition Center	Business & Industrial Trade Fairs 18/F., First Pacific Bank 51 Gloucester Road Hong Kong Tel: [852] 8652633 Fax: [852] 8661770 Tlx: 64882
International Trade Fair for Laboratory Equipment & Scientific Instruments (LAB CHINA) Last held: Oct. 14-18, 1992	Shenzhen International Exhibition Center	Shenzhen International Exhibition Center Shang Bu North Road Shenzhen Tel: (755) 2263838 Fax: (755) 2263753 Tlx: 420268
Shanghai International Light Industries Exhibition (SILIE) Last held: Sep. 17-22, 1992	Shanghai International Exhibition Center	Shanghai Int'l Trade Information & Exhibition Co. 817-837 Dong Da Ming Road Shanghai Tel: (21) 5463810 Fax: (21) 5455124 Tlx: 33046

Note: Country codes for telephone and fax numbers are not displayed unless they are *outside* of China. All country codes have square brackets around them, while city codes have parentheses. The country code for China is [86].

Trade Fair	Site	Contact

OTHERS Miscellaneous trade fairs

Trade Fair	Site	Contact
China Estate Last held: Jul. 14-18, 1993	Tianjin	CCPIT, Tianjin Sub-Council International Trade Bldg. 84 Jianshe Road, Heping District Tianjin Tel: (22) 301367 Fax: (22) 301344 Tlx: 23261
INTERAD **International Exhibition** **on Advertising** **Technology** Last held: May 26-30, 1993	Shanghai	Shanghai Int'l Trade Information & Exhibition Co. 817-837 Dong Da Ming Road Shanghai Tel: (21) 5463810 Fax: (21) 5455124 Tlx: 33046 Contact: Mr. Xu Zhiguo
International Exhibition **on Technology and** **Equipment for Banking** **and Finance Services** **(BANKING CHINA)** Last held: Dec. 7-12, 1993	Beijing China International Exhibition Center	Adsale Exhibition Services 14/F., Devon House Taikoo Place 979 King's Road Quarry Bay, Hong Kong Tel: [852] 5110511 Fax: [852] 5165204
International Trademark **Fair** Last held: Apr. 3-7, 1993	Guangzhou International Exhibition Center	Guangdong International Trade & Exhibition Corp. 33 Jichang Lu, Sanyuanli Guangzhou 510400 Tel: (20) 6678331 x1135 Fax: (20) 6678602 Tlx: 44476 Contact: Ms. Tang Ruiling CCPIT Guangdong Sub-Council 305 Dong Feng Zhong Lu Guangzhou, Guangdong Tel: (20) 3332756 Tlx: 44203 Organized with: NTD Patent & Trademark Agency
National Exhibition of **2000 Household** **Consuming Pattern** Last held: Jun. 18-26, 1993	Beijing China International Exhibition Center	China International Exhibition Center 6 East Beisanhuan Road Chaoyang District Beijing 100028 Tel: (1) 4678309, 4664433 Fax: (1) 4676811 Tlx: 210214
Sanitary Jun. 18-22, 1994	Shanghai	Glahe International Inc. 1700 K Street N.W. Washington, D.C. 20006, USA Tel: [1] (202) 659-4557 Fax: [1] (202) 457-0776 Tlx: ITT 440322
Tianjin World Bank **Funding** Last held: Nov. 1-5, 1993	Tianjin	Glahe International Inc. 1700 K Street N.W. Washington, D.C. 20006, USA Tel: [1] (202) 659-4557 Fax: [1] (202) 457-0776 Tlx: ITT 440322

Note: Country codes for telephone and fax numbers are not displayed unless they are *outside* of China. All country codes have square brackets around them, while city codes have parentheses. The country code for China is [86].

Business Travel

China is still confused about how travel is supposed to work, and it shows—in its official travel bureaucracies; airlines, railways and bus lines; its ticketing procedures; and in the levels of cleanliness and efficiency of many of its hotels and restaurants. In the recent past, the bureaucracies made group travel the only comfortable and remotely feasible way to visit China. Only since 1983 has China begun to accommodate the individual business traveler. Only recently has the government allowed foreign hoteliers and airlines with their world-class standards to enter the market.

Travel in China is rugged compared to travel in Japan, Korea, or Taiwan. Not everything works as it's supposed to, nor as any experienced, reasonable traveler would have supposed. Thus, a traveler in China needs much patience and humor, an equanimity that can take minor crises in stride, and a schedule padded enough to allow for delays. Nevertheless, with the right attitude—and the comfort of a deluxe hotel—travel in China can be almost as good as anywhere.

NATIONAL TRAVEL OFFICES WORLDWIDE

Don't bother with the overseas branches of the China National Tourism Office, the China Travel Service (CTS) and the China International Travel Service (CITS). They haven't reached the level of travel expertise and sophistication of China's East Asian neighbors. Chinese tourism officials are more difficult to communicate with and get answers from, and have fewer and less informative publications to distribute. They're likely to be as confused as you by the bewildering, duplicative array of agencies and forms. We've found travel books to be equally confusing, even out of date, concerning CITS and CTS.

You're much better off having your travel agent handle everything—airline tickets, hotels, airport transfers, visa, even a hired car and driver if you need one. However, make sure your travel agent has con-

siderable experience with China. Provided this is the case, the results are more likely to be what you expect than if you deal with CTS or CITS yourself.

However, the closer you get to China, the better the odds. The CITS office in Hong Kong can be valuable in arranging trips to China or making last-minute changes in your itinerary. The CTS Kowloon office is located at Peking Road opposite the car entrance ramp to the Hyatt Regency Hotel. CTS also has a check-in office at Hung Hom Railway Station. However, it's still probably best to go through a reputable Hong Kong travel agency and allow it to deal with CITS or CTS. Once in China, you may find you have to deal with CITS or CTS yourself. Both have offices in all major Chinese cities, often in one of the big hotels. Good luck.

China International Travel Service (CITS)
6th Floor, Tower II, South Seas Centre
75 Mody Road, Tsom Sha Tsui East
Kowloon, Hong Kong
Tel: [852] 7325888 Fax: [852] 7217154 Tlx: 38449

China Travel Service (CTS)
CTS House, 4/F.,
78-83 Connaught Road
Central, Hong Kong
Tel: [852] 8533533 Fax: [852] 5419777

China National Tourism Office
60 East 42nd St., Rm. 3126
New York, NY 10165, USA
Tel: [1] (212) 867-0271 Fax: [1] (212) 599-2892

TOURIST AND BUSINESS VISA/ PASSPORT REQUIREMENTS

Foreigners need valid passports and visas to enter China. A request for a tourist (or L, for *Lüxing*, meaning travel) visa request must be accompanied by a copy of your airline itinerary showing when and where you're entering and leaving the country. You'll also need a transit (or G, for *Guojing*) visa.

With one exception, freelance (as individual visas

are often called in China) tourist visas are easy to get: simply go to the Chinese embassy or consulate in the country you happen to be in at the time. Be aware, however, that the rules seem to vary from consulate to consulate, so if you run into problems, you can wait until you reach Hong Kong. In Hong Kong you can get a visa at the official state agencies—China Travel Service (CTS) or China International Travel Service (CITS)—or at a private travel agency. Wherever you get the visa, you'll need two passport-size photos; your application must be written in English. Because the visa is valid from the date of issue, not the date of entry, don't bother getting it too far ahead of time—they're good for three months, and it is easy to get one one-month extension—and more, depending on your skills at persuasion. It normally takes 10 days to get a visa, but in Hong Kong you can pay more and get it in three days, one day or even the same day—on a scale that slides upward, of course (China is nothing if not the cradle of capitalism.).

The lone exception is for citizens of South Africa, who may travel China only in group tours.

A request for a business (or F, for *Fangwen*) visa must be accompanied by an official invitation through the sponsor in China. This visa is not a simple matter. It is possible to do business in China on a tourist visa if you're doing it on a small scale, and if you're doing it in cash. But you're likely to be successful only if you already have experience in China and have solid contacts. If you're new at the game, or if you're doing business on a moderate or large scale, it's still best to follow the convoluted and time-consuming process of getting an official invitation from one of the Chinese Foreign Trade Corporations (FTC). This process begins with a business proposal, an involved process in itself which should include a Chinese translation. Just getting an answer can take anywhere from a month to a year, and there's no guarantee you'll get the invitation. If you do get one, then you can apply for a commercial business visa, and usually receive it within a week. Things are changing so fast in China that getting a business visa may soon not be so difficult.

A work (Z, for *ren Zhi*) visa is yet a different process, and again you'll need consular or corporate help. (Refer to "Important Addresses" chapter.)

IMMUNIZATION

Required Cholera if arriving from an infected area within five days (especially South America); yellow fever if arriving from an infected area within six days (tropical Africa and South America, and Panama).

Strongly advised Hepatitis A and B, influenza, tetanus, typhoid, typhus.

Recommended Polio booster, TB skin test.

Note If you plan to reside in China for a year or more, the law requires that you be tested for HIV, the virus that causes AIDS.

CLIMATE

China is a match for the United States or Europe (including European Russia) both in area and in the extreme range of climate such vast reaches create.

The region around Beijing has hot, wet summers; very cold, dry, sunny winters laden with coal dust; and a mild spring marked by sandstorms originating in the Gobi Desert. The January average daily temperature ranges from -23°C to 11°C (-9°F to 51°F); in July the range is 16°C to 40°C (61°F to 103°F). Winters in Shanghai and the Yangtse River valley are shorter, wetter and slightly warmer than Beijing's—Shanghai January temperatures match those of Madrid and Seattle—and the summers are longer, almost as rainy and even hotter. In fact, Chinese affectionately call Nanjing, Wuhan, and Chongqing "the three furnaces." And be forewarned: north of the Yangtse, people can burn coal for winter warmth, but south of the river they can't, meaning that there is usually no heat and your indoor comfort in southern winters depends on your clothes.

Further south in Guangdong Province, China's subtropical hotbed of capitalism, the summers are as hot (up to 38° C/100° F.) as in the north but even longer, stretching from April through September. July through September is typhoon season. Winters are milder but wetter than they are further north, but it can still dip to near freezing, so come prepared. And be ready for rain, which showers your suit with soot.

Your best chances for decent weather are in the spring and fall—if that particular spring or fall isn't cold and wet. China's weather isn't all dismal—there are many delightful spells with blue skies and mild temperatures. But the bottom line for China's climate is always caveat emptor.

BUSINESS ATTIRE

Business wear has changed in recent years as China's true nature—conservative and capitalist—has resurfaced. For business, Mao suits are out, power suits are in. If you're doing business on a small scale, especially in arts and crafts, jewelry, fashion, fabrics, and the like, you can probably get away with more casual, even flamboyant attire. But if you're in a higher-profile, larger-scale field, you must dress the part. Fine suits are a sign of status, dignity, success, and power, part of the Confucian concept of face. Whether you're male or female, you cannot go wrong dressing in classic business suits. (And, conveniently, Shanghai is justly renowned for its tailors.) In this male-dominated culture, women's wear needs to be especially conservative—in skirt and sleeve length, neckline and makeup. A business person loses face dressing in brown or light colors, or inexpensive synthetics. Stick with dark blue or dark gray in pinstripes or solids made of wool, linen, cotton, or finely-tailored blends. (An added advantage of dark colors is that they can hide sooty rain spatters.) Gold jewelry and watches are excellent face-creators, but avoid excess.

Be sure to match the weight of your attire to the season and region of China that you're visiting. If you're traveling in the winter and going to both Guangzhou in the south and Beijing in the north, you'll need two wardrobes: medium-weight clothing for the south, heavy clothes plus an overcoat, gloves and a fur hat with ear flaps for the north (the hats are easily found in Beijing). Conversely, you'll need lightweight attire and raingear in all regions to survive the summer. You can find raingear vendors on nearly every street corner or even right in front of your hotel.

AIRLINES

Although many international airlines fly to China, and the regional affiliates of the Civil Aviation Administration of China (CAAC)—China General, Southern, Eastern, Western, Northwest, Southwest, and Northern—have domestic flights, there is a severe shortage of seats as business travelers flock to this rapidly-awakening economic giant. The seat shortage is one reason for the hotel-room surplus: The would-be guest can't book a seat to China, and once within China, can't book a seat to a number of important cities. The cause of the seat shortage: China is very protectionist, and limits the international and domestic flights of competing airlines. The solution: Book early, confirm, and reconfirm, and only go through a travel agency. It is virtually impossible by telephone, and lines at local CAAC or Air China offices are endless.

An alternative solution: take a train or boat from Hong Kong.

Beijing (Capital Airport) This modern, massive, colorless, bustling, bureaucracy-rich capital city is served by, among others, CAAC, Air France, British Airways, Dragonair, El Al, Japan Airlines, Lufthansa, Northwest, SAS, Shanghai Airlines, Singapore Airlines, Swissair, Thai Airways, and United.

Guangzhou (Baiyun Airport) This southern business and manufacturing center is served by, among others, CAAC, Malaysia Airlines, Shanghai Airlines, and Singapore Airlines.

Shanghai (Hongqiao Airport) This largest, most cosmopolitan, and fastest-paced Chinese city and its industrial and shipping capital, is served by, among others, CAAC, Dragonair, Japan Airlines, Northwest, Shanghai Airlines, Singapore Airlines, and United.

AIR TRAVEL TIME TO BEIJING AND GUANGZHOU

Flying to China is not always a simple matter. Only a few airlines fly nonstop or direct to Beijing, Guangzhou or Shanghai. Most routes to China are on connecting flights through Hong Kong: Airlines fly into Hong Kong, where passengers catch connecting CAAC flights nonstop to Beijing (3 hours) or Guangzhou (35 minutes). So to use the tables in this section to figure total flight times, *add 3 hours* for flights stopping in Hong Kong en route to Beijing; *add 35 minutes* for flights stopping in Hong Kong en route to Guangzhou. The travel times listed here do not include time on the ground in layover cities waiting for connecting flights, which can vary from an hour to overnight. We've used the major airlines of each country, found as many nonstop flights to Chinese cities as we could, and selected the remaining routes because they're nonstop connecting routes. You may not be so lucky.

Hong Kong to Guangzhou by Train or Boat

The express train from Hong Kong to Guangzhou leaves Kowloon's Hunghom Station four times daily—twice in the morning in and twice in the early afternoon—and arrives at Guangzhou Station in about 2 hours 40 minutes. Ask your travel agent to book the tickets, or buy them from a travel agent in Hong Kong or at China Travel Service (CTS), China International Travel Service (CITS). The one-way fare is about HK$190 (about US$25).

You can also take a fast boat to China—to Guangzhou via hovercraft, which is almost as fast as the train. The 64-kph (40-mph) boats leave China Ferry Terminal in Kowloon several times daily and arrive at Zhoutouzui Pier in about three hours. You can buy tickets at the ferry terminal or at CITS. The fare is about HK$180 (about US$23) , although CTS adds a HK$25 (about US$3.25) service charge.

Another fast boat is the motorized catamaran, which takes about three and a half hours for the trip between the ferry terminal in Kowloon and Zhoutouzui Pier in Guangzhou. The fare is about HK$160 (about US$21); you can buy the tickets at the ferry terminal. The down side is that these boats leave only twice daily, at 8:15 am and 8:45 am. On the return trip, they leave Guangzhou at 1 pm and return to Kowloon by 4:30 pm. From the train station or ferry terminal in Guangzhou you can take a taxi.

AIR TRAVEL TIME

To Beijing

- From Auckland nonstop to Hong Kong on Air New Zealand: 11 hrs.
- From Bangkok nonstop on Thai Airlines: 4 hrs. 45 min.
- From Frankfurt nonstop on Lufthansa: 9 hrs. 25 min.
- From Hong Kong nonstop on China Southern: 3 hrs.
- From Jakarta nonstop to Hong Kong on Garuda Indonesia: 5 hrs.
- From Kuala Lumpur nonstop on Malaysia Airlines: 6 hrs.
- From London nonstop on British Airways: 9 hrs. 55 min.
- From New York nonstop to San Francisco on United: 6 hrs. 20 min. (see San Francisco below for remainder of route)
- From San Francisco nonstop to Tokyo on United: 10 hrs. 40 min.; from Tokyo nonstop to Beijing on United: 4 hrs. 20 min.
- From Seoul nonstop to Tokyo on Japan Airlines: 2 hrs. 15 min.; from Tokyo nonstop to Beijing on Japan Airlines: 4 hrs. 15 min.
- From Singapore nonstop on Singapore Airlines: 6 hrs.
- From Sydney nonstop to Hong Kong on Qantas: 9 hrs.
- From Taipei nonstop to Hong Kong on China Airlines: 1 hour 30 min.
- From Tokyo nonstop on Japan Airlines: 4 hrs. 15 min.

To Guangzhou

- From Auckland nonstop to Hong Kong: 11 hrs.
- From Bangkok nonstop to Hong Kong: 2 hrs. 40 min.
- From Frankfurt nonstop to Hong Kong: 12 hrs.
- From Hong Kong nonstop on China Southern: 35 min.
- From Jakarta nonstop on Garuda Indonesia: 5 hrs.
- From Kuala Lumpur nonstop on Malaysia Airlines: 2 hrs. 50 min.
- From London nonstop to Hong Kong on British Airways: 13 hrs. 15 min.
- From Manila nonstop to Hong Kong on Philippine Airlines: 1 hour 50 min.
- From New York nonstop to San Francisco on United: 6 hrs. 20 min. (see San Francisco for remainder of route)
- From San Francisco nonstop to Hong Kong on United: 14 hrs.
- From Seoul nonstop to Hong Kong on Korean Airlines: 3 hrs. 15 min.
- From Singapore nonstop on Singapore Airlines: 3 hrs. 50 min.
- From Sydney nonstop to Hong Kong on Qantas: 9 hrs.
- From Taipei nonstop to Hong Kong on China Airlines: 1 hour 30 min.
- From Tokyo nonstop to Hong Kong on Japan Airlines: 4 hrs.

TIME CHANGES

China is the size of four time zones but has only one—8 hours ahead of Greenwich Mean Time. It shares this zone with Taiwan, Hong Kong, the Philippines, Malaysia, Singapore, central Indonesia, and Western Australia. When you're in China, you can determine what time it is in any of the cities listed here by adding or subtracting the number shown to or from Chinese time.

Be forewarned: China goes on daylight savings time at 2 am on the first Sunday of the second 10 days in April, and off at 2 am on the first Sunday of the second 10 days of September (and not vice-versa). Maybe it's the first-Sunday-second-10-days formula, but despite years of practice, the Chinese haven't quite gotten used to it yet. For the first few weeks of both DST and standard time, expect people, planes, trains, buses, business hours, and meetings to be an hour late or an hour early, depending on each person's perception of what the time change means.

Time differences between China and

Auckland	+4
Athens	-6
Bangkok	-1
Chicago	-14
Frankfurt	-7
Hong Kong	0
Jakarta	-1
Kuala Lumpur	0
London	-8
Manila	0
Moscow	-5
New York City	-13
San Francisco	-16
Seoul	+1
Singapore	0
Sydney	+2
Taipei	0
Tokyo	+1

CUSTOMS ENTRY (PERSONAL)

Where you go through customs depends on how you enter China. If you arrive at an airport, the customs checks take place there. If you enter on the regular train from Hong Kong, you'll go through the formalities at the Shenzen border post. If you take the express train, hovercraft or catamaran from Hong Kong, you'll go through customs as you're boarding.

PRC customs has been streamlined considerably in recent years. Very often you'll be admitted with little or no scrutiny. Experienced travelers say it has much to do with how busy the checkpoint is—the busier the better—and the disposition of the inspector. You do need to declare your personal valuables such as cameras, watches, calculators, video cameras, computers, and jewelry; hold on to your declaration—when you leave China, customs inspectors will want to see it to make sure you haven't sold or given anything away. Foreign citizens of Chinese origin are in a different category from other foreigners, and can bring in certain items duty free that others cannot; Chinese consulates abroad have this information. (Refer to "Important Addresses" chapter for a listing of consulates.)

Duty-free
- Personal effects you don't plan to sell
- ATA carnet items—professional equipment, commercial samples and advertising materials you don't plan to sell (China has not formally signed on to the ATA carnet system, but plans to in the not-too-distant future.)
- Alcohol—2 liters
- Tobacco—600 cigarettes or the equivalent in other forms of tobacco
- Perfume—1 pint
- A calculator, camera, wristwatch, pocketwatch, radio, tape recorder, cassette player, 8-mm movie camera, 1/2-inch video camera, and film—all for personal use, and all must be taken with you when you leave or you will be charged duties (keep the customs declaration for proof)

Cash
- No limit on traveler's checks, bank drafts or letters of credit
- Declare Chinese and foreign currencies, including traveler's checks. Always keep your declaration forms and your money-changing receipts for your departure formalities. (Refer to "Currency and Foreign Exchange" chapter.)

Prohibited or restricted
- Arms, ammunition, explosives
- Counterfeit currencies
- Chinese domestic currency (*renminbi*—RMB)
- Publications and other media material that the Chinese deem offensive or detrimental to its economic, moral, cultural, or political interests
- Poisonous or narcotic drugs
- Animals, plants, or their products, infested with disease or pests
- Food, drugs, or other items, from areas of disease epidemics
- 16-mm or larger movie cameras and 3/4-inch or larger video cameras require special permission.

(Refer to "Import Policy & Procedures" chapter for information on commercial imports.)

FOREIGN EXCHANGE

The official PRC currency is the *renminbi* (RMB), known as *yuan*, and divided into *fen* and *jiao* (also called *mao*). Ten fen make up 1 jiao, and 10 jiao make up 1 RMB. There used to be two types of currency: *renminbi* ("people's currency"—RMB), and foreign exchange certificates (FEC). Chinese citizens could use only RMB, and although foreigners could use both RMB and FEC, depending on the situation, they usually were expected to use FEC. This situation changed as of January 1, 1994 when China abolished the FEC.

RMB coins come in denominations of 1, 2 and 5 fen; 5 jiao; and 1 RMB. RMB bills come in paper denominations of 1, 2, and 5 fen; 1, 2 and 5 jiao; and 1, 2, 5, and 10 RMB.

FEC currency, which came in denominations of 1 and 5 jiao and 1, 5, 10, 50, and 100 RMB only, is no longer legal tender.

Both RMB and FEC have the same official exchange rate—in fall 1993 it was 5.7 per US dollar (the government frequently devalues the RMB to stimulate exports and to face the reality that the RMB is severely overvalued). But FEC is actually more valuable than the RMB—by at least 10 percent and frequently 40 percent—which poses problems for the traveler and enriches the Chinese.

The Chinese invented FEC in 1980 to prevent foreigners from using foreign currencies to buy imported items such as liquor, cigarettes and publications. This maneuver was supposed to control the spread of foreign currencies in the economy, but all it really did was substitute FEC for dollars, pounds and yen. Most hotels, large restaurants and department stores, and transport agencies accepted only FEC from foreigners, but often give change in the less valuable RMB, claiming they did not have enough FEC to make change, which may or may not be true. Foreigners are now spared the machinations of dealing with China's two-tiered currency, although the change is so recent that it is uncertain what new difficulties will arise in operating within the new currency regime.

No matter how often you're asked, refuse to pay for anything with foreign currency—it's illegal. And never give in to the "Hello, change money?" invitations of black marketeers. Foreign currency is in great demand. Black market money-changers may offer you as much as double per dollar, but besides the illegality, there's a very good chance that you'll be cheated or robbed, since the business is dominated by truly nasty bona fide gangsters from Xinjiang.

You can buy RMB with foreign traveler's checks, bank drafts or currency at larger branches of the Bank of China—the first place to do this is at the airport if you fly into China—at larger hotels and at Friendship Stores (state stores that sell export items to foreigners). Whenever you change money, you'll receive a receipt. Keep all your receipts, especially for the large amounts, because you will be asked for them when you leave the country and want to change your RMB. RMB are not fully convertible, so don't let them pile up, do keep plenty of small denominations on hand so you don't get back large amounts in change, and try to spend them all before you leave.

Major credit cards are widely accepted, and the Bank of China will give cash advances on them, but only with a large service charge.

(Refer to "Important Addresses" chapter for listed banks. and "Currency and Foreign Exchange" chapter for commercial sums.)

TIPPING

The superiority of Chinese culture is shown in its prohibition of tipping. As the capitalistic economy gains strength, Chinese authorities disapprovingly note an increase in demands for tips. Unless you do your part to discourage this foreign scourge, it may well end up contaminating the country. Hotels and restaurants add service charges to their bills. If you offer tips to other people who help you, you may embarrass or offend them. A smile and a warm "thank you" (*xiè xiè*, pronounced shee-yeh shee-yeh) is sufficient. If a particular person has been particularly helpful, you might present a small gift—a pen, a book, a packet of picture postcards from your country—as a token of your thanks when you leave.

ACCESS TO CITY FROM AIRPORT

Beijing Shoudou Airport is 31 km (19 miles) northeast of the city, a long ride that should be made only by hotel limousine or taxi. Buses are crowded, unscheduled and inconvenient, especially with luggage. There are no trains.

Your travel agent should book your airport transfer at the same time you book your hotel room. Or arrange it on your own by phone call, letter, telex, cable, or fax, giving your exact arrival time and requesting an immediate reply. Many hotels have limousine or taxi services, but few have desks at the

airport or regular airport shuttles. The service isn't free—expect to pay up to RMB 100 (about US$11.50).

If you want to ask about hotels—or if you're looking for the hotel driver who didn't meet you at the gate—go to the information counter near the main ground floor exit.

Before you get a taxi, you must change money at the Bank of China counter in the customs area. Finding a taxi from the airport is easy enough. You can avoid the lines by submitting to the increasingly aggressive gypsy taxi drivers who will accost you as soon as you leave customs (they charge a hefty premium). Otherwise, line up with other travelers at the taxi stand inside the main exit doors, and hop into a cab when it's your turn. The ride takes at least 40 minutes, 60 minutes during rush hours. The fare will be at least RMB 50 (about US$5.75)—make sure the driver turns on the meter. (At least you won't have to tip him.)

An alternative to taxis is a van or mini-bus. Get together with some fellow passengers before you land, or as you're going through customs, and share a van to your hotels. The cost should work out to about RMB 10 (about US$1.15) per person.

Guangzhou Baiyun Airport is only 12 km (7.5 miles) north of the city, a 30-minute taxi ride (45 minutes in rush hours). Gypsy drivers will approach you as you leave customs; if you don't want to stand in the taxi queue, you can take a gypsy cab for a much higher rate than the normal RMB 40 (about US$4.60). Whatever the cab, make sure the driver uses the meter.

Only a few Guangzhou hotels have evolved to the airport-shuttle stage of the tourism era.

The bus is the cheapest way to town. For RMB 1 (about US$0.12), you get a ride to CAAC headquarters in the center of town; from there you can take a taxi. The bus stop is in the front parking lot; if you can't find it, ask, or follow other passengers who seem to know where they're going.

Shanghai Hongqiao Airport is 13 km (8 miles) west of the city. The best way to get to your hotel is to arrange a pickup ahead of time by travel agent, phone, fax, letter, telex, or cable specifying your exact time of arrival and requesting an immediate reply. The cost should be from RMB 15 (about US$1.75) to RMB 60 (about US$6.90) and take 30 to 45 minutes. Many Shanghai hotels have counters at the international terminal and can book a room for you and arrange your airport transfer.

A cheaper alternative is the Air China shuttle bus. which charges only RMB 2 (about US$0.25) and stops at the Air China office in the western part of the city, near the Hilton and Holiday Inn hotels and the Shanghai Trade Centre and Shanghai Exhibition Centre. From there you can take a taxi—if you can find one—to your hotel. Mini-buses are also an option—get together with your fellow passengers to split the cost, which should run to about RMB 10 (about US$1.15) each.

Taxis are legion at both the international and the domestic terminals. Drivers will approach you before you get to the exit doors, where lines of cabs are waiting for people, and lines of people are waiting for cabs. If your cab doesn't have a working meter, or if the driver doesn't use it, or doesn't reset it from the last passenger, get out and find another cab. The fare should be no more than RMB 50 or so (about US$5.75).

ACCOMMODATIONS

Although hotels in China are gradually reaching world standards of quality, service, and amenities, they can still present travelers with unwelcome surprises. For example, you arrive at your hotel only to find you don't have the reservation you thought you had. There's also the two-tiered rate structure—foreigners pay twice what Chinese pay—staff who enter your room without knocking while you're in it, varying levels of cleanliness, and business centers that will ruin your business if you rely on them.

The good news is that service has improved considerably in recent years, both from extensive training by international hotel management and from experience in handling foreign visitors. China has also set up a rating system that includes the Four Pests (rats, mosquitos, flies, and sparrows) and the political correctness of hotel movies, but doesn't yet include cleanliness or maintenance.

Room rates are also rising, but don't come near the rates for equivalent rooms in Tokyo, Seoul, or Hong Kong. One of the main reasons is that hotel rooms far outnumber airline seats. Your stay at a top-end or deluxe hotel in Beijing or Shanghai may be a little rough around the edges, but won't differ much overall from any other world-class hotel. Although most hotels will take reservations from individual travelers over the phone or by fax, you should get a confirmation in writing. Very often, the hotels either don't have computers or, if they do, they don't bother to enter your reservations. Your letter of confirmation may be the only proof you have of your reservation. It may be easier to have a travel agent do the work.

Request a room away from the street, or bring earplugs—Chinese streets resound with noise day and night.

Room rates cited here were accurate as of fall 1993, but rates in China are more subject to change than they are in many other countries. The government frequently devalues the RMB, as it did on January 1, 1994, which means that prices in RMB increase. Hotels often raise rates in efforts to milk the most from increasing tourism, and then cut them for fear of driving visitors to the competition (your room rate may thus depend on the greed rate or the panic rate of the hotel manager). Rates are for double rooms, single occupancy during peak periods (May and June, September to mid-November). At other times of the year rates drop considerably. The hotels listed add a 15-percent service charge to all room rates unless otherwise noted. You can pay your bill with credit cards, traveler's checks or RMB.

Beijing–Top-end

China World 1 Jianguomenwai Dajie, 100004; in China World Trade Center complex. 24-hour business center, business card printing, convention facilities, meeting rooms, banquet facilities, limousine service, fitness center, pools, tennis, bowling, squash, tourism office, restaurants, shopping. Rates: RMB 900 and up. Tel: (1) 5005258, 9005106 Fax: (1) 5005258 Tlx: 211206 CWH CN.

Palace Wangfujing Street, 100005; city center, one block from Tiananmen Square and the Forbidden City. Most prestigious, best all-around hotel in Beijing, managed by Peninsula Hotel Group of Hong Kong. 24-hour business center, executive business services, limousine service, hotel taxis, health facilities, pool, 12 restaurants. Rates: RMB 1,000 and up. Tel: (1) 5128899 Fax: (1) 5129050 Tlx: 222696 PALBJ CN.

Expensive

Capital 3 Qianmen Dong Dajie, 100006; city center at Tiananmen Square. 24-hour business center, office suites, health club, tennis, pool, 12 restaurants. Rates: RMB 450 and up. Tel: (1) 5129988 Fax: (1) 5120323 Tlx: 222650 CHB CN.

Great Wall Sheraton 6A North Donghuan Road, 100026; northeast city next to Agricultural Exhibition Centre. Favorite of business travelers. 24-hour business center, convention facilities, experienced staff, fitness center, tennis, pool, restaurants, Air China office, shopping. Rates: RMB 520 and up. Tel: (1) 5005566 Fax: (1) 5001938 Tlx: 22002 GWHBJ CN.

Jianguo 5 Jianguomenwai Dajie, 100020; in diplomatic quarter, near China World Trade Center. 24-hour business center, banks, pool, restaurants. Rates: RMB 500 and up. Tel: (1) 5002233 Fax: (1) 5002871 Tlx: 22439 JGHBJ.

Moderate

Beijing Exhibition Center 135 Xizhimenwai; northwest city near Beijing Exhibition Center, Foreign Trade Corporations, Trade Negotiation Building, universities, zoo, ancient temples, lake, and park. Business center, billiards, restaurants. Rates: RMB 350 and up. Tel: (1) 831-6633 Fax: (1) 8021450 Tlx: 222395 BECH CN.

Grace 8 Jiang Tai Road West; northeast city near Agricultural Exhibition Center and diplomatic quarter. Business center, conference rooms, shuttle bus to downtown and airport, restaurants, shops. Rates: RMB 350 and up. Tel: (1) 4362288 Fax: (1) 4361818 Tlx: 21599 BJGH CN.

Taiwan 5-15 Jinyu Hutung, Wangfujing, 100006; city center, in shopping district, near Tiananmen Square. Business center, health club, hotel doctor, banquet rooms, travel agency, shopping, limousine and shuttle services, restaurant. Rates: RMB 400 and up. Tel: (1) 5120593, 5136688 Fax: (1) 5120591.

Budget

Changchunyuan 5 Xiyuan Caochang, Haidian; northwest city, across from Beijing University, near Beijing Exhibition Center and Foreign Trade Corporations. Government run, small, comfortable, good service. Rates: RMB 85 and up. Tel: (1) 2561177, 288388 Fax: (1) 2562577 Tlx: 211119 CCYH CN.

Ritan Guesthouse 1 Ritan Road; overlooking Ritan (Altar of the Sun) Park in embassy district. Basic, comfortable, large rooms. Rates: RMB 160 and up. Tel: (1) 5125588 Fax: (1) 5128671 Tlx: 211129 RTH CN.

Xizhimen 14 Qixianxi, Haidian; northwest city near Beijing Exhibition Center and Foreign Trade Corporations. Business services, meeting rooms, taxis, foreign exchange, medical clinic, restaurants. Rates: RMB 100 and up. Tel: (1) 8021155 Tlx: 222364 BXZMH CN.

Guangzhou

Room rates triple or quadruple during the Guangzhou Trade Fair (April 15-30 and October 15-30). On the other hand, the city is both overbuilt with hotels and underserved by airlines, so rooms are readily available except during the Trade Fair. Because a deluxe hotel room normally costs what a lesser room costs in Beijing or Shanghai (or a far lesser room in Tokyo), we've listed more of the best hotels in Guangzhou.

Top-end

China Liu Hua Lu, 5100015; in Trade Fair District. Best business center in town; health club, Mercedes fleet, bank, medical clinic, bowling, tennis, pool, restaurants, shopping. Rates: RMB 450 and up. Tel: (20) 6666888 Fax: (20) 6677014, 6677288 Tlx: 44888 CHLGZ CN.

Garden 368 Huanshi Dong Lu; business district, near city center, short ride to Trade Center. Excellent business center, huge convention hall, limousines, fitness facilities, tennis, restaurants, formal gardens. Rates: RMB 550 and up. Tel: (20) 3338989 Fax: (20) 3350467 Tlx: 44788 GDHTL CN.

Holiday Inn City Centre Huanshi Dong, 28 Guangming Lu, 510060; in business district, near city center, next to large exhibition hall, short ride to Trade Center. Business center, convention facilities, government travel office, fitness center, pool, restau-

rants, shopping. Rates: RMB 600 and up. Tel: (20) 7766999, (800) 4488355 USA Fax: (20) 7753126 Tlx: 441045 HICCG CN.

White Swan 1 Nan Jie, Shamian Island, 510133; overlooking Pearl River, short taxi ride from Zhoutouzui Pier (hovercraft and catamaran from Hong Kong). Two business centers, conference rooms, multilingual staff, fitness facilities, balconies, Rolls Royce fleet, driving range, pool, 30 restaurants. Rates: RMB 570 and up. Tel: (20) 8886968 Fax: (20) 8861188 Tlx: 44688 WSH CN.

Expensive

Central 33 Ji Chang Lu, Sanyuanli, 510600; in International Exhibition Center, near Trade Fair complex. Business center, office rentals, fitness facilities, pool, restaurants, shopping. Rates: RMB 300 and up. Tel: (20) 6678331 Fax: (20) 6678331 ext. 1802 Tlx: 44664 GISCO CN.

Dong Fang 120 Liu Hua Road, 510016; across from Trade Fair complex. Old wing has more character. Excellent business center, government agencies and offices, fitness facilities, pool, bank, medical clinic, dozens of restaurants, shopping. Rates: RMB 300 and up. Tel: (20) 6662946 Fax: (20) 6681618 Tlx: 44439 GZDFH CN.

Parkview Square Yue Xiu Park, Jiefang Bei Lu, 510030; city center, across from Trade Fair Complex. Business center, offices, apartments, restaurants. Rates: RMB 285 and up. Tel: (20) 6665666 Fax: (20) 6671741.

Shanghai–Top-end

Shanghai Hilton International 250 Huashan Road, 200040; 15 minutes from city center, near Shanghai International Trade Center and Shanghai Exhibition Center. Shanghai's best. Top-rated 24-hour business center, health club, executive floors, limousines, pool, tennis, restaurants. Rates: RMB 850 and up. Tel: (21) 2550000, (800) 4458667 USA Fax: (21) 2553848 Tlx: 33612 HILTL CN.

Shanghai JC Mandarin 1225 Nanjing Road West, 200040; next to Shanghai Exhibition Center, near Trade Center. Business center, executive floors, health club, pool, tennis, limousines, airport desk, restaurants. Rates: RMB 850 and up. Tel: (21) 4335550 Fax: (21) 4335405 Tlx: 33346 SJCM CN.

Expensive

Portman Shangri-La 1376 Nanjing Road West, 200040; in Shanghai Center (businesses, offices, shopping), tallest building in city. 24-hour business center, conference rooms, exhibition facilities, executive floors, health club, tennis, racquetball, pool, putting green, restaurants, shopping. Rates: RMB 680 and up. Tel: (21) 2798888 Fax: (21) 2798999 Tlx: 33272 CPTCS CN.

Sheraton Hua Ting 1200 Cao Xi Bei Lu, 200030; in business district. Excellent 24-hour business center, meeting rooms, health club, tennis, pool, restaurants, free shuttle to downtown. Rates: RMB 570 and up. Tel: (21) 4396000, (800) 3253535 USA Fax: (21) 4391000 Tlx: 33589 SHHTH CN.

Westin Taiping Yang 5 Zun Yi Nan Road, 200335; in Hongqiao Development zone halfway between airport and downtown. 24-hour business center with rental offices, conference facilities, health club, rooftop tennis, pool, limousine and shuttle services, restaurants. Rates: RMB 680 and up. Tel: (21) 2758888, 800/2283000 USA Fax: (21) 2757576 Tlx: 33345.

Moderate

Holiday Inn Yin Xing 338 Panyu Road, 200052; midtown, part of Shanghai Film Arts Center. Business center, executive floors, conference and banquet facilities, health club, tennis, pool, medical service, limousine and shuttle service, restaurants, shops. Rates: RMB 400 and up. Tel: (21) 2528888, 2528711 Fax: (21) 2528545 Tlx: 30310 SFAC Cn.

Peace 20 Nanjing Dong Lu, 200002; Bund district, downtown, next to Bank of China, overlooking Huangpu River—busy, varied river traffic, park and morning Tai Ji classes. World-famous, faded glory, Art Deco, renovated, Shanghai's favorite gathering place. Business center, spacious rooms, shopping, restaurants, best old-time jazz in China. Rates: RMB 370 and up. Tel: (21) 3211244 Fax: (21) 3290300 Tlx: 33914 BTHPH CN.

Budget

Jing An Guest House 370 Huashan Lu; near Nanjing Road (main shopping street), short taxi or bus ride to downtown. Excellent service and restaurant, post office, shops, railway bookings. Rates: RMB 100 and up. Tel: (21) 255-1888 Fax: (21) 2552657 Tlx: 30022 BTHJA CN.

Shanghai 505 Wulumuqi Bei Lu, 200040; near midtown. New, a little grimy. Business services, liaison office for foreign companies, conference facilities, health club, shops, restaurants. Rates: RMB 270 and up. Tel: (21) 4712712 Fax: (21) 4331310 Tlx: 33295.

EATING

A not quite apocryphal saying about the Chinese holds that they will eat anything with four legs except the table. A product of frequent famines and a waste-not-want-not philosophy, Chinese culinary inventiveness is legendary, even mythical—such exotic fare as ducks' feet, fish lips and eyeballs, and bird saliva have saved countless Chinese lives. However, the Chinese no longer need to eat many of these things, and many Westerners may be offended by their continuing habit of eating such things as shark fins, bear paws, civet cats, dogs, and snakes for their allegedly aphrodisiac qualities or just for fun.

There are four basic regional types of Chinese cuisine:

- Beijing and Shandong—spicy, with noodles instead of rice; try Peking duck, beggar's chicken, Mongolian barbeque and hot pot, fried shrimp eggs.
- Shanghai—spicy, oily, heavy on seafood; lots of sweet snacks; try eels, sea cucumbers, abalone, drunken chicken, ham-and-melon soup, tofu and brown sauce.
- Sichuan—the spiciest of Chinese cooking; try frogs' legs, smoked duck, fish in spicy bean sauce, eggplant with garlic.
- Cantonese—the least oily, the least spicy, the most often steamed, boiled or stir-fried, the most familiar to Westerners. For the unfamiliar, try 1,000-year-old eggs, snake, squid, pig face soup.

Eating etiquette is pretty basic, at least for Chinese food: Don't leave your chopsticks sticking upright out of the bowl—it's a funeral-banquet gesture; do feel free to lift the bowl up to your mouth and shovel the food in, to drink the soup from the bowl, to belch appreciatively, to not touch food you don't like, and to make a mess. It's best to eat in a Chinese restaurant with someone who speaks Chinese and can order for you, to avoid unpleasant surprises in the food and, more particularly, the bill. Otherwise, just point to what someone else is eating that appeals to you. You can't always choose what you get at banquets, so keep in mind that if you don't know what you're eating, you just might like it. And remember that the more exotic the dish, the more expensive it is. A warning: If you order something that isn't on the menu, be it drink or food, ask how much it is before it's brought to you, or you may be unprepared for the charge.

The restaurant listing that follows is less than cursory but a good starting point for sampling the cuisine of each region. Each is among the finest restaurants in the city, and is priced accordingly—figure on spending up to RMB 100 (about US$11.50) per person. Most aren't in hotels, which themselves have many fine restaurants. The phone numbers in China are changing, so have your hotel make the reservations for you. In most of these restaurants, you will be steered to the foreigners' section, which looks nicer and costs twice what the Chinese pay. You can fight it, which won't do you much good, or you can relax and just enjoy yourself.

Beijing

Fang Shan On Qiong Hua Island in Bei Hai Lake. Most beautiful and sought-after restaurant in Beijing.

Varied menu. Specialty: minced pork stuffed in sesame buns, Spicy Whole Fish. Reservations required a week in advance.

Feng Ze Yuan 83 Zhushikou Xidajie. Northern Chinese and Shandong cuisine. Specialties: *Hongshao Yu*, fish in soy sauce and spices; "silver thread rolls", snowflake prawns.

Jin Yang 241 Zhu Shi Kou Road. Shanxi cuisine. Specialties: deep-fried prawns, diced chicken sauteed with hot pepper.

Kang Le 259 Andingmen Nei Road. Yunnan cuisine. Specialties: Jade Spinach Souffle, Shanghai shrimps with sizzling rice, deep-fried winter melon with dates and bamboo shoots.

Sichuan 51 Rongxian Xi Hutong. Sichuan cuisine. Specialties: Sichuan prawns, fish in red chili sauce, duck smoked in tea leaves and camphor.

Guangzhou

Ban Xi 151 Xiangyang Yi Road. Beautiful lakeside pavilions. Varied cuisine. Not as expensive as some. Specialties: quail eggs with green vegetables, dim sum, winter melon soup, stewed turtle.

Bei Yuan 320 Dong Feng Road. Most beautiful restaurant in Guangzhou; pavilions and tearooms in classic Suzhou garden style. Cantonese cuisine. Specialties: mixed stew (order a day in advance), mushrooms stuffed with shrimp, fish with pine nuts.

Guangzhou 2 Xiuli 2-Road. Set in big old teahouse; favorite for banquets. Cantonese cuisine. Specialties: Eight Treasures in Winter Melon Soup, braised chicken and frog legs, ducks feet stuffed with shrimp, roast goose.

Nanyuan 120 Qianjin Lu. Another extremely beautiful setting. Cantonese cuisine. Specialties: Assorted Cold Platter, mao-tai chicken, pigeon in plum sauce.

Vegetarian Fragrance 167 Zhongshan Liu Road. Completely vegetarian. Specialties: Dish of Six Treasures, Snow Mushroom Consommé.

Shanghai

Bai Yu Lan 3rd Floor Garden Hotel. Cantonese and Sichuan cuisine. Specialties: *chun cai* soup, sautéed beef with asparagus.

Friendship 5th Floor Shanghai Exhibition Centre, 1000 Yanan Zhong Lu. Cantonese cuisine. Specialties: braised shark's fin soup, pan-fried prawns.

Lily Hall 8th Floor Jing An Guest House, 370 Huashan Lu. Yangzhou cuisine. Inexpensive. Specialties: Jing An duck, sautéed shrimp, Lion's Head (pork medallions in soup). Inexpensive.

Sichuan Court 39th floor Shanghai Hilton International. Sichuan cuisine. Specialties: tea-smoked duck, hot-and-sour soup, *dan-dan* noodles. Very expensive.

Yangzhou 308 Nanjing Dong Road. Shanghai cuisine. Very popular—make reservations far ahead of time. Specialties: wild duck, seafood.

TRAVEL ADVISORY

China is a huge nation with a white elephant of a bureaucracy, often rudimentary facilities for visitors, and burgeoning corruption. A foreign visitor must take greater self-protective precautions than when visiting certain other East Asian nations.

- Always register with your embassy or consulate as soon as you arrive for an extended stay, and notify the embassy or consulate when you change your address in China.
- Always keep your passport and visa unquestionably current for the purposes of your travel. Chinese authorities sometimes use the pretext of visa violations to evict foreigners.
- Keep your passport and visa in a safe place, especially in crowded places, such as airports, train stations, and markets. China is one of the safest countries on the planet, but as elsewhere, the more capitalism the more crime.
- Be careful about carrying items the Chinese might deem pornographic, religious, or political. The authorities have been known to detain or even expel people they think crossed an indefinable line.

TRAVEL RESTRICTIONS

As of 1993 more than 700 cities were open to foreign travelers without special travel permits. Of these, maybe 150 have the ability to host visitors in any numbers. Even Tibet has been reopened to foreigners, but only with prior approval and official escorts.

LOCAL CUSTOMS OVERVIEW

Question: What happens when an irresistible force meets an immovable object?

When the force is Maoism and the object is Confucianism, the answer is: Modern China.

Confucius was born and raised in China. He died 2,500 years ago, but the Chinese behave as if he's still alive, watching them, making a list, checking it twice, finding out who's saving face and who's losing it. It was in China that the Confucian precepts—reverence for power, status, dignity, elders, and ancestors; preoccupation with image; and emphasis on the collective good—first gained sway in a reaction to centuries of invasion, warfare, flood, and famine. And it was from China that these precepts spread over all of East Asia. Wherever you find ethnic Chinese—Singapore, Thailand, Vietnam, the Americas, Europe—you find Confucian standards of behavior. China absorbs all conquerors, leaders and manifestos, dissipating their impact. Emperors, chairmen and ideologies can come and go, but Confucius lasts forever.

Mao came closest to replacing Confucianism. He tried to shuck these standards and impose his own on the Chinese, with mixed results—predictably, because he himself was raised in a Confucian culture. He elevated women's status above that typical of most Confucian societies. He devalued the idea of personal service, and it is readily apparent in hotels and restaurants. Mao's Red Guards even stepped on the concept of face by indulging in harsh public criticism. The outcome can be seen in standards of etiquette that don't match those in Japan, Korea, Taiwan, and other Chinese-influenced cultures.

But Maoism and Confucianism share similar paternalistic traits, for example, the government thinks public and personal manners are so bad that, father-like, it is trying to reeducate Chinese citizens about travel abroad—that it is not acceptable to scratch or spit or belch or pick their noses in public.

Confucianism runs deep; its basic values still dominate Chinese behavior—especially in business—and Westerners who want the best possible chances of success will honor them.

- Dignity, mutual respect, humility, courtesy, and deference are the most prized human traits. It's called face—you can create it, have it, and lose it, for yourself or for someone else. Face is part of every human interaction. If Westerners want to be able to develop the personal relationships essential to business success, they should take care to avoid typically Western directness, criticism, and sarcasm, especially in front of others. If anything, Mao's Red Guards, by subjecting the Chinese to brutal public humiliation, made them even more sensitive to loss of face. Be generous, but not effusive, with praise and thanks in front the recipient's peers or superiors.
- Confucius was paternalistic. Mao didn't change this trait; in fact, he reinforced it. Executives and managers are benevolent despots whose every word is law, whose behavior towards subordinates closely resembles that of a stern but loving father. The children are very obedient.
- Conformity is crucial to the survival of the group; individualism is selfish and subverts the group. Confucius and Mao agree wholeheartedly on these two points.
- Businesses and government agencies are like families. You are not a member of the family. You are a stranger. Strangers in China—even Chinese strangers—are treated rudely, pushed and shoved in crowds, ignored as being

unimportant. You must be invited to join the "family"—first to be introduced, next to dinner, then to meetings, negotiations, banquets, negotiations, banquets, negotiations.... You will need a matchmaker to make the first introductions, someone who has a personal relationship with whoever holds power.
- Gift giving is as important in China as it is in all Confucian societies, but Maoism has tempered this trait. Gifts should be modest—pens, chocolate, imported liquor, books—and given to the group or organization, not to the individual, and even then only after a promising relationship has begun. Wrap them in red, which signifies happiness.
- Learn to read between the lines. Yes can mean no, a word you will rarely hear. Instead, you must learn to ask the right questions. Press the Chinese to be direct, and they will retreat in confused if polite resentment.
- Approach all your dealings with the Chinese as they approach their dealings with you: with an attitude of utmost patience and all the time in the world.
- Communism weakened the work ethic in what was once an indefatigable workforce. You cannot expect the same work efficiency that you see in other Confucian countries; you will notice it most in the bureaucracy.
- Avoid political discussions, including criticism of your own government as well as China's. You'll find that's when the Chinese will stop talking, or say something like, "The situation is not very clear." To press the issue could cause trouble for your Chinese acquaintances in this totalitarian society.
- You need business cards, with your name, company and title—clearly indicating your responsibilities—printed on the reverse in Chinese. Give one to every business contact you meet upon first introduction. A handshake and a slight bow are proper greetings. Present and accept business cards with both hands; study the other's card carefully and respectfully, and then put it in a pocket above your waist.
- The Chinese love banquets. Even if you don't, you must learn to act as if you do, and you must reciprocate.

(Refer to "Business Culture" chapter for an in-depth discussion.)

DOMESTIC TRANSPORTATION

Air China is so big that the only time-effective way to travel long distances is by air, but air travel is problematic. The seven affiliated lines of the Civil

Aviation Administration of China (CAAC) fly all over the country, but don't have nearly enough seats for all the would-be travelers. If you want a seat, book early, confirm, and then reconfirm. And demand that the agent stamp your ticket with one of the big official-looking rubber stamps that seem as common in China as bicycles.

Then be prepared for impossibly crowded planes. Flights are often delayed or cancelled (experienced travelers say that CAAC also stands for "China Airlines Always Cancels") because of bad weather and antiquated technology (some say CAAC also stands for "China Airlines Almost Crashes"). There are so many cancellations that most airports have CAAC hotels, where CAAC puts entire planeloads of passengers up for the night and feeds them for free: Don't think you have to pay. But don't expect luxury either.

Airports are grim, even when new.

Domestic Airfares

Beijing-Shanghai	RMB 490
Beijing-Guangzhou	RMB 810
Beijing-Hong Kong	RMB 1,366
Guangzhou-Hong Kong	RMB 290
Guangzhou-Wuhan	RMB 355
Guangzhou-Kunming	RMB 470
Shanghai-Guangzhou	RMB 510
Shanghai-Hong Kong	RMB 959
Shanghai-Xian	RMB 560

The fares listed here are subject to change.

Train Unless you have a lot of time, trains aren't a good way to travel long distances. They're rather uncomfortable, not always very clean, and often extremely slow. The "express" train from Beijing to Guangzhou takes 34 hours to travel 2,313 kilometers (1,434 miles)—averaging 68 kph (42 mph). The cost of RMB 450 (about US$52) for the comfortable soft sleeper class doesn't include meals—which are often pretty bad. The soft sleeper class is the best, and only foreigners and high-ranking Chinese can use it. However, for shorter trips, trains are the way to go. The Beijing-Jinan run, for example, takes 9 hours and costs about RMB 75 (about US$8.65). Trains usually run on time, without the delays, crowding (at least in soft class) and cancellations common to air travel.

If for some bizarre or budgetary reason you must travel hard class, you may want to look under your seat before placing food or valuables there—the Chinese sometimes sleep (and, apparently, eat) there.

Don't try to buy a ticket on your own at a railroad station or CITS office. Besides the long lines,

you may find that you're not even at the right place, or a CITS agent may claim that all the trains leaving town are booked solid, no matter when you want to go. Instead, have your hotel buy the tickets for you. However (every situation in China always has at least one "however"), hotels in Beijing don't sell train tickets, so you have to go to the foreigners' booking window at the main railway station.

Bus Long-distance bus travel in China is not an option for foreigners with busy schedules. City buses can be an option, though, if you have a city bus map. (You can buy them in hotel gifts shops or in front of train stations.) The maps are in Chinese, but route numbers are in Arabic numerals. Ask someone—your hotel desk clerk, for example, or one of the many Chinese who will want to practice English with you—to point out where you are and where you want to go. Once you know the route, and you're on the bus (watch out for the stampede), the ticket seller will ask you where you're going. Say the name of your destination, hold out your palm with change in it, and let the ticket seller take what's needed—usually a few fen. The ticket seller will probably notice that you don't know where you are or where you're going and let you know when you've arrived.

Beijing also has a fleet of minibuses that seem to be everywhere. They are alleged to have routes, but their drivers can be very flexible, and it's also easier to hail them from the street than it is a taxi.

Taxi Taxis may not always be easy to get on the street, but big hotels often have their own fleets. The rates range from 50 to 80 fen per kilometer; you can't always trust the driver to charge you fairly, so note the mileage on the odometer when you get in. If you're going from your hotel to a restaurant, or to a meeting, it's better to have your driver wait for you for a small extra charge than to try to find a cab on the street afterwards. Pedicabs are also available; bargain for the fare.

Subway Beijing has a modern, cheap (RMB 1 - RMB 5) (up to about US$0.60), efficient, clean, and fast subway. Stops are noted both in Chinese characters and the Roman alphabet. The subway runs from the railroad station in the eastern part of the city to the far western area and the northern area near the zoo, with stops at convenient places such as the Jingguo Hotel, the Exhibition Centre, and Tiananmen Square.

Hired car Your hotel can arrange for you to hire a car or taxi and driver for the day. It's convenient and relatively inexpensive.

Bicycle There are at least one-quarter billion bicycles in China. Bicycling is one of the best ways to get around, since everyone else seems to be doing it—there's safety in numbers of that magnitude. Most of the cities are as flat as pancakes. With one of the good city maps printed in English and Chinese, you can go where and when you want, and lock and park your bike in a lot for a very low fee. If your hotel doesn't have its own bicycle fleet (they're yellow—easy to pick out in crowds of black bicycles), ask the desk clerk for the location of the closest rental outfit. You can rent a bike for a deposit and a low hourly, daily or 24-hour rate—probably at least RMB 5 (about US$0.60) per day, more at the big hotels. Avoid leaving your passport as security; instead leave money or your driver's license or some other official-looking document.

When you park your bike, leave a strip of brightly colored fabric or plastic tied to the handlebars—the lot attendants move the bikes around, and you may never be able to find your bike again. Park legally, or your bicycle may be towed—stick with the lots. Streets are packed with bikes (7 million in Beijing alone), but be careful in heavy car and bike traffic and walk your bike when the Chinese walk them. And watch out for cars: Drivers don't always look before turning, and don't have to stop before turning right on red lights.

Walking Walking in Chinese center cities is safe, easy, and fascinating. Your destinations will often be close enough to your hotel that you can walk.

HOLIDAYS/BANK HOLIDAYS

Unlike their fellow East Asians, the Chinese don't give themselves much time off. Official and bank holidays number only four. On Women's Day, agencies and banks somehow have to muddle through the afternoon without their female workers, who take off to celebrate. And although Spring Festival is supposed to last only three days, many Chinese take the entire week off. Foreign business travelers beware! The Chinese attempt to travel and stay in hotels during this week, but since hotel and transport managers and workers also take the week off, many hotels close down and railroads and airlines may cut their schedules. The result can be chaos, so if you're in China during this time, hang on to your hotel room, avoid travel and forget about doing business.

Chinese Official and Bank Holidays

New Year's Day	January 1
Spring Festival	3 days (Chinese Lunar New Year) in late January or early February
Women's Day	March 8 (half day)
Labor Day	May 1
National Days	October 1 (up to 3 days)

BUSINESS HOURS

Banks and government agencies are open Monday through Saturday, generally around 8 am, although it's unlikely you could make an appointment for earlier than 9 am. They close for two hours at noon, reopen at 2 pm, and close for the day at 5 pm or 6 pm But during a cold winter the lunchtime closing may be only an hour long, while during a summer heat wave it may be as long as three hours.

Stores and shops remain open on Sunday mornings, the official national rest day, and close down one weekday afternoon, usually Wednesday.

COMMUNICATIONS

China is still part of the Third World, and its communications systems are clear evidence. Try to do all your communicating from your hotel or a hotel business center.

Telephones The Chinese have not yet fully discovered the benefits of telephones, but they're trying. Many are paying up to RMB 5,000 or about US$575—the equivalent of two years' salary—to get private phones; some of the nouveaux riches are toting around cellular phones (RMB 30,000 apiece or about US$3,500), which are more reliable. Telephone companies hold auctions for numbers—the number 8 is a favorite because the Chinese word for 8, ba, is similar to fa, part of the verb meaning "to become wealthy." (Notice the number of 8s in the various lists we've given.)

There are few public telephones on Chinese city streets. It normally takes repeated efforts to make a successful local call, and clarity is poor—callers often have to shout to make themselves heard. And because the call will be automatically disconnected after 20 seconds of silence, if you're put on hold you must keep shouting, singing, whistling, or humming—to yourself. Thankfully, local calls are free.

The best place to use the phone is at your hotel. First-class hotels have the most reliable and static-free service, and often International Direct-Dial service in the rooms. Still, given the obstacles, it's best to talk with your Chinese contacts face to face.

Long-distance calling When you call long-distance within China, dial the 0 before the area code. You do not need to dial the area code when calling within that area. When you call China from a foreign country, omit the 0 before the area code.

International calling The quality of international calls varies from poor to crystal clear. Rates in China for international call rates high, so you may actually save money by making your international calls collect. Another tip for international calls: Give your prospective callers from abroad your hotel name and room number, because your hotel desk clerks often don't know your room number, and Chinese operators often cannot understand Western names. China's country code is 86.

To direct-dial internationally Dial the international access code—00—then the country code, then the area code (if there is one), and the local phone number. For example, to call World Trade Press direct, dial 00-1-415-454-9934. Hotels often impose sizable service charges on calls made from rooms. An alternative may be to call from a business center; public phones are often unreliable.

To use AT&T USDirect or AT&T World Connect China has AT&T World Connect service (known as Home Country Direct in some countries). A cooperative venture among large phone companies, including AT&T, the service allows you to bypass China's phone system (or the local system of the country you're in) and hook directly into the phone company of the country you're calling—if that country is also a member of World Connect. World Connect is much cheaper than IDD because you're not using your hotel's long-distance equipment, and so the hotel can assess only the local call surcharge (and in China local calls are free). You'll find out if your country is a member by trying to make the call. This is how to do it:

- Dial the access number: 800-1111.
- Wait for the recorded voice prompt, which offers you the option of using your home country calling card, a credit card (except US), or an operator for collect calls. Then follow the instructions for the option you choose.
- If you're calling the US on your calling card, follow the instructions for that procedure, then dial just the area code and the local phone number; you don't need to dial the country code.
- If you're calling another country that is a member of World Connect, dial 01, then the country code, then the area code, and then the local phone number.
- If you're making more than one call, don't hang up after the first call, or if there's a busy signal or no answer—simply press # and wait for the voice prompt and redial, or dial the new number.
- If you don't know if the country you want to call is a member of World Connect, wait for an operator to come on the line, and ask him or her.

USEFUL TELEPHONE NUMBERS

- AT&T World Connect: 10811
- AT&T Information: 01-5055566
- International Information: 115
- Domestic Long-Distance Information: 116
- Tourist Complaint Hotline
  Beijing: 5130828
  Guangzhou (Chinese-speaking): 6677422
  Shanghai: 4390630

Fax, telegram, telex, and cable Most hotels have fax machines, and many (along with the main post offices and telegraph offices) have telex machines. You can send cables from first-class hotel post offices or from the main telegraph office in each city.

Post Office China's postal system is remarkably good for a developing country. Domestic mail arrives quickly—usually within two days, and if within a city often the same day it's sent. Postage is absurdly cheap, even by Western standards. Nevertheless, it is best to have your hotel handle your mail needs.

English-language media The only English-language daily newspaper is the *China Daily*. *The Beijing Review* and *Ta Kung Pao* are weekly newsmagazines, and *China Today* is a monthly magazine. Foreign publications such as *Newsweek, Time, The Asian Wall*

China City Codes		Country Codes of Major Countries	
Beijing	01	Australia	61
Changchun	0431	Brazil	55
Changshu	0731	Canada	1
Chendu	028	France	33
Chongqing	0811	Germany	49
Dalian	022	Hong King	852
Fuzhou	0591	India	91
Guangzhou	020	Indonesia	62
Guilin	0773	Italy	39
Guiyang	0851	Japan	81
Hangzhou	0571	Korea	82
Harbin	0451	Malaysia	60
Hefei	0551	Mexico	52
Jinan	0531	New Zealand	64
Kunming	0871	Pakistan	92
Nanchang	0791	Philippines	63
Nanjing	025	Russia	7
Nanning	0771	Singapore	65
Shanghai	021	South Africa	27
Shenyang	024	Spain	34
Taiyuan	0351	Taiwan	886
Tianjin	011	Thailand	66
Wuhan	027	United Kingdom	44
Xi'an	029	United States	1

Street Journal, The International Herald-Tribune, and *The New York Times* are available in the lobbies of major hotels and foreign bookstores.

Most hotel rooms have TVs, and can receive CNN. If you bring along a portable shortwave radio, you can get Voice of America, BBC, Radio Japan, and Radio Australia broadcasts.

Courier services Most of the major international courier services operate in China.

Federal Express

Beijing Beijing Air Cargo Transportation Service Center, Inside Chao Yang Gymnasiums,Tuan Jie Hu Liu Litun Xi Kou, Chao Yan Qu, Beijing 100026; Tel: (1) 5011017, 5014888 Fax: (1) 5011015 Tlx: 211175

Guangzhou China National Foreign Trade Corporation, 20th Fl., 53 Hua Le Road, Guangzhou 510060; Tel: (20) 3805669, 3808747 Fax: (20) 3805674. TELEX: 44838 GZTRS

Shanghai Qian Tang Company, Room 460, Shanghai Center Building, 1376 Nanjing Xi Lu, Shanghai 200040; Tel: (21) 2798040 Fax: (21) 2798042 Tlx: 30155.

TNT World Express

Beijing TNT Skypak-Sinotrans Ltd., 14 Shu Guang Xi Li, Chao Yan Qu, Beijing 100028; Tel: (1) 4677877 (pickups), 4672517 (customer service) Fax: (1) 4677894 (customer service) Tlx: 211238 SKYPK CN (customer service).

Guangzhou Sinotrans Guangdong, Airfreight Department, 1131 Guang Yuan Road Central, Guangzhou; Tel: (20) 668092, 6680957/9, Fax: (20) 6680950, 6680971.

Shanghai TNT Skypak-Sinotrans Ltd., Shanghai Branch, Number 3 Lane, 211 Xin Hua Road, Shanghai 200052; (21) 2400819, 2521905 Fax: (21) 2400883 Tlx: 33668 ADSHA CN.

UPS

Beijing Sinotrans Ltd., 25 Xibinhe Road, An Dingmen Wai; Tel: (1) 4225670 Fax: (1) 4226694.

Guangzhou Sinotrans Ltd., Airfreight Department, 1131 Guang Yuan Road Central; Tel: (20) 6680964 Fax: (20) 6680971 Tlx: 44464 CGTRS CN.

Shanghai Sinotrans Ltd., Room 0201, Office Building, Hotel Equatorial, 65 Yanan Road West; Tel: (21) 2485760, 2487896 Fax: (21) 2485875.

LOCAL SERVICES

China is really just beginning its transition to modern business methods, and there is a paucity of business services for foreign travelers. The major hotels are the best places to find professional business services, such as secretarial and translation services, telex and fax transmission, business card printing, international calling, and liaison with government agencies and Foreign Trade Corporations. Always start your search for services at your hotel.

Business centers

The hotels on the list that follows have business services, from complete to rudimentary.

Beijing Asia, Beijing, Beijing Airport, Beijing Exhibition Center, Beijing Hotel Palace Tower, Beijing International, Capital, Chang Fu Gong (New Otani), China World, Dong Fang, Gloria Plaza, Grace, Grand, Great Wall Sheraton, Holiday Inn Crowne Plaza, Holiday Inn Downtown, Holiday Inn Lido, Hua Bei, Jianguo, Jinglun (Hotel Beijing-Toronto), Jing Guang New World, Jinlang, Kempinski, Kunlun, Novotel Song He, Olympic, Palace, Peace, Sara, Shangri-La, Swissôtel Beijing, Taiwan, Traders, Xin Da Du, Xizhimen, Yanshan, Yue Xiu, Zhaolung.

Also try the China World Trade Center at 1 Jianguomenwai Dajie (Tel: (1) 5052277); it has a wide range of business services.

Guangzhou Bai Yun, Central, China, Dong Fang, Equatorial, Garden, GITIC Plaza, Holiday Inn City Center, Holiday Inn Riverside, Landmark, Novotel Guangzhou, Ocean, Parkview Square, Ramada Pearl, Victory, White Swan.

The Central Hotel also has office space rentals.

Shanghai City, Cypress, Equatorial, Garden, Holiday Inn Yin Xing, Jinjiang, Jinjiang Tower, Jing An Guest House, Nikko Longbai, Novotel Shanghai Yuan Lin, Ocean, Park, Peace, Portman Shangri-La, Regal Shanghai, Shanghai, Shanghai Hilton International, Shanghai International Airport, Shanghai JC Mandarin, Sheraton Hua Ting, Westin Taiping Yang, Xijiao Guest House, Yangtze New World.

While in Shanghai, you should also take advantage of the Service Center for Overseas Traders (SCOT), a comprehensive business service center for business travelers. Located in the Jinjiang Hotel complex, (59 Maoming Nan Lu; Tel: (21) 2370115), SCOT can provide business introductions, trade consultants, translators, secretaries, guides, telex, photocopying, desks, daily financial reports, and foreign-language newspapers, and even office space in the Foreign Trade Building next door.

Fax, translation and secretarial services, and office space rentals are also available at the Shanghai Center, 1376 Nanjing Xi Lu; Tel: (21) 2582582.

Printers

You'll need business cards as soon as you land. If you haven't already had them made, a first-class hotel business center can usually arrange to have them done within a couple of days. They should be printed with your name, title, and company name in Chinese on the reverse—a translation of your address isn't necessary.

Stationery supplies

Beijing Friendship Store, 21 Jianguomenwai; Tel: (1) 5003311

Guangzhou Garden Hotel Shopping Arcade, 368-Huanshi Dong Lu.

Shanghai China Stationery Store, 505513 Chang Yang Lu; Tel: (21) 5460585.

Translators

Business centers are a best source of translators.

STAYING SAFE AND HEALTHY

Millions of people visit China each year, and few get seriously ill. Some will come down with ailments that are temporarily disabling and can make an arduous business journey even more difficult. So it's a good idea to be prepared.

Bronchitis This inflammation of the bronchial tubes is usually associated with a bout of the flu. Each year a new strain of the flu virus evolves in East Asia. A new vaccine is available in the West beginning about October, and you'd be wise to get an inoculation before you leave for China. Even the previous year's flu vaccine may provide some protection. The flu itself isn't dangerous for most people, nor is bronchitis, but bronchitis can lead to pneumonia, especially if aggravated by cold, dry winter air and coal dust and smog. A great many Chinese have chronic bronchitis—they get frequent colds and flus, they smoke too much and breathe too much bad air—and they help spread the bacteria and viruses that cause bronchitis by spitting all over the place. If you get bronchitis, have a doctor determine if the cause is viral or bacterial. Viral bronchitis has a clear phlegm; there is no drug for this type—only rest and avoidance of pollution can help. You'll need antibiotics for bacterial bronchitis, which is marked by a greenish phlegm.

Diarrhea Traveler's diarrhea is common for foreigners visiting China, as it is for foreigners visiting the United States or anywhere else. Your digestive system isn't ready for the strange food or intestinal flora it encounters and so tries to expel them.

Precautions are wise: Don't drink tap water or use it to brush your teeth; don't use ice cubes, since they may be made from tap water; don't eat raw fruits or vegetables unless you can wash them in boiled or bottled water and peel them yourself. If you're traveling for three weeks or less, you may want to take *Pepto-Bismol, Immodium* or *Lomotil* or an antibiotic (doxycycline or trimethoprim/sulfamethoxazole) as a preventive, but be careful—sometimes there are side-effects, and antibiotics especially increase the risk of your body developing resistant bacteria. Bring the drugs with you from your home country since you will not be able to find them in China.

Even with precautions, it's possible you'll have a bout of diarrhea. The best treatment is to ride it out as your body adapts and heals itself. The main danger is dehydration, especially in warm weather. Keep yourself well hydrated by drinking plenty of water, carbonated drinks, herbal teas, fruit juices and clear broth soups. Drink at least two glasses of liquid after each trip to the bathroom. Avoid solid foods for the first 24 hours, and then begin eating bland foods—such as bananas, rice, crackers, potatoes, fish, lean meat, beans, and lentils. Avoid dairy products; raw fruits (except bananas), and vegetables; fat, greasy foods; colas; and spicy foods. Also avoid caffeine and alcohol—both are diuretics (they cause your body to lose water).

If your diarrhea is accompanied by severe nausea or vomiting, don't try to eat anything, but focus on rehydration—drink small, frequent sips of liquid. If the vomiting doesn't stop in less than a day, see a doctor, and take an antinausea drug such as promethizine, which you can get from your hotel doctor or a pharmacy without a prescription.

If you must travel with traveler's diarrhea, Pepto-Bismol can usually handle mild or moderate diarrhea. If you have heavy-duty diarrhea, you'll need Immodium or Lomotil. Be aware, though, that while these drugs are very good at stopping you up, they're treating only the symptoms, not the cause, so take them only when absolutely necessary. At other times, follow the treatment regimen above and allow your body to heal itself.

Hepatitis Hepatitis is a mild risk in China. This liver infection comes in two main forms—A and B—and both preventable with vaccines. For extra protection against the A type, use disposable chopsticks for restaurant and street vendor food, or bring your own chopsticks—the disease is spread through contamination of food, water, and cooking and eating utensils. The main avenues of transmission for hepatitis B are sex and non-disposable needles used for intravenous drugs, tattooing, or acupuncture.

Crime China is one of the safest countries in the world. You can generally walk anywhere, even at night, without fear. But there are precautions you should take to avoid becoming a statistic.

- Check in with your embassy or consulate on your arrival.
- Avoid displays of flashy jewelry and watches; dress and behave conservatively.
- Be aware that pickpockets flourish in crowds, and don't give them a chance. Don't carry much cash, and do carry it in a money belt. Do conduct most of your transactions with credit cards or traveler's checks.
- Walk with your briefcase or shoulder bag to the side away from the street to keep bicycling or motorcycling thieves from grabbing it.

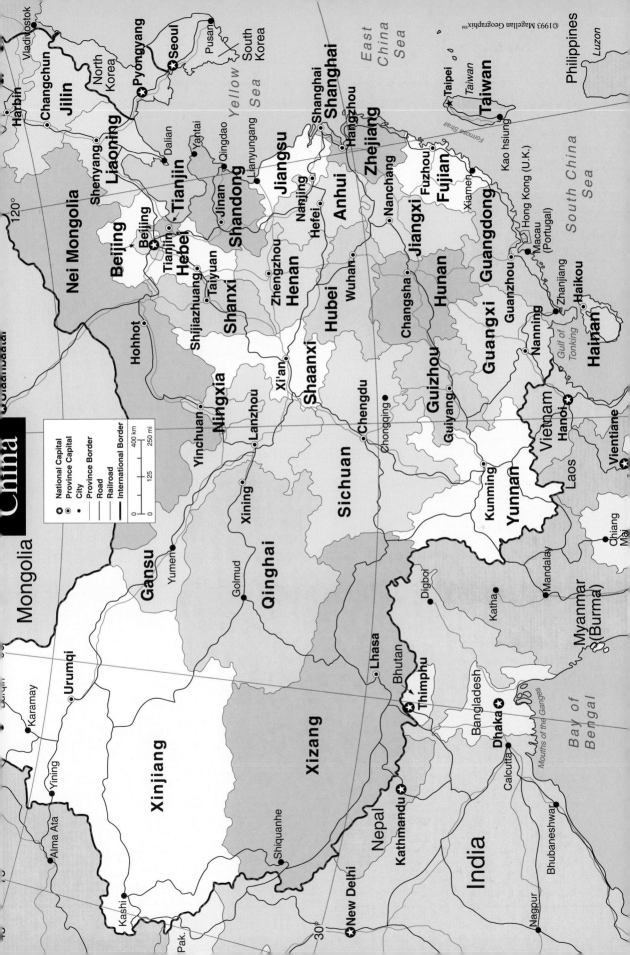

China

© 1993 Magellan Geographix℠

Legend:
- ⊛ National Capital
- ◉ Province Capital
- • City
- Province Border
- Road
- Railroad
- International Border

0 125 400 km
0 250 mi

Countries and regions:
Mongolia
Philippines
Luzon
Vietnam
Laos
Myanmar (Burma)
India
Nepal
Bangladesh
Bhutan
North Korea
South Korea

Provinces:
Nei Mongolia
Xinjiang
Xizang
Qinghai
Gansu
Sichuan
Yunnan
Guizhou
Guangxi
Guangdong
Hainan
Hunan
Jiangxi
Fujian
Zhejiang
Jiangsu
Anhui
Hubei
Henan
Shaanxi
Shanxi
Ningxia
Hebei
Shandong
Beijing
Tianjin
Liaoning
Jilin
Taiwan
Hong Kong (U.K.)

Seas:
Yellow Sea
East China Sea
South China Sea
Bay of Bengal
Gulf of Tonking
Formosa Strait

Cities:
Vladivostok
Harbin
Changchun
Shenyang
Dalian
Pyongyang
Seoul
Pusan
Yantai
Qingdao
Jinan
Lianyungang
Nanjing
Shanghai
Hangzhou
Nanchang
Fuzhou
Taipei
Kao hsiung
Xiamen
Macau (Portugal)
Zhanjiang
Haikou
Guanzhou
Hong Kong
Nanning
Hanoi
Vientiane
Kunming
Guiyang
Changsha
Wuhan
Hefei
Zhengzhou
Xi'an
Taiyuan
Shijiazhuang
Beijing
Tianjin
Hohhot
Yinchuan
Lanzhou
Xining
Golmud
Yumen
Urumqi
Karamay
Yining
Alma Ata
Kashi
Lhasa
Shiquanhe
Kathmandu
Thimphu
Dhaka
Calcutta
New Delhi
Bhubaneshwar
Nagpur
Chengdu
Chongqing
Digboi
Katha
Mandalay
Chiang Mai
Ulaanbaatar

120°
30°

Mouths of the Ganges

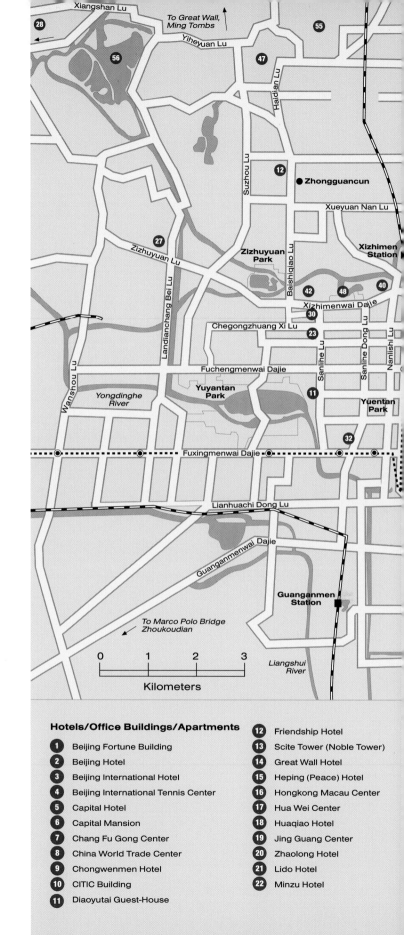

Hotels/Office Buildings/Apartments

1 Beijing Fortune Building
2 Beijing Hotel
3 Beijing International Hotel
4 Beijing International Tennis Center
5 Capital Hotel
6 Capital Mansion
7 Chang Fu Gong Center
8 China World Trade Center
9 Chongwenmen Hotel
10 CITIC Building
11 Diaoyutai Guest-House
12 Friendship Hotel
13 Scite Tower (Noble Tower)
14 Great Wall Hotel
15 Heping (Peace) Hotel
16 Hongkong Macau Center
17 Hua Wei Center
18 Huaqiao Hotel
19 Jing Guang Center
20 Zhaolong Hotel
21 Lido Hotel
22 Minzu Hotel

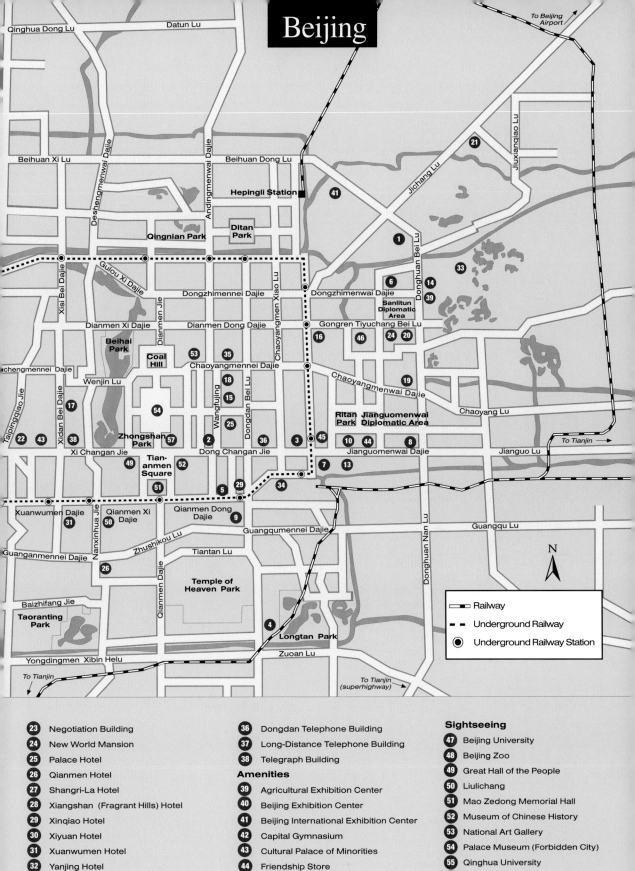

Beijing

Qinghua Dong Lu
Datun Lu
Beihuan Xi Lu
Beihuan Dong Lu

To Beijing Airport

Jiuxiangqiao Lu

Hepingli Station ■

(41)

(21)

Deshengmenwai Dajie

Andingmenwai Dajie

Jichang Lu

Ditan Park

Qingnian Park

Gulou Xi Dajie

(1)

Xisi Bei Dajie

Dongzhimennei Dajie

Chaoyangmen Xiao Lu

Dongzhimenwai Dajie

Donghuan Bei Lu

(33)

Dianmen Xi Dajie

Dianmen Jie

Dianmen Dong Dajie

(6)
(14)
(39)

Sanlitun Diplomatic Area

Beihai Park

Coal Hill

(53)

(35)

(16)

Gongren Tiyuchang Bei Lu

(46)
(24) (20)

Chaoyangmennei Dajie

Wenjin Lu

(18)

Wangfujing

(15)

Chaoyangmenwai Dajie

(19)

chengmennei Dajie

(54)

Dongdan Bei Lu

Chaoyang Lu

Taipingqiao Jie

(17)

(25)

Ritan Park
Jianguomenwai Diplomatic Area

Zhongshan Park

(57)

(2)

(36)

(3)

(45)

Xidan Bei Dajie

(22) (43)

(38)

Xi Changan Jie

Dong Changan Jie

(10) (44)

(8)

To Tianjin

(7) (13)

Jianguomenwai Dajie

Jianguo Lu

(49)

Tian- anmen Square

(52)

(5) (29)

(34)

Nanxinhua Jie

(51)

Xuanwumen Dajie

(31)

(50)

Qianmen Xi Dajie

Qianmen Dong Dajie

(9)

Guangqumennei Dajie

Donghuan Nan Lu

Guangqu Lu

Zhushikou Lu

Guanganmennei Dajie

(26)

Qianmen Dajie

Tiantan Lu

Temple of Heaven Park

Baizhifang Jie

Taoranting Park

(4)

Longtan Park

Yongdingmen Xibin Helu

Zuoan Lu

To Tianjin

To Tianjin (superhighway)

N

Railway

Underground Railway

Underground Railway Station

(23) Negotiation Building
(24) New World Mansion
(25) Palace Hotel
(26) Qianmen Hotel
(27) Shangri-La Hotel
(28) Xiangshan (Fragrant Hills) Hotel
(29) Xinqiao Hotel
(30) Xiyuan Hotel
(31) Xuanwumen Hotel
(32) Yanjing Hotel
(33) Yong An Apartments

Services

(34) Beijing Railway Station-Central Terminus
(35) CAAC Ticket Office

(36) Dongdan Telephone Building
(37) Long-Distance Telephone Building
(38) Telegraph Building

Amenities

(39) Agricultural Exhibition Center
(40) Beijing Exhibition Center
(41) Beijing International Exhibition Center
(42) Capital Gymnasium
(43) Cultural Palace of Minorities
(44) Friendship Store
(45) International Club
(46) Workers' Stadium

Sightseeing

(47) Beijing University
(48) Beijing Zoo
(49) Great Hall of the People
(50) Liulichang
(51) Mao Zedong Memorial Hall
(52) Museum of Chinese History
(53) National Art Gallery
(54) Palace Museum (Forbidden City)
(55) Qinghua University
(56) Summer Palace
(57) Working People's Palace of Culture

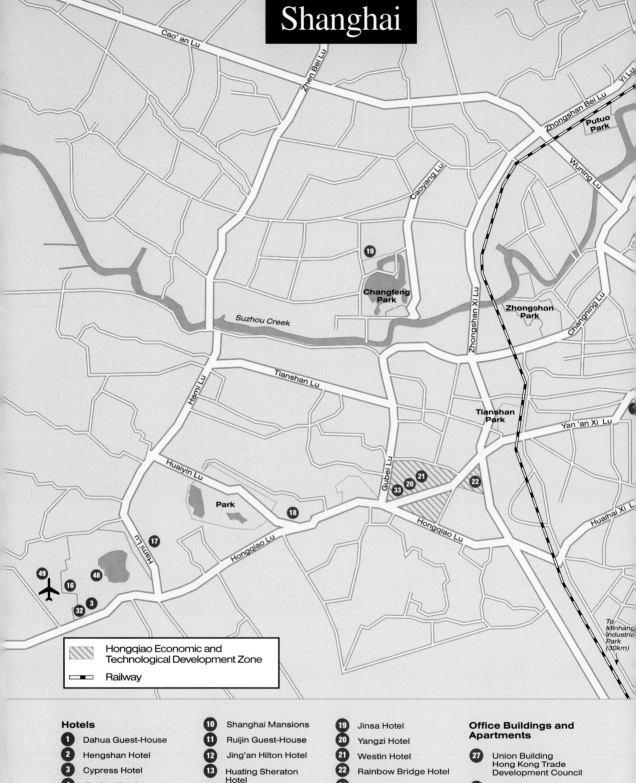

Shanghai

Hotels

1. Dahua Guest-House
2. Hengshan Hotel
3. Cypress Hotel
4. Jing'an Hotel
5. Jinjiang Hotel
6. Overseas Chinese Hotel
7. Park Hotel
8. Peace Hotel
9. Shanghai Hotel
10. Shanghai Mansions
11. Ruijin Guest-House
12. Jing'an Hilton Hotel
13. Huating Sheraton Hotel
14. Huaihai Hotel
15. Jinjiang Tower
16. Nikko Longbi Hotel
17. Shanghai Holiday Villa
18. West Suburb Hotel
19. Jinsa Hotel
20. Yangzi Hotel
21. Westin Hotel
22. Rainbow Bridge Hotel
23. Shanghai Jincang (JC) Mandarin Hotel
24. Garden Hotel
25. Ocean Hotel
26. Portman Shanghai

Office Buildings and Apartments

27. Union Building Hong Kong Trade Development Council
28. Huaihai Apartments
29. Jinjiang Club
30. Ruijin Building
31. Yandang Apartments
32. Cypress Apartments
33. International Trade Center

Hongqiao Economic and Technological Development Zone

Railway

Government and Business

34 Shanghai Patriotic Construction (Aijian Corp)

35 Shanghai Hongqiao United Development Company

36 Shanghai Foreign Economic Relations and Trade Commission

37 Customs Buildings

38 Shanghai Foreign Trade Corporation

39 Shanghai Industrial Exhibition Hall

40 Shanghai Investment and Trust Corporation

41 Shanghai Municipal People's Government

Sightseeing

42 Friendship Store

43 Jade Buddha Temple

44 Shanghai Natural History Museum

45 Site of First National Congress of the Chinese Communist Party

46 Dr Sun Yat-sen Museum

47 Yu Gardens

48 Shanghai Zoo

Services

49 Hongquaio Airport

50 Main Post Office

51 Shanghai Railway Station

52 Telecommunications Building

53 Huadong Hospital

Shenzhen

0   500   1,000
Meters

1 International Trade Center	**6** Shenzhen Railway Station
2 Development Center (under construction)	**7** Overseas Chinese Building
3 International Commercial Building	**8** Forum Hotel
4 Guangdong Hotel	**9** Hotel Oriental Regent
5 Golden Luster Hotel	**10** State Administration of Exchange Control

11 People's Government of Shenzhen City
12 Litchi Park
13 Renmin Park
14 Yayuan Hotel
15 Bamboo Garden Hotel

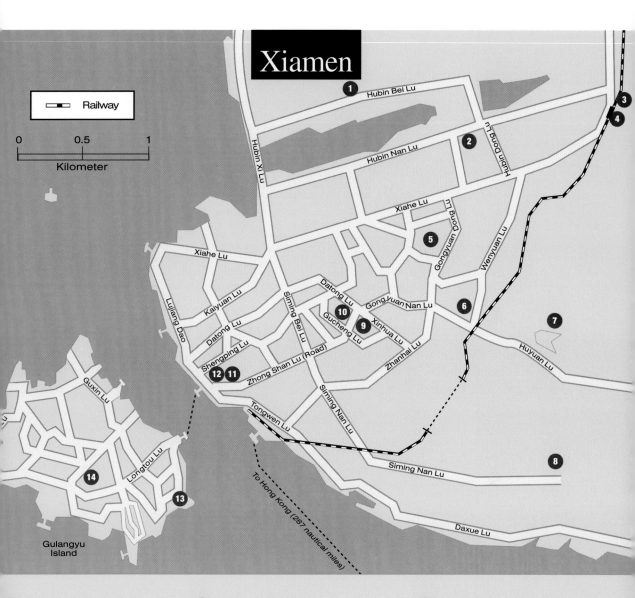

Xiamen

Railway

0   0.5   1
Kilometer

Hubin Bei Lu

Hubin Xi Lu

Hubin Nan Lu

Hubin Dong Lu

Xiahe Lu

Gongyuan Dong Lu

Wenyuan Lu

Xiahe Lu

Lujiang Dao

Kaiyuan Lu

Datong Lu

Siming Bei Lu

Datong Lu

Gong yuan Nan Lu

Gucheng Lu

Xinhua Lu

Shengping Lu

Zhong Shan Lu (Road)

Zhanhai Lu

Huyuan Lu

Tongwen Lu

Siming Nan Lu

Siming Nan Lu

Daxue Lu

Guxin Lu

Longtou Lu

Gulangyu
Island

To Hong Kong (287 nautical miles)

1 Xiamen City Government	**6** Xiamen Guest-House	**11** East Ocean Hotel
2 State Administration of Exchange Control	**7** Ten-Thousand Rock Botanical Garden	**12** Lujiang Hotel
3 South-East Asia Hotel	**8** South Putuo Temple	**13** Zheng Chenggong Statue
4 Xiamen Railway Station	**9** Overseas Chinese Mansion	**14** Zheng Chenggong Memorial Hall
5 Zhong Shan Park	**10** Posts and Telecommunications Building	

East Asia

LEGEND
✪ Capital
● Major City

1000 Kilometers
1000 Miles

RUSSIA

Okha
Yuzhno Sakhalinsk
Komsomol'sk
Svobodny
Skovorodino
Khabarovsk
Blagoveshchensk
Baley
Qiqian
Hailar
Vladivostok
Harbin
Qiqihar
Changchun
Jilin
Shenyang
Sapporo

JAPAN
Tokyo
Osaka
Fukuoka

Sea of Japan

NORTH KOREA
Pyongyang
SOUTH KOREA
Seoul
Pusan

East China Sea

MONGOLIA
Ulaan Baatar
Öndor Haan
Sayr Usa
Ongin
Jibhalanta
Jirgalanta

Baotou
Beijing
Tianjin
Qingdao
Shanghai

CHINA

Yinchuan
Xi'an
Chengdu
Wuhan
Chongqing
Guiyang
Guangzhou
Fuzhou
Xiamen

HONG KONG

TAIWAN
Taipei

Pacific Ocean

Tropic of Cancer

Philippine Sea

PHILIPPINES
Manila
Davao

South China Sea

Equator

PAPUA NEW GUINEA

Qamdo
Lhasa
Gar
Hami
Yumen
Qiemo
Urumqi
Kuqa
Qiemo
Shache

VIETNAM
Hanoi
Ho Chi Minh City

LAOS
Vientiane

KAMPUCHEA
Phnom Penh

THAILAND
Bangkok

MYANMAR
Mandalay
Yangon

BRUNEI

MALAYSIA
Kuala Lumpur

SINGAPORE

BORNEO

INDONESIA

Jakarta

KAZAKHSTAN

Lake Balkhash
Alma-Ata
Bishkek
KRGYSTAN
Dushanbe
TAJIKISTAN
Tashkent

UZBEKISTAN

TURKMENISTAN
Ashkhabad

Aral Sea

Kabul
AFGHANISTAN
Islamabad
PAKISTAN

IRAN

Muscat
OMAN

NEPAL
Kathmandu
BHUTAN
Thimphu
BANGLADESH
Dhaka

INDIA
New Delhi
Ahmadabad
Bombay
Calcutta
Madras

SRI LANKA
Colombo

Bay of Bengal

Arabian Sea

Indian Ocean

Personal-care products Bring everything you need from home. It's not likely you could find most personal care products in China, and even if you could, they would be very expensive. You can use the local toilet paper, but carry some along with you when you travel, even within cities, because public restrooms may not be well equipped.

EMERGENCY INFORMATION

Fire 09

Police 110

Doctors Your hotel is the first place you should ask about medical care. Major hotels usually have a doctor on call or even an in-house doctor. Chinese doctors are well trained and experienced.

Hospitals Chinese hospitals are not free. Bring cash to cover treatment and drugs. Nor do the hospitals resemble their Western counterparts. They are rather stark and off-putting, but the staff are competent.

Beijing

For a referral to a nearby clinic or hospital in Beijing, call (1) 505-3521.

Beijing Union Medical College Hospital, 1 Dong Shai Fuyuan Hutong (near Beijing Hotel); Tel: (1) 5127733

Friendship Hospital, Foreigners' Section; Tel: (1) 338671, extension 441.

Guangzhou

Foreign Guest Medical Clinic, Dong Fang Hotel, 120 Liu Hua Lu; Tel: (20) 6699900.

Guangzhou People's Hospital Number 1, 602 Renmin Bei Lu; Tel: (20) 3333090.

Shanghai

Huashan Hospital, 12 Wulumuqi Zhong Lu; Tel: (21) 4311600.

Shanghai People's Hospital Number 1 Outpatient Clinic, 410 Beisuzhou Lu; Tel: (21) 3240100.

DEPARTURE FORMALITIES

You cannot take out of China anything yo cannot bring in. You should keep all your money-changing receipts. Customs will subtract the amount shown on the receipts from the amount of foreign money you declared when you entered China. If somehow you end up with more foreign currency than the receipts say you should, it will be confiscated on the suspicion that you've been money-shopping at the black market.

You will have to pay the airport departure tax, which can be RMB 60 (about US$6.90) and more, depending upon which airport you're leaving from.

Customs officials keep a sharp eye out for antiquities that they consider to be cultural relics. An antique that is approved for export has a red seal (although the seal doesn't guarantee the item is a genuine antique). Keep your receipts, and be prepared to show the items and the receipts. And the inspectors will want to see you wearing your watch and carrying your camera and the electronic gear that you brought in.

Overall, getting through Chinese exit customs is usually easy. The officials are too busy, and they rarely give foreigners a thorough going-over.

BEST TRAVEL BOOKS

Although books on travel in China can't possibly keep up with the rapid changes in a travel situation that has been confusing from the start, three emerge from the crowd.

China, by Joe Cummings, Robert Storey, Robert Strauss, Michael Buckley, and Alan Samagalski. Hawthorn, Victoria, Australia: Lonely Planet Publications, 1991. ISBN 0-86442-123-0. 882 pages, US$19.95. Another Lonely Planet "travel survival kit." Informal, informative and geared to the budget-minded independent traveler, this book gives insights on the culture, the people and the places—not to mention the hassles of travel and how to navigate them. 186 clear maps. The typical Lonely Planet weakness in index, which is full of place names only. Needs updating, but still invaluable.

The China Guidebook, by Fredric M. Kaplan, Julian M Sobin, and Arne J. de Keijzer. Boston: Houghton Mifflin, 1993. ISBN 0-395-67028-4. 800 pages, US$19.95. Indispensable. Thick, detailed, insightful, matter-of-fact. 36-page "Doing Business with China" section, 17-page language section. Detailed table of contents, and a good index. Lists hotels, points of interest, covers 125 cities; lots of clear maps. Completely updated.

Fodor's China, by John Summerfield. New York: Fodor's Travel Publications, 1992. ISBN 0-679-02282-1. 593 pages, US$19.00. Fairly up-to-date; oriented towards the tourist and tour group, but also has a 44-page "Doing Business in China" section. Strong on hotels, restaurants, sight-seeing. Excellent maps.

Typical Daily Expenses in China

All prices are in renminbi (RMB) unless otherwise noted. As of January 1, 1994, the exchange rate was US$1 = RMB 8.65. B=Beijing, G=Guangzhou, S=Shanghai.

Expense	LOW			MODERATE			HIGH		
	B	G	S	B	G	S	B	G	S
Hotel	300	250	250	600	500	600	1150	800	1150
Local transportation *	5	5	5	30	30	30	75	75	75
Food	125	150	150	250	300	300	400	500	500
Local telephone †	0	0	0	0	0	0	0	0	0
Tips	0	0	0	0	0	0	0	0	0
Personal entertainment **	15	15	15	75	100	100	200	250	250
TOTAL	**445**	**420**	**420**	**955**	**930**	**1,030**	**1,825**	**1,625**	**1,975**
One-way airport transportation	10	2	2	100	40	10	100	60	60

USA Government per diem allowance as of December, 1993	lodgings (US$)	meals & incidentals (US$)	Total
Beijing	88	59	$147 = RMB 1,277
Guangzhou	92	61	$153 = RMB 1,330
Shanghai	116	60	$176 = RMB 1,529

Note: Guangzhou has a surplus of hotel rooms most of the year, making it less expensive than Beijing or Shanghai, except during the Chinese Commodities Trade Fair in the second half of April and October, when room rates double and triple.

* Based on 2 pedicab rides for low cost, 2 medium length taxi rides for moderate cost and 4 longer taxi rides for high cost.
† Pay phones are generally not available, and guests at better hotels may make local calls for free.
** Based on a visit to a cultural event for low cost, a visit to a club in a Western-style hotel with drinks for moderate cost and participation in a banquet for high cost.

Business Culture

CHINA'S DIFFICULT PAST

To fully appreciate China's booming economy and the mentality of Chinese businesspeople today, it is important to know the country's historical background. For centuries, China was a place where time seemed to stand still, an immense land of nobles and peasants bound by feudal tradition. The concept of business and trade in the Western sense scarcely existed, and the vast majority of the people were illiterate peasants concerned only with tilling the land and surviving. Foreigners called China a sleeping dragon.

Western Contact

The first Westerners to have a major impact on China were the British, who in the 1800s used it as a dumping ground for opium brought from India—an ignominious introduction to Western capitalism condemned by Chinese today as exploitive. The weak and ineffective Q'ing dynasty was brought to its knees by superior British firepower in the Opium Wars, and Hong Kong, Shanghai, and other ports were forcibly taken under foreign rule in a series of coerced treaties with the Q'ing.

Years of Chaos

The first half of the 20th century in China was full of turmoil. After the Q'ing dynasty fell in 1911, the country dissolved into chaos and people were subject to the brutal rule of petty warlords, Nationalists, Communists, and the Japanese. It was a time when intellectuals and patriots grappled for a definition of a "New China." The dragon stirred from its centuries-long sleep, but people could not coordinate their actions so that the nation could progress in any meaningful way.

Communist Victory

In 1949, the Communist Red Army under the leadership of Mao Zedong resolved China's identity crisis when the People's Republic of China (PRC) was proclaimed at Tiananmen Gate in Beijing. Many in China at this time supported the Communists and were op-timistic about the future. The Communists emerged victorious against overwhelming odds after 22 years of armed struggle, and the new leaders were disciplined, tough, and dedicated to rebuilding the country under revolutionary socialist principles. China's experiment with orthodox Marxism was more radical than any the world had seen, including the Soviet Union's. Land was redistributed to the peasants, then collectivized into huge communes where only the clothes on a person's back were privately owned. The state coordinated all economic interactions, and market competition and capitalism in any form were held to be crimes against the people. Foreigners were expelled, and China shut its borders to the outside world. It remained largely isolated for thirty years.

Early Years of the PRC

The Chinese people experienced a series of natural and man-made tragedies in the early years of the PRC. The Communists were fond of initiating "movements"—*huo dong* in Chinese—that turned society against various elements deemed dangerous to the general good. Every year brought new movements aimed at different targets, and often one movement contradicted the preceding one. People became wary of standing out in any way for fear of reprisals, and individual initiative and creativity were squelched. People were classified in economic terms, such as poor, middle, and rich peasant, petty bourgeois, or landlord. Those branded antirevolutionary were dispossessed of their material wealth and social standing, and they were often imprisoned or killed. Through a combination of poor economic planning and bad harvests, famine killed millions in the early 1960s. The leaders of the country, once close brothers in arms, fell to fighting among themselves for power, using ideology as much for personal gain as for the betterment of the nation.

The Lost Decade

In 1966, Mao Zedong unleashed the radical young Red Guards in a struggle to regain absolute leadership of the country, and the Great Proletarian Cultural Revolution began. For the next ten years, the Red Guards rampaged across China, destroying cultural reminders of the past and anyone who might have opposed them. Mao became a living god to the Chinese. Everywhere, people waved his *Quotations* (the so called "Little Red Book") and shouted his slogans. Schools were closed, and students were sent from the cities to the countryside to learn proletarian values and help educate peasants in Marxist principles. Competing factions of Red Guards took up arms against each other. In some places, the army was called in to quell riots and disorder.

Return to Normalcy

The death of Mao in 1976 sent a wake up call to the Chinese, who began collectively to realize the social insanity they had experienced in the Cultural Revolution. A month after Mao's death, moderate leaders in the Communist Party arrested Mao's wife, Jiang Qing, and three other radicals. They were branded the Gang of Four and blamed for most of the excesses of the Cultural Revolution. The trial of the Gang of Four was a national purge of conscience for a crime that millions had committed. But by scapegoating these few individuals, who certainly had favored radical and violent behavior, the Chinese nation as a whole could forgive itself for the Cultural Revolution and move ahead into a new era.

Deng, Reform, and Catching Mice

After Mao's death, a loose coalition of leaders arose who were unified in opposition to Maoist excesses but divided on the direction that the country should take. After a three-year power struggle, Deng Xiaoping emerged as China's new supreme leader. He brought to his position a new vision that again would remake the face of the nation.

Deng's vision of how things should work was based on practicality and the credo of "seeking truth from facts." The country had suffered for years in the name of ideals, and Deng himself had been purged twice for not being radical enough. The government of the PRC began in 1978 to carry out economic reforms designed to decentralize control and increase productivity through worker incentives. After decades of hostility toward the capitalist West, China made foreign companies welcome by extending special privileges, including tax breaks. When some hard-liners criticized Deng for moving away from orthodox Marxism, he replied that it doesn't matter whether a cat is black or white, so long as it catches mice. Deng's reply continues to be the unofficial guiding policy for macroeconomic decisions as well as business management in the PRC.

In the 1980s, many Chinese hesitated to undertake business ventures for fear of being purged if the political winds changed direction again. But after 15 years of reform and increased official encouragement, people have apparently decided that business for profit is safe. Even following the hard-line crackdown on protesters in 1989, the government only mildly criticized Chinese-style private enterprise. In 1992, Deng visited Shenzhen, the mecca of Chinese capitalism, and made his strongest statements ever in support of private enterprise. "To get rich," he said, "is glorious."

Today, tens of millions of would-be businesspeople are anxiously working out ways of going into business for themselves. This ground swell of business fever is unprecedented. It appears that after all the years of hardship and repression, the Chinese are embracing business as the only real outlet for individual initiative and skill. For the Chinese, business is new, exciting, and alive. The dragon has finally awakened.

The New Gods

Traditional Chinese religion has a flexible way of incorporating new ideas into its dogma and introducing new gods into its pantheon. Buddhism, imported from India, found a home in China about two millennia ago. Renowned kings and warriors were revered in death and eventually elevated to god status. Most of the figures seen on Taoist altars are representations of real people who have been deified.

When the Communists took control of China, they banned religion, which they derided as simpleminded superstition. Officially, China became a nation of atheists. But for all purposes, Communism itself became the state religion and Mao Zedong its god. Peasants could give up their religious beliefs, but not the underpinning habits that shaped those beliefs. Chief among these is the tendency to revere powerful persons.

After Mao's death and the official condemnation of most of his later policies, China fell into a sort of spiritual vacuum. For about a decade, the people had no overriding dogma or personality on which to focus their energies. However, a new god appeared in China recently, complete with an attendant messenger. The new god of China is money, and Deng Xiaoping is its prophet. Everywhere in China, people are grasping firmly to the notion that the be-all and end-all of life is to get rich.

Ironically, reverence for Mao has increased steadily over the past few years. His picture can be seen on t-shirts and buses and hanging from rearview mirrors in taxis. The Mao craze may be a popular fad, but in China a fad can soon become a tradition. Perhaps some day Mao's figure will be seen on Taoist altars as well!

UNDERSTANDING THE CHINESE MENTALITY

Chinese possess many characteristics that are difficult for Westerners to understand. Their world view has been shaped by very different experiences and cultural traditions. To operate successfully in China, foreigners must grasp the moral values and traditional concepts that shape the Chinese mentality.

Confucianism

Although the Communists officially banned his thought for many years, it is Confucius, who lived 2,500 years ago, who largely shaped the modern mentality of the Chinese people. Confucianism is not so much a religion as it is a code for social conduct. Its influence is so pervasive that people in China unconsciously function in a Confucian manner. The basic tenets of Confucian thought are obedience to and respect for superiors and parents, duty to family, loyalty to friends, humility, sincerity, and courtesy.

Age and rank are respected in China, and young people are expected to obey their elders unquestioningly. In the workplace, respect and status increase with age. Older foreign businesspeople have an advantage in this regard, and they are likely to receive more serious attention than younger people.

The family is the preeminent institution in China. One's first duty is to the welfare of one's family, and working family members often pool their financial resources. In many ways, Chinese view themselves more as parts of the family unit than as free individuals. Grown children typically live with their parents even if they are married (often with the husband's parents). The Chinese constitution even stipulates that children have a duty to support their parents in old age.

Confucianism honors humility and courtesy. Chinese are seldom overly boastful or self-satisfied, even if their accomplishments are laudable. When Chinese are being polite, they can be excessively self-deprecating. Chinese are among the most courteous people in the world toward their friends. Every detail of a guest's stay with a Chinese friend may be prearranged, and the guest may not be allowed to spend money on even the smallest items. For individualists from the West, this form of courtesy may be overwhelming.

However, the Chinese are often rude or uncaring when they deal with strangers. Such behavior is psychologically necessary in a country as overpopulated as China. Crowds are everywhere pushing and shoving; no apologies are given, and none are expected.

More than two millennia of Confucian indoctrination have made China an extremely conformist society. The word individualism has a decidedly negative connotation in the Chinese language, and people can create enemies simply by standing out of the crowd. To function as an individual is to invite criticism of being selfish and opportunistic. Together, Communist rule and Confucianism have homogenized Chinese culture and slowed development of new inventions and new ways of thinking. Unquestioning acceptance of the status quo is the norm.

Nevertheless, people in China do desire change and improved living conditions, as the protests of 1989 show. They look to the West for new ideas, particularly about technology and business management. But we can expect the basic social structure to remain the same regardless of economic or even political change.

Face Value

No understanding of the Chinese mentality is complete without a grasp of the concept of face—*mianzi* in Chinese. Having face means having a high status in the eyes of one's peers, and it is a mark of personal dignity. Chinese are acutely sensitive to having and maintaining face in all aspects of social and business life. Face can be likened to a prized commodity: it can be given, lost, taken away, or earned. You should always be aware of the face factor in your dealings with Chinese and never do or say anything that could cause someone to lose face. Doing so could ruin business prospects and even invite recrimination.

The easiest way to cause someone to lose face is to insult the individual or to criticize him or her harshly in front of others. Westerners can offend Chinese unintentionally by making fun of them in the good-natured way that is common among friends in the West. Another way to cause someone to lose face is to treat him or her as an underling when his or her official status in an organization is high. People must always be treated with proper respect. Failure to do so makes them and the transgressor lose face for all others aware of the situation.

Just as face can be lost, it can also be given by praising someone for good work in front of peers or superiors or by thanking someone for doing a good job. Giving someone face earns respect and loyalty, and it should be done whenever the situation warrants. However, it is not a good idea to praise others too much, as it can make you appear to be insincere.

You can also save someone's face by helping him to avoid an embarrassing situation. For example, in playing a game you can allow your opponent to win even if you are clearly the better player. The person whose face you save will not forget the favor, and he will be in your debt.

A person can lose face on his own by not living up to other's expectations, by failing to keep a promise, or by behaving disreputably. Remember in business interactions that a person's face is not only his own but that of the entire organization that he represents. Your relationship with the individual and the respect accorded him is probably the key to your business success in China.

It's Not What You Know...

Personal connections—or *guanxi* in Chinese— are the key element of doing business in China. As in Taiwan and Hong Kong, little or no distinction is made between business and personal relationships. This point cannot be overemphasized. To succeed in China, you must cultivate close personal ties with business associates and earn their respect and trust. Attempts to establish long-term businesses in the country have often failed because foreigners did not recognize that business relationships were also personal relationships.

"In China," someone said, "if you don't have *guanxi*, you don't have anything." This statement may seem extreme, but it is true. Everything in China seems to be in short supply, and to get things done, you need to know people. Any successful person in China will be a member of a loose network of personal friends, friends of friends, former classmates, relatives, and associates with shared interests. These people do favors for one another and always seek a rough balance between help given and received.

The importance of *guanxi* has its roots in the traditional concept of family. For the Chinese, individuals are parts of the collective family whole. The family is the source of identity, protection, and strength. In times of hardship, war, or social chaos, the Chinese family structure was a bastion against the brutal outside world, in which no one and nothing could be trusted. As a result, trust and cooperation were reserved for family members and extremely close friends. Moreover, China was and continues to be a land ruled more by decree than laws. A high official could act with impunity, and innocent people could get hurt unless they had powerful friends to protect them. By establishing close connections with other households and persons of higher rank, Chinese could survive and perhaps even prosper.

The social situation in China today is more secure than it was in the past, but the tradition of personal connections is as strong as ever. In essence, the Chinese possess a clan mentality under which those inside the clan work cooperatively and those outside the clan are seen as inconsequential or as potential threats. To be accepted into a network of personal or business relationships in China is an honor for foreigners. It entails responsibility and commitment to the members of the network.

In the new business environment of China, executives and entrepreneurs work constantly to maintain and expand their networks of connections. Networks extend to other companies and individuals, to Hong Kong, Taiwan, and even abroad to Europe, the US, and Southeast Asia. While the purpose of such contacts is often for mutual financial profit, the criteria are the same as for personal networks: trustworthiness and loyalty.

Cultivating Relationships

For the foreign businessperson, the difficulties in cultivating solid relationships can be the biggest obstacle to success in China. A Chinese who does not already know a potential associate will hesitate to do business with him until he has had time to get acquainted and size up the potential associate's character and intentions.

Find a Matchmaker The best way to make contact with potential Chinese business associates is to have a mutual friend serve as an intermediary and introducer. If the third party has close relationships with both sides, that alone may constitute solid grounds for the conduct of business. Finding a third party may be as simple as asking an overseas Chinese if he or she has any family members in China who could be potential associates. Anyone who has worked in China or who has cooperated with Chinese authorities in the past could be a key source of business contacts. There are also many business consultants who can provide assistance for a fee. Chambers of commerce, small business associations, and Chinese international trade offices may also help you to find contacts.

Go to the Source If finding a third party for introductions in your home country proves impossible, consider making a fact-finding trip to China and Hong Kong. Try to schedule your trip when there is a trade show in one of the major cities that allows you to display goods or services and gauge your business prospects, or you can simply spend your time meeting potential contacts in your area of business. Before leaving for China, fax businesses there in which you are interested and try to arrange a visit. Chinese companies are hungry for foreign investment, trade, and cooperation, so chances are good that at least some companies will be happy to meet you even if they don't know you. There are hundreds of branch offices of PRC companies in Hong Kong, so that may be the first place to visit.

Patience! On your first and perhaps even your second trip to China, you may accomplish nothing more than getting to know several possible candidates for business relationships. Rushing into business before you have established a personal relationship is an invitation to failure. After drawing up a list of possible candidates, take time to evaluate each party carefully, and weigh each one's strengths and weaknesses before you decide on who to follow up on. Don't underestimate your gut feelings or your comfort level with various individuals, but appraise their business abilities realistically and, of course, whom they know.

After making your first contacts with businesspeople in China, be prepared to spend a lot of time deepening and strengthening relationships through visits, dinners, gift giving, and many small favors. While this can be costly and time-consuming, Chinese appreciate all sincere efforts in this area, and no favor done goes unnoticed. Likewise, keep a running account of all favors done for you, all small gifts received, and the like. The odds are good that you will be expected to reciprocate in the future. Remember this aspect of Chinese business culture whenever someone offers you a favor, dinner, or gift. If you absolutely do not want to be in the person's debt, be creative and find some polite excuse for declining the offer. And decline it only if you have no intention of having a relationship, because declining offers can be insulting to Chinese.

Maintain Your Perspective Finally, foreign businesspeople will benefit from the process of cultivating personal connections by keeping in mind that it gives them an opportunity to learn about the people with whom they are dealing. Getting to know your business associates is practical regardless of your culture. Learning about the personality of an associate can make communication and understanding smoother, and the resulting knowledge can be critical when it comes time to decide how far to take the business relationship.

THE CHINESE WORK ENVIRONMENT

The transition to a market-based economy in China is fraught with obstacles, not the least of which is the structure of the work environment. Operating under Marxist principles, state employers have become caretakers for their workers, overseeing almost every aspect of their lives. The concept of business for profit, which now has official approval, must compete with entrenched interests and bureaucratic meddling.

The *dan wei*, or work unit, controls everything from housing to food coupons in China. (Refer to "Labor" chapter.) Under the previous system of strict socialism, the *dan wei* guaranteed workers security from cradle to grave, but today it is the greatest obstacle to people who want to start businesses of their own. If a person quits his job, he also must leave his work unit. As a consequence, he will often have to change apartments, and he will lose ration coupons for basic food staples. People with families are rarely willing to take such a risky step. Instead, creative people often keep their government jobs and take side jobs, working at both until the side job generates enough income to pay for daily necessities.

When you're looking for Chinese partners for joint ventures, keep in mind the difficulties of leaving a work unit. Ideally you will assist your Chinese partners with the transition.

For years, the Communist "iron rice-bowl" policy appeased workers by guaranteeing lifetime employment and food on the table. As in other socialist countries, the policy has resulted in low worker productivity. Without fear of being fired, many workers are content to dawdle their workday away. In joint ventures, employers may fire inefficient workers, but in fact many local government and party officials frown on the practice. Instead, officials encourage employers to provide positive incentives for increased productivity, preferring the carrot to the stick.

In China's more open areas, such as the Special Economic Zones in the south, the problem of bureaucratic meddling by party and government officials has been minimized. But in northern and inland areas, foreign businesspeople will often be frustrated by layers of bureaucracy. Local party bosses, municipal managers, tax officers, and the like can make establishing an operation difficult. Although there are specific guidelines for dealing with foreign businesses, China remains a country ruled by decree. For example, a local tax official can impose a tax on a company simply because the local coffers are low or, worse, because he doesn't like someone in the company. Chinese bureaucrats can engage in all kinds of intrigue, and have been known to sabotage projects for personal gain or revenge.

For these reasons, having powerful local officials for friends can be a major asset. Land-use rights, tax bases, and any number of regulations can be relaxed if the right people give their consent. This is especially true in more remote areas, where wages are lower, and the need for investment is greater.

Work units have a hierarchical structure, with a company supervisor at the apex directing the affairs of immediate assistants, who in turn direct the affairs of their subordinates. This structure is essentially Confucian in nature, and subordinates are not expected to question their superiors. In many ways, the work unit can be likened to a traditional Confucian family, with the supervisor acting as a father figure commanding the loyalty and respect of his subordinates. In return, he looks after their daily affairs and tries to take care of their basic needs.

Women in the Workplace

One of the first things the Communists did after gaining power in China was to give women legal rights equal to those of men. Officially, women have equal pay and equal status at jobs. They hold positions in factories, offices, government ministries, and the army right beside men.

However, Confucian male chauvinism lingers on, and today's reforms may actually mean that women are losing ground in the workplace. If a factory has economic difficulty, women are often laid off first, and some reports suggest that women of childbearing age are passed up for employment altogether. Few company leaders are women, though the exceptions may be found. However, attractive younger women are often given jobs in public relations or as front-desk secretaries.

Foreign businesswomen coming to China should not encounter any overt discrimination. Sexual harassment is virtually out of the question. Nevertheless, a woman on business in China should maintain a businesslike manner and her attire should be rather formal. By displaying self-confidence and poise, she may be able to accomplish things much faster than a male counterpart.

Chinese men sometimes feel in awe of tall, blond Western women. Women should not take this as a disadvantage. On the contrary, if a woman represents a company in China, the Chinese may feel that she is a person of exceptional competence to be given such an important job.

However, if two foreign business people are to visit China, it may not be wise to send two women together. There is the story of two women stationed in Beijing who for months could get nothing accomplished with their Chinese associates. Finally, word was leaked to the home office that the Chinese thought the two women were lesbians because they were not accompanied by men and therefore wanted nothing to do with them. After one of the women was replaced by a man, business resumed normally.

LEARNING THE CHINESE WAY

A knowledge of Chinese etiquette and rules for social behavior is a major asset for foreigners doing business in China. Body language, subtle remarks, and patterns of conduct can tell you more about a situation than blunt verbal communication. In contrast to Americans and other Westerners who value straight unambiguous dialogue, Chinese are masters of the oblique. In conversation, what is not said can be more important than what is said. Even the seating arrangements can tell you how the Chinese view a certain meeting. Knowing how to respond to situations appropriately can mean the difference between success and failure.

Chinese will not expect you to understand all the nuances of their behavior. But knowing how to read between the lines can give you an inside view into what is going on, whether the Chinese wish you to know it or not. And, by displaying a sensitivity to the native way of doing things, you can make the

Chinese respect you more and feel more comfortable interacting with you.

How Chinese View Foreigners

The vast majority of Chinese scarcely think of the outside world. Many Chinese have never even seen a foreigner. But with the government's new Open Door policy toward the West, foreigners are pouring into China in ever increasing numbers. In the past, Chinese citizens were forbidden to talk with foreigners. Today, a foreign guest can expect to be the object of much attention, often gathering crowds if pausing on the street long enough.

Many Chinese will regard foreigners with a mixture of awe, fear, and most of all, curiosity. Chinese often stare at foreigners in wide-eyed wonder. Visitors must come to accept this habit, however uncomfortable it makes them feel, and learn to ignore it. Otherwise, it will become a constant source of irritation.

Chinese generally consider any Westerner to be rich. This causes respect as well as resentment. Some Chinese cannot understand how foreigners could possibly have so much money, and probably some still believe it is a result of capitalist exploitation. But more and more people in China are coming to understand that free market economics is the real reason for the disparity between Chinese and foreign incomes.

While the Chinese accord foreigners a certain amount of respect, there is also a great pride in Chinese culture and a belief that Han Chinese, who comprise 92 percent of China's population, are the greatest race of people on earth. When coupled with xenophobia, this ethnocentricity can have ugly effects. Racism against Africans and other black people is widespread. This negative attitude may be due to physical differences and the intimidating large size of many blacks when compared to Chinese, but many observers believe that the real reasons are economic. For years, many small, poor African nations received substantial support from the PRC, and many African students were sent to China for training. This policy was in line with the Maoist theory of propagating Marxism in the Third World. This policy has been largely abandoned by the Chinese, who now are aware of their own relative poverty as compared to Westerners. The PRC increasingly shuns poor African nations, and Chinese citizens often regard Africans as poorer than they are and as having nothing to offer their own aspirations for development.

Chinese often view Americans in particular as having material strength but a shallow cultural foundation due to their short 200-year history. They view Europe as the cultural center of the Western world, but its continuous history is also short compared to China's reputed 5,000 years of civilization. The Western belief that individual freedom is paramount is totally alien in the collectivist culture of China. As a result, Chinese often see Western behavior as selfish and uncaring for the common interests of a group. Westerners visiting China should try to behave in ways that cannot be viewed as too self-centered.

The painful lessons of China's early exploitation by foreigners are still remembered today. The English are routinely reminded of the abuses they committed during the Opium Wars, and they are one of the background reasons for the less-than-hospitable negotiations over Hong Kong's future. But if the Chinese people had to single out one country for hostile feelings, it would be Japan. During World War II, the Japanese army committed atrocities in China on a grand scale. Although trade and economic cooperation between China and Japan is booming today, in private many Chinese will admit to negative feelings about the Japanese.

However, Chinese youth are increasingly entranced by foreign culture and they are likely to disregard old international animosities as things of the past. They are adopting styles that they believe are popular in the West, such as blue jeans, leather jackets, and a love for pop music. The PRC government has expressed concern over this Western influence, which it has termed "spiritual pollution." The press has countered the glamorous view of America with stories of robbery, murder, ethnic tensions, and drug addiction in that country.

Regardless of the mixed personal feelings that individuals may have, the Chinese people usually work hard to make foreigners feel wanted and appreciated when they visit the country. If personal affection is not an incentive for a welcoming attitude, the prospect of business and profit certainly is.

Meeting the Chinese

When meeting Chinese businesspeople, foreigners should display sincerity and respect. Handshaking, imported from the West, is generally the accepted form of salutation. However, Chinese handshakes differ in two ways from those common in the West. First, Chinese tend to shake hands very lightly, without the Western custom of gripping the hand firmly and pumping vigorously. Second, a handshake can last as long as ten seconds, instead of the brisk three-second contact common in the West.

The handshake is always followed by a ritualistic exchange of business cards. Foreigners should always carry an ample supply of business cards, preferably with English text on one side and Chinese on the other. Seek the advice of a knowledgeable person on the choice of characters for your name and company, as some characters have better meanings than others.

The proper procedure for exchanging business cards is to give and receive cards with both hands,

holding the card corners between thumb and forefinger. When receiving a card, do not simply pocket it immediately, but take a few moments to study the card and what it says, even if it is only printed in Chinese. The name card represents the person who presents it, and it should be given respect accordingly.

When the Chinese greet someone, they do not look a person straight in the eye, but lower their eyes slightly. This is a sign of deference and respect. A visitor should refrain from looking intensely into a person's eyes, as this can make a Chinese person feel uncomfortable.

Presenting letters of introduction from well-known business leaders, overseas Chinese, or former government officials who have dealt with China is an excellent way of showing both that you are a person of high standing and that you mean business. Chinese are very concerned about social standing, and anything that you can do to enhance their regard for you is a plus. But be careful not to appear arrogant or haughty, as Confucian morality condemns such behavior.

Appropriate Dress

Dress styles in China are changing rapidly. Little more than a decade ago, standard dress was the bland, unisex Mao jacket and baggy pants in solid blue, gray, or green. Today, businesspeople have adopted Western-style suits, sometimes with ties. Women have become fashion conscious and often wear modest skirts, high-neck blouses, and high-heeled shoes. Westerners are advised to dress somewhat formally in business dealings. Women should dress fashionably but avoid above-the-knee hemlines or low necklines.

Chinese today are impressed by wealth, and they consider Westerners to be rich. There is no reason to dissuade this opinion. Therefore, it cannot hurt to wear modest gold jewelry and a quality watch. Chinese will notice these adornments, which will help to make their evaluation of you positive. Excessive or gaudy jewelry is discouraged.

Giving and Receiving Gifts

Chinese are inveterate gift givers. Gifts express friendship, and they can symbolize hopes for good future business, the successful conclusion of an endeavor, or appreciation for a favor done. Foreign businesspeople should spend some time choosing appropriate presents before embarking on a trip to China. The Chinese consider the Western habit of simply saying thank you for a favor glib and perhaps less than sincere. Favors should be rewarded materially, although gifts can have more symbolic than monetary value. Avoid very expensive gifts unless the recipient is an old associate who has proved to be particularly important in business dealings. Gifts are not expected on the first visit, but they can be given if you feel that the beginnings of a relationship have been established.

Gift giving between Chinese and foreigners has been the subject of some controversy in PRC government circles in recent years. Before international business exchanges went into high gear, individuals receiving presents were ordered to turn them over to their work units, to be shared by all in a spirit of equality. The rationale was that rich foreigners might corrupt or use otherwise model workers. The official policy is still that expensive gifts should be turned over to authorities, but in fact this rule is often ignored. Essentially, there are no hard-and-fast rules concerning gifts, and the giver must use his or her best judgment when deciding what to give. In areas of rapid development, there have been reports of widespread graft disguised as gift giving, with "gifts" often being outright bribes involving several thousand dollars in hard currency. This behavior is risky in the extreme; convicted Chinese nationals are routinely executed.

To be on the safe side, foreigners visiting a place of business may present a single large gift to the company as a whole. The gift may vary in value from a nice piece of art to a coffee-table picture book. Gifts to individuals should be of lesser value, in the range of US$10 to US$15. If one gift is to be given, it should be presented to the head of the Chinese group at a dinner banquet or at the conclusion of a business meeting. If gifts are to be given to several individuals, make sure that each person receives a gift of roughly equal value. The gifts may be placed on the table at a dinner banquet or presented during an appropriately relaxed time. If you give many gifts, do not omit anyone present or anyone who has shown hospitality during your stay. Bring along extra gifts just in case.

If you are invited to a Chinese person's home, it is courteous to arrive with a small gift. Suitable presents include a basket of fruit, tea, flowers, or any memento from your home country that the host can associate with you. Picture books of your home area make good presents. Presenting a wife with perfume or children with toys is likely to be appreciated. Such presents show that you are concerned about the welfare of the entire family, not just the business relationship. Foreign liquor is another gift that is much appreciated. French cognac is the most prized, although it can be rather expensive, and it should only be given to those with whom you already have a personal relationship.

As in the case of business cards, the polite way to present and receive gifts is with both hands outstretched.

It is polite for the recipient to refuse a gift two or three times before finally accepting it. For Westerners, the process can be tricky. If the Chinese person appears embarrassed when he refuses your gift and says that he cannot possibly receive such a nice item, the proper thing to do is to insist that your gift is only a small token and to add that you would be honored if it were accepted. As a rule, after some hemming and hawing, the Chinese will accept the present graciously. If your attempts to give a present are rejected several times and it is evident that the intended recipient is serious about not wishing to accept it, it may be that he is sincere and that your offer should be withdrawn. He may refuse your gift because he does not want to be in your debt or because he has no intentions of having a relationship with you.

When a gift is offered to you, it is not necessary for you to refuse it ceremonially as the Chinese do. Humble acceptance and a few choice words of appreciation are enough. A gift from a Chinese businessperson may simply be a courtesy that he accords to all visitors, but it can also be an acknowledgment that a relationship with you exists. Or it may indicate that you will be asked for a favor. In any case, if someone presents you with a gift, you are expected to reciprocate in kind or through a favor.

If the gift is wrapped, it is considered impolite to open it in front of the giver unless he or she encourages you to do so. Tearing the wrappings off hastily is a sign of greediness. Any gift that you give wrapped to an individual should be wrapped in the traditional lucky colors of gold or red. White and black are considered colors of mourning.

Conversation

Cultural, political, and linguistic differences can cause trouble for Chinese and foreigners over the simple matter of small talk. Expect people whom you don't know well to ask questions concerning personal matters, such as your age, the amount of money you make, or the members of your family. It is obviously not polite to tell people such matters are none of their business, and with associates, frank answers are a sign of familiarity and closeness. The basic rule of thumb in conversation is not to say anything that the Chinese would find offensive or insulting.

Chinese are often curious about foreigners and their habits, and their questions are usually related to what they consider to be important in life. Often this involves money. For example, a Chinese may ask how much your watch cost or what kind of car you have and how much it is worth.

Family Matters Family members can be an important topic of conversation, because Chinese who are getting to know you may evaluate you as the member of a family as much as an individual. Asking Chinese about their families is readily acceptable, and they may go into great detail about the lives of brothers, sisters, parents, spouses, and children. If you are divorced or unmarried, the topic of family may be uncomfortable to you. It is a fact that many Chinese view the West as morally loose and full of homosexuals, which they find unacceptable. In a tense situation, it may be better to skirt the truth rather than to be open about something that could jeopardize a relationship.

Money Matters The subject of income often comes up in conversations with Chinese. If people ask you about your income, you may tell them the truth. However, many Chinese have difficulty comprehending how foreigners can earn so much money. With work partners, you may wish to avoid this topic, since knowing that you make twenty times as much as they do can cause resentment. To downplay incomes in the West, you may explain that things cost a great deal more in your home country than they do in China, so your purchasing power is limited even if you have a high income.

Political Matters One area of conversation about which you need to be particularly sensitive is politics. Avoid criticizing Communism, even if the Chinese initiate such talk. Nor should you talk about the Republic of China on Taiwan, although discussion of Taiwan as an economic entity or as a province of China is fine. The Tiananmen tragedy of 1989 is another topic that should be avoided, as are the situation in Tibet and human rights. The Cultural Revolution, now considered to be old history, may come up in conversation, but it is best not to bring it up yourself. Some Chinese may be willing to discuss that turbulent time freely and even to relate personal stories. Others may have misgivings about the Cultural Revolution, or they may be saddened or ashamed by personal memories, so the subject is best left alone.

Jokes It is fine to tell jokes in informal situations, but they are best avoided when you speak to a group. Sexual jokes are taboo. Also, cross-cultural humor is hard to find, and the point of a joke is often lost in translation. Puns, of course, are impossible, and jokes concerning persons or events specific to your country are not likely to be understood.

Saying No When asked for a favor, Chinese will usually avoid saying no, as to do so causes embarrassment and loss of face. If a request cannot be met, Chinese may say it is inconvenient or under consideration. This generally means no. Another way of saying no is to ignore a request and pretend it wasn't asked. Unless a request is really urgent, its best to respect these subtleties and not to press the issue.

Sometimes a Chinese will respond to a request by saying, "Yes, but it will be difficult." To a Westerner, this response may seem to be affirmative, but in China it may well mean no or probably not. If a person says yes to a question and follows by making a hissing sound of sucking breath between his teeth, the real answer could be no.

The Chinese also have the habit of telling a person whatever they believe he or she wants to hear, whether or not it is true. They do this as a courtesy, rarely with malicious intent, although it can be a real problem in the workplace. If bad news needs to be told, Chinese will be reluctant to break it. Sometimes they will use an intermediary for communication, or perhaps they will imply bad news without being blunt. To cut through such murkiness, it is best to explain to your Chinese coworkers that you appreciate direct communication, and that you will not be upset at bearers of bad news.

Body Language and Other Courtesies

Chinese often use body language that can be incomprehensible to unfamiliar Westerners, and some Western body language or positions can be misunderstood. This section reviews a few key examples to keep in mind when you visit China.

- When Chinese want someone to approach, they extend the hand palm down and curl the fingers, as if scratching an imaginary surface.
- Holding one's hand up near the face and slightly waving means no, or it can be a mild rebuke.
- Pointing at someone with the forefinger is an accusatory motion considered rude or hostile. When you point, use the entire hand, palm open.
- Winking is impolite and it can have a negative connotation.
- Laughing or smiling among Chinese can be confusing and means different things according to the situation. When nervous or embarrassed, Chinese will smile or laugh nervously and cover their mouths with their hands. This can be in response to an inconvenient request, a sensitive issue that has been brought up, or a social faux pas committed by the smiler or another person near by.
- While shaking hands is now the standard form of greeting, traditional etiquette calls for making a fist with the left hand, covering it with the right palm, and shaking the hands up and down. Some Chinese still do this, especially with close friends. It is also a formal way of saying thank you and a sign of reverence.
- When Chinese are embarrassed, they cover their faces with their hands.
- Hissing is a sign of difficulty or uncomfortableness.
- When Chinese yawn, cough, or use a toothpick, they cover their mouths.
- It is impolite to point one's feet at another

person. Chinese sit upright in chairs with both feet on the floor.

- In Chinese homes, people remove their shoes at the entrance. Be sure to wear clean socks!
- Chinese are not a "touchy" people, and they rarely hug in public. Lightly touching another person's arm when speaking is a sign of close familiarity. Men and women rarely hold hands in public, but it is not uncommon for friends of the same sex to hold hands or clasp each other by the shoulders.

Language

Language differences can, of course, be a big obstacle to meaningful dialogue between Chinese and foreigners. Few people in China speak English well, although English is now mandatory in most schools. People often want to try out their English on foreigners, so don't be surprised if you get cornered and have to deliver a quick English conversation course. When you speak English with a person who is not fluent, you must pay careful attention. Use short, simple sentences, and refrain from colloquialisms and slang.

It is an immense asset in China to know some Mandarin Chinese. Mandarin *pu tong hua* in Chinese is the official national language in China, although there are many dialects that are mutually unintelligible. The dialects of Chinese can be likened to the Romance languages in Europe. Like French, Italian, and Spanish, Chinese dialects are related, but each is an independent language. They differ from other languages, though, in that their writing systems use exactly the same characters; only the pronunciations of characters are different in each dialect. It is possible for a person who speaks Cantonese and a person who speaks Fujianese to communicate fluently in writing. But in conversation, they are most likely to communicate in Mandarin.

Spoken Mandarin is quite simple grammatically, and a few hours of study each week over a couple of months can prepare you for simple conversation and survival communication in China. Chinese are more likely to warm up to a foreigner who has taken the trouble to learn their language. If you are planning an extended stay in China, by all means take Chinese courses or hire a private tutor.

Names and Forms of Address

In Chinese, an individual's family name precedes his or her personal name. The family name is almost always monosyllabic, and the personal name usually has two syllables, although one-syllable personal names are not uncommon. For example, Deng Xiaoping's family name is Deng, and his personal name is Xiaoping. Lu Xun, a famous author of the early 20th century, has a one-syllable personal name:

Xun. Each syllable is the pronunciation of a single written character.

Chinese sometimes adopt English names, since they know it is difficult for foreigners to remember Chinese names. Sometimes they invert their names so that the family name follows the personal name. This can be confusing, since you may not know if a name has been inverted. As a general rule, assume that a name has not been inverted.

People outside the family almost never call each other by their personal names, often even if they are very close. Westerners should use Mister, Miss, or Mrs. when addressing Chinese, just as they do in Western society. Although a woman does not take her husband's family name when she marries, it is acceptable for Westerners to address a married woman in the Western form, such as Mrs. Hu if the woman's husband is Mr. Hu.

Another common form of address is to use a person's designated position in society. For example, a teacher with the family name Yuan can be referred to as Teacher Yuan. This form of address also applies to company managers, directors, and higher-ranking officials.

Trade Delegations

There are a few important points to remember when you send a trade delegation to China. First, keep in mind that the Chinese are a group-oriented people and that they are more comfortable functioning as members of a group than as individuals. Generally, they assume that this is true of all people. They are confused when members of a visiting group speak as individuals and make statements that are contradictory or inconsistent with the stated views of the group as a whole. Individual opinions are not wanted. Therefore, every trade delegation should have a designated speaker, who is also its most senior member. The Chinese will look to that member for all major communication and accept his words as the words of the entire organization.

Talk to the right people Before you send a delegation, make absolutely certain that the people with whom you will be talking have the authority to make decisions. Although Chinese companies are increasingly autonomous in their decision making, the vast majority are still state owned, and in some cases executives must get approval from superiors in either the government or the party before making a decision. If the person whom you meet is in this type of situation, concrete action may be slow, and you may have to make multiple trips to China before you know whether your endeavors will pay off. Therefore, be sure to talk with everyone who can make or break the deal, including local party and government leaders.

China is an enormous country, and business procedures vary from one province to another. Generally, businesses in the southern provinces of Guangdong and Fujian are the most likely to have authority to deal directly with foreigners. Shanghai is also relatively free of government interference. Beijing is still notorious for bureaucratic meddling in business affairs, and you should be prepared to deal with government and party representatives when doing business there. No matter where you are going, it is best to request to see a company's business registration documents verifying its right to do business with foreigners before you send a trade delegation.

The Importance of Status Chinese are really concerned about the status that an individual holds in a company or organization. They will evaluate the seriousness of a trade delegation by the rank of its members, and a delegation is not likely to succeed if the Chinese know that its head is a junior executive. Likewise, they will wish to match your delegation with executives of similar status from their own organization. It is wise to send them a list of the delegates who will attend that gives their ranks in the company and to request that they do the same. If the Chinese company sends someone to a meeting who is obviously of lower rank, the chances are good that it is not particularly interested in you, or that it is unaware of the status of the members of your delegation.

Delegation Leaders A trade delegation should be led by older members of the company who have at least middle-level executive rank. They should be patient, genial, and persistent, and have extensive cross-cultural experience. Ideally, they have already had some experience in China or Asia, and they have enough rank to make decisions on the spot without fear of repercussions from the home office.

Foreign Businesswomen In contrast to many other cultures, China accepts doing business with foreign women, and a trade delegation should have no problem having women members. However, women have not traditionally headed trade delegations. Outside of the cosmetic and fashion industries, companies should consider balancing delegations with men if the leader is a woman.

Your Interpreter is Crucial The interpreter is an important member of any trade delegation. While English is a mandatory course of study in schools, most Chinese speak little English. Even those who do speak English are not likely to put themselves at the disadvantage of having to speak a foreign language in serious negotiations. One member of the Chinese delegation will be their interpreter, but it is not wise to depend on that person for communication. There is little chance that the interpreter for the Chinese would intentionally try to mislead you, but there is a good chance that he will not be especially fluent in English will have virtually no understanding of the nuances and inflections that make English so expressive. Having an interpreter of your own can be expensive, but it is a real advantage and definitely worth the extra cost in sensitive, high-stakes negotiations. Your interpreter should be multicultural as well as multilingual, able to pick up on feelings and inflections in both English and Chinese. You can assist your interpreter by briefing him thoroughly in advance of negotiations and providing as much written material as possible. There are several translation and interpretation businesses in Hong Kong that can provide competent service for a visit to China.

First Day Protocol Little in the way of serious business will be accomplished on the first day of a delegation's visit to China. This is a time for getting to know one another and for feeling out the personalities who will be involved in later negotiations. Use this time to get to know the Chinese side, and try to determine the status of all the members and their likely relations with one other. The leader of the Chinese delegation will be the only spokesman for the group on substantive issues, but other members will probably have some say in decision making. Chinese place great stock in consensus. Most likely they will debate their position on the business at hand among themselves, but never in front of the foreign delegation.

As hosts, the Chinese will have an itinerary of events for your delegation, and most of your time will be taken up doing what they have planned. The first day may include a factory tour or visits to cultural landmarks, followed in the evening by a traditional Chinese banquet, which may be followed by a trip to a popular karaoke club.

Banqueting: A National Sport

It is fair to say that the number one pastime in China is eating. As one Chinese said, "When foreigners are happy, they dance. When we're happy, we eat!" If you like Chinese food, going to a traditional banquet may be your most pleasant experience in China. The form of the meal is ancient, and thus there are rules of etiquette which should be followed. Although your Chinese host will not expect you to know everything about proper banquet behavior, he will greatly appreciate your displaying some knowledge of the subject, because it shows that you have respect for Chinese culture and traditions.

Arrival Banquets are usually held in restaurants in private rooms that have been reserved for the purpose. All members of your delegation should arrive together and on time. You will be met at the door and escorted to the banquet room, where the hosts are likely to have assembled. Traditionally, and as in all situations, the head of your delegation should enter the room first. Do not be surprised if your hosts greet you with a loud round of applause. The proper response is to applaud back.

Seating and Settings   The banquet table is large and round and can seat up to twelve people. If there are more than twelve people, guests and hosts will have been divided equally among tables. Seating arrangements, which are based on rank, are stricter than in the West. This is another reason why you should give your host a list of delegation members that clearly identifies their rank. The principal host is seated facing the entrance and farthest from the door, usually with his back to the wall. The principal guest sits to the host's immediate right. If there are two tables, the second-ranking host and guest sit at the other table facing the principal host and guest. Interpreters sit to the right of the principal and second-ranking guests if there are two tables. Lower-ranking delegation members are seated in descending order around the tables, alternating with Chinese hosts. Guests should never assume that they may sit where they please and should wait for hosts to guide them to their places.

Each place setting at the table contains a rice bowl, a dish for main courses, a dessert dish, a spoon, and chopsticks on a chopstick rest; usually there is a napkin. Two glasses are customary: a larger glass for beer or soda and a small thin glass for hard liquor. In the middle of the table is a revolving tray on which entrees are placed. During the meal it can be spun at will to gain access to the dishes that it holds.

Chopsticks   Your host may politely ask if you are able to use chopsticks or if silverware would be more convenient. It is advisable to learn how to use chopsticks before you come to China. One good method of learning is to practice picking up peanuts from a bowl. If you are able to pick up a bowlful of peanuts with relative ease, then you should have no trouble at a banquet. If you absolutely cannot master chopsticks, silverware may be available.

Smoking and Drinking   It is probable that your host will offer cigarettes throughout the banquet. Most Chinese men smoke, but it is perfectly acceptable to decline the invitation to light up. It is rude to light a cigarette without first offering cigarettes to others. If at all possible, bear with the secondhand smoke. It would be rude in the extreme to ask the host not to smoke while enjoying a banquet.

Beer is the standard drink of choice at banquets, but you may feel free to substitute soda. Hard liquor, usually rice wine or perhaps brandy, is served ceremonially and is reserved for toasts. It is impolite to drink liquor alone.

Beginning the Feast   The first round of food at a banquet consists of small plates of coldcuts. They may already be on the revolving tray when you sit down. The dishes may contain pork, chicken, pick-

led vegetables, codfish, scallops, tofu, or any number of different foods. It is polite, but certainly not mandatory, to try a taste of each dish. It is better not to partake of foods that you cannot eat than to gag at the table, but if you find something on your plate that you dislike, you may simply push it around on your plate to make it look as if you have at least tasted it.

It is the host's responsibility to serve the guests, and at very formal banquets people do not begin to eat until the principal host has broken into the dishes by serving a portion to the principal guest. Or, the host may simply raise his chopsticks and announce that eating has begun. After this point, one may serve oneself any food in any amount, although it is rude to dig around in a dish in search of choice morsels. Proper etiquette requires that serving spoons or a set of large chopsticks be used to transport food to one's dish, but in fact many Chinese use their eating chopsticks for this purpose. Watch your host to determine which procedure to use.

After the first course of coldcuts comes a succession of delicacies. Waiters will constantly remove and replace dishes as they are soiled or emptied, so that it is hard to tell exactly how many courses are served through the event. Some banquets can include more than twelve courses, but ten is more likely. Remember to go slow on eating. Don't fill yourself up when five courses are left to go. To stop eating in the middle of a banquet is rude, and your host may incorrectly think that something has been done to offend you.

Manners   Table manners in China often have no relation to manners in the West. There are no prohibitions on putting one's elbows on the table, reaching across the table for food, or making loud noises when eating. Usually it is impolite to touch one's food with anything except chopsticks, but when eating chicken, shrimp, or other hard-to-handle food, Chinese use their hands. Bones and shells are usually placed directly on the tablecloth next to the eating dish. Waiters periodically come around and unceremoniously rake the debris into a bowl or small bucket. Although banquets have their prescribed methods for behavior, manners conform more to practicality than they do in the West. In fact, banquet time is when businesspeople tend to be the most relaxed and comfortable.

Liquor and Toasts   One reason is that drinking figures prominently in Chinese banquets. Toasting is mandatory, and the drinking of spirits commences only after the host has made a toast at the beginning of the meal. It is likely that he will stand and hold his glass out with both hands while saying a few words to welcome the guests. When he says the words *gan bei*, which means bottoms up (literally, dry glass), all present should drain their glasses. After this initial toast, drinking and toasting are open to all, but the head of the visiting group will be expected to toast the well-being of his hosts in return. Subsequent toasts can be made from person to person or to the group as a whole. No words are needed to make a toast, and it is not necessary to drain your glass, although to do so is more respectful.

Remember that hard liquor should never be drunk alone. If you are thirsty, you can sip beer or a soft drink individually, but if you prefer to drink hard liquor, be sure to catch the eye of someone at your table, smile and raise your glass, and drink in unison. Beer or soft drinks can also be used for toasting, but do not switch from alcohol to a soft drink in the middle of the banquet lest the host think that something has offended you.

Also, it is impolite to fill your own glass without first filling glasses of all others. This applies to all drinks and not just to alcohol. If your glass becomes empty and your host is observant, it is likely that he will fill it for you immediately. When filling another's glass, it is polite to fill it as full as you can without having the liquid spill over the rim. This symbolizes full respect and friendship.

It is a matter of courtesy for the host to try to get his guests drunk. If you do not intend to drink alcohol, make it known at the very beginning of the meal to prevent embarrassment. Even then, the host may good-naturedly try to goad you into drinking. One way to eliminate this pressure is to tell your host that you are allergic to alcohol.

In the course of drinking at banquets, it is not unusual for some Chinese to become quite inebriated, although vomiting or falling down in public entails loss of face. After a few rounds of heavy drinking, you may notice your hosts excusing themselves to the bathroom, from whence they often return a bit lighter and rejuvenated for more toasting! Also, many Asians are unable to metabolize alcohol as fast as Westerners do. The result is that they often get drunk sooner, and their faces turn crimson, as if they were blushing.

The Main Dish The high point of a Chinese banquet is often the presentation of a large whole cooked fish. In formal situations, the fish is placed on the revolving tray with its head pointing toward the principal guest. The guest should accept the first serving, after which everyone helps himself.

The final rounds of food follow, usually a soup followed by rice, concluding with fresh fruit. Chinese consider soup to be conducive to digestion. Rice is served at the end so that guests can eat their fill, as if the preceding courses had not been enough. It is polite to leave some rice and other food on your plate; to finish everything implies that you are still hungry and that you did not have enough to eat. Fruit is served to cleanse the palate.

Concluding the Banquet When the fruit is finished, the banquet has officially ended. There is little ceremony involved with its conclusion. The host may ask if you have eaten your fill, which you undoubtedly will have done. Then, without further ado, the principal host will rise, signaling that the banquet has ended. Generally, the principal host will bid good evening to everyone at the door and stay behind to settle the bill with the restaurateur. Other hosts usually accompany guests to their vehicles and remain outside waving until the cars have left the premises.

Reciprocity

After you have been entertained by your Chinese associates, it is proper to return the favor unless time or other constraints make it impossible. A good time to have a return banquet is on the eve of your departure from China or at the conclusion of the business at hand.

If possible, a third party should relay your invitations to the Chinese. If for some reason the Chinese must refuse the invitation, they will feel more comfortable telling the third party than speaking directly to you.

China has few decent Western-style restaurants, so it is advisable to make reservations at a Chinese restaurant where you are sure to get good service and food. Your Chinese guests are likely to appreciate it more than Western fare. Banquets are priced per person and cover all expenses except alcohol. There is no need to order specific dishes, although you may do so. Good restaurateurs know how to prepare adequately for a banquet.

Karaoke

After a banquet, a hardy Chinese host may invite you to go singing at a karaoke club (pronounced kala-okay in Chinese). Karaoke clubs began in Japan, but in recent years the craze has spread to all other countries in East Asia. For Chinese, the karaoke phenomenon is a technological extension of their natural propensity to sing with close friends.

Karaoke clubs feature a raised platform with a microphone above which is a monitor. The monitor displays preselected music videos with accompanying music but without vocals. The words of the song are displayed at the bottom of the screen. The designated singer will then sing the words. Most karaoke clubs have Chinese, Japanese, and English songs. Expect to be forced to sing at least one song when you visit a karaoke. For Chinese, being a competent singer enhances face, because one's close friends will be watching. Foreign guests are not expected to sing proficiently, and any attempt to sing will be greeted with much praise and applause. In higher-class karaoke clubs, large private rooms with big-screen television sets are the norm. Groups of friends can use these rooms to sing and drink until the sun comes up, attended the while by beautiful hostesses. It is an experience that you are not likely have in the West, although some foreigners find it rather boring unless they are a little drunk.

Many observers have wondered why karaoke has become so popular in the collectivist cultures of Asia. One answer is that singing in front of one's peers is one of the very few socially acceptable ways in which an individual can display his or her talent without being branded arrogant or self-centered. It fulfills the latent desire to gain credit as an individual without jeopardizing the need to be accepted by the whole group. Of course, no one goes to a karaoke club individually, and it usually is a meeting place for the closest of friends. If you wish to establish close relations with Chinese, going to karaoke is one of the best ways of doing it. However, some Chinese may regard karaoke as somewhat low-class, so you should avoid mention of karaoke unless you are invited to go.

BUSINESS NEGOTIATIONS

After banqueting and singing with Chinese businesspeople, foreigners may begin to believe that their business dealings will be equally smooth. This is possible but not likely. Chinese are known to be tough negotiators. Professional negotiators even attend a special boot camp at which they learn negotiation tactics. Most every aspect of a business deal between Chinese and foreigners is subject to the give-and-take of the negotiating process. Before going into negotiations, foreigners must be prepared for subtle and aggressive tactics from the Chinese side. In fact, the lavish entertainment heaped on foreign businesspeople before everyone sits down at the negotiating table is partly an attempt to soften up the delegation psychologically and gain maximum advantage in the process that arrives at a business agreement.

Negotiation Etiquette

When arranging for negotiations with Chinese, it is customary to give them as much detail on the issue to be discussed as reasonable, plus notice of all delegation members who will be present. The team leader's name should be listed first. Other members should be listed in order of seniority or importance for the deal. The number of negotiation members can vary from two to 10, depending on the nature of the business. The Chinese side will try to match their team members with the visiting team.

If the negotiations are to focus on a transfer of technology currently unavailable to the Chinese, be sure not to give away blueprints or any substantive knowledge of the technology. The Chinese have been known to use negotiations solely to gain free information to assist them in their effort to develop technology.

Beginning the Meeting

Negotiations are often held in meeting rooms at or near the Chinese place of business. A functionary escorts the members of the visiting delegation to the meeting room as soon as they arrive. The Chinese team is already there. The head of the visiting delegation should enter the meeting room first. This is Chinese custom, and not to observe it could confuse the Chinese about the identity of the delegation leader. If an interpreter escorts the visiting team, he or she should enter close behind the leader and remain by the leader's side throughout the negotiations.

After a round of handshaking and smiles, the visitors are seated at the negotiation table. The table is usually rectangular, and teams sit opposite each other, with the heads of delegations sitting eye to eye. Other team members are arrayed next to delegation heads, often in descending order of importance. Most likely, the guest delegation will be seated facing the door, a common Chinese courtesy. Tea or other drinks are provided.

Chinese are patient people and do not expect to jump into substantive negotiations right away. Some small talk is usually necessary in order to get the ball rolling, and this time can also be used to get a feel for those present. Chinese like to know with whom they are dealing. The subject of business usually comes up naturally after the participants feel comfortable enough to begin.

Entering Substantive Talks

After initial courtesies, the head of the host delegation usually delivers a short welcoming speech and then turns the floor over to the head of the guest delegation. Chinese customarily allow visitors to speak first in negotiations. In some ways, this can be to their advantage, but participants usually know enough about each other's positions through prior communication that there are few surprises. As noted earlier of trade delegations, Chinese look to the senior leader for all meaningful dialogue. Conflicting statements from different team members are to be avoided, and team members should speak only when they are asked to do so.

When speaking, the visiting delegation leader should look toward the head of the Chinese team, not at the interpreter. For clarity, he should speak slowly and not say too much before allowing the interpreter to speak. A couple of sentences at a time is enough. Interpreters need to rest at least every two hours. If negotiations are to continue for more than a day, you may need two interpreters. Using an interpreter can stretch a meetings to three times its normal length, so be patient with the flow of discussion.

The Chinese do not like surprises in negotiations, so it may be wise to lay out your basic position at this time. It can also be useful to distribute sheets stating your main points in Chinese. When tackling a business issue at the appropriate time, Chinese appreciate directness. Anything that you can do to clarify their understanding of your position is fine, but in the initial stage, your presentation may need to involve only the big picture. Details can be saved for later. However, in some forms of negotiations, the Chinese will expect a very serious and in-depth presentation, covering all the major details and answering all foreseeable questions at the very outset of talks. A typical opening statement highlighting the major topics that need to be discussed can last between five and ten minutes.

After the visitor outlines his team's position, the Chinese team leader takes the floor and answers point by point, remedying any perceived omissions. From this point on, the negotiation process runs with the rhythm of a controlled conversation, not an open-ended chat. The Chinese approach is often first to gain a holistic view of the entire proposal, then to break it down into specific chunks, at which time concrete issues and problems can be discussed. Use your own judgment in the talks, and adopt methods that are naturally suitable for your particular subject.

Chinese Negotiating Tactics

Chinese negotiators are shrewd and use many tactics. This section reviews some of the most common ones.

- Controlling the schedule and location. When negotiations are held in China, the Chinese are aware that foreigners must spend a good deal of time and money to come there and that they do not want to go away empty-handed. The Chinese may appear at the negotiating table seemingly indifferent to the success or failure of the meeting and then make excessive demands on the foreign side. It has been reported that in some cases, the Chinese team was not at all serious about making a business deal, but only wished to negotiate for practice.
- Threatening to do business elsewhere. Chinese may tell you that they can easily do business with someone else, for example, the Japanese or the Germans, if their demands are not met.
- Using friendship as a way of gaining concessions. Chinese who have established relations with foreigners may remind them that true friends would aim to out an agreement of maximum mutual benefit. Be sure that the benefits in your agreement are not one-way.

- Showing anger. Although the display of anger is not acceptable under Confucian morality, Chinese may show calculated anger to put pressure on the opposite side, which may be afraid of losing the contract.
- Sensing the foreigner's fear of failure. If the Chinese know that you are committed 100 percent to procuring a contract and that you are fearful of not succeeding, they are likely to increase their demands for concessions.
- Flattery. Chinese are not above heaping praise on foreigners either for personal attributes or business acumen. Don't let their skill at stroking your ego give them an advantage.
- Knowing when you need to leave. If the Chinese know the date of your departure, they may delay substantive negotiations until the day before you plan to leave in order to pressure you into a hasty agreement. If possible, make departure reservations for several different dates, and be willing to stay longer than anticipated if there is a real chance for success.
- Attrition. Chinese negotiators are patient and can stretch out the negotiations in order to wear you down. Excessive entertaining in the evening can also take the edge off a foreign negotiator's attentiveness.
- Using your own words and looking for inconsistencies. Chinese take careful notes at discussions and they have been known to quote a foreigner's own words in order to refute his current position.
- Playing off competitors. Chinese may invite several competing companies to negotiate at the same time, and they will tell you about it to apply pressure.
- Inflating prices and hiding the real bottom line. Chinese may appear to give in to your demand for lower prices, but their original stated price may have been abnormally high.

Tips for Foreign Negotiators

A number of tactics may be helpful for foreign negotiators dealing with the Chinese.

- Be absolutely prepared. The effective negotiator has a thorough knowledge of every aspect of the business deal. At least one member of your negotiating team should have an in-depth technical knowledge of your are and be able to display it to the Chinese. Be prepared to give a lengthy and detailed presentation on your side of the deal, but take care not to release sensitive technological information before you reach a full agreement.
- Play off competitors. If the going gets tough, you may let the Chinese know that they are not

the only game in town. Competition between Chinese producers is increasing, and there may be other sources in the country for what your counterpart has to offer. Also, if price is the problem, you may be able to strike a cheaper deal in Southeast Asia. If quality is the concern, Japanese and Taiwanese companies can generally outperform the Chinese.

- Be willing to cut your losses and go home. Let the Chinese know that failure to agree is an acceptable alternative to a bad deal.
- Cover every detail of a contract before you sign it. Talk over the entire contract with the Chinese side. Be sure that your interpretations are consistent and that everyone understands his duties and obligations.
- Take copious and careful notes. Review what the Chinese side has said, and ask for clarification on any possible ambiguities.
- Pad your price. Do as the Chinese do. Start out high, and be willing to give a little from there.
- Remain calm and impersonal during negotiations. Don't show your agitation, lest the Chinese know your sensitive areas. Even if you were good buddies the night before, a standoffish personal attitude in negotiations lets the Chinese know that your first priority is good business.
- Be patient. Chinese believe that Westerners are always in a hurry, and they may try to get you to sign an agreement before you have adequate time to review the details.
- State your commitment to work toward a fair deal. Tell the Chinese that your relationship can only be strengthened by a mutually beneficial arrangement.
- Be willing to compromise, but don't give anything away easily.
- Finally, approach negotiations and all business in China from the standpoint of long-term involvement. Giving some leeway to the Chinese over a specific issue can result in far greater benefit in the future.

The Chinese Approach to Contracts

China is just beginning to institute the rule of law in business. Nevertheless, many if not most Chinese executives view written contracts as virtually meaningless compared to personal commitments between associates. The power of the contract as a legally binding document is accepted in areas of concentrated foreign investment, but probably not in remoter areas.

In contrast to the Western view, some Chinese still consider a contract to be a loose commitment to do business, not a document outlining every aspect of the business relationship. Some head executives would rather sign a short agreement on the principle of doing business and allow subordinates to work out the details at a later time. Avoid this situation if you can, because it increases the chance of misunderstanding on both sides and necessitates further negotiations, which can be costly.

While negotiating a detailed contract is important, understand that the Chinese often view any deal with foreigners as only one component of a larger, ongoing relationship. The Chinese see the immediate issue as a sort of building block that allows them to measure and strengthen reliability and cooperation. This is a practical and realistic philosophy that any Westerner who wants to do business in China over the long term should appreciate and adopt for his own ventures.

FURTHER READING

The preceding discussion of Chinese business culture and etiquette is by no means complete. The books listed here can give the reader additional insight.

Dealing With the Chinese by Scott D. Seligman. New York: Warner Books, 1989. ISBN 0-446-38994-3. $12.95. A detailed examination of business relationships and etiquette between Chinese and foreigners whose author has extensive experience in mainland China and uses personal stories and examples to illustrate Chinese behavior and etiquette.

Chinese Etiquette and Ethics in Business by Boye De Mente. Lincolnwood, Ill.: NTC Business Books, 1989. ISBN 0-8442-8525-0. $14.95. A broad cultural survey of Chinese morals and values related to business interaction, mostly in mainland China but also in Hong Kong and Taiwan.

Do's and Taboos Around the World edited by Roger Axtell. New York: John Wiley and Sons, 1990. ISBN 0-471-52119-1. $10.95. A humorous and insightful bestseller compiled by the Parker Pen Company on different customs around the world that contains information on Taiwan, China, and Hong Kong.

Gestures: The Do's and Taboos of Body Language Around the World by Roger Axtell. New York: John Wiley and Sons, 1991. ISBN 0-471-53672-5. $9.95. A follow-up to the preceding book focused on body languages of different cultures.

Demographics

AT A GLANCE

The figures given here are the best available, but sources vary in comprehensiveness, in definition of categories, and in reliability. Sources include the United Nations, the World Bank, the International Monetary Fund, and the China State Statistical Bureau. Some figures may include Taiwan, and the agencies that gather the numbers do not always indicate this, but wherever we could discern it we subtracted Taiwan's numbers. Taiwan's population is small compared to all of China's, so it does not affect the statistics greatly. In any case, the value of demographics lies not just in raw numbers but in trends, and the trends illustrated here are accurate.

POPULATION GROWTH RATE AND PROJECTIONS

Average annual growth rate

1979-80	1980-91	1991-2000
1.8%	1.5%	1.3%

Age structure of population (percent)

	1991	2025
Under 15 years old	27.0%	21.2%
15 - 64 years old	66.4%	67.1%
Over 64	5.9%	11.7%

POPULATION

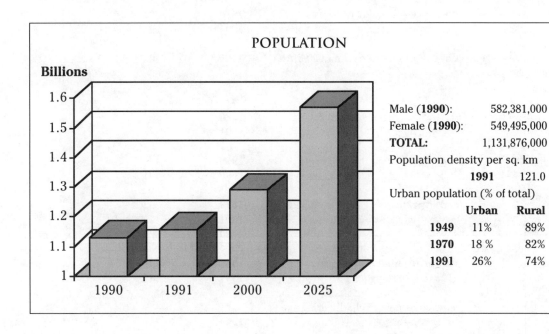

Billions

Male (**1990**):　　582,381,000
Female (**1990**):　　549,495,000
TOTAL:　　1,131,876,000
Population density per sq. km
　　1991　　121.0
Urban population (% of total)

	Urban	Rural
1949	11%	89%
1970	18 %	82%
1991	26%	74%

PRINCIPAL CITIES

(1990 official estimate)

Shanghai	7,830,000
Beijing	7,000,000
Tianjin	5,770,000
Shenyang	4,540,000
Wuhan	3,750,000
Guangzhou	3,580,000
Chongqing	2,980,000
Harbin	2,830,000
Chengdu	2,810,000
Xian	2,760,000
Nanjing	2,500,000
Zibo	2,460,000
Dalian	2,400,000
Jinan	2,320,000
Changchun	2,110,000
Qingdao	2,060,000
Taiyuan	1,960,000
Zhengzhou	1,710,000

POPULATION BY AGE AND SEX, 1990

Age	Total	Male	Female
All ages	1,131,876,000	582,381,000	549,495,000
0 - 1	23,274,000	12,279,000	10,995,000
1 - 4	93,350,000	48,873,000	44,477,000
5 - 9	99,439,000	51,688,000	47,752,000
10 - 14	97,455,000	50,332,000	47,123,000
15 - 19	120,402,000	61,814,000	58,587,000
20 - 24	125,877,000	64,364,000	61,513,000
25 - 29	104,268,000	53,481,000	50,786,000
30 - 34	83,805,000	43,604,000	40,201,000
35 - 39	86,314,000	44,475,000	41,840,000
40 - 44	63,845,000	33,369,000	30,476,000
45 - 49	49,181,000	25,886,000	23,294,000
50 - 54	45,664,000	24,117,000	21,547,000
55 - 59	41,753,000	21,866,000	19,887,000
60 - 64	34,055,000	17,515,000	16,541,000
65 - 69	26,395,000	12,938,000	13,457,000
70 - 74	18,119,000	8,368,000	9,751,000
75 - 79	10,971,000	4,699,000	6,272,000
80 - 84	5,371,000	1,997,000	3,375,000
85 +	2,338,000	716,000	1,622,000

VITAL STATISTICS

Live births:	**1990**	25 million
Birth rate (per 1,000 persons):	**1970**	33
	1991	22
Child mortality rate (per 1,000 births):	**1960**	210
	1975	85
	1990	43
Death rate (per 1,000 persons):	**1970**	8
	1991	7
Life expectancy at birth (years):	**1960**	43
	1990	69
Fertility rate:	**1970**	5.8%
	1991	2.4%
	2000	2.1%
Women of childbearing age:	**1965**	45
(% of all women)	**1991**	56
Married women of childbearing age using contraception:	**1989**	72%

China
Consumer Price Index (CPI)

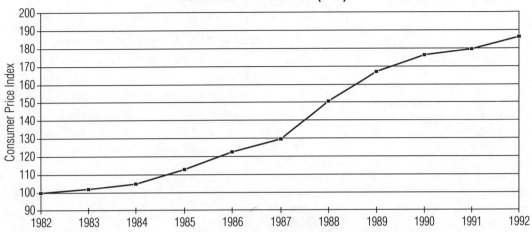

Note: 1993 nationwide inflation averaged 14.5%. Inflation was approximately 20% in the 35 largest metropolitan areas. Sources: Beijing Review, Handbook of Economic Statistics

NATIONAL INCOME

GNP per capita (1991): US$370
Average annual growth rate
1980-91: 7.8 percent
Income Distribution
Percent share of income (1990)

Lowest 20%	6.4
Second 20%	11.0
Third 20%	16.4
Fourth 20%	24.4
Top 20%	41.8
Top 10%	24.6

PRICE INDEX BY CATEGORY

(1980=100)

Category	1989	1990	1991
Food	209	211	216
Fuel	173	186	215
Clothing	138	150	156

AVERAGE ANNUAL
RATE OF INFLATION

1970-80	1980-91	1992	1993
0.9%	5.8%	5.3%	14.5%

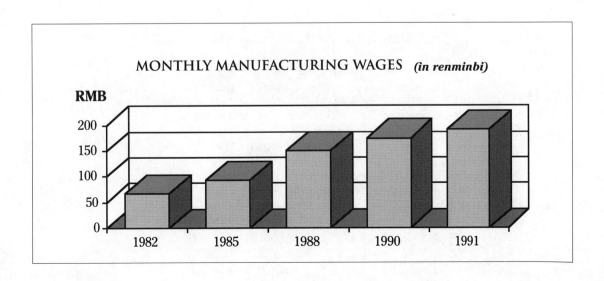

MONTHLY MANUFACTURING WAGES *(in renminbi)*

HEALTH

Health Expenditures **1990**:
 Total: US$13 billion
 Per capita: US$11.00
As a percentage of total GDP:
 3.5 (60% public, 40% private)

Tobacco consumption per year
 (kilograms per capita adult):
 1974-76   1.6
 1990   2.6
 2000   2.9

Chinese Nutrition

Individual Daily Average Consumption

Calories			% of Calorie Requirements			Protein (grams)		
1980	1986	1990	1980	1984/6	1990	1980	1986	1990
2,316	2,580	2,703	107%	119%	125%	54	62	66

EDUCATION—1990

Category	Institutions	Teachers	Enrollment
Kindergarten	172,322	750,000	19,722,000
Primary schools	766,072	5,582,000	122,414,000
General secondary	87,631	3,033,000	45,860,000
Secondary technical	2,956	176,000	1,567,000
Teacher training	1,026	59,000	677,000
Agricultural, vocational	9,164	224,000	2,950,000
Special schools	555	11,000	51,000
Higher education	1,075	395,000	2,063,000

ENERGY CONSUMPTION

kilograms per capita of coal equivalent

1980	1988	1990
557	787	837

MOTOR VEHICLES IN USE, 1989

Passenger	1.4 million
Commercial	3.1 million

COMMUNICATION CHANNELS

Daily Newspapers

Circulation (millions)		Number of dailies	
1986	**1988**	**1986**	**1988**
37.9	39.6	73	78

Televisions and Radios (millions)

	1980	**1985**	**1989**	**1991**	**1992**
TVs	4	10	30	85	125
Radios	55	120	206	250	300

Telephones

	Number (millions)			Per 100 Persons		
	1980	**1987**	**1990**	**1980**	**1987**	**1990**
	4.2	8.1	12.7	0.4	0.7	1.1

Marketing

Marketing China? Consumer goods? Chinese wearing Nike shoes and Esprit clothes and eating Kentucky Fried Chicken and watching TV soap operas? Is this the same China, land of subsistence-level peasants and mystic sages on mountaintops and US$353 annual per capita income and Mao's "Little Red Book" and 89-year-old dictators and the Massacre at Tiananmen Square?

Yes. Welcome to the New World Order, Chinese-style.

The new fact is that many people in China have enough money to spend on what they consider luxuries. Don't let that national per capita income figure throw you. The McKinsey management consulting firm figures that 60 million Chinese have a per capita purchasing power exceeding US$1,000, the magic number above which Chinese can start buying color TVs, washing machines and imported clothing. Five urban areas topped that US$1,000 threshold in 1992: Shenzhen with US$2,500, Shanghai with US$1,700, Guangzhou with US$1,500, Beijing with US$1,400, and Tianjin with US$1,100. The Hong Kong Trade Development Council has its own list, which includes these five cities plus two more in Guangdong Province near Hong Kong: Hangzhou in Zhejian Province near Shanghai, and the major port and open city of Dalian in Liaoning Province. Experts predict the list will grow to between 16 and 50 by the turn of the century and the number of Chinese above the US$1,000 threshold will hit 200 million.

That kind of income means that the Hualian Department Store in Shanghai sold 300,000 customers more than RMB 7 million (about US$700,000, pegged at swap market exchange rates) worth of goods in one day just before the Chinese New Year holidays. It means that people are standing in a line a mile long to get into the Kentucky Fried Chicken restaurant in Shanghai, one of 15 in China and that McDonald's is sure enough of the Chinese desire and ability to pay for a Big Mac that it's opened the world's largest McDonald's in Beijing. It means that Esprit, Playboy, and Nike are all players in the China market (Nike's list of retailers shot up fivefold to more than 200 between 1991 and 1993); that giant Hong Kong retailer Giordano opened more than a dozen stores in China in 1993 alone, stores 10 times the size of its Hong Kong outlets and offering three times the number of styles; and that Hong Kong's Goldlion high-end accessory stores in China have nearly doubled in sales each year since 1988.

Where are the Chinese getting all this money? For one thing, many Chinese don't report all their income—they have more than the government knows about, thanks to a booming black market in labor, goods, services, and foreign exchange. For another, government housing subsidies mean there are no mortgages in China. And look at the amount of household income the Chinese must spend on housing and utilities—between 5 and 10 percent, compared with 20 to 40 percent in other East Asian countries. Combine all this with a national savings rate of 38 percent of the GNP, almost no income taxes, and official restrictions on travel, and you have the individual Chinese citizen, some experts say, who has at least as much to spend as the individual Thai or Malaysian. The peasants are still mired in poverty with real incomes that haven't budged since 1987, but the urban Chinese have all the bicycles, watches and sewing machines they need, and many have refrigerators, TVs (80 percent in some areas) and washing machines. Now they are going after toilets and telephones, air conditioners and video cameras. Cars (and car parts) are not far down the road.

There are some cautionary notes. Retailers eager to break into the market are paying too much for space. China's official inflation rate in 1992 was 6.4 percent, but in July 1993 the real rate hit 15 to 25 percent in the cities. In addition, the government plans to abolish its official, unrealistic foreign exchange rate in 1994, and is probably preparing to make the RMB convertible at some time in the future, further roiling the markets. A new value-added tax (VAT) is also scheduled to go into effect in 1994. The inflation rate alone would be enough to cause a considerable shakeout in the retail market, so quite a few retailers could go belly-up in 1994, and Chinese consumers could find they don't have quite as much discretionary income as they thought. On the other hand, there's no denying the expansiveness and pent-up demand of the Chinese market. The government is trying to proceed cautiously enough to keep the economy from overheating, especially in construction of badly needed infrastructure. Meanwhile, Guangdong Province, China's richest, wants to catch up to Hong Kong, Singapore, Korea, and Taiwan by 2010, and has set annual goals of 13.4 percent growth in gross domestic product (GDP) and single-digit inflation (despite the current 14.5 percent level) until 2000. Guangdong's goals bode well for exports to China as what many observers are calling the greatest consumer boom in history takes hold in the biggest country on the planet.

So, are you ready to market in China?

HOW TO APPROACH THE CHINESE MARKET

Things are changing so fast in China that what was true a few years ago—the only way to export to China is through direct contact with one of the government's foreign trade corporations (FTCs)—is not true now. Gone are the old days when all a trader in a particular commodity had to do was visit Beijing and talk to the sole central government trader for that commodity. Now, independent, government, and semiprivate Chinese importers are spread all over the country—and foreign firms must pound a vast and complex market for sales. Since economic reforms began in 1979, the government has shattered the closed distribution system and allowed free market forces to develop systems that meet true market needs instead of bureaucratic wants. The Ministry of Commerce has relinquished its stranglehold, and now private individuals, collectives, producers, and government departments can buy and sell much more freely. The state has privatized or collectivized most of its small-scale commercial enterprises, and it has liberated its large-scale operations from the bureaucracies while maintaining ownership. And perhaps best of all, the government has given up its central planning role and now keeps price and allocation planning to a minimum.

The Chinese are quick to point out that the gradual dispersion and decentralization of trading rights have been less a case of enlightened top-down leadership than an acknowledgment that enterprises and producers have chipped away at the FTCs' central authority and monopolistic position. They say that the government's actions are largely pro forma recognition of what already exists. Growing gray and black markets are the result of the government's fail-

ure to keep pace with China's rapid economic development. These Chinese analysts are skeptical that the government will be able to anticipate the direction of change in China's trading system in time to be able to shape or mold it. Nor, for that matter, is there much confidence that the government's will be able to identify and adopt appropriate market-oriented policies. Most observers are confident that so much change has already taken place that the government will never regain control of the trading system. The breakdown of the old trade order will result in an increasingly confusing and complicated marketplace. As one academic put it, "The tiger is out of the cage, and government officials are clutching to its back while looking for riding instructions in Adam Smith's Wealth of Nations."

And so here we present instructions for riding the tiger.

NINE WAYS TO APPROACH THE CHINESE MARKET

As the number of state organizations obtaining trading rights soars and the number of goods subject to state trade management plummets, foreign firms in the PRC are finding more opportunities to establish direct contacts with buyers and sellers. These opportunities should continue to increase. Hundreds of foreign firms have set up offices in China since the early 1980s. The relatively high cost of maintaining these offices and staff has led others to use Hong Kong as their base of operations. Still others have chosen trading companies, banks, and consultants to represent their interests and send company personnel to China only when needed. And many firms are forming joint ventures with Chinese or Hong Kong partners to handle distribution and after-sales service.

Determining which Chinese enterprises or institutions you should deal with is sometimes difficult. Buyers include not only state trading corporations but also semiprivate Chinese producers, merchants, and agents. New trading firms are springing up everywhere, and foreign firms have a difficult time checking out the bona fides of these firms: Are these individuals and enterprises not only authorized to import into China but capable of it? For example, 100 Chinese scientific research institutes were granted trading powers at the beginning of 1993, but many of them are still trying to figure out how their own nation's trading system works. A director of a technical development institute said his organization was pleased that the year-long application process had resulted in trading powers for the institute. He confessed, however, that the process of importing and exporting is so complex (even for highly trained scientists) that they have yet to conduct a single transaction, relying instead on their old FTC links.

Ability isn't the only question that the new freedom raises. Another is integrity. The new importers can be "thieves and brigands" as much maybe more than the FTCs because they have little experience in international trading and, unlike the FTCs, no international reputation to uphold.

These are the choices you have in order to approach this market.

1. Go through Hong Kong for an agent, distributor or partner

Preferred for foreign firms with little or no (or bad) experience in dealing directly with China; by far the safest route to the China market, taken by most large and small firms.

Advantages: Government-sponsored Hong Kong Trade Development Council's programs; Hong Kong agents and distributors very active in China with extensive networks of Chinese contacts; wide range of professional support services—banking, insurance, legal, tax, office space, communications, accounting, advertising, shipping, packaging, personnel, translation, printing, marketing; simple and straightforward Hong Kong business and tax laws; freely convertible currency and no restrictions on foreign currency; free port, mostly duty free; agent can play a crucial role in keeping an eye out for evidence of disguised or open bribery, which is becoming increasingly widespread in the PRC, particularly in the southern part of the country.

Disadvantages: Middleman fees raise cost of product in market; marketing is limited by agent's preferences, experience and biases.

2. Go through a Government FTC

Preferred for suppliers of raw materials, telecommunications equipment, and heavy machinery, and for government procurement.

Advantages: Financial strength; governmental authority; long-term experience; have a memory and a sense of balance while individual enterprises may not; often push a miserly contract in one project and balance it off by a more generous reward in another.

Disadvantages: Excessively bureaucratic; often antiquated methods; extremely slow to respond; inexperienced in modern international trade.

3. Establish a representative office

Preferred for products needing heavy after-sales service and cultivation of close relationships with clients—for example, software, computers, appliances, sophisticated or large-scale equipment.

Advantages: Allows you to retain a competitive edge in prompt service, customer commitment, and consulting aspects of a sale; suggests to your buyers that you have a permanent presence in domestic markets, promoting an image of stability and long-term availability.

Disadvantages: Cost of office, plus added costs for specializing for customer's needs.

4. Exhibit at trade fairs

Preferred for promotion of existing products and introduction of new ones; available only if trade fair includes your product.

Advantages: Allows contacts with major and smaller buyers and foreign and local industry representatives; hands-on demonstration techniques increase product awareness.

Disadvantages: Market limited to attendees; competition with other products targeted for same industry may be intense.

5. Get a distributor or agent in China

Preferred for consumer products with well-established competitors or for nonconsumer products (i.e., business and vertical market applications software, industrial machinery, electronic parts) aimed at government or commercial institutions.

Advantages: Removes need to create your own marketing structure; knows local needs and customs; often aware of opportunities before bids are announced; knows ins and outs of bidding; monitors and promotes smaller sales, which can add up over time.

Disadvantages: Middleman fees raise cost of product in market; marketing is limited by agent's preferences, experience and biases; rapidly changing system in China means many middlemen are inexperienced, while others may be unauthorized, incompetent, or corrupt.

6. Do direct marketing

Preferred for consumer products (small appliances, consumer electronic products) but also common among industries (including factories) that want to avoid middleman costs.

One option is to contact local importers who market through warehouse stores or other retail outlets.

Advantages: direct access to large consumer market.

Disadvantages: extreme competition with other producers because such stores market a large number of products.

Another option is to advertise in industry-specific trade journals or magazines.

Advantages: Economical and effective means to increase product awareness among large number of consumers; good for testing the market.

Disadvantages: Limited time; costs of extended advertising can be high.

7. Open your own distributorship or retail stores

Preferred for companies with a large array of products to offer (for example, auto accessories).

Advantages: Direct market access, which allows you to keep prices low and competitive (by eliminating middlemen), control sales environment (type of building, training of sales personnel), and improves quality and service (by reducing the gap between you and the end user).

Disadvantages: High cost to establish, maintain, and staff; need to overcome bias of consumers towards already established local merchants; bureaucratic, language and cultural barriers.

8. Negotiate a joint venture with a local company

Preferred for high-tech products that must be modified for sale in local market, that are in growing international demand, and that are protected by copyright, patent, or similar intellectual property laws (for example, high-tech software).

Advantages: Direct resource for creating specialized products aimed at particular needs of consumers in domestic market; allows use of local company's marketing and other contacts; allows for good after-sales service.

Disadvantages: Bureaucratic delays and fumbling; allows technology transfer, potential infringement on design and technology rights, and resulting enforcement problems—a real problem in China.

9. Enter a bid on projects

Primarily for sales to public organizations.

Advantages: Successful bid may further your product's reputation in domestic markets.

Disadvantages: Price concessions may be needed for success; obstructionist, obfuscatory regulations for foreign firms; official corruption.

ADVERTISING

"Advertising in China" is not an oxymoron. No longer does the Communist government see advertising as a tool of capitalist running dogs out to subvert and swindle the masses into addiction to consumerism. No, the big advertising news in 1993 was a full front page of propaganda in Shanghai's biggest daily newspaper, *Wen Hui Bao*—a hard-sell ad on the benefits of household air conditioners.

How could such a drastic reversal take place so rapidly? The main reason is that the government has come down solidly on the side of a "socialist market economy" in which such practices are possible. This and the relative inexperience of Chinese firms in matters of advertising opens the door to such aggressive marketing. In this case, the pro-

ducer, Xileng ("Western Cold") Company wanted to promote its brand to fill a felt need in hot, humid Shanghai among newly affluent consumers, and was willing to pay for a prominent display ad to do so. The edges are rough, but the willingness to learn is definitely there.

Elsewhere in Consumerist, Marketist China, Beijing residents listen to radio cowboys tout the benefits of Marlboro cigarettes; consumer products commercials between popular TV soap operas in Xian feature blond, blue-eyed Westerners; government officials in Huaiyin drive around in cars that display—for free—signs advertising the particularly strong liquor of a local distillery that pays US$78 million in taxes annually; children sing the jingle from TV commercials featuring the high-tech superhero Captain Vermox, who, with his ray gun, metallic regalia and flowing cape, teaches children not to be afraid or embarrassed about having worms and that Vermox kills worms easily and painlessly.

Advertising in China has been reborn. It's grown beyond its infancy and toddler stages. It's now at the 9-year-old boy stage—hyperactive, loud, annoying, and eager to grow up—and, with billings jumping 30 to 50 percent a year, it's certainly doing just that.

In this section, you'll get a hard look at China's advertising system, and longtime consultant Xu Baiyi gives expert advice on how to reach the Chinese consumer.

Reality check

Not all in Chinese advertising is what it seems, and everything else is changing fast. The three main avenues of advertising—agencies, print and television—are widening their influence. It's through these avenues that you will probably advertise your product, so it's essential to be able to see through the hyperbole to the reality.

Advertising agencies

Currently, advertisers can employ ad agencies to produce their ads or commercials. But to buy time or space, advertisers themselves usually have to deal directly with the media, who are short on experience and swamped with clients. This situation developed because ad rates were so low that the media earned too little to make cost-effective use of agencies. The government plans—supposedly some time in 1994—to put an end to the chaos by making ad agencies the middlemen between advertisers and media and allowing the agencies to charge a 15-percent commission to take advantage of recently skyrocketing ad rates. Media companies will be able to form their own ad agencies, which will have to be entirely separate from the parent companies in management and budgets. The current system allows merged operations and budgets.

Although China has more than 15,000 ad agencies, more than 12,000 are divisions of government-owned media companies; about 3,700 are collectives; more than 600 are private; and about 100 are Chinese-foreign joint ventures. And only a very few could be called professional by international standards. Still, advertising expenditures rose 40 percent in 1992 and more than 30 percent in 1993, topping the US$1 billion mark. And leading the growth are the joint ventures with billings leaping 100 percent a year, although many have yet to see a profit because of rates that are still too low. These companies are the ones in China best suited to help advertise consumer products.

Newspapers and magazines

There is no Audit Bureau of Circulation in China, so advertisers must view circulation claims with some suspicion. So far there has been no hard evidence of fraud, as there has in Korea. But questionable circulation claims are just the tip of the print ad iceberg: most newspapers have only four pages, and ad space is often booked months in advance, so just getting your ad into a paper at all can be difficult, let alone at the right time and placement. This messy situation explains the stink that Hong Kong retailer Giordano created in 1992 when it not only bought all the space in a Guangzhou newspaper but paid extra to kick out previously booked ads. The newspaper in effect sold its space to the highest bidder, infuriating other advertisers, who rightly cried foul, and giving other newspapers a precedent that would be hard not to follow. Be ready to pay more than specified in your "agreement" and be grateful when your ad runs when and where you want.

Television

It's hard for print media to beat China Central Television's (CCTV) claim of 600 million viewers for its evening news show—except perhaps by telling an even bigger lie. If that figure were true, it would mean that more than 85 percent of the people in the country over the age of 20 watch the show. The rest—about 110 million—presumably either don't have good viewing habits or don't have televisions. Now for the truth. The 1992 estimate for number of TV sets in the PRC was about 125 million; for number of viewers, about 500 million. On the other hand, most Western advertisers would be deliriously happy to reach an audience one-tenth that size.

Such exaggerated claims have caused advertising rates to climb steeply in recent years. In 1993, CCTV and Shanghai Television (STV) each announced that they would raise ad rates for foreign advertisers by 30 percent and for joint ventures by 100 percent. They are getting what they ask. Commercials can be broadcast only between programs, and time is as short as newspaper space. Every day, representatives of more than 180 would-be advertisers jam CCTV headquarters clamoring for commercial time. Most don't get it. The ones who do are grateful to be able to pay whatever is demanded. The rate increases may seem extortionate, but if so, it's extortion on a Chinese scale—the rates pale in comparison to those in Western countries, especially given the size of the audience.

REACHING THE CHINESE CONSUMER*

Planning an advertising strategy to reach China's burgeoning consumer market can be a dizzying task; 1,076 newspapers, 2,197 magazines, 1,211 radio stations, and 747 television stations all accept advertising. Nearly a quarter of a million billboards, thousands of neon signs, illuminated street signs (commonly called light boxes), and window displays are also available to carry your message at reasonable cost. With so many options, the selection of the right media format is essential to the success of any company's advertising campaign.

Where to start

Major urban centers are the best places to introduce your name to the Chinese public. Given China's vast size, it is difficult to implement a nationwide marketing strategy from the outset. Instead, many foreign invested enterprises (FIEs) have scored success by using regional media first, concentrating on large cities such as Guangzhou, Shanghai, and Beijing. After acquiring a foothold and gaining market share for their products, they then expand their sales efforts to other cities and rural areas. S.C. Johnson & Son, Inc.'s joint venture, Shanghai Johnson Ltd., for example, used such a strategy: its Agree shampoo was first introduced and advertised in Shanghai in 1988, and has now become popular nationwide.

The most effective way to create an impression on Chinese consumers is to use more than one medium. Most FIEs employ a mix of television and newspaper advertisements to reach a large audience. For instance, Shanghai Santana's successful newspaper advertising campaign uses large Chinese characters, such as *qu* (fun), to describe the experience of driving their car. The companion television spot shows a famous calligrapher writing the big characters. Similarly, as part of a promotional campaign last year, Johnson & Johnson sponsored a baby care series on Shanghai TV and placed ads in the city's weekly TV guide and local dailies. This mix of media reinforces the advertiser's message and disseminates it

* *"Where To Place Your Ad For Maximum Effect,"* by Xu Baiyi (*The China Business Review, November-December 1992; reprinted with permission*)

more widely. Generally speaking, foreign companies are charged for advertisements in US dollars, while domestic firms and most joint ventures pay in *renminbi*.

Fit to print

Most foreign companies advertising in China should include at least some advertisements in newspapers. While no exact circulation figures are available, the high readership rates of Chinese newspapers make them the country's most popular advertising medium—currently, they run about $15.6 million worth of ads every year. Because of late printing and delivery times, these papers—all published by central or provincial-level governments—are not read at the breakfast table or on the way to work. Instead, most dailies are sent to offices where they circulate among quite a few people.

The titles of Chinese newspapers usually give a clear indication of their intended audience, making it easy to identify whether a publication is an appropriate advertising vehicle. Among the leading publications, *Renmin Ribao* (People's Daily), the official organ of China's Communist Party, is read by Party members and those who work in government, industrial and commercial organizations. This paper is often the first choice for advertisers who wish to reach top decision makers and a national audience. Shanghai's *Jiefang Ribao* (Liberation Daily), also read by decision makers, is another favorite place to advertise both capital and consumer goods. Other good newspapers for advertisements include *Jingji Ribao* (Economic Daily), which is read in economic circles, and *Gongren Ribao* (Worker's Daily), which is read by over a million workers.

Evening newspapers, which are usually delivered to homes and read during leisure hours, can also be good advertising vehicles. Local and foreign consumer goods manufacturers advertise heavily in *Xin Min Evening News*, a Shanghai publication that has about 1.5 million readers, many of whom reside in other cities. Afternoon regional newspapers provide an effective and economical way to reach specific local populations through print.

China also has newspapers that attract audiences by specific interests. *Wen Hui Bao,* read mostly by intellectuals, is good for advertising cultural events. *Zhongguo Tiyu Bao* (China Sports), in contrast, caters to sports fans, while *Zhongguo Qing Nian Bao* (China Youth Gazette) is read by young people. All these publications provide a relatively inexpensive way to reach a highly targeted audience.

Magazines are another cost-effective advertising medium for foreign companies in China. Most of the magazines that accept advertising have national circulations. Copies are sold by subscription and through retail news stands. Most Chinese magazines clearly fall into professional, trade, or consumer categories, making it easy to identify which magazines might be effective advertising vehicles.

Another type of print ad, direct mail advertising, is still a novelty in China. Because Chinese people do not receive many fliers in the mail, they read and consider direct mail more carefully than do Westerners. The Chinese government appears open to the idea of direct mail; in 1991, the Shanghai post office launched a campaign to encourage firms to mail commercial messages. These messages can be mailed only at first class rates; businesses are not entitled to the cheaper bulk rates common in other countries. High international postage rates, moreover, generally make it uneconomical to send mass mailings from overseas. The best method is to hire a local Chinese advertising agency to address wrappers and mail fliers. Currently underused, direct mail is an area with strong potential for future advertising efforts.

On the air

Since the first television commercial aired in China in 1979, TV has assumed more and more of companies' advertising budgets and is now closing in on newspapers as the most popular advertising medium in China. Viewership has rapidly expanded—China Central Television (CCTV) now claims an audience of 600 million for its evening news. Consequently, TV ad rates and revenues have risen steeply over the past few years. In addition to nationwide Central TV, 746 municipal and provincial television stations also accept advertising.

Television ads are generally used to establish brand recognition and highlight the special characteristics of a product to set it apart from its competition. The ads for Boeing Co., for example, have helped the company gain a reputation for safety and comfort among the Chinese population, many of whom may never even ride in a plane.

The format for television advertising in China is partially responsible for this emphasis on unique qualities. TV commercials can be broadcast only between programs when viewers are likely to switch channels, get a snack, or engage in other activities. Ads for similar products are often aired together so that the audience can compare claims. Eye-catching ads, therefore, are a must if a company's products are to stand out from its competition's.

One ploy used by advertisers to eliminate competing ads is to sponsor a program, an approach used by Shanghai Johnson & Johnson, Ltd., which backed a prime time baby care series. The four, five-minute vignettes featured a young couple puzzling over care for their newborn infant. Each ended with a Johnson & Johnson baby-care expert dispensing advice. Aided by tie-in print ads, the series garnered much consumer attention and boosted product sales. Similarly,

HELPING YOUR COMPANY LEARN TO LOVE EXPORT MARKETING
Five In-house Rules

1. Eliminate as much guesswork as you can

Expert export consultation is usually time and money well spent. You need a well thought out marketing plan. You cannot get into successful exporting by accident. It's not a simple matter of saying, "Let's sell our product in China." You need to know that your product will, in fact, sell and how you're going to sell it. First, do you need to do anything obvious to your product? Who is your buyer? How are you going to find him? How is he going to find you? Do you need to advertise? Exhibit at a trade fair? How much can you expect to sell? Can you sell more than one product? A plan may be the only way you can begin to uncover hidden traps and costs before you get overly involved in a fiasco. While you may be able to see an opportunity, knowing how to exploit it isn't necessarily a simple matter. You must plot and plan and prepare.

2. Just go for it

We're not suggesting you throw caution to the winds, but sometimes your "plan" may be to use a shotgun approach - rather than the more tightly targeted rifle approach- and just blast away to see if you hit anything. You can narrow things down later. If your product is new to the market, there may be precious little marketing information, and you may have essentially no other choice. Two scenarios illustrate these points: Two companies decide to begin selling similar products in East Asia, which has never seen such products before. Company A hires a market research firm, which spends six months and US$50,000 to come up with a detailed plan. Company Z sends its president to a trade fair—not to exhibit but just to look around and meet people. He follows that trip up with two others. On the last one his new associates present him with his first order. Company Z also spent six months and US$50,000 investigating doing export business, but it has an order to show for it, while Company A only has an unproven plan.

3. Get your bosses to back you up and stick with the program

Whether your company consists of 10, 50, 500, or 5,000 people—or just you— and whether you're the head of the company, the chief financial officer, or the person leading the exporting charge, there must be an explicit commitment to sustain the initial setbacks and financial requirements of export marketing. You must be sure that the firm is committed to the long-term: Don't waste money by abandoning the project too early.

International marketing consultants report that because results don't show up in the first few months, the international marketing and advertising budget is *invariably* the first to be cut in any company that doesn't have money to burn. Such short-sighted budgetary decisions are responsible for innumerable premature failures in exporting.

The hard fact is that exports don't bring in money as quickly as domestic sales. It takes time and persistence for an international marketing effort to succeed. There are many hurdles to overcome—personal, political, cultural, and legal, among others. It will be at least six to nine months before you and your overseas associates can even begin to expect to see glimmers of success. And it may be even longer. Be patient, keep a close but not a suffocating watch on your international marketing efforts, and give the venture a chance to develop.

4. Avoid an internal tug-of-war

Consultants report that one of the biggest obstacles to successful export marketing in larger companies is internal conflict between divisions within a company. Domestic marketing battles international marketing while each is also warring with engineering, and everybody fights with the bean counters. All the complex strategies, relationship building, and legal and cultural accommodations that export marketing requires mean that support and teamwork are crucial to the success of the venture.

5. Stick with export marketing even when business booms at home

Exporting isn't something to fall back on when your domestic market falters. Nor is it something to put on the back burner when business is booming at home. It is difficult to ease your way into exporting. All the complex strategies, relationship-building, legal and cultural accommodations, and financial and management investment, and blood, sweat, and tears that export marketing requires means that a clear commitment is necessary from the beginning. Any other attitude as good as dooms the venture from the start, and you may as well forget it. We can't overstress this aspect: Take the long-range view or don't play at all. Decide that you're going to export and that you're in it for the long haul as a viable money-making full-fledged division within your company.

McDonald's Corporation spokesperson Brad Trask, commenting on his company's overwhelming international success, notes, "We're a very long-term focused company. We do things with patience; we're very deliberate. We're there to stay, not to take the money and run." And Texas Instruments, which has suffered recent losses in its semiconductor business, has made a considered move into long-term joint ventures in East Asia, banking that these investments will provide a big payoff five years down the road.

Marlboro sponsors programs such as "Marlboro Sports World," which display the company's logo despite a national ban on TV cigarette ads.

Television-related publications are also good advertising vehicles, as viewers often consult their local TV listings for program information. These publications have large circulations and, given their week-long lifespan, are inexpensive. For example, the 8-page Beijing tabloid *Zhongguo Dianshi Bao* (China TV Weekly) has a readership of 3 million, while its Shanghai counterpart, *Meizhou Guangbo Dianshi* (Weekly Radio Broadcasting and TV) has a circulation of 2.8 million. China's 80-plus TV guides have a combined circulation of over 40 million. All accept advertising, but each one must be approached individually.

Despite the growth of the TV audience in China, radio remains a popular and important medium. Radio's broadcast area—basically the entire country—is larger than that of television, and radio programs reach consumers unable to read newspapers. Currently, around 1,200 regional and national broadcast stations accept advertising. Though radio's percentage of total advertising revenue dropped from 7.7 percent in 1983 to 4 percent in 1991, audiences are still large and ad rates remain a bargain (see table).

While consumer goods make up the bulk of Chinese radio ads—the Coca-Cola Co., for instance, broadcasts a 10-second message every morning before the 6:15 weather forecast on Shanghai Radio—other products can also be marketed effectively. Da An Real Estate sold all of its available apartments in two months after advertising on Shanghai Radio, though previous advertising efforts in national and overseas newspapers had yielded disappointing results. Much of the success of the campaign was attributed to being able to reach consumers relaxing at home.

Taking it to the streets

The heavy traffic and bustling crowds typical of most Chinese cities guarantee large audiences for outdoor ads such as billboards. Although it is impossible to obtain precise data, several million people are estimated to pass through Shanghai's main thoroughfares every day. Other urban areas offer similarly heavy street traffic. This exposure,

NEWSPAPER AD RATES, LATE 1992

TITLE	CIRCULATION	DISTRIBUTION	RATE PER COLUMN CM.		
			Local	Joint Venture	Foreign
People's Daily	4.5 million	national	RMB 220	RMB 275	US$130
Economic Daily	1 million	national	RMB 90	RMB 90	US$60
Beijing Daily	700,000	Beijing	RMB 76	RMB 114	US$50
Wenhui Bao	970,000	Shanghai	RMB 150	RMB 150	US$50
Guangzhou Daily	510,000	Guangzhou	RMB 125	RMB 150	HK$380
China Daily (English)	150,000	national	RMB 50	US$26	US$26

RADIO AD RATES, LATE 1992

STATION BROADCAST	AREA	RATE FOR 30 SECONDS		
		Local	Joint Venture	Foreign
CPBS	national	RMB 600	RMB 690	US$400
Beijing Radio	Beijing	RMB 250	RMB 325	US$238
Shanghai Radio	Shanghai	RMB 400	RMB 400	US$140
Guangzhou Radio	Guangzhou	RMB 115	RMB 115	US$102

OUTDOOR ADVERTISING RATES

TYPE	RATE (US$)	RENTAL PERIOD
Billboards	35-80 per square meter per month	6 months
Neon signs	60-80 per square meter per month	3 years
Bus shelter*	7,000 per shelter	1 year
Buses, trolleys*	10,000 for three vehicles	6 months
Light box	negotiable	negotiable

* Shanghai only
Source: Xu Baiyi, The China Business Review, Nov.–Dec. 1992

combined with low prices and the long life of bill-board ads (usually six months), makes billboards the most popular mode of outdoor advertising.

Most domestic advertising agencies rent out bill-boards, which are often constructed in rows of 10 or more. Because billboards in China are of various sizes, paste-on posters are not usually used; instead, most billboards are hand painted. Cut-outs (portions of the ad that extend beyond the frame of the bill-board), three-dimensional effects, and simple ad copy are often utilized to attract the fleeting attention of pedestrians.

In addition to large billboards, other ad sites dot downtown cities. Light boxes, which hang from build-ings as shop signs, are rented out to advertisers by store owners. Pedestrian bridges and sidewalk rail-ings in Guangzhou and Shanghai sport advertise-ments designed to keep product names in shoppers' heads. Arrangements for these ads can be made through almost any Chinese ad agency. Some of the most dramatic street advertisements are window displays, which are created by advertisers who rent the window space. The facade of Shanghai No. 1 De-partment Store, for instance, contains a row of 18 picture windows that can be leased from the store.

Another advertising option is plexiglass bus shel-ters; Coca-Cola's Sprite and Fanta, the first shelter advertisers, are still placing ads in these locations. The company credits its initial Shanghai bus shelter ads with helping boost sales in the city. Following Shanghai's lead, Beijing and Tianjin municipalities, and the provinces of Guangdong, Zhejiang, Jiangsu, and Sichuan are also introducing bus shelter ads. The local municipal planning bureau in each loca-tion generally handles advertising requests. Adver-tisers not content with the shelters may want to con-sider advertising on the buses and trolleys them-selves. Pepsi Cola International, one of the first ad-vertisers on Shanghai's trolleys, says the novel place-ment of its ads on trolley fronts drummed up cus-tomer awareness and hence sales of Pepsi and 7-Up. Salem cigarettes and other advertisers are now also placing such ads.

Companies looking for a little more flash may want to consider neon signs, which have sprouted up in Chinese cities over the last few years. More than 60 large neon signs now light up Shanghai's skyline. As the number of skyscrapers in China's major cities in-creases, their roofs should be considered ideal loca-tions for neon signs, which can be seen for miles.

TELEVISION AD RATES, LATE 1992

STATION	BROADCAST AREA	DAY	RATE FOR 30 SECONDS		
			Local Firm	Joint Venture	Foreign Firms
CCTV2	national	Mon-Fri	RMB 4,000-10,000	RMB 6,000-13,000	US$4,000-8,000
		Sat-Sun	RMB 5,000-11,000	RMB 7,500-14,000	US$5,000-9,000
CCTV8	Beijing	Mon-Sun	RMB 4,000	RMB 5,500	US$3,000
BTV6	Beijing	Mon-Fri	RMB 4,500	RMB 4,500	US$1,600
		Sat-Sun	RMB 5,700	RMB 5,700	US$2,000
BTV21	Beijing	Mon-Sun	RMB 1,500	RMB 1,500	US$1,000
STV8, 20	Shanghai	Mon-Fri	RMB 1,200-3,000	RMB 1,800-4,500	US$500-1,800
		Sat-Sun	RMB 1,400-3,500	RMB 1,800-5,250	US$500-2,160
			50% premium	50% premium	20% premium
GDTV14	Guangdong	Mon-Fri	RMB 300-2,200	RMB 450-3,300	HK$1,800-12,900
		Sat-Sun	RMB 345-2,530	RMB 518-3,795	HK$1,800-16,770
GDTV2	Guangdong	Mon-Fri	RMB 500-1,000	RMB 750-1,500	HKS1,800-9,100
		Sat-Sun	RMB 575-1,150	RMB 863-1,725	HK$1,800-11,830
			50% premium on holidays	50% premium on holidays	30% premium on holidays

Source: Saatchi & Saatchi Advertising China; reprinted with permission

English awareness now

A carefully planned advertising campaign does bring results. For instance, Raid insecticide's summer 1990 inaugural ad campaign used well-coordinated television and newspaper ads, billboards, neon signs, bus panels, light boxes, window displays, and posters to create a strong and immediate impact on consumers. An autumn 1991 survey of Shanghai pedestrians revealed that 92 percent of the sample knew the Raid brand name.

The growing popularity—and sophistication—of ad campaigns in China is attracting more large names in the business. Ogilvy & Mather; Dentsu, Young & Rubicam; J. Walter Thompson; and Saatchi & Saatchi have already opened offices or established joint ventures in China. They have brought the advanced technology and modern advertising and marketing techniques needed to further develop China's advertising industry. They are not without competition, however; 20 other foreign advertising firms have entered China this year, and domestic advertising agencies, such as Guangdong White Horse Advertising and Shanghai Advertising & Decorating Corp., are rapidly improving their services.

Xu Baiyi, an advertising writer, lecturer, and consultant, has over 60 years experience in the industry. He is the author of Marketing to China: One Billion New Customers *(National Textbook Co., 1989), and has lectured as a visiting scholar at the University of Illinois and Michigan State University.*

MAJOR MARKETS

China is too vast and varied a country to market to as a whole. With 22 provinces, three municipalities and five autonomous regions to choose from and a wide range of per capita disposable income, exporters seeking success need a careful pick-and-choose approach. One important thing to remember is that supply, not demand, drives the Chinese market. Creating demand is not a problem; even a third-rate ad campaign can tell enough people all they want to know. The problem is getting your product to them, at the right time and the right place. Distribution is the weak link here. That's one major reason why you should focus your marketing and distribution efforts. Don't try to take on the whole country; not even the biggest multinationals do that. Instead, focus on one or a few of the richest cities and provinces. This section reviews China's major markets.

CHINA'S MAJOR CITIES AND SPECIAL ZONES*

Where to Invest?

Would-be investors in China face many difficult questions. One of the earliest choices that must be made is that of where to look for business opportunities. This is a crucial decision, which bears heavily on the eventual selection of Chinese partners, whether for joint ventures, trade or other forms of cooperation.

Deciding where to locate a business depends upon the particular needs of the business. Important considerations may include infrastructure, availability or proximity of raw materials, nature and strength of the industrial base, quantity and quality of labor, intellectual infrastructure—access to universities or research institutions and cultural factors. This is a matter of common sense and the economics of different industries.

In China, for example, the Pearl River Delta is an increasingly attractive location for light industry. The economy of this area is becoming more and more closely integrated with that of Hong Kong. With labor in short supply in Hong Kong, hundreds of thousand of jobs have been created in towns and cities such as Shenzhen, Zhuhai, and Zhongshan, as well as in Guangzhou itself, as manufacturing of a wide range of light industrial products, including notably textiles and toys, has been transferred across the border to take advantage of plentiful, lower-cost labor.

China's northeastern provinces, notably Liaoning and Jilin, are foremost in heavy industry, partly be-

---

Excerpted from China Perspectives (Fourth Edition, August 1993) by Arthur Andersen & Co, SC; reprinted with permission.

cause of abundant coal and partly because of substantial investment by the Japanese during their occupation of Manchuria in the 1930s and 40s. Other areas famous for heavy industry include Shanghai and the cities of the middle Yangtze, notably Wuhan and Chongqing.

If intellectual infrastructure is an important consideration, Beijing is the main rival to Shanghai. The capital enjoys the greatest concentration of seats of higher learning and is increasingly turning to new technology, notably computer hardware and software development in the high-technology zone at Haidian in the northwest part of the city, which is also the university quarter. Other universities and research institutes in different parts of the country also have strong reputations in specific fields.

With the completion of the Beijing-Tianjin-Tanggu Expressway, northern China's two largest cities are now only one-and-a-half hours apart. The time taken to travel from Beijing's city center to Tianjin's city center is little more than it takes from Beijing's further suburbs to Tiananmen Square. It will soon be realistic to treat the Tianjin-Beijing area as one massive metropolis, bringing together the intellectual, administrative, commercial, and cultural resources of the capital, the solid industrial base and long trading experience of Tianjin, and some of the finest port facilities in China at Tanggu. This will surely offer a formidable investment environment at the front door of the vast hinterland of the North China Plain.

REGIONAL POLICY

History of the Zones

The creation of four Special Economic Zones (SEZs) at Shenzhen, Zhuhai, Shantou, and Xiamen was announced in July 1979. This was billed as an experiment to allay the worst fears of the skeptics and the doubters. The policy of creating special zones had the advantage of confining any dangerous developments within narrowly delimited geographical bounds. It was easier to justify a limited experiment to those who were initially nervous about departing from old policies.

Nor was the choice of the sites an accident. The location of three of the four zones at sites adjacent to Hong Kong, Macao and Southeast Asia, and one facing Taiwan 165 nautical miles across the Taiwan Strait, would make it easier to reach the international market, to introduce foreign capital and advanced technology, and to build up an export-oriented economy.

In April 1984 the government held a seminar to evaluate the achievements of the SEZs. Apparently satisfied with their performance, it decided to open up a further 14 Coastal Cities, Dalian, Qinhuangdao, Tianjin, Yantai, Qingdao, Lianyungang, Nantong, Shanghai, Ningbo, Wenzhou, Fuzhou, Guangzhou, Zhanjiang, and Beihai. Special privileges were accorded to these cities generally and a particularly favorable climate offered within the Economic and Technological Development Zones (ETDZs), which were to be established in each city to facilitate the introduction of foreign capital and technology. Most of these so-called 14 Coastal Cities have a history of commerce and trade.

Except for Wenzhou and Beihai, all the other 12 coastal open cities set up ETDZs. In Shanghai, three ETDZs were established, in Minghang, Hongqiao and Caohejing respectively. These ETDZs are otherwise known as Small SEZs (SSEZs). They are small, compared with Shenzhen, Zhuhai, Shantou, and Xiamen. And they are special, because they implement preferential policies similar to those available in the SEZs.

In 1988 Hainan Island was designated as an SEZ, bringing the total number of SEZs to five. After the designation of the SEZs and the open Coastal Cities, a series of other zones were created. Open Economic Zones were designated in the three major deltas, the Yangtze River Delta, the Pearl River Delta and the Southern Fujian Delta. Not long afterwards followed the opening of the Liaodong Peninsula, Shandong Peninsula and the Bohai Bay rim area. So with the designation of the SEZs, the 14 Coastal Cities and the open deltas and peninsulas, three different tiers of open coastal economic development belts have come into shape, covering a total area of 320,000 square km (123,550 square miles) and including 291 cities and countries, with a population of 200 million. In April 1990 the Chinese government approved the stepping up of the development of the new Pudong Development Zone in Shanghai. The Pudong Development Zone is a triangular area to the east of the Huangpu River, covering an area of 350 square km (135 square miles), roughly the same size as the present city proper of Shanghai. The Chinese government subsequently designated additional ETDZs, bringing the total number to 27.

Aside from the above open economic development areas, a number of new and high-technology development zones and tourism zones have been established in many major cities. In addition, all the provinces and autonomous regions, except for Tibet, are open to foreign investment. It is important that the investors carefully check the environment and incentives available because conditions change rapidly.

Hinterland Cooperation

There is little doubt that while China as a whole has become more prosperous as a result of reform, the gap between the rich coastal strip and the relatively impoverished interior has widened. Take Yunnan Province for example. In 1989 the province's economy grew at about 5.5 percent as opposed to11.6 percent for the country as a whole.

The government has reacted to the mounting pressure from the interior in a number of ways. It has started to open up trade and set up special zones along China's long inland borders, notably with the former Soviet Union, and it has placed great emphasis on horizontal cooperation between cities and enterprises in the interior and their counterparts on the coast.

Inland Economic Zones Along the northeastern border with Russia, in Heilongjiang Province and the Inner Mongolia Autonomous Region, the cities of Manzhouli, Suifenhe, Heihe, and Tongjiang are reviving their cross-border commercial contacts. And in 1988 a further seven border towns—Huichun, Mishan, Hulin, Raohe, Luobei, Jiaqin, and Mohe—were authorized as commercial ports for cross-border trade.

Similar arrangements are also made for the western sector of the border in Xinjiang. The border and adjacent provinces such as Jilin and Gansu are now permitted to conduct trade, barter and other types of countertrade, technology transfer agreements, and joint ventures with the former Soviet Union.

In 1991, there were 16 Chinese cities and towns along the 7,000 km-long border doing cross-border business with the former Soviet Union. The border trade volume between the two countries reached US$1 billion in 1990, 10 times as much as in 1987.

Joint ventures have also been set up in both China and Russia. During the 1987-1990 period the former Soviet Union set up seven joint ventures in China, with a total Soviet investment of US$8.6 million, while China established 34 joint ventures in the former Soviet Union, investing US$28 million in total.

Another area for cooperation is labor export. The former Soviet Far East is critically short of labor and, in the past few years, 100,000 workers, notably forestry workers, have been brought in from North Korea, Vietnam, and Cuba. China is now beginning to meet this need, particularly because China desperately needs timber. By mid-1991 45 labor-cooperation or contracting companies specializing in labor export to the former Soviet Union had sprung up in China. Compensation trade deals involving Soviet resources, Japanese technology, and Chinese labor are also contemplated.

With the improvement of China's relations with Vietnam, trade, barter, and other types of countertrade as well as technology transfers between Chinese border provinces and Vietnam are being resumed.

Horizontal Economic Links In a further response to the problems of the interior, the government is placing greater emphasis on cooperation both among the interior provinces themselves and between the interior and the coast.

In mid-1988 the government drew attention to the types of cooperation between the coast and inland

areas and set up examples for others to follow. It cited the fact that since 1985, RMB 3 billion and 34,000 skilled or trained personnel had moved from Beijing, Shanghai, Tianjin, Liaoning, Jiangsu, Guangdong, and Zhejiang to the western provinces of Xinjiang, Tibet, and Ningxia, Qinghai, Gansu, Shaanxi, Guizhou, Yunnan, and Sichuan. It further announced that 15,800 cooperation projects had been concluded during the same period.

In a report in June 1988, the *China Daily* raised the example of "interregional economic cooperation between six provinces and three cities in Central and Southern China." The six provinces—Guangdong, Hunan, Hubei, Henan, Hainan, and the Guangxi Zhuang Autonomous Region—together with the cities of Wuhan, Guangzhou, and Shenzhen were reported to have set up 260 joint ventures.

Since the mid-1980s the eight provinces and autonomous regions in the Yellow River Delta—particularly Shandong, Henan, and Shaanxi—have cooperated closely in trade, economic development, and tourism.

The southwestern provinces—Sichuan, Guizhou, and Yunnan provinces and the Guangxi Zhuang Autonomous Region—have also banded together in an organization headquartered in Chongqing to coordinate economic development.

In order to improve their own prospects, many of the interior provinces have been investing along the coast, notably in port facilities. Thus, Shaanxi is investing RMB 30 million in Tianjin. Further south, Henan, Shaanxi, Gansu, and Anhui are investing in the port at Lianyungang. More than 85 percent of provinces have companies set up in Shenzhen.

In a further initiative, the provincial and municipal governments are promoting economic cooperation along the length of the Lunghai railway, a corridor stretching from Urumqi in the far northwest to Lianyungang in Jiangsu. When the new cross-border link between China and the former Soviet Union is completed in the early 1990s, the belt should be in a strong position to take advantage of possibilities for trade. It is estimated that shipment by existing rail lines is not only much quicker but also 20 to 30 percent cheaper than ocean shipping. These advantages will be increased still further with the new Urumqi-Usu-Alma Ata route.

Perhaps the most remarkable experiment to date, however, was the creation of the Central China International Group, which was announced in June 1988. This joint stock company, with a registered capital of RMB 500 million and US$10 million in foreign currency, was sponsored by major agencies of the Henan provincial government, including the Commission of Foreign Trade and Economic Cooperation and the provincial branches of the People's Bank of China (PBOC) and the Bank of China (BOC). A num-

Five Ways to Build a Good Overseas Relationship

1. Be careful in choosing overseas distributors

This is crucial. Whether you choose to go with a subsidiary, agent, export trading company, export management company, dealer, distributor, or your own setup, you must investigate the potential and pitfalls of each. Pay personal visits to potential partners to assure yourself of their long-term commitment to you and your product, and their experience, ability, reputation, and financial stability. Many Chinese trading companies are relatively small, and, while they are often reputable and competent on their own level, they may not measure up to your needs. Rather than relying on bank or credit sources for information on a prospective distributor's financial stability and resources, hire an independent expert to advise you.

The keys to the McDonald's Corporation's foreign success, says spokesman Brad Trask, is a meticulous search for partners that focuses on "shared philosophies, past business conduct, and dedication. After all, we're asking a businessman to give up two years to be absorbed into the McDonald's way of business. We want to be sure we're right for each other."

2. Treat your overseas distributors as equals of their domestic counterparts

Your overseas distributors aren't some poor family relations entitled only to crumbs and handouts. They are part of your company's future success, a division equal to any domestic division. Offer them advertising campaigns, discount programs, sales incentives, special credit terms, warranty deals, and service programs that are equivalent to those you offer your domestic distributors and tailored to meet the special needs of that country.

Also take into account the fact that distributors of export goods need to act more independently of manufacturers and marketers than do domestic distributors because of the differences in trade laws and practices, and the vagaries of international communications and transportation.

McDonald's partners in China adhere to the company's overall standards of consistency and quality,

Trask says, but in all other ways, the McDonald's restaurants in China are thoroughly Chinese—Chinese owned, staffed and operated. "We're not operational police," Trask says. "Those partners have purchased the rights to a formula for proven success. We've never found anyone foolish enough to fly in the face of success. Instead, they've adapted the formula to suit their needs." Kentucky Fried Chicken sees things the same way. "We mandate that our partners or licensees have the Colonel up on the logo, and they have to serve original recipe chicken and cole slaw," says Steve Provost, KFC's vice president of International Public Affairs. "Beyond that it's up to them."

3. Learn the dos and taboos

Each country does business in its own way, a process developed over years to match the history, culture and precepts of the people. Ignore these practices and you lose. "McDonald's system has enough leeway in it to allow the local businessmen to do what they have to do to succeed," Trask says. Thus every new McDonald's in Thailand holds a "staff night" just before the grand opening. The families of the youthful employees descend en masse to be served McDonald's meals in an atmosphere that they can see for themselves is clean and wholesome. [Refer to" Business Culture" chapter for a detailed discussion.]

4. Be flexible in forming partnerships

American companies in particular are notoriously obsessed with gaining a majority share of a joint venture, the type of partnership most favored by East Asian governments. One reason is accounting. Revenue can show up on the books at home only when the stake is more than 50 percent. Another reason is the US Foreign Corrupt Practices Act, which makes US citizens and companies liable for the conduct of their overseas partners; the idea, presumptuous at best, is that majority control translates into control of the minority partner.

Here, again, Japanese practices are illuminating. Ownership is yet another area where the Japanese have succeeded; they see a two-sided relationship where Americans see themselves as the superior partner in

Five Ways to Build a Good Overseas Relationship (cont'd.)

knowledge, finances, technology, and culture—in other words, know-it-alls. Westerners, and Americans in particular, have a lot to learn about flexibility in business relationships. McDonald's Corporation has chosen the 50-50 joint-venture route, with great profitability—more than half its income now comes from outside the US. KFC is another American company that has found enormous success by being flexible. "We have a philosophy of relying heavily on our joint venture or franchise partners to guide us," says KFC's Trask. "We'd never dream of trying to impose our attitudes on them."

Finally, keep in mind that there is more than one way to do business overseas and that changing laws or market conditions will often force you to consider other options. Where a distributorship may be best at first, a joint venture or a licensing agreement may be the way to go later.

5. Concentrate on the relationship

We cannot emphasize this point too greatly. The Confucian culture of East Asia emphasizes personal relationships above all else. Building a good relationship takes time, patience, courtesy, reliability, dignity, honorable conduct, and farsightedness; a poorly developed relationship dooms even your best marketing efforts to failure. One US computer maker made a great mistake when it fired its Asian distributor after a falling-out. The dismissal, handled in a typically abrupt American way,

caused the man to lose face, and ruined all the relationships the company had built through this man. For three years afterward, company executives couldn't find another distributor because no one would talk to them. Not only did the company lose untold millions of dollars in sales, but it took US$40 million in advertising to create enough consumer-driven demand for local distributors to even consider meeting with the firm.

So do your very best to build a sound, trusting and profitable relationship with your overseas partners. They are putting themselves on the line for you, spending time, money and energy in hopes of future rewards and a solid, long-term relationship.

And by all means, don't expect your foreign distributors to jump through hoops on a moment's notice. For example, they need price protection so they don't lose money on your price changes. If they buy your product for US$100 and a month later you cut your price to US$90, you have to give them credit so they don't get stuck with inventory at the higher price. If you raise your price, you have to honor your prior commitment while you give ample notice of the increase.

With their focus on long-term personal relationships and on mutual respect and trust, East Asians, in particular, make honorable partners once you have gained their confidence by showing them they have yours.

---

ber of existing companies, including four involved in trading, finance and technological cooperation and 72 other enterprises are combined in this enterprise. Of these, 27 are overseas entities and a number of the others are located along the coast. The company's role is to act as a bridge between the central provinces and foreign enterprises.

These initiatives and the industrial links at both governmental and enterprise levels that they promote would have been unthinkable just a few years ago. At present, interregional economic cooperation between the less-developed provinces, with rich resources and raw materials, and the more developed coastal provinces and cities, notably Shanghai, Beijing, and Guangzhou, which are starved for raw materials, is expanding rapidly.

MAJOR CITIES

Beijing

Beijing (Peking), the capital of China, is situated at the northwestern corner of the North China Plain, just inside the Great Wall, which cuts through the municipal area and approaches to within sixty km of the city center. Beijing lies on the edge of the heartland of the majority Han ethnic group. To the north and east lies Manchuria and to the west, beyond the mountains, only some 400 km (250 miles) away, are the vast open plains of Mongolia. Indeed it was the Mongolian RMB dynasty that first made Beijing, then known as *Dadu*, the capital of the empire in the 13th century, and capital it has remained, with only brief interruptions, ever since.

The western part of the city occupies the mountains, the Western Hills, that mark the edge of the North China Plain. Much of Beijing is flat, resting on the plain itself and flanked on the east by the Chaobai and Jixun Rivers and on the south by the Yongding River.

In spite of these rivers, Beijing, in common with other parts of the semiarid North China Plain, is chronically short of water. There has been excessive pumping to ground water, lowering the water table, and has become an important constraint upon industrial development.

According to the 1990 general census, metropolitan Beijing has a population of 10.8 million, with about 7 million living in the city proper. It is certainly the political and cultural capital of China. Its claim to be the economic capital may be disputed, although the fact remains that its GDP is the second largest of China's major cities after Shanghai. The ministries are all located in Beijing, as are the headquarters of all but one of the major banks and all the foreign trade corporations.

The city is not, however, a great center of industrial production nor is it the forefront of commercial innovation. It is rather conservative, though this is hardly surprising, considering it is the seat of Party and government bureaucracies.

Beijing serves as a major hub of China's transportation system. From the main railway station, trains depart for every corner of this vast country, and indeed for Pyongyang, Moscow, and indirectly to the capitals of Europe. From Capital Airport, flights link with every province and autonomous region. Many of the world's largest international airlines now fly to Beijing, connecting China directly with cities in Africa, Asia, Australia, Europe, and North America.

Government is Beijing's most important industry, but it has a diversified economy. There is coal to the west of the city in the Mentougou District, and heavy industry is also strongly represented: iron and steel, coal mining, machine building, petroleum, chemicals, building materials, car manufacturing, and heavy engineering. Light industry is still more important, including textiles, food processing, electricals and electronics, glass, and pharmaceuticals. Its chemicals, electronics, machinery, pharmaceuticals, metallurgy, arts and crafts, and textiles industries occupy an important position in the national industry.

Investment in heavy industry is discouraged because of growing concern about pollution. However, the capital is zoned for light industry, service industries, entertainment, and cultural development. In 1988 the new Haidian High-Technology Zone was created to foster the development of high-technology industries, particularly electronics and information technologies to the northwest of the city. Beijing has perhaps the most highly educated workforce of any Chinese city with more than 70 universities and colleges, and more than 500 research institutes, mostly within the Haidian district.

By April 1993 more than 4,970 foreign investment enterprises had been approved to set up in Beijing with a total foreign direct investment of more than US$12.24 billion. A number of large industrial joint ventures have also been established, notably in the auto, TV picture tube, and boiler-making industries. Investment in property is being discouraged, but investment is welcome in light industry, electronics, food processing, building materials, automotive manufacturing, and textiles, and, especially, in high-technology fields.

In addition to direct foreign investment, Beijing recorded more than 1,400 advanced technology licensing agreements between 1979 and 1990. Trade—both imports and exports—attributable to Beijing-based enterprises was US$1.76 billion in 1990.

Beijing is important to any would-be investor or trader, because it is the seat of political power, a fact that assumes enormous importance when doing business in a centralized socialist state. It is also a good place for making contacts and for getting a start in China, whether through exhibitions held there or in discussions with ministries or others who can help to identify specific possibilities to follow up over the length and breadth of the country.

Tianjin

Tianjin is just 140 km (87 miles) southwest of the capital, yet the contrast between the two is striking. Away from the brooding presence of the national Party and government bureaucracies, informality breaks out and with it a certain element of spontaneity.

Situated where the North China Plain meets the Bohai Sea, Tianjin lies a little upstream of the mouth of the Haihe River, close to its confluence with a number of tributaries, including the Yongding River, which flows down from Beijing.

The 1990 general census shows that the Tianjin metropolitan area had a population of 8.5 million, of which 5.8 million live in the city proper. The city is an important transportation center. The port of Tianjin, Xingang (New Harbor), is the largest man-made harbor in China, serving Beijing as well as much of the northern part of China and a number of inland provinces. Tianjin also has the largest container wharf in China. Nearly 30 shipping routes link the city with 150 countries. Tianjin also sits astride the main railway line between Beijing and the northeast, and is on the line from Beijing to Shanghai, enjoying regular services to all parts of China. The airport, which lies to the northeast near Tanggu, has daily flights to Hong Kong and regular connections to many Chinese cities. Now that the new highway to Beijing has opened, discussions are under way to build a new international airport to serve both cities in the open plains that flank the road. The city's major roads network consists of about 100 highways, providing a link with many different parts of the country.

Tianjin is one of China's oldest industrial cities, with a long history of manufacturing and commerce. Opened up to foreign business in the late 19th century, it quickly established itself as the foremost trading city of northern China. Most of the foreign powers of the day, including Great Britain, Russia, Germany, France, Austria-Hungary, and Japan established their concessions there—slices of land that they developed and administered like colonies. These concessions have left their mark on the face of the city to this day. For the businessmen with a spare moment, it is interesting to walk through the old concessions, noting where one ends and the next begins from the distinctive architectural styles.

Tianjin has a well-developed and broad industrial base. Famous traditionally for bicycles, watches, and carpets, it is especially strong in light industry, including light engineering, cosmetics, detergents, garments, cameras, textiles, textile machinery, food processing, and electricals. Heavy industries are also well represented, including metallurgy, machinery, automobile manufacturing, chemicals, and shipbuilding. Tianjin has some oil and natural gas resources and refineries.

The city has ample resources of highly skilled labor and, in common with Beijing, a relatively well-educated population. Foremost among its many research institutes and institutions of higher education is Nankeen University, founded from the old Nankai School, of which Zhou Enlai is the most celebrated alumnus.

Tianjin is a pro-business city, strongly wedded to the Open Door policy, and municipal authorities have done a great deal not just to attract investment, but to ensure its success. Former mayor Li Ruihuan, who has played a major part in framing and improving the investment environment, is a national leader of considerable distinction and serves as a member of the ruling Politburo.

As of June 1991 there were 685 FIEs in Tianjin, accounting for a total contracted investment of US$1.26 billion. More than 81 percent of these enterprises are industrial in nature, including machine building, textiles, electronics, chemicals, garments, light industry, and construction.

Shanghai

Shanghai is the largest city in China. It had a metropolitan area population of around 13.4 million with the city itself numbering 7.8 million in 1990. The population of Chongqing has reportedly surpassed that of Shanghai but this claim is widely disputed.

Situated near the mouth of the Huangpu River, close to its confluence with the Yangtze Delta, Shanghai enjoys a remarkable position. It is the largest port not just for oceangoing vessels but for river craft that ply the Yangtze and its tributaries (not to mention the Grand Canal and other manmade arteries) pushing deep into the heart of Asia.

Shanghai's airport is China's busiest after Guanzhou and Beijing, controlling a comprehensive domestic network as well as an increasing number of international flights linking it directly to North America and Europe as well as to Asian destinations. Rail connections are also good, and passenger services on China's slow trains were improved by the time the new railway station was opened in 1988.

Shanghai does not have the appearance of a typical Chinese city. It looks like a European city populated by Chinese. Before the Europeans came it was a small settlement, but by the end of the 19th century it had grown into the preeminent industrial, trading, commercial, and financial center in Asia. Its eclipse by Tokyo, Hong Kong, and Singapore did not come until the late 1960s when the tide of the Cultural Revolution finally overtook it.

The European influence is evident in the magnificent old buildings, notably those along the Bund, the riverfront promenade in the old city center. The International Settlement, dominated by the British, and the French Concessions can still be distinguished. Not for nothing was Shanghai known as the Paris of the Orient.

Following the 1960s Shanghai fell on hard times. Always feared by Beijing as a rival power center, it produced more than 8 percent of China's industrial output, becoming the cash cow of the central government, and yielding no less than 16 percent of national revenue. Staggering under this huge burden, the city was unable to modernize its infrastructure. Many beautiful old buildings and houses fell into disrepair, and deteriorating transportation and housing became increasingly serious problems. This load has now been lightened by the central government in order to facilitate the regeneration of Shanghai's economy. Shanghai since 1988 has contributed a fixed percentage of its income to the treasury, and any money it collects in excess can be retained to finance its own development.

With the appointment of two distinguished mayors in succession, Shanghai appears to have overcome some problems. Jiang Zemin, previously mayor, is now Communist Party general secretary. Another former mayor, Zhu Rongji, is now vice premier and governor of the central bank, having served as vice chairman of the State Economic Commission. These men have done much to revitalize this great city. New projects include an underground railway, modernization of the sewage system, improved roads and telecommunications, expansion of the airport, and housing development.

Despite its problems, Shanghai has never been seriously challenged as China's leading industrial city. It was and remains especially strong in light industry, including textiles, light engineering, and food processing. It has a diversified industrial base with heavy industries, including chemicals, petrochemicals, metallurgy (notably iron and steel), machine building, automobile manufacturing, and shipbuilding. Its best-known products include cotton, silk fabrics, knitwear, bicycles, and sewing machines.

Shanghai remains preeminent in trade, drawing on long years of experience, its geographical position, and a highly skilled and educated work force. The city's colleges and universities are second only to Beijing's. The Shanghainese are undoubtedly clever people—some say too clever by half, the New Yorkers of China. They are known as very tough negotiators. But they are good, cooperative partners once they enter into an agreement with foreign investors. Their street smarts and the highly skilled work force partly account for the high success rate of the ventures in Shanghai.

Shanghai remains a cosmopolitan, international city, perhaps more so than any other in China. The larger industrialized countries all maintain consulates there, and there are significant foreign business and diplomatic communities.

Foreign investment is strongly encouraged in the city, which has been strikingly successful in attracting some of the world's best-known companies. Investors in Shanghai are typically substantial companies, making large investments in contrast to the small, family-based investments from Hong Kong that form a large proportion of joint ventures in Guangzhou. Several dozen large, wholly foreign-owned enterprises have also been set up.

Cooperation with foreign firms covers a wide range of industries, notably electronics, textiles, light engineering, automobiles, machine building, airplane assembly, and glass. Also prominent are joint venture real estate projects, including hotels, offices, and apartments.

By the end of 1990 more than 400 FIEs had gone into operation, of which 70 percent are entering the profit-making stage. Those which have already made substantial profits are expanding their business and injecting additional investment in Shanghai.

Guangzhou

Guangzhou (formerly known as Canton) is the political, economic and cultural capital of southeast China. Situated at the head of the Pearl River Delta and facing the South China Sea, it is both a sea and river port. Baiyun Airport commands a comprehensive domestic network, as well as international flights to Hong Kong, Manila, Singapore, Sydney, and other cities. A new international airport is under construction 28 km (17.5 miles) north of Guangzhou, and is set for a 1996 or 1997 completion. Baiyun is currently China's busiest airport, so the new international gateway is particularly important to the country.

Railway and inland waterway transport is well developed, linking Guangzhou with the major cities and most of the river ports in China. Oceangoing shipping has easy access to 500 ports worldwide, with Huangpu Harbor serving most foreign trade. It has 30 berths, and its international container dock has an annual handling capacity of 29.72 million tons. The city has a long trading history; it was the first Chinese port open to foreign trade.

Since the inauguration of the Open Door policy, Guangzhou has increasingly fallen under the sway of Hong Kong. Guangzhou stands at the far end of a corridor of development that begins in Shenzhen on the Hong Kong border and stretches north up the Pearl River. This is one of the most prosperous parts of China, grown rich on investment and processing work from Hong Kong.

Distinct in dialect and to a certain extent in culture from the rest of China, Guangdong and its capital have very strong affinity with Hong Kong. The influence of the territory upon the province is likely to increase still further once the Guangzhou-Kowloon express railway and the new highway connecting Hong Kong, Macao, Shenzhen, and Zhuhai with the city are completed. Much of the outside investment is from Hong Kong and based partly on the strong family connections that have survived for nearly a century across the political boundaries.

Guangzhou remains China's foremost window on the outside world. In the early 1970s when China was almost completely sealed off, the twice-yearly Canton Trade Fair kept alive a tradition that had begun centuries before.

The city has a broad industrial base, with particular strength in the light industrial sector, including oil refining, building materials, leather tanning, rubber making, textiles, electronics, pharmaceuticals, and—as befits the center of one of China's most fertile agricultural area—food processing. It is also a major base for oil exploration in the South China Sea.

Like China's other major cities, the educational and technical level of the population is relatively high. Because of this, the city is especially anxious to attract investment in high-technology industries.

Seven Rules for Selling Your Product

1. Respect the individuality of each market

The profit motive generally operates cross-culturally and the nationals of most countries, especially within a given region, will have much in common with one another. However, there will also be substantial differences, enough to cause a generic marketing program to fall flat on its face and even build ill-will in the process. You may have some success with this sort of one-size-fits-all approach, but you won't be able to build a solid operation or maximize profits this way. "Japan proves this point phenomenally," says Steve Provost, KFC's vice president of International Public Affairs. "Our first three restaurants in Tokyo were modeled after our American restaurants, and all three failed within six months. Then we listened to our Japanese partner, who suggested we open smaller restaurants. We've never looked back." What works in Japan doesn't necessarily work in China. Chinese tastes may be more similar to US tastes than to Japanese, or may differ in other ways.

2. Adapt your product to the foreign market

Markets are individual, and you may well need to tailor your products to suit individual needs. As the United States' Big Three automakers have yet to learn, it's hard to sell a left-hand-drive car in a right-hand-drive country. Black may be a popular color in your country, but may also be seen as the color of death in your foreign market. Dress, styles, and designs considered fashionably tasteful at home can cause offense abroad. One major US computer manufacturer endured years of costly marketing miscalculations before it realized that the US is only one-third of its market, and that the other two-thirds required somewhat different products as well as different approaches.

You can avoid this company's multi-million dollar mistakes by avoiding lazy and culturally-biased thinking. A foreign country has official regulations and cultural preferences that differ from those of your own. Learn about these differences, respect them, and adapt your product accordingly. Often it won't even take that much thought, money, or effort. Kentucky Fried Chicken offers a salmon sandwich in Japan, fried plantains in Mexico, and tabouleh in the Middle East — and 450 other locally specific menu items worldwide. And even the highly standardized McDonald's serves pineapple pie in Thailand, teriyaki burgers and tatsuda sandwiches (chicken with ginger and soy) in Japan, spicy sauces with burgers in Malaysia (prepared according to Muslim guidelines), and a seasonal durian fruit shake in Singapore.

3. Don't get greedy

Price your product to match the market you're entering. Don't try to take maximum profits in the first year. Take the long-term view. It's what your competitors are doing, and they're in it for the long haul. The Chinese are very price-conscious. When you're pricing your product, include in your calculations the demand for spare parts, components, and auxiliary equipment. Add-on profits from these sources can help keep the primary product price down and therefore more competitive.

4. Demand quality

A poor-quality product can ambush the best-laid marketing plans. The Chinese may look at price first, but they also want value and won't buy junk no matter how cheap. And there's just too much competition to make it worth your while to put this adage to the test. Whatever market you gain initially will rapidly fall apart if you have a casual attitude towards quality. And it is hard to come back from an initial quality-based flop. On then other hand, a product with a justified reputation for high quality and good value creates its own potential for market and price expansions.

5. Back up your sales with service

Some products demand more work than others — more sales effort, more after-sales service, more hand-holding of the distributor, and more contact with the end user. The channel you select is crucial here. Paradoxically in this age of ubiquitous and lightning-fast communications and saturation advertising, people rely more than ever on word of mouth to sort out the truth from hyperbole. Nothing will sink your product faster than a reputation for poor or nonexistent service and after-sales support. US firms in particular need to do some serious reputation building for such after-sales service. Although the Chinese see US products as generally superior in quality and performance, they rate Japanese after-sales service as vastly better. And guess whose products they buy.

Consider setting up your own service facility. If you're looking for a Chinese agent to handle your product, look for one who has qualified maintenance people already familiar with your type of product or who can handle your service

Seven Rules (cont'd.)

needs with a little judicious training. And make sure that this partner understands how important service and support are to you and to your future relationship with him.

6. Notice that foreigners speak a different language

Your sales, service, and warranty information may contain a wealth of information but if it's not in their language, you leave the foreign distributors, sales and service personnel, and consumers out in the cold. It's expensive to translate everything into Chinese, but it's absolutely necessary.

7. Focus on specific geographic areas and markets

To avoid wasteful spending, focus your marketing efforts. A lack of focus means that you're wasting your money, time, and energies. A lack of specificity means that your foreign operations may get too big too fast. Not only does this cost more than the local business can justify or support, it also can translate into an impersonal attitude towards sales and service and the relationships you've working so hard to build. Instead concentrate your time, money, and efforts on a specific market or region, and work on building the all-important business relationships that will carry you over the many obstacles to successful export marketing.

ADDITIONAL CITIES

Chongqing (formerly know as Chungking) in the middle Yangtze area now boasts first place amongst China's major cities with a population of more than 14 million, pushing Shanghai with 13.4 million people into second place. Much of Chongqing's population, however, is rural; indeed, cynics claim that its boundaries were extended to cover a vast rural area in order to make it China's largest city and its urban population was listed at under 3 million in 1990, seventh in the country. In spite of its well-developed and diversified industrial base, which partly stems from its period as capital of China during the Japanese occupation, and partly from Mao's "third front" development policy, it cannot rival Shanghai's industrial and commercial supremacy.

Nevertheless, this vibrant metropolis contributes no less than one-twelfth of China's GDP. Indeed, it was Chongqing's physical isolation and inaccessibility that made it an ideal wartime fortress for Chiang Kai Shek (known as Jiang Jieshi in China) and for the industries that Mao dispersed from the east coast for fear of their vulnerability if war should come again. Chongqing has a sound claim to the title of capital of southwest China.

Other important cities include Wuhan, located right in the central part of China and also in the middle Yangtze River Valley, and Nanjing, the lowest bridging point of the Yangtze and capital of China in the early Ming dynasty and again under Chiang Kai Shek. In the northwest, Xian is the linchpin. The capital of China for many more years than Beijing, it retains vital strategic importance and is the home of a substantial part of China's aerospace industry. In the northeast, the cities of Shenyang (Mukden) and Changchun (the capital of the Japanese puppet state of Manchukuo, where China's last emperor, Pu Yi, briefly resumed his throne) are important centers of heavy industry. Shenyang can fairly claim to be the economic capital of the northeast. The Coastal Cities, which play such a dominant part in China's economic life, are reviewed later in this section.

SPECIAL ECONOMIC ZONES

Shenzhen, Zhuhai, Shantou, and Xiamen were designated in 1980. In April 1988 the National People's Congress raised Hainan Island to the level of a province and declared that it was also to enjoy the status of an SEZ.

The investment environment in Hainan is still being shaped. The stated intention is that Hainan should have the most liberal regime of all the special zones, the sea providing a *cordon sanitaire* around the island. Local officials stress the parallel with Taiwan—Hainan is China's second largest island after Taiwan.

Preferential treatment is granted to foreign investors in the SEZs. With the exception of the tax incentives, which are prescribed in national legislation, most such preferential treatment is set out in local regulations, which vary from zone to zone. Potential investors should obtain copies of appropriate rules covering business registration, land management, labor management, administration, and import and export regulations by contacting the authorities of the zone in question.

Shenzhen

Shenzhen SEZ is bounded by Hong Kong on the south and by an equally well-policed northern frontier to prevent the entry of unauthorized mainland Chinese. Its total area is 327 square km (126 square miles), including the 2-square-km (.75-square-mile) Shekou Industrial District, which is under the management of the China Merchants' Steam Navigation Company.

Profiting from its proximity to Hong Kong—it is less than an hour by train, and not much more than an hour by road and sea—the zone has developed more quickly than the others. Shenzhen's population, less than 30,000 in 1980, exceeded 1.8 million by 1990.

In the 10 years ending in October 1990, more than 5,000 joint ventures or wholly foreign-owned enterprises were set up, with the total foreign investment actually received exceeding US$4.2 billion, which accounted for one-ninth of the direct investment throughout China. Between March 1992 and May 1992 more than 100 new FIEs per month were registered in Shenzhen. Major industries include electronics (accounting for 40 percent of output value), light industries, beverages, textiles, and medicines. The industrial export output value made up about 62.7 percent in 1990. In 1989 Shenzhen's exports amounted to US$2.2 billion, making it China's second largest foreign exchange earner next to Shanghai.

In the 1980 to 1990 period, Shenzhen's average annual GDP growth rate was 47.8 percent; its average growth in industrial output was 6.2 percent; and its average growth in exports was 72.5 percent.

Shenzhen is divided into a commercial area, three industrial areas (including Shekou), a warehousing district, a residential zone, and an area dedicated to tourism. It has been a front-runner in sales of land use rights in China. Infrastructure is relatively good. Road communications will be greatly improved when the Hong Kong-Guangzhou-Macao Expressway (a joint venture with Hong Kong participation) is completed. Port facilities are also good. Electricity supplies are better than in most parts of China. The first phase (700 megawatts) of the Shajiao Power Station is already in operation, and work is under way on the 600-megawatt second phase. Completion of the joint venture Nuclear Power Station at nearby Days Bay is expected in 1994.

Other infrastructure projects under construction include the Yantian deep-water port, the Shenzhen Railway Station, an additional water supply system, sewage drainage system, highways, and city roads.

Because the border between Shenzhen and mainland China beyond is policed, it is possible to obtain a special visa good only in the zone only by applying to the immigration authorities at the Hong Kong border.

Zhuhai

The city of Zhuhai consists of the Zhuhai SEZ, Xiangzhou District, and Doumen County, covering a total area of 7,555 square km (2,917 square miles), of which 1,630 square km (629 square miles) is land area. Like Shenzhen, though on a smaller scale, there are areas reserved for commerce, residential development, and tourism. The city of Zhuhai has a population of 635,000.

Bordered on the south by Macao, Zhuhai is only 36 nautical miles from Hong Kong and 140 km (87 miles) from Guangzhou. The Guangzhou-Shenzhen-Zhuhai Expressway will be completed shortly, and the port facilities are being upgraded for 30,000-ton vessels. A communications network consisting of direct-dial telephones, telex, and special delivery services, links the city with 138 countries and regions and more than 600 Chinese cities and countries.

Industries in Zhuhai include electronics, textiles, foodstuffs, and other light industries, as well as building materials. As of October 1990 around 1,100 joint ventures and foreign enterprises had been set up with foreign investment actually received coming to more than US$1 billion. Since 1990 the development of FIEs has gained added momentum, with an average of nearly one venture being set up daily. During the early years the majority of the projects were labor-intensive, small in scale and limited to tourism, textiles, electronics, building materials, and light industries. Now there are now many technology-intensive projects not only in electronics and light industries, but also in energy, petrochemicals, and telecommunications. Due to Zhuhai's attractive geographic location, foreign investors are showing increasing interest in infrastructural projects, such as communications, port construction, power plants, and transportation. The majority of the FIEs are export oriented, and as the profitability of foreign investment rises, the number of wholly foreign-owned projects is increasing notably. While there were only 45 wholly foreign-owned enterprises in 1989, in the first half of 1991 alone more than 90 foreign enterprises were set up in Zhuhai, bringing the total to more than 200.

Over the past decade, the GDP of Zhuhai has grown at an average annual rate of 35 percent. Aside from manufacturing, Zhuhai has been rather successful in developing a thriving tourist industry as well as substantial trade in farm produce, exporting fruits and vegetables to Hong Kong and Macao.

Shantou

Shantou, a city of just under 800,000, lies close to the border between Guangdong and Fujian. This "capital of the Chiu Chow People" is the ancestral home of many overseas Chinese; there are 1.2 million Chiu Chows in Hong Kong, 4 million in Thailand, and other sizable communities in Indonesia, Malaysia, Singapore, and the Philippines, as well as in Europe and North America. Foreign investment has come largely from this source, notably from Hong Kong, and this justified the original decision to designate Shantou as an SEZ.

The zone itself covers 53 square km (20 square miles) and is divided into two areas of approximately equal size: Lunghu, which borders the eastern edge of the city proper, and Guangao, which is a little further out. Guangao is earmarked for heavy industry, electrical power generation, and perhaps petrochemicals. Lunghu is designated as a light industrial area. In 1991 the Chinese government gave approval for the Shantou SEZ to expand into the whole city, covering 234 square km (90 square miles).

The infrastructure in Shantou is improving rapidly. The airport is newly expanded, and airlines link the city with Hong Kong, Bangkok, and Singapore, as well as a dozen major cities inside China. Highways extend in all directions. The expressway connecting Shantou with Shenzhen and the railway from Shantou to Guangzhou are both under construction. Programmed telephone systems directly link the city with more than 200 cities in China, and direct-dial telephone, telex and fax systems are available. An additional 290,000-kilowatt power generating plant and four 5,000-ton docking berths have been recently completed. However, in view of the expansion of the SEZ in the coming years, the infrastructure in Shantou still needs improvement.

By the end of 1990 there were more than 8,000 enterprises in the zone, more than 300 of them funded by foreign investment. As a result of the rapid improvement of the infrastructure, foreign investment in the whole city has grown fairly quickly. From January to July 1991, direct foreign investment in Shantou came to more than US$95 million, an increase of greater than 70 percent over the same period in 1990.

Major industries include textiles, ceramics, machinery, electrical products, food processing, arts and crafts, and agricultural and aquatic products (including high-quality foodstuffs such as prawns, shrimps, eels, mushroom, fruits, and vegetables). Gross industrial output value of the zone was RMB 5.3 billion for the first half of 1991.

Shantou boasts that it can compete with Shenzhen and the other zones on the basis of costs and on the flexibility of its bureaucracy. Factory rents and labor costs are also much lower than elsewhere.

Xiamen

The Xiamen SEZ now includes the whole of Xiamen Island, which is located at the mouth of the Jiulong River across the straits from Taiwan. The 130 square km (50 square miles) island is linked to the mainland by a causeway, which carries both the road and the railway. The city of Xiamen (formerly known as Amoy) sits at a corner of this island and straddles both sides of the strait between the main island and a smaller island, Gulangyu, where the foreign concessions were located. Xiamen has a metropolitan area population of 1 million in the metropolitan area.

Xiamen is undoubtedly one of China's most attractive cities, exhibiting fine examples of both Chinese and European architecture. Its narrow cobbled streets have great charm. It is the ancestral home of millions of overseas Chinese and also of many Taiwanese who left the mainland in earlier centuries.

The mountainous terrain is picturesque, contributing to Xiamen's enormous tourist potential. The well-known Gulangyu Island is often referred to as the Garden on the Sea or Music Island. Aside from the great number of visitors from Taiwan, tourism from Singapore, Thailand, Malaysia, Indonesia, and the Philippines is also increasing annually. In the first half of 1991 tourist arrivals from these five countries alone reached 23,000, an increase of 115 percent over the same period in 1990.

Overseas Chinese have been the source of much of Xiamen's foreign investment to date, while the Taiwanese are the most active investors.

In the past, Xiamen's proximity to Taiwan was not a blessing. For military reasons, the port was not developed, although there is a fine natural harbor. Thousands of soldiers were quartered in and around the city. Now the troops have largely gone, and the trading of propaganda by high powered loudspeakers across the narrow channel that separates Xiamen from the Taiwanese-controlled island of Quemoy, a few miles off the coast, has ceased.

The zone boasts two industrial districts, Jiangtou and Huli. Major industries include textiles, agricultural production, food processing, arts and crafts, shipbuilding, chemicals, machinery, electronics, and tourism. Foreign investment in Xiamen has now exceeded US$1 billion. Much of this investment is in electronics, textiles, and food processing. In common with the other SEZs, Xiamen is now particularly keen to attract investment in high-technology sectors. The 1991 statistics show that 565 FIEs are operating, more than 90 percent of which are making profits.

As a fine harbor in the southern part of China, Xiamen has 22 medium-sized and small docks, including the Heping dock with an annual handling capacity of 1.5 million tons. The newly built Dongdu dock, consisting of two deepwater berths for 50,000-ton vessels, another berth for 10,000-ton container ships, and still another for 15,000-ton ships, is earmarked for oceangoing freighters. Currently Xiamen is linked by sea with Hong Kong, Singapore, Australia, and Japan. Its airport has flights to most of the major domestic cities and to Hong Kong, Singapore, Japan, and the Philippines. Electricity supplies in Xiamen are better than in many other parts of China, and because Fujian has great potential for hydroelectric power, the situation should continue to improve steadily.

The telephone system in Xiamen is adequate, and direct-dialing service is available to major countries.

Hainan

Hainan is China's fifth and largest SEZ, covering the entire island of 33,000 square km (20,500 square miles). It was raised to the level of a province and concurrently to the status of an SEZ in April 1988.

At that time the island was almost completely

underdeveloped, with agriculture the mainstay of the economy. The education and technical skill levels of the population were low. Likewise, the infrastructure was poor with few roads, no railways to speak of, and infrequent air services. Electricity was also in short supply, and power cuts were common.

Nevertheless, Hainan clearly has great potential, and there is tremendous political will to ensure the development of the economy.

The Hainan provincial government has adopted a system characterized as "a small government and a greater society." It has set up a macroeconomic control system based on indirect administration, giving market forces an ever-increasing role to play.

Hainan offers China's most flexible regulatory regime for foreign investors. The widest participation in the economy by foreign concerns is encouraged, including investment in infrastructure, agriculture, extractive industries, and the service sector. Many of these activities are closed to foreigners in other parts of China. Land use regulations are flexible and land leasing common. Immigration and customs procedures are simplified, as are business registration and import and export administration.

Sensibly, the government of the island has now settled upon a realistic development program, having initially attracted criticism for overambitious talk of a high-technology paradise that many commentators dismissed as castles in the air. During the first five years—1988 to 1993—the authorities concentrated on development of the infrastructure, including new airports at both Haikou and Sanya to replace the existing inadequate facilities. Hainan is currently linked to Guangzhou and Hong Kong by daily flights and to Beijing three or four times weekly. Flights from Haikou to Malaysia were recently initiated.

Also included are plans for new harbors and the upgrading and expansion of existing facilities at Xuyin, Haikou, Macun, Yangpu, Basuo, Qinglart, and Sanya. The Macun development is linked to the construction of new power stations close by, burning coal from Guizhou. The first phase of the Macun Power Station, with a capacity of 150 megawatts, was commissioned in 1988, and the second 250-megawatt phase was completed in late 1989. These new facilities have doubled the island's pre-1988 generating capacity. A third station with a capacity of 200 megawatts is planned for Basuo; it will burn natural gas from the offshore fields south of Hainan, which will be exploited through a gas-gathering system to be built by Atlantic Richfield. A third 1,000-megawatt station is also planned for Yangpu, but details have not yet been settled. To improve road links, a Haikou-Sanya Expressway is being planned; the route is expected to run down the east side of the island.

While this infrastructure is being constructed, Hainan will concentrate on encouraging the devel-

Checklist for Choosing an Agent or a Distributor

Although China is modernizing rapidly, its business practices are in many ways less than efficient and reliable by Western standards. This is especially true of agents and distributors. Many Chinese agents and distributors don't care much for the lower profit margins and relatively few after-sales services offered by foreign suppliers. The suppliers, in turn, recount nightmare stories of late deliveries, nondeliveries, slipshod sales and service, short-term profit making instead of long-term investment, inadequate experience and financing, and blatant misrepresentation of abilities and commitment. Honor-bound Confucian ethics dominate Chinese business, and Western-style iron-clad contract law is still largely unknown and underappreciated, so what you may consider to be clearly understood, the Chinese may see as wide open to interpretation—in their favor.

Don't be scared off by the tales of woe. Sometimes true, sometimes apocryphal, they can serve as guidelines in selecting a competent, committed agent or distributor. Investigate your prospective partner's:

✓ **experience**—in distributing, selling or servicing foreign goods in general and your product line in particular;

✓ **financial status**—get an independent analysis;

✓ **reputation**—with other clients and his bankers;

✓ **strength**—many Chinese companies with impressive names are only mom-and-pop operations;

✓ **goals**—you want someone who has long-term objectives, not a grab-the-money-and-run type; and

✓ **conflicts of interest**—you want someone who isn't involved with other companies or organizations whose interests compete with yours.

opment of industry that is not heavily dependent on good infrastructure. Given the island's tropical climate, agriculture will be prominent among these. Hainan is rich in tropical produce, such as coconuts, pepper, coffee, cocoa, tea, pineapples, and sugar cane. It is the largest producer of natural rubber in China, accounting for more than 70 percent of total production. The coffee produced there is of very high quality. There is plenty of good virgin land, and plantation companies would be welcomed there to help upgrade existing production. A Thai joint venture has already established shrimp farms, and a major US multinational corporation is looking into pineapple production and processing as well as possibilities for the cultivation and processing of other fruits and vegetables. Other light industries are also encouraged. Foreign investment pledged as of 1991 has totaled US$600 million, of which about US$322 million has actually been paid up. Altogether 1,575 FIEs had been established by early 1991.

Foreign investment is primarily made in manufacturing, construction, transportation, public facilities, culture, and education

Once the infrastructure has been established, Hainan will actively promote the development of heavier industry, including chemicals, petrochemicals, glass, cement, and building materials. The island produces 300,000 tons of iron ore per year from reserves estimated at 300 to 400 million tons. There are also large deposits of titanium sands, and the authorities are keen to secure foreign participation in mining and processing these reserves to produce titanium dioxide.

Because of the natural beauty of Hainan, with its white sands and clear, blue seas, there is a good potential for tourism. A tourist industry is now being developed, but infrastructure improvements are essential before tourism can really take off.

In an interesting development, in early 1989 Hainan authorities agreed to lease a large slice of land at Yangpu in the northwest of the island to a group of Japanese companies in the nearest approach to the old foreign concessions since 1949. These companies plan to develop a separate industrial area with all supporting facilities. Investment for the initial phase is estimated at more than US$70 million.

The five-year period since the designation of Hainan as a Special Economic Zone has witnessed quite rapid growth of its economy. The province's GDP rose by 27.4 percent between 1987 and 1990, while total income jumped by 24.5 percent.

THE FOURTEEN COASTAL CITIES

In April 1984 the government designated 14 Coastal Cities that were to be allowed greater autonomy in economic policy making and permitted to offer special incentives to encourage foreign investment. Each city would set aside a special district—called an Economic and Technological Development Zone (ETDZ)—where a particularly favorable climate would be created. The zones were to enjoy special rights to approve projects involving foreign investments and to offer tax incentives independent of central authorities.

Different incentives are available in each zone and city, and different regulations are in force. It is important that would-be investors consult the specific legislation in the area concerned in order to make a detailed evaluation of the climate for investment. These regulations may cover a wide range of issues, including land use, land use fees, business registration, labor matters, and foreign trade administration.

In 1992 Beijing was granted coastal city status, bringing the total number to 15.

During the early 1990s many more cities have been designated as development zones, providing various degrees of preferential treatment to attract foreign investment. However, the 14 cities designated in 1984 generally remain more developed and preferred by foreign investors. The following sections describe these cities.

Dalian

Dalian is a huge industrial city that also boasts the second largest harbor in China after Shanghai. This important ice- and silt-free deepwater port serves as the main route for almost all goods going into and coming out of northeast China. Currently massive construction projects designed to enlarge and modernize harbor facilities are under way.

The town, which was built by the Japanese, still maintains close cultural and even closer commercial ties with Tokyo. A new international airport was recently opened, and there are good railway links with Beijing and Harbin. But, even more important, a new 375-km (232 mile) expressway links Dalian with the provincial capital, Shenyang.

A new power station with a 700-megawatt capacity has already been completed. Some 40,000 lines of program-controlled automatic telephones have been installed, and direct dialing is available to all major cities in China and more than 200 foreign countries.

The Dalian ETDZ, which is named Maqiaozi, is 33 km (20 miles) from the center of the city. The construction of the ETDZ began in 1984, and a fairly good infrastructure and set of public facilities have been constructed in the zone. As of July 1991 300 enterprises had been approved to set up in the ETDZ; of these 242 were FIEs with a total investment of US$1.2

billion. Some 60 percent of the investment came from foreign sources. Foreign investment in both the city and the ETDZ concentrates on the production of petrochemicals, shipbuilding, machine tools, and textiles.

Nine interdependent functional districts, including bonded warehouses, industry, finance and trading, storage, manufacturing, port, and science and technology facilities will gradually take shape, covering an area of 64 square km (25 square miles).

Qinhuangdao

Qinhuangdao is a famous ice- and silt-free deepwater port situated on the northern edge of Bohai Bay in Hebei Province. With a population of 2.35 million, the town is a picturesque summer resort where the Great Wall runs down from the mountains to meet Bohai Bay. Tourists are accommodated in a variety of hotels at the nearby Beidaihe and Nandaihe resorts.

With developed offshore fishing and aquaculture, the city abounds in prawns, jelly fish, sea cucumber, and crabs, as well as agricultural products such as corn, peanuts, wheat, sweet potatoes, and sesame seeds. The mountainous areas to the north of the city produce apples, grapes, peaches, pears, walnuts, and Chinese chestnuts.

Mineral resources include coal, gold silver, iron, uranium, manganese, marble, granite, graphite, and limestone, as well as large deposits of high quality sandstone. Coal reserves amount to over 2 billion tons.

Large quantities of coal and oil pass through the port. Presently Qinhuangdao port has 24 deepwater berths, with an annual cargo-handling capacity of 92.4 million tons. Rail links are good, because the city is on the trunk line from Beijing and Tianjin to northeast China. It is, moreover, the terminus of the new 652-km (405 mile) heavy-duty railroad designed to speed the transport of coal from the rich coal fields at Datong in Shanxi Province to the coast. Highways extend to different parts of the country, while four domestic airlines connect the city with major cities in China.

A power plant with a generating capacity of 1.1 million kilowatts is under construction, and another massive gas plant went into operation in 1992. With the completion of the water diversion project, the daily water supply capacity of the city is now double that of the actual need. Direct-dial telephone service is available.

The new ETDZ is nearby. As of mid-1991 78 FIEs had been approved with a total investment of US$642 million. Foreign investment is welcome in the development of the glass making, machinery, textiles, and chemical industries, as well as in tourism, finance, port construction, ocean shipping, and export trading.

Tianjin

The Tianjin ETDZ is in Tanggu, 50 km (31 miles) from the city center. The zone covers 40 square km (25 square miles) and is adjacent to the port of Tianjin at Tanggu; to Xingang, China's largest container terminal; and to Tianjin's international airport. The main railway line from Beijing and Tianjin and to North Korea and the Soviet Union also passes through Tanggu.

Foreign investment in the ETDZ is mainly in light industries, including medical instruments, pharmaceuticals, cosmetics, and building materials. Owing to the remoteness of the zone from the city, many foreign investors have chosen locations closer to the city center, but this is changing now that the new expressway has been completed.

The Tianjin ETDZ is zoned for different purposes, including residential, administrative, and industrial. The authorities are also keen to secure foreign investment for the development of heavier industries, including metallurgy.

As of mid-1991, more than 290 FIEs had been established in the Tianjin ETDZ with a total investment of US$720 million. The Tianjin ETDZ has distinguished itself as having high economic efficiency.

Many inland provinces and cities as well as Beijing have also set up more than 60 projects in the zone. CITIC has built its own industrial facility there covering an area of 0.78 square km (0.3 square mile). The Tianjin ETDZ is, moreover, among the first to assign the right to lease large tracts of land to foreign investors for development. Among those that have entered into land leasing contracts with the zone are MGM, Motorola, and Delaware Electronics Co., all US companies.

Yantai

Yantai is situated on the eastern part of the Shandong Peninsula. It is a well known tourist resort famed for its charm and natural beauty, and has a prosperous fishing industry and a reputation for the production of fruit and nuts.

The associated ETDZ, Fulaishan, is 10 km (6 miles) from the city, and is scheduled to reach 20 square km (7.75 square miles). Its major industries are food processing, machinery, chemicals, textiles, and building materials. More than 150 FIEs are now in operation in the whole city, while 65 operate in the ETDZ.

The city has good road and rail links with Qingdao, Jinan, Beijing, and Nanjing, and has had international direct dialing since 1988.

The port of Yantai, which has a history of 130 years, was updated not long ago, with the dock being extended by more than 2,400 meters. The port has built China's largest base for transshipping imported chemical fertilizer and alumina in bulk. The port of Yantai provides shipping services that link with more than 100 ports throughout the world as well as 20 major cities in China. As of 1991 almost 80 percent of the cargoes handled by this port are destined for foreign ports.

Aside from introducing foreign investment in the ETDZ, the local authorities have tried to direct foreign investors deep into the rural areas by carrying out such activities as wine festivals, art festivals, and fruit festivals to promote contacts between the township enterprises and the outside world. Due to the rich resources and sound development of many of these township enterprises, a fair number of projects have been set up jointly by these township enterprises and foreign investors.

To promote foreign trade, Yantai has set up a large number of agricultural export bases for the further improvement of its famous native products, including apples, pears, peanuts, silk, asparagus, mink, and aquatic products. These products are exported to more than 50 countries and regions.

Qingdao

Qingdao is situated in the southeastern part of the Shandong Peninsula facing the Yellow Sea. It is well known in many parts of the world because of its Tsingdao beer, which uses the equally celebrated Laoshan Mineral Water. But the city, with a population of nearly 2.1 million, is important both for industry and as a tourist center. Indeed, the name means Green Island, and it is famous in the heat of summer for cool breezes and cold currents at sea. In the early part of the century, the Germans took over a small village and constructed the present city with its splendid harbor. It is among the most attractive towns in China, retaining a strong Teutonic flavor. Unique in China, there is also a development zone for the tourist industry.

Textiles and light industries are well developed together with building materials, machinery, rubber, electronics, precision instruments, and chemicals.

Qingdao harbor ranks fourth in China. It is deep, wide, and ice- and silt-free. In addition to the new port that is being constructed at Qianwan, Qingdao Harbor is also under expansion. Air services link Qingdao with Japan, Hong Kong, and Singapore as well as with a dozen major cities in China. Qingdao is, moreover, directly linked by rail with Beijing, Shanghai, Wuhan, Lanzhou, Jinan, Yantai, and Shenyang. The port, which handled 27 million tons of cargo in 1985, is heading for 100 million tons within the next decade. Huangdao, situated outside the city, is the ETDZ.

Qingdao is under review for industrial development as well as in the areas of wine and foodstuffs.

Lianyungang

Lianyungang is situated in the northeastern part of Jiangsu Province in the middle of China's long eastern coastline, facing the Yellow Sea. Its favorable geographic position at the eastern end of China's principal east-west railway line has made it the major port for the coal-producing areas of central and northwest China. As a city located at the eastern end of the new Asia-Europe Continental Bridge, which connects Asia with Europe (with Rotterdam at the western end), Lianyungang is stepping up its efforts to create the conditions necessary for the Continental Bridge concept to become a reality by increasing its own container shipment and port handling capacity. Lianyungang's port has already opened container shipping routes to Kobe, Osaka, Nagoya, Hong Kong, South Korea, Singapore, Malaysia, and Thailand, and maintains shipping links with 176 ports in more than 50 countries. The city also has river access to the Beijing-Hangzhou Grand Canal, and the Yangtze River system. Its development is naturally focused around its role as a port whose annual capacity is planned to reach 50 million tons by the year 2000.

The area is rich in natural resources, including grain, cotton, peanuts, soybeans, fruit, aquatic products, and dozens of kinds of minerals.

The ETDZ, Zhongyuntai, lies 19 km (12 miles) to the southwest of the city. The basic infrastructure is now in place over a small area, but it is eventually planned to expand the zone to 35 square km (13.5 square miles). The major industries are chemicals, textiles, machinery, building materials, paper, plastics, and electronics. Since the completion of the new Asia-Europe Continental Bridge, the number of foreign investors coming to Lianyungang has been increasing. They have come not only from neighboring countries but also from Germany, Spain, the Netherlands, the USA, and Singapore.

Nantong

Nantong developed as a trading port on the north side of the Yangtze River estuary in the southeastern part of Jiangsu Province, and is now the third largest port on the river. Nantong is rich in agricultural, freshwater, and offshore aquatic resources. It is an important production base for commodity cotton in China. Its output of silk cocoons, goat skin, spearmint, and peppermint ranks the first in the province, and the city is the major supplier of pork and eggs for Shanghai. The city is famous for its silk and textile industries, particularly the blue cotton fabrics traditionally produced in Jiangsu. Most of its industry is light, but includes such heavy industry as shipbuilding.

Situated at the confluence of several rivers and linked to many canals, Nantong has easy access to 15 provinces, including Jiangsu, Anhui, Hubei, Hunan, and Sichuan, and regular ferry service covers the 130-km (81-mile) route to Shanghai. The fine natural harbor has two berths for 10,000- to 20,000-ton vessels and 10 berths for 3,000- to 5,000-ton vessels. The port has a current annual capacity of more than 20 million tons of cargo, and it is scheduled to increase its capacity to 40 million tons by 2000. Currently, container and regular cargo shipping services are available to Hong Kong and Kobe. High-speed river passenger liners connect the city with Shanghai. Regular flights are available to Beijing, Nanjing, and Guangzhou. The city has a daily water supply capacity of 300,000 tons, and its power supply capacity has recently been increased by 700,000 kilowatts per hour.

The ETDZ, Fumin, is 10 km (6 miles) southeast of the city, and is planned to cover about 5 square km (2 square miles). In addition, there is a new high-technology development zone, the second one to have been set up in Jiangsu.

Local incentives exist to encourage foreign investment. There are currently about 57 FIEs, operating in the city, 12 of which have an investment of more than US$5 million each. Most are involved in machinery, electronics, and chemicals.

Shanghai

Within the Shanghai Metropolitan Area, there are three ETDZs: the Minhang ETDZ, the Hongqiao ETDZ, and the Caohejing High-Technology Park (HTP). Minhang ETDZ and Hongqiao ETDZ were designated in 1984, while Caohejing HTP was sanctioned by the central government in 1988.

Minhang ETDZ, which lies some 30 km (19 miles) southeast of the city center and 27 km (17 miles) from the airport, is zoned for industrial development. There are currently more than 45 FIEs operating or being built in the zone, representing a total investment of US$210 million. Well-known international companies that have set up operations there include Xerox, Squibb, Union Carbide, Seagram, Coca-Cola, Mitsubishi Elevator, Unilever, and Johnson & Grace.

Hongqiao ETDZ, which lies only 6.5 km (4 miles) from the heart of the city and adjacent to the airport, is zoned for service industries, including trade, tourism, and property development. It was the first zone in Shanghai opened to assign land use rights for terms of more than 50 years. Infrastructural facilities in the zone are adequate. Aside from tourist hotels and commercial and office buildings, many foreign consulates are also located in this zone.

Caohejing High-Technology Park, as its name implies, is charged with fostering high-technology industries, including computers, fibers optics, large-scale integrated circuits, microelectronics, robots, biotechnology, lasers, and precision instruments. There are 20 universities and colleges and more than 120 research institutes in its vicinity. The park is planned to cover 5 square km (2 square miles) and is located 11 km (6.9 miles) from the city center and 7 km (4.3 miles) from the airport. Infrastructure there is good and, moreover, there is a 20-meter by 1 km (65 feet by 0.6 mile) green belt in the park.

The development of the much larger and more significant Pudong Development Zone was encouraged and approved by the central government in 1990. The Pudong Development Zone is the triangular zone to the east of the Huangpu River. It covers an area of 350 square km (135 square miles), roughly the same size of the present city proper and much larger than any of the existing Chinese ETDZs. The Pudong area currently has a population of 930,000, of which the urban population is 410,000. It has been described as the "pearl of Shanghai" and "one of the real treasures for land development in the world."

The development of Pudong is a long-term undertaking that will extend well into the next century. It is aimed to strengthen the multiple functions of Shanghai and bring about the concerted growth of the primary, secondary, and tertiary industries, but the early focus will be on industry.

Aside from the renovation and upgrading of existing enterprises, direct foreign investment will be encouraged in Pudong to turn out export-oriented and technologically-advanced products and import substitutes. Special efforts will be made to attract investments by international corporations for large industrial projects. In the meantime, finance, trade, services for foreign investors and businessmen, real estate, oceangoing shipping, and information and consulting businesses will be developed in this new area.

Partial infrastructure is already in place, including 711 port berths, 17 ferry lines, two cross-river tunnels, 7.5-km-long (4.7-mile-long) trunk roads, a 550,000 tons per day general sewage pipeline project, a gas plant (1 million cubic meters per day), a water plant (400,000 tons per day), a city telephone bureau, and high-voltage transmission and transformer facilities. The Nanpu Bridge spanning the Huangpu River is about to be completed. The construction of many more infrastructural projects is under way.

Currently there are around 2,400 industrial enterprises in the area. Major industries include petrochemicals, shipbuilding, iron and steel, textiles, building materials, and machinery.

Preferential policies, which are followed by the ETDZs and some SEZs, are implemented in the Pudong Development Zone. They include, for example:

- levying of enterprise income tax at a reduced rate of 15 percent;
- exemption of customs duty and industrial and commercial consolidated taxes of imports of raw materials, equipment, transportation vehicles,

and office supplies for the enterprises' own use;

- permission to operate the tertiary industries by foreign investors, and establishment of financial operations and commercial retail sales on an experimental basis in the area;
- permission for foreign banks to set up branches in the area;
- permission for foreign operations to engage in entrepôt trade in the bonded area or to act as agents for the import and export of raw materials and spare parts for FIEs in the area; and
- permission for foreign investors to develop land through the assignment of land use rights with compensation for a term of 50 to 70 years.

The key to Pudong's development is financing. In the start-up stage, investment in infrastructure alone will require billions of dollars. Although the Chinese central government agreed to grant a moderate amount of several billions of loans over five years, it is falling far short of the targeted contribution. Shanghai will have to rely on foreign soft loans and commercial loans and, above all, foreign direct investment.

Ningbo

Ningbo is the second largest city in Zhejiang Province. It lies south of Shanghai across Hangzhou Bay. Blessed with a spacious modern harbor and an efficient small airport, the inhabitants have overcome the isolation they suffered between the two world wars when its most famous citizen, the Hong Kong billionaire Sir Y. K. Pao, was a child there.

Today a massive development plan is in progress. The Ningbo Beilun Port Industrial Area, set up in 1986 and designated by the Chinese government as an important base for the economic development of Zhejiang, covers an area of 70 square km (27 square miles) and extends along the 13-km-long (8-mile-long) golden coastal line. In the last decade, the central and provincial governments have invested RMB 6 billion in building the infrastructure. A host of deepwater berths, including 14 berths for 10,000-ton vessels, have been completed. Other infrastructure projects put into commission include a transportation network comprising an airport, railways, and highways centering around Beilun Port; a 1.05-million kilowatt power plant; a number of large- and medium-sized water reservoirs with a storing capacity of more than 100 million cubic meters; and an international and domestic direct-dial telephone system with a capacity of 59,000 telephone lines. At present, the construction of the Ningbo-Hangzhou-Shanghai Expressway and the second phase of Beilun Port, which includes six berths for 30,000- to 50,000-ton container ships, a 97,000-line direct-dial telephone system, and fiber optic communications lines, are under way.

With the infrastructure initially in place, industrial joint ventures are being established. The first four large enterprises involve a total investment of RMB 602 million.

Beilun Port is only 130 nautical miles from Shanghai. Because the existing capacity of the Shanghai port cannot meet the rising demand, and the Yangtze River navigation channel near the Shanghai docks is only 7 meters deep, Beilun Port is well qualified to serve as Shanghai's subsidiary deepwater port.

Moreover, investors in Ningho, have the advantage of being able to draw on the skilled work force and expertise of nearby Shanghai. Currently about 170 FIEs, of which more than 150 are industrial in nature, are operating in Ningbo City.

Industries in Xiaogang, the small ETDZ in Ningbo, include petrochemicals, food processing, textiles, shipbuilding, and raw materials industries. The infrastructure in the ETDZ is adequate, and efficiency is high. It has been said that it can take only two weeks to complete the necessary approvals for a new project here.

Wenzhou

Wenzhou is an ancient city on the lower reaches of the Oujiang River in southern Zhejiang Province. It has abundant aquatic products, timber, and more than 30 kinds of minerals. Oil and natural gas resources are also rich on the coastal continental shelf. Its major farm products include rice, wheat, tea, rapeseed, jute, spices, and oranges.

The infrastructure of the city is inadequate, but is improving. There are direct-dial telephone and facsimile systems connecting different parts of China and more than 170 countries and regions. Apart from the old port facilities, there are two new berths for 10,000-ton vessels at the Longwan port. The new airport, completed in 1991, links the city with 14 major cities in China. Its passenger turnover exceeds that of the airports in Jinan, Nanchang, and Hefei, capitals of the neighboring provinces. There are regular passenger and cargo liners between Wenzhou and Hong Kong.

It has been the remarkable initiative of the local people that has turned this otherwise quiet backwater into a dynamic industrial and commercial center. The mobility of the local people is very high. Currently an estimated 650,000 Wenzhou people (the city's population is 6 million) are doing business in different parts of China, while every year about 200,000 businesspeople coming from every corner of the country to do business in Wenzhou. The city is particularly known for the private financial institutions that have sprung up to meet the needs of burgeoning private and individual industrial and commercial sectors.

Moreover, the city is the well-known ancestral

home of many overseas Chinese. There are more than 220,000 overseas Chinese of Wenzhou origin living in about 53 different countries and regions. Of the 117 FIEs operating in Wenzhou, 90 percent have been either directly formed or recommended by overseas Chinese.

The ETDZ is 14 km (8.7 miles) from the city center and close to the site of the new airport. In absorbing foreign investment, priority has been given to the development of chemicals (alumina and food additives), machine building (printing and packaging machinery, electronic components, energy-saving electric motors), building materials (fiberglass, reinforced plastics, and granite slabs), shoe making, garment manufacture, and food processing (fruit and aquatic products).

Fuzhou

Fuzhou is one of the most charming cities in China and the ancestral home of millions of overseas Chinese. Isolated from the interior by steep inhospitable mountain ranges, its inhabitants became merchants or fishermen. By the end of the 13th century, Marco Polo described the town as a place where "great trade is done." He also mentioned that the inhabitants "make sugar" and "produce pearls." This is still true. Immediately after the First World War there were more than 20 foreign companies in the city dealing in timber—which was floated down the river—tea, lychees, silks, lacquerware, and handicrafts. The railway, which then as now connects Fuzhou with Beijing and Shanghai, changed the city from its purely maritime role to an industrial center.

Today there is a large and efficient harbor, and an airport, but the coastal road remains narrow and bumpy. Meanwhile, the telephone system is adequate, with direct-dial connections to more than a dozen countries and a local population more friendly and better educated than that in many Chinese provincial cities.

Because ancestral Fuzhou is the home of many overseas Chinese, and the city is geographically very close to Taiwan, the city has become a favorite place of investment for overseas Chinese of Fujian origin, notably the Taiwanese. There is a special Taiwanese investment zone in Fuzhou.

Mawei is the ETDZ, about 4.5 square km (1.75 square miles) in area and situated some 13 km (8 miles) from the city center. The ETDZ has its own port with berths for six ships. The major industries are iron and steel, machinery, electronics, chemicals, foodstuffs, textiles, shipbuilding, and handicrafts. At the end of 1990, 82 FIEs were operating in the ETDZ accounting for more than US$100 million in foreign investment. As of March 1991 430 FIEs were operating in the city.

Guangzhou

The Guangzhou ETDZ is in the historic Huangpu (Whampoa) district, about 35 km (22 miles) downstream on the Pearl River from the city center. The total area of the zone is 10 square km (3.9 square miles), but a 2.5-square-km (1.0-square-mile) area adjacent to the river is being developed first. Here new port facilities are under construction, financed by soft loans from the World Bank.

The ETDZ has been among the most successful of its kind as a result of substantial investment, notably from Hong Kong. Major industries within the zone include food processing, canning, textiles, and the assembly of electronic components.

Zhanjiang

Zhanjiang is situated in a pleasant area of southern Guangdong Province only 80 nautical miles by sea from Haikou, capital of Hainan Island. It is the southernmost port in China and the starting point of the shortest route from the Chinese mainland to Africa, Europe, and Southeast Asia. It includes a minor naval base and residential and recreation areas constructed for the many foreigners who, in the early 1980s, were using Zhanjiang as a headquarters for offshore oil exploration.

Apart from frequent ferry service to Haikou, there is an airport with regular flights to Hong Kong, Guangzhou, Haikou, and Sanya, and a major highway constructed to facilitate the movement of goods. Zhanjiang has international direct-dial telephone service.

The Litang-Zhanjiang and Hunan-Guangxi railways connect the city with the Beijing-Guangzhou Railway.

Xiashan is the ETDZ. It is situated only 2 km (1.25 miles) from the center of the town. Harbor development is planned and the area is earmarked for light industry. Donghai, a tourist site some 22 km (14 miles) away, is more prosperous. Priority for foreign investment in Zhanjiang is given to building materials, machinery, food processing, home appliances, cereals and edible oils, and fertilizers.

Beihai

Beihai is an attractive small port situated in the subtropical sector of the Guangxi Zhuang Autonomous Region in the southernmost part of China. With a population of around one million, the town has abundant aquatic resources (more than 500 kinds), pearls, and hippocamous (a rare Chinese medicinal herb). The continental shelf of the adjacent Beibu Gulf is rich in oil, with reserves of 350 to 500 million tons. Quartz sand, a kind of quality glass material, is also abundant along the coast. In the vicinity of the city, large reserves 20 to 30 meters thick of high-grade pottery clay, an excellent material for industrial ceramics, have been found.

Industries include textiles, paper-making, chemicals, food processing, porcelains, and pharmaceuticals. Priority is given to the development of off-shore oil, marine chemicals, marine biomedicines, building materials, steel, processing of aquatic products and other foodstuffs, power generation, and petrochemicals.

Beihai harbor currently has a port handling capacity of 800,000 tons, but that could be doubled. Regular flights link the city with Banning (capital of Guangxi Autonomous Region) and Guangzhou. Some 1,860 microwave telecommunications lines connect Beihai with Nanning. A railway linking the city with Qinzhou, an extension of the existing Kunming-Nanning Railway, is slated to begin construction in the near future.

OPEN ECONOMIC ZONES (OEZ)

In 1985 the Chinese government designated three delta areas as open economic development zones, and soon afterwards two peninsulas were added to the list. These three Delta areas, from north to south, are the Yangtze Delta, the Southern Fujian Delta and the Pearl River Delta. The two peninsulas are Shandong and Liaodong. These five regions are among the most developed areas in China. They are rich in grain and fruits, subtropical cash crops, and

aquatic products. Handicraft industries are also well developed, and the deltas are otherwise characterized by their ready accessibility, superior education levels, and traditional ties with foreign countries. The incentives and privileges available in the OEZs generally resemble those found in the 14 Coastal Cities. They enjoy considerable flexibility in foreign trade and investment. Infrastructure projects are also going ahead to improve transport, communications, energy supply, and other services. As in the Coastal Cities, the aim appears to be to develop export-oriented processing business and to concentrate on technological improvement of industry.

The boundaries of the OEZs change frequently and it is difficult to define the areas with any precision.

The Yangtze Delta

The Yangtze River Delta OEZ covers an area of about 30,000 square km (11,580 square miles), comprising the cities of Suzhou, Wuxi, and Changzhou in Jiangsu Province, the cities of Jiaxing and Huzhou in Zhejiang Province, 10 suburbs in counties under Shanghai jurisdiction, and some additional areas. Like the 14 Coastal Cities, the Yangtze Delta is one of the most developed and important economic areas in China.

The delta has long been known as "the land of fish and rice," with abundant supplies of grain, fruits,

Five Ways to Help Your Local Agent

1. Make frequent visits to China to support your agent's efforts. They help to build the relationship, without which no amount of effort can succeed in China. Keep in mind that your competitors are also paying personal visits to their agents and customers. And invite your agent to your country to reciprocate his hospitality and to familiarize him with your country and your company.

2. Hold many demonstrations and exhibits of your products. If you're a supplier to Chinese manufacturers, the value of sales presentations at factories cannot be overemphasized. Factory engineers and managers are directly responsible for the equipment and machinery to be purchased, and they have a great deal of influence over the decision to buy. This is so highly effective—and so cheap—a sales booster that it's irresponsible for an exporter to ignore it.

3. Increase the distribution of promotional brochures and technical data to potential buyers, libraries and industry associations. When your agent makes personal sales calls, your potential customers won't be completely in the dark.

4. Improve follow-up on initial sales leads. Let your agent know you're backing him or her up with whatever it takes to pursue the lead. "All our foreign partners know that they have the support of a large system behind them," McDonald's spokesman Brad Trask says. "The support system is available on request."

5. Deliver on time. If you don't, you can believe that someone else will. Failure to deliver on time not only makes your agent lose face and thereby undermines your relationship, but it jeopardizes your sales. There's not much you can do to make ships go faster or airlines schedule more flights, but you can stockpile your products in China to ensure that your agent has a steady supply. When you have to (and it's possible) forget the expense and airfreight the product for two-day delivery: The extra effort will go a long way in establishing and fortifying your reputation.

silk, and aquatic products. Considerable foreign investment has been attracted to the area, and foreign technology and equipment have been introduced for various industries.

Priorities include the development of maritime trade, technical upgrading of textiles and other light industries, machine building, chemicals, electronics, plastics, building materials, and food processing.

The announcement of the opening up of the new Pudong Development Zone in Shanghai has recently led to a series of reactions in the Yangtze Delta. Seven major industrial cities at the lower reaches of the Yangtze River—Nantong, Suzhou, Wuxi, Changzhou, Yangzhou, Zhenjiang, and Nanjing—have decided to bill themselves as an interdependent industrial belt with an outward-oriented economy to take advantage of the development of Pudong. Other major cities along the upper reaches of the river have decided to create a Shanghai-Nanjing-Wuhan-Chongqing Yangtze Economic Corridor. Currently, infrastructural development activity is being stepped up to pave the way for the implementation of these programs.

The Southern Fujian Delta

Known sometimes as the Xiamen-Zhangzhou-Quanzhou Open Economic Triangular Zone, the Southern Fujian Delta is situated in southeast Fujian Province. It comprises Xiamen City's Tongan County, Zhangzhan City, Longhai County, Zhangpu County, Dongshan County, Quanzhou City, Hui'an County, Nan'an County, Jingjiang County, Anxi County, and Yongchun County. In 1986 the Fujian provincial government designated 13 satellite towns to be included in the zone. In November 1987 another 18 towns were added to list.

Known as the golden delta, the area is famous for its rich natural resources and fertile land. It enjoys an abundance of subtropical crops, fruits, aquatic products, and flowers, most of which are exported. There are also mineral and timber resources. The major industry is textiles. The OEZ also has the advantage of being the ancestral home of very large numbers of overseas Chinese.

Priorities include technical renovation of existing enterprises, the development of packaging techniques, the expansion of the export of various products, and the establishment of a comprehensive industrial system linking the production of textiles, chemicals, and electronics to those of building materials and machinery.

The Zhujiang (Pearl River) Delta

The Zhujiang Delta also covers an area of about 30,000 square km (11,580 square miles) surrounding the mouth of the Zhujiang River in the southern part of Guangdong Province. It comprises Panyu and Zengcheng Counties in Guangzhou municipality; Foshan City and its three counties, Nanhai, Gaoming and Shunde; Zhongshan City; Jiangmen City and its five counties, Heshan, Xinhui, Kaiping, Enping, and Taishan; Baoan County in Shenzhen City; Doumen County in Zhuhai City; and Dongguan City in Huiyang Prefecture.

The Zhujiang Delta OEZ is the richest area in Guangdong with many cash crops, subtropical fruits, and aquatic products. It also has mineral resources, including deposits of nonferrous and nonmetallic minerals. Oil and natural gas reserves have been discovered along the continental shelf of the offshore areas.

The Zhujiang Delta OEZ has been one of the most prosperous in China, and was also one of the earliest open to the outside world. Traditionally, the delta was primarily a supplier of farm produce, poultry, and vegetables to Hong Kong, Macao, and the southern part of China. In the 1980s it became a processing area for textiles, garments, electronics, home appliances, and other light industries, with more than a million jobs dependent upon investment or processing contracts from labor-starved Hong Kong. Due to the implementation of preferential policies in the delta and its geographic proximity to Hong Kong, it soon thrived, with the economy of the Four Tigers of Guangdong (Zhongshan, Dongguan, Xinde, and Nanhai) growing even more quickly than the Four Little Dragons in Asia (Hong Kong, Taiwan, South Korea, and Singapore). During the 1990s the economy of this area has taken on a new look. Technology and capital-intensive projects are on the rise. For example, an advanced textiles production system has been shaping up in the delta centering around Enping, Xinhui, and Kaiping, where no textile industry existed in the past. With the rapid absorption of foreign investment, the tertiary industries, particularly the property, tourist, and telecommunications industries, are also developing at a considerable pace. As an extensive hinterlands area for Hong Kong's economy, this OEZ is helping to alleviate Hong Kong's labor and raw materials shortage.

The increasing integration of the economy of the British territory with that of the Zhujiang Delta is regarded as encouraging for the future of Hong Kong as 1997—the year in which the territory will be handed back to China—approaches.

Shandong Peninsula

Situated on China's northeast coast, Shandong Peninsula is the largest peninsula in the country. It consists of the seven cities of Qingdao, Jinan, Yantai, Weihai, Weifang, Zibo, and Rizhao, along with 50 surrounding counties under their jurisdiction. It covers an area of about 50,000 square km (19,300 square miles), almost one-third of Shandong Province, and has a population of 27 million.

The peninsula has more than 20 large and small ports, including Qingdao and Yantai, with an annual cargo-handling capacity of 50 million tons. There is a good basic network of railways and highways reaching every corner of the peninsula. Regular domestic air flights carry both cargo and passengers to Qingdao, Jinan, Yantai, Weihai, and Weifang.

The peninsula is one of China's most populous regions, noted for its long coastline, abundant farm production, aquatic, and mineral resources, as well as cheap labor. Agricultural products include peanuts, tobacco, fruits (apples, grapes, pears, and dates), silkworm cocoons, and vegetables, while industries include machinery, electronics, textiles, building materials, and chemicals.

Many of Shandong's industrial products enjoy good reputations both in China and abroad, including Tsingdao beer, Yantai wine, cotton and wool textiles, chinaware, and garments. Currently priority in attracting foreign investment is given to the development of energy, raw and building materials, chemicals, and high technology.

In the first half of 1991 396 FIEs were approved to set up in the zone, with contracted foreign investment of US$210 million, nine times as much as in the corresponding period in 1990.

Liaodong Peninsula

The Liaodong Peninsula lies on the northeast coast of China facing the Pacific Ocean. It covers an area of 43,000 square km (16,600 square miles), consisting of the eight cities of Dalian, Shenyang, Anshan, Panjin, Yingkou, Liaoyang, Dandong, and Jingzhou, along with 16 outlying countries under their jurisdiction. The peninsula is comprised of two major economic belts: the coastal belt, with Dalian as its center and including the port cities of Dandong, Yingkou, and Jingzhou; and the inland industrial belt, with Shenyang, the largest industrial city in the northeast, as its center, and including industrial cities such as Anshan and Liaoyang.

The peninsula is rich in agricultural and aquatic products, including rice, corn, soybeans, sorghum, peanuts, apples, prawns, fish, and shellfish. Its prawn catch makes up one-third of the country's total. Moreover, the peninsula boasts very rich reserves of coal and minerals. Industries include machinery, metallurgy, electric power generation, chemicals, petroleum, and building materials. It used to be one of the most important industrial areas in China. However, from the mid-1960s to the late 1970s the Liaodong Peninsula was reduced to a low priority position for development. But its favorable geographic location, its rich natural resources, its solid industrial foundation, and its skilled work force make it an ideal investment environment, leading the central government

designated it an open coastal economic region in the early 1980s. Since its opening, more than 250 foreign invested ventures have been set up, with an actual input of about US$1.93 billion in foreign investment. Dalian, in particular, has become a favorite place for Japanese investment. During the 1990s foreign trade and export of technologies on the peninsula have made great headway, with cumulative export value reaching US$6.52 billion.

Currently, the opening of the peninsula is expanding from the Coastal Cities to inland areas and from urban enterprises to township and rural enterprises. Although past exports from the peninsula consisted mostly farm products and primary products, there are many more manufactured goods and downstream processed products being exported now.

According to the local government plan to attract foreign investment, priority will be given in the coming decade to the development of energy, metallurgy, petrochemicals, building materials, raw materials, and textiles. Haicheng, Yingkou, and Benxi will be built into production bases for talc and talc products; Shenyang and Haicheng into ceramic production centers; Dandong and Benxi into marble and granite production centers; and Dalian, Ansham, Liaoyang, and Fuxun into cement export bases. Five hundred categories of advanced technology will be introduced into the peninsula to upgrade existing enterprises during the next five years. And a large, new, high-tech industrial development belt will be created in the Shenyang, Dalian, Anshan, Liaoyang, and Yinkou areas designed to follow development in the two original high-technology development districts in Dalian and Shenyang.

Business Entities & Formation

FORMS OF BUSINESS ORGANIZATION

China offers Chinese and foreign nationals several options for establishing a business in China. Alternatives include forming a joint venture, operating as a wholly foreign-owned enterprise, or setting up a representative office. Between 1979 and 1986 almost 98 percent of the entities that foreign investors set up in order to do business in China were joint ventures, and only about 2 percent were wholly foreign-owned enterprises. By the end of 1992 equity joint ventures accounted for 65 percent of approved foreign investment by number and 47.7 percent by value, followed by contractual joint ventures with 18.5 percent by number and 28.6 percent by value. Wholly foreign-owned enterprises represented 16.5 percent by number and 23.7 percent by value. Other formats are gaining in familiarity and popularity, but the joint venture remains the most common vehicle for overseas participation in the Chinese economy. In May 1992 Chinese authorities authorized foreign firms to organize as companies limited by shares, but this format is still in the experimental stage and lacks clear implementing regulations. Additional ways of doing business involve special contractual trade arrangements, including countertrade, compensation trade, assembly and processing, and technology transfer contracts.

The specific type of business selected will be determined by the investor's objectives, circumstances, the anticipated duration, the importance of limiting bureaucratic involvement—which electing to operate through contractual agreements can curtail to some extent—and other business, investment, and personal considerations. This discussion reviews the various forms of foreign business operations that China allows under current rules.

Recognized Entities

China recognizes a variety of business entities as appropriate for foreign investors who want to operate in its jurisdiction. These entities include both equity and cooperative joint ventures, wholly foreign-owned enterprises, and representative offices. China does not recognize some other types of business entity that are common elsewhere. Businesses cannot use branch or liaison offices to operate in China and they generally are not allowed to organize as partnerships or sole proprietorships.

Joint Ventures

A joint venture is a business arrangement in which the participants create a new business entity or official contractual relationship and share investment and operation expenses, management responsibilities, and profits and losses. Most Asian legal systems do not recognize a joint ventures as a separate legal entity. However, Chinese joint venture law accords the special status of a legal person to ventures formed under its terms. The joint venture is the form of organization that PRC authorities encourage foreigners to use when they do business in China. To underline this preference, the PRC has stated that it will not nationalize or expropriate any foreign joint ventures except under extraordinary circumstances and with compensation.

Participants technically can be Chinese or foreign individuals or one or more corporations, although official China is still uncomfortable dealing with individuals and prefers that they represent some corporate entity. Joint ventures may also be formed through and with institutions, such as the China International Trust and Investment Corporation (CITIC), China Venturetech Investment Corporation, and China Everbright Holdings Co. Ltd., all entities that have been specifically designed to arrange such partnering, or with other Chinese entities at virtually any level of organization.

A joint venture has the right to conduct business independently within the scope of the provisions of Chinese laws and rulings according to the terms of its contract agreement and articles of association. This stipulation frees a joint venture from having to comply with certain work rules and from some over-

Glossary

Bank of China (BOC) The Bank of China has overall responsibility for China's foreign exchange system. Beyond implementing domestic policies and regulating currency, the BOC also serves as the primary focal point for foreign business conducted in China. In addition to providing investors with assistance in the form of feasibility studies, loans, and credit guarantees, it offers other services which include consulting on joint ventures, compensation trade, and other types of business.

China International Trust and Investment Corporation (CITIC) The semi-private China International Trust and Investment Corporation carries ministry status and is able to advise foreigners on joint venture formation, technical cooperation agreements, and investment insurance, among other areas of concern.

Foreign Trade Corporations (FTCs) As distinct legal entities under the supervision of the MOFTEC, foreign trade corporations provide the focus for foreign trade at both national and local levels. Individual FTCs are responsible for the goods or services provided by industry or sector. These corporations have the authority to approve technical and commercial agreements between Chinese and foreign entities. FTCs have traditionally served as a primary point of contact for enterprises wishing to make contacts or conduct business in China, although more entities are now authorized to deal directly with foreigners.

Ministry of Foreign Trade and Economic Cooperation (MOFTEC) The Ministry of Foreign Trade and Economic Cooperation, formerly the Ministry of Foreign Economic Relations and Trade (MOFERT), has primary authority to approve and regulate foreign business activity in China.

Special Economic Zones (SEZs) Located in the southern provinces of Guangdong and Fujian and on Hainan Island, the Special Economic Zones (SEZs) were established in the early 1980s to promote foreign investment by offering tax, land use, and import duty incentives to facilitate China's overall modernization and expansion of international markets. SEZ investment incentives have been extended to designated Economic and Technological Development Zones (ETDZs) in various Coastal Cities.

State Administration for Industry and Commerce (SAIC) The State Administration for Industry and Commerce is the office generally responsible for the registration of businesses in China. All foreign business must register for a business license with the provincial or local Administration for Industry and Commerce after receiving foreign investment approval from the MOFTEC.

---

sight with which domestic firms and firms using other forms of organization must deal. However, foreign entities must still abide by most rules and there is some evidence that they are facing increased enforcement of the rules that apply.

Chinese law recognizes two types of joint venture: The equity joint venture and the cooperative joint venture.

Equity Joint Venture The organizational structure of an equity joint venture is that of a limited liability company registered in China in compliance with joint venture law. It thus has the status of a separate legal entity the liability of which is limited to the value of its assets, apportioned by the percentage of capital contributions that individual parties have made. Management of the enterprise is a shared responsibility, and profits and losses are allocated by the percentage of capital contribution that the respective partners have made. About 40 percent of the joint ventures in China are equity joint ventures.

Foreign investors can legally own 100 percent of the entity, but in practice they are usually limited to about a 50 percent share. Before reforms were enacted in 1990, a joint venture agreement could run for a maximum period of 30 years. After reform, the maximum life of a joint venture has been extended to 50 years. With special permission, certain businesses can be allowed to register for longer terms. Extensions are judged on a case-by-case basis.

Equity joint ventures enjoy preferential tax treatment, although the Chinese have announced their intention to phase out this incentive by dropping the tax rate paid by local firms to the level paid by foreign joint ventures to enhance the competitiveness of the local firms. However, joint ventures are often exempt from customs duties levied on goods imported as inputs, depending on the business activity conducted, its location, and the nature of the foreign contribution.

Because the Chinese government favors this arrangement, legal provisions defining it are the most extensive of any governing business formation. This is both a blessing and a curse. On the one hand, substantive law tells operators what they can and cannot do, which eliminates some uncertainty. On the other hand, the fact that there is extensive legal coverage attracts official attention to such operations, which can be unwelcome.

Remittance of earnings is allowed, but in practice it is a chronic problem in China, where foreign exchange is always in short supply and the local currency is effectively inconvertible. As part of the 1990 reform, joint ventures were allowed to establish accounts with banks authorized to deal in foreign exchange, so such firms have some limited access to foreign exchange for remittances. However, remittances can be made only from direct net cash earnings.

Cooperative or Contractual Joint Ventures Under the Chinese-foreign cooperative joint ventures law, partners are not required to form a new company, but can carry on a joint venture based on contractual agreement. If the contract is executed under the terms of the governing statute, it gains the status of a separate legal entity without the necessity of forming a separate company. The rules for this type of joint venture are somewhat looser than they are for equity joint ventures. Usually of shorter duration than equity joint ventures—the majority are for periods of five to ten years—cooperative joint ventures define the terms of participation by contract. As a result, they are often more flexible than the more heavily regulated equity joint ventures. About 60 percent of the joint ventures in China are cooperative joint ventures.

The areas to be negotiated include capital contribution, ownership and management, rights, and liabilities. Distribution of earnings or products is also

Joint Ventures

China's voluminous but often sketchy, arbitrary, and contradictory laws and regulations pose a constant challenge to foreign investors. In recognizing joint ventures as one of the better-defined business forms, a Chinese employee of a government-owned import-export corporation stated, "For starting up a joint venture company, there is no minimum amount required. It depends on what type of joint venture is formed. For example, some amounts may be more than US$10,000, while others may need less than US$100. However, foreign investment must be a minimum of 25 percent of the total amount."

Capital contributions do not necessarily have to be made in money. Investment on the foreign side can take the form of such contributions as cars, office supplies, equipment, or raw materials. For example, automobiles are currently a scarce and highly desirable import item, and importing vehicles for use in a joint venture can not only make an otherwise unobtainable resource available for company use but also lend prestige to the venture. Promises of terms for disposal of the asset can also provide a bargaining chip when permits and other concessions are being negotiated. Chinese partners often contribute land, factory buildings, or equipment as their part of the investment. All capital contributions are imported duty free and contributed tax free.

Foreign investors may start a joint venture with a Chinese entity or a Chinese individual. For investors looking for non-specific business opportunities in China, an alliance with a local entrepreneur can be a flexible and advantageous way of gaining a foothold in China business. However, this area can be tricky, because China often does not recognize contracts between individuals. Its system is geared to dealing with entities represented by individuals, not with individuals acting on their own. Much of the new entrepreneurialism that lies at the heart of China's present-day boom results from the efforts of individuals acting on their own behalf, but the official status of such enterprises has yet to be defined.

When entering into specific ventures, investors must not only consider such factors as location, availability of incentives, logistics, and levels of outlay, expense, and projected profits but also whether their proposed partner is authorized and able to conduct the business activities envisioned. Such considerations involve an examination not only of the partner's relevant business expertise and resources but also of its local influence. Because *guanxi*—connections, or more bluntly, clout—are often critical in gaining official approval, authorization, and ongoing favor, an influential Chinese partner can be the most valuable intangible asset that a business can have.

determined by contractual agreement, not by percentage of capital contribution. Management responsibility can be shared, separate, assigned exclusively to one party, or even assigned to a third party.

In accordance with the state's goal to promote the acquisition of new technology, growth in exports, and the expansion of activities that produce foreign exchange, this form of venture is often used for the joint development of energy resources and infrastructure for tourism. The contractual nature of a cooperative joint venture gives the parties more flexibility in dealing with earnings than does an equity joint venture, in which earnings are divided on a strict percentage-of-ownership basis. Moreover, in

an equity joint venture earnings can only be paid out of net cash profits while those in a cooperative joint venture can consist of noncash items. For example, returns in a cooperative joint venture can be arranged via countertrade or other means of compensation rather than limited to net income and the vagaries of access to foreign exchange.

Because there is no separate company in a cooperative joint venture, each party is taxed separately. (In an equity joint venture, the taxable entity is the company as a whole). Domestic partners are liable for taxes under domestic law and foreigners are liable under the Foreign Enterprise Income Tax Law (FEITL). By law, all fixed assets revert to the

Companies Limited by Shares and Limited Companies

In May 1992 China announced that it would allow foreigners as well as locals to do business in China organized as corporations, either as companies limited by shares or as limited companies. The State Economic Commission promulgated the "Share Enterprise Trial Measures," the "Opinion for Companies Limited by Shares," and the "Opinion for Limited Companies." The first two cover limited liability joint stock companies and the last covers limited companies that would not issue transferable shares but would otherwise operate as corporations. Local authorities in Shanghai and Shenzhen have also prepared standards and regulations to govern companies issuing shares on their stock exchanges. The impetus for these regulations appears to be the need to regularize the concept of joint stock companies in order to provide a legitimate supply of shares for China's growing stock exchanges.

The exact relationship between these new rules and existing foreign investment rules remains unclear. In the past foreign firms have not been authorized to organize as joint stock companies or offer shares to either domestic investors or to other foreigners. This had the effect of freezing ownership which could then only be altered by special application that amounted to seeking reauthorization for the investment as a whole. Since about 1990 domestic firms have been allowed to issue stock and have been able to acquire foreign invested enterprise (FIE) status by placing their shares with foreign investors, but foreign firms have not been allowed to issue shares. To date no FIEs have organized as Chinese joint stock companies.

The company limited by shares raises its capital by issuing shares of equal value. Shareholders have a proportional vote in matters regarding corporate governance and operations as well as the right to a proportional share of earnings. A limited company is effectively similar to a joint venture in that although it is organized as a corporation it does not offer negotiable shares to the general public but apportions ownership proportionally among the contracting parties. However, the limited company structure allows for greater input from the stakeholders in matters of corporate governance than does the traditional joint venture structure in which decsions were left to the designated managers. Participants in a limited company also have access to an ongoing share in the earnings of the enterprise. Both formats are designed to convey separate legal person status on the entity and limit the liability of the shareholders to the proportion of ownership represented by their shareholdings. This represents a significant theoretical shift for China, where corporate responsibility has traditionally been viewed as absolute.

Under the rules advanced in Shanghai and Shenzhen such corporations must appoint a quasi-independent supervisory authority responsible for monitoring the actions of the board of directors and management. In accord with listing rules, incorporated firms can issue up to 25 percent of their total capitalization as B shares available for purchase by foreign investors. Such entities are eligible for incentives and preferential treatment as FIEs. (Refer to "Financial Institutions" for a discussion of Chinese stock markets and listing rules).

Doing Business Through Hong Kong

The costs and difficulties of doing business in China are substantial, and many foreign investors prefer to gain access to China through an office in Hong Kong. Access to China is easy from Hong Kong—most foreigners desiring to do business in China enter via Hong Kong anyway—and access to Hong Kong itself is even easier. In fact, it is often easier to arrange travel, even in outlying areas of China, from Hong Kong than it is from Beijing. And Hong Kong is geographically adjacent to Guangdong and Fujian, the main locations for foreign business in China.

Despite the fact that nominal costs in China are a fraction of what they are elsewhere, the actual costs of maintaining a foreign business there can be astronomical—as high as anywhere else in the world. Hong Kong may actually compare favorably in terms of the cost of maintaining foreign personnel, and a Hong Kong location is likely to improve staff morale.

Hong Kong itself has a laissez faire atmosphere, few regulations on business, and minimal bureaucracy. It also offers excellent communications and business infrastructure, including a pool of experts and English-speaking staff people.

All major Chinese governmental agencies and organizations maintain offices in Hong Kong, and they are often more accessible there than they are in their home venues. The fact that these different entities are in competition gives the foreign operator a chance to shop projects among various Chinese units in order to obtain the best deal. Some of these offices lack the authority to close deals, but the main ones can handle all aspects of negotiations, and some can even sign contracts.

Foreign businesses looking to exploit this opportunity must remember that home offices in China usually have veto power over arrangements made by their representatives. Businesspeople must also remember that such representatives can get carried away and make promises on which they cannot deliver. The representative's desire to close the deal, inexperience, or outright incompetence or fraud are all possible explanations for such behavior.

Hong Kong also supports hundreds of firms that act as agents, middlemen, and facilitators for foreign entities interested in doing business in China. The foreign business can sometimes obtain most of the benefits that it is seeking from China through such an agent without ever having to set foot in China. There are limits on what such agents can accomplish, and they do take an often substantial cut of the profits, but they may allow a firm with a less than total commitment to doing business in China or a relatively short-term need to gain certain benefits while minimizing its liabilities.

The buyer must beware of Hong Kong-based China business agents. Many are experienced, and some are even miracle workers, but others lack experience, ability, and perhaps even integrity. It is important to investigate the credentials of these people.

For firms uncertain about whether to go to China or stay in Hong Kong, there remains the possibility of having it both ways. An office established in Hong Kong now will automatically become a Chinese office in 1997.

Chinese partner at the end of the contract. If foreign partners negotiate such a provision into the original contract, they may receive a larger share of interim profits during the operation of the venture to allow them to recover their initial investment.

Capital Requirements No general minimum or maximum limits have been placed on the amount that can be contributed to an equity joint venture, although since 1987, joint ventures with foreign participants in the Shenzhen Special Economic Zone (SEZ) have been required to have a minimum capital of RMB 1 million—about US$115,000.

Foreign investors are required to provide at least 25 percent of the registered capital. In practice, most foreign contributors supply closer to 50 percent. Officials often try to get a greater foreign contribution, but this desire to maximize inputs is offset by a fear of foreign control, and most deals end up with some sort of balance between domestic and foreign parties.

Some foreign participants have tried to reduce their actual contribution by obtaining national currency on the informal swap markets where the exchange rate is more favorable. However, this procedure is unreliable, and is at best only tolerated by officialdom. It is better used at a later stage for obtaining operating funds than it is for providing the initial capital contributions, which the government scrutinizes more closely.

In either type of joint venture arrangement, contributed capital may consist of funds, property rights, machinery and equipment, capitalized labor, or technical knowledge in any combination. These forms of investment are contingent on the comparative advantage of each side, established need, indispensability to production, domestic inability to produce the needed inputs, current international market prices, and considerations of resource and raw materials allocation. The foreign participant usually is expected to contribute hard assets, such as actual cash and fixed assets, while the Chinese expect to be allowed to furnish soft assets, such as property rights, access to power grids, and capitalized labor.

A semiofficial rule-of-thumb sliding scale sets a certain ratio of hard assets to soft assets as the necessary condition for investment approval. In general, the smaller the total investment, the larger the percentage of hard assets required. For example, if the total investment is under US$3 million, the authorities generally require that 70 percent of the sum be in hard assets, while for large investments—those exceeding US$30 million—only about one-third of the commitment needs to consist of hard assets.

Contributions of capital must be made on a timely basis. A 15 percent down payment must be made within three months after the contract has received official approval. The remainder is due within six months. Failure to comply could result in loss of the entity's license and recognition of the entity. Moreover, the defaulting party is also liable for compensating the other party if the joint venture folds because the defaulter failed to make its agreed upon contribution. As a practical matter, such a claim would be limited to assets on hand, which are likely to be minimal if they were inadequate to comply with the terms of the agreement in the first place. However, such a default could prejudice a foreign entity's ability to operate in China in the future.

Shareholders, Directors, Officers, and Corporate Governance As a result of the 1990 reform, a foreigner may serve as the chairman of the board of a joint venture. (Before reform, only Chinese were allowed to lead joint ventures). The chairman and the vice-chairman are chosen in consultation by the participants in an equity joint equity venture or by the board of directors. If the Chinese side provides the chairman, the vice-chairmanship devolves to the foreign side and vice versa.

Both sides of a joint venture choose the board of directors in a manner that they agree upon and specify in the initial contract. A cooperative joint venture may appoint a joint management committee in place of a board of directors. The board must have a minimum of three members. Directors serve a four-year term, and they can serve multiple consecutive terms. Few specific regulations govern the powers and responsibilities of board members.

A board must meet at least once a year, and two-thirds of the board members must be present to establish a quorum. Most decisions are by simple majority, but changing the articles of incorporation requires the unanimous accord of the members in attendance at an official board meeting. Decisions to terminate the venture; increase capital or the assigned share of capital; or to merge with another entity must also be unanimous. Internal disputes among participants must be submitted to arbitration.

The board appoints a general manager and deputy managers to handle the day-to-day operations of the venture. There is currently no provision for the issuance of stock or other transferable securities by entities in which foreigners hold equity. However, approved enterprises can issue stock which foreigners are allowed to buy, effectively converting such entities into foreign invested enterprises.

Liquidation Most joint ventures dissolve at the end of the term specified in their agreement. Such firms can also petition to extend the life of the venture but must do so before its scheduled expiration. The conditions under which an agreement can be terminated before the time specified in the agreement include insolvency; the failure of one party to fulfill the terms of the agreement; war, natural disaster, or other circumstances that make continuation of operations impossible; inability to reach the objectives of the agreement; or other reasons or conditions specified in the contract.

Management can agree to terminate the operation and liquidate assets, but the general requirement for mandatory arbitration to settle disputes means that such a mechanism rather than a strict, court-administered process would prevail if the participants disagree. In dissolutions, a management committee has the right to allocate assets to current claimants before apportioning any remaining assets among the participants.

Equity capital cannot be repatriated during the life of an equity joint venture. The remaining assets are distributed in proportion to the percentage of original capital contributions. In a cooperative joint venture, all fixed assets revert to the Chinese partner at the end of the contract. The foreign partner retains the right to only such property as the terms of the contract accord to it as profits.

Wholly Foreign-Owned Enterprises

A wholly foreign-owned enterprise (WFOE) is a business formed in China entirely with foreign capital, totally under foreign control, and without any formal Chinese ownership participation. WFOEs are set up as limited liability entities represent separate legal persons, and have the right to remit earnings. To date, such businesses have been mostly subsidiaries of foreign parent firms, usually large firms with international name recognition that have been willing to risk going it alone in China. This type of entity is still comparatively new and unfamiliar. It has legal status, but in practice its functional status remains undefined.

Virtually all such businesses are located within Special Economic Zones (SEZs) or Economic and Technological Development Zones (ETDZs) in coastal areas, although it is legal for such entities to operate elsewhere in the country. These pioneering outfits represented less than 2 percent of the foreign contractual entities established in China between 1979 and 1986. However, it is expected that more such entities will be set up and in other locations as the rules become better established and the entities become more familiar to the members of the local business community.

WFOEs are similar in concept and organization to US corporations, and most function like wholly owned subsidiaries. They differ from foreign branch offices in that they are legally independent entities that carry out all their own business operations, not dependent entities that derive their standing from the parent. The life of a WFOE is generally limited to a period of no more than 50 years, and the average life is much shorter, around 20 years. Any change in ownership or operations is strictly controlled. Approval must be granted by the Administration for Industry and Commerce. However, reasonable business requests are usually approved.

WFOEs can generally control their own governance through articles of association, although they are subject to all relevant Chinese laws. As legally recognized entities, they are protected from seizure except through due process and with compensation. Such entities are eligible for incentives, but incentives are not granted automatically, and they must be justified to the granting authorities.

The authorities will allow business entities of this type only if the ventures are deemed advantageous to China's economic development. Enterprises that provide new advanced technology or increase exports are the most likely to be approved, but entities that promote import substitution, production of approved new products, or improved quality are also favored. Moreover, WFOEs generally are not allowed to participate in such areas as national defense, public utilities, banking, insurance, real estate, media and communications, shipping, domestic service businesses, or exports for which there are established quotas. However, the government reserves the right both to make exceptions and allow limited participation for special opportunities that it deems to be particularly advantageous as well as to further restrict the areas in which such entities can operate.

Many foreign investors are likely to find the idea of a WFOE attractive because of the control that 100 percent ownership offers in theory. However, this control comes at a cost, because a WFOE does not enjoy the moderating influence provided by a local partner in dealing with bureaucracies, suppliers, and labor; in setting up physical and service infrastructures; and in gaining local acceptance while establishing a domestic presence.

As with all types of business conducted in China, the authorities expect foreign entities to fill virtually all positions with Chinese. Foreign personnel may occupy only a limited number of management and technical slots. It is especially useful for a WFOE to employ a local Chinese general manager above and beyond the official requirements simply to smooth the way.

The foreign investor contributes 100 percent of the capital. The assets of a WFOE cannot be disposed of except by liquidation. After liquidation by established procedures, the foreign investor may repatriate all legitimate residuals, earnings, and profits.

Branch Offices

A branch office is any office maintained for business purposes for which the company's main office holds ultimate responsibility. Because the PRC does not want to be in the position of not being able to control an entity, as it would not in the case of an offshore parent, China does not officially recognize branch offices of foreign parent firms or allow them to operate in China. The exceptions are branches of international banks which are allowed to operate as such.

Branch offices of domestically organized firms, including joint ventures that have foreign participants and of WFOEs, are recognized as long as both the parent and the branch operate in China and are thus accessible to control by Chinese authorities. The authorities can also grant permission for Chinese organized entities to operate branches outside China. Because of these difficulties, restrictions, and lack of legal standing, branch offices are not considered an appropriate vehicle for foreign investment in China.

Representative Offices

A representative office is an entity involved in business activities that do not result in a direct profit being earned by the office. All representative offices must be formally sponsored by a Chinese organization, which assumes official responsibility for the foreign enterprise. Essentially, the Chinese host serves as a proxy parent from whom the government can demand official satisfaction if the guest office misbehaves. As such, the host becomes something of a hostage and is in a position to demand certain considerations from the foreign parent for its services.

The restrictions on its income-earning ability relegate a representative office to such tasks as conducting market research, providing customer information, coordinating the execution of existing contracts, and arranging contacts and local travel for visiting personnel.

All funds needed to establish and operate a representative office are supposed to be channeled through the parent company. Because no income is generated, a representative office has no tax liability. The head office can be either the parent company or a designated subsidiary, although offices lower down in the hierarchy for which a representative office may provide services are somewhat narrowly defined. Local offices that collect fees as agents of a parent or intermediate business entity are subject to income tax on such revenues.

Although the Chinese allow non-earning representative offices while prohibiting profit-making branch offices, in practice they allow some representative offices to function as quasi-branch offices. Many representative offices—some observers estimate the number at around half of all the representative offices in China—function as de facto branches engaged in income-earning activities, although representative offices still cannot operate directly in production, buying, or selling. The Chinese implicitly recognize that some representative offices earn income by having fairly detailed regulations for calculating the taxes due on such revenues.

Liaison Offices

Chinese law does not recognize liaison offices as separate business entities, and as such they do not exist in China. The limited functions that such offices fulfill elsewhere are usually accomplished in China by representative offices.

Partnerships and Sole Proprietorships

The General Principles of Civil Law, Articles 26, 33, 41, and 42 recognize individual, partnership, and similar private enterprises. However, in practice con-

---

Advantages and Disadvantages of Doing Business in China

Many firms go to China for the prestige. In and of itself, this is a poor reason. However, an established presence in China indicates a commitment on the part of the foreign business that can impress and help to gain the confidence of the Chinese. It is also usually easier to deal with people face to face than it is long distance or through intermediaries. Even if the information available locally is incomplete, it is still going to be fresher and carry with it the local context that is lacking when it is relayed across the globe.

Because so much business in China is based on relationships, a physical presence in China can be important because it allows the entity to cultivate such contacts. On-site personnel will also be able to find out about market shifts, capacity and competitive developments, and regulatory changes sooner than others, and they may be in a position to respond more appropriately. A regularized business presence also implies on site decision making for many aspects of operations, which is more efficient. There is also the possibility of developing useful relationships within the local Chinese and expatriate business communities. Finally, operations are best monitored by an interested party who is present on a permanent basis.

On the debit side, China can be one of the most expensive places in the world to do business. Local costs are usually low, but costs to foreigners will usually be quite high, especially the costs of maintaining expatriate personnel. In all but a very few areas, facilities are at a premium and often well below international standards, and infrastructure is undeveloped and poor.

Foreign businesses are expected to employ local workers and managers and to keep foreign managerial and technical personnel to a minimum. Despite regulations that free foreign entities from some of the more onerous labor standards, control over the work force, which may not have adequate qualifications, is tenuous. Communication, language, and cultural differences can also play a major role in lessening the effectiveness of foreign personnel.

The main drawback is bureaucracy, which is omnipresent. It may also be incompetent, corrupt, or both. Regulation is often what a local official says it is, and there is little recourse. Interference can prevent foreign businesses from operating in desired areas or prevent them from conducting profitable operations in others. Rules can change without notice, and unsuspected taxation issues can come out of nowhere. Finally, the lack of foreign exchange—a chronic problem—can make getting one's profits and investment out of the country problematic.

temporary Chinese legal and social theory recognizes no role for the individual other than as a representative of a duly constituted group. Thus, there is no acceptance of partnerships between individuals or of sole proprietorships. Joint ventures, especially cooperative joint ventures, can be considered as a form of partnership, but partnerships as such do not exist in China.

Although there is no accepted legal framework for these entities, they do operate around the edges of the economy as informal, officially unrecognized, entrepreneurial operations. As such, they account for much of the most dynamic activity in the economy, and it is therefore to be expected that, over time, there will be some official recognition and regulation of this area within the burgeoning private sector. However, foreign investors should be extremely wary of entering into agreements with individuals, because they lack official status. The advantages to be gained from dealing with such freewheeling entrepreneurs can be outweighed by the absence of enforcement mechanisms for performance and by the liabilities that could arise from official challenges to deals that they have made with foreigners.

Cooperative Trade Arrangements in Lieu of Formal Business Entities

A variety of recognized contractual trade arrangements exist that allow businesses to obtain the benefits of operating in China without incurring the liabilities and headaches of establishing onshore facilities and formal business entities. Trading is subject to government regulation, but there is less of it than there is in the setting up and operating of onshore business entities. Of course, foreigners could simply import their goods into China and sell them, a fairly complicated task in itself. They could also purchase Chinese goods for export to their home or other countries. Or they could undertake two consecutive, separate transactions. Contractual trading agreements are designed to regularize and elaborate on this buy-sell balancing act.

China is most likely to embrace trade proposals that boost exports and that, because they are self-financing, require no foreign exchange. Areas targeted by the current Five-Year Plan include high technology, energy, transportation, communications, and infrastructure development.

Trading options include countertrade, which can involve such variations as counterpurchase, coproduction, evidence accounts, switch, and barter arrangements; compensation trade; and processing and assembly agreements. Investors may also wish to consider contractual licensing and technology transfer arrangements as a means of doing business with China.

Countertrade Agreements

Countertrade usually involves the import by Chinese entities of foreign machinery, equipment, goods, services, or commodities in exchange for other commodities or products rather than cash. A sale is contingent on an equivalent and offsetting purchase. Chinese officials usually favor such agreements because they do not require chronically scarce foreign currency. However, the Chinese authorities also do not want to cannibalize the sales of established export goods that bring in foreign exchange, and they have limited the development of countertrade arrangements in the product areas that would be of greatest interest to foreigners.

Countertrade operations have traditionally been conducted on a government-to-government basis. However, foreign companies can engage in countertrade activities with smaller official units, either provincial or municipal governments, or with Chinese business entities. Much countertrade activity is carried on by large foreign firms with considerable market power. Japanese trading companies in particular have developed this tactic and used it successfully in recent years. However, smaller firms can also operate profitably in this arena.

Countertrade is not for the faint of heart or for those who depend on a rapid turnaround and a quick profit to get the cash that they need to stay in business. But for those with deep enough pockets and a commitment to develop the necessary expertise and relationships it can still provide a valuable way to do business in China.

Types of Countertrade Arrangements There are numerous variations on the theme of countertrade and many ways in which it can be carried out. These ways are themselves fluid, and different practitioners may employ different twists and use different terms to describe them. All countertrade techniques are designed to offset sales and purchases so that the actual funds that change hands are kept to a minimum. Even if funds do change hands, countertrade minimizes or eliminates the need to obtain foreign exchange in order to bring the returns home.

Counterpurchase arrangements involve the purchase of offsetting items that are not related to the type of items offered for sale. Coproduction involves the provision of certain inputs—which can include management or technical expertise—by one party, usually the foreign trader, who then takes part of the resulting production in return.

An evidence account involves a balancing of sales and purchases over a period of time—which can be as short as a few months or as long as several years—so that the exchanges are equalized. In essence, the traders run a tab, and an agency such as the Bank of China keeps track of the balances.

Switching is the practice of accepting in payment goods that then are sold by a third party on behalf of the recipient. Barter is the swapping of items on a par basis. These last two varieties, barter and switching, usually involve commodities rather than finished goods, and they are the province of large corporate or government entities.

Countertrade Opportunities and Problems Countertrade offers the opportunity to make sales to China while sidestepping many of the obstacles associated with the country's chronic lack of foreign exchange. Companies engaging in countertrade face the problem of finding usable or salable commodities at acceptable prices, terms, and imputed rates of exchange in return for their goods. Firms that engage in countertrade must be sure that their goods are acceptable under current Chinese policy, that they can negotiate a deal on favorable terms, that they can complete the deal including delivery and export of the goods, and that they can turn over the goods received in a timely and profitable manner.

The absence of generally accepted guidelines on procedures and valuations and drawn out, complicated negotiations can be substantial hurdles. The Chinese are shrewd bargainers, but except for a few high government officials used to dealing with other governments, they have relatively little experience in this sort of commercial transaction. Foreign traders have complained of difficulties due to inexperience on the part of the Chinese. It is also axiomatic that the difficulty in closing a deal increases exponentially with the number of parties involved especially when there are several Chinese entities involved at different levels and in different jurisdictions. As with any kind of trade, establishing a price is critical, and there can be wide variations between local and world market prices. Other problems include delayed delivery of goods and quality problems.

Compensation Trade

Compensation or buyback trade refers to a trade agreement in which a foreign firm agrees to sell raw materials, equipment, or technology and buys back the manufactured product or another substitute product. Labor and production facilities are usually provided by the Chinese side. Large-scale compensation trade projects are usually undertaken through direct agreement with state entities on the ministerial, provincial, or municipal level, but foreign entities are often able to made compensating arrangements with small- and medium-sized Chinese enterprises, particularly in areas of light manufacturing.

Compensation trade is generally considered to be easier than countertrade to arrange because fewer Chinese entities are involved. The foreign trader is generally expected to pay a processing fee for production of the goods. The receipt of the goods by the foreign trader is usually accounted for as a loan payment or as an installment sale. Both of these types are tax exempt. However, if the deal involves technology transfer, the proceeds are taxable. Because the foreign trader exits with goods, there is no need to obtain foreign exchange.

High domestic demand can result in a shortage of the desired manufactured goods or acceptable substitutes available for exchange. And the government can intervene if the end products exchanged will lessen export earnings or put the foreign trader in direct competition with the Chinese producer in overseas markets. In fact, items offered in compensation trade agreements are often those that the Chinese have had a hard time marketing abroad on their own, so traders engaging in this sort of arrangement must be sure of both products and markets. To date, the Chinese have resisted the idea of discounting goods traded in this manner to make them more attractive to foreign business people.

Compensation trade has several other problems. The most notable is that the foreign partner has little or no control over such issues as quality, shortages of necessary skilled labor or components, and poor equipment or maintenance of equipment in manufacturing operations. Although the foreign trader often supplies materials, equipment, and specifications for its use, the lack of direct control can mean that the product delivered is unacceptable, and the foreign partner has little recourse in such cases.

Processing and Assembling

Processing and assembling agreements are those in which foreign enterprises place Chinese factories under contract to manufacture goods to specifications. Generally, the Chinese side provides facilities, basic equipment, and labor, and the foreign trader provides raw materials, parts or components, and specifications. No customs duties are levied on imported materials and components to be processed and assembled for export.

Foreigners usually provide machinery and technology if the product requires specialized types. The foreign entity also pays a processing fee. Sometimes, it can opt to pay with part of the finished product. In return, it receives finished or semifinished goods and export rights for them. In essence, a foreign entity provides most of the inputs that it would have to supply if it were producing the items in its own facilities. But instead of establishing a dedicated facility, it rents the Chinese facility on a job lot basis, paying only the much lower local labor and overhead costs plus a fee.

Such processing and assembly arrangements are considered favorable to China's economic goals, and China has set up special operating zones for such

Finding a Chinese Partner

The choice of a Chinese joint venture partner is the most critical element in creating a successful business operation in China. It is difficult to find and evaluate Chinese partners, despite official offers from the CITIC to provide suitable candidates. Most foreign entities prefer to find their own rather than take a chance with an official matchmaker.

Because the Chinese partner actually makes the submission for project approval to the government, the foreign partner must have confidence in its Chinese compatriot. Investors can waste time and resources in pursuing partners and projects that have little hope of working out.

The foreign partner must determine whether the proposed project is desirable and in accord with local, provincial, and national development plans to a degree that it can be virtually certain of gaining approval, or whether it is just the pet project of the local partner, in which case it may have little hope of being approved and, if approved, even less hope of being profitable. Good chemistry between the participants is also important. Initial contacts can be expected to involve sparring and testing, but prolonged belligerency should suggest incompatibility.

Foreign investors must make sure that their goals are in line with those of PRC officials. It will do them little good to buck the tide. They must also make sure that their goals are congruent with those of their local partners. Projects must be mutually beneficial in order to work, and each partner must understand the benefits that the other partner needs in order for the business to prosper.

Location is even more important in China than it is elsewhere. Favorable location is necessary to obtain inputs, such as raw materials, labor, power, and transport. Regulatory environment is another important consideration. A good partner cannot make a bad location work, and a bad partner can sink a good location.

Some foreign investors try to eliminate the local partner wild card by going it alone and forming a wholly foreign-owned enterprise (WFOE). This structure has its advantages, the main one being control, but it also raises problems. A local partner may be difficult to deal with, but he and the foreign partner are in the deal together, he has expertise in operating in the local environment, and he has an incentive to operate as effectively as possible. These factors can prove to be critical for success, and they are unavailable to a business organized as a WFOE.

---

activities in Guangdong and Fujian provinces. The majority of processing and assembly facilities are located close to Hong Kong, which provides much of the management and intermediary support for this type of activity. Government incentives also serve to encourage such business arrangements. This type of arrangement has proved to be popular with both the Chinese and foreign businesspeople, and it is expected to be extended throughout larger areas of the country in the future.

Arrangements of this type give foreign investors increased control over specifications and quality, require minimal capital investment, and provide access to a low-cost, flexible work force. Moreover, they eliminate several areas and sources of bureaucratic interference. Finally, they do not require any long-term commitment by either party. Foreigners using this type of arrangement point out that careful monitoring is required to assure quality control and that specifications and schedules are met. Problems can also arise if the deal relies on domestic raw materials or components, because supplies are often unreliable.

It is recommended that foreign participants arrange to supply as many of the critical inputs as they can.

Technology Transfer

Despite the fact that the actual volume of technology transfers has been falling since the late 1980s, China remains eager to acquire advanced technologies, and officials will approve a variety of technology transfers, leasing, and licensing agreements. However, China expects to receive extremely favorable terms in such transactions. And this official interest in technology has the drawback that anything that falls under the rubric of technology is regulated by Chinese officials. Items brought into China under technology transfer agreements are usually allowed to enter duty free, but earnings from such transfers are taxable to the provider in China.

At present, all contracts that involve the following are regulated: Assignments or licensing of product rights, such as patents; technical service contracts; cooperative production contracts that specify technologies to be employed and stipulate design, technical data, or technical specifications; sales of turnkey operations that involve technology; and any other contracts that authorities decide fall under the general heading of technology.

In order for a contract involving technology to be approved, China requires that it must serve the following goals: result in new products; improve quality; reduce costs, energy, or materials use; increase resource utilization efficiency; increase exports; increase foreign exchange earnings; reduce environmental damage; increase process safety; improve management efficiency; or allow an advance in scientific achievements. Specific proposals must demonstrate the feasibility and cost-effectiveness of the technology to achieve its stated ends.

The Ministry of Foreign Trade and Economic Cooperation (MOFTEC), or its authorized designee must approve all technology-related contracts. Contracts are rejected if they contain conditions that require the recipient to purchase additional inputs exclusively from the foreign entity providing the technology, restrict the recipient from modifying the technology, prevent the recipient from acquiring technology from other sources, place restrictions on the production and sale of products made using the technology, limit the distribution of resulting products, prevent the recipient from continuing to use the technology after the agreement expires, or require tie-in purchases. Technology-related contracts generally may not run more than ten years.

Such stipulations effectively mean that a foreign entity transferring technology to a Chinese entity is giving the Chinese permanent rights to that technology. Although China has improved its record on protection of intellectual property, the terms of transfer contracts do little to protect patents and technology. Foreign entities must rely on the weak and largely unenforceable nondisclosure clause included in most technology contracts. This clause only prevents the Chinese entity from transferring the technology to other unrelated entities. It does not restrict the firm from making whatever internal use it sees fit of the technology.

REGISTERING A BUSINESS

Businesses cannot start operations in China until they have completed approval and registration procedures. Registration certification is needed before a business can legally employ Chinese nationals, open a bank account, import business materials duty-free, obtain telephone lines, advertise or put up signage, obtain a multiple-entry commercial visa, and, usually, sign a lease for office or other commercial space, although landlords are often more flexible on this item. Moreover, enterprises are usually restricted to specifically authorized activities. The

particular rules that define the process depend on whether the business is foreign or domestically owned and to what degree, how the business is organized, what industrial sector it operates in, where in the country it operates, and how the relevant authorities feel at the moment. Doing business in China not only involves learning the shifting complexities of the official Chinese system but also requires an aptitude for interpreting unwritten rules.

Joint ventures are formed under joint venture law, WFOEs under wholly foreign-owned enterprise law, and representative offices under representative office interim and supplementary provisions, but generally applicable nationwide rules with acknowledged statutory authority governing all types of foreign investment and business entity formation either do not exist or are being continuously modified in China's rapidly changing economic environment. In practice, a great deal of procedure and regulation is on an ad hoc and ad hominem basis, and local influence (*guanxi*) can be required to obtain necessary approvals, operating authorizations, and protection from subsequent reversals or modifications.

Individuals or firms should seek professional legal and accounting assistance in addition to consulting with government authorities to ensure that they are in compliance with regulatory requirements and procedures. (Refer to "Important Addresses" chapter for listing of government agencies, legal offices and accounting firms.)

Licensing Most forms of business require a certificate of approval and a business license in order to operate.

Restrictions The Chinese prohibit foreign projects with objectives that have been determined not to further the goals established in official planning documents. Prohibited and restricted areas of endeavor—there is little real distinction between the two categories—are subject to change and interpretation. Restricted investments currently include, but are not limited to film processing; maintenance and repair of household electric appliances; processing of cigarettes, alcoholic beverages, and foods and beverages targeted at China's domestic market; and assembly of specified products, such as computers, watches, refrigerators, and washing machines.

Fees Commercial enterprises must pay a registration fee equal to 0.1 percent of total registered capital for projects under RMB 10 million (about US$1.15 million), with a minimum fee of RMB 50—about US$5.75, and 0.05 percent for projects over RMB 10 million, up to a maximum fee of RMB 30,000—about US$3,500. Registration fees for joint ventures are paid by the participants in proportion to their capital contributions.

Fees for registering a representative office are minimal: RMB 600—about US$69—to register and

RMB 300—about US$35—to reregister. A fee of RMB 100—about US$11.50—is levied to amend an existing registration.

Basic Authorizations Needed and Applications Procedures

Specific provisions exist for the formation and registration of each type of organizational entity. However, all entities must generally obtain investment approval from the Ministry of Foreign Trade and Economic Cooperation (MOFTEC), formerly known as the Ministry of Foreign Economic Relations and Trade (MOFERT). The MOFTEC exercises final approval authority over the terms of all contracts concluded between foreign and Chinese entities and thus over the creation of new entities.

Foreigners must establish whether their proposed operations can be approved before they ask for official approval. Unofficial consultations with Chinese authorities, are the usual means of doing so, and some entities are now requesting a "nonbinding preliminary approval" before submitting final documents. Specific approvals can also be obtained from the appropriate provincial or municipal authorities acting for and under the supervision of the MOFTEC. All necessary approvals for joint ventures, WFOEs, and representative offices are ultimately under the administrative authority of the MOFTEC, although it often delegates effective responsibility to either its local offices or other entities. All foreign business entities must also register with the State Administration for Industry and Commerce (SAIC), presenting their certificate of approval from the MOFTEC or its designee. Finally, all entities must register with local tax authorities.

Summary of Procedures by Type of Entity

Joint Ventures Joint ventures must receive approval from either the MOFTEC or its local designee. The MOFTEC has published a lengthy model joint venture contract, and adherence to the terms of the model contract are supposed to improve chances for acceptance; any significant departure from these terms is likely to impede approval. The new venture must register with the local office of SAIC and apply for a business license within 30 days of receiving approval. The entity must then register with local tax authorities and any special permit granting authorities.

Wholly Foreign-Owned Enterprises The procedures for wholly foreign-owned enterprises are similar to those for joint ventures. WFOEs must receive approval from either the MOFTEC or its local designee. WFOEs located within a SEZ should apply to the zone committees for authorization. The entity must then register with the local SAIC office and afterwards with local tax and any special permit granting authorities.

Representative Offices Representative offices must apply for approval to the MOFTEC, the Ministry of Finance, or the local trade bureau office dealing with the specific area of business in which the entity wishes to operate. When approval has been received, the representative office is established under the required sponsorship of a Chinese host entity. The representative office must then register with the local SAIC office and with local tax authorities. Registration must be renewed annually.

Contractual Trade Arrangements All varieties of contractual arrangement must be negotiated with authorized organizations, such as the import and export administrations, foreign trade corporations (FTCs), foreign trade bureaus, or investment and trust corporations at the national, provincial, or municipal levels. No additional approval or registration is usually required.

Technology Transfers Technology transfer contracts must be approved by the MOFTEC or its designee before the contract is implemented. The foreign partner must then register with local tax authorities.

Chinese-language translations of all materials in a foreign language must be submitted along with originals or certified copies. All items must be submitted in multiple copies; the number varies with the particular submission. Requirements can be changed at the ministerial level for any or all procedures without notice, and many local authorities have their own special requirements in addition to or in place of established procedures. The applicant must check with local authorities to determine the authorizations, approvals, and permits needed and the materials necessary for a specific submission.

Different or additional requirements and documentation can apply to businesses operating within the special economic, technical, and coordinating zones and in designated coastal areas. Additional permits may be required as determined by various authorities, especially for entities involved in restricted sectors or activities. In practice, authorities at any level are free to require business entities to obtain additional approvals and licenses without prior notice or review. All amendments to existing authorizations and registrations must be reported promptly in accordance with procedures.

One critical task for an entity seeking to do business in China is to convince authorities that the operations to be undertaken are desirable. Applicants must demonstrate that the project helps to realize national and local policy and planning goals and that they are capable of carrying out the project to the benefit of all. Another factor that is crucial to approval and over which applicants have no direct control is the assessment that authorities reviewing the project make of its priority and where it sits in the queue vis-a-vis other projects. China still operates with central planning, and once quotas have been filled, no additional projects can be undertaken without machinations that most often have nothing to do with the applicants.

Basic Procedures

Foreign Investment Approval Requirements Foreign investors intending to form a joint venture must locate a Chinese partner and negotiate a contract before approaching the authorities for approval. Once the local partner has been located, the next step is to send the partner a letter of intent. Although this letter is not a legally binding document, many Chinese entities see it in practice as a firm commitment. The potential partners must then undertake a detailed feasibility study of the proposed project. An optional agreement or preliminary contract is then negotiated. After this document has been finalized, the partners must submit it to the authorities for approval.

Foreign entities intending to use a WFOE structure must prepare the project feasibility study, but they do not need to locate or reach an agreement with a local partner.

Larger projects must obtain approval from the MOFTEC. Small projects should seek approval from the appropriate provincial or municipal authorities that have authority to act for the MOFTEC. The Chinese partner makes the official submission on behalf of the proposed joint venture. WFOE proposals are submitted directly by the foreign investor. The documentation required includes, but is not limited to, the following:

- Project proposal
- Preliminary feasibility study of the business operations to be carried out by the proposed entity
- Financial or technical feasibility studies certified by the appropriate authorities, such as the Chinese Engineering Consulting Corporation, where necessary; this submission demonstrates that the project fits national and local planning priorities
- Business agreement or contract between the parties
- Bank or other financial institution references
- Lists of candidates for board positions.

The contract submitted must include the following information:

- Particulars on the entities and individual representatives participating in the contract
- Name of the joint venture, its legal address, purpose, and scope of business
- Investment, portion contributed by each participant, form of contribution, schedule for contribution, stipulations regarding contribution, and allotment of ownership
- Apportionment of profits and losses among participants
- Roster of board of directors and statement of members' responsibilities
- Assets and technology to be used
- Means of acquiring inputs and distributing products
- Foreign exchange arrangements
- Principles to be used in finance, accounting, and auditing
- Labor policy
- Duration of the venture
- Liabilities for breach of contract
- Methods of dispute resolution
- Conditions established to ratify the contract and begin operations

Approval is to be granted or denied within 90 days of submission for equity joint ventures and within 45 days for cooperative joint ventures. There is no specific period of time for the review of WFOE submissions, but it usually takes between 45 and 90 days as well. Cooperative joint ventures and WFOE proposals must include essentially the same information, but their submissions usually do not need to observe such a rigid format. The authorities can require amendments, which must be made within a limited specified time. When the venture is approved, the MOFTEC issues a certificate of approval.

Foreign investors interested in forming a joint venture but who do not have a local partner can submit a proposal directly to authorities and authorize the China International Trust and Investment Corporation (CITIC) or other comparable organization to assist them in their search for potential Chinese partners.

Entity Registration Requirements Within 30 days of receiving approval from the MOFTEC, the entity must register with SAIC to obtain necessary licenses and proper registration for joint ventures and WFOEs. Smaller entities must register with the appropriate local authorities. Larger entities must register at the ministerial level. This registration approval is not automatic. Applications for registration usually require the following documentation:

- Official request for registration signed by venture officials, including chairman, vice-chairman, general manager, and deputy manager
- Approved name, location, and form of business
- Scope of business
- Location of the head office and any branch offices
- Certificate of approval issued under MOFTEC authority

- Project proposal and feasibility studies
- Agreements, contracts, and articles of association
- Documentation and certification of all assets
- Commercial business license
- Written application signed by key individuals in the business, plus their credentials and authority to act on the entity's behalf
- Name, address, and nationality of directors and other responsible persons authorized to represent the company
- Roster of all employees

To obtain a commercial business license, an entity must submit an application to conduct business, certification that it has received authorized working capital, a list of key individuals in the business and their credentials, and any other documentation that local authorities choose to require.

Representative Office Approval and Registration Procedures Approval for a representative office must be obtained from the MOFTEC or the local organization responsible for the specific industry in which the office expects to operate. The process usually involves making contact with the appropriate office, explaining the operations envisioned, and documenting the existence of the parent and the parent's authorization to set up an office in China for these purposes. The approving office will specify the procedures and documentation that it requires.

After this initial approval has been granted, the prospective representative office must secure a Chinese sponsor. Many groups interested in establishing a representative office will have been working with a potential Chinese sponsor during the preliminary stage, but others will need to secure sponsorship at this stage. Once sponsorship has been arranged, the sponsor submits a formal application for registration to SAIC on behalf of the representative entity. This submission includes:

- Certificate of approval from the MOFTEC or another authority
- Application with appropriate signatures of the entity's chairman or general manager
- Authorization from the parent entity to form the office
- Copy of the home office's business license and certificate of incorporation
- Detailed proposal for office operations
- Bank references
- Details regarding the Chinese sponsor

When the submission has been approved, the office must register with local tax authorities.

Technology Transfer Contract Approval Application Procedures An entity wishing to transfer technology to a Chinese entity must submit its contract to the MOFTEC or its local designee for approval

within 30 days after the contract between the parties has been concluded. The submission must include the completed application, the contract, documentation certifying the legal status of the contracting parties to undertake the transaction, and technical feasibility studies documenting the appropriateness of the technology to be transferred and the means to be used in paying for it. The contract must include the following information:

- Names of contracting entities
- Detailed description of the technology
- Standards, time limits, maintenance requirements, assessment measurements, and liability assignments
- Assignment of any relevant patent rights
- Confidentiality agreements
- Financial details
- Arrangements for liquidation of the contract and proposed measures for dispute resolution
- Definition of specific relevant technical terms

The approving authority must accept or reject the contract within 60 days, or it can send it back to the parties for amendment, in which case the time period will be considered to have started over when the revised contract is submitted. If the contract is approved, the contracting parties will receive a certificate of technology contract approval, and the contract goes into effect on the date of such approval. If the approval has been granted by a designee, the designee is responsible for registering the approval with the MOFTEC within 10 days.

Cooperative Trade Agreement Approvals and Licensing Procedures Until relatively recently, the central government controlled all import and export trade and exercised direct control over the items and arrangements allowed through the foreign trade corporations (FTCs). Now individual entities and local authorities have considerably more say in these matters. This is a mixed blessing, because it multiplies the number of separate agreements and approvals needed in order to conclude a cooperative trade agreement.

There is no standard set of procedures and no standard set of approvals for a cooperative trade deal. Traders are responsible for negotiating contracts and finding out whether their deal requires any specific authorizations. To simplify matters, it is generally best to limit the number of entities and agencies involved. For this reason, compensation trade is generally preferred over other forms of cooperative trade, because relatively few parties are involved.

Imports are still subject to licensing, although the number of items requiring prior authorization continues to shrink. Traders need to make sure that their items will not need such authorizations and that licenses can be obtained if required. Finished goods do not generally require export licenses; some raw materials require approvals. Traders must also ascertain that their proposed deal does not involve items limited by international quotas or, if the items are subject to quotas, that the products to be exported fall within existing allotments.

Registration with Local Tax Authorities All entities must register with local tax authorities, but there is no specific procedure for doing so. Generally, to establish its tax status, an entity should be prepared to submit copies of all approvals, certificates, licenses, and other documentation explaining its presence and form of organization.

TEN REMINDERS, RECOMMENDATIONS, AND RULES

1. Little or no distinction is made in practice between business relationships and personal ties. The cultivation of connections is therefore crucial to doing business in China. Having the ear of the appropriate local official can be of more practical value than scrupulously following the letter of the law in a given situation.
2. There is a chronic shortage of foreign exchange. Issues of rights to obtain foreign exchange and repatriate capital and earnings are critical. In practice, these issues are settled on a case-by-case basis.
3. Devaluation of Chinese currency can cut the profits of foreign investments drastically. To protect themselves, foreign firms negotiating to establish businesses in China should specify that valuations be in terms of hard currency, specify the exchange rate to be used when financial contributions are evaluated, make investment contributions only as required, change funds into local currency only as needed, repatriate funds as soon and as often as possible, depreciate assets over as long a period as is allowed, and leverage operations to the maximum extent possible.
4. As an alternative to establishing a business in the People's Republic of China, investors should consider the advantages and disadvantages of operating through an office in Hong Kong.
5. Investors must be aware that unwritten rules and ad hoc determinations often represent the operating norm for Chinese officials maneuvering in an unfamiliar and rapidly changing environment where local officials have considerable latitude in which to operate and there is little concrete regulation, precedent, or supervision.
6. Because past contracts often become models for future ones, as many issues as possible should be settled up front, and every contract should be made as detailed as possible. Handshake and general principle agreements are not appropriate for doing business in China because cultural norms are so different. However, even the most closely negotiated contract can be inadequate because of changed conditions or a willful partner.
7. Joint ventures and compensation trade arrangements are the formats that Chinese business entities use most often in their dealings with foreigners. The forms preferred by and most frequently used by foreign businesses are equity and cooperative joint ventures.
8. Personal contacts established through the exchange of foreign experts between Chinese and foreign organizations, joint ventures, WFOEs, and individuals play an important role in setting the direction of economic liberalization and developing business practice in China.
9. The Chinese consider technology transfer agreements to include an implied commitment by the foreign investor to help the Chinese entity sell or promote the resulting products manufactured in overseas markets.
10. Of the three types of factory ownership in China—state-run, collective, and private—all types may allow partial to full ownership by foreign entities. State entities are least susceptible to foreign participation and ownership, even on a minority basis. In practice, even when 100 percent foreign ownership is theoretically possible, such participation is usually kept to around 50 percent.

USEFUL ADDRESSES

In addition to the organizations listed here, individuals or firms should contact other government agencies with special jurisdiction, chambers of commerce, embassies, banks and financial service centers, local consultants, lawyers, and resident foreign businesses for assistance and information. (Refer to "Important Addresses" for a more complete listing.)

China Council for the Promotion of International Trade (CCPIT)
1 Fu Xing Men Wai Dajie
Beijing 100860, PRC
Tel: [86] (1) 8013344, 8013866 Fax: [86] (1) 801137

Ministry of Foreign Trade and Economic Cooperation (MOFTEC)
Foreign Trade Department
2 Dongchangan Jie, Dongcheng Qu
Beijing 100731, PRC
Tel: [86] (1) 5197420, 5198328, 5198504
Fax: [86] (1) 5129568 Tlx: 22168

Beijing Foreign Trade Corporation
Building 12, 17 Yong An Dong Li, Jian Guo Men Wai
Beijing 100022, PRC
Tel: [86] (1) 5001315 Fax: [86] (1) 5001668
Tlx: 210064

Beijing Foreign Economic Law Office
Working People's Cultural Palace
Beijing 100006, PRC
Tel: [86] (1) 5513167/8 Fax: [86] (1) 5126406

FURTHER READING

The preceding discussion is provided as a basic guide for individuals interested in doing business in China. The resources described here provide further information on company law, investment, taxation and accounting procedures, and procedural requirements.

Doing Business in China, by Ernst & Young. New York: Ernst & Young International, 1988. Available in the United States from Ernst & Young, 787 Seventh Avenue, New York, NY, USA; Tel: [1] (212) 773-3000. Available in China from Ernst & Young, Suite 6E, CITIC Building, Jianguomenwai Da Jie, Beijing, PRC; Tel: [86] (1) 5002255 x3665. Available in Hong Kong from Ernst & Young, China Division, 1501 Hutchison House, Hong Kong. Provides an overview of the investment environment in China and information on taxation, business organizational structures, business practices, and accounting requirements.

Doing Business in the People's Republic of China, by Price Waterhouse. Los Angeles: Price Waterhouse World Firm Limited, 1988 and 1990. Available in the United States from Price Waterhouse, 400 South Hope Street, Los Angeles, CA 90071-2889, USA; Tel: [1] (213) 236-3000. Available in China from Price Waterhouse, 3063/5 Beijing Hotel, Beijing, PRC; Tel: [86] (1) 5137293, 5137766 x3063/5. Available in Hong Kong from Price Waterhouse, Prince's Building, 24th Floor, P.O. Box 690, Hong Kong. The 1988 edition and the 1990 supplement cover the investment and business environment in China as well as audit, accounting, and taxation requirements.

Perspectives on China, Fourth Edition, by Arthur Andersen & Co. Chicago: Arthur Andersen & Co., 1993. Available in the United States from Arthur Andersen & Co., 69 W. Washington Street, Chicago, Il 60602, USA; Tel: [1] (312) 580-4000. Available in China from Arthur Andersen & Co., Room 2525-2529, China World Trade Center, No. 1 Jian Guo Men Wai Avenue, Beijing, PRC; Tel: [86] (1) 5053333. Available in Hong Kong from Arthur Andersen & Co., Wing On Centre, 25th Floor, 111 Connaught Road, Hong Kong; Tel: [852] 8520222. Provides an overview of the official structure in China and information about foreign trade and investment and taxation and accounting issues.

Labor

THE LABOR ECONOMY

China is a country of enormous proportions. Its labor force is twice the size of the combined populations of the United States and Canada. Although about two-thirds of all Chinese workers are engaged in agriculture, the agricultural sector produces only about 28.4 percent of the country's gross domestic product (GDP). Slightly more than half of China's inhabitants have received no more than a primary education. There are approximately 144 million workers in China's cities and an additional 80 million workers employed in village and township enterprises, many seasonally. About 433 million Chinese are under the age of 20 and about 126 million are between the ages of 20 and 24, representing nearly half of the population. The members of this second group are faced with the task of entering the labor force at a time of unprecedented economic change and uncertainty.

A visit by Chinese leader Deng Xiaoping in early 1992 to the prosperous Shenzhen Special Economic Zone in southern China touched off a wave of optimism for the prospects of economic reform. Meanwhile, Chinese reformers have renewed efforts at labor reform with a new slogan: Break the three irons and the one big pot. The iron rice bowl, the iron chair, the iron salary, and the one big pot respectively symbolize the major tenets of China's inflexible labor system: guaranteed lifetime employment, protection from demotion, and a virtual lack of salary differentials on either a skills or performance basis. And a conference on labor in October 1991 set a national goal of implementing the labor contract system in all enterprises by the start of the 21st century.

Population

According to the most recent census, which was conducted in 1990, there are 1,132 million people in China, and the population is growing at an annual rate of 1.3 percent. Han Chinese comprise 91.2 percent of the population. Some 56 recognized ethnic groups, including Zhuang, Manchu, Hui, Miao, Uygur, Yi, Tujia, Mongolian, and Tibetan, are also represented. Approximately 300 million people live in urban areas. Overall life expectancy is 69 years, 67.2 years for males and 70.6 years for females.

Labor Force and Distribution by Sector

China's civilian labor force is easily the largest of any country in the world: 647.2 million people in 1990. Males account for 55 percent and females 45 percent of the total. According to the 1990 census, 60.2 percent of the labor force was engaged in agriculture, 21.6 percent in industry, and 18.2 percent in services. Figures are not likely to be reliable, because of the difficulty of conducting censuses in China as well as because many Chinese in recent years have taken second or even third jobs, often in unrelated fields.

Labor Availability

In China, government employment offices are charged with assigning people to positions in work units (dan wei), where they may remain for a lifetime. College and university graduates typically have little choice of jobs, despite recent reforms that seek to dismantle the largely inefficient job assignment system. Nevertheless, an increasing number of university students look for jobs with joint venture enterprises by attending so-called talent fairs or by applying in person during their last year of school. Advertising is gradually becoming an accepted means of matching people with job openings.

Due to the job assignment system and the fact that work units provide comprehensive benefits, including housing, health care, child care, retirement pay, and even coupons that can be used to purchase scarce goods, foreign-owned and joint venture businesses can be hard-pressed to find suitable workers. Private enterprises that seek to hire a worker away from his or her work unit can expect to encounter many hurdles. The most obvious is the residence permit, which can prevent rural people from moving to a city and urban dwellers from moving to from one city to another. The work unit must grant the worker permission to leave. Even then, the worker may be required to pay a release fee. The unit may attempt to charge a foreign-owned business for a worker's training. Finally, because work units usually provide housing and other benefits, foreign enterprises should be prepared to offer similar benefit packages when seeking to recruit experienced workers.

Officially-sponsored labor markets have been established in many cities to aid in the recruitment and placement of middle and high school graduates, unemployed workers, and those wishing to change jobs. Joint venture enterprises often find it more feasible to hire inexperienced high school graduates than individuals with university degrees or prior experience. In most cases, it is necessary to provide the training needed for a job in-house. In the absence of significant reform in housing and social security and an end to the job assignment system, real labor mobility is not likely to occur any time soon.

Foreign Workers

Information on foreign workers in China is very difficult to obtain, because the Chinese government does not provide statistics on immigration. Foreigners working in China are not required to have work permits, but they must obtain residence permits. Normally, a foreigner affiliated with a registered enterprise located in China, either foreign-owned or Chinese—for example, a foreign individual providing technical assistance to a Chinese enterprise or a representative of a foreign company's subsidiary office—is automatically granted a residence permit. The residence permit must be issued by the local public security bureau; it is usually valid for six months.

Ministry of Public Security
14 Dongchangan Jie
Beijing, PRC
Tel: [86] (1) 5122831, 5121176 (Foreign Affairs Bureau)

Unemployment Trends

Despite sustained growth rates that have been among the highest in the world, unemployment and underemployment have become pressing problems for China. Although the official unemployment rate hovered around 2.5 percent in the early 1990s, off-the-record estimates by officials and even some published reports put the real urban unemployment rate to be two to four times that level, which means that there are anywhere from 7 to 14 million unemployed in the cities alone. Guangdong Province has a reported 5 million unofficial surplus migrant workers out of a total population of 65 million. Most are rural refugees seeking pickup employment in the cities.

A 1990 Ministry of Labor report states that 12 million people sought work that year but that the state sector could only provide six million new jobs. Moreover, the official figures exclude some six million youths waiting for employment—that is, young people who have never held a job, are not working, and are not in school.

Underemployment is another significant problem among urban workers. Estimates of the proportion of surplus workers who are kept on as full-time employees in urban enterprises range from 10 to 30 percent. Some enterprises may be overstaffed by a factor of two to three times the number of workers actually needed. The term tertiary industry is a favorite of Chinese officials trying to solve the underemployment problem. The term refers to the service sector. In pro-

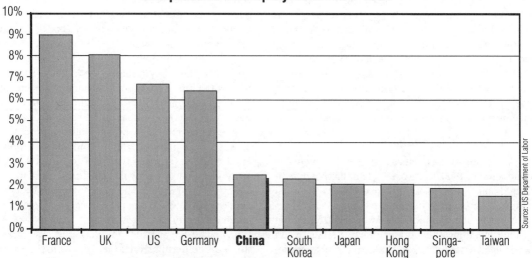

Comparative Unemployment 1990-1991

Source: US Department of Labor

moting tertiary industry, officials have been known to urge a steel plant to open a restaurant or beauty parlor in order to absorb surplus labor.

Many urban workers who cannot earn enough in their primary jobs find a second or even a third job. In Beijing and Guangzhou, almost one-third of the state workers have second jobs. In Chongqing and Shanghai, the proportion is estimated at 40 percent. Workers often earn as much or more at their second jobs, where their services are more in demand. They show up at their overstaffed state work unit once a month to collect their pay, usually having bribed the work unit executive committee to keep them on the books. Moonlighting consists of anything from street peddling to financial consulting. This quasi-free labor market appears to be gaining acceptance among the more innovative employers and young people just entering the labor market. But the government sends conflicting signals: It simultaneously supports the notion of increased job mobility while maintaining regulations that prevent it.

Unemployment and underemployment are even more critical in China's rural areas. With the introduction of new technology, the doubling of the rural population since the 1950s, and slowed growth of rural industries, the agricultural work force has more than twice as many people as it needs. Between 1957 and 1985, the average land area available to rural laborers declined from 0.52 hectares (about 0.2 acres) to 0.27 hectares (about 0.1 acres) per person. Since one farmer can till about 0.6 hectares (about 1.5 acres), agriculture can fully employ only about 175 million people. Official figures place the number of people currently in the sector at roughly 390 million, and there may be as many as 90 to 100 million more.

Shrinking rural employment opportunities have driven people into urban areas—as many as 100 million, according to some estimates. The phenomenon has become known as the *floating population*, and government officials and urban communities fear rising crime and social unrest as a result. Typically, rural workers take the dangerous, temporary, or menial jobs that no one else will accept. However, rural youths are beginning to demand better positions. Many Chinese policymakers support expansion of the private sector as a way of decreasing unemployment. This view is apparently not shared by all. A more efficient private sector could result in even greater unemployment. At any rate, the government continues to prop up inefficient and oversized state enterprises in the hopes curbing rising unemployment.

In 1993 the government announced a plan to reduce employment in official bureaucracies by 25 percent, about 2 million jobs. Not only does this present the specter of a large number of unemployed bureaucrats, but it also raises the issue of who will be left to administer the sweeping changes anticipated in an economic system that is already overwhelmed by change.

HUMAN RESOURCES

As with many other aspects of China, it is difficult to generalize about the quality of the education and training that Chinese receive. While not officially recognized under Communism, the traditional Asian philosophies of life, such as Confucianism, Buddhism, and Taoism, form an unwritten code of conduct for Chinese society. All three philosophies make hard work and the pursuit of knowledge two of their highest ideals. Since 1979 the Chinese government has designated increased education and vocational training for the Chinese people as one of the main priorities for modernization.

Education

Access to primary and secondary education is open to everyone in China. Nominal fees of up to RMB 10 (about US$0.25) per term are charged at all levels. As living standards have risen, schools known for good facilities and teachers have begun to charge higher fees, thus in essence creating a two-tiered system.

Estimates by the United Nations Educational, Scientific, and Cultural Organization (UNESCO) placed adult illiteracy in 1990 at 16 percent for males and 38 percent for females—a testimony to Mao Zedong's crusade against illiteracy, which used to be the norm throughout China.

Primary education begins for most children at seven years of age and lasts for five years. Secondary school begins at 12 years of age and lasts for another five years. Free higher education was abolished in 1985, and prospective college students now undergo a rigorous competition for scholarships awarded on the basis of academic ability. (Of course, *guanxi*—connections—help too.)

As a result of the Tiananmen Square disturbances of May and June 1989 students are now required to complete one year of political education before entering college. The government also announced in 1989 that candidates for postsecondary education would be selected on the basis of moral and physical fitness as well as academic ability.

In general, foreign invested enterprises (FIEs) are able to recruit workers who have completed high school and received at least some university education, if not a university degree. The caliber of such education varies widely, although it is generally high in the major schools.

Training and Attitudes Toward Work

The task of training, educating, and motivating workers in China falls mainly to the country's only union, the All China Federation of Trade Unions (ACFTU). In contrast to unions elsewhere, the ACFTU concerns itself primarily with means of increasing production rather than with promoting the interests of workers, and its interest in worker training is geared accordingly.

All China Federation of Trade Unions (ACFTU)
10 Fu Xing Men Wai Je
Beijing100865, PRC
Tel [86] (1) 8012200 Fax [86] (1) 8012933
Tlx: 222290

The Ministry of Labor has become active in retraining and in job creation for unemployed workers. It is encouraging young people to seek more vocational training before entering the job market. Whether or not this policy has had an effect on young Chinese, the ACFTU and the Ministry of Labor report that high school and college graduates are more aware that they need to acquire skills than they were a decade ago. State work units also play an important role in training workers. On joining a work unit, a worker will often enter a training program. Its duration and focus vary widely.

Ministry of Labor
12 Hepinglizhong Jie, Dongcheng Qu
Beijing 100708, PRC
Tel: [86] (1) 4212454, 4213431 Fax: [86] (1) 4211624

State-run enterprises are constantly trying to motivate workers to work harder. But because in most state-run and collective enterprises pay is not based on performance and workers have traditionally had little fear of losing their jobs, there is little incentive for workers to respond. Partly for this reason, the government has declared that private enterprises operating on the basis of profit maximization should serve as models for state-run and collective enterprises. However, such a strategy could increase the instability in Chinese society as workers compete for the best jobs and experience the uncertainties of potential job loss.

Women in the Work Force

Although official policy calls for working women and men to be treated equally, a disproportionate number of women are still concentrated in lower-paying positions. China is a traditionally patriarchal society. However, some advances have been made: women hold roughly 30 percent of the jobs in government and 20 percent of the seats in the legislative body. Ironically, given China's official policy of protecting women from heavy labor, they constitute only 26 percent of the office workers, but perform a substantial percentage of farm work and of some industrial jobs.

The Women's Protection Law, enacted in September 1988, gives women three months of maternity leave and additional child-care benefits. However, the expense to enterprises of providing these benefits to female workers is generally believed to have increased discrimination against them. With reforms giving employers greater freedom to hire workers of their choice, employers admit that they prefer to hire men because it means that they do not have to pay maternity leave and child-care benefits.

In response to these developments, the Chinese government passed additional legislation in March 1992 known as the Law on the Protection of Rights and Interests of Women. This law specifically outlaws consideration of pregnancy, maternity leave, or child-care issues in hiring or firing decisions. However, the law leaves open a broad area defined as "work or physical labor not suitable to women."

Despite the government's strong stance against gender discrimination, both the ACFTU and the All China Women's Federation are reluctant to deal with discrimination unless it is blatant. For example, they choose to ignore that although women entering the work force are generally better educated than men they often lack specific technical skills, because work units give most vocational training slots to men.

CONDITIONS OF EMPLOYMENT

One of the most significant recent developments in the area of labor in China was the introduction in 1986 of a labor contract system. This system was designed to allow enterprises to hire new workers for fixed-term periods on a contractual basis rather than as permanent employees. Progress in this area stalled in the wake of the Tiananmen Square events in 1989. Even so, some enterprises have tentatively adopted the labor contract system.

The government has also encouraged state enterprises to reform the compensation system by introducing merit pay raises and promotions, piecework wages, and performance review committees. In theory, state enterprises may also fire a worker or decline to renew a worker's contract, but in practice many enterprises are reluctant to dismiss employees. While the push toward increasingly flexible conditions of employment seems to be gaining acceptance, progress remains slow if for no other reason than that changes in a system create uncertainty. The continued proliferation of private enterprises in China is likely to do the most to dispel feelings of job insecurity among workers by providing viable outside options.

Introduction of Labor Contracts

The introduction of labor contracts is one element of a larger campaign to break the three irons and one big pot policy, which has been in place since 1949. Labor contracts cover salaries, bonuses, subsidies, and the individual worker's job requirements for a fixed term of anywhere between 6 months and 10 years. Such contracts normally tie bonuses to the performance of the individual as well as the enterprise. At the end of the contract period, both worker and employer are theoretically free not to renew the contract. While the extent to which enterprises will be in fact allowed to release workers is as yet unclear, it is clear that dissatisfied workers can now choose to leave without having to obtain permission from the work unit, which for skilled workers often proved an impossible task. The vast majority of cases brought to labor arbitration involves contract workers, an indication that a written contract makes both employer and employee clearer about the ground rules and thus more likely to object when they are breached.

Working Hours and Vacations

Government offices and state enterprises are open six days a week, Monday through Saturday, from 8 am to noon and from 1 to 4:30 pm. For workers, these hours mean a 45-hour workweek. The official workweek is 48 hours, unchanged since 1949. Four to six hours of this time each week are supposed to be spent in political education or in the study of current social issues, but few workers do so. The government has announced that it will lower the official workweek to 44 hours on March 1, 1994, giving state workers Saturday afternoons off. There are no regulations governing the hours of operation of private enterprises. Generally, they keep the same hours as state enterprises.

Vacation leave varies widely by location and industry. The only official regulations concerning vacations are for government personnel: a government employee who has worked for 15 years or more receives 10 days of paid vacation a year. Those who have worked less than 15 years get six days.

State-run enterprises and collectives typically do not grant vacation time. However, an individual who works continuously over a period of time can accumulate days off that he or she would normally have taken each Sunday. In addition, workers with immediate family members in other parts of China can arrange to take time off from work to visit them. Such special leaves have become relatively common and are almost always given during summer months.

Foreign-owned and joint venture businesses are not obligated to grant vacation time. However, more and more foreign employers are instituting paid vacation as a benefit.

Special Leave

Apart from the special leave for visits to family members and maternity leave for female workers, there are no regulations pertaining to special leave. Foreign business owners are free to grant special leave and vacation time at their discretion.

Termination of Employment

The only accepted reason for firing a worker in China is flagrant absenteeism without a medical excuse—generally 30 working days of unexplained absences during one year. To date poor performance has not been seen as grounds for dismissal. As labor

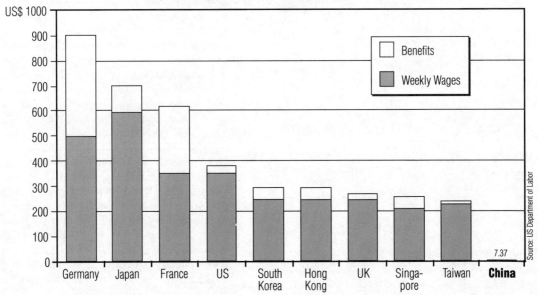

Comparative Average Weekly Wages - 1991

Source: US Department of Labor

Average Monthly Earnings of Employees of Joint Venture Companies - 1992

Job Category	Base Salary (RMB)	Allowances (RMB)	Total (RMB)	Total (US$*)
Deputy General Manager	1,434	876	2,310	397
Manager	542	434	976	168
Supervisor	446	402	848	146
Secretary	299	390	689	118
Engineer	405	382	787	135
Buyer	312	388	700	120
Salesman	325	388	713	123
Customer Service	347	352	699	120
Translator	290	370	660	113
Storekeeper	280	367	647	111

Source: Arthur Andersen & Co.
* US$1.00 = RMB 5.816
Note: This data represents a survey of joint venture companies in Shanghai in August 1992. Costs may be substantially higher or lower in other locations.

Average Weekly Earnings by Occupation - 1991

Occupation	RMB	US$*	% Change from 1990
All	45.5	8.40	10.5
Laborer	45.0	8.31	7.1
Technician	45.0	8.31	7.1
Professional	45.0	8.31	18.4
Commercial	91.0	16.81	10.3

Source: US Department of Labor
*US$1.00 = RMB 5.414

Average Weekly Earnings by Industry - 1990

Industry	RMB	US$*	% Change from 1989
Industry	42.46	8.11	10.3
Agriculture	30.33	5.79	11.3
Construction	45.98	8.78	10.1
Transportation	48.46	9.26	10.1
Commerce	35.25	6.73	9.5
Public Services	42.48	8.12	12.8
Education	40.71	7.78	12.4
Technical	46.21	8.83	13.5
Finance	40.33	7.70	12.3
Government	40.63	7.76	12.7
Joint Venture Companies	55.87	10.67	8.8
Foreign Invested Enterprises	65.60	12.53	-4.5

Source: US Department of Labor
*US$1.00 = RMB 5.235

reform proceeds, firms can expect to have increased freedom to fire surplus or incompetent workers or at least to release workers when their contracts expire. Although government officials tend to realize that it is desirable to release excess workers, many are wary of the social instability that could result.

The trend has been for state enterprises to take bolder action in laying off excess workers. In many cases, large state-run firms employ two to three times as many people as they really need. However, the tendency has been to lay people off according to who has the least seniority, and the result is that the unemployed tend to be the newest hires, that is young people. Although not the most experienced, they are not necessarily the least competent workers. At the same time, the fact that firms are increasingly awarding bonuses on the basis of individual performance gives workers a strong incentive to look for work only in enterprises where they will actually be used.

WAGES AND BENEFITS

Chinese work units have traditionally provided subsidized housing, medical benefits, retirement pay, and in some cases even education for the worker's children. Many enterprises also provide some meals. In 1990 the average state worker in a city received 50 percent of his or her total income as base salary, 23 percent as bonuses and cash subsidies for such things as transportation and fuel and 27 percent as subsidized housing, health insurance, and other benefits.

As increasing numbers of Chinese look to private and joint venture enterprises for employment opportunities, they are willing to forgo some subsidized benefits in exchange for the higher base salaries that they often receive. In addition, rising unemployment rates, inflation, and other factors place workers in a relatively unfavorable bargaining position with private enterprises. However, because there is often no real market for housing and benefits, independent workers may have difficulty functioning outside of an officially recognized work unit no matter how well they are paid.

Foreign invested enterprises (FIEs) still experience difficulties in recruiting Chinese workers, who must usually obtain permission from their work unit or risk losing all their state benefits. FIEs often find that they must pay a Chinese individual's work unit an average of about RMB 1,000 (about US$115) in order for the unit to agree to release the individual. To attract the

Average Monthly Earnings of Employee of Foreign Invested Enterprises - 1992

Wage Category	Management	Sales	Production
Base Pay	473	328	289
Bonus	268	277	186
Housing Subsidy	71	64	54
Retirement Fund	101	83	72
Other Subsidies	103	96	87
Total Pay	RMB 861	RMB 677	RMB 549
Total Pay	US$157	US$123	US$100

Unit: Renminbi (US$1.00 = RMB 5.5)
Source: The China Business Review, September-October, 1992

most qualified Chinese workers, FIEs also find it necessary to offer comprehensive benefits packages. As a result, many FIEs have found that basic wages and salaries account for between 49 and 55 percent of the total cost of employing a Chinese worker.

Reform of the social security system, including health insurance, retirement plans, subsidized housing, and unemployment benefits (a new feature in China), is a crucial component of overall labor reform. Unfortunately, the pace of the government's progress in this area too often lags behind the pace of ongoing economic change.

Wages and Salaries

In the state sector, Chinese workers earn very low wages by international standards. In urban areas, the average total income in 1992 was RMB 2,597 (about US$447), and it was only about RMB 770 (about US$132) in rural areas. Low incomes that fail to keep pace with inflation are clearly one of the main reasons for the recent exodus of people from the countryside to the cities.

In an effort to increase productivity through monetary incentives, wage schemes have become increasingly diverse. While a Chinese worker typically receives a base monthly wage and then a bonus based on the performance of the enterprise (not the individual), other methods, such as a piece rate wage, are becoming common, especially in the southeast which is more influenced by business practices in Hong Kong where piecework is prevalent. A piece rate factory usually pays higher average wages than an enterprise that pays salaries, but managers are finding that increased productivity more than pays for the additional payroll costs. Salary-based state enterprises are also adopting free market techniques to increase productivity, including raises and promotions based on merit and bonuses based on actual production. However, differentials based on skill and managerial responsibility are still minimal in most industries, making it difficult to recruit effective supervisory personnel.

Wages and salaries at FIEs vary by region and occupation. Total average monthly compensation, including base pay, bonuses, housing subsidies, retirement payments, and other subsidies, for production workers in Guangdong Province was RMB 845 (about US$145), RMB 614 (about US$106) in most other coastal regions, and RMB 322 (about US$55) in the upper northeastern and inland regions of China in 1992. Average total monthly compensation for Chinese production workers at FIEs was RMB 549 (about US$94). Salespeople at FIEs received an average monthly compensation of RMB 677 (about US$116), while Chinese managers typically receive RMB 861 (US$148). In Guangdong Province, salespeople and managers tend to receive about 25 percent more than similar workers at FIEs in other coastal regions of China.

It cannot be overemphasized that conditions in China change rapidly. A variety of factors, including rising unemployment, inflation, failing state enterprises, and the expanding private sector, make accurate wage rate compilations and comparisons all but impossible. These rates will certainly change in the near future. But at least one thing seems clear: market mechanisms are increasingly playing an important role in determining the cost of labor in China.

Minimum Wage

There is no legal minimum wage in China, but administrative regulations appear to fix the minimum at RMB 40 (about US$6.88) per month, a rate at which foreigners are unlikely to attract any labor, making the issue moot.

Health Insurance

Traditionally, work units have provided 100 percent health care coverage for workers and a single child. (There is no coverage or credit for additional children.) As better quality medical care has become available, hospitals have raised their charges to levels that have caused the cost of health care coverage to skyrocket as it has elsewhere in the world. Enterprises have attempted to control costs by requiring copayments from employees, by making contracts with hospitals for set fees, and even by paying bonuses to employees who use less than a certain level of health care each month.

When private enterprises first emerged in the 1980s, there were no regulations requiring them to provide health care coverage and other benefits. Of course, few workers were then willing to take a position with a private firm, regardless of pay, without at least some of the benefits that work units offered. Officially, private firms still have no requirement to provide employees with health care coverage. But in most cases, firms are well advised to offer benefits packages both to forestall possible

Chinese Labor Cost Update

A study by the American Chamber of Commerce in Beijing released in January 1994 indicates that the cost of doing business in China is rising, although the labor component is still substantially lower than it is elsewhere in Asia and most of the world. A survey of 42 US wholly foreign-owned enterprises (WFOEs) and eight Sino-foreign joint ventures showed that wages rose an average of 17 percent during 1993. The Chamber predicted that such costs will rise by an additional 16 percent during 1994. These figures lag behind the urban inflation rate, which reached 24 percent in some large cities. Many domestic firms hiked wages to match this figure.

In Beijing US WFOEs paid up to US$780 per month for deputy general managers, while wages for lower level staff such as drivers, interpreters, secretaries, and receptionists were less than US$345 per month. Joint venture salaries were lower, with joint venture deputy general managers making an average of US$552 per month, while support and technical personnel earned no more than US$260 per month.

In addition, all operations paid bonuses and provided monthly allowances for food, housing, transportation, and clothing as part of prevailing labor arrangements. Three-quarters of the joint ventures provided health care for employees and their children, although not for spouses or other family members.

Most employees worked between 40 to 45 hours per week and most had no overtime arrangements. The standard seven day national holiday schedule applied. However, foreign invested firms are introducing a new nonstandard benefit: most firms reported giving annual paid vacation of between 16 and 23 days. Traditionally Chinese workers have received no vacation, although they have been able to take unpaid or partially paid leave and save up their Sundays to take as a block of time off.

Workers employed by foreign firms—often university graduates with language, technical, or other specialized skills—are likely to be better educated than the work force as a whole. Although the potential supply is virtually boundless, the effective supply is highly limited, and firms can expect to pay more as demand picks up. Foreign firms must also expect to have to raise compensation to match inflation and the rising standard of living, especially if they are to attract labor from the limited pool of skilled workers.

government intervention and to prevent unrest among workers.

Unemployment Insurance

China's unemployment insurance program has been in place since the mid-1980s. Despite rising unemployment, it remains largely unused. State enterprises contribute 1.5 percent of total wages to local or provincial funds. Most recipients of unemployment insurance benefits to date have been young people who signed the first labor contracts in 1986. They chose to look for other work when their three-year contracts expired, innocent of the implications of the economic retrenchment that had started by the late 1980s. Since unemployment insurance is paid no matter who terminates the employment relationship, these individuals all received payments. Those who are laid off, as opposed to those whose contracts expire, are paid by their employers and not out of the general unemployment fund.

Unemployment insurance is available only to those who have been employed in the state sector, but apparently some of the money from the unemployment fund has been given as one-time grants to youths waiting for employment who wish to start a business of their own. Essentially, this means that for the time being private firms are exempt from paying unemployment insurance, a situation that is unlikely to last. Government officials are currently investigating how to expand benefits beyond the state sector to collective enterprises, foreign-owned businesses, and joint ventures.

Retirement Plans

The Ministry of Labor made significant progress toward establishing a program for national retirement insurance in 1991. In October of that year, the State Council published new regulations creating a three-tiered system of national social security for urban workers.

The first tier is a nationally mandated but provincially administered retirement fund, into which enterprises and contract workers pay a percentage of their current wages. Because the percentage paid into the fund varies widely by region and individual enterprise, foreign businesses are advised to contact the Ministry of Labor to make sure that they are in compliance. Permanent employees do not pay, although they, too, receive retirement benefits. This burden to employers will decrease as permanent employment is phased out. The second tier enables enterprises to establish plans of their own, which an insurance company, another financial institution, or the firms themselves may administer. The third tier allows individuals to form their own retirement plans through an insurance company or bank.

Since the union-based retirement insurance fund failed during the Cultural Revolution (1966-1976), enterprises have been paying for their own retirees' benefits out of current funds. The government only recently stepped in with a mandatory national program after it became clear that voluntary programs would favor newer firms with fewer retirees and leave established enterprises with heavy retirement expenses.

Authorities in Guangdong Province recently announced a plan to establish a social security trust fund system modeled on Singapore's mandatory Central Provident Fund retirement scheme. However, it remains to be seen whether such a system can be set up to function in a single jurisdiction.

LABOR RELATIONS

As with so many other aspects of labor in China, labor relations are now undergoing fundamental changes. New reforms have been announced, but not all have been embraced wholeheartedly. Significantly, independently instituted changes that do not always have the approval of the government are occurring. This is especially true of the independent worker organizations that are now emerging and of the increased willingness of labor to demand better working conditions.

Unions and the Labor Movement

China's only union, the ACFTU, is closely controlled by the Communist Party, although the organization is nominally independent. Union membership is voluntary for individuals, but every enterprise (including private enterprises) must have a union. Virtually all state-sector workers and almost 90 percent of all urban workers belong to a chapter of the ACFTU. If a worker is unemployed, he or she is no longer considered to be a union member. Workers are allowed to organize other groups independently, but once they have decided to form a union, they must affiliate with the ACFTU and accept its leadership.

The ACFTU views its primary role as one of improving labor discipline and increasing production, rather than championing workers' rights. After the

demonstrations in June 1989, China's leaders attributed much of the unrest to incorrect political thinking among Chinese workers and students. A move to improve party discipline and political training in enterprises was instituted, and press reports in 1991 indicated that a number of union officials had lost their positions for political reasons.

According to foreign and domestic press reports, a number of independent workers' unions have formed in recent years. The reports describe some of these organization as modeled after the Solidarity movement in Poland. Because independent unions are outlawed, they must operate underground, making it virtually impossible to evaluate how prevalent and effective they are or the success of the government's reported attempts to suppress them.

Many involved in the protests centering around the Tiananmen Square protests were expelled from their work units and banned from state jobs as punishment for their dissent. At first, those who found themselves without the security of a state-assigned job were horrified at their situation. Many have of necessity become entrepreneurs and in the process emerged as some of the country's most innovative businesspeople.

Worker Congresses

All employees are supposed to attend worker congresses, which are held once or twice a year. In practice, workers are usually represented by delegates. Participants discuss union plans, the enterprise budget, factory management, and the distribution of benefits. Since 1989 China's union leaders have attempted to make the worker congresses more responsive to the basic welfare concerns of ordinary workers. While the actual influence of worker congresses can vary widely, many serve simply as rubber stamps for agreements reached between the factory manager, the union, and the party secretary.

Strikes and Work Slowdowns

The right to strike was included in China's 1975 and 1978 constitutions. It was dropped from the 1982 constitution on the grounds that the socialist political system had eradicated contradictions between workers and the owners of enterprises. However, the 1992 Union Law states that if a local union and its safety officers find a workplace to be dangerous and the enterprise does not address the problem, the union has the right to suggest that the staff or workers withdraw from the site of the danger.

Chinese leaders appear to view strikes as justified only when they respond to such problems as a sudden critical deterioration in safety conditions. Nevertheless, informal work slowdowns to express worker discontent are not counted as official strikes and they are not uncommon. They are tolerated for brief periods as long as vital services and national security industries are not affected. Although there are no known formal regulations regarding strikes in Special Economic Zones, the authorities there seem to be slightly more tolerant of them than authorities elsewhere in the country.

For several years running, Chinese officials have maintained that there have been no strikes in China. Nevertheless, foreign press reports routinely document strikes, work stoppages, and even work-related riots or other disturbances around the country.

Labor Relations in Joint Ventures and Foreign-Owned Enterprises

Despite assertions by the Ministry of Labor that foreign ventures have access to the cream of the Chinese labor force, foreign-owned and joint venture enterprises in China face problems of discipline, motivation, and low educational levels.

Like Chinese state-run and collective enterprises, joint ventures and foreign-owned firms are required to have unions and to provide facilities for union activities. In practice, unionization in these enterprises is only about 20 percent. Some especially large joint ventures, including many involving US firms, are fully unionized. Meanwhile, many small foreign-owned enterprises in southern China are not unionized at all. In addition to the blanket central government mandate, almost all coastal provinces and cities have passed regulations specifically requiring foreign ventures to allow unions.

In mid-1993 10 foreign firms in southeastern China were reportedly given heavy fines for labor infractions. The violations involved the failure to sign proper contracts with workers. No details were given in the local press other than that one of the those involved was a Taiwanese shoe factory. Other local press reports have indicated that foreign enterprises have experienced labor problems from time to time.

The Role of Manager

As the economic reforms introduced in the 1980s continue to evolve, production decisions have seen a partial decentralization. The Law on State-Owned Industrial Enterprise or Enterprise Law of 1988 states that the manager, rather than the factory's Communist Party committee, is responsible for day-to-day management of the enterprise. The law speaks in general terms about the *managerial responsibility* system, which gives managers ultimate decision-making power over production and management.

In practice, many factory managers consult with the factory party committee and union representatives. The wisdom of such cooperation is reinforced by the fact that, under the Enterprise Law, worker congresses may remove factory managers for incompetence. Moreover, in almost all cases, union and party committee officials are all members of the Communist Party committee.

It is hoped that eventually management will exercise prerogatives, including profit and loss responsibility and hiring and firing discretion, comparable to those found in developed countries. Although some of the more recent official pronouncements on business relations pay lip service to this concept, it is expected to be some time before management has effective control, and managers must learn to work within the system as it exists.

Child Labor

Regulations promulgated in 1987 prohibit the employment of minors who have not completed the compulsory 10 years of education. Statistics on school attendance indicate that approximately 20 percent of the school-age children in cities do not attend school and are presumed to be working. The percentage may well be higher in poorer, isolated regions, where child labor in agriculture is believed to be widespread. In connection with a campaign against vice, the press and public security officials reported that female minors were being sold into prostitution or to factories as manual workers.

In 1991 the State Council issued a regulation prohibiting the employment of children under the age of 16. It imposes heavy fines, withdrawal of business licenses, or imprisonment for employers who hire child laborers. The regulation seems for the most part not to be enforced, although there have been occasional spot checks in southern China, where the problem is assumed to be the most pronounced.

International Labor Affiliation

Since China joined the International Labor Organization (ILO) in 1983, an ACFTU official has served as China's delegate to the body. The ILO opened a Beijing office in 1985, and it runs various programs in China. Most concentrate on worker safety and health issues. China has ratified 17 ILO resolutions, but it has refused to ratify several of the most important, including Resolution No. 87 (Freedom of Association), Resolution No. 98 (The Right to Organize and Conduct Collective Bargaining), and Resolution No. 105 (Abolition of Forced Labor).

Business Law

INTRODUCTION

China is reforming its business laws, particularly as they relate to the activities of foreign businesses. Changes are frequent, and the trend is to improve the climate for foreign investment. In addition, many rules and regulations that significantly affect foreign businesses are in unpublished government advisories and internal policy statements, rather than in the statutes. You should investigate the status of the legal requirements that may affect your particular business activities. The information in this chapter is intended to emphasize the important issues in commercial law, but it should not replace legal advice or council. You should be certain to review your business activities with an attorney familiar with international transactions, the laws of China, and the laws of your own country. Refer to "Important Addresses" chapter for a list of attorneys in China.

BASIS OF CHINA'S LEGAL SYSTEM

China is primarily a civil code country, and therefore its legal system is based on codified laws. However, the courts recognize principles based on custom in specific instances, provided such principles do not conflict with written statutes. Case precedents are not generally recognized, although interpretations of the law by the highest government organ with appropriate authority are considered binding on lower courts and subordinate government entities.

All laws in effect before October 1, 1949, were abrogated when the People's Republic of China was established. At that time, China became a socialist state, based largely on the Soviet system. Since then, the political system has been variously revised and reformed as part of a continuing effort to modernize the country's industry, agriculture, science, and defense. Legal reform has accompanied social and political change, and written laws have become increasingly important in ordering business and nonbusiness relationships.

STRUCTURE OF CHINA'S GOVERNMENT AND LAWS

China's constitution proclaims that Chinese Communist ideology controls in all matters. The National People's Congress is the highest government body with legislative powers. The Congress appoints a State Council, which is the highest government body with administrative powers. China's highest judicial body is the Supreme People's Court, which is held responsible to the Congress. An independent body, the Supreme People's Procuratorate, is authorized to enforce the constitution and laws. In addition to setting forth the government's organization and powers, China's constitution describes the rights and duties of citizens. In practice, the Chinese Communist Party dominates the government, although its authority is not explicitly written into the constitution.

As the country's supreme law, the constitution controls over any conflicting domestic laws, regulations, or decrees. In 1979, the Standing Committee of Fifth National People's Congress reaffirmed all laws passed and not repealed since October 1, 1949. Since 1979, substantial legislation has also been adopted. Numerous regulations and administrative rules affecting foreign trade have been promulgated since 1989 in an effort to regulate the domestic economy.

LAWS GOVERNING BUSINESS IN CHINA

Principal-agency and Chinese-foreigner relationships are governed by general principles in China's Civil Code. (*See* Civil Code.) Imports and exports must meet consumer protection standards under the Laws on Inspection of Import and Export Commodities and

---

Introduction based on interviews with Frankie Leung, of Lewis, D'Amato, Brisbois & Bisgaard, in Los Angeles, California; and John Lo, of Lewis, D'Amato, Brisbois & Bisgaard, in San Francisco, California.

BUSINESS LAW
TABLE OF CONTENTS

Foreign Corrupt Practices Act 238
Legal Glossary 239
International Sales Contract Provisions 240
Trademark Law Developments 243
Exchange Control Regulations 243
New Consumer Protection Law 244
New Regulations Regarding Land
   Use Rights in Guangzhou 246
Restructuring Government Ministries
   and Renaming of MOFERT 247
Law Digest **247**
   Acknowledgements 247
   Actions 247
   Administrative Law 248
   Advertising 249
   Affidavits 249
   Aliens 249
   Arbitration and Award 250
   Assignments 251
   Associations 251
   Attachment 251
   Attorneys and Counselors 252
   Bankruptcy 252
   Bills and Notes 254
   Civil Code 254
   Commercial Code 256
   Commercial Register 256
   Conflicts of Law 256
   Consumer Protection 256
   Contracts 257
   Copyright 262
   Corporations 263
   Customs (Duty) 265
   Damages 266
   Environment 267
   Executions 268
   Foreign Trade 268
   Frauds, Statute of 269
   Fraudulent Sales and Conveyances 269
   Health Regulations 269
   Insolvency 269
   Interest 269
   Joint Stock Companies 270
   Joint Ventures 273
   Judgments 273
   Mines and Minerals 274
   Monopolies and Restraint of Trade 274
   Notaries Public 275
   Partnership 275
   Patents 275
   Principal and Agent 277
   Private Enterprise 278
   Sales 278
   Seals 279
   Sequestration 280
   Statistics, Standards and Quality
      Control 280
   Trademarks 281
   Trade Zones 282

regulations promulgated to implement those statutes. (*See* Consumer Protection.) Business contracts are subject to various statutes and regulations, including the Foreign Economic Contract Law, Economic Contract Law, Joint Venture Law, Environmental Protection Law, Regulations on Administration of Contracts for Acquisition of Technology, and local regulations for particular economic zones. (*See* Contracts and Trade Zones.) Specific industries, including textiles, are also controlled by foreign trade agreements. (*See* Foreign Trade.) In addition, China has ratified the United Nations Convention on Contracts for International Sales of Goods, which provides requirements for sales contracts and transactions. (*See* Sales.)

Foreign enterprises with representative offices in China must be registered under the Provisional Regulations for Handling of Long-Term Representatives of Foreign Enterprises. (*See* Aliens.) Formation and operation of business entities in China must be in compliance with general statutes in the Civil Code, as well as any applicable special statutes or regulations, such as the Joint Venture Law, Law on Wholly Foreign Owned Enterprise, Regulations Governing the Registration of Resident Office of a Foreign Enterprise, Regulations Governing the Administration of the Registration of Enterprise Names, and Regulations for Registration of Enterprises Having Foreign Investment. (*See* Civil Code, Corporations, and Joint Stock Companies.) Private enterprises are separately regulated by the Provisional Regulations for Private Enterprises and Regulations on Private Enterprise Income Tax. (*See* Private Enterprises.)

Commercial advertising is subject to government regulations on content, including registration for use of trademarks and prize offers. (*See* Advertising.) Intellectual property and trademark rights are protected generally under China's Civil Code and more specifically under the Copyright Law, Regulations for the Protection of Computer Software, Patent Law, and Trademark Law, and several international conventions. (*See* Copyright, Patents, and Trademarks.) Firms doing business in China must comply with numerous environmental laws and regulations that protect the air, water, oceans, mineral resources, forests, grasslands, animals, natural historical remains, relics, and scenic and historical regions. (*See* Environment.) Labor relations are governed by such laws and regulations as the Trade Union Law and Labor Insurance Regulations.

GEOGRAPHICAL SCOPE
OF CHINESE LAWS

Laws and regulations digested in this section apply throughout China, except as noted otherwise. The country is divided into provinces, autonomous regions, and cities controlled directly by the central government. Provinces are further subdivided into prefectures, autonomous prefectures, districts, administrative areas, and leagues, and these are again subdivided into county organizations. Local people's congresses in all the various subdivisions have significant self-governing powers. Therefore, a business owner may need to comply with additional local requirements when transacting business within a particular region.

PRACTICAL APPLICATION OF CHINESE LAWS

Contracts Contracts are typically short and vague, with statements designed to provide guidelines for a long-term relationship between the contracting parties. Foreign business owners may negotiate to add more specific contract language and, after some resistance, Chinese companies will often agree. The addition of specific terms may make it easier for a foreign business owner to insist on compliance and to negotiate changes should a dispute arise.

Although Chinese business enterprises consider contracts to be binding and enforceable, they also allow frequent modification of contract terms as circumstances change. A business transaction is thus a continuing negotiation, not necessarily fixed once a contract is reduced to writing. Despite this flexibility in terms, written contracts are an important means of documenting agreements and constitute proof of an agreement should litigation become necessary.

Chinese companies do not expect damages as a primary remedy for a contract breach. Indeed, the concept of damages on breach of contract has been introduced only as a result of transacting business with Western countries. Within their own legal traditions, negotiation of amended contract terms, or a demand for specific performance, is generally more acceptable than enforcing damages against a Chinese business.

Dispute Resolution Chinese business enterprises prefer to negotiate first, arbitrate second, and litigate only in extreme situations. Litigation is rare and is considered a disruption of social harmony, even a personal insult. Arbitration within China is generally satisfactory to all parties, including foreign businesses. (*See* Arbitration and Award.)

Role of Attorneys Foreign companies seeking legal advice should retain an attorney knowledgeable in both Chinese law and international commercial transactions. Locating such an attorney, however, is difficult because only a small percentage of the few attorneys in China are sufficiently familiar with such transactions. Foreign attorneys who work in China may provide legal services only with respect to non-Chinese law; they are not permitted to practice Chinese law.

With increasing industrialization, particularly in Southeastern China, an increasing number of Chinese attorneys are handling commercial transactions. Awareness is growing among Chinese business enterprises of the need for legal counsel in forming commercial relationships and in protecting Chinese nationals in business deals with foreign companies. (*See* Attorneys and Counselors.)

Role of Notaries Notaries are trained government officials who legalize entire documents, as opposed to only verifying signatures. A notary will investigate and certify the truth of representations made in an acknowledged document. (*See* Notaries Public.)

Property Infringement Intellectual property rights, copyright, and patent protection in China are increasing, but trade secrets remain vulnerable. Trademark protection has been available since 1963, with substantial changes made in 1982. For several decades, the primary impetus to improve laws protecting these property rights and prohibiting unfair competition has come from the United States. Protection of intellectual property rights is included in various agreements between China and the United States, including the 1979 United States-China Trade Agreement and the 1992 Memorandum of Understanding on Intellectual Property Rights. Under these agreements, China has committed to improving protection for inventions and copyrighted works, including computer software and sound recordings.

Copyrights for domestically produced work arise without registration, and emphasis is therefore on enforcement of a copyright after infringement. In October 1992, China joined the Berne Convention and the Universal Copyright Convention and committed to joining the Geneva Phonograms Convention. Substantial regulations for the protection of computer software and documentation were adopted in 1992. China has agreed to amend its copyright laws and regulations to conform to international conventions. (*See* Copyright.)

China's 1992 amendments to its patent laws greatly improved protections and extended the scope of these laws to processes for pharmaceutical, chemical, food, and beverage products. (*See* Patents.)

Trade secrets remain unprotected by law, and therefore must be protected by contract. Financial recovery for disclosure of a trade secret is available only through proceedings for breach of contract. China is committed to passing unfair competition laws by 1994 to improve trade secret protection.

RELATED SECTIONS

Refer to "Taxation" chapters for a discussion of tax issues, and "Business Travel" chapter for details on immigration and visa requirements.

Foreign Corrupt Practices Act

United States business owners are subject to the Foreign Corrupt Practices Act (FCPA). The FCPA makes it unlawful for any United States citizen or firm (or any person who acts on behalf of a US citizen or firm) to use a means of US interstate commerce (examples: mail, telephone, telegram, or electronic mail) to offer, pay, transfer, promise to pay or transfer, or authorize a payment, transfer, or promise of money or anything of value to any foreign appointed or elected government official, foreign political party, or candidate for a foreign political office for a corrupt purpose (that is, to influence a discretionary act or decision of the official) and for the purpose of obtaining or retaining business.

It is also unlawful for a US business owner to make such an offer, promise, payment, or transfer to any person if the US business owner knows, or has reason to know, that the person will offer, give, or promise directly or indirectly all or any part of the payment to a foreign government official, political party, or candidate. For purposes of the FCPA, the term *knowledge* means *actual knowledge*—the business owner in fact knew that the offer, payment, or transfer was included in the transaction—and *implied knowledge*—the business owner should have known from the facts and circumstances of a transaction that the agent paid a bribe but failed to carry out a reasonable investigation into the transaction. A business owner should make a reasonable investigation into a transaction if, for example, the sales representative requests a higher commission on a particular sale for no apparent reason, the buyer is a foreign government, the product has a military use, or the buyer's country is one in which bribes are considered customary in business relationships.

The FCPA also contains provisions applicable to US publicly held companies concerning financial record keeping and internal accounting controls.

Legal Payments

The provisions of the FCPA do not prohibit payments made to *facilitate* a routine government action. A facilitating payment is one made in connection with an action that a foreign official must perform as part of the job. In comparison, a corrupt payment is made to influence an official's discretionary decision. For example, payments are not generally considered corrupt if made to cover an official's overtime required to expedite the processing of export documentation for a legal shipment of merchandise or to cover the expense of additional crew to handle a shipment.

A person charged with violating FCPA provisions may assert as a defense that the payment was lawful under the written laws and regulations of the foreign country and therefore was not for a corrupt purpose. Alternatively, a person may contend that the payment was associated with demonstrating a product or performing a preexisting contractual obligation and therefore was not for obtaining or retaining business.

Enforcing Agencies and Penalties

Criminal Proceedings The Department of Justice prosecutes criminal proceedings for FCPA violations. Firms are subject to a fine of up to US$2 million. Officers, directors, employees, agents, and stockholders are subject to fines of up to US$100,000, imprisonment for up to five years, or both.

A US business owner may also be charged under other federal criminal laws, and on conviction may be liable for fines of up to US$250,000 or up to twice the amount of the gross gain or gross loss, provided the defendant derived pecuniary gain from the offense or caused pecuniary loss to another person.

Civil Proceedings Two agencies are responsible for enforcing civil provisions of the FCPA: The Department of Justice handles actions against domestic concerns, and the Securities and Exchange Commission (SEC) files actions against issuers. Civil fines of up to US$100,000 may be imposed on a firm; any officer, director, employee, or agent of a firm; or any stockholder acting for a firm. In addition, the appropriate government agency may seek an injunction against a person or firm that has violated or is about to violate FCPA provisions.

Conduct that constitutes a violation of FCPA provisions may also give rise to a cause of action under the federal Racketeer-Influenced and Corrupt Organizations Act, as well as under a similar state statute if enacted in the state with jurisdiction over the US business owner.

Administrative Penalties A person or firm that is held to have violated any FCPA provisions may be barred from doing business with the US government. Indictment alone may result in suspension of the right to do business with the government.

Department of Justice Opinion Procedure

Any person may request the Department of Justice to issue a statement of opinion on whether specific proposed business conduct would be considered a violation of the FCPA. The opinion procedure is detailed in 28 C.F.R. Part 77. If the Department of Justice issues an opinion stating that certain conduct conforms with current enforcement policy, conduct in accordance with that opinion is presumed to comply with FCPA provisions.

Legal Glossary

Agent The person authorized to act on behalf of another person (the principal). Example: A sales representative is an agent of the seller.

Aliquot Fractional share. Example: Several parties who breach a contract may be held responsible aliquot, and therefore each is liable for a proportionate share of the damages.

Attachment The legal process for seizing property before a judgment to secure payment of damages if awarded. This process is also referred to as sequestration. Example: A party who claims damages for breach of contract may request a court to issue an order freezing all transfers of specific property owned by the breaching party pending resolution of the dispute.

Authentication The act of conferring legal authenticity on a written document, typically made by a notary public who attests and certifies that the document is in proper legal form and that it is executed by a person identified as having authority to do so.

Bill of exchange A written instrument signed by a person (the drawer) and addressed to another person (the drawee), typically a bank, ordering the drawee to pay unconditionally a stated sum of money to yet another person (the payee) on demand or at a future time.

Distrain The detention or seizure of a person's property to secure that person's performance of an obligation. For example, a court may order that a person's property be distrained to ensure that the person will appear before the court at a hearing.

Execution The legal process for enforcing a judgment for damages, usually by seizure and sale of the debtor's personal property. Example: If a court awards damages in a breach of contract action and the breaching party has failed to remit the sum due, the party awarded damages may request the court to order seizure and sale of the breaching party's inventory to the extent necessary to satisfy the award.

Force majeure clause A superior force clause. A contract clause that excuses a party who breaches the contract because performance has been prevented by the occurrence of an event that is beyond the party's reasonable control. Example: A force majeure clause in a contract may excuse performance on the occurrence of such events as natural disasters, labor strikes, bankruptcy, or the failure of subcontractors to perform.

Negotiable instrument A written document that can be transferred merely by endorsement or delivery. Example: A check is a negotiable instrument.

Locus A place. Example: The locus of arbitration is the place where arbitration proceedings are held.

Power of attorney A written document by which one person (the principal) authorizes another person (the agent) to perform stated acts on the principal's behalf. Example: A principal may execute a special power of attorney authorizing an agent to sign a specific contract or a general power of attorney authorizing the agent to sign all contracts for the principal.

Principal A person who authorizes another party (the agent) to act on the principal's behalf.

Promoter of corporation The individual or entity that organizes a corporation.

Sequestration *See* Attachment.

Turnkey contract An agreement under which a builder agrees to complete a building so that it is ready for occupancy when it is delivered to the other contracting party.

Void ab initio Invalid from the time of initiation. Example: A contract that violates law or public policy is void ab initio, that is, it is invalid when it is made.

International Sales Contract Provisions

When dealing internationally, you must consider the business practices and legal requirements of the country where the buyer or seller is located. For a small, one-time sale, an invoice may be commonly accepted. For a more involved business transaction, a formal written contract may be preferable to define clearly the rights, responsibilities, and remedies of all parties. The laws of your country or the foreign country may require a written contract and may even specify all or some of the contract terms. Refer to Contracts and to Sales for specific laws on contracts and the sale of goods.

Parties generally have freedom to agree to any contract terms that they desire. Whether a contract term is valid in a particular country is of concern only if you have to seek enforcement. Thus, you have fairly broad flexibility in negotiating contract terms. However, you should always be certain to come to a definite understanding on four issues: the goods (quantity, type, quality); the time of delivery; the price; and the time of payment.

You need to consider the following clauses when you negotiate an international sales contract.

Contract date

State the date when the contract is signed. This date is particularly important if payment or delivery times are fixed in reference to it—for example, "shipment within 30 days of the contract date."

Identification of parties

Designate the names of the parties, and describe their relation to each other.

Goods

Description Describe the type and quality of the goods. You may simply indicate a model number, or you may have to attach detailed lists, plans, or drawings. This clause should be clear enough that both parties fully understand the specifications and have no discretion in interpreting them.

Quantity Specify the number of units, or other measure of quantity, of the goods. If the goods are measured by weight, you should specify net weight, dry weight, or drained weight. If the goods are prepackaged and are subject to weight restrictions in the end market, you may want to provide that the seller will ensure that the goods delivered will comply with those restrictions.

Price Indicate the price per unit or other measure, such as per pound or ton, and the extended price.

Packaging arrangements

Set forth packaging specifications, especially for goods that can be damaged in transit. At a minimum, this provision should require the seller to package the goods in such a way as to withstand transportation. If special packaging requirements are necessary to meet consumer and product liability standards in the end market, you should specify them also.

Transportation arrangements

Carrier Name a preferred carrier for transporting the goods. You should designate a particular carrier if, for example, a carrier offers you special pricing or is better able than others to transport the product.

Storage Specify any particular requirements for storage of the goods before or during shipment, such as security arrangements, special climate demands, and weather protection needs.

Notice provisions Require the seller to notify the buyer when the goods are ready for delivery or pickup, particularly if the goods are perishable or fluctuate in value. If your transaction is time-sensitive, you could even provide for several notices to allow the buyer to track the goods and take steps to minimize damages if delivery is delayed.

Shipping time State the exact date for shipping or provide for shipment within a reasonable time from the contract date. If this clause is included and the seller fails to ship on time, the buyer may claim a right to cancel the contract, even if the goods have been shipped, provided that the buyer has not yet accepted delivery.

Costs and charges

Specify which party is to pay the additional costs and charges related to the sale.

Duties and taxes Designate the party that will be responsible for import, export, and other fees and taxes and for obtaining all required licenses. For example, a party may be made responsible for paying the duties, taxes, and charges imposed by that party's own country, since that party is best situated to know the legal requirements of that country.

Insurance costs Identify the party that will pay costs of insuring the goods in transit. This is a critical provision because the party responsible bears the risk if the goods are lost during transit. A seller is typically responsible for insurance until title to the goods passes to the buyer, at which time the buyer becomes responsible for insurance or becomes the named beneficiary under the seller's insurance policy.

Handling and transport Specify the party that will pay shipping, handling, packaging, security, and any other costs related to transportation, which should be specified.

Terms defined Explain the meaning of all abbreviations—for example, FAS (free alongside ship), FOB (free on board), CIF (cost, insurance, and freight)—used in your contract to assign responsibility and costs for goods, transportation, and insurance. If you define your own terms, you can make the definitions specific to your own circumstances and needs. As an alternative, you may agree to adopt a particular standard, such as the Revised American Foreign Trade Definitions or Incoterms 1990. In either case, this clause should be clear enough that both parties understand when each is responsible for insuring the goods.

Insurance or risk of loss protection

Specify the insurance required, the beneficiary of the policy, the party who will obtain the insurance, and the date by which it will have been obtained.

Payment provisions

Provisions for payment vary with such factors as the length of the relationship between the contracting parties, the extent of trust between them, and the availability of certain forms of payment within a particular country. A seller will typically seek the most secure form of payment before committing to shipment, while a buyer wants the goods cleared through customs and delivered in satisfactory condition before remitting full payment.

Method of payment State the means by which payment will be tendered—for example, prepayment in cash, traveler's checks, or bank check; delivery of a documentary letter of credit or documents against payment; credit card, credit on open account, or credit for a specified number of days.

Medium of exchange Designate the currency to be used—for example, US currency, currency of the country of origin, currency of a third country.

Exchange rate Specify a fixed exchange rate for the price stated in the contract. You may use this clause to lock in a specific price and ensure against fluctuating currency values.

Import documentation

Require that the seller be responsible for presenting to customs all required documentation for the shipment.

Inspection rights

Provide that the buyer has a right to inspect goods before taking delivery to determine whether the goods meet the contract specifications. This clause should specify the person who will do the inspection—for example, the buyer, a third party, a licensed inspector; the location where the inspection will occur—for example at the seller's plant, the buyer's warehouse, a receiving dock; the time at which the inspection will occur; the need for a certified document of inspection; and any requirements related to the return of nonconforming goods, such as payment of return freight by the seller.

Warranty provisions

Limit or extend any implied warranties, and define any express warranties on property fitness and quality. The contract may, for example, state that the seller warrants that the goods are of merchantable quality, are fit for any purpose for which they would ordinarily be used,

International Sales Contract Provisions (cont'd.)

or are fit for a particular purpose requested by the buyer. The seller may also warrant that the goods will be of the same quality as any sample or model that the seller has furnished as representative of the goods. Finally, the seller may warrant that the goods will be packaged in a specific way or in a way that will adequately preserve and protect the goods.

Indemnity

Agree that one party will hold the other harmless from damages that arise from specific causes, such as the design or manufacture of a product.

Enforcement and Remedies

Time is of the essence Provide that timely performance of the contract is essential. The inclusion of this clause allows a party to claim breach merely because the other party fails to perform within the time prescribed in the contract. Common in United States contracts, a clause of this type is considered less important in other countries.

Modification Require the parties to make all changes to the contract in advance and in a signed written modification.

Cancellation State the reasons for which either party may cancel the contract and the notice required for cancellation.

Contingencies Specify any events that must occur before a party is obligated to perform the contract. For example, you may agree that the seller has no duty to ship goods until the buyer forwards documents that secure the payment for the goods.

Governing law Choose the law of a specific jurisdiction to control any interpretation of the contract terms. The law that you choose will usually affect where you can sue or enforce a judgment and what rules and procedures will be applied.

Choice of forum Identify the place where a dispute may be settled—for example, the country of origin of the goods, the country of destination, a third country that is convenient to both parties.

Arbitration provisions Agree to arbitration as an alternative to litigation for the resolution of any disputes that arise. You should agree to arbitrate only if you seriously intend to settle disputes in this way. If you agree to arbitrate but later file suit, the court is likely to uphold the arbitration clause and force you to settle your dispute as you agreed under the contract.

An arbitration clause should specify whether arbitration is binding or nonbinding on the parties; the place where arbitration will be conducted (which should be a country that has adopted a convention for enforcing arbitration awards, such as the United Nations Convention on Recognition and Enforcement of Foreign Awards); the procedure by which an arbitration award may be enforced; the rules governing the arbitration, such as the United Nations Commission on International Trade Law Model Rules; the institute that will administer the arbitration, such as the International Chamber of Commerce (Paris), the American Arbitration Association (New York), the Japan Commercial Arbitration Association, the United Nations Economic and Social Commission for Asia and the Pacific, the London Court of Arbitration, or the United Nations Commission International Trade Law; the law that will govern procedural issues or the merits of the dispute; any limitations on the selection of arbitrators (for example, a national of a disputing party may be excluded from being an arbitrator); the qualifications or expertise of the arbitrators; the language in which the arbitration will be conducted; and the availability of translations and translators if needed.

Severability Provide that individual clauses can be removed from the contract without affecting the validity of the contract as a whole. This clause is important because it provides that, if one clause is declared invalid and unenforceable for any reason, the rest of the contract remains in force.

Trademark Law Developments

Several changes have been made in the trademark area, as China continues to modernize its intellectual property laws.

Introducing service marks and multi-class filings

Amendments to the Trademark Law of the People's Republic of China were adopted by the Standing Committee of the National People's Congress (the "NPC") on February 22, 1993. The amendments were effective from July 1, 1993. One major change is the introduction of registration of service marks (trademarks used for services). Provisions of the Trademark Law relating to trademarks for goods shall apply to trademarks for services. Service marks will be registered in the same way as trademarks. The International Classification system will also be applied to services.

Cancellation procedures

The amendments formalize proceedings for cancellation actions against registered trademarks and facilitate the cancellation of registrations obtained deceptively or fraudulently.

Licensee requirements

In addition, a new provision requires anyone using a registered trademark pursuant to a license to mark on the goods the name of the licensee and place of origin of the goods.

Prohibition of foreign geographical names

The law now formally prohibits the registration of foreign geographical names known to the public and the registration of Chinese place names at the county level and above, except for names that have other meanings. Existing registrations of geographical names shall remain valid.

Passing off registered trademarks

Supplementary Regulations Concerning Punishment of the Crime of Passing Off Registered Trademarks were passed by the Standing Committee of the NPC on February 22, 1993 and were effective from July 1, 1993. The Regulations provide heavier sanctions against counterfeiters of trademarks.

In serious cases of unauthorized use of a registered trademark on the same type of goods, counterfeiters are now subject to fines and imprisonment for a period of between three and seven years. Sellers of such goods who are aware that the goods are counterfeits of a registered trademark are subject to fines and imprisonment. Where the offender is an enterprise, the person bearing direct responsibility may be subject to fines and imprisonment.

Reprinted from Asia Pacific Legal Developments Bulletin, vol. 8, no. 3, Baker & McKenzie, Sept. 1993, with permission of the author, Lim Mei Yin, Hong Kong, and the law firm of Baker & McKenzie, Hong Kong.

Exchange Control Regulations

New measures have been introduced for controlling the movement of money in and out of China.

"Measures of the People's Republic of China for Administration of the Entry and Exit of the National Currency" were issued by the State Council on January 20, 1993 and became effective on March 1, 1993. The new measures supersede the old "Measures of the People's Republic of China Prohibiting the Entry and Exit of the National Currency," issued by the State Council on March 6, 1951.

The new measures stipulate that the People's Bank of China (the "PBOC") shall impose limits on the amount of renminbi that individual Chinese citizens may take into or out of China. According to the "Announcement of the People's Bank of China Concerning the Maximum Amount of National Currency That May Be Carried Across the Border," issued on February 5, 1993 and effective from March 1, 1993, the PBOC set the initial individual limit at RMB 6,000. This limit may be adjusted for the purpose of low-volume trading between inhabitants of open border areas.

Reprinted from Asia Pacific Legal Developments Bulletin, vol. 8, no. 3, Baker & McKenzie, Sept. 1993, with permission of the author, Sara Y. Bosco, Hong Kong, and the law firm of Baker & McKenzie, Hong Kong.

New Consumer Protection Law

In an effort to protect consumers, China recently enacted a "product quality law." The details are described in this article.

The Product Quality Law of the People's Republic of China was adopted by the National People's Congress on February 22, 1993 and will come into effect on September 1, 1993. The Product Quality Law is intended to protect the rights and interests of consumers.

Under the Product Quality Law, producers and sellers are prohibited from engaging in the following activities:

- counterfeiting or passing off quality marks, such as certification marks, marks of fame and marks of excellence;
- falsifying the place of origin of products, and falsifying or passing off of the name and/or address of another's factory;
- adulterating products or mixing improper elements with products;
- passing off spurious products as genuine products;
- passing off products of poor quality as quality products; and
- producing products which the government has pronounced obsolete.

The Product Quality Law stipulates that industrial products which may be hazardous to health, personal safety or the safety of property must conform to national and industrial standards. In cases where no national or professional standards have been formulated, the products must conform to the requirements of the safeguarding of health, personal safety and the safety of property.

Supervision and control of product quality

The State Council's department of supervision and control of product quality is responsible for the nationwide supervision and control of product quality. Relevant departments of the State Council and governments at and above the county level are responsible for the supervision and control of product quality within their administrative jurisdictions. The government will rely mainly on spot checks to supervise product quality, and the results of such checks shall be made available to the public. Users and consumers are given the right to make inquiries of producers and sellers concerning product quality problems.

The Product Quality Law sets forth provisions for the government to establish two certification systems. The first is a certification system for enterprise quality systems based on international quality control standards. The second is a product quality certification system established by reference to international advanced product standards and technological requirements. Enterprises may apply to an approved certification institution to issue a certificate to verify that the system or product is up to standard.

Obligations of producers

Under the Product Quality Law, producers are responsible for ensuring that their products:

- pose no unreasonable danger to personal safety or the safety of property, and comply with applicable State or industrial standards relating to the protection of health, personal safety and safety of property;
- possess the properties for use that they should possess, except where flaws in their properties for use are clearly indicated;
- conform to the standards indicated on the product itself or its packaging;
- have a product quality inspection certificate;
- display the product name and the producing factory's name and address in Chinese;
- display the product specifications, grade and main ingredients where required by a product's characteristics and usage requirements;
- carry the production date, period of safe use or date of expiry, if applicable; and
- carry a warning mark or a warning in Chinese where improper use might result in damage to the product or endanger the use or the user's property.

Product marks need not be affixed to unpackaged foodstuffs and other products to which it is difficult to affix marks due to the special characteristics of the product. Hazardous, toxic and fragile products must conform to the relevant requirements and carry warning marks written in Chinese indicating the procedures for storage and transport.

New Consumer Protection Law (cont'd)

Obligations of sellers

Sellers are subject to the same responsibilities as producers with respect to product marks, place of origin, the passing off of the name or address of another's factory, the mixing and adulteration of products, and the passing off of spurious or poor quality products. In addition, sellers must:

- implement a quality control and maintenance system for their products;
- not engage in the sale of expired or deteriorated products; and
- ensure that their products carry the necessary marks.

Liability

Under the new law, the seller of a product is responsible for its repair, replacement or return and is responsible for losses incurred by the purchaser of the product where:

- the product, without prior and clear indication, does not possess the properties for use that it should;
- the product does not meet the product standards carried on the product or its packaging; or
- the product does not conform to the quality indicated by the product description or physical sample.

If the seller fails to take responsibility for inferior products, the department in charge of supervising product quality or the relevant administrator of industry and commerce must resolve the matter. Where the producer or supplier of the product is responsible for the product defect, the seller has a right to recover damages.

The producer is liable to provide compensation in cases where a defect in a product causes physical injury or damages other property, except where the producer is able to prove one of the following:

- it has not put the product into circulation;

- the defect did not exist when the product was put into circulation; or
- the level of science and technology at the time the product was put into circulation was insufficient to detect the existence of the defect.

The seller is liable to provide compensation in cases where the producer or supplier of the defective product cannot be identified. Claims for compensation for damages caused by a defect in a product must be brought within two years from the date on which the party knew or should have known that its rights and interests had been infringed, and within ten years from the date of delivery of the defective product to the first user or consumer.

Civil disputes arising over product quality may be settled through consultation or mediation between the parties. If the parties are not willing to settle a dispute through consultation or mediation, or if consultation or mediation is unsuccessful, the dispute may be submitted for arbitration on the basis of agreement between the parties. If the parties do not reach an arbitration agreement, proceedings may be instituted in a People's Court.

Penalties

The Product Quality Law stipulates that producers and sellers found guilty of profiteering from defective products are subject to fines of between two and five times the amount of income generated from the production or sale of the substandard, unsafe, adulterated, obsolete, expired, or deteriorated products. Administrative sanctions are imposed upon violators of the provisions of the Product Quality Law. In serious cases, the business license of the producer or seller may be revoked. Criminal offenders will be subject to prosecution.

Reprinted from Asia Pacific Legal Developments Bulletin, vol. 8, no. 3, Baker & McKenzie, Sept. 1993, with permission of the author, Tan Loke Khoon, Hong Kong, and the law firm of Baker & McKenzie, Hong Kong.

New Regulations Regarding Land Use Rights in Guangzhou

In an attempt to keep pace with the increasing investment in China, the Guangzhou Economic and Technological Development Zone is allowing foreign investors to acquire land use rights for value and to transfer, lease or mortgage such rights. This article summarizes these amendments.

In view of the increasing interest in investing in southern China, particularly in real estate development, the Guangdong Provincial People's Government and the local People's Governments within the Province have issued regulations allowing foreign investors to acquire land use rights for value and, further, to transfer, lease or mortgage such rights. The Guangzhou People's Government promulgated the *Measures for the Grant and Assignment for Value of Land Use Rights in the Guangzhou Economic and Technological Development Zone* ("ETDZ Measures") on 9 March 1988 and amended them on August 25, 1992 in an effort to keep pace with the changing investment environment.

The major amendments are as follows:

• The amended ETDZ Measures now expressly stipulate that grantees, assignors and assignees of land use rights may not only be companies, enterprises, other economic organizations and individuals within or outside China, but may also be from Hong Kong, Macao and Taiwan.

• The Management Committee of the Development Zone (the "Management Committee") has been empowered to determine the length of the term of land use in accordance with relevant regulations and the practical needs of the project. The 50 year-term limitation has been abolished and more flexibility is now allowed in granting land use rights on the basis of actual circumstances.

• Under the amended ETDZ Measures, land use right transfer contracts executed within Guangzhou are not required to be notarized. For such contracts executed outside China, legalization by the relevant Chinese embassy or consulate is no longer necessary.

• Important new provisions are:

—no state land use certificate can be obtained before full payment of the land use fee is made, but the Management Committee may issue a document evidencing the entitlement to the land when effecting the registration of transfer; and

—if the land use rights are used as a capital contribution for the establishment of a Chinese-foreign equity joint venture, cooperative joint venture or domestic joint venture and the rights are to be passed to such joint ventures, the land use rights are considered to have been transferred.

Commentary on the amendments

The aim of the first amendment is to legitimize the investments made by individuals and companies from Hong Kong, Macao and Taiwan who have already invested in real estate in the Guangzhou ETDZ. The second amendment is simply a confirmation of the provisions of the *Regulations of the People's Republic of China Concerning the Grant and Assignment of the Right to Use State Land in Urban Areas* issued by the State Council in 1990. Under these regulations, land use rights for residential use can be granted for up to 70 years.

The more important amendment is the third amendment. Under the *Provisional Regulations of the People's Republic of China Concerning Notarization* promulgated in 1982, notarization is effected on the basis of the relevant parties' own volition and is intended to prevent disputes and minimize the possibility of litigation. In remote areas where there are fewer lawyers and legal awareness of the residents is low, it may be necessary to involve the notary officers in economic transactions. On the contrary, the Guangzhou ETDZ is an area quite open to the outside world and its property law is relatively sophisticated. Furthermore, the ETDZ has established a special department, the Management Committee, to supervise and control land grants and transfers. Eliminating the requirement of notarization will simplify the relevant procedures, reduce administrative costs and encourage foreign investment.

With respect to the two amended provisions, the first is one which facilitates the transfer of land use rights. Under similar regulations, land use rights cannot be transferred until the state land use certificate is issued. However the ETDZ Measures allow the Management Committee to issue a document evidencing the ownership to facilitate the transfer. This is particularly encouraging to interested investors. The latter provision further specifies that contribution of land use rights shall be considered to be a transfer, and thus shall be subject to completion of transfer procedures and payment of a land appreciation fee.

Reprinted from Asia Pacific Legal Developments Bulletin, vol. 8, no. 3, Baker & McKenzie, Sept. 1993, with permission of the author, David Y.W. Ho, Hong Kong, and the law firm of Baker & McKenzie, Hong Kong.

Restructuring Government Ministries and Renaming of MOFERT

China's central economic bureaucracy has been restructured.

In its March 1993 session, the National People's Congress of the PRC adopted in principle a plan to reform the State Council and its ministries by the end of 1993. Seven ministries are to be dissolved or divided and renamed. These include: the Ministry of Energy Resources, the Ministry of Machine-Building and Electronics Industry, the Ministry of Aeronautics and Astronautics Industry, the Ministry of Light Industry, the Ministry of Textile Industry, the Ministry of Commerce, and the Ministry of Materials and Equipment.

Under the plan, six new ministries are to be created: the State Economic and Trade Commission, the Ministry of Power Industry, the Ministry of Coal Industry, the Ministry of Machine-Building Industry, the Ministry of Electronics Industry, and the Ministry of Internal Trade. The Ministry of Aeronautics and Astronautics Industry is to be divided into two specialized semi-autonomous corporations, provisionally named the China National Aviation Industry Corporation (CNAIC) and the China National Space Industry Corporation. The China National Aero-Technology Import and Export Corporation will report to CNAIC.

In addition, the Ministry of Foreign Economic Relations and Trade ("MOFERT") was renamed the Ministry of Foreign Trade and Economic Cooperation.

Reprinted from Asia Pacific Legal Developments Bulletin, vol. 8, no. 3, Baker & McKenzie, Sept. 1993, with permission of the author, John V. Grobowski, Hong Kong, and the law firm of Baker & McKenzie, Hong Kong.

LAW DIGEST

ACKNOWLEDGEMENTS

See Notaries Public.

ACTIONS

Citizens' rights to lodge administrative complaints against malfeasance or to initiate legal proceedings to protect their rights are safeguarded by Constitution and Administrative Law. (Art. 41). In addition, international contracts may specify tribunal having jurisdiction over dispute, normally arbitration tribunal, and law that will govern any disputes. Said tribunal and law need not be local but may be non-Chinese. Agreement on Trade Regulations signed on July 7, 1979 between US and China specifically provides that arbitration is permitted and provides that competent authorities in each jurisdiction will enforce arbitration awards. Treaty also expresses intent of parties to be bound by customary international trade practices. In addition, Foreign Trade Arbitration Commission established in China on May 6, 1954 provides for arbitration of disputes arising from foreign trade. By decision of State Council of Feb. 26, 1980 Foreign Trade Arbitration Commission was renamed Foreign Economic and Trade Arbitration Commission, and its jurisdiction enlarged to include taking cognizance of international disputes such as those arising from joint ventures with foreign firms, foreign investment disputes and disputes over credit and loans between Chinese and foreign banks, etc. Obviously, this tribunal's jurisdiction depends initially upon agreement between parties. Arbitral panels have been established in Shenzhen, which include Hong Kong barristers and solicitors.

Art. 8 of Environmental Protection Law, adopted on Sept. 13, 1979 confers upon Chinese citizens right to commence lawsuit against organization or individual that violates provisions of this draft Act.

Organic Law of People's Courts promulgated on July 1, 1979 (C. I, Art. 5) specifies that Chinese citizens, regardless of race, sex, occupation, social status, religion, education, economic circumstances or length of residence will be treated equally before law. There is no specification in this statute that foreigners may have access to courts, or that they are denied access to courts, but in fact cases initiated by foreigners have been brought in courts and Chinese courts have accepted jurisdiction over said proceedings. Furthermore, Code of Civil Procedure, Part IV, provides that foreigners have access equal to Chinese citizens to courts for purposes of civil and commercial litigation, so does Administrative Law.

Part IV. Special Regulations on Civil Procedure Concerning Foreign Matters

Chapter XXIV. General Principles Civil litigation concerning foreign matters in territory of People's Republic of China should utilize regulations of this Part. Where this Part lacking in regulations, then they should utilize other relevant provisions of this statute. (Civ. Pro. Code, Art. 237).

Those foreign persons and organizations, or international organizations, which give rise to civil litigation, but enjoy exemption from legal process, are to be handled by courts according to laws of People's Republic of China, or treaties entered into by China, or regulations provided in international conventions entered into by China. (Civ. Pro. Code, Art. 239). Where treaties of People's Republic of China or international agreements to which China a signatory have provisions different from those provided in this statute, provisions of international agreement should be applied, except where China has reserved its rights in provision of said agreement. (Civ. Pro. Code, Art. 238).

When court tries case concerning foreign matters, written and spoken language normally used in China should be utilized. If parties request interpreter, such can be provided, but said party must be responsible for paying fees of interpreter. (Civ. Pro. Code, Art. 240). Foreign nationals, stateless persons, foreign enterprises and organizations that bring or respond to suits, and who need to entrust attorneys to represent them in litigation, must employ attorneys of People's Republic of China. (Art. 241). Foreign nationals or stateless persons who do not reside in People's Republic of China and foreign enterprises and organizations who entrust attorneys to represent them in litigation, must have powers of attorney notarized in country where they reside and obtain Chinese embassy or consulate attestation thereto or verification through procedures provided in relevant treaty between China and foreign entity's country of origin who mail to Chinese attorneys or Chinese citizens powers of attorney must, in order for said powers to have legal effect, have such powers of attorney documented by notary public in nation where they reside and have Chinese embassy or consulate attestation thereto. (Civ. Pro. Code, Art. 242).

ADMINISTRATIVE LAW

Administrative law of China was adopted on Apr. 4, 1989 at second session of seventh national Congress. Since citizens have authority to sue government, this statute ensures courts try administrative cases correctly and promptly, so as to protect legitimate rights of citizens, legal persons and other organizations, and ensure administrative organizations exercise powers in accordance with law.

Citizens, legal persons or other enterprises and organizations whose legitimate rights are infringed by concrete actions of administrative organization and their staff have rights to bring suit against said organizations. (Art. 2).

In administrative proceedings, courts utilize system of collegiate bench, public trial and two levels of appeal in accordance with law. (Art. 6). Mediation is generally not utilized. (Art. 50).

Courts shall accept litigants for following concrete administrative actions: (1) contesting administrative punishments as detention, fine, revoking business license, instructions to stop production or operations, confiscating capital, etc.; and (2) contesting such forcible administrative measures as limit of personal freedom or in sealing up, distraining, freezing assets; and (3) infringement on decision-making power in operations and management by administrative organizations and staff; and (4) administrative organizations failure to issue business license or to reply to persons who conform to lawful provisions for application for licenses; and (5) refusal to perform or failure to reply to applications to administrative organization for liability for personal rights, property rights and the like; and (6) failure to pay pensions for disabled or for family of deceased; and (7) illegally requiring parties to undertake liability for matter they have no responsibility for; and (8) infringement on personal rights and property rights. (Art. 11).

Courts are directed not to take cases concerning national defense, diplomatic affairs, and rules or regulations and concrete administrative acts where administrative organizations have final decision making authority pursuant to law.

Foreigners, stateless persons, foreign enterprises and organizations within territory of China can all undertake suit except those actions governed by other laws. (Art. 70). Foreigners enjoy same rights and obligations as citizens and organizations of China in commencing administrative action. (Art. 71).

Court is to apply principle of reciprocity to right to administrative proceedings by citizens, enterprises and organizations of those countries that impose restrictions on rights of administrative proceedings by citizens, enterprises, and organizations of China. (Art. 71).

Where provisions of international treaties, which China has concluded or to which China is party are different from those of this law, former shall be applicable, except as to clauses where China has declared reservation. (Art. 72).

Citizens, legal persons or other enterprises and organizations have rights to claim for compensation when their legitimate rights are infringed upon and they suffer loss as result of actions by administrative organizations or staff. In case of claims for compensation only, disputes shall be decided first by administrative organization. Litigant contesting decision rendered by administrative organization may bring action.

ADVERTISING

On Feb. 17, 1982 State Council promulgated Provisional Regulations Concerning Supervision of Advertising, consisting of 19 articles, effective May 1, 1982. On Oct. 26, 1987, these were replaced by new Regulations, consisting of 22 articles, effective Dec. 1, 1987. State Administration of Commerce and Industry and its local bureaus are responsible for regulation of advertising. (Art. 5). All specialized advertising enterprises and individual enterprises of industry and commerce must register under these most recent regulations. (Art. 6). Regulations define advertising broadly to include all promotional activity through media, as well as putting up billboards, etc. (Art. 2).

Truth In Advertising Regulations require that contents of advertisements be factual, have proper purpose, be clear and in no way deceive consumers. (Art. 3).

Various types of advertisements require special authority, e.g., use of trademarks must have certificate of trademark registration. (Art. 11[5]). Similarly, use of patent requires possession of patent certification (Art. 11[4]); if advertisements offers prizes, certification must also be obtained. (Art. 11[2]).

Prohibition and Restrictions Proscribable contents in advertisement are as follows: Anything which violates laws or regulations (Art. 8[1]); damages dignity of any Chinese nationals (Art. 8[2]); involves national flag, emblem or song (Art. 8[3]); has reactionary or superstitious content (Art. 8[4]); defrauds or deceives consumers (Art. 8[5]); or belittles product of another company (Art. 8[6]). Regulations also prohibit advertisement of tobacco through radio, television, newspapers or magazines. (Art. 10). Furthermore, news agencies must not print or broadcast any advertisement during news report. (Art. 9). Companies may only advertise in posters that information which is relevant to their business and permitted by State for their business. (Art. 7). Local Administration of Industry and Commerce must authorize all posting of handbills on government buildings or protected cultural sites. (Art. 10).

Fees Advertising agencies may set their own standards for fees and then must file these with both local Administration of Industry and Commerce and Organization of Price Control. (Art. 14). Standard agency fees shall be jointly determined by State Administration of Commerce and Industry and Organization of Price Control. (Art. 15). Other fees shall also be fixed by these two departments, subject to approval by People's Government. (Art. 15).

Administration Advertising agency and advertiser shall enter contract which clearly defines responsibilities of both parties. (Art. 17). State Administration of Commerce and Industry is responsible for interpretation of regulations and promulgation of detailed plans for enforcement of said regulations.

(Art. 21). All advertising agencies must keep books of account and pay taxes according to law. (Art. 16).

Penalties If advertiser or advertising agency violates regulations, Administration of Industry and Commerce will, depending on circumstances, invoke following sanctions: Suspend published advertising, compel modifications, criticize, confiscate illegal income, levy fine, or revoke business license or license to advertise of party at fault. (Art. 18). If violation is particularly egregious and with serious repercussions, judicial body with responsibility for criminal punishment shall prosecute guilty party. (Art. 18). If advertiser or advertising agency contests penalties imposed by Administration of Commerce and Industry, it may, within 15 days of its notification, apply to superior Administration of Commerce and Industry for review. If still dissatisfied, it may, within 30 days of receiving decision of superior administration, file suit with People's Court. (Art. 19).

If advertiser or advertising agency causes damage to consumer due to violation of aforementioned regulations, responsible party must compensate said consumer. (Art. 20). Alleged victim may apply for compensation at Superior Administration of Commerce and Industry. If dissatisfied with decision of Superior Administration, alleged victim may contest decision directly at People's Court. (Art. 20).

AFFIDAVITS

Affidavits in China may be sworn and signatures acknowledged by notaries public.

ALIENS

Regulations Governing Entry, Exit, Transit, Residence and Travel of Aliens were originally promulgated by State Council in China on Apr. 13, 1964. Law on Control of Entry and Exit of Aliens was adopted by Standing Committee of National People's Congress and promulgated on Nov. 22, 1985 effective as of Feb. 1, 1986. Aliens, pursuant to these latter regulations, must have prior permission of competent Chinese agencies for their entry, exit, transit, residence and travel in China. (Art. 2) viz. Ministry of Public Security and Foreign Affairs and agencies in China handling entry and exit of aliens. (Art. 25). Chinese diplomatic and consular missions abroad handle applications from aliens for entry, exits and travel in China (Art. 6), as authorized by Ministry of Foreign Affairs, as does China Travel Service in certain locations such as Hong Kong. Diplomatic, consular and other officials of foreign diplomatic and consular missions who apply for entry, transit or exit from China are processed by Ministry of Foreign Affairs or local bureaus of foreign affairs.

Visas are required by aliens to enter, exit and transit in China (Art. 6) except when they are covered by agreements between states for mutual exemption from visas. (Art. 6). Residence in China requires application and residence registration, normally with local public security, organs. (Art. 13). . . . .

General Ministry of Staff of Foreign Affairs and State Travel Bureau classify travel areas into four types: (a) 29 specified cities where aliens can travel without credentials, or any advance notice (Art. 3[1]); (b), areas opened to aliens or where aliens may travel with travel permits routinely granted (Art. 3[2]); (c) non-open areas where aliens may go with travel permits for investigation, scientific exchange, construction or other official business (Art. 3[3]); and (d) all areas except aforesaid three types of areas where aliens are not permitted travel until host organization obtains agreement of said province's autonomous region's government or great military region, then makes application to security unit for traveling permit.

Provisional Regulations for Handling of Long Term Representatives of Foreign Enterprises were promulgated on Oct. 30, 1980 by State Council. These representative offices must, pursuant to regulations (Art. 2), apply for long term status, obtain approval and be registered. Different organizations in China are afforded authority to approve these applications. Thus, Ministry of Foreign Trade would handle applications from foreign trading organizations, transportation companies, factories, etc. (Art. 4[1]), while insurance companies would apply to Bank of China. (Art. 4[2]). Within 30 days of approval of application foreign firm must register with Office of General Administration for Industry and Commerce (Art. 5), and thereafter employees of said enterprise must apply to local public security office for residence permits in China. (Art. 6). Hiring local personnel to assist in said office must proceed through appropriate Chinese government offices. (Art. 11).

Subsequent to promulgation of these regulations, various localities promulgated detailed procedures for implementing these rules. Thus, on May 11, 1981 Guangdong province published procedures for registration of foreign corporations on long term basis in Guangdong and on July 21, 1981 Bureau of Labor of Guangzhou City published procedures for hiring local personnel by said foreign entities. Shanghai is about to publish detailed procedures for registering foreign corporations on long term basis, at time of this writing, while Beijing's (Peking) rules have been in force for some time.

Consular Relations Agreement of Jan. 31, 1979 between China and US provides that US citizens having visas to China are insured consular access and protection. (Art. 3). Similarly, if American citizen is arrested in China, consular or embassy notification must be without delay. (Art. 5).

ARBITRATION AND AWARD

Arbitration, after conciliation, is favored Chinese means of resolving international commercial disputes. On May 6, 1954 then Government Administrative Council established Foreign Trade Arbitration Commission, now entitled Foreign Economic and Trade Arbitration Commission . . . . Commission, under aegis of China Council for the Promotion of International Trade, is authorized by decision of May 6, 1954 to settle disputes between foreign firms and Chinese firms (Art. 1), pursuant to terms of contracts between parties (Art. 2), as well as disputes arising from joint ventures and foreign commercial credit and loans (State Council's Notice, Feb. 26, 1980). In 1988, State Council changed name of this Commission to China International Economic and Trade Arbitration Commission and Rules of said Arbitration Commission were adopted on Sept. 12, 1988 at Fourth Session of China Council for Promotion of International Trade. According to these Rules, Arbitration Commission is to consist of one chairman, one vice-chairman and several members. (Art. 3). China Council for Promotion of International Trade initially selects group of Chinese and foreigner arbiters, based on their professional knowledge and practical experience in international economic trade, scientific technology and law; from this group, Arbitration Commission must make list of potential panelists. (Art. 4). Disputing parties may either select arbitration panel from Commission's list or authorize chairman of Arbitration Commission to appoint said panel from aforementioned list and name presiding arbiter. (Art. 14). If disputing parties prefer to have their case handled by single arbiter, then they may jointly select, or authorize chairman to appoint for them, individual from said list. (Art. 15).

One disputing party must submit written application to Arbitration Commission (Art. 2), along with initial fee (Art. 7), before arbitration may commence. Panel determines award by majority vote (Art. 33) which is final and not subject to appeal. (Art. 36). Chinese Courts are authorized to enforce said award (Art. 38) but, alternatively, one party may request enforcement by foreign court according to jurisdiction rights granted foreign courts at Convention on Recognition and Enforcement of Foreign Arbitral Awards or international treaties to which China is signatory. (Art. 38). Trade Agreement between US and China of July 7, 1979 permits arbitration by rules of U.N. Committee on International Trade or other international rules acceptable to parties. American Arbitration Association rules are sometimes acceptable to Chinese parties.

Regulations on Arbitration of Economic Contracts were promulgated by State Council on Aug. 22, 1983. These regulations, promulgated pursuant to Economic Contract Law, are designed to handle domestic disputes concerning economic contracts executed pursuant to said Law. (Art. 8).

Statute of limitations to commence arbitration proceeding under these regulations is within one year from time complainant knew or should have known of infringement of his rights. (Art. 6; cf. Foreign Economic Contract Law).

Arbitration organization where economic contracts were executed or where they are implemented have jurisdiction over these disputes, or if difficult to administer tribunal at respondent's residence may have jurisdiction. (Art. 9).

Construction contracts are under jurisdiction of arbitral organization where structure is located; disputes where contracts involving railway, highway and water freight transportation are under jurisdiction of arbitration organizations where transport administrative department responsible for handling disputes are located; air transport disputes are to be handled where contract was signed, or where goods were dispatched or their destination or scene of accident. (Art. 9).

Normally arbitration organizations in counties (cities) or municipal districts have jurisdiction over contract disputes, but if amount in controversy is between 500,000 to 5,000,000 yuan, or matter relatively significant, it is to be handled by panels in cities under provincial governments, or self-governing prefectures, or prefectures; if matter is of major significance or involves disputed sum of 5,000,000 to 10,000,000 yuan then arbitration panels in provinces, cities directly under central government or autonomous regions have jurisdiction. If matter is of national significance, or is between certain designated government entities or in value more than 10,000,000 yuan is in controversy then it is to be arbitrated by panel affiliated with State Administration for Commerce and Industry. (Art. 10). Lower level panels can request higher level panels to handle certain disputes. (Art. 11).

Economic contract arbitration committees are formed at various levels under administration for commerce and industry, which in turn appoints full time arbitrators to handle disputes. (Art. 14). Normally panels are composed of two arbitrators and referee, decisions are by majority and difficult cases can be submitted to arbitration committee for decision. (Art. 16). Parties can apply to have panel members recuse themselves and arbitration committee chairman or vice-chairman decide issue. (Art. 18).

Arbitration is commenced by petition (Art. 19) and if petition is in conformity with law then copy of petition should be sent to respondent within 15 days of receipt of copy of petition. (Art. 20). Panel is given authority to conduct thorough investigation from departments concerned, to collect evidence, and relevant departments should where necessary produce evidence required. (Art. 21). Panel can ask for guarantees from petitioners or respondents, can seal goods, distrain goods, sell goods difficult to maintain and keep proceeds, etc. (Art. 24).

After hearing and accord either party may within 15 days appeal to people's court if not satisfied with ruling. (Art. 33). State Administrator of Commerce and Industry sets standard arbitration fees for disputing parties. (Art. 36).

Aside from arbitration before Chinese Arbitration Commissions, numerous contracts with American and other foreign firms provide for arbitration outside of China according to foreign laws and procedures. For some time Stockholm, Sweden had been favored locus of arbitration in accordance with Swedish Arbitration Procedures and with reference to Swedish arbitration laws. Switzerland, and in past Holland, were also typical third nations chosen for locus of arbitration. Arbitration in respondent's country is another typical clause in Chinese contracts with foreigners. Chinese presently do not object to having arbitration in US pursuant to AAA. rules, on some sort of reciprocal basis, such as that specified above, viz. respondent's country. Contracts specifying arbitration in Hong Kong are becoming more common. China has acceded to United Nations Convention on the Recognition and Enforcement of Foreign Arbitral Awards, effective as of Apr. 22, 1987.

ASSIGNMENTS

See Civil Code.

Chinese law at present does not prohibit assignments of claims of creditor to another person, unless contrary to contractual provisions.

ASSOCIATIONS

Foreign Chambers of Commerce Several nations have established chambers of commerce in China. Provisional regulation concerning administration of foreign chambers of commerce were promulgated on Apr. 28, 1989. Foreign chambers of commerce refer to nonprofit making bodies established in China by foreign business organizations and individuals. Foreign chamber of commerce in China shall not engage in business. (Art. 2).

ATTACHMENT

See Civil Code.

Once civil proceedings are commenced party can make application to have its claim secured prior to issuance of judgment, and courts presently have authority to attach property to secure civil claim. (Code of Criminal Procedure, Art. 53).

Attachment can be commenced by application of one of parties prior to court adjudicating claim if there is reason to believe that it will be difficult or impossible to make execution after adjudication because of acts of one of parties or for some other reason. Normally, court would be concerned with sale, transfer or secreting of property in question. Under extraordinary circumstances court should provide written decision within 48 hours from party's application for preservation of certain property, and should commence immediate execution on said property. Application to preserve property in question, provides scope of relief that may be granted, unless it is property which is subject matter of litigation in which case said property determines scope of relief. If after application for relief, party is not satisfied with decision, application can be made for reconsideration, but during reconsideration original decision stands.

Court can use numerous means of preserving property including: Attaching or sealing property, distraining property or freezing asset (Code of Civil Procedure, Arts. 92-99). Latter form of freezing asset is normally applied to monies or property in bank, or cooperative trust, etc. Sealing involves placing notice of sealing where property is located or property can be moved to another location. If property is distrained, said property can be placed in other persons hands for safe keeping or if property is perishable it can be sold.

In addition court can request guarantee such as deposit of money in bank, bond, etc.

In disputes involving foreign property or foreign parties, courts have same authority to act on petition of party to preserve property. Provisional attachment is available where monetary claims or claims for property are made, or claims are made that can be converted into monetary claims.

Courts in which litigation is taking place, normally basic level courts, or economic trial courts of intermediate level courts, have jurisdiction to act on provisional attachments, etc. If property to be attached, distrained or sealed is not in court's jurisdiction, court where property is located, at behest of trial court, shall act to attach property pursuant to order of trial court.

ATTORNEYS AND COUNSELORS

See Civil Code.

Attorney's unit of employment is Legal Counsel Office which is under supervision and authority of national judicial administrative organizations. (Art. 13). These offices exist throughout China, although they are understaffed with competent legal personnel as result of lack of law school training in most locations during so-called Cultural Revolution (1966-1976). Cultural Revolution also saw termination of publication of most books and magazines dealing with Law, as well as de-emphasis upon legal procedures. Presently there are over 300 legal counsel offices in China, five political science and law institutes, 32 university law faculties and approximately 15,000 law students. There are several legal journals, legal newspapers and numerous law treatises and books being published. There is thus major effort to reestablish legal profession, and importance of law and attorneys is manifest in country's media.

Fees for attorneys may be established by Ministry of Justice, according to Provisional Regulations Concerning Attorneys (Art. 20) but State Council on July 20, 1956 promulgated Provisional Rules Concerning Attorneys' Fees which established principle that fees are to be directly related to quality and quantity of work involved. There are number of cases where counsel need not charge, such as when persons do not have means to pay fees, etc. Different fees are established for separate types of cases but presently legal offices do not all have uniform fee schedules. Foreign nationals, foreign enterprises and foreign organizations seeking counsel to represent them in litigation in China must employ attorney of People's Republic of China, or can entrust private persons to represent them.

Foreign attorneys recognized by Chinese arbitral law, etc. and in practice foreign firms have been permitted to utilize their counsel in China during business negotiations. American attorneys have offices in Beijing, Shanghai and Guangzhou, etc. Certain American law firms have agreements with local Chinese law firms, which are approved by Provincial Bureau of Justice, for cooperation in legal matters both in China and elsewhere. New draft regulations may permit foreign firms to operate to China to advise on foreign law on reciprocal basis.

BANKRUPTCY

See Civil Code; Joint Stock Companies.

Introduction With exception of certain local trial regulations, those of Shenyang being most prominent, China enacted no bankruptcy legislation until latter part of 1986. On Nov. 29, of that year Standing Committee of Guangdong Provincial Congress enacted bankruptcy regulations for companies with foreign participation in Shenzhen Special Economic Zone (hereinafter SEZ Bankruptcy Law) and on Dec. 2, 1986, Standing Committee of Sixth National People's Congress enacted, for trial implementation, Enterprise Bankruptcy Law of China, effective as of 1 Nov. 1988.

SEZ Bankruptcy Law only has effect in Shenzhen and is only applicable to corporations in Shenzhen having foreign equity participation (Art. 2), whereas Enterprise Bankruptcy Law is applicable only to state owned enterprises in all of China. (Art. 3). Nevertheless these are first serious statutes to deal with bankruptcy matters.

Definition Both regulations define bankruptcy as inability to repay debts as they fall due. (Art. 3 of both statutes).

Intermediate court in Shenzhen handles all bankruptcy matters and determines bankruptcy (Arts. 7, 3) as do state courts pursuant to Enterprise Bankruptcy Law. (Art. 5).

Petition for Bankruptcy In Shenzhen creditors of bankrupt and debtor itself may petition court, but debtor's petition requires resolution of its shareholders or board of directors. (Art. 8). In national legislation creditors may petition for bankruptcy (Arts. 3, 7) or debtor may petition after approval of senior department in charge of enterprise. (Art. 8).

Creditor's Meeting Enterprise Bankruptcy Law provides that creditors of bankrupt may hold meeting in which all unsecured creditors have right to vote and court has power to appoint chairman of creditors' committee. (Art. 13). Creditors' committee adopts resolutions by majority vote of those attending, so long as they represent more than half of unsecured debt. (Art. 15). If there is agreement between creditors and bankrupt this can be approved by court and bankruptcy proceedings suspended or terminated. (Art. 19).

In SEZ Bankruptcy Law, court can appoint liquidation committee, to be paid by debtor, which acts under court supervision and in turn convenes and presides over creditors' meetings. (Arts. 12, 13, 14). Creditors' committee itself elects representatives to work with liquidation committee and represent creditors. (Art. 16). Similarly decisions are made at creditors' committee by majority of members present at meeting who represent more than half of unsecured creditors. (Art. 18). Agreement between creditors and bankrupt can be approved by court. (Art. 18).

Bankruptcy Declaration SEZ Bankruptcy Law provides that upon adjudication of bankruptcy, court shall make public announcement specifying time limit for creditors to register their claim, providing date for first creditors' meeting, etc. (Art. 27). Enterprise Bankruptcy Law provides after declaration by court of bankruptcy (Arts. 23 and 3) court shall appoint liquidation committee (as in SEZ Bankruptcy Statutes), who shall appraise and allot assets of bankrupt. (Art. 24). Under Enterprise Bankruptcy Law, liquidation committee, which is responsible to court, is to be appointed from senior general agency in charge of bankrupt, Ministry of Finance and related departments. (Art. 21).

Bankrupt's Assets Assets of bankrupt are defined in both statutes. SEZ statute lists assets as all property belonging to bankrupt at time of bankruptcy declaration, other rights to property, rights to assets surrendered by bankrupt within 180 days

of declaration of bankruptcy that should not have been released (e.g., advance payments of certain debts, etc.). (Arts. 31, 11).

Enterprise Bankruptcy statute defines assets of bankrupt to include all assets of bankrupt at time of declaration of bankruptcy and those acquired prior to liquidation, as well as other rights and interests of bankrupt. (Art. 28). Statute also gives liquidation committee authority to determine whether or not to perform contracts of bankrupt not yet performed. (Art. 26). Enterprise statute also has provision for recalling assets wrongfully released within six months of bankruptcy. (Art. 25).

Non-Bankrupt Assets and Unacceptable Claims SEZ Bankruptcy Law provides that debts occurring after declaration of bankruptcy are not normally part of claims that can be made (Art. 34); Enterprise Bankruptcy Law has similar provision. (Art. 30). Both statutes deny creditors fees for participation in bankruptcy proceedings as claims against bankrupt estate. (Enterprise Law, Art. 30; SEZ Law Art. 34[2]).

Priorities SEZ statute provides that secured debts shall have prior claim up to amount of debt or if value of asset securing debt is less than claim than up to value of asset. (Art. 35). Enterprise Bankruptcy statute provides priority to secured assets (Art. 32) pursuant to similar terms.

Enterprise Bankruptcy Law provides that bankruptcy fees are to be first appropriated from bankrupt estate, then salaries of staff and workers, labor insurance fees, tax payments, and unsecured debts are to have priority in that order. If assets do not suffice to cover debts then they are to be paid off proportionately. (Art. 37).

Similarly SEZ regulations provide that bankruptcy fees including legal costs have certain priority; thereafter salaries, labor insurance, national taxes and unsecured debts, in that order, have priority.

Subsequent Legislation Statutes will have to be supplemented by detailed legislation and administrative rules. National legislation, affecting as it does only State owned enterprises, is naturally very carefully drawn so as not to appear too harsh or hasty. Thus there are provisions making this law only trial legislation, for short period, with steps for trial implementation to be separately stipulated. (Art. 43). Declaration of bankruptcy requires acquiescence of superior government agency in charge (Art. 3), state is to arrange jobs for employees thrown out of work as result of bankruptcy (Art. 4), government organizations are encouraged to subsidize state enterprises in financial difficulty having significant national importance (Art. 1) etc. Law has yet to be implemented.

SEZ Bankruptcy statute only applies to enterprises in Shenzhen partially or fully owned by non-Chinese interests, thus it is less tentative and immediately effective.

National legislation applicable to enterprises partly or wholly owned by foreign entities and enterprises other than state enterprises may be promulgated in future.

BILLS AND NOTES

See Corporations.

Chinese law does not at present time make clear provisions for promissory notes or bills of exchange. Nevertheless, checks are clearly recognized; generally on bank as drawee. Checks can be made to individuals, corporations, units or to cash. Checks on foreign currency accounts can only be paid to those in China who have rights to utilize foreign currency within China.

CIVIL CODE

General Rules of Civil Law ("Civil Law") were adopted by Sixth National People's Congress on Apr. 12, 1986, effective as of Jan. 1, 1987. Chinese law is held applicable to civil activities in China, as is Civil Law, which is applicable to foreigners, stateless persons and citizens unless otherwise specified. (Art. 5). Opinion of Supreme Court adopted on 26 Jan. 1988 provides details regarding Civil Law.

Civil Rights and Capacity of Natural Persons
Individual may register sole proprietorship for industrial or commercial business (Art. 26) and rural collectives engaged in sales of commodities may register rural contracting operations (Art. 27), but individuals are responsible for debts of said business. (Art. 29).

Partnership may be formed on basis of agreements for capital contribution, distribution of profits, termination, withdrawal, etc. (Art. 30); property accumulated by partnership is jointly owned (Art. 32); each partner is responsible for debts in accordance with partnership agreement, but joint and several liability exists. However, where one assumed greater share of debts than provided in partnership agreement they can look to other partners for contribution. (Art. 35).

Civil Rights and Capacities of Legal Persons Entity which has civil rights and capacities, enjoys those rights from time of establishment of said legal person (Art. 36); to be considered legal person entity must have its own name, structure, premises, property, be established according to law and able to independently undertake civil liability. (Art. 37). Legal representative of legal person is person designated by law or articles of association of said legal person to act on behalf of said legal person. (Art. 38). Legal person is considered resident of location of its major office. (Art. 39).

In order for enterprise to obtain status of legal person, if it is Chinese-foreign joint venture, cooperative venture, or wholly owned foreign entity, it needs government approval and registration with relevant division of General Administration of Commerce and Industry. (Art. 41).

As for state enterprises and collective enterprises, who meet capital requirements, have articles of association, premises, organizational structure, and ability to undertake civil liability, they will obtain status of legal person upon approval of organization in charge and registration. (Art. 41).

Scope of business operations of enterprise is operational limits approved for its registration (Art. 42), and it shall operate through its legal representative or other personnel. (Art. 43). If enterprise merges, or branches split off, separate registration is required (Art. 44), and if it terminates operation it must go through termination procedures to revoke its registration. (Art. 46). In cases of dissolution, bankruptcy, and like, enterprise shall establish organized group to liquidate all accounts under jurisdiction of relevant department of court or organization in charge of enterprise. (Art. 47).

Social organizations, groups and governmental organizations having their own independent funds have status of legal persons from time of their establishment, except for those social organizations and groups required to register, whose status as legal person shall only commence after approved registration. (Art. 50).

Principal and Agent Agent may within scope of its authority undertake legal act in name of its principal. (Art. 63). Agents include those entrusted with certain acts, statutory agents and designated agents. Designated agents are those designated either by courts or designating unit. (Art. 63). Where agent is entrusted with specific acts, document shall specify agent's name, items upon which he will act, limits of his authority and time period within which document has effect. (Art. 65).

If document authorizing agency of entrustment is unclear then principal and agent shall have joint liability to third parties (Art. 65); principal is only responsible for acts exceeding document granting agency if he retroactively ratified or acknowledges said acts, or, if principal knows another is acting in his name, and does not renounce said act such scheme shall be deemed to be consented to. (Art. 66). Agent is liable for acts he is entrusted with if he knows said acts are in violation of law. (Art. 67). Where agent entrusted with task must in turn entrust another person, he must obtain consent of his principal (Art. 68), else, save in emergency, agent shall be liable for acts of subsequent agent. (Art. 68).

Termination of agency of entrustment occurs where either principal or agent dies, or either principal or agent terminate agency, or agent loses his capacity to act civilly or period of agency expires or acts to be performed by agent are completed. (Art. 69).

Relation of statutory or designated agents with their principal terminates if either dies, agent loses its capacity to act civilly, principal on whose behalf agent acts loses its capacity to act civilly or court or organization designating agent cancels appointment. (Art. 70).

Creditor's Rights Debt is specific relationship of rights and obligations created between parties pursuant to contract or by law. (Art. 84). Person enjoying such rights is creditor, person having obligation is debtor, and creditor has right to demand debtor's performance pursuant to contract or provisions of law. (Art. 84).

Contract is agreement where parties establish, alter or terminate civil relationships (Art. 85); parties to contract should fully perform their obligations in accordance with contractual terms (Art. 88); where terms of contract are not clear and parties cannot reach agreement through negotiations regarding quality, time limits, location or cost then as to: (1) Quality, contract will be performed in accordance with national quality standards, but if there are none then pursuant to usual standards; and (2) time limit, debtor can perform at any time and creditor can demand performance at any time, giving debtor necessary time to prepare performance; and (3) location of performance, unless otherwise indicated, party making payment shall make it in location where party receiving payment is located; and (4) cost, if not clearly specified, payment shall be made pursuant to state specified prices, or if there are none then with reference to market prices or standard prices for similar type goods or remuneration for similar work. (Art. 88).

Where contract contains no arrangement as to right of application for patent, party making invention or creation enjoys that right. (Art. 88).

Debts may be guaranteed in following manner: (1) Guarantor may give creditor assurance that debtor will fulfill debt obligation, and where debtor fails to do so, pay said debts and thereafter look to creditor for reimbursement, or (2) debtor or third person may provide certain property as pledge, and pursuant to law creditor shall have right to value of pledge or money from sale of pledge, or (3) party may pay deposit to another party and if one paying deposit does not fulfill its debts, then it may not ask for return of deposit, or if party receiving deposit does not fulfill its obligation then it must return twice value of deposit; or (4) where party pursuant to contract occupies property of other party, and latter party does not make timely payment of its obligations, person in control of property has lien on said property which it can levy upon. (Art. 89).

Transfer of portion of or all of rights and obligations under contract to third party, except where contract or law otherwise provides, requires consent of other party and approval of state organization that approved initial contract. (Art. 91).

If person is unjustly enriched without lawful basis and causes losses to others, he shall return said unjust enrichment to person suffering said loss. (Art. 92). Where person undertakes services or management without legal obligation to do so, to prevent loss to others, he shall be entitled to obtain repayment from beneficiary for necessary expenditures. (Art. 93).

Civil Liability—General Persons who breach contracts and those who trespass on other's property are civilly liable (Art. 106), except if due to force majeure. (Art. 107). Debts shall be repaid in full, and only with consent of creditor or by court ruling can debt be repaid in late installments. (Art. 108).

Civil Liability—Breach of Contract Where party fails to perform or its performance does not conform to contractual terms, other party has right to demand performance or to take remedial measures and demand compensation for any losses. (Art. 111). Compensation for breach of contract should make injured party whole (Art. 112), though parties may have liquidated damages clause in contract or may specify means of computing loss for breach. (Art. 112). Where there is breach of contract by both parties they should separately undertake civil liability for their own breach. (Art. 113). Party must promptly attempt to mitigate its damages if other party breaches contract. (Art. 114). Where losses are caused by one party breaching because of acts of higher level organization, contracting party is liable under contract for its breach but it may claim compensation from higher level organization. (Art. 116).

Tortious Conduct If plagiarism, infringement, and like occur with regard to copyright, patents, trademark or discoveries then injured party may demand cessation of such tortious conduct and compensation for loss. (Art. 118).

Where there has been infringement of use of person's name, image, or defamation, then person has right to stop such tortious conduct, eliminate its effect, obtain apology and demand compensation for loss. (Art. 120).

Where persons or property have been damaged by product's quality not meeting standards, manufacturer and distributor of product are both liable for damages. Where storage or transportation groups are responsible for damage product manufacturer and distributor have right to demand compensation from these parties. (Art. 122).

Those who violate environmental protection regulations shall have civil liability pursuant to law. (Art. 124).

If two or more parties commit tort they have joint

liability (Art. 130) and if injured party contributed to damage then defendant's liability will be proportionately reduced. (Art. 131).

Statute of Limitations Civil case to enforce civil rights must be brought within two years unless otherwise specified in law. (Art. 135). Following cases have one year statute of limitations: (1) Where there is demand for compensation for bodily injury; and (2) where commodities, not up to standard are sold without notice of said fact; and (3) where there is delay or refusal to pay rents; and (4) where property in storage has been lost or damaged.

Calculation of commencement of (Art. 136) running of statute of limitations commences from time infringement of rights was or should have been known. (Art. 137). Where there is agreement to perform obligations which are subject of suit, period of limitations shall be suspended and only commence again if there is failure to perform. (Art. 140).

Civil Relations Involving Foreign Parties Where there are conflicts between treaties to which China is participant and civil law, unless reservations to said treaty have been made, provisions of treaty prevail. (Art. 142). If there are no provisions in either domestic Chinese law or in treaties to which Chinese are parties then customary international practice shall prevail. (Art. 142).

Law of country wherein real estate is located shall be applicable to issues relevant to ownership of real estate. (Art. 144). Unless law otherwise provides, parties may choose law applicable to contract disputes, involving foreign party, or if they do not so choose, national law having closest link to contract shall apply. (Art. 145).

Where application for damages for tortious conduct is made, law of country where such acts occur shall apply (Art. 146), but if both parties reside in same country or have same nationality, national laws or laws of country of residence shall also be applicable. (Art. 146). Where Chinese law does not deem act occurring outside its territory as tortious act, it shall not be determined as tort. (Art. 146).

Where foreign or international law is applicable pursuant to this chapter it shall not violate social or public interest of People's Republic of China. (Art. 150).

Supplementary Principles and Definitions Force majeure referred to herein refers to objective circumstances which are unforseeable, irrevocable, and insurmountable. (Art. 153).

For enterprise existing prior to this law coming into force, of state organization, approved by department in charge above level of province, autonomous region or city directly under control of central government, already registered with General Department of Commerce and Industry, no additional registration is necessary to be classified legal person. (Art. 152).

COMMERCIAL CODE

No actual commercial code exists but commercial transactions are widespread. Some commercial transactions will be covered by Civil Code now in draft form, some are governed by private international law and custom (*See* Actions), some by specifics of approved contracts and Economic Contracts Law (*See* Contracts; Joint Stock Companies) and some by specific legislation such as Joint Venture Law. *See* Joint Stock Companies.

COMMERCIAL REGISTER

See Corporations; Joint Stock Companies.

CONFLICTS OF LAW

See Contracts; Joint Stock Companies; Civil Code.

International contracts can and do specify which law is to govern particular transaction, and where they fail to so specify, then unless otherwise provided in Chinese law, e.g., contracts pursuant to Joint Venture Law are by statute governed by Chinese law, then law of country most closely related to contract will apply. (Foreign Economic Contracts Law, Art. 5). Inheritance of property within China is governed by Chinese law; however, wills may be governed by law of decedent's domicile. Some of these conflicts questions have yet to be resolved in statutory law or by judicial fiat, but contracts themselves can specify governing law except when in conflict with Chinese laws or regulations.

CONSUMER PROTECTION

Goods sold by state organizations, as well as those imported, are subject to inspection by Import and Export Commodity Inspection Bureau. There are 29 bureaus in all provinces except Taiwan, municipalities directly under central government (Beijing, Shanghai, Tienjin) and autonomous regions. Role of Bureau is to undertake inspection of goods being exported and imported to ensure quality control, so that goods meet national standards and conform to contractual specifications. There is Bureau of Weights and Measures that inspects imported weighing and measuring apparatus. In addition, there is Animal and Plant Quarantine Center for quarantine of imported plants and animals. Ministry of Health is responsible for inspecting imported foodstuffs and drugs and Ship Inspection Bureau is responsible for inspecting ships, etc. Import and Export Commodity Bureau has right to inspect certain commodities specified in "List of Commodities Subject to Inspection," 196 in number, as well as right to inspect animal products and foodstuffs subject to inspection. If contracts require certificate of inspection from

Bureau, it obviously has right to inspect said products. Inspection of other foodstuffs and drugs involves quality, specifications and packing conditions, and where satisfied, certificate is issued releasing goods from Customs. Provisional Regulations Governing Inspection and Testing of Import and Export Commodities were promulgated as of Jan. 3, 1954. State Council replaced said Regulations on Jan. 28, 1984 with Regulations on Inspection of Import and Export Commodities. These latter regulations were also later replaced by Laws on Inspection of Import and Export Commodities, adopted on Feb. 21, 1989, effective Aug. 1, 1989.

According to latest Regulations, State Council will establish Inspection of Import and Export Commodities Department. (Art. 2). Violators of regulations will be fined by Commodity Inspection Organization; in cases resulting in serious loss, responsible party will be penalized according to Art. 187 of Criminal Code. (Art. 26). In addition to this Bureau there is National Bureau of Standards whose work is being expanded to include development of standards at each level of production pursuant to Regulations Governing Standardization promulgated by State Council on July 31, 1979.

Foreign inspection institutes which invest in Chinese territory to set up import/export commodity inspection organizations must obtain approval by China National Commodity Inspection Bureau. Without such approval, relevant economic and trade departments and other organizations will not handle examination procedures. Administrative department of industry and commerce will not handle registration for organizations of Import/Export Commodity Inspection without getting such approval.

CONTRACTS

See Joint Stock Companies; Trade Zones; Civil Code; Sales.

Traditional Chinese law, as reflected by law and practice of last imperial dynasty, Ching (1644-1911), permitted extensive scope for freedom of contract. Ching code itself was addressed in only small part to civil law matters, and civil contracts were buttressed by customary law and practice.

In international trade, contracts and tribute dominated commercial practice. Transactions in People's Republic of China, particularly in international field, have until recently been relatively unfettered by domestic regulations and thus contracts determined not only normal rights and obligations of parties, but also provided for things such as patent protection, etc. Contracts thus at times established law to govern particular transaction.

Chinese publicists have for some time recognized importance of contracts. Chinese authors have rec-

ognized that in order to have binding contract there must be mutuality of interest, and recognize that legal consequences of contract are those parties intend. Chinese authors of legal texts have recognized that parties to contract have equal status, and those who breach contracts will be liable for damages flowing therefrom. Chinese recognize need for offer, and acceptance within terms of said offer, in order for there to be standard contract. Chinese legal experts hold that contracts must be based on free intention of parties and yet state that contracts should be fair and reasonable. If portion of contract is unreasonable it may be deemed void. Under Joint Venture Law contracts must be reviewed by certain Chinese government agencies and most complicated international agreements made at local level must be approved by provincial authorities which to some extent examine said contracts for reasonableness.

Chinese authorities have recognized sales contract as being bilateral contract, consensual in nature, and being non-gratuitous.

Chinese international contracts normally contain force majeure provision. Chinese international contracts are frequently denominated in hard currencies. Contracts are often in English or Chinese and English, although not infrequently executed only in Chinese language.

Joint Venture Law, Environmental Protection Law, Trademark Law, Patent Law, tax laws and other recent legislation limit ability of parties in international transactions to freely contract.

China has promulgated legislation directly concerned with contract law e.g., Government Administrative Council on Sept. 27, 1950 promulgated Provisional Rules for Contracts by Organizations, National Enterprises and Cooperative Societies. It provided for type of arrangements in which contracts were necessary, including sale and purchase of goods, loans, rental agreements, joint ventures, etc. Rules also provided for responsibility of guarantors of contracts; thus, e.g.,, if contract for bank loan is involved, there must be guarantor, in principle goods themselves acted as guarantors, but if there were no such goods lending unit, superior organization or principal organization was to guarantee loan. When signing contract there should be person, normally in superior organ, who undertakes to review contractual terms. Contract must be executed by legal entity, since individual cannot undertake to execute or guarantee contract if organization he represents refuses to execute contract.

Once contract is executed both sides must undertake to carry out their duties pursuant to its terms, and if for some reason one side or other cannot conform to its terms, any changes must be made with consent of other side to have legal effect. If one side is damaged by failure of other side to perform its terms, then they must be compensated by other side for damage; guarantor also has such obligation. If contracts are between domestic entities in China, administrative units can be utilized to compel performance of contractual terms and if that is ineffective, then one can bring judicial proceedings before court.

On Nov. 10, 1963 State Council promulgated Rules Regarding Strictly Implementing Economic Contracts which concerned strict adherence to said contractual terms, including time of delivery, quantity and quality of goods, time of payment, etc. Those failing to adhere to said contracts would have economic responsibility for losses of other side.

In 1963 National Economic Committee promulgated Provisional Regulations Regarding Basic Provisions of Contracts for Purchase of Industrial and Mining Products. These regulations also call for strict performance of contracts. They provide that contracts should include specific technological standards for products and packing which is subject matter of contract, viz., name, specification, measurements, amount, packing standard, weight, shipping instructions, time of delivery, price calculations and economic responsibility. Latter is in nature of penalty clause to ensure performance.

Various governmental commercial agencies in China also promulgated their own regulations to ensure performance of contracts and meeting of national plans. E.g., Ministry of Textile Industry on Oct. 17, 1953; and on Apr. 11, 1955 Ministry of Heavy Industry, promulgated regulations regarding contracts. Primary intent of these provisions was to ensure meeting of goals embodied in national plan. These contracts call for inclusion of provisions making reference to national plan, employees, wages, incentives, etc.

National Economic Contracts Law Fourth Session of Fifth National People's Congress, on Dec. 13, 1981, effective July 1, 1982 (Art. 57), adopted Law of Economic Contracts. Art. 55 of said statute provides that regulations governing international trade contracts will, based on principles of this statute and international practice, be separately promulgated. Statute provides some guide to present practice of contract law, although is primarily designed to regulate contracts between state enterprises, as well as contracts between private individuals and legal entities in China. Joint venture or other commercial entity having foreign participation, incorporated in China, will be bound by relevant provisions of this law. Statute defines economic contract as agreement between persons specifying their rights and obligations under agreement in order to achieve specific economic goal. (Art 2). Purchase and sales agreements, construction contracts, transportation contracts, processing contracts, supply of utilities such as electricity, warehouse storage agreements, rental agreements, loans, insurance, scientific and techni-

cal cooperation agreements, etc. are all subsumed under term economic contracts . (Art. 8).

Formation In general, said contracts should be in written form (Art. 3), formulated in accordance with laws of nation and requirements of national policy and plans. (Art. 4). Contracts drawn according to law are legally binding and cannot be unilaterally terminated or breached. (Art. 6). Contracts are to be formulated according to free intentions of parties. (Art. 5). Contracts are deemed invalid and without binding force from their inception if executed under coercion or fraud, or if they violate law, national policy or national plans, or if executed by agent in excess of his authority, or if they violate national or public interests. (Art. 7). Valid, severable provisions of contract do not necessarily fall if parts of contract invalid. Courts and units administering contracts have authority to determine invalidity of contract. (Art. 7).

Contract should be executed only after parties have agreed on major provisions of contract (Art. 9), which should include following: Subject matter of contract, quantity end quality, prices or commissions, time, place and form of performance, responsibilities on breach, etc. and such other provisions as parties deem important. (Art. 12). Specific provisions for different types of contracts are provided in statute, e.g., product packaging and quality must meet state standards (Art. 17[2]); construction contracts require substantial detail; including specifics as to time to provide design data, time for construction, times to commence and complete intermediate work projects, and quality of work provisions (Art. 18); leases should explicate size, use, period of lease and rental price of property concerned, stipulate times for payment of rent and include stipulations as to maintenance responsibilities and responsibilities in case of breach. (Art. 18).

Breach On breach of contract where deposit was involved, breaching party has no right to return of deposit if it does not fulfill its obligations under contract. However, if receiver breaches contract, he must return twice sum of deposit. (Art. 14). If one party breaches contract and if losses exceed any penalty provisions, breaching party must pay consequential damages (Art. 35) within ten days after determination of quantum of breach. (Art. 37). If contract deemed invalid, property should be returned and party at fault should compensate other party for any losses that occurred. If both parties at fault, each must bear its (aliquot) responsibility for its corresponding breach. (Arts. 16, 32). If major accidents or serious losses occur as result of wrongdoing, or illicit contracts entered into, criminal responsibility may result. (Arts. 32, 53).

Cancellation/Alteration Contracts may be altered or canceled when agreed by mutual consultation, through written novation (Arts. 27[1], 28), as result of force majeure (Art. 27[4]) apparently including closing of enterprise or plant, or cessation of production. (Art. 27[3]). Breaches of specific types of contracts at times require payment of penalties, as well as consequential damages, e.g., breach of buy and sell agreement when buyer cancels order. (Art. 38[2][a]).

Dispute Settlement If disputes cannot be settled by consultation, any of parties may request government, or organization in charge of managing contract, to apply for mediation or arbitration within one year of discovering breach, or may directly commence litigation. (Art. 48). In cases of arbitration, parties may appeal decision of arbitrator to court within 15 days after judgment. (Art. 49).

Shenzhen SEZ Foreign Economic Contract Regulations On Feb. 7, 1984 Guangdong government promulgated Shenzhen SEZ Regulations Concerning Foreign Economic Contracts, which had been approved by Standing Committee of People's Congress of Guangdong Province on Jan. 11, 1984.

Scope of these contractual regulations encompasses: (1) Agreements between Chinese enterprises or other organizations in SEZ and foreign enterprises, economic organizations or individuals, entered into in order to develop economic and technical cooperation in SEZ, that have agreements under Chinese law establishing relationships of mutual rights and obligations; and (2) between following entities which execute agreements to be undertaken in SEZ: foreign and Chinese-foreign joint venture or joint agreement enterprises registered and doing business in SEZ; SEZ enterprises and foreign enterprises or other economic organizations or individuals; and SEZ enterprises and Chinese enterprises or other economic organizations established in SEZ. (Art. 2).

Approvals Required These contracts must have approval of SEZ government or its authorized representative (Art. 5), and applications for approval to be determined within three months of submission. (Art. 5). Those contracts in violation of Chinese law, or doing damage to Chinese sovereignty or social public interests, or employing fraud or coercion are null and void ab initio; however, if portion of confirmed contract which does not influence efficacy of remainder is null and void, rest of contract still has effect. (Art. 5).

Elements of Contract Contracts must be in written form, clearly specify parties' rights and obligations and be signed by parties or their authorized agents. Cables, letters, or telexes sufficient to provide written form of contract if both parties agree not to execute formal contract. (Art. 7).

Authority to Contract and Guarantee Parties executing contract should present following documents to each other for examination: (1) Copies or photocopies of documents of registration with local

or other governmental agency; (2) evidence of financial status re responsibility; (3) notarized documents of guarantee; and (4) documents evidencing authority of agents. (Art. 9).

Parties to contract should provide guarantees, which can take following form: (1) Deposit of cash; or (2) pledge of property; or (3) bank guarantee; or (4) corporate or enterprise guarantee; or (5) other guarantee. (Art. 12).

Provisions of Different Forms of Contracts

Joint venture is contract or written agreement whereby both parties invest, and divide profit or losses in proportion to said investment, in limited liability entity. Such contracts should contain following elements: (1) Names of parties, registered address, legal address and name of legal representative, nationality; (2) name of joint venture enterprise, address, scope of its activities and size, amount of land to be used; (3) total amount of investment, registered capital, each party's contribution to capital, form of contribution to capital, and provisions for time period to pay in said capital; (4) important equipment and technology to be used for production, and its origins; (5) means of purchase of raw materials and sales of products; (6) each party's responsibility for preparatory work, construction, production, operations, etc.; (7) time limit of joint venture, procedures for computation and windup, division of capital on termination of venture; (8) principles of accounting, auditing and finance; (9) provisions of labor management, salaries, social benefits, labor protection and insurance, etc.; (10) organization, duration of office and of responsibilities of board of directors; (11) means of selecting general and assistant general manager, personnel organization, and their responsibilities and authority; (12) limitations of liability and division of profits and losses; (13) guarantees and responsibility for breach of contract; (14) arbitration agreement or other means of resolving disputes; (15) time and place of execution of contract; and (16) other provisions parties deem necessary. (Art. 15).

Cooperative venture is written contract for venture in which SEZ party provides use of land, buildings, labor, labor services, authority to exploit resources, and foreign party provides capital, equipment, materials, technology, etc. Contract also provides for cooperation in production or operations, etc., and specifies each party's share of profits or products, and each party's assumption of risk, etc. Essential contents of this type of contract similar to joint venture. (Art. 16).

Compensation Trade (Art. 17) *and Assembly and Work-Added Contracts* (Art. 18) also outlined by statute. Contracts for wholly-owned foreign entities (Art. 19), and contracts for land use, labor, importation of technology, leasehold pledges or mortgages, etc. are not outlined by this statute, but reference made to other unspecified regulations of SEZ. Contracts for sales of goods, utilities products, insurance, construction, and transportation are not outlined by statute, but reference made to unspecified Chinese national statutes. (Art. 19).

Breach of Contract and Dispute Resolution Shenzhen City Bureau of Industry and Commerce designated as supervisory agency for contracts, and after approval of said contracts, copy should be sent by parties to this agency for registration, as well as to tax bureau. (Art. 31). This agency can supervise contracting parties, conciliate disputes, restrain parties from unlawful acts, and can fine parties for serious violations. (Art. 32). When entering into joint ventures, cooperative ventures, cooperative ventures to exploit natural resources, and contracts closely connected with matters of Chinese sovereignty, parties must apply Chinese law in resolution of disputes through arbitration. (Art. 35). Arbitration of these contracts should take place in China, but need not utilize arbitral organization in SEZ if parties agree to another arbitral body. (Art. 36). If contract has no arbitral provision, parties can bring suit in Chinese courts having jurisdiction over said disputes. (Art. 36). There are also various specific penalty provisions for breach of certain contracts; thus, where there is failure to ship goods on time, in addition to breaching party's responsibility to compensate plaintiff for its losses, statute requires breaching party to pay for each day's delay one-thousandth of value of goods that were to be shipped on said day. (Art. 21). Statute also contains force majeure provision (Art. 24) permitting avoidance of liability if breach caused by war, serious natural disaster, or other force majeure specified in contract, etc.

Technology Transfer, etc. Contracts Shenzhen SEZ also has Temporary Regulations for the Importation of Technology, promulgated by Standing Committee of People's Congress of Guangdong on Feb. 8, 1984, covering all importation of technology from abroad by enterprises, etc. in SEZ. (Art. 2). These contracts for technology transfer must be in writing (Art. 4), and said technology must be modern, all clearly economically effective. Scope of technology covered includes patented technology, patent-pending technology and trade secrets. (Art. 5). Shenzhen City Scientific Technology Development Center, or other Chinese national scientific research organization, can verify level of modernity or important economic effectiveness of technology; thereafter, tax bureau, land bureau, etc. must approve in order to obtain special advantageous provisions for importation of such technology. (Art. 6). If technology has already been patented or is pending patent approval, evidence of such approval must be proffered. (Arts. 7, 8). Those involved in technology transfer of trade secrets must

proffer evidence, including designs, forms, samples, models, etc. (Art. 9). Party applying for technology transfer should: (1) Provide Shenzhen city government with application, letter of intent, and feasibility study report; (2) after approval of project application, application for technology transfer should be obtained, contract signed, and application for approval of contract made to Shenzhen City government. (Art. 15). Said contract in triplicate, together with application for technology transfer in triplicate, evidence of lawful status of parties (each in triplicate), and purchaser's operations license in triplicate should all be submitted to Shenzhen City government for approval. (Art. 15). Decision on approval should be made within three months of application and once said contract is approved, it is effective as of date of approval. (Art. 16). Thereafter, said contract must be submitted to Shenzhen Bureau of Commerce and Industry and to tax bureau for registration. (Art. 16). Contract should include following important provisions: (1) Name of project, parties, and their addresses; (2) definition of key terms; (3) scope and contents of technology; (4) trademark used; (5) technological training and technological service to be undertaken; (6) operational plans; (7) guarantees of technology; (8) secrecy agreement; (9) provisions for rights and duties of the parties; (10) means of calculating value of technology; (11) breach provisions; (12) force majeure clause; (13) arbitration or dispute settlement clause; (14) time period of contract; (15) location of execution of contract; (16) means of calculating royalty and payment rights and duties of parties, and other provisions parties deem necessary. (Art. 17). Statute further provides that other than for investment purposes, these contracts normally do not exceed five years, but they can be extended with approval of Shenzhen City government, provided application made within six months of expiry of contract, and decision made within one month of submission. (Art. 19). Transfer of patented, technology must not exceed period of validity of patent, unless contributed as investment. (Art. 19). If technology invested in joint venture, its value should not exceed 20% of registered capital of joint venture. (Art. 23).

Regulations on technical imports to Xiamen S.E.Z. promulgated Feb. 24, 1985. These regulations are applicable to imports of technology from abroad or from Hong Kong, Macao or Taiwan where payment is made to foreign entity concerned. (Art. 2). Technology must be practical, advanced, have clear economic benefit and includes technology: (1) With valid patent rights; (2) with patent pending; and (3) proprietary technology. (Art. 3).

Forms of contracting include licensing, consultancy or service contracts, investment of proprietary technology, coproduction, compensation trade, turnkey projects, and other forms. (Art. 5).

Domestic organization acquiring technology will enjoy benefits provided by SEZ including possibility of receiving low interest loan or other financial assistance from domestic bank in SEZ if: It is of world advanced level as certified by state scientific organizations; it can markedly improve competitiveness of products in international market; it will markedly improve economic results of existing local enterprise, or SEZ City government recognizes its special need for technology. (Art. 6).

Procedures to go to contract involve submitting letter of intent and feasibility study to SEZ City government; once approved parties may go to contract. Approval of contract should be within 44 days of submission. (Art. 7).

Contracts are to include: Definition of terms, subject and scope of technology, list of technical information, date of delivery, implementation plan, technical service and training provisions, use of trademark, warranty and acceptance of technology procedures, rights and obligations of parties to improve technology, secrecy clause, means and amount of payment, responsibility for breach of contract. (Art. 8).

Provisions of Contracts for Purchase and Sale of Industrial and Mineral Products were promulgated by State Council pursuant to Economic Contract Law on Jan. 23, 1984, effective as of promulgation. These Provisions cover both industrial and mineral products used in production and for human consumption. (Art. 1). These Provisions cover contracts for sale of industrial and mineral products between all enterprises having status of legal persons, rural communes and brigades, national organizations, commercial and noncommercial units, and social organizations, etc. (Art. 2). Individual households and rural commune members, specialist households and important households must, when signing contracts with legal persons for purchase or sale of mineral products do so with reference to these regulations. (Art. 2). Principles of contracting require parties contracting for essential supplies to emphasize Economic Plan first and free market as supplementary. (Art. 3). Except where urgent necessity to wind up activities of one party, contracts must be in writing and signed or sealed by person with legal authority to represent party, and sealed with official seal, or seal used for contracts by parties. (Art. 4).

Essential elements of said contracts include: Name, type, specifications, article numbers, technical standards and specifications, quantities, packaging, shipping specifications, date of shipment, inspection methods, price, bank, responsibility for breach and other agreed-upon matters. (Art. 6). Each of these items spelled out in some detail in statute.

Regulations of property insurance contracts promulgated on Sept. 1, 1983 pursuant to Economic Contracts Law. This statute is particularly relevant to various types of insurance concerning property and other interests. Liability of insurance company is for actual loss at time of occurrence as limited by coverage of policy. (Art. 16). Property insurance contracts involving foreign parties are to apply these regulations by reference.

Regulations of construction, installation engineering contracts promulgated Aug. 5, 1983 by State Council pursuant to Economic Contract Law. These contracts which must be in writing (Art. 3), are to include documents for design and agreed design alteration, data, charts, negotiating records all of which are components of this contract. (Art. 3). Said contracts shall include limits of contents of project, commencement and termination dates, quality guarantees, costs, terms of payment, methods of inspection and approval, dates for providing design, budget and technical data, provision for material and equipment, delivery schedule, and responsibilities for breach. (Art. 6).

Regulations of survey and design engineering building contracts promulgated by State Council Aug. 5, 1983 pursuant to Economic Contract Law require affixing of seals of parties to be valid. (Art. 6). Deposit is required, either 30% of survey fee or 20% of design fee. (Art. 7).

Foreign Economic Contract Law promulgated by Standing Committee of People's Congress on Mar. 21, 1985 effective as of July 1, 1985 is now paramount piece of legislation regarding foreign contracts. This statute is applicable to economic contracts between Chinese enterprises or other economic organizations and foreign enterprises, institutions, or individuals. (Art. 2).

Law permits parties choice of law in dispute settlement (Art. 5) or if they make no choice law of country most closely related to contract shall apply (Art. 5), except for those joint, cooperative or prospecting contracts operating within boundaries of China to which Chinese law is applicable. (Art. 5). International customary rules may be applied where Chinese law lacks provisions.

Compensation for breach of contract should be actual compensation foreseeable at time contract was made (Art. 19), though parties can limit their liability for breach. (Art. 20). One must mitigate damages (Art. 22), when confronted with breach of contract.

Dispute settlement by arbitral tribunal agreed to by parties, is acceptable. (Art. 38). Statute of limitations for commencing action is four years from knowledge of or when one should know of breach of contract for contracts concerning purchase and sale of commodities. (Art. 38). Other limitations for bringing action to be provided in separate legislation.

Joint venture, cooperative venture, joint exploration contracts undertaken within China with approval of relevant Chinese government authorities can be governed by provisions of approved contract even if there is subsequent intervening legislation. (Art. 40).

On 19 Oct., 1987 Supreme Court issued Notice Regarding Answers to Several Problems in Application of Foreign Economic Contract Law.

Notice pointed to broad scope of use of Foreign Economic Contract Law (Art. 1[a], [b]), but stated that in China, for contracts between Chinese entities and joint ventures, applicable statute is Economic Contract Law (Art. 1[c]). Joint ventures, cooperative ventures, joint exploration agreements in China, must apply Chinese law and their domestic contracts cannot select foreign law for dispute settlement. (Art. 2[c]). See further Art. (2)(f)(i)ff for various conflicts of laws application.

Regulations on Administration of Contract for Acquisition of Technology, promulgated by State Council May 24, 1985. These regulations apply to acquisition of technology from abroad (Art. 2), including contracts for licensing of or transfer of patents or other industrial property rights (Art. 2[1]); supply of technical know-how in form of management, quality control, or through supply of drawings, technical materials, technical specifications, etc. as to provide product design, formulae or process specifications (Art. 2[2]) or supply of technical services (Art. 2[3]).

Acquired technology must be advanced, applicable (Art. 3) and should conform to at least one of following: (1) Development and production of new products; (2) improve quality and performance of products, reduce cost and consumption of energy or materials; (3) maximize use of Chinese resources; (4) increase exports of product and foreign currency earnings; (5) benefit environmental protection; (6) improve production safety; (7) improve management operations; or (8) assist in raising scientific technology standards. (Art. 3).

These contracts must be approved by Ministry of Foreign Economic Relations and Trade or its designated agency, which contracts must be acted on by said agencies in 60 days or they shall be regarded as approved. (Art. 4).

These contracts must specify content, scope and description of technology and list of patents and trademarks, technical goals to be reached within specified time period and means of achieving said goals, and means of payment. (Art. 5).

Supplier should guarantee that it owns technology, that it is complete, without faults, effective and able to meet objective specified in contract. (Art. 6). Purchaser shall within scope and time period agreed to by parties maintain secrecy of confidential portion of technology. (Art. 7).

These contracts shall not be longer than ten years without special approval of approving authority. (Art. 8). In addition, following restrictions require special permission of approving recipient: Restrictions on freedom of choice to purchase raw material, intermediate products or equipment from different sources; restrictions on purchaser developing or improving technology; restrictions on requisition of similar or competing technology; nonreciprocal exchange of improvements of technology; restrictions on volume, variety or sales price of products produced; unreasonable restrictions on sales channels or export markets; restrictions on use of technology after expiration of contract or requiring recipient to take or pay for patents that will not be used or have expired. (Art. 9).

Thus China has promulgated several sets of regulations concerning contracts, and Chinese legal experts have written about contracts. Many of these regulations emphasize domestic contracts although they embrace concepts applicable to private international agreements. Trade Agreement of July 7, 1979 between China and US calls for commercial transactions to be concluded on basis of customary international trade practice and commercial considerations. Contracts approved by proper legal authorities at times contain provisions contrary to statutes. For example, tax relief may be granted by contract despite statutory provisions, for standards of payment. *See* Joint Stock Companies.

COPYRIGHT

See Civil Code.

Chinese copyright law was enacted in Sept., 1990 effective as of 1 June, 1991.

Irrespective of whether their works are published or not, Chinese citizens, legal persons, units with legal personality have copyright protection pursuant to this law. (Art. 2).

Foreigners have copyright protection according to this law if their works were published in China first. (Art. 2). Foreigner's books that are published out of China enjoy copyright protection pursuant to agreements executed between their country and China or international conventions. (Art. 2).

Works protected by this statute include literature, art, natural science, social science and technical engineering work including written works, oral works, music, drama, opera, fine art, dance, arts and crafts, photographs of film, television, video, engineer designs, production designs, papers, illustrations, maps, sketch maps, computer software, other works protected by law and administrative principles. (Art. 3).

According to law, works prohibited publication are not protected by this law. (Art. 4).

Protective measures for copyright of folk literature and art will be separately provided by State Council. (Art. 6).

Scientific technical works that should be protected by patent law, technical contract law, etc. are protected by applicable provisions of said statutes. (Art. 7).

Copyright administrative management department of State Council is in charge of national copyright administrative management. Copyright administrative management bureau of province, autonomous region and municipality are in charge of copyright administrative management of own administrative region. (Art. 8).

Those with copyright protection enjoy right to publish work or determine whether or not to license protected work to others. (Art. 10).

Right to copyright extends to life of individual plus 50 years. (Art. 21).

Registration of work is not required, and legal protection is afforded by statute, which provides for redress in courts or if provided for by contract in arbitration tribunals, and there can be resort to administrative sanctions.

CORPORATIONS

See Foreign Trade; Joint Stock Companies; Civil Code; Trade Zones.

Office of General Administration for Industry and Commerce has broad responsibilities over private and public enterprises. On Dec. 30, 1950 General Administrative Council promulgated Provisional Regulations for Private Enterprise. These regulations provided for private enterprises' forms of organization, labor regulations, registration of said enterprises, and scope of authority and business activity of said entities. On Dec. 1, 1962 State Council promulgated trial Rules for Registratin of Commercial and Industrial Enterprises. These rules were in force until July 7, 1982, when Standing Committee of State Council approved and promulgated Regulations for the Handling of Registration of Industrial and Commercial Enterprises, which superseded original regulations. (Art. 22).

Regulations on Registration of Legal Representative of enterprise were adopted on May 13, 1988. Administration of Commerce and Industry is responsible for handling said registration (Art. 4) and its Registration Authority must decide, within 30 days of receiving application, whether or not to approve registration. (Art. 14).

Steps for implementation of aforementioned Regulations were adopted on Nov. 3, 1988. Accordingly, all state enterprises, collectively owned enterprises, private enterprises, jointly operated enterprises, and enterprises having foreign investment in China (including Chinese-foreign joint ventures, Chinese-foreign cooperations and enterprises operated exclusively with foreign capital) must register with Administration of Commerce and Industry. (Art. 2). Foreign representative offices must also register. (Art. 5).

Enterprise having foreign investment must also register legal representative with Administration of Commerce and Industry. (Art. 7). Said registration requires enterprise having foreign investment to demonstrate properly authorized and approved name, location, contract and Articles of Association; their equipment, working capital, scope of business and employees must be registered and approved, and it must use authorized system of finance and accounting, etc. (Art. 16). Similarly, aforementioned approvals are required for said enterprise to obtain business registration. (Art. 17).

Specifically, enterprises having foreign investment must use system of unified accounting. (Art. 17). They must register name, location, identity of individual in charge, etc. (Art. 18). Name of enterprises must include name of firm, line of business (or feature of business) and form of organization. (Art. 24). Said name must be approved before enterprise may sign contracts or obtain Articles of Association. (Art. 25).

Regulations for Registration of Enterprises Having Foreign Investment requires submission of following documents: Application duly signed by chairman and vice-chairman of Board of Directors; contract; Articles of Association approved by proper authority; project proposal; preliminary feasibility study with certified documents; license to conduct commercial business; certified approval of all assets; list of board members; certified approval of appointing members of board, general manager and vice-general manager; names of all Chinese employees; and any other relevant documents and certifications. (Art. 35).

Registration of commercial business requires submission of following: Application to conduct commercial business, evidence of approval of operation capital, credentials of individual in charge, certified approval to use operation site and any other relevant documents and certified statements. (Art. 36).

Registration of branch or office requires submission of following documents: Application signed by chairman of board; evidence of approval and notice from original registration authority; decision by Board of Directors to establish branch or office; copy of business license; evidence of certification of individual in charge; and any other relevant documents and certified statements. (Art. 36).

If application meets aforementioned regulations, then certified business license and registration, etc., will be issued. These can be used to open bank accounts, obtain official seal, and conduct other relevant business activities. (Arts. 38, 39). To change registration, application signed by legal representative of enterprise, and all other relevant documents, must be submitted. (Art. 40). Upon receipt of said documents from applicant, registration authority must, within 30 days, approve or deny request. (Art. 49).

Foreign investment enterprise must apply to cancel its registration within three months from expiry date of business term, which is when all business ceases, business certification becomes automatically invalid and original examination authority approves decision to terminate contract. (Art. 51).

Registration fee for commercial business is 10% of all registered capital. If this amount is greater than RMB 10 million, 0.5% of sum exceeding RMB 10 million must be paid. If this amount exceeds RMB 100 million, registration fee is not levied on sum exceeding RMB 100 million. Registration fee shall not be less than RMB 50. State Administration of Industry and Commerce will stipulate fee for change of registration and annual examination. (Art. 26).

Sanctions Registration authority may administer one or more of following sanctions, depending on circumstances, for violation of aforementioned regulations: Admonishment, fine, notification to enterprise's bank to cease payments, temporary closing of business for modifications, permanent closing of business, revoking business license, confiscating all illegal income, etc. (Art. 66). Violations include: Commencing business without proper authorization; concealing factual circumstances or blatant deception upon registration; illegally changing enterprise's name, address, nature of business, legal representative, director or amount of business capital; operating beyond permitted scope of business; forging, altering, leasing, lending, transferring, selling, or illegally copying business license; unlawfully protecting against examination by registration authority, etc. (Art. 67). In cases of criminal law violations, violator must be sent to judicial branch for punishment. (Art. 68).

Hong Kong, Macao and Taiwan enterprises are those of overseas Chinese and compatriots from Hong Kong, Macao and Taiwan who establish either joint ventures or enterprises operated exclusively with their own capital must also register pursuant to aforementioned regulations. (Art. 72).

Regulations for Registration of Industrial and Commercial Enterprises require registration of following manufacturing and management units: Industrial, communications and transportation, construction, commercial, foreign trade, food and drink, service, travel, handicrafts, repair (Art. 2), whether state enterprises, cooperatives or other collectively owned enterprises, jointly operated and federated enterprises, public service units belonging to indus-

trial and commercial enterprises, viz. railroads, civil air transportation, postal and telecommunications (Art. 2[1], [2], [3]). Provincial level industrial and commercial enterprises deemed by relevant governments to require registration must register. (Art. 2[4]). Registration of foreign enterprises within China must be handled with reference to these regulations. (Art. 19). Chinese-foreign joint venture enterprises and foreign long term representative offices must register pursuant to those regulations. (Art. 19).

Organization responsible for handling registration of enterprises is Bureau of Administration of Commerce and Industry of relevant level of government. (Art. 3). Registration requires providing information about enterprise, such as name, address, persons in authority, date of commencement of business, nature and scope of commercial or industrial activity, capital, number of employees, etc. (Art. 5). Company name may only be used by one company in any given field of commerce or industry in city or county. (Art. 6). If basic construction required to engage in particular commercial or industrial enterprise, then application should be made within 30 days of approval of construction project for registration; preparatory to construction, if necessary. After construction, but 30 days prior to commencement of production or commencement of business, enterprise should apply for registration to commence business. In applying for registration to commence business, following documents, depending on circumstances, should be submitted: (1) Approved application from relevant departments to commence business, (2) approval of county or above planning organization, or people's government, and other relevant documents. (Art. 9). In addition, enterprise's business regulations should also be submitted. (Art. 9). If application conforms to these regulations, then business license or construction permit should be issued, which then can be used to open bank account and commence other relevant activities. (Art. 10). Those industrial and commercial enterprises who have not received approval to commence construction or business may not register their trademarks, have official seals engraved, execute contracts, place advertisements, nor may banks open accounts for such enterprises. (Art. 10). If there are changes in scope of production, form of business, nature of enterprise or economic character, then within 30 days of approval of such changes, application should be made for alterations in registration. (Art. 11). If there are other changes, they should be put in writing, prior to year end, to relevant Industrial and Commercial Administration Bureau. (Art. 11). Regulations also require that within 30 days after approval received to close business, then procedures should be undertaken to cancel registration and turn in business license for cancellation. (Art. 11). Similar procedures should be undertaken to terminate, alter or initiate registration if production or business ceases for a year or more (Art. 12), or if enterprise moves to new location, transfers its business, merges, or establishes separate branch. (Art. 13).

Registration fees, as determined by Administration of Industry and Commerce, paid at time of registration. (Art. 14). Relevant Administration of Industry and Commerce has authority to supervise and examine all enterprises under its jurisdiction, and said enterprises must produce for examination required documents, books of account, statistical tables and reports, and other relevant materials. (Art. 17).

Sanctions by Administration of Commerce and Industry for violating these regulations include, depending on circumstances, educational criticism, or if circumstances severe, admonishment, fine, notifying bank to freeze company's deposits or to cancel its bank account, legally compelling closing down or actual winding up of business, or revoking enterprise's preparatory construction or business license. (Art. 18). Administration of Commerce and Industry should invoke one of above sanctions for following violations: (1) Commencing preparatory construction or business without authorization, i.e. having not yet registered; (2) commencing production or business in violation of approved provisions of registration and not accepting exhortations to abide by said provisions, or failing within time limit permitted to correct said violations; (3) concealing factual circumstances when registering, or resorting to deception; (4) forging, altering, or transferring possession of permit to commence construction or business license. (Art. 18). If enterprise uses its business license according to legal form to engage in illegal enterprise, its illegal income should be confiscated. (Art. 18).

Company regulations for corporations having foreign interest in Special Economic Zone ("SEZ") in Guangdong, were promulgated on Sept. 28, 1986, effective as of Jan. 1, 1987. These regulations are applicable in SEZ to foreign-Chinese joint venture and cooperative ventures and foreign corporations and Chinese-foreign stock companies. (Art. 2).

Minimum registered capital requirements for company under these regulations is RMB 1,000,000 of which at least 25% must be initially paid in (Art. 7), management and technology must be modern, and portion or all of products of venture must be exported in international markets. (Art. 2). Registration of said company must be with city bureau of commerce and industry after approval by city government in SEZ. (Art. 9).

Registration of Chinese-foreign joint or cooperative ventures and foreign corporations require submission of feasibility report (Art. 12), including scope of production, operation or services, form of capital

or cooperative terms, investment amount and time framework, length of time for existence of company operational capacity or international market requirements, sales of product or services, and balancing of foreign currency economic projections, environmental impact, labor, safety and health programs, land use, overall plan, etc. (Art. 13).

Chinese-foreign limited stock corporations require at least five promoters of which half or more should be from SEZ. These promoters should execute contract and prospectus and articles of association. (Art. 16). In addition promoters should present to city government application, financial reports on promoters, feasibility study and prospectus. (Art. 17). Regulations also provide for organization and winding up of these corporations.

CUSTOMS (DUTY)

General Administration of Customs, directly under highest administrative organ, State Council has approximately 93 branches in China. All cargo and vessels must pass through Customs and be released by Customs when entering or exiting from China. Foreign trade organs issue import, and export licenses against which Customs officials check cargo. Customs officials also check for damage to cargo. Cargo can be examined either at warehouses, wharves and the like under customs control, or at ultimate destination of cargo if Customs so permits. In addition, Customs officials have responsibility for preventing smuggling or illegal transportation of precious metals and foreign currency. . . . Customs officials have authority to confiscate goods that are brought into China illicitly, to impose fines, not exceeding value of said goods, and/or send offender to judicial authorities for punishment.

Goods for exhibitions are governed by Rules Governing Supervision and Control of Importation of Goods for Exhibitions by Customs, promulgated by Ministry of Foreign Trade on Nov. 3, 1975. Under said rules organization responsible for reception of incoming foreign exhibitions shall present copies of authorizing documents to Customs. (Art. 3). Customs formalities must be adhered to, but said goods are essentially exempt from customs duties, except for those sold in China, for which foreign trade control organs must grant import license and duties must be paid. (Art. 15).

Import duties on passenger baggage are governed by Rules Governing Levying of Import Duty on Articles in Passengers' Baggage and Personal Postal Parcels approved by State Council on June 16, 1978 and promulgated by Ministry of Foreign Trade on Aug. 1, 1978. These rules provide for ad valorem duties, assessed on c.i.f. value or where not ascertainable, domestic price (Art. 5), and run as high as 100% on foodstuffs, beverages, clothing made of cotton or linen, radio sets and record players. (Art. 3). Wristwatches, tobacco, wine, spirits, and cosmetics are taxed at 200%. (Art. 3). Appeals as to levy can only be made after paying duty. (Art. 6). Passengers entering China as tourists or for brief visits are not subject to these levies pursuant to regulations, unless they are carrying unusually large quantity of items beyond what appears to be normal personal usage. See Provisional Customs Regulations for Supervision and Control over Baggage and Articles Accompanying Incoming and Outgoing Overseas Chinese and Other Passengers, promulgated by Ministry of Foreign Trade on Apr. 5, 1978. See also Customs Guide for Passengers Entering and Leaving China, which provides that articles and baggage carried by incoming passengers, in reasonable quantities for personal use, shall be released duty free, but there are limits on certain articles, e.g., wristwatches, bicycles and radios, which are to be limited normally to one per person.

Customs duties on commercial goods are provided for in official publications pursuant to official categories. See Order of Government Administrative Council of May 10, 1951. Customs Schedule on Imported Goods, and Provisional Regulations on Levying Import and Export Duties approved by Government Administrative Council on May 4, 1951, effective as of May 16, 1951, which have been amended several times subsequently; Regulations on Import Export Custom Duties promulgated by State Council 7 Mar., 1985, and revised 12 Sept., 1987, effective 15 Oct., 1987, pursuant to Customs Law.

All imported and exported goods should have duties imposed on them by customs according to customs regulations except those which have been accepted. (Art. 2). Customs schedule is part of these rules. (Art. 2).

Customs taxpayer is consignee of imported cargo and consignor of exported cargo. Agent who is entrusted to proceed with cargo concerned, shall abide by these rules. (Art. 4). Certain items are free of import duties, but not export duties including those with value of less than ten renminbi; of no commercial value such as advertising materials and samples; gifts from foreign governments and international organizations; goods originally exported from China and returned. (Art. 24).

Certain other statutes provide for evaluation of customs duties as noted above including goods imported pursuant to approved joint venture or compensation trade contract, pursuant to application with customs services. (Art. 31). Customs duties fall into two categories, those with favored nations and normal duties. (Art. 6). (*See* Joint Stock Companies.) In addition, appeal can be made to reduce or eliminate customs duties pursuant to joint venture regulations.

Under compensation trade agreements normally no customs duties are levied. Goods from US pursuant to Trade Agreement obtain most favored categories of duty levy. If party objects to customs levy then said party can make application within 30 days on customs form to appeal said levy (Art. 32), which should be decided in 15 days, which is reviewed by Management Bureau of Customs Agency. (Art. 13). There can be yet another review demanded by exporter or importer (Art. 14) if second decision is unfavorable. If there is continued disagreement about said levy, then party contesting duty can post bond, or make deposit, normally in amount of duty, or such other amount as Customs may decide, and thereafter customs officials must release goods; and application made to court. (Art. 34). Normally duties are levied on costs of goods plus freight to port of entry. Said costs include proper wholesale price of goods, plus export tax, cost of transportation to China, cost of packaging, foreign domestic transportation to foreign port, insurance costs, and local licenses, etc. (Art. 9). If said normal wholesale price at place of purchase cannot be determined by customs officers, then they should calculate duty on basis of average wholesale price in Chinese domestic market where goods eater Chinese market, less import fees and enterprise fees (or taxes) as basis for determining duties. (Art. 10). If domestic wholesale price in China cannot be ascertained, or transaction has particular or unusual circumstances, then customs administrator is to estimate and determine value for tax purposes based on wholesale prices of imported goods to China port of same type. (Art. 10).

See also Trade Zones.

DAMAGES

See Arbitration and Award; Contracts; Environment; Civil Code.

Concept of damages for breach of contract is known, understood and not infrequently explicated in Chinese contracts, including international contracts which may have penalty clauses or clauses that call for compensation for breach thereof. In addition, certain statutes provide for damages. Thus statute promulgated on Aug. 17, 1959 by Government Administrative Council, entitled Provisional Regulations for Protection of Inventions, Patent Rights and Patents, provided in para. 3 of Art. 7 that those who do not obtain permission of patent holder, may not use invention; and those who violate this provision will according to law compensate patent holder for his loss. On Oct. 15, 1959 Ministry of Communications promulgated Several Rules Concerning Compensation for Loss at Sea, whereby negligent acts of ship employees resulting in loss require owners of said ocean vessels to make compensation; if cause of loss is carrier, however, then carrier should be responsible for compensation. Similarly, Art. 32 of trial Law on Environmental Protection provides that organizations or individuals who violate provisions of law may be called upon to make compensation for losses.

ENVIRONMENT

See Joint Stock Companies; Trade Zones.

Constitution provides that state protects and improves environment, ecology, prevents and eliminates pollution and other hazards to public. State organizes and encourages people to grow and protect forests. (Const. Art. 26). Also provides that state protects places of scenic or historical interest and cultural relics, etc. (Const. Art. 22). On Sept. l3, 1979 Standing Committee of Fifth National People's Congress, pursuant to Art. 11 of Constitution, in principle adopted extensive piece of legislation on trial basis entitled; Environmental Protection Law of People's Republic of China, which was promulgated on date of adoption. Statute is quite broad in scope, encompassing in its legal responsibilities reasonable use of natural environment, prevention and elimination of pollution, prevention of ecocide, creation of clean and salubrious environment in which to live and work, protection of people's health, and promotion of economic development. (Art. 2). Term "environment" is broadly defined by statute to include air, water, land, mineral reserves, forests, grasslands, wild animals, wild plants, aquatic life, places of antiquity, scenic spots, hot springs, health resorts, protected natural regions, residential areas, etc. (Art. 3). Law provides that State Council, in establishing national economic plan, must encompass environmental considerations which strive to improve environment, and must establish plan to solve existing problems of pollution. (Art. 5).

Statute requires that environmental impact statement must accompany all proposed construction plans, including alteration or expansion of existing construction. . . . Foreign persons, aircraft, vessels, vehicles, animal or biological material from abroad, entering or passing through Chinese territory, territorial waters or air-space are required to abide by Environmental Protection Statute. (Art. 9).

Industrial Wastes and Pollutants Pursuant to National Standard GBJ4-73, effective Jan. 1, 1974, amended 1984, 1987, trial standards enacted for release of three industrial wastes, which standards designed to prevent pollution caused by industrial gas, water and water residues. (Art. 1). All factories, mines and other enterprises required to diminish or eliminate these three pollutants. Industrial noxious water and gas which cannot be re-used must proceed to purification and recovery treatment pursuant to national standards of release. (Art. 3). All plans

for new construction, expansions or reconstruction projects for factories, mines or other enterprises must incorporate purification installations for three waste products. Such installations must meet national standards and be put into operation concurrently with primary project. Existing factories, mines and other enterprises causing pollution must provide plan of elimination of said pollution within approximately five years, depending on severity of pollution. (Art. 4). All relevant industrial departments required, pursuant to standards of these draft regulations, to lay down design criteria for enterprises and administrative norms for consumption of raw materials and fuels, as well as water to be discharged. (Art. 5).

Seas and Oceans On Aug. 23, 1982 Standing Committee of State Council promulgated Law of Environmental Protection of the Seas and Oceans.

Jurisdiction This law, effective Mar. 1, 1983 (Art. 48), covers all sea waters under jurisdiction of China, including inland seas and territorial waters (Art. 2), and covers virtually all activities of shipping, underwater and aviation apparatus, platforms, including scientific research, production, exploration, development, navigation, and any other activities of commercial and noncommercial enterprises and individuals. (Art. 2). Sea waters outside jurisdiction of China, where there is discharge of noxious substances, or dumping of discarded materials that damage seas under Chinese jurisdiction are covered by this statute. (Art. 2).

Pesticide Registration Pursuant to Environmental Protection Act regulations were promulgated, effective Oct. 1, 1982, requiring registration of all technical and formulated products of chemical pesticides and biological pesticides used to control plant diseases, insects, pests, weeds, and other harmful living beings in agriculture, forestry and animal husbandry. (Art. 2). Regulations prohibit production, distribution or use of pesticide without registration. (Art. 4). Even pesticides used for demonstration purposes must apply for temporary registration. (Art. 4[3]). in addition to providing samples for registration (Art. 6), regulations require four copies of information on toxicology, residues, effect upon environment, products standard, application technique, production technique and description of product. (Art. 5). Pesticides produced by foreign companies must be registered before marketing (Art. 7), but information on techniques of production need not be provided. Registration requires certification by relevant authorized organizations of Ministries of Chemical Industry, Public Health, Urban and Rural Construction and Environmental Protection, Agriculture, Animal Husbandry and Fishery.

Ministry of Commerce may set packaging standards, and Evaluation Committee on Pesticide Registration shall make overall evaluation and certificate shall be issued by Ministry of Agriculture, Animal Husbandry and Fishery. (Art. 6).

EXECUTIONS

Pursuant to Trade Agreement between US and China certain foreign arbitral awards and judgments embodying said awards can be enforced in Chinese courts. *See* Arbitration and Award.

Legally effective decisions, judgments, orders, and conciliation agreements concerning property are to be executed by court of first instance. (Code of Civil Procedure). Courts having jurisdiction can also enforce arbitral awards. (Code of Civil Procedure, Art. 217). If property to be executed upon is outside jurisdiction of court, court where property is located can be entrusted with execution of said judgment, which should commence within 15 days of receipt of petition and should not be refused. (Code of Civil Procedure, Art. 210).

Marshall of court should undertake enforcement of judgment. Compulsory execution commences with service of process by marshal of document of execution. Record should be made of circumstances of execution and someone at location, etc. should sign or place his seal on said record, as witness thereto. (Art. 209). Where notarial offices have legal authority and undertake execution on behalf of creditors they may do so but if there is resistance to execution, application to basic level court can be made for enforcement of said document reflecting indebtedness. (Code of Civil Procedure, Art. 218). If both parties are natural persons they have one year in which to apply for execution, while if both parties are legal persons they have six months to apply for execution. Time for execution is calculated from last day of time limit specified in legal document upon whose provisions execution is sought. (Code of Civil Procedure, Art. 219).

Party upon whose property execution is to take place by sealing or distraint should be notified or adult of his family should be notified to appear at location of execution. Their failure to appear will not delay execution. In addition work unit and basic governmental organization where property is located should also send representative to location. List of property executed upon must be made and one on location should sign or put his seal on list, and thereafter said list should be given to person upon whose property execution has taken place. (Code of Civil Procedure, Art. 173). Marshall should notify person whose property was distrained or sealed that he has specific time to meet legal obligations provided in court decision. When time expires property is to be turned over for sale. (Code of Civil Procedure, Art. 175).

If there is execution on realty (land or buildings), then person on whose property execution is to take place should be given notice, and if he fails to perform within that time marshal should use compulsory process to compel performance. (Code of Civil Procedure, Art. 172).

FOREIGN TRADE

See Advertising; Arbitration and Award; Contracts; Copyright; Corporations; Customs; Joint Stock Companies; Trade Zones.

Trade Agreement of July 7, 1979 between US and China expresses intent of contracting parties to expand trade primarily by contracts between companies. Said contracts are to be concluded on basis of commercial considerations and customary international trade practice. Each country must afford other most-favored-nation treatment on products originating from other. Quantitative restriction on certain products applied by either contracting party shall be applied on equitable basis, with other countries so restricted. Parties expressed their intent to reciprocate satisfactory concessions with regard to tariff and non-tariff barriers to trade. Agreement declares intent of parties to promote visits by commercial persons, to support holding of fairs, exhibits and technical seminars, to permit and facilitate stationing of representatives or establishment of business offices by firms and corporations of party trading in other party's territory. Art. V of Trade Agreement provides that there are to be no restrictions, except in time of declared national emergency, on payments or transactions to be effected in freely convertible currencies mutually acceptable to parties executing contracts or otherwise agreed by parties. Industrial property rights including patents, trademark and copyright are to be protected.

Textile agreements were originally executed between China and US on July 23 and 25, 1980 by exchange of letters, and Sept. 17, 1980 by executed Agreement. July exchange of letters, proposed visa system for textiles, which Chinese accepted, for cotton, wool and man-made fiber textiles and textile products from China. Each commercial shipment of said products from China is to be accompanied by export visa issued by official of Chinese government. Said visa, stamped in blue ink on customs invoice Form 5515 or commercial 'invoice will have visa number and date. Agreement of July 23, 1980 reaffirmed Agreement on Trade Relations (Art. 1) which provided for three-year agreement from Jan. 1, 1980 through Dec. 31, 1982 (Art. 2) and provides for categories of goods (Art. 3 and Annex. A) with restrictions on exports from China to US in certain categories. (Art. 4 and Annex. B). There is provision for exceeding specific limits by stipulated percentage in any year provided said expansion is compensated for by equivalent decreases in one or other specific limit for that Agreement year. (Art. 5). China is to use its best efforts to space exports, within each category, evenly throughout year, taking into consideration normal seasonal factors. (Art. 6). If government of US believes that imports from China in any category not covered by specific limits are, due to market disruption, threatening to impede orderly development of trade between two countries, then consultations, based on detailed factual statements for reason for same, may be requested by US (Art. 8). Contracting parties agree to supply each other with data of imports and exports in categories for which levels have been established. (Art. 10). Annex. B contains specific limits on cotton gloves, knit shirts and blouses, non-knit blouses, trousers and sweaters. This Agreement successfully renegotiated in early Aug. 1983; and renegotiated again in 1990.

In July, 1980 legislation authorizing OPIC operations in China was passed. On Aug. 8, 1980 President Carter determined that it was in national interest for OPIC to do business with China. Agreement of Oct. 30, 1980 provides final link in preliminary procedures necessary for OPIC to commence activity regarding China projects; thus, OPIC has now started its China activity. OPIC insurance, loan guarantees, direct loans, preinvestment assistance, construction insurance and insurance for contractors' guarantees are all theoretically available for China projects. In addition, Ex-Im Bank has full authority to institute its programs in China, but will only finally approve project after it has been approved by Bank of China. Treaty on investment protection still under discussion between U.S, and China although China has signed treaties on promotion and protection of investment with Sweden, Belgium, West Germany, Luxembourg and Romania.

Export Administrative Regulations in US were amended in May, 1980 creating new group category (Group P) for China, permitting more liberalized policy toward China than other non-market economies. . . . On Nov. 23, 1983 China was removed from Country Group P to Group V under Export Administration Regulations, US Department of Commerce emphasizing that sales to China should be on similar basis as most other friendly nations. On Dec. 27, 1985 export control regulations were further amended (50 FR 52900-01) to require end user's certificates from technology import-export department of MOFERT.

Foreign firm's activity in China is governed by Trade Agreement and applicable Chinese law. Upon receipt of visas issued-by Chinese embassy in Washington, or any Chinese consulate, embassy or related institution elsewhere, representatives can proceed to China to negotiate, execute and carry out agreements. Permanent offices in China require applica-

tion by foreign firms active within country. US citizens in China for extended periods and companies having long-term representative offices are subject to Chinese tax laws.

FRAUDS, STATUTE OF

Contracts may have to be notarially certified where title to buildings, or building rights are conveyed, and will have to be registered with local authorities. Normally all international commercial contracts are evidenced by writing as matter of practice.

FRAUDULENT SALES AND CONVEYANCES

Sale concluded under influence of fraud is generally regarded by Chinese legal authorities as invalid, with wrongdoer being required to return what was received under contract. (See topics Contracts; Civil Code.) Details of Chinese concepts of fraudulent sales will be further explicated in Civil Code when said draft is promulgated.

HEALTH REGULATIONS

On Nov. 19, 1982 Trial Regulations on Foodstuffs Sanitation were promulgated effective as of July 1, 1983. These regulations, which cover all persons engaged in production of foodstuffs, provide for enforcement measures ranging from providing time limit in which to come up to standards, to confiscation, loss of health certificate, fines up to RMB 30,000, etc. (Art. 37). Any individual may bring complaint against violator. (Art. 3). Specific requirements are provided for production and supply of foodstuffs (Art. 6) and restrictions are enumerated (Art. 7) applying not only to all food items but also to materials, tools, equipment, location, environment, packing, containers, and additives. (Art. 3). These regulations are comprehensive, providing standards, inspection, regulations concerning additives and packaging, and enforcement.

INSOLVENCY

See Bankruptcy.

INTEREST

Interest is charged by Bank of China and all other Chinese banks on loans they extend, and interest is given to those maintaining savings accounts with relevant banks in China. Chinese Organizations borrowing money from foreign banks likewise pay interest, often at commercial rates.

JOINT STOCK COMPANIES

See Advertising; Corporations; Statistics, Standards and Quality Control; Trade Zones.

Law on Joint Ventures Using Chinese and Foreign Investment (Joint Venture Law of China) was adopted by National People's Congress on July, 1, 1979, and permits foreign companies to enter into joint ventures with Chinese companies or other entities, subject to authorization by Chinese government. (Art. 1). Statute provides that Chinese government protects resources invested by foreign investor, as well as any profits due. (Art. 2). Parties to joint venture originally to apply to Foreign Investment Commission in China for approval of agreements and contracts between parties, and articles of association. (Art. 3). Commission had three months to reject or approve these documents, and if approved, joint venture shall register with General Administration for Industry and Commerce (GAIC) and pursuant to license obtained, commence operations. (Art. 3). This has been modified by Regulations for the Implementation of the Law on Joint Ventures Using Chinese and Foreign Investment ("JV Implementation Regs."), promulgated by State Council on Sept. 23, 1983. These Regulations formulated with view to facilitating implementation of Joint Venture Law. (JV Implementation Regs. Art. 1). Pursuant to said Regulations promulgated subsequent to Joint Venture Law, joint venture is normally subject to approval of Ministry of Foreign Economic Relations and Trade ("MOFERT"), which issues certificate of approval. (JV Implementation Regs. Art. 8). However, MOFERT can and does designate government organizations of provinces, autonomous regions, and municipalities directly under central government, or relevant ministries or bureaus under same Council, to examine and approve establishment of joint ventures complying with certain specific conditions. Chinese partner to joint venture submits to its department in charge project proposal and preliminary feasibility report of joint venture which, on approval of department in charge, must be submitted to approval authority for final approval. Thereafter, work can be commenced on relevant feasibility study and joint venture agreements based on such preliminary feasibility report. (JV Implementation Regs. Art. 9[1]).

Regulations on Registration of Joint Ventures Using Chinese and Foreign Investment ("Joint Venture Registration Regulations") approved by State Council on July 26, 1980 provide that joint venture should within one month of receiving Foreign Investment Commission approval register with GAIC. (Joint Venture Registration Regulations, Art. 2). Local administrative bureaus of industry and commerce are authorized to register joint ventures, but licenses shall be issued only after examination by GAIC. (Joint Venture Registration Regulations, Art. 2).

Joint venture is limited liability company, in general foreign partner contributing not less than 25% of registered capital, wherein parties share profits and risk of loss in proportion to their registered capital. (Joint Venture Law, Art. 4). Investment of party may be cash, capital goods, industrial property rights, use of site, etc., but technology and equipment contributed by any foreign partner "shall be truly advanced and appropriate to China's needs." (Joint Venture Law, Art. 5). Joint venture's board of directors shall have chairman appointed by Chinese participant and one or two vice-chairmen appointed by foreign participants, amended on Apr. 4, 1990 to allow foreign party to provide Chairman of Board of Directors. If one party to joint venture assumes position of board chairman, then vice-chairman of board of directors shall be assumed by other party (Art. 6), thus no longer requiring Chinese party be chairman of board. Board is empowered to discuss and take action, pursuant to articles of association, on all venture's fundamental issues, viz., budget, production programs, business programs, distribution of profit, pay scales, termination of business, expansion projects, appointment and hiring of president, vice-president(s), chief engineer, treasurer and auditors, as well as their functions, power and remuneration, etc. (Joint Venture Law, Art. 6). President, vice-president(s), general manager and assistant-general manager(s) in factory shall be chosen from among parties to venture. (Art. 6). Within scope of joint venture contract, articles of association, and Chinese laws and decrees, joint venture has right to do business independently. (JV Implementation Regs. Art. 7). However, governmental department in charge of Chinese participant in joint venture will be in charge of joint venture and responsible for guidance and assistance, and will exercise supervision over joint venture. (JV Implementation Regs. Art. 6).

Length of Term of Joint Venture Contract term of joint venture shall be decided according to its particular line of business and circumstances. Some lines of business of enterprise with foreign investment shall provide term of joint venture, some may or may not provide term of joint venture. Those enterprises with foreign investment which have decided term of joint venture, if parties have agreed to extend term, shall apply to examination and approval authority six months before expiration of term of joint venture. Upon receipt of application for extension of contract, examination and approval authority shall, within one month decide whether to approve or disapprove it. (Art. 12). Before expiration of joint venture contract in cases of heavy losses aside from failure of party to fulfill obligations prescribed by contract and articles of association, force majeure etc., contract may be terminated through consultation and agreement by parties to joint venture, subject to approval by authority in charge of national foreign economic trade and to registration with General Administration for Industry and Commerce. In case of losses caused by breach of contract financial responsibility shall be borne by party that breaches contract. (Art. 13).

Balance of Foreign Exchange Receipts and Disbursements Ministry of Foreign Economic Relations and Trade promulgated Measures Concerning the Purchase of Domestic Products for Export by Enterprises with Foreign Investment to Balance Foreign Exchange Receipts and Disbursements on Jan. 20, 1987. In principle; enterprises with foreign investment shall achieve balance of foreign exchange receipts and disbursements through export of products of such enterprises.

With regard to production enterprises with foreign investment for which temporary difficulties exist, they may, within fixed period of time, apply to purchase domestic products (except commodities subject to unified control according to state regulations) for export so as to balance foreign exchange receipts and disbursement of such enterprises. (Art. 2). If enterprise with foreign investment, meeting requirements of Art. 2 herein, needs to purchase domestic products for export to balance foreign exchange receipts and disbursements, it shall file application in advance with foreign economic relations and trade department at provincial level in locality where enterprise is located. (Art. 3). Quantity of domestic products for export approved for purchase by enterprise with foreign investment shall be limited to amount required in that year to make up for foreign exchange required for production and operation of enterprises and remittance of profits to foreign party, or foreign exchange required to be remitted upon winding up and liquidation of enterprise. (Art. 4). Domestic products approved for purchase by enterprise with foreign investment to balance foreign exchange receipts and disbursement must be transported out of Chinese territory for distribution and sale and shall not be resold within Chinese territory. (Art 6).

Labor Regulations promulgated on Nov. 26, 1986 by Ministry of Labor and Personnel limit autonomy of enterprises having foreign investment in hiring personnel, setting wages and paying insurance and welfare expenses of employees.

Enterprise having foreign investment may, according to its production and operational needs, independently determine its organizational structure and personnel system and, with assistance from local Department of Labor and Personnel, it may recruit and select employees using its own criteria. (Art. 1[a]).

Senior management personnel selected by Chinese party in enterprise for work in said enterprise must be capable of grasping concepts, be knowledgeable about technology, have management skills, be innovative and able to cooperate and work with foreign investors. Supervisors in their respective departments must support said senior personnel in their position and generally not transfer them during their term of office. If said transfer becomes necessary, Board of Directors must consent. (Art. 1[c]).

Enterprises having foreign investment may dismiss those employee who prove unqualified for their posts after probationary or training period or who have been rendered unnecessary by changes in technology or new methods of production. Employees who violate regulations of enterprise with damaging consequences may be sanctioned accordingly, with maximum sanction being discharged. (Art. 1[d]).

Wages of employees of enterprise having foreign investment will be set by its Board of Directors but may not be less than 120% of average wages paid workers of state-owned enterprises with similar conditions, in same field and in same area; said level must be adjusted periodically, mainly in response to improved economic performance of enterprise. (Art. 2[a]).

Enterprise having foreign investment must pay retirement and pension funds and employment insurance premiums for Chinese employees according to regulations of local People's Government. Insurance and welfare plans must also meet government requirements set for state-owned enterprise and must be funded strictly by said enterprise. (Art. 2[b]).

Enterprise having foreign investment must pay housing subsidy funds according to regulations of local People's Government. Chinese party to enterprise shall apply said funds to expenses incurred in building and purchase of housing for employees of said enterprise. (Art. 2[c]).

Labor Relations Contract between parties' shall, pursuant to law, cover employment and discharge of workers and staff members. (Joint Venture Law, Art. 6). On July 26, 1980 State Council approved Regulations on Labor Management in Joint Ventures Using Chinese and Foreign Investment ("Joint Venture Labor Reg."). Regulations require that labor contracts be signed either collectively with trade union, or if venture is small, with individual members of staff and laborers, specifying conditions of employment, dismissal, resignation, production tasks, other work, wages, awards, punishment, working hours, vacations, labor insurance, welfare insurance, labor protection and labor discipline. (Joint Venture Labor Reg., Art. 2). This contract must be submitted to labor management department of province, autonomous region or municipal people's government for approval. (Joint Venture Labor Reg., Art. 2). Where there are surplus workers as result of changes in production and technical conditions of joint venture, said workers, pursuant to labor contract, can be discharged, but enterprise must compensate these workers. (Joint Venture Labor Reg., Art. 4). Workers violating rules and regulations of enterprise with resulting bad consequences can be discharged, but such discharge must be reported to authorities having jurisdiction over joint venture, and to labor management department for their approval. (Joint Venture Labor Reg., Art. 5). Trade union can object to dismissal or punishment of workers and staff, and send representatives to board of directors for consultation. (Joint Venture Labor Reg., Art. 6). If said consultation fails, then either party can seek to have matter arbitrated by labor management department of people's government of province, autonomous region or municipality where venture is located, and if arbitration decision is not acceptable either party can file lawsuit. (Joint Venture Labor Reg., Art. 14). Wage level of workers and staff members in joint venture will be determined at 120% to 150% of real wages of workers and staff members in state-owned enterprises of same trade in locality. (Joint Venture Labor Reg., Art. 8).

Joint venture must pay for Chinese workers' labor insurance, cover their medical expenses and provide various kinds of subsidies in line with prevailing standards in state-owned enterprises. (Joint Venture Labor Reg., Art. 11). Joint ventures are also required to implement relevant rules and regulations of Chinese government regarding labor production to ensure safe and civilized production. (Joint Venture Labor Reg., Art. 13). Labor management department of Chinese government is authorized to supervise and inspect implementation of these rules. (Joint Venture Labor Reg., Art. l3).

Loans from Bank of China Bank of China promulgated regulations on Apr. 24, 1987, concerning loans to enterprises with foreign investment. In granting loans, Bank of China must sign loan agreements with borrowing enterprise. (Art. 4). Bank of China grants following types of loans to enterprises; (1) Fixed asset loan, which may be medium or short-term, on buyer's credit, syndicated or for project financing; (2) working capital loan, in form of production reserves and revolving funds, temporary credit or overdraft limit on current account; (3) Renminbi loan against mortgage; (4) stand-by credit loan. (Art. 5).

Net profit of joint venture shall be distributed between parties to venture in proportion to their respective shares in registered capital, after paying joint venture income tax on gross profits pursuant to China's tax laws, and after deducting, as stipulated in articles of association, monies for reserve funds, bonus and welfare funds and expansion funds. (Joint Venture Law, Art. 7). Said net profit received by foreign participant, funds received when joint venture terminates, and other funds may be remitted abroad

through Bank of China, in currencies specified in contract. (Joint Venture Law, Art. 10). Applications for income tax reduction by joint ventures having up-to-date technology, for first two or three profit-making years may be made, as can application for restitution of portion of taxes paid be made by foreign entity which reinvests any part of its share of net profit in China. (Joint Venture Law, Art. 7). Joint ventures exempt from customs duty and Industrial and Commercial Consolidated Tax on certain imported materials, such as raw materials, auxiliary materials, components, parts and packing materials imported by joint venture for production of export goods, machinery, equipment, parts and other materials imported with funds which are part of joint venture's total investment or are part of foreign partner's shares of investment according to provisions of contract. (JV Implementation Regs., Art. 71).

Settlement in Foreign Currency Regulations promulgated by State Administration of Exchange Control, effective Mar. 1, 1989, were attempt to control use of foreign currency by foreign investment enterprises to settle debts in China and to assist said enterprises in their balance of payments in foreign currency.

Foreign investment enterprises who wish to sell products for foreign currency in China must apply to State Administration of Exchange Control or one of its branches. (Art. 1).

Enterprises having foreign investment which meets following requirements may apply for permission to do business in foreign currency: (1) Whose products are necessarily imported based on government plan; (2) whose products are marketed in Special Economic Zones, Economic and Technical Development Zones and to other foreign investment enterprises; (3) materials and parts of whose products must be imported by Chinese manufacturing enterprises. (Art. 2).

To apply for permission to do business in foreign currency, enterprise must submit application report including reasons for request, name of product, quantity sold, total amount, term requested, certificate of approval of capital issued by registered accounts office, and any other documents required by State Administration of Exchange Control. (Art. 3).

Investment Certificates, Contributions to Capital, Registered Capital, etc. Joint venture corporation empowered to issue investment certificates to parties who invest in joint venture. (JV Implementation Regs. Art. 32). In order for party to assign all or part of its investment to third party, other party to joint venture has preemptive rights, and must consent to such assignment if not to itself. (JV Implementation Regs. Art. 23). Thus, investment certificates not negotiable documents. Contributions to joint venture can be in cash, buildings, premises, materials, industrial property, know-how, right of use of site, etc. (JV Implementation Regs. Art. 25). Investment of know-how or industrial property rights must be verified by documentation and serve as annex to joint venture contract. (JV Implementation Regs. Art. 29). Joint Venture bank accounts are to be opened with Bank of China or bank approved by Bank of China, although in business operations venture can obtain funds directly from foreign banks. (Joint Venture Law, Art. 8). Insurance appropriate to joint venture shall be furnished by Chinese companies. (Joint Venture Law, Art. 8). In its purchase of required raw and semi-processed materials, fuels, auxiliary equipment, etc., joint venture should give first priority to Chinese sources, but may also acquire them directly from world market with its foreign exchange funds. (Joint Venture Law, Art. 9). Said venture can market its produce in and out of China, and it may set up affiliates outside of China. (Joint Venture Law, Art. 9). Contract period of joint venture may be agreed between parties, and may be extended by agreement between parties and application, six months prior to expiration, to Foreign Investment Commission. (Joint Venture Law, Art. 12). Termination of joint venture can take place before expiration date if there are heavy losses, or if any party fails to execute its obligations under contract, or by force majeure, etc. (Joint Venture Law, Art. 13). Parties must agree to said early termination and obtain authorization of Foreign Investment Commission. (Joint Venture Law, Art. 13).

Law On Chinese Foreign Contractual Joint Ventures Law on Contractual Joint Ventures, promulgated on 13 Apr. 1988, provides for establishment of terms of joint venture including distribution of profit on basis of agreement of parties rather than by operation of law. (Art. 2). Contractual joint venture entity can acquire status of independent legal person under Chinese law. (Art. 2). These agreements must be approved by relevant government examination and approval authority within 45 days of receipt of application (Art. 5); modification requires same approval procedure as does assignment. Board of directors or management committee shall be established to manage venture pursuant to contract and/or articles of association. (Art. 12). Hiring and firing of staff shall be specified in contracts with said employees (Art. 13) though union can be established. (Art. 14). Contractual joint ventures permit foreign parties to recover their investment on priority basis prior to payment of income tax, provided such is approved by financial and tax authorities. (Art. 27).

Dispute Resolution and Legal Status Validity, interpretation, formation and execution of contract, as well as settlement of disputes under joint venture contract, governed by Chinese Law. (JV Implementation Regs. Art. 15). Joint venture contract, articles of association and amendments to either come into

force after approval by examination and approval authorities. (JV Implementation Regs. Art. 17). Disputes between parties to joint venture may be settled through conciliation or arbitration by Chinese arbitral body or through arbitral body agreed upon by parties. (Joint Venture Law, Art. 14). In cases of losses caused by breach of contract by party to venture, financial responsibility shall be borne by said party. (Joint Venture Law, Art. 13).

Expropriation Joint Venture Law of China was amended on Apr. 4, 1990. Amendments provide China will not nationalize and requisition enterprises with foreign investment. In case of special circumstances according to demand of social public interest, enterprises with foreign investment may be requisitioned by legal procedures; corresponding compensation will be granted. (Art. 2).

Accounting Regulations for Joint Ventures Using Chinese and Foreign Investment were promulgated on Mar. 4,1985. These regulations, applicable to all Chinese-foreign joint ventures established in China (Art. 2), can be supplemented by public finance bureaus of provinces, etc. (Art. 3). Joint ventures must have separate accounting offices; if large or medium size, controller and auditor which offices and persons are to fulfill their responsibilities with care, make accurate calculations, reflect faithfully actual conditions, and strictly supervise all economic transactions. (Art. 7).

Joint ventures are to adopt debit and credit double entry bookkeeping (Art. 11) and books of account and accounting statements are to be prepared accurately and promptly (Art. 12), to be kept in Chinese language and if parties wish concurrently in foreign language. (Art. 13).

Accrual basis of accounting is to be used; all revenues realized and expenses incurred during current period shall be recognized in current period. (Art. 15). Assets are to be stated in their original costs and accounting methods are to be consistent from one period to other, changes to be submitted to local tax authorities. (Arts. 17, 19).

JOINT VENTURES

See Joint Stock Companies.

JUDGMENTS

See Arbitration and Award.

Enforcement, of Foreign Judgments, Court Orders, etc. on basis of treaties or international conventions to which People's Republic of China is signatory, on principle of reciprocity Chinese and foreign, courts can mutually entrust each other to undertake certain litigation action. Where matter foreign court wishes to entrust is incompatible with sovereignty or security of People's Republic of China, it should be rejected; where it is not within scope of authority of court, reasons should be clearly explicated and matter returned to foreign court. (Civ. Pro. Code, Arts. 262-267).

Where court of People's Republic of China is presented with judgment having legal effect, or definitive decision of arbitration tribunal and petitioner wishes to compel enforcement thereof, and said petition involves property which is not in Chinese territory, court can, pursuant to treaties or international conventions to which China party, or in accordance with principles of mutuality, entrust foreign court to assist in execution of said judgments, etc. (Civ. Pro. Code, Arts. 262-270). With regard to judgments and final arbitral decisions which foreign courts authorize Chinese courts to enforce, Chinese courts should, according to treaties and international conventions to which China signatory, or on basis of principle of mutuality, commence examination of said judgment and if they consider it does not violate basic principles of laws of People's Republic of China or China's social interests, and ascertain that said decision has validity, execute judgment according to procedures provided in this statute. If these conditions not met, then matter should be referred, back to foreign court. (Civ. Pro. Code, Arts. 262-270).

Documents of foreign courts entrusting courts of People's Republic of China to assist in execution, or to represent said foreign court in delivery, and documents entrusting Chinese court to undertake specific legal action, must have appended Chinese translation. Documents of courts of China entrusting foreign court to represent it in serving papers or assist in execution of Chinese decree, etc. and document wherein China entrusts foreign court to undertake specific legal action, must have appended foreign language translation. (Civ. Pro. Code, Arts. 262-270).

China became signatory on 2 Dec., 1986 to Convention on the Recognition and Enforcement of Foreign Arbitral Awards, agreed to in New York on 10 June, 1958. *See* Arbitration and Award.

MINES AND MINERALS

Mineral resources are owned by state (Const., Art. 9) and are exploited by state enterprises or jointly with foreign enterprises.

MONOPOLIES AND RESTRAINT OF TRADE

State has until recently monopolized foreign trade, and through its control over exchange controls and approval of joint ventures, still plays major role in foreign trade and in domestic economy. Nevertheless, it is clear that joint foreign-Chinese enterprises, and small private businesses and agricultural free market are playing increasingly larger role in international and domestic trade in China.

State also has established monopolies pursuant to regulations such as Tobacco Monopoly Regulations, promulgated by State Council on Sept. 23, 1983. Said monopoly includes cigarettes, cigars, smoking tobacco, flue-cured tobacco, air and sun dried tobacco, cigarette paper and filters, cigarette manufacturing equipment (Art. 2), all under State Tobacco Monopoly Administration (Art. 3), which exercises overall administrative management of tobacco monopoly, and National Tobacco Corporation, which manages production, supply, sales, personnel, finances, materials, domestic and foreign trade. (Art. 3). Imports of technology, associated materials, cigarette manufacturing equipment, import and export of leaf tobacco, cigarettes and cigars all under National Tobacco Corp. (Art. 20), as are all activities within tobacco industry regarding use of foreign materials, compensation trade, co-production and joint ventures. (Art. 21). Planned production (Art. 8) and national standards of quality provided. (Art. 11). Retailers require permit (Art. 14) and all cigarettes and cigars require registered trademark. (Art. 16). Prices fixed by National Tobacco Corp. (Art. 15).

Economic Combination and Socialist Competition Provisional Regulations Concerning the Promotion of Economic Combination, adopted by State Council on July 1, 1980, designed to encourage certain types of economic combination. These Regulations, particularly applicable to state enterprises, encourage voluntary participation, In economic combinations. Combination of various enterprises not restricted by trades, territory or ownership, or relationship of subordination. (Prov. Regs. Promotion Economic Combination, Art. 1). Combination, of producers and processors of raw material promoted. (Art. 3). Combined enterprises may obtain raw materials, for example, directly from enterprises with which it combined, bypassing intermediate supply and marketing distribution departments. Combination agreement normally executed contract. Breach of contract settled through mediation between parties, under jurisdiction of department in charge, or if that fails, by arbitration by court.

On the other hand, Provisional Regulations Concerning the Development and Protection of Socialist Competition, adopted by State Council on Oct. 17, 1980, obviously designed to promote competition. To that end, these Regulations provide that enterprise must be granted greater power to make its own decisions (Art. 2) without interference of local authorities or departments in rights to which enterprise entitled by law, particularly regarding production, supply and marketing, personnel, finance and materials. Agreements and contracts between enterprises must be honored by both parties and protected by laws of state. Party breaching contract held legally and economically responsible for said breach. (Art. 2). Clause three states that in economic activities no monopoly of commodity allowed, other than those State, has specified to be handled exclusively by certain departments and units. While Regulations give priority to production for Plan targets, enterprises may market products in excess of Plan targets for those allocated for state use. (Art. 4). Departments not permitted to forbid sale of outside products in own locality or department, and regional monopoly should be restrained. (Art. 6). Compensation should be made for transfer or possession of important technological achievements to encourage technological innovation and inventions. (Art. 7). Thus, Chinese policy and law provide dual goals for both combination and competition. In licensing joint ventures, or other entities including foreign participants, Chinese at times offer to protect market for new joint venture, and in licensing other ventures with similar technology or products are sometimes careful to protect existing enterprises.

NOTARIES PUBLIC

Notaries public existed in China before "Cultural Revolution" and have been gradually restored to active role in legal system. . . . Notarial work encompasses not merely attestation of signature, but also evidences legality of document or act. It is based on application by party and evidence brought forth and examined. At times special forms and careful examination of law are required for notary seal to be properly affixed. Notarized documents have many applications, but not meant to be used to resolve legal disputes that should be settled in court of law, but rather to lessen need for, litigation.

On Apr. 13, 1982 State Council promulgated Temporary Regulations for Notaries Public, consisting of six chapters and 30 regulations. Regulations also apply to foreign citizens living in China (Art. 28), as well as applications by Chinese citizens to Chinese embassies and consulates abroad. (Art. 15). Notarial duties undertaken only upon application of party to evidence, according to law, legal act, fact or document. (Art. 1). Fourteen separate duties conferred upon notaries by Art. 4 of Regulations, including those of evidencing: Contract, . . . ; that signature or seal on document correct, and that copies, photocopies, portions or translations of document identical with original document. Also, notarial office can evidence that document reflecting compensation due on debt or for goods is undoubtedly authentic, and that it can be compulsorily enforced . . . .; Notarial office can also, upon application and in accordance with international custom, handle other notarial responsibilities.

Notaries public are Chinese citizens with rights to vote and having legal education or training (Art. 4), who should not act as notary to close relations. (Art. 17). Notaries must examine applicant's status and capacity and factual and legal basis of application and documents submitted. (Art. 18). They must maintain confidentiality of notarial work. (Art. 19). Where notary public has determined pursuant to Art. 4(i) that document reflecting debt, etc. can be enforced by compulsory process, if necessary, party can then apply to basic level court having jurisdiction for enforcement. (Art. 24).

PARTNERSHIP

See Contracts; Corporations; Joint Stock Companies; Civil Code.

Since domestic private enterprises exist, and cooperative ventures with foreign entities can be with individual foreign person(s), partnerships can exist. Small private partnerships in urban areas would have to be registered and licensed for certain purposes, such as establishing restaurant. Foreign ventures with local entities also must be licensed but are unlikely to be partnerships in that other than partnerships between two entities, viz., joint ventures, partnerships with individual Chinese persons will not be common in normal international transactions.

PATENTS

In 1984 China signed Paris Convention for the Protection of Industrial Property and in 1983 joined World Intellectual Property Organization.

On Mar. 12, 1984 Standing Committee of People's Congress promulgated China's Patent Law ("Law"), effective Apr. 1, 1985.

On Jan. 19, 1985 State Council promulgated Implementing Regulations of the Patent Law ("Regs").

Inventions, utility models and exterior designs may be patented. (Law. Art. 2).

Invention is defined as any new technical solution relating to product, process or improvement thereof (Regs 2); utility model is any new technical solution relating to shape, structure or combination for product fit for practical use (Regs 2); and design means any new design of shape, pattern, color or their combination of product, which creates aesthetic feeling and is fit for industrial application. (Regs 2).

No patent may be issued for: (1) scientific discoveries, rules and processes of mental activities, (2) methods of diagnosis or treatment of disease, (3) food, beverages and flavorings, (4) pharmaceutical products, (5) substances obtained by means of chemical process, animal and plant varieties, (6) substances derived by means of nuclear transformation. (Law Art. 25). However, patents can be granted for processes used in producing products stipulated in items (3), (4) and (5). (Law Art. 25).

Microbiological processes, products thereof and microorganisms will be patentable (Regs 25 and 26), and computer software while not clearly excluded by statute, is said by some officials to be covered by forthcoming legislation and if software is closely related to operation of hardware for which patent application is made then software may now be patentable.

Authority to examine patent applications and issue patents is held by Patent Office. (Arts. 20, 34). China has established Patent Office, which is reported to have staff of several hundred persons, including attorneys, examiners and administrators. This office has headquarters in Beijing and offices throughout China. Patent application by nonresident foreigners or foreign businesses without offices in China is to be made either to Patent Agency of China Council for the Promotion of International Affairs, Hong Kong based China Patent Agent (HK) Ltd. or Shanghai Patent Office. Foreign persons resident in China can make patent application through local patent offices where they have residence. Chinese have also established offices in New York and California to assist in registration in China.

Patent Office shall maintain Patent Register (Regs Art. 51) and publish Patent Gazette (Regs Art. 51) continuing abstract of invention or utility model, and information on all proceedings by Patent Office regarding application, e.g., approval, registration, request for examination, etc. China Patent Agent (HK) Ltd. will publish bilingual quarterly entitled China Patents and Trademarks.

Within six months of first application for utility model, or 12 months from first application for patent in foreign country, applicant should make application for registration in China. (Law Art. 19).

Said inventions and utility models must have characteristics of newness, originality and practicality. (Law Art. 22). Newness is defined as where prior to date of patent application no similar invention or practical new model has been published or otherwise made known either in China or in foreign countries. Originality of utility model means it must have substantial distinguishing features and represent improvement, while originality of invention is defined as it having substantial distinguishing features and representing marked improvement over prior inventions. Practicality is defined to mean utility model or invention can be made to produce effective results. Any exterior design to be patentable, must not be identical with or similar to any design published in foreign or Chinese publications or publicly used in China prior to date of application to be patentable. (Law Art. 23).

No other entity or individual may exploit patent after issuance of patent without authorization of patentee. Patent marking can be placed on patented products.

From third year of application for patent of invention where application has not yet been granted, applicant must commence paying maintenance fee, said fee payable annually is 100 yuan (100 renminbi). In addition, once patent has been issued annual fee shall be paid. For inventions said fee varies according to years, thus from first to third year it is 200 yuan, 300 yuan from fourth to sixth year, 600 yuan from seventh to ninth year, 1,200 yuan from tenth to 12th year and 2,500 yuan from 13th to 15th. Utility model patents annual fees start at 100 yuan per year and go to 200 yuan from fourth to fifth year and 300 yuan from sixth to eighth year. Exterior design patents start at 50 yuan, go to 100 yuan from fourth to fifth year and 200 yuan from sixth to eighth year.

Where two or more applicants file applications for patents for identical inventions, utility models or exterior designs, patent right shall be granted to applicant whose application was first filed, though if both file on same day inventors may negotiate mutual agreement as co-inventors. Exhibition of patentable product, six months prior to application at international exhibition sponsored or recognized by Chinese government, at prescribed academic or technical meeting or disclosure without consent of applicant, shall not result in loss of novelty. Receipt of priority shall be counted from date above events occurred for patent on invention or utility model. Where foreign applicant filed application in China within 12 months from first filing in foreign country (or within six months for exterior design) pursuant to reciprocity or treaty, priority date will be date application first was made in foreign country. Claim of priority by filing in foreign country requires applicant to within 15 months of said filing submit filing number in China.

Failure, without justified reason, after three years from grant of patent right, to exploit patent, can, pursuant to application by entity capable of exploiting product, result in order by Patent Office of compulsory license. Person receiving compulsory license cannot license others and shall not have exclusive right to exploitation of patent. Award of compulsory license can be appealed to courts within three months of notification of decision.

Patent Office, within 18 months of date of filing of patent for invention, or earlier at request of applicant, if after preliminary examination finds application in conformity with law, shall publish application. Substantive examination can be made within three years from date of filing, provided that request is made by applicant; failure of applicant without justified reason to make such request in three year period will result in application having been deemed withdrawn. Patent Office can on its own initiative proceed to examine any application of invention for substance. If, in application for patent for utility model or exterior design, Patent Office upon preliminary examination finds it in conformity with patent law, it shall immediately so announce.

Within three months of date of announcement, any person may file opposition to Patent Office, copy of which Office shall transmit to applicant. Applicant must respond in three months of receipt of opposition and if it is found to be justified by Patent Office then application shall be rejected. Within three months from receipt of notification applicant can appeal said rejection to Patent Application Board, and if still not satisfied with decision on patent application for invention, legal proceedings can be commenced. Decisions of Patent Application Board as to utility models or exterior designs are final. Where no opposition is filed or where after examination opposition is found unjustified, patent shall be granted. Applications must be submitted in duplicate. Invention and utility model applications require abstract on main points, description and claims and title, name of inventor, name and address of applicant and description in manner sufficiently clear to permit person skilled in relevant technology to carry it out. Where necessary, drawings should be provided. Applications for exterior design require drawings or photographs of design; statement as to class to which product belongs shall also be included. Relevant materials about priority of earlier applications should be included.

Normally as to invention or utility model following should be provided: Title, technical field, description of relevant prior art, task it is to perform, its merits compared to prior art, description in drawings, best mode for carrying it out, claims in clear and precise manner explaining protection sought, dependent or independent nature of claim, if involving microbiological process or product thereof, deposit sample shall be provided.

Drawings or photographs that must be submitted shall be no longer than 19 cm by 27 cm and no smaller than 3 cm by 5 cm. Where necessary Patent Office may require application for patent design to submit sample or model of product incorporating design, and if design seeks protection of colors drawing or photograph in color and black and white shall be submitted.

Inventor or creator may apply for Patent as individual or entity or if discovered in course of duty or during work entrusted to said person by entity for whom he works, then entity may make application. Right to apply for patent can be assigned, pursuant to written contract, though assignment of right to apply by Chinese entity or individual to foreigner must be approved by relevant Chinese government authorities.

Patent Office is able to issue: (1) Exclusive patents to foreign firms for 15 years from application (Law Art. 45); (2) five-year renewable industrial design, patents and five-year renewable utility model patents (Law Art. 45). Latter two patents can be extended for three to five-year periods.

Adjudication of Patent Disputes Measures of Patent Administrative Authorities on Adjudicating Patent Disputes have been implemented effective as of Dec. 4, 1989. Patent administrative authorities shall mediate and adjudicate following patent disputes: (1) patent infringement; (2) license fees for use of invention or creation between time of publication of patent application for invention or public announcement of patent application for utility model or design and time when patent is granted; (3) right to apply for patent and disputes over ownership of patent; and (4) other patent disputes, which may be mediated or dispose of by patent administrative authorities. (Art. 5). Disputes over right to apply for patent and disputes over ownership of patents shall be mediated and adjudicated by patent administrative authorities where respondents are located. (Art. 7). If any party to dispute has instituted proceedings in court, patent administrative authorities shall not accept petitions for mediation and adjudication. (Art. 12[4]). In mediating and adjudicating patent disputes, patent administrative authorities shall abide by principle that matter once-decided shall not be subject to readjudication. (Art. 4). If party is not satisfied with decision of patent administrative authorities, then institution of proceedings in court can be commenced within three months after receipt of such decision. Where no proceedings have been instituted upon expiry of this time limit, decision shall become effective immediately. (Art. 24).

See Civil Code.

PRINCIPAL AND AGENT

See Civil Code.

Representation by agent is generally permitted and some standard form Chinese contracts are drafted with agent as executing entity. Agent may not be bound if he clearly is not principal to contract. Power of attorney must be in writing and may have to be notarized at times before Chinese entity like embassy or consulate.

Power of Attorney To entrust another to represent one in litigation, one must present written power of attorney to court, containing signature or seal of individual entrusted. Power of attorney must specify matter and scope and time limit of such authority. Specific authority required for attorney in fact to conciliate, counterclaim, admit, abandon litigation or alter its object. (Civ. Pro. Code, Art. 51). Power of attorney to represent citizens of China living out of China must be attested to by Chinese embassy or consulate in that country or, if none, by patriotic overseas Chinese organization. (Civ. Pro. Code, Art. 51). Parties required to inform court in writing of any alterations or termination in power of attorney and through court inform other parties. (Civ. Pro. Code, Art. 52). Divorce cases require presence of parties even though power of attorney issued, unless special circumstances. (Civ. Pro. Code, Art. 54). Foreign nationals or stateless persons not residing in China who mail Chinese attorneys powers of attorney must have said power of attorney documented by notary public in their country and attestation by local Chinese embassy or consulate. (Civ. Pro. Code, Art. 191).

PRIVATE ENTERPRISE

Provisional Regulations were promulgated on June 25, 1988, by State Council, effective as of July 1, 1988, where "private enterprise" refers to privately funded economic entity which employs at least eight persons. (Art. 2). Private enterprise may be (1) sole investment enterprise; (2) partnership enterprise; or (3) limited liability company. (Art. 6). Sole investment enterprise is funded and managed by one person; said owner assumes unlimited liability for obligations of enterprise. (Art. 7). Partnership enterprise is jointly funded and managed by two or more persons who share its profits and losses, based on written agreement. Partners share unlimited liability for obligations of enterprise. (Art. 8). Limited liability company is one in which investor is only liable for company only up to amount of his investment; said company is liable only up to amount of its total assets. (Art. 9).

Following persons may apply to form a private enterprise: Villagers; persons awaiting employment in urban areas; operators of individual industrial and commercial ventures; persons who have resigned or were dismissed from previous posts; retired cadres, retired workers and other persons authorized under State laws, regulations and policies. (Art. 11).

Private enterprise may engage in production and business operations, as permitted by State laws, statutory regulations and policies, in fields such as industry, construction, transportation, commerce, catering, public service, repair and scientific and technological consultancy. Private enterprise may not engage in production and business operations related to war industry or finance and may not produce, market, or purchase products proscribed in China. (Art. 12).

Investors in private enterprise must hold legal title to its property and said property may be inherited according to law. (Art. 20). Private enterprise must open account with bank or other financial institution in compliance with State regulations and may apply for loan if it can prove its ability to repay said loan.

Registration Business operations of private enterprise may commence only after application for registration is approved by local Administration of Commerce and Industry and business license is procured. (Art. 15). Private enterprise which successfully registers as legal person must additionally register commencement of its operations and any amendments or cancellation of registration, according to Administrative Regulations governing Registration of Corporations. (Art. 19).

SALES

See Statistics, Standards and Quality Control; Contracts.

Generally, no particular form is required for purchase of personal property, but most of Chinese corporations engaged in international sales have standard form purchase and sales agreements that conform to standard international practice including provisions for price, quantity, method of payment, date of shipment, means of shipment, etc. Sales of buildings require notarial stamps and registration with local authorities, as well as payment of taxes.

China has ratified United Nations Convention on Contracts for the International Sale of Goods ("Sales Convention") which is now in force and effect as of 1 Jan. 1988. China had two reservations to "Sales Convention," namely Art. 1(b), which permits application of treaty beyond Contracting States via operation of law; and pursuant to Art. 96 have reserved provisions of Arts. 11, 29 or Part II that give effect to sales contracts other than in writing.

Sales Convention also ratified by US, applies to sale of goods between, parties whose places of business are in different States, when States are Contracting States. (Art. 11[a]). Convention does not apply to sales for personal, family or household use, auction, by authority of law, securities, negotiable instruments, ships, vessels or aircraft, or to electricity (Art. 2), nor to processing contracts. (Art. 3). Parties to contract can exclude application of Sales Convention to contract or vary terms of any of its provisions by contract. (Art. 6).

Offer under Sales Convention is good if party making it intended to be bound, and if it indicates goods and makes provision for determining quantity and price or specifies them (Art. 14); it is effective when reaching offeree (Art. 14); acceptance is statement or conduct by offeree indicating acceptance, silence is not sufficient (Art. 18).

Sales Convention provides for specific performance, remedies for delivery of nonconforming goods (e.g., repair), if there is fundamental breach buyer can void contract, and of course sue for damages. (Arts. 4.5-5.2). Damages for breach of contract are measured as sum equal to foreseeable loss, including loss of profit suffered by party damaged as result of breach. (Art. 14). If contract has been voided, party claiming damages can claim difference between contract price and cost of substitute goods it purchased. (Art. 75). Party must attempt to mitigate its losses. (Art. 22).

State Council promulgated Provisional Regulations for the Administration of Commodity Prices (July 7, 1982), which provide regulations for administration for said prices under State Council policies and plans. State Council has authority additionally to establish prices on important industrial and agricultural commodities, transportation, and on noncommodity fees. (Art. 4). Relatively important commodities and fees are under jurisdiction of local government bureau in charge of prices and other commodities and fees are to be established by industrial and commercial enterprises within ambit of national policy and regulations. (Art. 4).

Unless there are other regulations to contrary, administration of imported and exported commodities as well as those commodities of joint venture enterprises with foreign firms, enterprises with foreign investment, and those sold to foreigners, overseas Chinese and Hong Kong and Macao compatriots are all governed by these regulations. (Art. 26). Regulations combine principles of planned economy and those of market economy, taking into account market forces. (Art. 3). There are three forms of price determination, namely, national, which is principal form and within scope of national regulations, prices established by rural markets and by enterprises. (Art. 3).

National Price Bureau proposes general price policy, as well as specific price policies, regulations and plans for approval by State Council. (Art. 9). Provincial level price departments carry out national plans and enforce regulations and formulate and enforce price standards within their jurisdiction. (Art. 10). Prices are differentiated on basis of wholesale, retail, region, standards, quality, season, purchase, sales, allocated goods, and supplies for principal commodities. (Art. 10[3]).

Industrial and commercial enterprises can establish prices on defective goods, within limits of regulations establishing gross profits on foodstuff enterprises, where said foodstuffs have no governmentally fixed, unified price, establish prices for foodstuffs; according to type of commodity and range of fluctuation, establish basic prices for commodities whose prices fluctuate; pursuant to administrative procedures approved by State Council, establish negotiated prices for agricultural products and by-products purchased and, sold on negotiated basis;

based on restrictions in regulations of relevant commodity pricing organizations, establish trial sales prices for new products; establish pursuant to regulations, inter-enterprise prices on specialized products made by joint efforts; establish prices on products where there are no prices fixed by Government, as well as establish charges for noncommodity and handicraft items produced by joint efforts; and pursuant to regulations as to type and pricing principles, negotiate prices on small, light industrial, textile and handcrafted industrial products. (Art. 14).

Prices on heavy industrial products already established by government cannot be negotiated, but where necessary temporary prices can be fixed pursuant to regulations. (Art. 28).

In many cases prices of goods on both fixed commodity price market and free market fluctuate within certain price ranges.

Trial Provisions on Fixing Prices of Machinery Products According to Their Qualities and Grades, issued by State Economic Commission, Price Bureau and Ministry of Machinery Industry, effective Jan. 1984. These Trial Provisions permit state enterprises manufacturing general machinery products recognized as top quality by State Economic Commission to set prices for said products at 20% higher than state price lists. In general, quality products can be sold at prices from 8% to 12% higher than state list prices, and products with energy-saving attributes at prices 15% higher. Prices of products technically backward to be gradually lowered. This considered first step in modification of rigid price controls for state enterprises.

SEALS

Seals in China, having long history, are normal means of execution of contracts, though foreign trade contracts are at times not sealed, but signed by responsible parties.

In 1986 memorandum was issued by Supreme Court of China entitled "Regarding Concepts of Several Problems of Operation of Economic Contracts." While a discussion document, this memorandum has influenced practice in courts, and it in general requires that seal of organization be placed on economic contracts. In addition as noted below certain statutes specially provide that seal is required.

General Principles of Civil Law provide that, pursuant to law or articles of association of legal person, responsible individual who acts on behalf of said person is its legal representative. Only legal representatives can execute contracts. Clearly if not legal representative or not acting with authority on behalf of said representative, signature would normally not be effective to execute contract. Normally document appointing legal representative is in writing.

There are provincial regulations such as Regulations of Guangdong People's Government Regarding the Execution of Economic Contracts, which provide for certificate of legal representative which must contain organization's seal or certificate of entrustment of authority of legal person, latter of which also normally requires seal of organization. At time of signing economic contract these documents, in original, must be exchanged between parties, else prior to actual commencement of performance, contract is not enforceable. If contract has been partially performed, regulations do not specify what will occur if there is dispute and document has yet to be exchanged. Different judges appear to have different opinions, e.g., in San Shui County in county court, Guangdong Province—judges during trial disagreed as to need for these documents after contract was partly performed and dispute arose.

Regulations of Contracts for Lending of Money, Art. 5 (promulgated by State Council and effective as of 1 Apr. 1985) provides loan contracts must be signed by legal representatives of both parties or by legal person who was entrusted to sign contract. Organization seal must be placed on contract.

Several other regulations provide for similar requirements such as early Trial Regulations on Industrial and Mining Product Contracts, 1981, which states that legal representative, e.g., factory head, manager or important responsible production chief should sign contract, and if legal representative of organization must entrust signing of contract to another person, then said person should present other party with certificate of authority given to him.

Regulations for Contracts for Purchase of Industrial and Mine Products 1984, state that in execution of these contracts, legal representative must sign (by using his personal seal) and seal of organization must be placed on contract for it to have legal effect.

Regulations of Contracts for Construction, Survey and Design provides that responsible persons of parties must sign contract and official seal of organizations be placed on contract for it to be executed.

Similarly, Regulation of Contracts for Property Insurance provides for placing of seal by insurer for execution to be effective in certain contracts.

Thus in summary, placing of seal, and signature of organization's legal representative are required by several statutes and when not specified are frequently required by custom and practice, as legally effective means of executing contract. While certain contracts may be executed by signature of organization's legal representative or parties, this generally requires document entrusting this authority which itself will contain organization seal.

SEQUESTRATION

Court, on its own initiative or on request of party, may take measures to assure availability of property of defendant to satisfy potential judgment.

STATISTICS, STANDARDS AND QUALITY CONTROL

See Sales.

Effective Jan. 1, 1984, new law on statistics implemented whereby statistical departments to be set up at and above county level, and statistical officials to be employed at lower levels under State Statistical Bureau. All government organizations, mass organizations, enterprises, self-employed individuals, foreign firms in China and joint ventures must report designated statistics to departments concerned. Falsification, fabrication and misrepresentation not permitted.

Provisional Regulations for Total Quality Control in Industrial Enterprises promulgated by State Economic Commission on Mar. 18, 1980, which provided in principle that high prices to be paid for high quality, low prices for low quality (Art. 27), providing also rewards for quality (Art. 28) and cessation of enterprises whose products are consistently inferior, and reduction in salaries of leading cadres and suspension bonuses for workers producing inferior goods . (Art. 30).

On July 31, 1979 State Council promulgated Regulations on Standardization Control, requiring that technical standards be established and implemented for all industrial goods in regular production, major farm products, engineering projects, environmental protection, safety, sanitation and other areas where technical requirements should be unified. (Art. 2). Internationally accepted standards and advanced foreign standards should be studied as far as possible. (Art. 7). Export products and engineering projects undertaken in foreign countries by Chinese organizations to have standards geared to needs of foreign markets. (Art. 8). Three standards provided: State, ministry and enterprise (Art. 11), lower standards not to contravene higher and ministry standards to be replaced by specialized standards. (Art. 11). Standards to be drafted by departments in charge under State Council, e.g., State Administration of Standards (for industrial and agricultural products), State Capital Construction Commission (for engineering projects and environmental protection) and Ministry of Public Health. (Art. 13). Once standards endorsed and promulgated, they become technical decrees which must be strictly observed by all and are not to be altered without authorization. (Art. 18). Where violation causes serious accidents, economic sanctions and court action can be undertaken. (Art. 18). Award system provided and higher price allowed for better quality products. (Art. 29).

Several implementing regulations promulgated; e.g., State Bureau of Standardization and Metrology, on Nov. 16, 1981, promulgated Procedures for the Administration of Standardization of Industrial Enterprises (Provisional Implementation), and on Mar. 14, 1981 State Bureau of Standardization, State Economic Commission and State Commission of Machine Building promulgated Procedures for the Examination and Administration of Standardization of New Mechanical Electrical Products. On Mar. 17, 1982 Provisional Procedures for the Administration of the Adoption of International Standards promulgated, providing that ". . . vigorous adoption of international standards or advanced foreign standards is an important technical and economic policy" of China. (Art. 2). Reference made to standards of International Standard Organization (ISO) and International Electrotechnical Commission (IEC). (Art. 3). Guiding Rule three of ISO and Guiding Rule 21 of IEC should be conformed to in adopting standards. (Art. 13). Annotations of Provisional Procedures recognize various American standards such as those of American Society of Testing Material (ASTM), American Petroleum Institution (API), Electronics Industry Association (EIA), US Military Standards (MIL), American Underwriters Laboratory Safety Standards (UL), as well as various European standards, e.g., Lloyd's Ship Classifications, British Standards (BS), standards provided by Comite Europeen de Normalization (CEN), etc.

TRADEMARKS

Regulations Governing Trademarks (Trademark Regulations) were originally promulgated by State Council on Apr. 10, 1963 and Implementing Rules under Regulations Governing Trademarks were promulgated by Central Administration Bureau of Commerce and Industry on Apr. 25, 1963, which regulations effective until Mar. 1, 1983 and replaced by new regulations discussed below.

Under old regulations, China Council for Promotion of International Trade (CCPIT) had Trademark Registration Agency which handled trademark applications on behalf of foreign applicants. Trademark Department within General Administration of Commerce and Industry acted on all trademark applications and issued rejections and certificates of registration. Trademark registrations were valid for period of ten years from date of registration and could be renewed upon application, for ten year periods. Infringement actions could be brought by complaint to administration agencies or courts. Penalties included injunctive relief, monetary penalty, compensation for losses and confiscation of infringer's goods.

Under old regulations, right to exclusive use of trademark was acquired by registration, not mere usage. Foreigners could apply for trademark registration if applicant's country also accepts Chinese applications for trademarks, as does US, or if agreement on reciprocal registration of trademarks has been concluded, which US and China have done, as have most western European countries, Thailand, Japan, Romania, Hungary, East Germany, Czechoslovakia and Argentina.

Local organizations of Administration of Commerce and Industry promulgated directives requiring publication of trademarks. For example, in Guangzhou trademark directive was issued by city Administration of Commerce and Industry requiring that all approved registered trademarks in Guangzhou be published, with registration number, in Guangzhou Daily.

On Aug. 23, 1982 new Trademark Law promulgated by Standing Committee of People's Congress, which regulations took effect Mar. 1, 1983, superseding prior 1963 legislation. (Art. 43). Trademarks registered under prior law will remain in effect. (Art. 43). Trademark Bureau of State Council's Administration of Commerce and Industry department will supervise work of trademark registration for entire nation. (Art. 2). On Mar. 10, 1983 State Council, pursuant to Trademark Law, Art. 42, promulgated Implementing Regulations under Trademark Law (Implementing Regs.) effective as of date of promulgation. (Implementing Regs. Art. 34).

Trademarks approved for registration by Trademark Bureau are registered trademarks; registrant enjoys benefits of exclusive use and legal protection. (Art. 3). Trademark users responsible for quality of commodities bearing their trademarks, and relevant departments of Administration of Commerce and Industry must supervise quality of said commodities through trademark control, to prevent acts that deceive consumers. (Art. 6). Foreign persons must employ this Trademark Law pursuant to treaties between their nation and China, or international conventions of which both nations signatory, or in accordance with principal of reciprocity. (Art. 9). Foreigners, to entrust all trademark applications to CCPIT (Implementing Regs. Art. 29), said applications to include specific power of attorney (Implementing Regs. Art. 30), which should be notarized (Implementing Regs. Art. 31), and Chinese language should be used in applications. (Implementing Regs. Art. 31). Trademark's duly registered valid for ten years from said approval. (Art. 23). Six months prior to termination of validity of said trademark, application must be made for extension of registration which, if approved, will be valid for ten years. (Art. 24).

Regulations provide that words and designs, or their form, must have manifest characteristics easy to distinguish. (Art. 7). Symbol of registration, or words "registered trademark" should accompany registered trademark. (Art. 7). Trademarks should not bear certain words or symbols, such as common symbol or name of commodity in question (Art. 8[5]); those that directly indicate quality, important raw material, functions, uses, weight, quantity or other characteristics of commodity (Art. 8[6]); those that contain exaggerated claims and are of deceptive nature (Art. .8[7]); those that are same as or similar to state names, flags, emblems, military flags or medals of China or other nations (Art. 8[1], [2]) or those same as or similar to banners, emblems or names of international organizations (Art. 8 [3]), those of discriminatory nature (Art. 8[7]), or those that harm socialist morality or have other bad influence. (Art. 8[9]). Substantial enforcing authority granted to relevant administrative authority for industry and commerce regarding quality of goods under trademark (Implementing Regs. Arts. 19, 20, 21, 22, 23) and regarding infringement. (Implementing Regs. 24, 26).

On Jan. 3, 1988 State Administration of Industry and Commerce promulgated new Implementing Regulations which replaced those promulgated on Mar. 10, 1983. Pursuant thereto foreign persons or foreign enterprises shall use Chinese language applications for registration of trademarks or other trademark related matters, and shall submit document of entrustment which is to include specific authority and nationality of entrustor. (Implementing Regs. Art. 14). Foreign persons or enterprises shall entrust all trademark application and other trademark matters to organizations specified by State Administration of Industry and Commerce. (Implementing Regs. Art. 3).

TRADE ZONES

See Contracts; Corporations.

Standing Committee of National People's Congress, on Aug. 26, 1980 approved Regulations on Special Economic Zones in Guangdong Province, (Regulations on SEZ's of Guangdong) governing Guangdong and three special economic zones in Shenzhen, Zhuhai and Shantou (Swatow). Within Shenzhen, Shekou Industrial Zone has been established. Hainan Island has been granted some of advantages of special economic zone, e.g., two year tax holidays pursuant to application and thereafter income taxes at same rates as those prevailing in SEZ's.

Fujian Province has been granted special economic status, as has Xiamen City within province. Xiamen SEZ, under jurisdiction of Administrative Commission of Xiamen SEZ of Fujian Province, has designated 2.5 sq. klmtrs. in region of Huli for development of export processing zone. This zone, immediately adjacent to Dongdu wharf, contains factory buildings for investors to rent or purchase, as well as office buildings which are being developed. Subsequently entire city was made SEZ Recently, Xiamen airport opened for traffic.

Standing committee of 6th Fujian Provincial Congress on July 14, 1984 approved several statutes relating to Xiamen SEZ which regulations were promulgated, on Feb. 25, 1985 including:

Regulations on Registration of Enterprises in Xiamen Special Economic Zone Normal operations of foreign resident office requires registration (Art. 5) with Xiamen City Administration for Commerce and Industry. (Art. 2). Prior to registration approval of foreign entities application must be received from Xiamen City Government or its authorized department. (Art. 3[1]). Foreign enterprises, resident offices and the like are considered to have been established only after their business license or registration certificate has been issued (Art. 6), only then can local bank account be opened. (Art. 7). Resident certificates are renewable annually. (Art. 9).

Regulations on the Use of Land in Xiamen SEZ promulgated on Feb. 24, 1985. Enterprise when in need of land must make application to Xiamen Urban and Rural Construction Commission (Art. 4), and within nine months of issuance of land use certificate enterprise must submit blueprints of overall design and construction plan, and within one year of said issuance commence construction (Art. 5) and complete construction on schedule, though extensions of time may be applied for. (Art. 5).

Beijing, Shanghai, and Tianjin are also to be leaders in trade decentralization. Many provinces and localities have been given authority to independently approve commercial projects with foreign entities up to maximum amount of investment without need to obtain central government, or even provincial approval where locality is involved of said projects. Recently, new regulations with particular regard to Shenzhen have been approved by central government to facilitate ease of entry and exit by foreign visitors, to simplify customs and to create almost open border with Hong Kong.

Special Administrative Organization Guandong Provincial Administration of Special Economic Zones was established to exercise unified management over said zones. (Regulations on SEZ's of Guangdong, Art. 3). Guangdong Provincial Administration can issue registration licenses and land use permission for approved projects of foreign investors. (Regulations on SEZ's of Guangdong, Art. 7). Normally these areas are regarded as export oriented. (Regulations on SEZ's in Guangdong, Art. 9). Foreign investors are permitted to operate their enterprises independently in Special Economic Zones (Art. 10) and employ foreign personnel for technical and administrative work. (Art. 10).

Tax Relief Means of production such as machinery, spare parts and raw materials, vehicles and other means of production which are imported from abroad are exempt from import duties. (Art. 13). Rate of income tax levied on enterprises in special zone is to be 15%. (Art. 14). Further preferential tax treatment is to be accorded enterprises established within two years of promulgation of these regulations with investment of US $5,000,000 or more and enterprises involving high technology or having relatively long cycle of capital turnover. (Art. 14).

Remittance of Profits After taxes, profits and salaries of foreigners and overseas Chinese of enterprises in zone can be remitted out of China. (Art. 15). Investors who reinvest profits in special zone for five years or longer can apply for exemption from income tax on such reinvestment. (Art. 16).

Preferential prices will be offered enterprises in special economic zone that use Chinese machinery, raw materials and other goods. (Art. 17).

Labor Service Companies are established in special economic zones and enterprises can test Chinese personnel before hiring them. (Art. 19). Said employees can be dismissed, pursuant to terms of labor contract, if necessary, since enterprises are to be managed according to their business requirements. (Art. 20).

State Council approved establishment of Huli Special Economic Zone in May, 1980. Huli, which is within Xiamen municipality, has access to harbor facilities of Xiamen, including prospective container berth. It is anticipated that materials imported into Huli Special Economic Zone for construction and production will be exempt from duty. Three to five year tax holiday will be granted to enterprises located in zone. All utilities in Huli zone to factory door will be without cost. Foreign firms, in factories already constructed for them, will have full control of factories, subject only to Chinese law, which factories may be 100% owned, except for land and buildings which are to be leased, by foreign companies. Leases will be offered up to 30 years.

Entry and Exit Regulations Provisional Entry and Exit Regulations of Guangdong SEZ's adopted at Fifth Guangdong Provincial Congress, 13th Session, Nov. 7, 1981. Foreigners, overseas Chinese, Hong Kong, Macao and Taiwan compatriots who enter SEZ's via country's open ports, or ports designated for SEZ, are subject to these regulations and subject to inspection on entering and leaving. (Art. 2). Those entering from Hong Kong or Macao who are foreign nationals or overseas Chinese should use their passports to obtain visas in Hong Kong or Macao before entering border check points. Foreign nationals and overseas Chinese who need to travel regularly to and from SEZ, or who have set up factories there, work or live there or purchased home there may apply for multiple exit-entry visas.

Economic Laws Shenzhen approved regulations on contracts, etc. relating to foreign matters.

Fourteen Coastal Cities, Hainan and Four SEZs Fourteen cities of Dalian, Qinghuangdao, Tianjin, Yantai, Qingdao, Lianyungang, Nantong, Shanghai, Ningbo, Wenzhou, Fuzhou, Guangzhou, Zhanjiang and Beihai, have been declared cities open to foreign trade with flexible economic policies similar to special economic zones.

Legislation for Development Zones has been promulgated, first by Guangzhou City government on Apr. 9, 1985.

Interim Regulations on the Guangzhou Economic and Technological Development Zone provide development zone is comparatively independent, located in east Huangpu district, and is designed to establish productive enterprises, implement policy of introducing foreign investment together with domestic enterprises, introducing advanced scientific technology and the like. (Art. 2). Domestic Chinese entities outside zone are also encouraged to invest in zone. (Art. 4).

Administrative Committee of Guangzhou Economic and Technological Development Zone has been established to manage zone. (Art. 8). It has authority to formulate development plans, approve investment projects, approve income and consolidated industrial and commercial tax reductions, manage land in zones, supervise enterprises, coordinate with Guangzhou City government, protect legitimate rights and interests of workers, establish educational, cultural, health and public welfare functions, promulgate administrative management rules, and represent Guangzhou city government in foreign matters regarding zone. (Art. 9).

Special income tax treatment is specified for enterprises in zone . . . . Registration is required of enterprises in zone. (Art. 23).

Interim Regulations of the Guangzhou Economic and Technical Zone concerning introduction of technology were promulgated on Apr. 9, 1985.

These rules require technology introduced by foreign entities to be advanced, applicable and having tangible economic efficiency. (Art. 5). Advanced is defined to be more advanced than same technology in China, being used or developed in industrially developed countries, or that it is of benefit domestically so as to raise domestic industry or product to world levels. (Art. 5). Technology is defined to include patented, patent pending, know-how and software. (Art. 6).

There are in addition Tentative Procedures for Land Management in the Guangzhou Economic and Technological Zone, promulgated Apr. 9, 1985 that classify land by use and provide standard land use fees ranging from one yuan to 12 yuan per square meter per month. Land use fees for industrial use, or for communications and transportation industry is calculated at two yuan per square meter per year.

Special Administrative Zone Pursuant to treaty with Great Britain, Chinese government has agreed that commencing from 1997 when Crown Colony of Hong Kong will revert to full Chinese jurisdiction, Hong Kong will become special administrative zone, retaining most facets of its present legal and economic structure. Basic Law has been drafted for Hong Kong, which is equivalent of constitution, under Chinese constitution. There is presently negotiation over enactment of legislation to establish Supreme Court of Hong Kong to hear highest appeals from Hong Kong lower courts.

In establishing commission to consult on policy for new Hong Kong airport at Lantou Island, Hong Kong government has included representatives from China on commission and guaranteed to leave certain quantum of reserves in Hong Kong government coffers on turnover of Hong Kong to China in 1997.

Shanghai's Pudong Special development zones in Shanghai, particularly in Pudong, have been given substantial authority and substantial infrastructure funds to develop this location for foreign investment. Central government has put great emphasis on increasing foreign investment in Shanghai. Regulations to Reduce or Eliminate Enterprise Income Tax and Industrial and Commercial Tax to Encourage Foreign Investment in Shanghai's New Pudong District were promulgated in 1990. Enterprise income tax of 15% was highest level subject to application accepted to eliminate said taxes on first tow years of profit. (Art. 2)/ Companies with foreign investment exporting more than 70% of their productions or having been certified as having modern technology can reduce tax to 10% of profits. (Art. 3)./ There are numerous other regulations which encourage investment.

Hainan Province Hainan, new province, has been given very substantial authority and has promulgated numerous regulations to encourage foreign investment.

Financial Institutions

China's economic reform is now well into its second decade; however, certain key elements necessary for the completion of a modern economic structure have yet to become firmly established. In the financial sector, banks and financial markets remain plagued by lack of expertise, government mismanagement, corruption, and unclear legal status. While progressive reformers have generally won out over conservative opponents in pressing ahead with modernization, heated debates over just how far reforms should be allowed to deviate from the socialist path continue. Nowhere is this controversy more apparent than in the area of financial liberalization and reform.

The majority of China's leaders are convinced that the nation must restructure itself as a modern economy, changing the traditional centrally planned economic system and its hierarchical command structure at least enough to enable China to function in the modern world. Changes in the financial system—both those already accomplished, which are numerous and substantial, and those that are pending—are designed to facilitate smooth and effective interactions with the rest of the world. They are also designed to induce the populace to inject a high percentage of their savings into a revamped financial system for use in funding growth. An estimated RMB 1.4 trillion (about US$160 billion) in savings currently exists in private hands outside the formal system.

Foreigners interested in operating in China need to understand the country's present financial system in order to do business there. However, there is no comprehensive national financial legislation, and the system is confusing and often contradictory, having evolved largely through local responses to highly specific circumstances. Financial matters are governed through more than 800 decrees and provisional regulations promulgated since 1978 alone. The once-monolithic financial edifice, formerly a tool of the central state government, has become increasingly decentralized as it struggles to become modern. Provinces have enjoyed a great deal of effective autonomy from the central government during the reform period. Local offices of national entities, such as banks and agencies, have tended to identify with the local authorities and have gone their own way, often in open disregard of instructions from the head office. And rules and regulations on foreign financial activities have tended to vary from place to place, often rather widely.

The old center-periphery tensions evident in China from its beginnings are resurfacing with a vengeance in the financial sector. The central government wants to allow the development of independent units but finds it difficult to relinquish the centralized controls that help it manage the total system. Ironically, the pragmatic reformers are currently in the forefront of attempts to recentralize the financial system in hopes of overcoming the anarchy that local option financial rules have produced and in order to craft a more rational structure before again entrusting the system to the locals.

In the very near future, reformers will face the crucial challenge of restructuring banks and financial markets to suit the needs of an economy that increasingly resembles the capitalist model. If banking and financial reform is successful, China's prospects for continued advances will receive a critical boost. If it is not, many analysts believe the country will fall into a situation where chronic inflation and widespread unemployment lead to general economic and social chaos.

The present discussion focuses on the current state of China's financial institutions and markets, their influence on foreign businesses and joint ventures, and the likely direction of developments during the next few years. But the financial system, like everything else in China, is in flux, with radical changes occurring with unsettling frequency. Those interested in doing business in China should expect to deal with change and a high degree of uncertainty.

THE BANKING SYSTEM

China's banking system consists of the People's Bank of China (PBOC); specialized banks including the Bank of China (BOC), the People's Construction Bank of China (PCBC), the Agricultural Bank of China (ABC), and the Industrial and Commercial Bank of China (ICBC); local credit cooperatives; and various other quasi-official, unofficial, and illicit private financial institutions. Under the Chinese banking law reform of 1978 the entire banking system was removed from the control of the Ministry of Finance and given more autonomy. The PBOC became responsible for the banking system, and its president gained ministerial rank, reporting directly to the State Council, the country's highest administrative body. However, the BOC subsequently gained a status almost coequal with the PBOC, being allowed to report directly to the State Council as well. Officially the PBOC retains supervisory authority over all banking activity, including the BOC, and bureaucratic turf battles between the two major banking entities have resulted. The 1978 reform also created the climate for the establishment or reestablishment of specialized banks designed to serve specific sectors, again partially as arms of state policy and partially as profit-making enterprises, leading to greater competition, which is welcome, and greater confusion, which is not.

In addition to those institutions established with explicit government approval, a host of unapproved yet quasi-official financial institutions have sprung up in recent years to function as the investment arms of various government ministries, agencies, local governments, and state-owned enterprises, which use them to facilitate their own financial operations and often to speculate in developing financial markets in hopes of generating additional funds. Some private financial institutions have also appeared, primarily in Shanghai and the Special Economic Zones (SEZs) in the south.

Foreign-owned and joint-venture banks have again been allowed to operate in China since the economic reforms began in the late 1970s. The number of foreign bank branches and representative offices has grown dramatically since the late 1980s. Their allowable activities are currently somewhat limited, but the scope of their authorized business, geographic as well as functional, is expected to expand as China's economy becomes more fully integrated with that of the rest of the world.

The People's Bank of China

The People's Bank of China (PBOC) was established by the Chinese Communist Party (CCP) in 1948 to serve as the country's central bank. Within the context of a planned economy, the PBOC functioned as the rubber-stamp organization charged with dol-

ing out the funds allocated to enterprises by the government's State Planning Commission (SPC). Because the government controlled fiscal appropriations, the PBOC's role in financial policy matters was severely limited, as were its operational activities.

Loans extended to businesses during the early years of Communist rule represented grants of working capital to operate the enterprise—capital for plant and equipment came from the industrial bureaus—and all profits generated were expected to be handed over to the government, not as interest on or as amortization of the so-called loan, but as part of the state ownership system. Such permanent loans were never paid off, called, or otherwise removed from the books, and the PBOC's role was primarily that of a cashier.

During the 1980s the government resolved to limit its intervention in the economic sphere and particularly in the financial sector. It allowed the PBOC greater autonomy to actually manage the financial system. All budgetary appropriations were henceforth advanced by banks in the form of interest-bearing and repayable loans. As a result of this key reform, banks took on added importance in the economy, and the PBOC assumed even greater authority in setting interest rates and determining the amount of lending by the specialized banks.

In practice, thousands of state-owned companies chronically operate in the red and have been unable to service, much less repay, these loans. Perhaps 40 percent of all loans simply cannot be repaid, and an estimated 70 percent of all enterprises, including those that report profits, have hidden losses that sap their ability to service their debt and put them in need of additional support. This situation continues to worsen, creating a major policy problem with more than financial implications: If the banks call the loans and force the insolvent enterprises into bankruptcy, they can move toward rationalizing and modernizing the financial and economic system. To do so, however, will result in massive unemployment, social dislocation, and social unrest, a prospect that the government has been unable to face to date, as it continues to funnel available funds into the inefficient state sector in hopes of buying labor peace.

In 1986 the State Council enacted the Provisional Regulations of the PRC on the Control of Banks. This law reaffirmed the PBOC's role as the central bank and defined the duties of the bank in relation to the government. The PBOC decreased its role as a direct lender with the ICBC taking over responsibility for actual lending operations that previously had been administered by the PBOC. The PBOC's primary duties under the provisional regulations shifted from micro-level operational to macro-level operational and policy concerns. These include researching and proposing laws and guidelines governing financial activities; implementing and administering such laws following State Council approval; regulating issuance and circulation of currency and maintaining currency stability; managing interest rates on deposits and loans; managing exchange rates between the domestic renminbi (RMB) and foreign currencies; and controlling credit extended to state enterprises. Also among the PBOC's concerns are managing foreign exchange and gold reserves; regulating the establishment, merger, and dismantling of banks and financial institutions; auditing the operations of banks and financial institutions; managing the State Treasury and issuing government bonds; regulating financial and capital markets; and engaging in international financial operations on behalf of the government. In a bureaucratic coup in 1992 the PBOC gained primary control over the management of China's foreign exchange reserves, which had previously been the exclusive preserve of the rival BOC.

The PBOC is playing a crucial role in the transformation of China's banking system into a market-driven sector, although its power is considerably less in practice than it is on paper. Under the leadership of reformist central bank governor and chairman Zhu Rongji, who also holds the title of vice premier in the government and has been mentioned as a possible future head of state, the PBOC is attempting to pattern its operations after central banks in developed capitalist nations such as the United States and Japan. However, Zhu has offended many constituencies in his attempts to rationalize the system and he will have an uphill struggle to consolidate his position and continue the reforms. In early 1994 there were renewed rumors that he was set to resign as head of the PBOC. Nevertheless, additional legislation advancing banking reform is expected in the near future.

The Bank of China

Formerly little more than the foreign exchange department in the Chinese financial system, the influential Bank of China (BOC) has been delegated to handle virtually all international banking operations as the overseas agent for the PBOC and the State Council. As the agency responsible for handling foreign trade transactions, international interbank deposits and loans, international remittances, deposits and loans in foreign currencies, RMB deposits relating to foreign exchange activities, and the buying and selling of foreign currencies and gold on international markets, the BOC is the face of Chinese finance that most foreigners see and deal with. As the nation's chief investment bank, the BOC also participates in international syndicated loans and the financing of joint ventures with foreign banks. The BOC bears the responsibility for issuing government

bonds and other securities denominated in foreign currencies in overseas markets.

The BOC has 522 domestic offices, at least one in every duly constituted governmental jurisdiction in China. It has been rapidly expanding its RMB deposits and other domestic operations to compensate for the loss of its external financial monopoly as the PBOC has increasingly authorized other agencies to deal directly in foreign exchange operations. It has also been striving to become more professional and recently announced the appointment of Wang Xuebing, a 41-year-old former chief of the BOC's New York branch and an up-and-coming technocrat, as its new president.

In the past, foreign-invested enterprises (FIEs) were required to open foreign currency accounts with the BOC as the exclusive means of managing foreign exchange transactions and receiving authorized foreign exchange for the repatriation of earnings. These enterprises now have a few more options outside the BOC for such accounts. Foreign exchange funds for investment in foreign countries and repatriation of profits must be channeled through these accounts. All such transactions require approval from the BOC and the State Administration of Economic Control (SAEC), a unit of the PBOC. The BOC is slowly losing its monopoly position as the PBOC and SAEC have authorized more financial institutions to conduct certain foreign exchange transactions.

The BOC has embarked on a campaign to upgrade it international operations. It has a network of 430 overseas branch offices, including offices in all major and most minor world financial centers and tax havens, two representative offices (Moscow and Seoul), and correspondent relations with more than 1,400 banks in 155 countries. It has targeted Southeast Asia, the former Soviet republics, the Middle East, and Latin America in particular for expansion. At the end of 1991 the BOC's foreign assets stood at US$95.3 billion, about one-third of its total assets, and its foreign-based deposits had reached more than US$42 billion.

The bulk of these deposits are located in Hong Kong, where it was reported in 1991 that the BOC and its affiliates held 21 percent of the colony's US$178 billion in bank deposits. The BOC's Hong Kong and Macao operation is its most elaborate. It runs the second-largest banking operation in Hong Kong, controlling 14 banks with more than 330 branches. The BOC plans to merge this entire network under its own flag during 1994 in preparation for assuming its role as one of the currency-issuing banks in Hong Kong.

Since economic reform began in the late 1970s, the BOC has participated in a variety of Chinese-for-

Refer to "Important Addresses" chapter for names and addresses of financial institutions in China.

Recent Financial Sector Developments and Trends

In the 1990s China's financial system has been plagued by excessively rapid credit growth, rampant corruption, and stubbornly high inflation. These acute problems are interrelated and will abate only when a comprehensive restructuring of the country's financial system is successfully implemented.

The most pressing need is reform of the way state banks extend loans. At present more than 70 percent of state banks' allocations and loans are made to state-owned enterprises, as dictated by the State Planning Commission, without regard to the beneficiaries' ability to repay such loans. Many of these loans will never be repaid, because losses at state-owned enterprises have more than doubled over the past few years. No one really knows what percentage of bank loans are nonperforming or uncollectable, but some analysts estimate the amount to be as much as 40 percent of all loans made by Chinese banks.

Excessive credit growth in the nonplan sector—the lending not accounted for by specifically directed policy loans—has threatened China with economic turmoil. Nonplan lending exceeded private deposits by RMB 429.5 billion (about US$79.5 billion) in January 1992. The state has traditionally made up the difference by printing money to cover the shortfall. Credit growth since 1990 has exceeded annual targets by 50 to 100 percent, and the money supply rose by 54 percent during the first half of 1993 alone.

To maximize profits on loans many local bank branches have established unauthorized and at best semilegal finance company subsidiaries to attract deposits. These so-called back door financiers offer deposit interest rates substantially above the limits dictated by the PBOC and in turn make loans for nonplan development at even higher rates, that calculated on a daily basis amount to a usurious 20 to 30 percent annual rate. It is an open secret that most government ministries operate de facto investment branches that attract private deposits by offering higher-than-authorized rates of return. Such deposits are then speculatively invested, often in real estate and stocks both at home and abroad, providing increased working capital for the ministries,

rake-offs for many of the officials involved, and huge potential losses for the institutions should anything go wrong, which is almost inevitable.

In their eagerness to make high-margin loans and investments, some banks have diverted government funds earmarked for such activities as purchasing grain from farmers into more lucrative opportunities. The result has been a shortage of cash balances to pay peasants for their crops. Ingenious bank officials attempted to offer peasants elaborately printed IOUs, a discredited central government expedient that had been used in the past but was officially forsworn. Peasants rioted in several locations across the country during the summer of 1993 over the issue of such scrip. In Sichuan Province, irate peasants even attacked local Communist Party offices, causing damage and beating up cadres.

The frenzy of excessive loans and investments has served to worsen the already high inflation in the overheated economy. Inflation resurfaced in 1993 following a three-year hiatus and by the second half of the year was running at more than a 20 percent annual rate in larger cities. By year's end, the government had acknowledged that the rate was almost 20 percent in the 35 largest urban areas, and 13 percent in the countryside, although it calculated that the nationwide average rate at closer to 14.5 percent. Much of this inflation was due to commodity speculation and hoarding, with grain prices leading the way. In certain areas of the southeast, grain prices were up by more than 30 percent during November 1993 alone as peasants held supplies in anticipation of higher prices. With the announcement of price controls in late 1993 food prices in Beijing jumped by 40 percent and in Shanghai and Guangzhou by 20 percent virtually overnight. Inflation appears to be poised to reassert itself in 1994.

In response to the sharp drop in real purchasing power, citizens have rushed to pull their savings out of banks where they were earning a negative return due to low officially-controlled interest rates and gone on a buying spree, stocking up on consumer goods in anticipation of shortages to come and as an investment for resale. As an example, one man reportedly spent his life savings on four refrigerators, figuring that their resale value would at least keep up with the rate of inflation whereas his financial savings would not. Many consumers are opting to buy gold to hedge against inflation. The World Gold Council estimates China's 1993 gold demand at 700 tons of imports, a 40 percent jump above the 1992 figure.

The 1993 Austerity Program

Sensing an impending economic disaster, the central government acted in early summer 1993 to tighten credit, crack down on corruption, and rein in inflation. On July 2, 1993, Vice Premier Zhu Rongji assumed command of the country's financial sector as governor of the PBOC. Zhu replaced Li Guixian, who was accused of mismanagement and a lack of resolve in dealing with the country's financial difficulties.

Zhu's arrival was initially viewed as a welcome sign that the government was at last acting decisively to reform the banking industry and clean up provincial-level mismanagement and corruption. Perhaps not coincidentally, on the same day Zhu became PBOC governor, the president of a local bank branch was sentenced to death for taking bribes and extending unauthorized loans. In the second half of 1993 at least eight financial officers were executed for corruption. In response to the peasant riots demanding cash payment for crops, Zhu declared that he would "cut off the head" of any financial officer found to be handing out scrip.

The hard-headed former mayor of Shanghai, Zhu is immensely popular among China's urban intelligentsia and more progressive members of the Communist Party. He is also regarded as one of the most adept of China's "barbarian handlers," that is one of the best outside people to deal with foreigners, although his outspokenness has earned him enemies at home. There is a common belief that if Zhu cannot control the economy, no one can. As a progressive and practical technocrat, Zhu is expected to accelerate financial reform in China. However, in the short term he appears to be concentrating on rectifying economic instability through a combination of authoritarian central planning edicts and manipulation of macroeconomic levers. His stated goals

are to slow annual inflation to 10 to 12 percent, cut government spending by 20 percent, put the brakes on the growth of the money supply, and call and reallocate as much as RMB 100 billion (about US$17.25 billion) in unauthorized bank loans.

In the short term the austerity program appears to have had limited success. As of late 1993 currency valuations had stabilized somewhat; the rate of inflation had stabilized at around 20 percent in the largest cities, and growth in the money supply had eased marginally from 26 percent at the beginning of the austerity campaign in June to 22 percent in September. However, no more than 60 percent of targeted unauthorized loans have been retrieved. The country is sure to experience another bout of inflation and speculation in 1994 unless substantial structural reforms are implemented.

The Real Estate Situation

Real estate development and speculation in China has generated a great deal of interest, a great deal of profit, and more recently a great deal of concern and loss for domestic and foreign investors and banks. All land in China is owned by the state, and the buying and selling of even use rights was banned in 1949, with land not even being assigned an imputed value. This situation changed in 1986 when the State Land Administration instituted a market in land use rights. The real estate business grew rapidly, resulting in the development of RMB 103 billion (about US$27.75 billion) of property between 1986 and 1990. During this period the industry was growing at an average annual rate of 27 percent. Investment rose to a cumulative RMB 400 billion (about US$69 billion) in 1992 with much of the impetus coming from Hong Kong investors.

The property market fueled by foreign interest and capital began in Shenzhen in 1988. Nationwide there are an estimated 10,000 real estate-related enterprises. In Guangzhou alone some 55 development corporations, mostly run by different and often competing offices of the municipal government, and more than 150 private property development companies operate. Over the past several years, real estate development fever has extended to Shanghai, Beijing, Tianjin, Shenyang, Harbin, Wuhan,

Recent Developments (cont'd)

Chengdu, and other secondary centers where the foreign presence is as yet a minimal.

The market is hardly perfect and often barely legal, with most activity occurring on the district level where officials are interested primarily in making a financial killing rather than in supporting sustainable development. Planning, infrastructure, and aftermarket support are often nonexistent. During the late 1980s foreigners put up numerous luxury hotels, leading to a glut in such properties in large cities such as Shanghai. More recently, a surge of speculative building has occurred in the Pearl River Delta and other areas in the more wide open southeast, resulting in a glut of new construction in some areas where no market for the upscale properties developed exists. Projects already in the pipeline have also led to a shortage of building materials and a sharp rise in costs. And existing residents displaced by all this new construction not designed with them in mind now constitute an increasingly large and vocal disgruntled minority. Such displaced residents recently rioted in Xian, refusing to vacate their homes to make way for a development project. Relocation costs can account for 30 percent of total development costs, with land representing 5 percent, and construction 65 percent of project outlays.

The official market, such as it is, is driven by an underground market consisting of unofficial uses of official funds and activity by marginal private operators. This underground market is in turn fueled primarily by foreign speculative money. Even the official market has functioned using extreme amounts of leverage and informal letters of intent and options to develop in place of contracts, an unusual approach in this bureaucratic society where everything is usually required to be spelled out in detail. One developer boasted that he could buy all of China for as little as US$2 billion, US$3 billion tops.

As a result of the austerity crackdown in summer 1993, many Chinese joint-venture partners have been unable to fulfill their parts in real estate deals. The PBOC instructed banks to call their unauthorized real estate loans in August 1993. Even without this official edict, many banks were already reassessing their policies regarding such lending. And as lending has dried up, prices have begun to slide, especially for the large luxury projects favored by foreign investors.

In early 1994 officials banned new luxury projects such as golf courses and race tracks. They also instituted a campaign to deny permits, licenses, land allocation, and lending for development not approved at the national level. Bankers operating in China have been arguing that prices, which are already down by 20 percent in some areas, will fall substantially into 1994, declining by as much as 50 percent in some overbuilt areas, and that new deals will be difficult to arrange anywhere during the coming year.

Easing the Austerity Program

By early fall of 1993 the tightening of credit under the austerity program was causing companies nationwide to how as they were unable to obtain working capital and investment funds, and economic activity was being choked off even as the excesses that austerity was designed to eliminate continued largely unabated. As a result, the PBOC began to ease credit, announcing its intention to double lending to RMB 200 million (about US$34.5 billion) in the fourth quarter and to raise total lending for 1993 to RMB 400 billion, a 13 percent increase over the 1992 level. However, lending was to continue to be earmarked primarily for the support of state enterprises and infrastructure projects rather than allocated by the free market. By the end of November 1993 the austerity program had died a quiet and unmourned death.

Because of the unpopularity of the austerity program, coupled with the resistance of municipal and provincial authorities to a proposed tax-sharing arrangement by which they would have to make a fixed percentage contribution of locally collected tax revenues to the central government, there was speculation that Zhu Rongji had fallen from favor. Public calls by Deng Xiaoping and Li Peng for continued rapid growth and Zhu's absence from the press and public appearances, which in China often means that the absent one has been purged, gave credence to this speculation.

However, Zhu reappeared in December following

the annual Central Committee meeting, having apparently survived challenges to his authority and announcing additional reform proposals. Some observers contend that Zhu is merely being publicly set up as the scapegoat if reform programs fail. Others argue that his continued championing of reform indicates that the progressives have essentially won out.

Future Reform Plans

In November 1993 the government announced a rather sketchy blueprint for financial reform. Party leaders agreed to allow the PBOC a freer hand in formulating monetary policy through the use of macroeconomic levers such as reserve requirements on deposits, independent control of interest rates, and the revolutionary—for China—idea of the use of open-market operations (the official buying and selling of government securities to manipulate credit and the money supply). Promotion of the use of checks, bills of exchange, and credit cards, which can be more easily monitored and controlled than cash, is expected eventually to reduce the amount of cash in circulation and provide an additional lever with which to implement monetary policy. Interest rates will also be allowed to float more freely within a specified range.

China's specialized banks are expected to be converted into for-profit full service commercial banks that will compete with each other for banking business across the board instead of servicing policy goals in specific areas. They will be relieved of the responsibility of extending special policy loans at the behest of the State Council. To allow the existing financial entities to concentrate on market competition without having to divert resources in policy considerations, the government will create three new development banks to handle policy lending to otherwise commercially nonviable projects in industry, agriculture, and infrastructure. Details of how this proposal is to be funded and operated remain sketchy.

In order to improve banking efficiency, the government has also announced a pilot scheme for a national interbank clearing system. The project, estimated to cost around US$750 million, will reduce the time needed for clearing interbank transactions from several weeks to a few days. The project is being funded in part by the World Bank.

On the issue of foreign exchange, the November announcement stated that Chinese currency should gradually become convertible, at least for foreign investment and external trade purposes, with the abolition of FEC and the unification of the currency system as the first step in this eventual decontrol program, a step which was implemented on January 1, 1994. As the RMB becomes more convertible, foreign banks will be allowed to engage in domestic banking business, and foreign invested enterprises will find it easier to operate and repatriate profits.

Free convertibility of the RMB is expected to be an especially slow and balky process. The government uses tight control over its currency to manage its economic affairs, largely because its economic performance in the past has been inadequate to clear its trade with the rest of the world on an open market basis. By keeping the RMB at artificially high levels, China has been able to manipulate the system to get more bang for its overvalued buck. A convertible currency would remove such machinations from China's bag of tricks and could lead to a prodigious outflow of financial and other assets.

Rumor has it that local officials were offered more leeway in approving investment projects and lending on the local level in return for their acquiescence to the reform package. Much of the vagueness in the reform proposals is said to be intentional, allowing the central authorities room to negotiate details with specific groups of locals. However, observers note that local officials are in a good position to short-circuit reforms by the simple expedient of ignoring or reinterpreting central directives largely at will. Provincial and municipal authorities have become accustomed to exercising a considerable degree of initiative in defiance of central policy. Others worry over the ominous implications generated by the prospect of 1993 representing China's first trade deficit since 1989 which could cause a bad case of official nerves and further serve to derail the loosening of traditional controls.

eign joint ventures. The BOC owns a substantial share in several key joint ventures in China, and foreign businesses actively seek BOC participation in Sino-foreign joint ventures because of the stability of funding and the official imprimatur that such participation represents. BOC participation is perhaps the best way there is to reduce financial risk for foreign investors. In addition to investing directly in joint ventures for an equity position, the BOC can also lend to approved joint ventures.

The BOC also makes investments through a variety of its own joint ventures with external financial institutions. For example, the BOC owns 30 percent of CCIC Finance Limited, which acts as a merchant bank to finance foreign investments in energy, communications, and light industrial projects in China. Another foreign joint venture, Trilease International Ltd., finances the purchase of foreign equipment by Chinese enterprises and promotes the sale of Chinese equipment abroad by financing lease arrangements. In one of its more nontraditional ventures, the BOC helped form China Development Finance Co. (HK) Ltd. to underwrite and trade in negotiable certificates of deposit (CDs), stocks, and other securities on international markets.

The BOC also extends foreign currency loans to domestic enterprises wishing to obtain advanced foreign technology. This service is crucial to many domestic enterprises that need to upgrade their technology but lack the hard currency necessary to obtain foreign goods and services. The BOC is a critical link for foreigners desiring to export goods to China because it can make the necessary determination that the foreign products are actually needed in China and further state plans, and that they are therefore eligible for import and allocation of foreign to pay for them. The government places a high priority on advanced technology transfers from abroad, and the BOC is the agency with the responsibility for assuring that such transfers are facilitated and properly handled from the financial standpoint.

To assist in foreign trade and investment, the BOC provides flexible forms of settlement and payment, including international payments and settlements with foreign banks and businesses. Standard international payment practices such as letters of credit (L/Cs) are written and sometimes guaranteed by the BOC. The BOC also has the authority to grant credit guarantees to foreign lenders that provide financing to Chinese or Sino-foreign joint enterprises.

The BOC provides consulting services to international and domestic clients, providing introductions to many business connections both within China and overseas. Foreign investors can also consult with the BOC for assistance in establishing operations in China.

The Industrial and Commercial Bank of China

The Industrial and Commercial Bank of China (ICBC) was created in 1983 to take over the PBOC's credit operations. The largest and most influential of the specialized banks and the largest commercial bank in China, it handles almost half of all legal deposits and loans in the country. In the late 1980s the ICBC held 75 percent of the nation's RMB 700 billion (about US$167 billion) in official savings deposits. These balances have increased dramatically in recent years, as the money supply has more than doubled in the 1990s.

The ICBC's main functions are to accept savings deposits from individuals and enterprises in urban areas, to provide working capital for businesses in urban areas, to provide payroll management services for state enterprises, and to make loans for capital equipment. The bank also operates in the securities business and in trust and real estate areas. It issues its own VISA credit card as well as a domestic credit card called the Peony card. The ICBC has also been authorized to deal in foreign exchange in its branches in areas of major foreign activity, mostly in the Special Economic Zones (SEZs) and the open Coastal Cities. Approved foreign exchange transactions include accepting deposits, making loans, handling remittances, financing foreign trade, and providing foreign exchange guarantees. The ICBC has a network of 208 correspondent banks in 50 countries and maintains its own overseas branch office in Singapore.

The ICBC supervises the Urban Credit Cooperatives (UCCs), which represent the lowest level of officially approved financial institution and the only one that most individual Chinese are likely to come in contact with. As the name suggests, these cooperatives operate in urban areas and provide loans and payment services for individual enterprises and small collectives. A reserve percentage of UCC deposits are held with the ICBC.

Similar to credit unions, UCCs are designed to accept deposits, make loans, and handle transactions for so-called urban street collective organizations or individual industrial and commercial households, euphemisms for locally formed non-work-unit cooperative organizations and private enterprises respectively. UCCs specifically exclude state and foreign enterprises from participation.

The Agricultural Bank of China

The Agricultural Bank of China (ABC) was established in 1979 to finance rural farm and business activity and facilitate the production and distribution of agricultural products. The second-largest specialized bank in China, holding about 12 percent of all deposits in the country, the ABC took over the operations of the PBOC in rural areas. It serves the same function in rural areas as the ICBC serves in urban areas—running rural credit cooperatives (RCCs) to provide banking services for individuals—while operating as a supposedly independent commercial bank and assuming responsibility for all agricultural purchases by state-owned trading companies. In essence, the ABC is responsible for handling the financial end of seeing that the country gets fed. It also exercises a substantial policy role in the area of agricultural finance and procurement, albeit usually without the wherewithal to implement its decisions. The ABC-operated RCCs are the only connection that the bulk of China's peasant population has to the formal financial sector. Altogether, the ABC operates more than 100,000 "branches," most of them local rural credit cooperatives.

The ABC has been allowed to deal in foreign exchange since 1985, and it operates branches in centers of major foreign activity, mainly in the SEZs and open Coastal Cities, to gather deposits and make loans in its function as a commercial bank. In 1992 it had US$114 billion in foreign exchange-denominated loans outstanding and total deposits of RMB 661.7 billion (about US$114 billion). The ABC has ties to 112 banks in 21 foreign countries. It has borrowing authority abroad, mostly from international agencies that use it as a conduit for agency lending and grants for rural development projects, and has linked up with computerized international bank clearing systems.

The ABC's main functions are to manage the money supply in rural areas, to accept deposits from and extend credit to farmers and rural enterprises, and to assist in the procurement and distribution of agricultural products. It works closely with the several state bureaus entrusted with managing aspects of agriculture. It has also been designated to spearhead the development of rural enterprises in order to alleviate rural poverty, unemployment, and underemployment. However, it has been largely unable to come up with the funds to do so adequately.

Rural credit cooperatives were established as part of the household responsibility system that in 1985 shifted agricultural production from a system in which the state simply took the produce of collectives to one in which the state contracted with the individual farmer to produce specified types and quantities of product. RCCs accept deposits, extend loans, and handle transactions for peasant households that become members by purchasing shares through depositing nominal sums. In 1991 such cooperatives accepted RMB 9 billion (about US$1.7 billion) in deposits. RCC loans provide the main vehicle for peasants to finance their agricultural operations and purchase such necessary items as fertilizer and pesticides. In the late 1980s approximately 80 percent of peasant households were RCC members.

The ABC and the RCCs have suffered from a chronic shortage of operating funds and have often been in the position of offering scrip instead of cash for purchases. The rural economy, which is still largely cashless, has been unable to provide an adequate deposit base to supply the demand for credit, and scarce government funds have been channeled into higher-return development projects and stop-gap lending in urban areas to hold back the rising tide of unrest caused by economic dislocation. As a result, the ABC and the RCCs have largely been unable to fulfill their mission to modernize the financial system, upgrade production and distribution, underwrite rural business development, and generally improve the lot of the three-quarters of China's population who live in the rural hinterlands. Through the issuance of scrip, they have even on occasion added to the problem.

The People's Construction Bank of China

The People's Construction Bank of China (PCBC) was created in 1954 to handle government investments in large capital construction projects. Nominally under the State Council construction committee, the PCBC is in effect the investment arm of the Ministry of Finance and is accountable to both it and the PBOC.

The PCBC's main functions include setting allocations and administering loans for large-scale capital and technological construction projects, holding and regulating the investment funds of state enterprises, and supervising the financial aspects of approved construction projects. It directs funds to targeted industries by offering special low-interest policy loans to high-priority sectors of the economy. The PCBC also supervises the China Investment Bank (CIB) for the Ministry of Finance. The CIB channels loans from the World Bank and the PCBC to small- and medium-sized enterprises wishing to import foreign capital equipment. These enterprises receive foreign currency loans to pay for the imported equipment and domestic currency loans to pay for domestic modernization projects. Because of its role in raising foreign capital, the CIB often finds its activities overlapping with those of the BOC in the increasingly decentralized banking arena.

The PCBC is slowly transforming itself from an old-style bureaucracy into a more modern commercial banking entity. It is now funding itself through deposits, overseas borrowings, and foreign and domestic bond issues and offers its own MasterCard in 33 cities. The PCBC has 70 branches, several of which have been authorized to conduct foreign exchange business since 1987. It is working to expand this business by setting up an international department to channel and facilitate overseas business activity.

Refer to "Important Addresses" chapter for names and addresses of financial institutions in China.

The Communications Bank of China

The Communications Bank of China (CBC) was reestablished in 1987, resurrecting an entity that had been dormant for more than 30 years. It is China's newest specially organized domestic bank and the closest thing the system has to a Western-style commercial bank. Like China International Trust and Investment Corporation (CITIC), the CBC is jointly owned by the government and private investors, but receives no government funding. Various government entities purchase the securities issued to fund the bank's activities, although private enterprises and individuals are accounting for an increasing share of the CBC's ownership.

The CBC's main function is to support the modernization of the economy through development of domestic and foreign enterprises in China. Its broad charter allows it to deal in both RMB and foreign currency loans and deposits, operate in securities markets, and branch internally and externally virtually at will. The CBC provides full banking services to its customers, including deposit and transactions accounts, trade financing, international remittances and other foreign exchange transactions, insurance, and real estate investment services. Foreigners may open accounts with the CBC denominated in either RMB or foreign currency. As an indicator of its independence, the CBC is the only major financial institution to be headquartered in Shanghai instead of in Beijing. It operates 70 domestic branches, 467 service centers that are more than representative offices but less than full branches, and a Hong Kong office. Although still small by Chinese standards, it is growing rapidly.

Provincial Banks

To date the authorized national financial institutions cast a long shadow, dominating financial activity on the local level through their branch offices. Provincial officials have generally been unwilling to formally challenge the authority or market power of these entities by setting up their own official banks, although they have often coopted these local offices into making common cause with them against their masters in Beijing.

An exception is the semi-official provincial Guangdong Development Bank, which opened in 1988. This bank was financed by the original issue of 1.5 million shares. The majority of these were subscribed by local branches of the PBOC, BOC, and ABC, although it is thought that as many as one-third of the shares may have gotten into the hands of foreign investors. This fledgling bank, sponsored by the provincial authorities, offers services in both RMB and foreign currencies.

Foreign Banks in China

After the Communists came to power in 1949 all but four foreign banks were forced to close down. The Hongkong and Shanghai Banking Corporation, the Standard Chartered Bank, the Overseas Chinese Banking Corporation, and the Bank of East Asia, all headquartered in Shanghai, stuck it out and have enjoyed a special relationship ever since.

Beginning in the late 1970s foreign banks were allowed to establish representative offices. In the mid-1980s the establishment in the SEZs of foreign branches, wholly foreign-owned banks, and banking and finance company joint ventures followed. Foreign banks are the only type of business currently allowed to establish branches in China, and branches are the most common type of foreign banking presence. Wholly foreign-owned banks are uncommon because they require a much greater financial commitment. Joint-venture banks are relatively common, while finance companies are similar but more restricted entities that operate in fewer areas but also require less capital.

More recently, foreign banks have been allowed to move to Shanghai, the rapidly developing financial hub of China. Many of the world's largest banks have entered the Chinese market, including banks from Japan, the United States, England, France, and Germany. The presence of these banks is often crucial to the success of foreign enterprises operating in areas that require trade finance and foreign currency loans. As of mid-1993 more than 50 foreign bank branches were operating in 13 Chinese cities, with 239 representative offices of banks from 29 foreign countries operating in 15 Chinese cities. There are also several Sino-foreign joint-venture banking operations. Most are located in Shanghai, although some also operate in SEZs. In January 1994 Chinese authorities announced plans to add more cities to the list of those in which foreign bank branches can operate, although they did not say which cities would be involved or when the opening would occur.

Foreign branches are allowed to book loans denominated in foreign currencies, discount foreign exchange bills, collect bills and remittances from overseas, handle documentary credit arrangements, act as agents in foreign exchange transactions, offer safe deposit services, conduct credit checks, and accept consulting engagements. The ability to offer RMB-denominated deposits and loans has been promised but has yet to materialize, although many foreign banks indirectly handle such business by steering clients to domestic bank offices for such loans. Foreign banks can also lend hard currency funds to FIEs that then convert the funds into local currency at the local BOC branch, although this poses a problem of hard currency repayment (parent organizations will sometimes make arrangements to reimburse the bank offshore). Foreign banks usually lend to FIEs or to official state bank entities in what amounts to a nascent interbank market. They cannot lend to private Chinese enterprises or individuals although this is under discussion.

Foreign lending has shifted from the funding of hotel projects in the early years to working capital and development loans in recent years. Foreign banks have experienced more than their share of loan write-offs as enterprises supposedly operating with state guarantees have defaulted, leading many foreign banks to shift to services other than lending. US-based banks have specialized in trade financing, while Hong Kong and European banks tend to focus on project lending.

All loans made by a foreign bank must be registered with the State Administration for Exchange Control (SAEC), a unit of the PBOC, and can be declared void if they fail to meet technical or policy requirements, with the bank being held liable for unrecovered funds. Banks are given an annual quota for foreign exchange business, and all short-term working capital loans are charged against this quota, which cannot be extended to serve additional clients. Medium- to long-term foreign currency lending is not so limited, but only loans for necessary technology or those that are expected to generate foreign exchange for repayment are allowed by the SAEC.

Foreign banks can lend for longer terms, but most prefer a five- to 10 year horizon, and most insist on a state agency guarantee, usually from the BOC or CITIC. Banks have limited options for collateral because they cannot put a lien on cash flow or future earnings. Although they can gain the rights to certain assets, they usually choose to call loan guarantees, renegotiate the loan, or try to pressure the state enterprise partners in joint ventures for repayment. Mortgage lending has been allowed in a limited fashion in Shenzhen since 1986; however, because land cannot be owned the market in use rights has been slow to take off. Broader geographic mortgage lending authority is also under discussion.

Despite high costs and a poorly developed financial system, most foreign banks see China as an essential market for the long haul. They argue that they can charge relatively high fees and almost always get some return even on bad loans, provided they watch the entity that guarantees the loans. Although this sounds suspiciously like the specious sovereign risk rhetoric (countries can't go bankrupt) commonly heard from banks during the 1980s, some observers estimate that even at the height of the 1990 austerity campaign when business was exceedingly bad, most foreign banks were still profitable. Nevertheless, foreign banks control few of the levers that lead

to profitability elsewhere: They cannot deal in local currency, must operate with low caps on the interest rates that they can charge and minimal spreads, must fund large reserve balances, and are subject to high taxes and operating expenses.

Foreign banks may establish representative offices in Beijing, designated Coastal Cities, and various other locations with authorization from the PBOC. These offices may engage in non-profit-producing operations such as negotiations, liaison functions, and consulting activities. They are not allowed to engage in direct profit-making activities such as taking deposits and making loans. A bank wishing to open a profit-making branch office must first have maintained a representative office in the country for at least three years before it is eligible to obtain branch-operating approval.

It is also possible to form Sino-foreign joint-venture banking companies. Such entities often have better access to potential customers because of the local contacts of the Chinese partner and can offer a wider range of services. However, the risks have generally been seen as outweighing the advantages. Such joint ventures cannot operate in some areas of trade, such as the issuance of letters of credit, or engage in commercial banking activities, and they have heavy initial capital requirements—a minimum of US$20 million. Few foreign banks have wanted to make that much of a commitment, especially when they have relatively little control over the Chinese partner, who usually does not have anything near that amount at risk. The lack of infrastructure, systems, and qualified personnel has also put a damper on foreign expansion. These factors have also kept banks from opening wholly foreign-owned operations, especially when they can gain most of the same autonomy and benefits from operating using a branch structure.

Sino-foreign finance companies are allowed to engage in some or all of the following activities: extending foreign currency loans; accepting foreign exchange deposits in excess of US$100,000; discounting foreign currency bills; handling foreign currency-denominated investments; making foreign currency guarantees; trading bonds and securities; performing credit investigations and related financial consulting; and performing such other business operations as may be specifically authorized by the PBOC.

Although the presence of foreign bank branches was authorized in 1985, China still does not have a unified law governing the establishment of such operations. Local authorities have adopted regulations for allowing the establishment of foreign banks in Shanghai and 12 Coastal Cities in conjunction with the PBOC. The regulations governing the operation of foreign banks vary with the venue in which they wish to do business. However, the local legal variations are not so important as the local variations in regulatory practice. A national law governing foreign and domestic bank activities has been promised for 1994 but similar promises have also been made in the past.

Banking in Shanghai

There were 26 foreign bank branches and several joint-venture finance companies operating in Shanghai at the end of 1993. In August 1993 Citibank announced that it would relocate its China area headquarters from Hong Kong to Shanghai, and other major banks are expected to follow suit. This move reflects a growing conviction that Shanghai will emerge as the country's preeminent financial and business center during the ensuing decade, especially for domestic business.

Foreign banks in Shanghai concentrate their activities on trade finance and cash settlement of stocks traded on the Shanghai exchange, but many hope to have access to a more open RMB market in the near future, which would give them added scope to do business in China. Bankers speculate that this liberalization will be driven by China's desire to participate in the General Agreement on Tariffs and Trade (GATT).

Regulations on foreign financial institutions in Shanghai cover foreign banks incorporated in Shanghai or operating there as branches of overseas parent organizations, Sino-foreign joint-venture banks, and Sino-foreign joint-venture finance companies. Foreigners establishing joint-venture banks or wholly foreign-owned banks in Shanghai must meet the following requirements: The foreign investor must have maintained a representative office in China for at least three years; the foreign investor's primary business must be as a financial institution; and the total assets of the foreign parent bank must exceed US$10 billion.

Foreign banks that want to establish a branch office must have maintained a representative office in China for at least three years prior to applying to operate as a bank; have total assets in excess of US$20 billion; and have a system of supervising and regulating the Shanghai branch from the home country of the foreign bank, so that the branch is under the direct control of the parent organization rather than operating as an autonomous unit. Joint-venture finance companies seeking to operate in Shanghai must have maintained a representative office in China for a period of time that is unspecified by rule but must satisfy authorities of the institution's solidity, expertise, and good intentions. Both the Chinese and the foreign partners must be financial institutions. There are no established minimum asset requirements for nonbank financial firms.

Foreign Banks in Special Economic Zones and Other Cities

During the 1980s foreign banks and Sino-foreign joint-venture banks were allowed to establish operations in Special Economic Zones (SEZs) in south China. Presently, there are five SEZs: Shantou, Zhuhai, and Shenzhen in Guangdong Province, the island Province of Hainan, and Xiamen in Fujian Province. In 1992 seven other Coastal Cities, ranging from Tianjin in the north to Guangzhou in the south, were permitted to allow the operation of foreign banks. Some observers foresee the eventual merger of the financial operations of Shenzhen and Hong Kong, making the combined regional entity the international financial center of China, while Shanghai becomes the domestic financial center.

SEZs and other Coastal Cities have patterned their regulations for foreign banks after the regulations in Shanghai. The PBOC must give its permission for foreign banks and Sino-foreign banks to operate profit-making operations in these areas before local authorities are allowed to approve any activities, but the possibility remains that various localities could offer foreign banks the opportunity to engage in wider areas of business than some of their cohorts elsewhere, generating a bidding war for foreign banks.

Foreign banks are generally allowed into areas where there is a high concentration of wholly foreign-owned and Sino-foreign joint-venture investment activity. These banks service international clients primarily in the areas of trade financing and foreign exchange operations. The scope of foreign bank participation is expected to increase as other foreign business activities develop. Within the next decade, foreign banks are also expected to be able to enter inland areas of China as foreign investors seek out cheaper overhead and wage costs in less-developed parts of the country.

NONBANK FINANCIAL INSTITUTIONS

Trust and Investment Corporations

There are more than 600 trust and investment corporations in China. These are regulated by the PBOC and the SAEC. About 100 of them are authorized to conduct foreign exchange operations. These entities began in 1979 with the founding of the China International Trust and Investment Corporation (CITIC), the most prominent. They are identified by a name which includes "trust and investment" or "investment and trust" corporation and are often referred to collectively as the ITICs.

Trust and investment corporations were de-

Refer to "Important Addresses" chapter for names and addresses of financial institutions in China.

Financial Aspects of Foreign Operations in China

Domestic lending facilities for foreign business operations are extremely limited in China. A large proportion of loans continue to be earmarked for state-owned enterprises, which soak up most available credit. The small remainder is usually put into high-margin, high-risk speculative real estate or securities market lending. Private enterprises are still not officially recognized as bankable entities. Recognized Sino-foreign joint-ventures are sometimes able to secure funding from specialized banks. However, until banking reform is successfully implemented, foreign businesses will continue to rely primarily on foreign banks for basic operational loans and trade financing. International banks operating in China and Hong Kong are the preferred source of such foreign currency loans.

Bank Accounts

All foreign businesses must set up an account with either the BOC or another foreign exchange-authorized bank through which they must channel all foreign exchange-related business. These accounts are characterized as either fixed or current accounts. Fixed accounts are for set terms—usually three, six, 12 or 24 months—and pay interest at either fixed or floating rates. Demand transaction accounts are characterized as either current—paying no interest—or deposit, which pay a floating rate of interest on balances. Such accounts must be maintained in an approved foreign currency, usually the US or Hong Kong dollar, yen, deutsche mark, or British pound. Special arrangements can be made for renminbi-denominated accounts, but these were actually FEC accounts, and required proceeds to be converted to local renminbi as needed. Now that FEC have been abolished, there may be greater freedom to use such accounts in the future.

Balancing Requirements

Foreign invested enterprises are required by law to ensure that their foreign currency revenues cover their hard currency expenditures so that the two net out and create no foreign exchange obligation for China. This requirement highlights a basic contradiction between the goals of foreigners operating in China and the goals of the government. China wants foreign investment prima-

rily to enable it directly or indirectly to generate more exports and foreign exchange, while many foreigners invest in China primarily to gain access to the country's huge developing domestic market.

Under certain circumstances, balancing requirements can be waived for joint ventures. For instance, joint ventures that manufacture technically advanced products for which there is a high demand in the Chinese domestic market may be allowed to sell their products in China without regard to balancing requirements because of strategic needs and because onshore production effectively acts as import substitution, canceling out foreign exchange that would have been lost anyway.

Chinese investment authorities usually prefer foreign enterprises to rely on exports to generate foreign currency, but this is not always possible, especially if the manufacturer is selling most of its goods inside China. Despite an ambivalence—the Chinese do not want foreign-generated Chinese goods competing with their own exports—authorities often push for a contractual agreement requiring that a percentage of products be exported to reduce foreign exchange liabilities. Most foreign invested enterprises usually sign such an agreement but stipulate that export targets are nonbinding goals rather than enforceable contractual quotas. In practice, most businesses have failed to meet such imposed export targets and have not been penalized inordinately for doing so.

Accessing Domestic Funds

For foreign businesses producing and marketing goods in China, the lack of available domestic financing poses a serious problem because their profits are generated in RMB, yet foreign bank loans are repayable in foreign currency. Conversely, the necessity of converting hard currency into RMB to pay for operating expenses such as payroll and the purchase of domestic inputs exposes foreign businesses to exchange rate risk and steep service charges from banks. It is therefore desirable for foreign businesses to earn enough RMB through domestic sales to cover operational costs. At the same time, most businesses wish to export enough goods to generate hard currency earnings as well.

Instead of attempting to secure domestic loans in

Financial Aspects (cont'd.)

RMB, foreign businesses may try to enlist the participation of a domestic institution in a joint-venture deal. On the national level, the BOC, CITIC, and the CBC have all made renminbi loans to joint ventures. Provinces and municipalities also have investment institutions that may be able to finance joint-venture projects with foreigners. In Guangdong Province, the Guangdong International Trade and Investment Corporation (GITIC) has been especially active in such joint-venture financing. Similar institutions in other coastal provinces and in the cities of Shanghai and Tianjin have also provided domestic financing for foreign operations.

Foreign producers can establish joint ventures with successful domestic companies engaged in similar endeavors. By enlisting domestic joint-venture support, foreign producers can repay loans using shared profits. In addition, domestic banks give Sino-foreign joint ventures priority over foreign businesses for such funds as are available.

Swap Centers and Foreign Exchange

Chinese authorities have established foreign exchange-adjustment enterprises, better known as swap centers, to allow foreign invested enterprises to gain access to at least some of the foreign currency or RMB necessary to support their Chinese operations. Swap centers have been established in the SEZs, Shanghai, Guangdong, and in various other areas where foreign investment activity is substantial. As of late 1993 such centers accounted for nearly 80 percent of all foreign exchange activity in China.

At swap centers, foreign businesses are allowed to arrange foreign currency and RMB transactions directly with other foreign and with some domestic enterprises under careful government supervision. Exchange rates at these swap centers have usually been about 50 percent above the official rate, which prior to January 1, 1994 had been frozen at RMB 5.8 to the US dollar. Swap markets formed a shadow free-foreign-exchange-rate market. The rate on the swap markets has usually been about 50 percent higher than the official rate. When the RMB and FEC were unified on January 1, 1994, with the FEC being abolished, the official rate fell to that prevailing on the swap markets. It remains to be seen whether the swap market rates will continue to be at significant variance from the official rate. Rates do range higher and, on rare occasions, lower depending on supply and demand.

Swap centers are the primary vehicle available to businesses wishing to acquire hard currency. Foreign invested enterprises that have an oversupply of foreign currency may also purchase RMB at a favorable rate to meet domestic needs. In a recent 1993 survey, individual swap center transactions were found to range from US$10,000 to US$1 million, with an average of US$250,000 per transaction.

Other Sources of Foreign Exchange

Although swap centers are the primary means of obtaining foreign exchange in China, they are rarely able to clear demand due to official restrictions and limits on hard currency availability, which is inadequate under the best of conditions. At times when foreign currency is particularly tight, businesses have found that they needed to buy foreign currency on the black market at a substantially higher exchange rate. Although black-market dealings are illegal, many foreign businesses argue that they have no other recourse. This was widely considered to be the case in late 1993.

Foreign invested enterprises have used a variety of creative ways to earn an adequate supply of foreign currency. In addition to regular exports, swap center transactions, and the black market, businesses have used the following methods: Export components and parts produced in their Chinese facilities to parent companies or subsidiaries overseas for transfer payments in hard currency; use RMB earnings to purchase products in China, exporting such products for sale abroad for hard currency; earn commissions in foreign exchange by selling an overseas company's products in China as an ancillary operation; or, if the product made in China is of foreign-origin quality, selling the product in China for foreign exchange or, more frequently, a combination of foreign exchange and RMB. Chinese buyers are frequently willing to participate in this last type of import substitution arrangement because they can save some foreign exchange and get the product at a lower cost than if they had to import the item for 100 percent foreign exchange.

For accounting purposes, companies can also purchase imported production inputs from a Chinese trading company. In this way RMB can be used to purchase foreign components and parts that can be book valued in foreign currency because they are of foreign origin.

Various other arrangements, including countertrade deals such as counterpurchase, co-production, evidence accounts, switches, and barter arrangements, are also used to finesse the need for foreign exchange. However, most of these arrangements represent ways to avoid having a presence in China rather than ways to do business in China.

Protecting Against Devaluation

China's artificial exchange rate has meant that the currency is heavily overvalued at its official levels. Because of this the government has regularly been forced to devalue the renminbi, often rapidly and without notice, leaving foreign businesses with considerable exchange rate risk with regard to their Chinese operations. Foreign businesses should make sure that any contracts stipulate initial investment values in hard currency, not in RMB. Otherwise, Chinese partners might try to get by with a lesser contribution in devalued local currency, making the success of the venture more problematical, or reducing the value of the residual assets on termination of the venture. Foreign investors should stipulate the exchange rate to be used to evaluate transactions. They are also advised to advance the minimum amounts necessary, exchanging hard currency into RMB only as needed. Most China-based enterprises will also wish to leverage their investment as much as possible and elect the longest depreciation schedule possible to limit exposure from currency depreciation.

Repatriation of Profits

Repatriation of earnings from authorized wholly foreign-owned and joint-venture foreign invested enterprises is permitted by law. However, the Equity Joint Venture Law only provides for repatriation of capital upon the suspension or termination of a joint-venture agreement. In March 1989 the SAEC passed a provisional regulation designed to favor Chinese control of foreign exchange profits in a joint venture, the first article of which states that the Chinese investor in a joint venture may retain all the foreign exchange it earns during the first five years of operation and 50 percent of foreign exchange after the initial five year-period.

Persons experienced in joint-venture operations stress that although foreign entities have limited leverage with the government, all aspects of profits and repatriation are negotiable with the Chinese partner. They further note that if you don't ask, you don't get, and that even if foreign negotiators are not successful on this particular issue it can become a bargaining chip for other concessions. Foreign investors are strongly advised to reach a specific, detailed agreement on the repatriation of hard currency profits before signing a joint-venture agreement.

Regulations governing repatriation of wholly foreign-owned enterprise profits remain vague, and therefore negotiable, although the basic principle that requires the balancing of foreign exchange inflows and outflows applies. Foreign employee incomes and other profits may be repatriated upon payment of applicable Chinese taxes.

---

signed to promote investment, and they have been granted broader powers than banks in order to be able to do so. Specific financial transactions involve making foreign exchange guarantees and raising funds through overdrafts, making short-, medium-, and long-term loans, and floating bonds and debentures to support investment activities. ITICs are barred from local currency lending except as working capital loans to entities in which they have an equity stake. They are usually prohibited from taking regular deposits, although some are authorized to accept large deposits for periods of greater than one year. In 1988 their total deposits were RMB45 billion (about US$12.1 billion) and total capitaliza-

tion RMB 107 billion (about US$28.8 billion).

Trust and investment corporations are owned and run primarily by banks, ministries, and provincial, municipal, or local governments. The various corporations exist primarily to raise capital to promote the areas of investment connected with their specific sponsoring entities. National-level trust and investment companies must have minimum capital of RMB 50 million (about US$5.75 million); provincial-level entities must have capital of RMB 10 million (about US$1.2 million), and local-level entities must have capital of RMB 5 million (about US$600,000).

CITIC is the oldest, largest, and most influential trust corporation in China. In 1993 its total capitalization was RMB 45 billion (about US$5.2 billion), and it operated 30 subsidiaries. Although it is a quasi-private company owned jointly by the state and individual shareholders, CITIC effectively functions as a government ministry. As an indication of its stature, CITIC was authorized in 1992 to undertake onshore investments of up to RMB 200 million (about US$23 million) and offshore investments of up to US$30 million without seeking government approval. CITIC's founder, Rong Yiren, enjoys close relations with Deng Xiaoping and is a vice-president of the PRC. Known as the Red Capitalist, Rong comes from a wealthy Shanghai family and, despite the fact that he is not a party member, has been very influential in China's economic reform efforts.

CITIC is a major conduit for international investments to and from China. It is a partner in many joint ventures in China and overseas and has made several major investments in Hong Kong. CITIC has invested billions of dollars in more than 300 projects, including more than 65 overseas projects in more than 15 countries. It is China's largest overseas investor, holding title to 18 percent of the country's overseas assets.

Half of CITIC's estimated US$9 billion in hard assets consist of production facilities in China in the areas of energy, machinery, textiles, metallurgy, chemistry, construction materials, and transportation, although CITIC prefers to operate in higher-margin financial areas rather than industrial sectors. CITIC's headquarters are in Beijing, but it is moving heavily into the Shanghai market and much of its activity is conducted from offices in Hong Kong. Its Hong Kong subsidiary, CITIC Pacific, is among the 20 largest companies listed on the Hong Kong Stock Exchange.

CITIC borrows funds from foreign banks, issues foreign currency bonds overseas, and accepts foreign exchange deposits from overseas Chinese. It has established overseas joint-venture financial institutions designed to raise foreign capital to fund investments in China. Between 1982 and 1992 CITIC raised more than US$2 billion from such overseas bond issues. CITIC also assists foreigners in planning and establishing private businesses in China.

In 1987 CITIC's bank department was spun off and incorporated as CITIC Industrial Bank. The hybrid CITIC Industrial Bank offers most commercial bank services, such as accepting deposits; lending in RMB as well as in foreign currencies; services such as trade finance, documentary credits, foreign exchange, and leasing; and issuing bonds and dealing in securities. It also operates a trust department and offers financial consulting services. The CITIC Industrial Bank primarily funds the modernization projects of CITIC itself, but it has also participated in syndications abroad, including funding of the English Channel tunnel project.

In addition to CITIC's substantive contribution to China's development, the organization plays an important role as a training center for the nation's promising young financial professionals. Foreign companies looking for local talent in China often recruit CITIC alumni because the center is one of the few sources of Chinese personnel skilled in Western business and financial practices.

CITIC's success has not left it without critics. As the favored recipient of special dispensation to operate in areas forbidden to others, CITIC has made enemies. Some argue that were CITIC to lose its special status and other organizations allowed to break the rules as well, as is anticipated, its record would quickly look less impressive. Others speculate that CITIC has simply grown too fast and too indiscriminately and is riding for a fall. CITIC has also been given the unenviable task of turning around a variety of money-losing state enterprises, a task that will eat into its reserves and take up valuable management energy. Rong's impending retirement is also expected to be a blow to the corporation.

China Everbright International Trust and Investment Corporation (CEITIC)

In 1991 the Everbright Finance Company and the China Industry Commerce Trust and Investment Corporation merged to form CEITIC. CEITIC is part of China's attempt to set up the equivalent of investment banks. It can arrange lease financing, equity investments, and loans and is allowed to take deposits in Chinese and foreign currency, issue securities, and borrow in Chinese or overseas markets. CEITIC has so far focused on real estate and securities trading to fund its activities. Its deposit base quadrupled from RMB 900 million (about US$167 million) in 1991 to RMB 4.2 billion (about US$725 million) in mid-1993.

China Venturetech Investment Corporation

Founded in 1985, China Venturetech Investment Corporation (CVIC), or Venturetech as it is usually known, is a venture capital entity owned by a variety of cooperating ministries. Its mission is to raise capital for high-tech development, applications, and marketing. Like CEITIC, it is authorized to take direct equity positions, arrange lease financing, lend, provide guarantees, and issue stocks or bonds in domestic or foreign markets.

Venturetech specializes in small- to medium-sized start-ups, and it can invest in foreign-invested enterprises. So far, it has been most active in the biotechnology, information technologies, and materials sciences areas. It has offices in Wuxi and Foshan in southeastern China as well as in Hong Kong and plans to open additional offices in the open Coastal Cities.

China Investment Bank

The China Investment Bank (CIB), which operates under the authority of the Ministry of Finance and under the direct supervision of the PCBC, is not a bank. Its primary function is to administer funds from international agencies, such as the World Bank, and some overseas commercial bank lenders. It lends, but only to state-approved priority projects. Because of the CIB's limited role, it is not a source of funding for foreign businesses and operates in a relatively restricted niche.

State Investment Companies

In an attempt to modernize its economy, China created six new investment companies in 1988: the China National Energy Investment Corporation; the China National Transportation and Communications Investment Corporation; the China National Raw Materials Investment Corporation; the China National Machinery, Electronics, Light Industry, and Textile Investment Corporation; the China National Agricultural Investment Corporation; and the China National Forestry Investment Corporation. These entities are designed to allocate the budgetary funds of the State Planning Commission.

The revolutionary aspect of this scheme is that individual projects will have to compete among themselves for funding allotted in their areas, even though central planners will continue to decide which sectors will receive funding. The funding is supposed to be awarded based on the rate of return projected for the specific project, much as it is in free-market corporate capital budgeting exercises. The administering investment companies are also expected to turn a profit on their operations. Observers wonder about the degree to which these investment companies, which are still in the process of getting set up to fulfill their mandates, will be allowed to substitute market for political criteria, especially given the fact that they report directly to a central planning authority used to making politically-based decisions and getting its own way.

The Insurance Industry

The People's Insurance Company of China (PICC), until recently the state insurance monopoly, resumed offering insurance products in 1979 after being out of business since 1958, when insurance was deemed inappropriate to a socialist system. Traditionally, insurance has been a hard sell in Confucian-based societies in Asia, because many of its savings and indemnity functions are considered to be the responsibility of the family or community unit. However, recognition of its role in spreading risks and providing investment funds in modern economies is growing, and of-

ficials have accelerated authorizations for insurance activity in hopes of preventing the lack of insurance from becoming a roadblock in the development of the new economic system. Although the insurance industry is making great strides in the provision of coverage and products in China, it has not yet developed to the point that it offers a source of investment funds that can be tapped by foreign investors.

PICC offers a variety of products to more than 600,000 enterprises and 60 million households. Some 81 million individuals have bought life insurance policies, which are also sold to foreigners for coverage of risks incurred in China. The PICC operates two subsidiaries, the China Insurance Company (CIC) and the Tai Ping Insurance Company (TPIC), that deal specifically in international business, mostly trade and shipping. The PICC operates nationwide and has several overseas offices, including one in London, the international insurance center. Premium income was more than RMB 18 billion (about US$3.1 billion) in 1992.

The PICC had a monopoly on insurance services in China until 1988, when the PBOC authorized China National Chemicals Import and Export Corporation (SINOCHEM), CBC, the Pingan Insurance Company (in Shenzhen only), and a handful of other entities to begin insurance operations. These upstart competitors were allowed special opportunities to form joint ventures and other cooperative arrangements with foreign insurers, primarily in order to gain insurance expertise. The same year, foreign insurers were provisionally authorized to open branches in the SEZ on Hainan Island, although this experiment did not generate substantial interest. At the end of 1992 US-based American International Group (AIG) was allowed to open a branch in Shanghai to offer life insurance products. Additional developments are expected to occur after new insurance regulations are drafted. At present foreign and joint-venture firms are required to deal with authorized Chinese entities for in-country insurance needs, although this situation is rapidly changing as alternate onshore providers become available.

China's foreign trade corporations (FTCs) usually write their own insurance through the PICC to cover trade activities. Coverage is usually standard and limited: marine risk for total loss only, plus average, all risks, and war risk, at up to 110 percent of invoice value. Claims are to be filed within 30 days of receipt of goods. This standard coverage is referred to as the China Insurance Clause (CIC).

Insurance covering processing with supplied materials reimbursing the holder for certain losses incurred due to failure of suppliers to provide needed inputs is also available. This coverage can be elected with Chinese, British, or United States terms on op-

---

Refer to "Important Addresses" chapter for names and addresses of financial institutions in China.

erations in Guangzhou. The PICC will also, in theory, write coverage for political risks including inability to remit funds, war, riot, and expropriation, although experience is nonexistent.

Pension Funds

There are no effective funded pension schemes operating in China. State enterprises are responsible for paying pensions to retired workers, but, although deductions are made for such payments, they have tended to be funded out of operating revenues on a pay-as-you-go basis. There was a union-operated retirement insurance plan, but it failed during the Cultural Revolution.

The Ministry of Labor moved to set up a framework for a pension system in 1991, but it has not yet become well established. Guangdong Province recently announced a plan to establish a social security trust fund system modeled on Singapore's mandatory Central Provident Fund retirement scheme. However, it remains to be seen whether such a system can be set up to operate in a single jurisdiction. Even if it comes to pass, it will take a considerable time to build up reserves before it becomes a significant source of investment capital.

Private Financial Institutions and the Underground Economy

By definition, all private institutions are part of the underground economy and, as such, lack legal status and are subject to closure by the authorities. However, a number of curious hybrid quasi-legal entities are gaining official recognition, while others remain entirely outside the fold. As noted, many official agencies operate their own free wheeling finance arms, many of which lend and offer financial services to the sponsoring agency's immediate constituents, other recognized entities, and private enterprises as an extension of their primary activities. Others speculate blatantly using public funds, either to buttress their operating funds or to line the pockets of officials. Some of these investment activities have been simply naive, although others have been Ponzi schemes or outright frauds.

In the land of *guanxi*, where the connections and the favors the term implies are critically important and resources are scarce, fiscal abuses are rampant. There are few reports of kickbacks being demanded in order for companies to receive official financing, but bribery has been known to influence the diversion of funds from one project to another, and other forms of graft and corruption are commonplace. In mid-1993, it was rumored that perhaps as much as US$28 billion was missing from PBOC accounts, and that much of it had ended up outside the country in private accounts. Officials denied it, but knowledgeable observers, while questioning the magnitude of the amount, were less ready to dismiss the tale.

In recent months there has been a crackdown on this category of official corruption, with authorities for the first time acknowledging the existence of venal officials. In mid-1993 the authorities detained 100 financial officials, including officers of banks, credit cooperatives, and insurance branches on charges of using their positions for corrupt purposes in Sichuan Province alone. About the same time, 20 suspects led by Li Xiaoshi, a vice minister of the State Science and Technology Commission, were charged in the Changcheng bond fraud case. In this case, officials floated US$175 million in fraudulent bonds, swindling 200,000 investors. Penalties for such fiscal malfeasance includes death. Two BOC employees in Kunming reportedly created a dummy account, crediting it with US$4.3 million and transferred the funds before fleeing. In another reported incident, a student used a computer to loot an overseas account maintained by the People's Liberation Army.

Some private banks have developed to serve needs that have been ignored by duly constituted institutions. For example, in Zhejiang Province at least 53 private banks are purported to be operating in the province, 26 of them in the capital of Wenzhou. These enterprises operate informally to provide funds and services to the dynamic private sector. State institutions do not officially recognize the private entities and usually dedicate their funds to shoring up state-run enterprises.

State banks have taken the position that the unofficial institutions divert funds away from them, adding to the general shortage of funds and skewing the efficient allocation of such funds as are available, a largely disingenuous argument. So far the Wenzhou operations have skirted the edge of illegality by arguing that their activities are experimental and therefore theoretically authorized under the terms of special rules that allow for private operations. Similar private entities are rumored to exist elsewhere as well, as is money lending by individuals and groups of individuals for speculative and private business activities.

At present it is unlikely that foreigners would be able to access funds through such unofficial entities, nor that they would want to take the risk of doing so. However, unless there is a total reversal of the liberalization process, more such outlets will likely appear and they can be expected to gain greater respectability and official standing in the future.

FINANCIAL MARKETS

Chinese capital markets are in their infancy, but they have been developing with surprising rapidity in recent years. There now exist two government-approved stock exchanges and several other informal ones, and although still tightly controlled foreign participation is steadily growing. Government and corporate bond and money markets have become linchpins of financial stability, both as a means of raising capital and as a way to manage, if not control, the nation's money supply. As reforms progress over the next decade, foreign businesses are expected to be allowed to participate in the bond market as well as to operate with greater freedom in stock markets.

Because capital markets are basically so antithetical to Chinese Communist thought, the existing examples have developed in a catch-as-catch-can, bottom-up fashion rather than from a well thought out top-down model, as has the spotty regulation of them. PBOC regulators are trying to think through a comprehensive securities law reform, but they are lacking in expertise, somewhat overwhelmed by it all, and caught up in more pressing issues and ideological battles, so that real reorganization and regulation of the markets is probably still some way off.

Equities Markets

Stocks have long been considered a bugaboo of capitalism in China, although to raise funds during the 1930s the Communist Party issued shares in confiscated companies within the areas it controlled; some of these certificates were even signed by Mao Zedong. When the Communist Party came to power in 1949, it closed down existing stock exchanges, including the one in Shanghai, the predominant equities market in Asia at the time.

As part of its economic opening and in an effort to raise funds, the Chinese government began experimenting with the idea of equity ownership in 1986, issuing shares in some state-run firms. There was no understanding of the stocks and no demand, and cadres ended up peddling the shares door to door without being able to sell out the offering. However, in 1989 dividends on some issues began to rise significantly above the yields available from bank accounts, and share prices rose as much as 800 percent in a short period of time, introducing stock speculation to a new generation of Chinese.

Chinese equities markets deal in plain vanilla buying and selling. There are no futures, options, short selling, or other derivative securities operations allowed. Technically, no limits exist on holdings by any investor, including foreigners, although acquisitions of more than 5 percent of a company's shares must be reported to the PBOC in advance (the authorities have reversed an attempted hostile takeover of one domestic firm by another on the grounds that the buyer failed to follow the 5 percent notification rule). Further, the government has stated its intention of retaining majority state ownership in all listed firms, preventing independent control. While it encourages firms to clean up their operations in order to be allowed to list shares and broader ownership of such shares by individuals, it continues to subscribe to the ideology that the state should retain control of the means of production. Privatization of state holdings is not a goal of the Chinese stock market system.

The lack of effective regulation, investor protection, and acceptable financial statements and disclosure has also hampered the further development of Chinese markets. Observers note that to become fully established, the Chinese markets must increase the number of shares listed; enforce greater disclosure rules; draft national securities and companies laws to regularize operations; and establish an effective independent regulatory body. Chinese markets must encourage more national companies to list on the exchanges, which currently serve only firms operating in their own immediate geographic areas, partly because of the fact that the local governments derive added revenues from locally listed firms, but do not benefit directly from the listing of firms outside their jurisdictions.

Currently the PBOC has regulatory oversight, but even the responsible officials acknowledge their lack of expertise and ability to regulate effectively. Chinese brokers have formed the self-policing Securities Association of China, modeled on the National Association of Securities Dealers (NASD) in the United States, which was called in to consult; however, the industry still operates at a fairly rudimentary level. At the end of 1992 there were 85 securities companies, 386 trust and investment companies, and more than 2,000 bank and credit cooperative units authorized to handle securities transactions. The Shanghai exchange had 171 members, while the Shenzhen exchange had 151.

Authorized Stock Exchanges

The Shanghai Securities Exchange was officially opened at the end of 1990, with the Shenzhen Stock Exchange opening about six months later in 1991. The Shanghai over-the-counter market had been trading debt securities since 1986, while the Shenzhen market began over-the-counter equities trading in 1990, prior to its official authorization by national authorities. By June 1992 total market value of shares listed on the two exchanges had grown to RMB 70.6 billion (about US$12.2 billion), with foreigners—mostly from Hong Kong and Taiwan—holding an estimated one-third of that. By the end of 1992 market capitalization had grown to US$18.4 billion for the 53 issues listed on the two exchanges.

Price-earnings ratios were in the high 80s in Shenzhen and many were above 300 in Shanghai; comparable ratios, which were considered high, were around 20 on the New York and Hong Kong stock exchanges. Despite volatility and setbacks, listings and their value have continued to grow, albeit at a reduced rate, and novice investors have found that prices can go down as well as up, often sharply.

The two exchanges operate in somewhat different economic environments. The Shanghai market is dominated by large companies heavily involved in the domestic market, and the performance of these shares tracks the performance of the domestic economy. Most observers consider that the Shanghai exchange, which operates under heavy influence from Taiwanese investors, will eventually become the premier equities market in China, and it has been somewhat grudgingly designated as the primary financial center in official plans. The Shenzhen exchange lists mostly medium-sized, export-oriented companies, many of which represent foreign-invested joint ventures, and it has closer ties to the Hong Kong and international markets.

Some firms have already begun overtures to either list on both exchanges or transfer their listings from the Shenzhen to the Shanghai exchange. In fall 1993 a Shenzhen-listed firm bought a large position in a Shanghai-listed firm in China's first example of a stock market-effected merger. One of the stated objectives of the move was to obtain a proxy listing on the larger Shanghai exchange.

Currently both markets are small, operating with limited daily turnover, which exacerbates volatility. For a while the markets operated with daily trading limits, but this led to reduced activity and sluggish price action, and limits were removed in May 1992. Authorities can still step in to halt trading at their discretion. Shanghai trades in round lots of 10 shares tied to par value minimums; Shenzhen round lots consist of 2,000 usually lower priced shares. Although both use relatively advanced computer-based paperless systems (which function largely thanks to a low turnover that places few strains on their capabilities), procedures are somewhat tortuous, and technicalities restrict many foreign investors from operating on the exchanges. Exclusionary Chinese rules are less responsible for this situation than is the failure of the Chinese exchanges to meet standards prescribed by foreign home-country regulators. So far, foreign investment in Chinese markets is only for the brave.

Other Trading Venues

To date, the national authorities have authorized the opening of only the two exchanges in Shanghai and Shenzhen, despite a clamor from other areas to operate their own bourses. Shenyang, Guangzhou, Fuzhou, Hainan, Xiamen, Hangzhou, Chongqing, Chengdu, and Kunming have all gone through the preliminaries; some have even set up trading floors. Shenyang has a physical exchange, but no equities and no authorization to trade. Hainan has a gray market that trades unofficially over the counter in the stocks of three property developers. Hangzhou has solved the problem of not being able to open its own exchange by setting up computer links that allow its traders to deal on the Shanghai and Shenzhen exchanges. In Sichuan local officials set up a local exchange in defiance of the national government, charging a fee to traders to meet in a public park to deal in unlisted "shares" of local firms.

The national government has allowed limited over-the-counter trading in certain shares through the Securities Trading Automated Quotation system (STAQ) and the National Electronic Trading system in Beijing, but it has resisted authorizing more exchanges because it wants to concentrate on developing the two that exist and doubts its ability to manage additional ones. The government also fears that robust local exchanges—with the added revenues they produce for the local entities—could provide the provincial centers with strong enough local economies to allow them effectively to resist central directives once such exchanges are established. In turn, locals argue that the existing exchanges constitute unfair monopolies that do not serve their areas or needs. The exchanges do not list the provincials' stocks, and locals are unable to use the market mechanism to mobilize capital or derive benefits from the system.

Problems have also arisen with the allocation of shares for sale. Demand has grown so great among Chinese that the exchanges instituted a lottery system to allocate shares to potential buyers. Potential investors have to buy a lottery ticket, essentially a warrant allowing them to buy newly issued shares at the issue price. The possessors of the tickets drawn are then allocated a portion of the issue. Illegal unofficial secondary markets quickly developed in these warrants, as did counterfeit warrants, and there have been protests, mob scenes, and even riots over alleged misconduct in the manipulation of such warrants. A riot involving thousands of disappointed would-be buyers occurred in Shenzhen in 1992, and in 1993 an estimated 10,000 people took part in a two-day sit-in to protest warrant irregularities in Kunming, which does not even have an authorized stock exchange.

The PBOC announced in late 1993 that it was setting up a procedure to eliminate some of the anarchy and exert control over speculation by prequalifying buyers. Future potential buyers will have to demonstrate that they hold an unspecified minimum balance in fixed-term savings accounts in an official bank in order to be eligible to buy the lottery warrants. This procedure is expected to cut down on the number of bidders and therefore on the level of confusion.

Classes of Shares

Between 1981 and 1992 Chinese entities issued RMB 15.9 billion in equities. Two-thirds of this, RMB 10.9 billion (about US$1.8 billion), was issued in 1992 alone. China has experimented with a variety of shareholding systems, but it has largely standardized holdings into Class A and B shares. The A shares are available only to local investors, while the B shares can only be purchased by foreigners. B share dividends must be paid in foreign currency, either US or Hong Kong dollars. A and B shares carry the same rights and responsibilities, including voting rights. All shares are quoted in renminbi, however B share trades must be settled in foreign exchange. Because of currency restrictions, Chinese B shares are more subject than most to foreign exchange risk, and market risk in the thin emerging markets is already high to begin with.

Companies must first issue A shares and then meet stricter requirements to offer B shares. Each exchange has its own listing criteria, but all companies regardless of their venue are required by national authorities to prepare a feasibility study detailing the proposed uses of capital raised through the issue. To issue B shares companies must submit a proposal detailing how they expect to gain the foreign exchange to support their issues. They must also submit board resolutions to pay dividends 20 days in advance of the payment date, which payment can implicitly be overruled by the PBOC.

In Shanghai companies need only demonstrate to the satisfaction of the governors of the exchange that they possess adequate foreign exchange to cover the annual dividend payment in order to issue B shares, although the unofficial discretionary rules of this larger and more sophisticated exchange are considered adequate to prevent listings by unqualified companies. Shenzhen has stricter nominal rules, although it is generally considered to be the less heavily regulated market. Companies wishing to list B shares on the Shenzhen exchange must have a three-year record of profitability; must have capital of at least RMB 20 million (about US$2.3 million); a ratio of net tangible assets to total assets of at least 38 percent; a ratio of after-tax profit to issued share capital of at least 10 percent during the previous year, and at least 8 percent for the two years preceding that year; and a minimum of 1,000 shareholders.

Currently only state-owned companies—not private Chinese or wholly foreign-owned enterprises—are eligible to list shares, although foreign-invested joint ventures with state firms can list, and listed firms can officially become foreign-invested joint ventures through foreign portfolio investment in their shares.

There are substantial incentives for companies to list B shares. If the Chinese can sell 25 percent of their shares to foreign investors, they are eligible to be considered foreign-invested joint ventures, which allows them more management autonomy in such areas as personnel and investment. Workers (and other interested parties, often local officials whose approval is needed to list) usually must be given shares, warrants, or phantom shares—so-called C and D shares—that can later be sold, resulting in huge profits. In fact, one current investment strategy views the stock markets not as a means of investing in Chinese firms but as exit vehicles, allowing those with interests in such firms to cash out.

There are also disincentives to listing. Firms are supposed to arrange to buy out the state's interest in at least the portion of the company that is taken public, liquidating any debt—usually state-advanced loans—and paying off the imputed value of land, plant and equipment, inventory, and any goodwill which were not previously considered separate assets. The government, as well, sees the listing of stocks as a way of cleaning up the books on a variety of state obligations, hence the required disclosure on the use of funds to be realized from listing. However, companies have been less than honest about their actual use of such funds, which often go not to paying off debt or into operations, but to funding real estate or stock market speculations or distributions to interested parties. Offering prospectuses detailing the nature and extent of indebtedness can make for hair-raising reading.

Because of these requirements, it is estimated that only about 5 percent of all state companies would currently be able to list shares, a fact that international investment bankers are confirming during their search for Chinese underwriting business. Nevertheless, this small percentage still leaves approximately 3,750 potential issuing firms out of the roughly 75,000 state-run entities in China, 13,000 of which are classed as large- and medium-sized firms that should eventually be eligible to issue stock. Although reformers argue that listing will provide the carrot necessary to get companies to clean up their acts, hard-liners protest that listing that is available only to the strongest companies, those that are already doing well, will leave the government to continue supporting the basket cases while depriving it of its control over and participation in the more-productive firms.

Refer to "Important Addresses" chapter for names and addresses of financial institutions in China.

At the end of June 1993 10 B issues were listed on the Shanghai exchange with a market capitalization of US$392 million (in addition, there were 64 A issues), and 17 B issues were listed in Shenzhen, with a market value of US$467 million (plus 34 A issues). By late 1993 at least 34 foreign investment mutual funds with US$1.5 billion in capital were designed to invest in Chinese equities, specifically B shares. This has resulted in the bidding up of the prices of the limited number of available shares. B shares shot up shortly after they were first introduced for foreign consumption, but fell by 50 percent within six months, as their underlying prospects dimmed somewhat. As of June 1992 B shares on both exchanges were down more than 20 percent since the first of that year, and they have traded in a volatile range since then, remaining largely flat in real terms.

Equally ominous was a late 1993 crash of A shares on the Shanghai market. The A share index fell by 13 percent overnight to a 52-week low, more than 50 percent below its February high. Authorities sparked the sell-off by announcing a calendar of new offerings that is expected to inundate the Shanghai exchange with a reported additional 1.2 to 1.5 billion new shares in the first quarter of 1994 alone. Subsidiary rumors told of plans for capital gains taxes and other new levies on share transactions. Investors doubt that the market can absorb this volume of stock without giving up substantial value in existing shares. The lack of linkage between the Shanghai and Shenzhen exchanges was demonstrated by the fact that Shenzhen exchange A shares, where the new listing calendar is less ambitious, lost only about 5 percent. The almost total disconnection between the skittish local A shares and the B shares with their support provided by an excess of foreign money was confirmed by the failure of the B shares to react on either exchange.

In May 1993 23 foreign brokerage firms were authorized to trade directly in B shares on the Shanghai exchange; in August eight foreign brokerage houses were allowed to trade on the Shenzhen exchange. Transaction costs are relatively high, especially the minimum fees on foreign transactions.

Overseas Listings

Foreigners interested in Chinese equities can also trade H, or so-called Red Chip, shares that are listed on the Hong Kong or other international exchanges outside China. At the end of 1993 six such issues traded in Hong Kong, where listing rules are stricter than in China. An additional three have been authorized, and in early 1994 the government announced plans to allow perhaps another 20 firms to list overseas.

Hong Kong rules include the requirement that an issue retain a sponsor and market maker for three years after its initial public offering. Listed Chinese companies must maintain two sets of books, one using the less developed Chinese accounting standards and one using stricter Hong Kong or other recognized international standards, with an explanation of any differences between the two sets of figures. Semiannual statements to foreign investors must contain the relevant points recorded in these sets of books and be available in English. H shares must make up at least 10 percent of total capitalization, with at least 25 percent of all shares, including B and H shares, being available for purchase. A and H shares must represent different voting classes, with a mechanism for resolution of disputes in case of a tie. Dividends on H shares must be payable in foreign currency.

In addition to the Hong Kong-listed issues, three Chinese proxy issues trade directly on the New York Stock Exchange (NYSE), the main one being the Bermuda-incorporated financial subsidiary of a Chinese auto maker. As of fall 1993 there were plans to list four issues on the Vancouver Exchange and at least one each on the London and Singapore exchanges.

The early 1994 announcement calls for as many as 20 new issues to be listed worldwide during the year. These new listings are expected to represent large state-run heavy industrial enterprises including firms in the utilities, airline, and steel industries. Most were expected to list in Hong Kong, but others were planning to list on the NYSE. A series of proprietary put and call warrants on an index of Hong Kong-listed Chinese issues has also been introduced on the American Stock Exchange.

Some observers worry that the exaggerated demand for Chinese shares will result in a crash when disappointing results undermine the overly optimistic prices commanded by the scarce shares. Others express concern that the Hong Kong and other foreign exchanges will cherrypick the best Chinese shares for overseas listing, leaving the majority of B shares to wither on the vine at home. In general, these are short-term concerns, as China's growing market has more than enough potential power to provide additional securities in the future. Most observers expect growing sophistication on the part of the Chinese in developing their markets eventually to overcome the disadvantages of the current situation.

Money and Debt Markets

The PBOC began issuing treasury bills in 1981, the first such debt securities to be issued since 1949. In 1982 local enterprises were allowed to issue bonds, and in 1984 state-owned financial entities began issuing bonds. In 1986 state-run enterprise short-term corporate bonds were authorized, forming the basis for the development of a money market. Lower level government entities still are not authorized to issue debt, however. Between 1981 and 1992 a total of RMB 381.7 billion in securities was issued: RMB 148.1 billion in treasury bills and notes (almost 40 percent of the total), RMB 96 billion in enterprise bonds (25 percent), RMB 61 billion in finance bonds (16 percent), 60.7 in other types of bonds (15 percent), and RMB 15.9 billion in stocks (4 percent). The value of bonds issued in 1992 was double that of issues in 1991, and by the end of 1992 there was about US$25 billion in government and about US$10 billion in "corporate" debt outstanding.

Treasury bills started as forced savings instruments because purchase was mandatory and the instruments were not tradable but had to be held to maturity. Transferability was allowed in 1988 in 61 localities nationwide, providing the basis for the development of a debt market. The Shanghai exchange began its modern operation in 1986 as an over-the-counter bond market. It continues to trade treasury instruments, financial bonds, and enterprise bonds, although debt securities make up a small and shrinking portion of its total activity. The government has also set up over-the-counter markets—the Securities Trading Automated Quotation system (STAQ) and the National Electronic Trading system—which allow trading in treasury issues and some stocks through about 3,000 local outlets nationwide. A small but growing secondary market for trading debt has also emerged in industrial Wuhan.

The government was accustomed to placing its debt forcibly with state-owned enterprises and official entities and has in the past even required payroll deductions to make individual workers the owners of public debt. These practices were resented because such issues have tied up scarce capital and the yields offered have been low. Now moves are afoot to issue debt that is more attractive to investors to get them to channel some of the estimated US$175 billion in informal savings into the financial system. The China Investment Bank (CIB) has been authorized to issue US dollar denominated bonds domestically in an attempt to capture reserves of privately held currency. Bonds linked to the price of gold that could serve as an inflation hedge have also been discussed.

More and more borrowing is being done overseas, and some 119 separate Chinese entities are authorized to borrow and issue debt securities abroad. These entities raised about US$1.7 billion overseas in 1993 and have plans to borrow at least US$1 billion more in 1994. Although much borrowing has been done in the form of barely securitized syndicated loans from international commercial banks that hold the resulting paper for their own ac-

counts, the PCBC, ABC, BOC, and CITIC have all become active in issuing floating- and fixed- rate straight bonds in Japan, the United States, and Europe. In December 1993 international rating agencies upgraded the debt of the BOC, PCBC, and CITIC to investment-quality levels, making the offerings of these institutions more attractive. However, underwriters are beginning to balk at the concessionary rates that they have had to give Chinese issuers, and investors are beginning to look for higher yields to compensate for what they see as the risks of lending to an out-of-control Chinese economy.

Money markets are still primitive in China. In 1986 the government began to develop an experimental money market among the regional cities of Guangzhou, Chongqing, Wuhan, Shenyang, and Changzhou, hoping to distribute capital based on supply and demand as determined by the interest rate differentials bid by these cities spread across the country. During the first half of 1986 total transfers amounted to RMB 14 billion, about nine times the roughly RMB 1.5 billion that the PBOC allocated to the cities to provide liquidity.

This pilot project has grown to encompass 20 cities and serves as a de facto interbank market. Some 10 additional regional money markets have developed, led by those in Wuhan and Shenyang, which have started to act as trading centers for and market makers in other debt as well. So far there is no nationwide system linking these thriving centers, which compete in some areas and fail to serve others entirely. Two other regional centers anchored by Shanghai have also grown up: the Wuxi system and the Yangtze River system, which together can handle lending of up to RMB 10 billion (about US$1.15 billion) on a short-term basis.

In 1988 the government allowed Shanghai firms to issue commercial paper, a privilege that has since been extended to firms in Shenzhen, with the promise of similar authorizations in additional areas in the future. So far no formal market exists for the trading of such short-term debt, which tends to be privately placed. A market for such commercial paper can be expected to develop once the amount of such paper reaches critical mass. The Shanghai branch of the BOC has already been authorized to discount and trade in bills of exchange, paving the way for such an eventual development.

To date, foreigners have not been allowed to participate in any of these markets. However, the government anticipates that the debt markets will take off much as the stock markets have, and it recognizes that China will need to tap overseas expertise and capital to develop a more comprehensive debt management system in the future.

Refer to "Important Addresses" chapter for names and addresses of financial institutions in China.

Despite China's proverbial shortage of foreign exchange, it has a financial sector surplus due to export sales and foreign investment inflows, much of which is invested in offshore debt securities, mostly in Hong Kong. Observers state that Chinese institutions regularly take 10 to 20 percent of bonds offered in regional sales, and they took 30 percent of an offering by General Electric Credit Corporation in fall 1993. The same observers note that Chinese bond traders are rapidly gaining expertise, and are already much more aggressive than some other Asian traders, although they prefer high-rated paper. The BOC, ICBC, and CBC are the most active players.

Other Financial Markets

There are no formal futures or commodities markets operating in China for either hedging or speculative purposes. However, informal markets are springing up, with private entrepreneurs offering and trading in contracts in various Chinese cities and on Hong Kong markets. In early 1994 authorities announced that they would set up an official meat futures market in Chengdu, the center of pork production in China. The market is set to begin operations in April.

Due to currency restrictions, no market in foreign exchange exists, although a type of forward foreign exchange contract is available on the Shanghai swap market in which foreign exchange is contracted for at a time in the future rather than on the spot.

Gold is in great demand as a store of wealth. However, it is difficult to obtain formally and no organized market exists for transactions in the metal.

China has not expressed any interest to date in developing markets in derivative financial instruments.

FURTHER READING

This discussion is provided as a basic guide to money, finances, financial institutions, and financial markets in China. Those interested in current developments may wish to consult the *Far Eastern Economic Review, Asia Money,* the *China Business Review,* the *Beijing Review,* and the *Wall Street Journal,* all of which frequently cover economic and financial developments in China.

Currency & Foreign Exchange

INTERNATIONAL PAYMENT INSTRUMENTS

China does not subscribe to the International Chamber of Commerce (ICC) Uniform Customs and Practices for Documentary Credits, the international standard for payment instruments and procedures. However, it normally follows these conventions. Chinese sellers will generally accept only confirmed, irrevocable letters of credit (L/C) at sight. If they have a long-standing relationship with the buyer, sellers may grudgingly accept documents against acceptance (D/A) or documents against payment (D/P) arrangements. Unless arranged otherwise in advance, any costs associated with the operation of payment instruments—advisories, negotiation, cables, confirmations, or amendments—are expected to be paid by the foreign party abroad in order to avoid expenditures of foreign exchange.

The Bank of China (BOC) is the agency responsible for handling all such transactions, although it regularly delegates actual negotiations to correspondent banks. A BOC or other official bank L/C usually cannot be issued unless all other necessary permits have been authorized, which serves as a cross-check on the deal in question.

Chinese firms do not normally acknowledge acceptance of amendments, although they are quick to make their nonacceptance known. If the other party does not hear anything to the contrary, it can usually assume that amendments have been accepted.

The Chinese usually do not sign off on specific documents, such as bills of lading, insurance policies, and invoices. Rather they use a rubber stamp, making authentication of specific documents difficult. Also, documents are commonly issued as a single unit rather than as separate items. For instance, invoices often incorporate certificates of origin, packing, weight, and measurement all in a single document unless the credit specifies otherwise. Sanitary specifications and quality certificates are usually issued together. Requesting separate documents can become a major issue.

Large sales are often made on the basis of a 10 to 20 percent down payment, with a 70 to 80 percent payment being made at the time of delivery, and the remaining 10 to 20 percent being paid on an installment basis over time. Chinese buyers often require a standby letter of credit to cover the return of their down payment if the deal falls through.

The problems occasioned by the lack of foreign exchange are often circumvented by using a variety of other arrangements such as countertrade, compensation trade, licensing, and leasing.

Refer to the "International Payments" chapter for a full discussion of letters of credit and documentary collections.

CURRENCY

China's currency is the renminbi (RMB), or "People's money." Renminbi is divided into units known as *yuan*, or "dollars," and colloquially known as *kuai*, or "money." Each yuan is divided into 100 *fen*. Ten fen constitutes a unit known as a *jiao*, colloquially *mao*; thus, 20 fen is referred to as 2 jiao or 2 mao. Coins are issued in denominations of RMB 0.01, RMB 0.02, and RMB 0.05, although these will be seen and used infrequently by foreigners. Notes are issued in denominations of RMB 0.10, RMB 0.20, RMB 0.50, RMB 1, RMB 2, RMB 5, RMB 10, RMB 50, and RMB 100. The RMB 50 note is worth about US$5.75 at the official rate. Taking renminbi out of the country has been illegal, but it is now possible to take up to RMB 6,000 (about US$690) out of the country legally, although bringing RMB into China is still legally questionable. Some retail outlets in Hong Kong are now accepting RMB, and the BOC and Po Sang Bank in Hong Kong have exchanged RMB for foreign currencies. The renminbi is not a convertible currency and many of the difficulties experienced by foreigners trying to do business with China come from the country's lack of foreign exchange and hurdles in getting their money out of the country. The government has been taking tentative steps toward making the renminbi somewhat more convertible and user-friendly.

FOREIGN EXCHANGE CERTIFICATES

Until January 1, 1994 foreigners were generally required to use a separate currency, the foreign exchange certificate, or FEC. FEC were first issued in 1980 in notes of RMB 0.10, RMB 0.50, RMB 1, RMB 5, RMB 10, RMB 50, and RMB 100. Although foreigners were legally allowed to use renminbi for all but a few types of transaction, many outlets would accept only FEC from foreigners. Theoretically, the outlets had to be licensed to accept FEC, and such licenses were relatively few, but the premium for FEC made it difficult for foreigners to get by with anything other than FEC. Merchants usually attempted to give change in renminbi, which was often useless to foreigners, rather than in FEC. As the renminbi became somewhat more convertible and acceptable, there was less insistence on the use of FEC, although many outlets that did accept RMB from foreigners charged a premium amounting to as much as 50 percent.

FEC were originally issued to eliminate the black market use of foreign currency in China. Foreign currency cannot legally be used in China, but foreigners are allowed to possess it, and there is great local demand for it. Hong Kong dollars enjoy a substantial circulation in southeastern China, and they can sometimes be used—illegally—for retail purchases there. A black market quickly developed in FEC, which were more valuable than RMB because they could be used to buy goods not available to ordinary Chinese and could be used indirectly to gain access to hard currency.

Because of the burgeoning black market in FEC, the government announced in 1986 that FEC would be abolished. This announcement was renewed in 1988, and again in 1990, with the State Administration of Exchange Control (SAEC), the unit of the PBOC responsible for regulating foreign exchange activity, stating again in May 1993 that the government would phase out FEC as a prelude to establishing convertibility of the RMB. In December 1993 PBOC governor Zhu Rongji announced plans to eliminate FEC, but most observers remained skeptical until the government actually announced the immediate abolition of the FEC and unification of the RMB and the FEC as a single currency as of January 1, 1994. This left companies and individuals scrambling to unload their FEC during the last days of the year and resulted in an effective devaluation of the renminbi by 50 percent to a new year's rate of RMB 8.69 to US$1.

REMITTANCE AND EXCHANGE CONTROLS

All foreign exchange is tightly controlled under the Provisional Regulations for Exchange Control of the PRC of 1981, as modified in 1985. These regulations consist of more than 30 separate articles grouped under seven headings.

Only authorized outlets are allowed to change money. No wholesale business rate exists, although foreign businesses should attempt to establish an understanding with Chinese partners as to the specific rates that will be used in calculating the financial aspects of arrangements and may be able to negotiate a somewhat more favorable effective rate with these partners. Most foreigners involved in business will deal with banks, particularly the BOC. Foreigners can usually change foreign currency for personal use at airports, some large stores, Friendship stores (national tourist stores), and major hotels, most of which usually charge a commission, resulting in a somewhat less-favorable overall rate.

Foreigners receive a receipt when they exchange foreign currency for RMB, and they must present this receipt in order to reconvert currency later. Usually, no more than half of the amount of currency accounted for by receipts will be redeemed.

A thriving and highly illegal black market operates in most urban areas but especially in the southeast where US and Hong Kong dollars are traded openly. However, black-market money changers are reported to be unreliable and readily cheat on rates and amounts given. They may also work in conjunction with muggers who rob you of the funds you have just changed.

Traveler's checks issued by major banks and other recognized financial entities are readily negotiable in China at banks and at some retail outlets. Major credit cards are also accepted by outlets used to dealing with foreigners, although the BOC, which processes most of these payments, charges a hefty premium when converting the charges on such purchases. The BOC will also issue cash advances on credit cards, again at a hefty commission rate. It is not practical to wire or otherwise receive funds from home though the Chinese financial system. Bank transfers are error-prone and can take several weeks, and no other accepted channels for such transfers exist due to the primitiveness of the system and the rigorousness of the exchange controls.

Businesses are expected to generate the foreign exchange necessary for purchases of foreign imported items and the repatriation of profits earned from operations in China. They can sometimes buy such foreign exchange on the swap markets, although doing so greatly reduces real profits. Foreign exchange generated by certain export sales is effectively exempt because foreign businesses are allowed to retain such proceeds abroad.

FOREIGN EXCHANGE
OPERATIONS

Renminbi are basically inconvertible, being bought and sold only as needed for authorized purposes, such as for commercial and travel requirements, and only by authorized entities under strict controls. Foreigners wishing to do business in China must receive authorization from the Ministry of Foreign Trade and Economic Cooperation (MOFTEC), or other appropriate authority, in order to be eligible to participate in foreign exchange transactions.

Formerly, only the BOC was authorized to conduct foreign exchange transactions. However, authority to handle foreign exchange transactions has been steadily expanded to include a variety of additional state and foreign banks, although the range of outlets through which foreign exchange transactions can be handled is still relatively narrow. Foreign businesses must open an account with the BOC or other authorized institution to handle official foreign exchange transactions. Such accounts are literally deposit accounts: Actual sums of foreign currency are deposited in them with the bank taking and converting the currency as needed, charging a commission on each transaction. All foreign exchange receipts must be placed in these accounts, where they can be held essentially in escrow without being converted into renminbi as is the general rule for domestic businesses. Business expenses are to be paid out of these accounts, and foreign businesses are also expected to deposit the proceeds of offshore foreign currency-denominated borrowings in their onshore accounts unless other arrangements have previously been made.

Foreign Exchange Adjustment Centers, known as swap centers, are quasi-official markets in which for-

eigners can trade for foreign currency and RMB outside the official procedures but still under the official supervision of the BOC and SAEC. Operations are considered a privilege rather than a right, and the authorities have broad discretion as to whether they will allow a particular transaction to go through. Good relations with the local authorities can be important in getting funds through the swap centers.

The first such centers were authorized in 1986, and there are currently more than 10 authorized markets, although the markets in Shenzhen and Shanghai remain the most important. Most of the others operate infrequently and at low levels of activity. The Shanghai market deals mostly in US dollars, while Shenzhen trades in a wider variety of currencies but handles mostly US and Hong Kong dollar transactions. Shanghai also allows some limited forward foreign exchange purchases. Operating rules vary widely. For instance, Shanghai allows large entities to handle their own deals, while small firms must use brokers; in Guangzhou all entities can do their own deals; and in Shenzhen all entities must go through brokers. Only authorized entities are allowed to trade in the swap markets, although individuals may be allowed to participate under special circumstances.

In order to trade, foreign entities must submit an annual plan demonstrating sources and uses of foreign exchange, justifying their need for the funds to be obtained through the swap. They must also show that such funds will be applied in a legal manner. Foreign exchange purchase rates in the swap markets are theoretically determined by supply and demand but have usually represented about a 50 percent premium over the official rate. With devaluation, this differential is expected to contract substantially.

China's Foreign Exchange Rates - Year End Actual
Chinese Renminbi (RMB) to United States Dollar (US$)

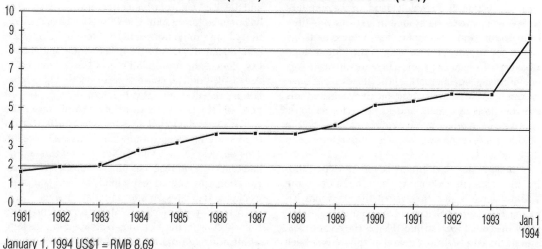

January 1, 1994 US$1 = RMB 8.69

Swap markets are funded through the foreign exchange earned by Chinese exporters. Exporters are currently required to sell 20 percent of their hard currency funds to the PBOC for RMB at the official rate, but they are allowed to retain their remaining foreign exchange, held not as cash but as quotas to buy foreign exchange from the PBOC in the future at the then prevailing rate. These quotas can be sold to authorized entities, such as other Chinese entities involved in external trade, or to foreign firms with operations in China. Proposed reforms would allow exporters to keep 100 percent of hard currency earnings in cash for operations, investment, or sale in swap markets, loosening the government's grip on foreign exchange transactions.

In June 1993 the government temporarily removed all controls on swap market prices, and the effective swap market exchange rate shot up to RMB 11 from RMB 8.2 to the US dollar. By November 1993 the swap rate had returned to a more reasonable level of about RMB 8.7, still an indication that the RMB was significantly overvalued (the official rate was around 5.8). The government worked to maintain currency stability by pumping about US$200 million into the Shanghai swap center, the country's largest such foreign exchange market. These funds came from the PBOC managed foreign currency reserves and established the PBOC as the main formulator of foreign exchange policy. Before this intervention, most observers had believed the BOC exercised de facto control over exchange policy. However, the BOC now seems to be acting more or less as an agent carrying out PBOC directives.

RATES OF EXCHANGE

The SAEC, a unit of the PBOC, began setting exchange rates using a managed float system on January 1, 1994. The system will nominally set rates based on basic supply and demand for foreign currency, although its is unlikely that demand for the renminbi will be adequate to maintain it in a strong position. Prior to this announcement, rates were ostensibly based on the daily performance of the RMB against a basket of foreign currencies. In reality the rate was heavily managed, fluctuating little. Its level has been more a political than an economic decision, and this situation is likely to continue despite reforms. In recent years the government has been keying on the US dollar rate to maintain stability with reference to that currency.

The RMB has been progressively devalued during the years since China began to open up to the world, falling 70 percent against the US dollar between 1981 and 1990. It was devalued at the end of 1981, the end of 1985, in mid-1986, at the end of 1989, and at the end of 1990. Since that time it has been allowed to slowly ease further against the US dollar, and frequent flurries of activity, including local hoarding, occur based on rumors of additional official devaluations.

The elimination of the FEC on January 1, 1994 resulted in an effective immediate devaluation of 50 percent from an official rate of 5.8 to 8.7, the prevailing rate on the swap markets. Some observers note that even at this rate the RMB is overvalued and that it would have to fall an additional 15 to 25 percent to between 10 and 11 to the dollar to reach parity and clear the market. However, despite frantic activity as companies rushed to dump their FEC prior to the change, there was little immediate instability. The PBOC counted on the fact that nearly 80 percent of all foreign exchange activity was already occurring on the swap markets at roughly the 8.7 rate to counteract any major dislocation, an assumption that seems to have been borne out, at least during initial trading.

FOREIGN RESERVES AND FOREIGN DEBT

China has a chronic shortage of foreign currency, which, more than ideological factors, accounts for some of its more restrictive operating policies. Despite a favorable balance of trade with many of its principal trading partners—the United States in particular—China's foreign reserves have continued to drop since reaching a high in the late 1980s. During the first half of 1993 total reserves fell 14 percent to US$38.4 billion, down from about US$45 billion at the beginning of 1993. However, by the end of the third quarter of 1993 international reserves had risen to US$41.4 billion. China runs a substantial budget deficit and has numerous calls on its shrinking hoard of hard currency which it draws on to shore up its ailing state sector.

China's foreign reserves are held by the PBOC and the BOC, each of which has control over roughly half of the total amount. The World Bank has decreed that China should not count the amount held by the BOC because it theoretically is an independent entity. Hence, the mid-1993 drop of US$640 million in the PBOC's official share of reserves to US$18.8 billion represented a relatively minor drop of about 3 percent. However, the drop of US$6 billion in the BOC's share of unofficial reserves to US$19.6 billion represented a steep drop of more than 23 percent. This suggests that China is attempting to keep its use of its foreign reserves off the books. Such deteriorating ratios could result in China being required to pay higher rates on international lending.

A temporary freeze on international lending to China following the Tiananmen incident in 1989 kept China's foreign debt position from growing for a while. However, the resumption of lending in 1990 has led to increased sovereign debt accumulation. Foreign debt was reported to equal US$73 billion at the end of 1993, after having risen 15.2 percent to US$60.6 billion in 1991, and 27.2 percent in 1990. China also has a time bomb ticking away in that large amounts of medium-term loans taken out during the mid- to late-1980s are scheduled to fall due en masse during the mid-1990s. China has been paying the interest on these obligations but will need to roll over the principal.

The Ministry of Finance and the Bank of China have waged an internal bureaucratic battle over which agency will handle the nation's foreign debt. Whichever entity gains control—and there is little reason to predict victory for either or to assess pluses or minuses depending on which wins out— some changes in the way such borrowing is used must occur. Currently, 119 separate official and semi-

official entities have borrowing authority, authority which the state planning commission is expected to rein in by the use of quotas. Too many entities have used such debt to fund current operations or projects that cannot generate the foreign exchange needed to pay off the loans, putting added pressure on China's foreign reserves to maintain the country's acceptable credit rating.

FURTHER READING

This discussion is provided as a basic guide to money in China. Those interested in current developments may wish to consult the *Far Eastern Economic Review, Asia Money,* the *China Business Review,* the *Beijing Review,* and the *Wall Street Journal,* all of which frequently cover economic and financial developments in China.

Exchange Rates—RMB/US$

Note: The official exchange rate was RMB 8.69=US$1 at the beginning of January 1994

	Jan	Feb	Mar	Apr	May	Jun	Jul	Aug	Sep	Oct	Nov	Dec
1981	1.552	1.613	1.613	1.666	1.727	1.760	1.765	1.800	1.754	1.758	1.741	1.740
1982	1.771	1.820	1.843	1.856	1.812	1.901	1.930	1.943	1.957	1.989	2.000	1.944
1983	1.924	1.965	1.983	1.994	1.989	1.995	1.997	1.984	1.987	1.966	1.994	1.992
1984	2.049	2.063	2.065	2.093	2.187	2.218	2.299	2.372	2.547	2.649	2.678	2.795
1985	2.816	2.835	2.853	2.848	2.856	2.869	2.881	2.909	2.972	3.078	3.209	3.209
1986	3.209	3.215	3.220	3.214	3.201	3.211	3.643	3.713	3.715	3.726	3.731	3.731
1987	3.731	3.731	3.731	3.731	3.731	3.731	3.731	3.731	3.731	3.731	3.731	3.731
1988	3.731	3.731	3.731	3.731	3.731	3.731	3.731	3.731	3.731	3.731	3.731	3.731
1989	3.731	3.731	3.731	3.731	3.731	3.731	3.731	3.731	3.731	3.731	3.731	4.182
1990	4.734	4.734	4.734	4.734	4.734	4.734	4.734	4.734	4.734	4.734	4.971	5.235
1991	5.235	5.235	5.235	5.277	5.357	5.367	5.369	5.372	5.387	5.392	5.399	5.414
1992	5.462	5.478	5.487	5.510	5.518	5.489	5.456	5.442	5.505	5.586	5.613	5,816
1993	5.780	5.787	5.745	5.720	5.739	5.750	5.775	5.791	5.801	5.801	5.805	5.800

Source: US Federal Reserve System

International Payments

International transactions add an additional layer of risk for buyers and sellers that are familiar only with doing business domestically. Currency regulations, foreign exchange risk, political, economic, or social upheaval in the buyer's or seller's country, and different business customs may all contribute to uncertainty. Ultimately, however, the seller wants to make sure he gets paid and the buyer wants to get what he pays for. Choosing the right payment method can be the key to the transaction's feasibility and profitability.

There are four common methods of international payment, each providing the buyer and the seller with varying degrees of protection for getting paid and for guaranteeing shipment. Ranked in order of most security for the supplier to most security for the buyer, they are: Cash in Advance, Documentary Letters of Credit (L/C), Documentary Collections (D/P and D/A Terms), and Open Account (O/A).

Cash in Advance

In cash in advance terms the buyer simply pre-pays the supplier prior to shipment of goods. Cash in advance terms are generally used in new relationships where transactions are small and the buyer has no choice but to pre-pay. These terms give maximum security to the seller but leave the buyer at great risk. Since the buyer has no guarantee that the goods will be shipped, he must have a high degree of trust in the seller's ability and willingness to follow through. The buyer must also consider the economic, political and social stability of the seller's country, as these conditions may make it impossible for the seller to ship as promised.

Documentary Letters of Credit

A letter of credit is a bank's promise to pay a supplier on behalf of the buyer so long as the supplier meets the terms and conditions stated in the credit. Documents are the key issue in letter of credit transactions. Banks act as intermediaries, and have nothing to do with the goods themselves.

Letters of credit are the most common form of international payment because they provide a high degree of protection for both the seller and the buyer. The buyer specifies the documentation that he requires from the seller before the bank is to make payment, and the seller is given assurance that he will receive payment after shipping his goods so long as the documentation is in order.

Documentary Collections

A documentary collection is like an international cash on delivery (COD), but with a few twists. The exporter ships goods to the importer, but forwards shipping documents (including title document) to his bank for transmission to the buyer's bank. The buyer's bank is instructed not to transfer the documents to the buyer until payment is made (Documents against Payment, D/P) or upon guarantee that payment will be made within a specified period of time (Documents against Acceptance, D/A). Once the buyer has the documentation for the shipment he is able to take possession of the goods.

D/P and D/A terms are commonly used in ongoing business relationships and provide a measure of protection for both parties. The buyer and seller, however, both assume risk in the transaction, ranging from refusal on the part of the buyer to pay for the documents, to the seller's shipping of unacceptable goods.

Open Account

This is an agreement by the buyer to pay for goods within a designated time after their shipment, usually in 30, 60, or 90 days. Open account terms give maximum security to the buyer and greatest risk to the seller. This form of payment is used only when the seller has significant trust and faith in the buyer's ability and willingness to pay once the goods have been shipped. The seller must also consider the economic, political and social stability of the buyer's country as these conditions may make it impossible for the buyer to pay as promised.

DOCUMENTARY COLLECTIONS (D/P, D/A)

Documentary collections focus on the transfer of documents such as bills of lading for the transfer of ownership of goods rather than on the goods themselves. They are easier to use than letters of credit and bank service charges are generally lower.

This form of payment is excellent for buyers who wish to purchase goods without risking prepayment and without having to go through the more cumbersome letter of credit process.

Documentary collection procedures, however, entail risk for the supplier, because payment is not made until after goods are shipped. In addition, the supplier assumes the risk while the goods are in transit and storage until payment/acceptance take place. Banks involved in the transaction do not guarantee payments. A supplier should therefore only agree to a documentary collection procedure if the transaction includes the following characteristics:

- The supplier does not doubt the buyer's ability and willingness to pay for the goods;
- The buyer's country is politically, economically, and legally stable;
- There are no foreign exchange restrictions in the buyer's home country, or unless all necessary licenses for foreign exchange have already been obtained;
- The goods to be shipped are easily marketable.

Types of Collections

The three types of documentary collections are:
1. Documents against Payment (D/P)
2. Documents against Acceptance (D/A)
3. Collection with Acceptance (Acceptance D/P)

All of these collection procedures follow the same general step-by-step process of exchanging documents proving title to goods for either cash or a contracted promise to pay at a later time. The documents are transferred from the supplier (called the remitter) to the buyer (called the drawee) via intermediary banks. When the supplier ships goods, he presents documents such as the bill of lading, invoices, and certificate of origin to his representative bank (the remitting bank), which then forwards them to the buyer's bank (the collecting bank). According to the type of documentary collection, the buyer may then do one of the following:

- With Documents against Payment (D/P), the buyer may only receive the title and other documents after paying for the goods;
- With Documents against Acceptance (D/A), the buyer may receive the title and other documents after signing a time draft promising to pay at a later date;

- With Acceptance Documents against Payment, the buyer signs a time draft for payment at a later date. However, he may only obtain the documents after the time draft reaches maturity. In essence, the goods remain in escrow until payment has been made.

In all cases the buyer may take possession of the goods only by presenting the bill of lading to customs or shipping authorities.

In the event that the prospective buyer cannot or will not pay for the goods shipped, they remain in legal possession of the supplier, but he may be stuck with them in an unfavorable situation. Also, the supplier has no legal basis to file claim against the prospective buyer. At this point the supplier may:

- Have the goods returned and sell them on his domestic market; or
- Sell the goods to another buyer near where the goods are currently held.

If the supplier takes no action the goods will be auctioned or otherwise disposed of by customs.

Documentary Collection Procedure

The documentary collection process has been standardized by a set of rules published by the International Chamber of Commerce (ICC). These rules are called the Uniform Rules for Collections (URC) and are contained in ICC Publication No. 322. (See the last page of this section for ICC addresses and list of available publications.)

The following is the basic set of steps used in a documentary collection. Refer to the illustration on the following page for a graphic representation of the procedure.

(1) The seller (remitter, exporter) ships the goods.
(2) and (3) The seller forwards the agreed upon documents to his bank, the remitting bank, which in turn forwards them to the collecting bank (buyer's bank).
(4) The collecting bank notifies the buyer (drawee, importer) and informs him of the conditions under which he can take possession of the documents.
(5) To take possession of the documents, the buyer makes payment or signs a time deposit.
(6) and (7) If the buyer draws the documents against payment, the collecting bank transfers payment to the remitting bank for credit to the supplier's account. If the buyer draws the documents against acceptance, the collecting bank sends the acceptance to the remitting bank or retains it up to maturity. On maturity, the collecting bank collects the bill and transfers it to the remitting bank for payment to the supplier.

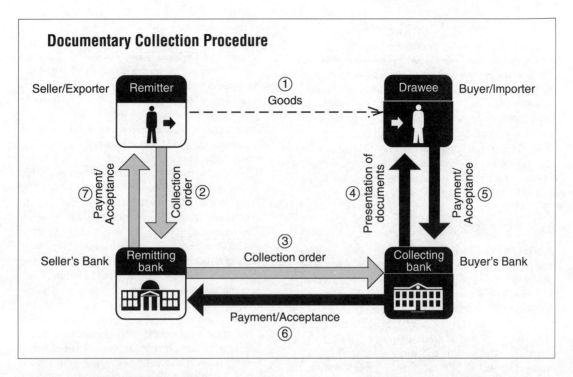

Documentary Collection Procedure

Seller/Exporter — Remitter

① Goods

Drawee — Buyer/Importer

⑦ Payment/Acceptance

② Collection order

④ Presentation of documents

⑤ Payment/Acceptance

Seller's Bank — Remitting bank

③ Collection order

Collecting bank — Buyer's Bank

⑥ Payment/Acceptance

TIPS FOR BUYERS

1. The buyer is generally in a secure position because he does not assume ownership or responsibility for goods until he has paid for the documents or signed a time draft.
2. The buyer may not sample or inspect the goods before accepting and paying for the documents without authorization from the seller. However, the buyer may in advance specify a certificate of inspection as part of the required documentation package.
3. As a special favor, the collecting bank can allow the buyer to inspect the documents before payment. The collecting bank assumes responsibility for the documents until their redemption.
4. In the above case, the buyer should immediately return the entire set of documents to the collecting bank if he cannot meet the agreed payment procedure.
5. The buyer assumes no liability for goods if he refuses to take possession of the documents.
6. Partial payment in exchange for the documents is not allowed unless authorized in the collection order.
7. With documents against acceptance, the buyer may receive the goods and resell them for profit before the time draft matures, thereby using the proceeds of the sale to pay for the goods. The buyer remains responsible for payment, however, even if he cannot sell the goods.

TIPS FOR SUPPLIERS

1. The supplier assumes risk because he ships goods before receiving payment. The buyer is under no legal obligation to pay for or to accept the goods.
2. Before agreeing to a documentary collection, the supplier should check on the buyer's creditworthiness and business reputation.
3. The supplier should make sure the buyer's country is politically and financially stable.
4. The supplier should find out what documents are required for customs clearance in the buyer's country. Consulates may be of help.
5. The supplier should assemble the documents carefully and make sure they are in the required form and endorsed as necessary.
6. As a rule, the remitting bank will not review the documents before forwarding them to the collecting bank. This is the responsibility of the seller.
7. The goods travel and are stored at the risk of the supplier until payment or acceptance.
8. If the buyer refuses acceptance or payment for the documents, the supplier retains ownership. The supplier may have the goods shipped back or try to sell them to another buyer in the region.
9. If the buyer takes no action, customs authorities may seize the goods and auction them off or otherwise dispose of them.
10. Because goods may be refused, the supplier should only ship goods which are readily marketable to other sources.

LETTERS OF CREDIT (L/C)

A letter of credit is a document issued by a bank stating its commitment to pay someone (supplier/exporter/seller) a stated amount of money on behalf of a buyer (importer) so long as the seller meets very specific terms and conditions. Letters of credit are often called documentary letters of credit because the banks handling the transaction deal in documents as opposed to goods. Letters of credit are the most common method of making international payments, because the risks of the transaction are shared by both the buyer and the supplier.

STEPS IN USING AN L/C

The letter of credit process has been standardized by a set of rules published by the International Chamber of Commerce (ICC). These rules are called the Uniform Customs and Practice for Documentary Credits (UCP) and are contained in ICC Publication No. 400. (See the last page of this section for ICC addresses and list of available publications.) The following is the basic set of steps used in a letter of credit transaction. Specific letter of credit transactions follow somewhat different procedures.

- After the buyer and supplier agree on the terms of a sale, the buyer arranges for his bank to open a letter of credit in favor of the supplier.
- The buyer's bank (the issuing bank), prepares the letter of credit, including all of the buyer's instructions to the seller concerning shipment and required documentation.
- The buyer's bank sends the letter of credit to a correspondent bank (the advising bank), in the seller's country. The seller may request that a particular bank be the advising bank, or the domestic bank may select one of its correspondent banks in the seller's country.
- The advising bank forwards the letter of credit to the supplier.
- The supplier carefully reviews all conditions the buyer has stipulated in the letter of credit. If the supplier cannot comply with one or more of the provisions he immediately notifies the buyer and asks that an amendment be made to the letter of credit.
- After final terms are agreed upon, the supplier prepares the goods and arranges for their shipment to the appropriate port.
- The supplier ships the goods, and obtains a bill of lading and other documents as required by the buyer in the letter of credit. Some of these documents may need to be obtained prior to shipment.
- The supplier presents the required documents to the advising bank, indicating full compliance with the terms of the letter of credit. Required documents usually include a bill of lading, commercial invoice, certificate of origin, and possibly an inspection certificate if required by the buyer.
- The advising bank reviews the documents. If they are in order, the documents are forwarded to the issuing bank. If it is an irrevocable, confirmed letter of credit the supplier is guaranteed payment and may be paid immediately by the advising bank.
- Once the issuing bank receives the documents it notifies the buyer who then reviews the documents himself. If the documents are in order the buyer signs off, taking possession of the documents, including the bill of lading, which he uses to take possession of the shipment.
- The issuing bank initiates payment to the advising bank, which pays the supplier.

The transfer of funds from the buyer to his bank, from the buyer's bank to the supplier's bank, and from the supplier's bank to the supplier may be handled at the same time as the exchange of documents, or under terms agreed upon in advance.

Parties to a Letter of Credit Transaction

Buyer/Importer  Buyer's bank

Seller/Supplier/Exporter 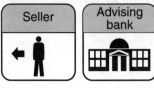 Seller's bank

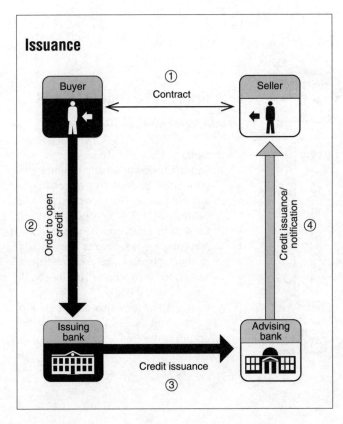

Issuance of a Letter of Credit

① Buyer and seller agree on purchase contract.
② Buyer applies for and opens a letter of credit with issuing ("buyer's") bank.
③ Issuing bank issues the letter of credit, forwarding it to advising ("seller's") bank.
④ Advising bank notifies seller of letter of credit.

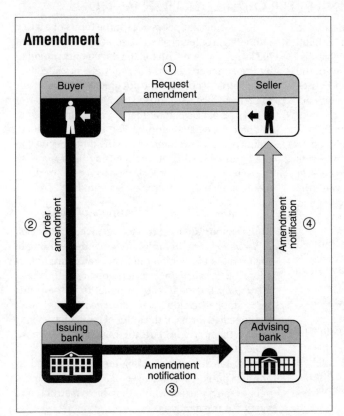

Amendment of a Letter of Credit

① Seller requests (of the buyer) a modification (amendment) of the terms of the letter of credit. Once the terms are agreed upon:
② Buyer issues order to issuing ("buyer's") bank to make an amendment to the terms of the letter of credit.
③ Issuing bank notifies advising ("seller's") bank of amendment.
④ Advising bank notifies seller of amendment.

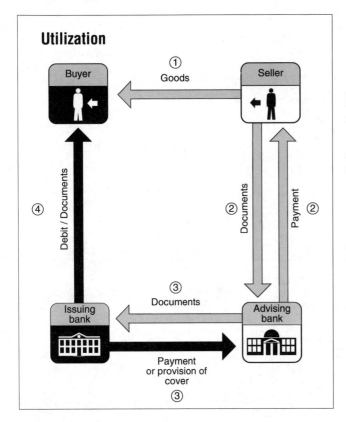

Utilization

Utilization of a Letter of Credit

(irrevocable, confirmed credit)

① Seller ships goods to buyer.
② Seller forwards all documents (as stipulated in the letter of credit) to advising bank. Once documents are reviewed and accepted, advising bank pays seller for the goods.
③ Advising bank forwards documents to Issuing bank. Once documents are reviewed and accepted, issuing bank pays advising bank.
④ Issuing bank forwards documents to buyer. Seller's letter of credit, or account, is debited.

COMMON PROBLEMS IN LETTER OF CREDIT TRANSACTIONS

Most problems with letter of credit transactions have to do with the ability of the supplier to fulfill obligations the buyer establishes in the original letter of credit. The supplier may find the terms of the credit difficult or impossible to fulfill and either tries to do so and fails, or asks the buyer for an amendment to the letter of credit. Observers note that over half of all letters of credit involving parties in East Asia are amended or renegotiated entirely. Since most letters of credit are irrevocable, amendments to the original letter of credit can only be made after further negotiations and agreements between the buyer and the supplier. Suppliers may have one or more of the following problems:

• Shipment schedule stipulated in the letter of credit cannot be met.
• Stipulations concerning freight cost are deemed unacceptable.
• Price is insufficient due to changes in exchange rates.
• Quantity of product ordered is not the expected amount.
• Description of product to be shipped is either insufficient or too detailed.
• Documents stipulated in the letter of credit are difficult or impossible to obtain.

Even when suppliers accept the terms of a letter of credit, problems often arise at the stage where banks review, or negotiate, the documents provided by the supplier against the requirements specified in the letter of credit. If the documents are found not to be in accord with those specified in the letter of credit, the bank's commitment to pay is invalidated. In some cases the supplier can correct the documents and present them within the time specified in the letter of credit. Or, the advising bank may ask the issuing bank for authorization to accept the documents despite the discrepancies found.

Limits on Legal Obligations of Banks

It is important to note once again that banks *deal in documents and not in goods*. Only the wording of the credit is binding on the bank. Banks are not responsible for verifying the authenticity of the documents, nor for the quality or quantity of the goods being shipped. As long as the *documents* comply with the specified terms of the letter of credit, banks may accept them and initiate the payment process as stipulated in the letter of credit. Banks are free from liability for delays in sending messages caused by another party, consequences of Acts of God, or the acts of third parties whom they have instructed to carry out transactions.

TYPES OF LETTERS OF CREDIT

Basic Letters of Credit

There are two basic forms of letter of credit: the Revocable Credit and the Irrevocable Credit. There are also two types of irrevocable credit: the Irrevocable Credit not Confirmed, and the Irrevocable Confirmed Credit. Each type of credit has advantages and disadvantages for the buyer and for the seller. Also note that the more the banks assume risk by guaranteeing payment, the more they will charge for providing the service.

1. Revocable credit This credit can be changed or canceled by the buyer without prior notice to the supplier. Because it offers little security to the seller revocable credits are generally unacceptable to the seller and are rarely used.

2. Irrevocable credit The irrevocable credit is one which the issuing bank commits itself irrevocably to honor, provided the beneficiary complies with all stipulated conditions. This credit cannot be changed or canceled without the consent of both the buyer and the seller. As a result, this type of credit is the most widely used in international trade. Irrevocable credits are more expensive because of the issuing bank's added liability in guaranteeing the credit. There are two types of irrevocable credits:

a. The Irrevocable Credit not Confirmed by the Advising Bank (Unconfirmed Credit) This means that the buyer's bank which issues the credit is the only party responsible for payment to the supplier, and the supplier's bank is obliged to pay the supplier only after receiving payment from the buyer's bank. The supplier's bank merely acts on behalf of the issuing bank and therefore incurs no risk.

b. The Irrevocable, Confirmed Credit In a confirmed credit, the advising bank adds its guarantee to pay the supplier to that of the issuing bank. If the issuing bank fails to make payment the advising bank will pay. If a supplier is unfamiliar with the buyer's bank which issues the letter of credit, he may insist on an irrevocable confirmed credit. These credits may be used when trade is conducted in a high risk area where there are fears of outbreak of war or social, political, or financial instability. Confirmed credits may also be used by the supplier to enlist the aid of a local bank to extend financing to enable him to fill the order. A confirmed credit costs more because the bank has added liability.

Special Letters of Credit

There are numerous special letters of credit designed to meet specific needs of buyers, suppliers, and intermediaries. Special letters of credit usually involve increased participation by banks, so financing and service charges are higher than those for ba-

sic letters of credit. The following is a brief description of some special letters of credit.

1. Standby Letter of Credit This credit is primarily a payment or performance guarantee. It is used primarily in the United States because US banks are prevented by law from giving certain guarantees. Standby credits are often called non-performing letters of credit because they are only used as a backup payment method if the collection on a primary payment method is past due.

Standby letters of credit can be used, for example, to guarantee the following types of payment and performance:

- repayment of loans;
- fulfillment by subcontractors;
- securing the payment for goods delivered by third parties.

The beneficiary to a standby letter of credit can draw from it on demand, so the buyer assumes added risk.

2. Revolving Letter of Credit This credit is a commitment on the part of the issuing bank to restore the credit to the original amount after it has been used or drawn down. The number of times it can be utilized and the period of validity is stated in the credit. The credit can be cumulative or noncumulative. Cumulative means that unutilized sums can be added to the next installment whereas noncumulative means that partial amounts not utilized in time expire.

3. Deferred Payment Letter of Credit In this credit the buyer takes delivery of the shipped goods by accepting the documents and agreeing to pay his bank after a fixed period of time. This credit gives the buyer a grace period, and ensures that the seller gets payment on the due date.

4. Red Clause Letter of Credit This is used to provide the supplier with some funds prior to shipment to finance production of the goods. The credit may be advanced in part or in full, and the buyer's bank finances the advance payment. The buyer, in essence, extends financing to the seller and incurs ultimate risk for all advanced credits.

5. Transferable Letter of Credit This allows the supplier to transfer all or part of the proceeds of the letter of credit to a second beneficiary, usually the ultimate producer of the goods. This is a common financing tactic for middlemen and is used extensively in the Far East.

6. Back-to-Back Letter of Credit This is a new credit opened on the basis of an already existing, nontransferable credit. It is used by traders to make payment to the ultimate supplier. A trader receives a letter of credit from the buyer and then opens another letter of credit in favor of the supplier. The first letter of credit is used as collateral for the second credit. The second credit makes price adjustments from which come the trader's profit.

OPENING A LETTER OF CREDIT

The wording in a letter of credit should be simple but specific. The more detailed an L/C is, the more likely the supplier will reject it as too difficult to fulfill. At the same time, the buyer will wish to define in detail what he is paying for.

Although the L/C process is designed to ensure the satisfaction of all parties to the transaction, it cannot be considered a substitute for face-to-face agreements on doing business in good faith. It should therefore contain only those stipulations required from the banks involved in the documentary process.

L/Cs used in trade with East Asia are usually either irrevocable unconfirmed credits or irrevocable confirmed credits. In choosing the type of L/C to open in favor of the supplier, the buyer should take into consideration generally accepted payment processes in the supplier's country, the value and demand for the goods to be shipped, and the reputation of the supplier.

In specifying documents necessary from the supplier, it is very important to demand documents that are required for customs clearance and those that reflect the agreement reached between the buyer and the supplier. Required documents usually include the bill of lading, a commercial and/or consular invoice, the bill of exchange, the certificate of origin, and the insurance document. Other documents required may be copies of a cable sent to the buyer with shipping information, a confirmation from the shipping company of the state of its ship, and a confirmation from the forwarder that the goods are accompanied by a certificate of origin. Prices should be stated in the currency of the L/C, and documents should be supplied in the language of the L/C.

THE APPLICATION

The following information should be included on an application form for opening an L/C.

(1) **Beneficiary** The seller's company name and address should be written completely and correctly. Incomplete or incorrect information results in delays and unnecessary additional cost.

(2) **Amount** Is the figure a maximum amount or an approximate amount? If words like "circa," "ca.," "about," etc., are used in connection with the amount of the credit, it means that a difference as high as 10 percent upwards or downwards is permitted. In such a case, the same word should also be used in connection with the quantity.

(3) **Validity Period** The validity and period for presentation of the documents following shipment of the goods should be sufficiently long to allow the exporter time to prepare his documents and ship them to the bank. Under place of validity, state the domicile of either the advising bank or the issuing bank.

(4) **Beneficiary's Bank** If no bank is named, the issuing bank is free to select the correspondent bank.

(5) **Type of Payment Availability** Sight drafts, time drafts, or deferred payment may be used, as previously agreed to by the supplier and buyer.

(6) **Desired Documents** Here the buyer specifies precisely which documents he requires. To obtain effective protection against the supply of poor quality goods, for instance, he can demand the submission of analysis or quality certificates. These are generally issued by specialized inspection companies or laboratories.

(7) **Notify Address** An address is given for notification of the imminent arrival of goods at the port or airport of destination. Damage of goods in shipment is also cause for notification. An agent representing the buyer may be used.

(8) **Description of Goods** Here a short, precise description of the goods is given, along with quantity. If the credit amount carries the notation "ca.," the same notation should appear with the quantity.

(9) **Confirmation Order** It may happen that the foreign beneficiary insists on having the credit confirmed by the bank in his country.

Sample Letter of Credit Application

Sender	Instructions to open a Documentary Credit
American Import-Export Co., Inc. 123 Main Street San Francisco, California USA ____ Our reference AB/02	San Francisco, 30th September 19.. Place / Date

Please open the following

[X] irrevocable   [ ] revocable documentary credit

Domestic Bank Corporation
Documentary Credits
P.O. Box 1040
San Francisco, California

Beneficiary	Beneficiary's bank (if known)
① China Trading Corporation 12 Xichangan Jie Beijing 100804 PEOPLE'S REPUBLIC OF CHINA	④ China Commercial Bank Beijing Main Branch Beijing/CHINA

Amount
② US$ 7,200.--

Date and place of expiry
③ 25th November 19.. in San Francisco

Please advise this bank
[ ] by letter
[X] by letter, cabling main details in advance
[ ] by telex / telegram with full text of credit

Partial shipments	Transhipment	Terms of shipment (FOB, C & F, CIF)
[X] allowed [ ] not allowed	[ ] allowed [X] not allowed	CIF Oakland

Despatch from / Taking in charge at	For transportation to	Latest date of shipment	Documents must be presented not later than
China	Oakland	10th Nov. 19.. ③ 15	days after date of despatch

Beneficiary may dispose of the credit amount as follows

[X] at sight upon presentation of documents ⑤

[ ] after ....days, calculated from date of ....

[ ] by a draft due ....
drawn on [ ] you [ ] your correspondents
which you / your correspondents will please accept

against surrender of the following documents ⑥

[X] invoice   (....3.....copies)

Shipping document
[X] sea: bill of lading, to order, endorsed in blank
[ ] rail: dublicate waybill
[ ] air: air consignment note
[ ]

[X] insurance policy, certificte   (................. copies)
covering the following risks:
"all risks" including war up to
[ ] Additional documents final destination in USA

[X] Confirmation of the carrier that the ship is not more than 15 years old

[X] packing list (3 copies)

Notify address in bill of lading / goods addressed to	
American Import-Export Co. ⑦ 123 Main Street San Francisco, California USA	Goods insured by [ ] us [X] seller

Goods ⑧

1,000 "Record players ANC 83 as per proforma invoice
no. 74/1853 dd 10th September 19.."

at US$70.20 per item

Your correspondents to advise beneficiary [ ] adding their confirmation [X] without adding their confirmation ⑨
Payments to be debited to our...US Dollar......................account no 1032679150

NB. The applicable text is marked by [X]

E 6801 N 1/2 3.81 5000

American Import-Export Co., Inc.

Signature _____

For mailing please see overleaf

[Left margin vertical text:] This credit is subject to the «Uniform customs and practice for documentary credits» fixed by the International Chamber of Commerce. It is understood that you do not assume any responsibility neither for the correctness, validity or genuineness of the documents which will be remitted to you nor for the description, quality, quantity and weight of the goods thereby represented.

TIPS FOR PARTIES TO A LETTER OF CREDIT

Buyer

1. Before opening a letter of credit, the buyer should reach agreement with the supplier on all particulars of payment procedures, schedules of shipment, type of goods to be sent, and documents to be supplied by the supplier.
2. When choosing the type of L/C to be used, the buyer should take into account standard payment methods in the country with which he is doing business.
3. When opening a letter of credit, the buyer should keep the details of the purchase short and concise.
4. The buyer should be prepared to amend or renegotiate terms of the L/C with the supplier. This is a common procedure in international trade. On irrevocable L/Cs, the most common type, amendments may be made only if all parties involved in the L/C agree.
5. The buyer can eliminate exchange risk involved with import credits in foreign currencies by purchasing foreign exchange on the forward markets.
6. The buyer should use a bank experienced in foreign trade as the L/C issuing bank.
7. The validation time stated on the L/C should give the supplier ample time to produce the goods or to pull them out of stock.
8. The buyer should be aware that an L/C is not failsafe. Banks are only responsible for the documents exchanged and not the goods shipped. Documents in conformity with L/C specifications cannot be rejected on grounds that the goods were not delivered as specified in the contract. The goods shipped may not in fact be the goods ordered and paid for.
9. Purchase contracts and other agreements pertaining to the sale between the buyer and supplier are not the concern of the issuing bank. Only the terms of the L/C are binding on the bank.
10. Documents specified in the L/C should include those the buyer requires for customs clearance.

Supplier

1. Before signing a contract, the supplier should make inquiries about the buyer's creditworthiness and business practices. The supplier's bank will generally assist in this investigation.
2. The supplier should confirm the good standing of the buyer's bank if the credit is unconfirmed.
3. For confirmed credit, the supplier should determine that his local bank is willing to confirm credits from the buyer and his bank.
4. The supplier should carefully review the L/C to make sure he can meet the specified schedules of shipment, type of goods to be sent, packaging, and documentation. All aspects of the L/C must be in conformance with the terms agreed upon, including the supplier's address, the amount to be paid, and the prescribed transport route.
5. The supplier must comply with every detail of the L/C specifications, otherwise the security given by the credit is lost.
6. The supplier should ensure that the L/C is irrevocable.
7. If conditions of the credit have to be modified, the supplier should contact the buyer immediately so that he can instruct the issuing bank to make the necessary amendments.
8. The supplier should confirm with his insurance company that it can provide the coverage specified in the credit, and that insurance charges in the L/C are correct. Insurance coverage often is for CIF (cost, insurance, freight) value of the goods plus 10 percent.
9. The supplier must ensure that the details of goods being sent comply with the description in the L/C, and that the description on the invoice matches that on the L/C.
10. The supplier should be familiar with foreign exchange limitations in the buyer's country which may hinder payment procedures.

GLOSSARY OF DOCUMENTS IN INTERNATIONAL TRADE

The following is a list and description of some of the more common documents importers and exporters encounter in the course of international trade. For the importer/buyer this serves as a checklist of documents he may require of the seller/exporter in a letter of credit or documents against payment method.

Bill of Lading A document issued by a transportation company (such as a shipping line) to the shipper which serves as a receipt for goods shipped, a contract for delivery, and may serve as a title document. The major types are:

Straight (non-negotiable) Bill of Lading Indicates that the shipper will deliver the goods to the consignee. The document itself does not give title to the goods. The consignee need only identify himself to claim the goods. A straight bill of lading is often used when the goods have been paid for in advance.

Order (negotiable or "shippers order") Bill of Lading This is a title document which must be in the possession of the consignee (buyer/importer) in order for him to take possession of the shipped goods. Because this bill of lading is negotiable, it is usually made out "to the order of" the consignor (seller/exporter).

Air Waybill A bill of lading issued for air shipment of goods, which is always made out in straight non-negotiable form. It serves as a receipt for the shipper and needs to be made out to someone who can take possession of the goods upon arrival—without waiting for other documents to arrive.

Overland/Inland Bill of Lading Similar to an Air Waybill, except that it covers ground or water transport.

Certificate of Origin A document which certifies the country of origin of the goods. Because a certificate of origin is often required by customs for entry, a buyer will often stipulate in his letter of credit that a certificate of origin is a required document.

Insurance Document A document certifying that goods are insured for shipment.

Invoice/Commercial Invoice A document identifying the seller and buyer of goods or services, identifying numbers such as invoice number, date, shipping date, mode of transport, delivery and payment terms, and a complete listing and description of the goods or services being sold including prices, discounts, and quantities. The commercial invoice is usually used by customs to determine the true cost of goods when assessing duty.

Certificate of manufacture A document in which the producer of goods certifies that production has been completed and that the goods are at the disposal of the buyer.

Consular Invoice An invoice prepared on a special form supplied by the consul of an importing country, in the language of the importing country, and certified by a consular official of the foreign country.

Dock Receipt A document/receipt issued by an ocean carrier when the seller/exporter is not responsible for moving the goods to their final destination, but only to a dock in the exporting country. The document/receipt indicates that the goods were, in fact, delivered and received at the specified dock.

Export License A document, issued by a government agency, giving authorization to export certain commodities to specified countries.

Import License A document, issued by a government agency, giving authorization to import certain commodities.

Inspection Certificate An affidavit signed by the seller/exporter or an independent inspection firm (as required by the buyer/importer), confirming that merchandise meets certain specifications.

Packing List A document listing the merchandise contained in a particular box, crate, or container, plus type, dimensions, and weight of the container.

Phytosanitary (plant health) Inspection Certificate A document certifying that an export shipment has been inspected and is free from pests and plant diseases considered harmful by the importing country.

Shipper's Export Declaration A form prepared by a shipper/exporter indicating the value, weight, destination, and other information about an export shipment.

GLOSSARY OF TERMS OF SALE

The following is a basic glossary of common terms of sale in international trade. Note that issues regarding responsibility for loss and insurance are complex and beyond the scope of this publication. The international standard of trade terms of sale are "Incoterms," published by the International Chamber of Commerce (ICC), 38, Cours Albert Ier, F-75008 Paris, France. Other offices of the ICC are British National Committee of the ICC, Centre Point, 103 New Oxford Street, London WC1A 1QB, England and US Council of the ICC, 1212 Avenue of the Americas, New York, NY 10010 USA.

C&F (Cost and Freight) Named Point of Destination The seller's price includes the cost of the goods and transportation up to a named port of destination, but does not cover insurance. Under these terms insurance is the responsibility of the buyer/importer.

CIF (Cost, Insurance, and Freight) Named Point of Destination The seller's price includes the cost of the goods, insurance, and transportation up to a named port of destination.

Ex Point of Origin ("Ex Works" "Ex Warehouse" etc.) The seller's price includes the cost of the goods and packing, but without any transport. The seller agrees to place the goods at the disposal of the buyer at a specified point of origin, on a specified date, and within a fixed period of time. The buyer is under obligation to take delivery of the goods at the agreed place and bear all costs of freight, transport and insurance.

FAS (Free Alongside Ship) The seller's price includes the cost of the goods and transportation up to the port of shipment alongside the vessel or on a designated dock. Insurance under these terms is usually the responsibility of the buyer.

FOB (Free On Board) The seller's price includes the cost of the goods , transportation to the port of shipment, and loading charges on a vessel. This might be on a ship, railway car, or truck at an inland point of departure. Loss or damage to the shipment is borne by the seller until loaded at the point named and by the buyer after loading at that point.

Ex Dock—Named Port of Importation The seller's price includes the cost of the goods, and all additional charges necessary to put them on the dock at the named port of importation with import duty paid. The seller is obligated to pay for insurance and freight charges.

GLOSSARY OF INTERNATIONAL PAYMENT TERMS

Advice The forwarding of a letter of credit or an amendment to a letter of credit to the seller, or beneficiary of the letter of credit, by the advising bank (seller's bank).

Advising bank The bank (usually the seller's bank) which receives a letter of credit from the issuing bank (the buyer's bank) and handles the transaction from the seller's side. This includes: validating the letter of credit, reviewing it for internal consistency, forwarding it to the seller, forwarding seller's documentation back to the issuing bank, and, in the case of a confirmed letter of credit, guaranteeing payment to the seller if his documents are in order and the terms of the credit are met.

Amendment A change in the terms and conditions of a letter of credit, usually to meet the needs of the seller. The seller requests an amendment of the buyer who, if he agrees, instructs his bank (the issuing bank) to issue the amendment. The issuing bank informs the seller's bank (the advising bank) who then notifies the seller of the amendment. In the case of irrevocable letters of credit, amendments may only be made with the agreement of all parties to the transaction.

Back-to-Back Letter of Credit A new letter of credit opened in favor of another beneficiary on the basis of an already existing, nontransferable letter of credit.

Beneficiary The entity to whom credits and payments are made, usually the seller/supplier of goods.

Bill of Exchange A written order from one person to another to pay a specified sum of money to a designated person. The following two versions are the most common:

Draft A financial/legal document where one individual (the drawer) instructs another individual (the drawee) to pay a certain amount of money to a named person, usually in payment for the transfer of goods or services. Sight Drafts are payable when presented. Time Drafts (also called usance drafts) are payable at a future fixed (specific) date or determinable (30, 60, 90 days etc.) date. Time drafts are used as a financing tool (as with Documents against Acceptance D/P terms) to give the buyer time to pay for his purchase.

Promissory Note A financial/legal document wherein one individual (the issuer) promises to pay another individual a certain amount.

Collecting Bank (also called the presenting bank) In a Documentary Collection, the bank (usually the buyer's bank) that collects payment or a time draft from the buyer to be forwarded to the remitting bank (usually the seller's bank) in exchange for shipping and other documents which enable the buyer to take possession of the goods.

Confirmed Letter of Credit A letter of credit which contains a guarantee on the part of both the issuing and advising bank of payment to the seller so long as the seller's documentation is in order and terms of the credit are met.

Deferred Payment Letter of Credit A letter of credit where the buyer takes possession of the title documents and the goods by agreeing to pay the issuing bank at a fixed time in the future.

Discrepancy The noncompliance with the terms and conditions of a letter of credit. A discrepancy may be as small as a misspelling, an inconsistency in dates or amounts, or a missing document. Some discrepancies can easily be fixed; others may lead to the eventual invalidation of the letter of credit.

D/A Abbreviation for "Documents against Acceptance."

D/P Abbreviation for "Documents against Payment."

Documents against Acceptance (D/A) *See* Documentary Collection

Documents against Payment (D/P) *See* Documentary Collection

Documentary Collection A method of effecting payment for goods whereby the seller/exporter instructs his bank to collect a certain sum from the buyer/importer in exchange for the transfer of shipping and other documentation enabling the buyer/importer to take possession of the goods. The two main types of Documentary Collection are:

Documents against Payment (D/P) Where the bank releases the documents to the buyer/importer only against a cash payment in a prescribed currency; and

Documents against Acceptance (D/A) Where the bank releases the documents to the buyer/importer against acceptance of a bill of exchange guaranteeing payment at a later date.

Draft *See* Bill of exchange.

Drawee The buyer in a documentary collection.

Forward Foreign Exchange An agreement to purchase foreign exchange (currency) at a future date at a predetermined rate of exchange. Forward foreign exchange contracts are often purchased by buyers of merchandise who wish to hedge against foreign exchange fluctuations between the time the contract is negotiated and the time payment is made.

Irrevocable Credit A letter of credit which cannot be revoked or amended without prior mutual consent of the supplier, the buyer, and all intermediaries.

Issuance The act of the issuing bank (buyer's bank) establishing a letter of credit based on the buyer's application.

Issuing Bank The buyer's bank which establishes a letter of credit in favor of the supplier, or beneficiary.

Letter of Credit A document stating commitment on the part of a bank to place an agreed upon sum of money at the disposal of a seller on behalf of a buyer under precisely defined conditions.

Negotiation In a letter of credit transaction, the examination of seller's documentation by the (negotiating) bank to determine if they comply with the terms and conditions of the letter of credit.

Open Account The shipping of goods by the supplier to the buyer prior to payment for the goods. The supplier will usually specify expected payment terms of 30, 60, or 90 days from date of shipment.

Red Clause Letter of Credit A letter of credit which makes funds available to the seller prior to shipment in order to provide him with funds for production of the goods.

Remitter In a documentary collection, an alternate name given to the seller who forwards documents to the buyer through banks.

Remitting Bank In a documentary collection, a bank which acts as an intermediary, forwarding the remitter's documents to, and payments from the collecting bank.

Sight Draft *See* Bill of Exchange.

Standby Letter of Credit- A letter of credit used as a secondary payment method in the event that the primary payment method cannot be fulfilled.

Time Draft *See* Bill of Exchange.

Validity The time period for which a letter of credit is valid. After receiving notice of a letter of credit opened on his behalf, the seller/exporter must meet all the requirements of the letter of credit within the period of validity.

Revocable Letter of Credit A letter of credit which may be revoked or amended by the issuer (buyer) without prior notice to other parties in the letter of credit process. It is rarely used.

Revolving Letter of Credit A letter of credit which is automatically restored to its full amount after the completion of each documentary exchange. It is used when there are several shipments to be made over a specified period of time.

FURTHER READING

For more detailed information on international trade payments, refer to the following publications of the International Chamber of Commerce (ICC), Paris, France.

Uniform Rules for Collections This publication describes the conditions governing collections, including those for presentation, payment and acceptance terms. The Articles also specify the responsibility of the bank regarding protest, case of need and actions to protect the merchandise. An indispensable aid to everyday banking operations. (A revised, updated edition will be published in 1995.) ICC Publication No. 322.

Documentary Credits: UCP 500 and 400 Compared This publication was developed to train managers, supervisors, and practitioners of international trade in critical areas of the new UCP 500 Rules. It pays particular attention to those Articles that have been the source of litigation. ICC Publication No. 511.

The New ICC Standard Documentary Credit Forms Standard Documentary Credit Forms are a series of forms designed for bankers, attorneys, importers/exporters, and anyone involved in documentary credit transactions around the world. This comprehensive new edition, prepared by Charles del Busto, Chairman of the ICC Banking Commission, reflects the major changes instituted by the new "UCP 500." ICC Publication No. 516.

The New ICC Guide to Documentary Credit Operations This new Guide is a fully revised and expanded edition of the "Guide to Documentary Credits" (ICC publication No. 415, published in conjunction with the UCP No. 400). The new Guide uses a unique combination of graphs, charts, and sample documents to illustrate the Documentary Credit process. An indispensable tool for import/export traders, bankers, training services, and anyone involved in day-to-day Credit operations. ICC Publication No. 515.

Guide to Incoterms 1990 A companion to "Incoterms," the ICC "Guide to Incoterms 1990" gives detailed comments on the changes to the 1980 edition and indicates why it may be in the interest of a buyer or seller to use one or another trade term. This guide is indispensable for exporters/importers, bankers, insurers, and transporters. ICC Publication No. 461/90.

These and other relevant ICC publications may be obtained from the following sources:

ICC Publishing S.A.
International Chamber of Commerce
38, Cours Albert Ier
75008 Paris, France
Tel: [33] (1) 49-53-28-28 Fax: [33] (1) 49-53-28-62
Telex: 650770

International Chamber of Commerce
Borsenstrasse 26
P.O. Box 4138
8022 Zurich, Switzerland

British National Committee of the ICC
Centre Point, New Oxford Street
London WC1A QB, UK

ICC Publishing, Inc.
US Council of the ICC
156 Fifth Avenue, Suite 820
New York, NY 10010, USA
Tel: [1] (212) 206-1150 Fax: [1] (212) 633-6025

Corporate Taxation

This chapter refers only to the taxation of entities and business establishments with foreign investment and wholly foreign-owned entities.

AT A GLANCE

Corporate Income Tax Rate (%)	33 (a)
Capital Gains Tax Rate (%)	33
Branch Tax Rate (%)	33
Withholding Tax (%)	
Dividends	20 (b)
Interest	20
Royalties from Patents, Know-how, etc.	20 (c)
Branch Remittance Tax	0
Net Operating Losses (Years)	
Carryback	0
Carryforward	5

(a) Lower rates may apply to establishments operating in specified locations in China (see Taxes on Corporate Income and Gains).
(b) Dividends remitted abroad by foreign investment enterprises and foreign enterprises are exempt from withholding tax.
(c) A reduced rate of 0 to 10 percent may apply to certain qualifying royalties that have preferential transfer terms.

TAXES ON CORPORATE INCOME AND GAINS

Corporate Income Tax

The People's Republic of China (PRC) income tax system discussed below refers to rules specially applicable to business operations with foreign investments including Sino-foreign equity joint ventures, cooperative ventures and wholly foreign-owned subsidiaries and other business activities and operations. Domestic state-owned enterprises, subject to a different set of rules which are not disclosed publicly, are not discussed in this chapter.

Generally, all foreign investment enterprises and foreign enterprises are subject to the Income Tax Law of the People's Republic of China on Enterprises with Foreign Investment and Foreign Enterprises. This unified tax law replaces the Joint Ventures Income Tax Law and the Foreign Enterprises Income Tax Law, effective from July 1, 1991. Under the new law, a joint venture is defined as a foreign investment enterprise.

Foreign investment enterprises include equity joint ventures, cooperative and contractual enterprises and entities wholly owned by foreigners. A foreign investment enterprise is subject to tax on its worldwide income. However, a foreign tax credit is allowed for income taxes paid to other countries by branches of the foreign investment enterprise, limited to the PRC income tax imposed on the same income. If cooperative and contractual joint ventures are not legal persons, the parties to the joint ventures may elect to be taxed separately on their share of the taxed as a single entity.

The term "foreign enterprises" refers to foreign companies, enterprises and other economic organizations such as representative offices, contracted projects and royalty arrangements. Foreign enterprises are subject to tax only on their income from PRC sources. The taxation of foreign enterprises depends on whether the enterprise has an establishment in China. Foreign enterprises with establishments in China are subject to tax on all income derived from the PRC; however, those without establishments in the PRC are only subject to withholding tax on income from PRC sources.

The term "establishment" is broadly defined to include a place of management; a branch; an office; a factory; a workshop; a mine, an oil or gas well, or any other place of extraction of natural resources; a building site; a construction, assembly, installation or exploration project; places that provide services; and business agents.

Note: *This section is courtesy of and © Ernst & Young from their Worldwide Personal Tax Guide, 1993 Edition. This material should not be regarded as offering a complete explanation of the taxation matters referred to. Ernst & Young is a leading international professional services firm with offices in 100 countries, including China. Refer to "Important Addresses" chapter for addresses and phone numbers of Ernst & Young offices in China.*

Recent Changes in the Chinese Corporate Tax Code

In late 1993 Chinese authorities announced plans for a substantial revision of their tax system to be implemented on January 1, 1994. Details of the changes are not yet available. However, the basic provisions and some of their implications can be outlined. Stephen Lee, senior manager of Ernst & Young's China division, was quoted in the *Wall Street Journal* as saying, based on available preliminary information, that the changes would probably result in little net increase in businesses' overall tax burdens. Interested parties should consult tax specialists in the area for specifics, which may not be settled for some time. In early January 1994 the new tax system had already resulted in such confusion that Chinese authorities were mobilizing officials and an estimated one million "tax tutors" in an attempt to explain the new tax arrangements to local authorities, businesses, and the populace at large.

Central authorities have hastened to state that the overall changes are designed to be revenue neutral, and that the shift in the amounts and types of taxes paid could actually result in net savings to a variety of business operations. They have further left open the possibility that individual businesses will be able to make deals on their tax situation to offset negative impacts. To calm the fears of foreign invested enterprises (FIEs) the central government has gone so far as to offer to refund any extra taxes paid by FIEs under the new rules for a period of five years. This offer applies to FIEs that had approval to operate in China as of the end of 1993. Future FIEs will be subject to the new rules, but they may still be eligible for tax incentives, especially if they are involved in high priority areas such as advanced technology. Investors should plan for tough negotiations on the issue of tax concessions when they apply to do business in China.

The primary focus of the new tax regime is the lowering of the business tax rate on domestic state-run enterprises from the preexisting 55 percent average rate to an estimated 33 percent, ostensibly to allow them to compete on a more equal basis with FIEs that usually have been given concessionary tax rates. Such lower rates have commonly been around 15 percent in Special Economic Zones (SEZs) and 24 percent in designated Coastal Cities (CCs) and have seldom risen above an effective 33 percent rate in any venue or activity where FIEs were allowed to operate. Under the new rules tax rates are expected to be unified at the higher 33 percent level for both foreign and domestic firms.

The new tax code also calls for the immediate implementation of a 17 percent value-added tax (VAT) on goods, services, and imported items. This universal tax will replace the preexisting patchwork arrangement of sales taxes. Authorities point out that the new rules should actually benefit firms because they will be given a tax credit for VATs already levied on inputs and charged the VAT only on their net contribution to total value. They received no such benefits under the old system. Although authorities argue that the VAT should be relatively neutral for businesses because of offsetting credits, it could result in higher consumer prices, including those paid by expatriate staff.

The government also announced a series of new business taxes to be levied on nine specific sectors and activities. These include recreation (5 to 20 percent), transportation (3 percent), construction (3 percent), telecommunications (3 percent), financial services (5 percent), the sale of fixed assets—effectively a capital gains tax (5 percent), royalties and other payments on intellectual property (5 percent), insurance operations (5 percent), and other service enterprises (5 percent). Additional levies on capital gains and on securities transactions have been rumored but not confirmed.

Personal tax rates for expatriate staff are also expected to rise substantially. The preexisting effective rate for expatriates topped out at 22.5 percent, while the maximum rate for nationals reached 60 percent above certain income levels. However, this tax on nationals was effectively applied primarily to nationals employed by FIEs that were required to withhold income taxes. The new unified personal tax rate structure is reported to range from a minimum of 5 percent to a maximum of 45 percent, although there are provisions for certain offsetting allowances. These higher personal taxes are of concern to businesses that gross up or otherwise adjust the income of their expatriate staff or provide other subsidies to compensate them for overseas earnings differentials.

The new tax system is designed to ensure more stable funding for the central government, although some provincial authorities worry that they will lose out in the process. Part of the sensitive negotiations between central and local authorities prior to implementation involved assurances that locals would have the freedom to adjust levies to provide adequate funds for their own needs in the face of larger fixed contributions due to the central government. This has caused fears in the business community that local authorities will institute new taxes and fees to make up for any shortfall or use the new system as a pretext to hike levies, resulting in higher business costs.

Taxes are collected by provincial authorities and actual tax rates are set by those local authorities, so the universal rates given are subject to modification. As part of the new tax regime, the provincial authorities are expected to forward a fixed percentage of tax receipts to the central authorities. This percentage is supposed to be set at 60 percent as opposed to the 40 percent average that had prevailed under the old system in which each province annually negotiated its contribution to the central government and was allowed to keep any funds collected over and above that base amount. Revenues to the central government derived from taxes have been falling since 1978 when China began its Open Door policy which involved greater provincial autonomy. Tax receipts of the central authorities dropped from an amount equivalent to 36 percent of gross domestic product (GDP) at the beginning of the period to an estimated 18 percent in 1993, leaving central authorities with inadequate funds to manage the national budget which has run a growing deficit in recent years.

There exist concerns that local officials will raise new fees and levies to augment their own take now that they have to give up more to the central authorities. There is also pressure to tax some of the outsized gains of domestic private businesses, either through special business or personal income taxes. However, because most of these enterprises operate outside the system the problem of effectively tapping them is a complicated one. And foreigners worry that they themselves will represent easier and more tempting targets.

Rates of Corporate Tax

In general, for 1993, foreign investment enterprises and foreign enterprises with establishments in China are taxed at an effective rate of 33 percent (30 percent plus a local surtax of 10 percent of national tax).

A reduced rate of 15 percent applies to foreign investment enterprises and foreign enterprises with establishments in China located in Special Economic Zones (SEZs), which are Shenzhen, Shekou, Zhuhai, Shantou in Guangdong Province, Xiamen in Fujian Province and Hainan Province. The reduced rate of 15 percent also applies to foreign investment enterprises engaged in production or manufacturing activities located within the Pudong Development Zone in Shanghai and within the Economic and Technology Development Zones of the 14 Open Cities, which are Beihai, Dalian, Fuzhou, Guangzhou, Lianyungang, Nantong, Ningbo, Qingdao, Qinhuangdao, Shanghai, Tianjin, Wenzhou, Yantai and Zhanjiang. Foreign investment enterprises engaged in infrastructure projects including energy, transportation and port development are also taxed at the reduced rate of 15 percent.

Foreign investment enterprises engaged in production and manufacturing activities located within the Coastal Open Economic Regions and within the 14 Open Cities are taxed at a reduced rate of 24 percent.

Tax holidays and significant reductions in the tax rate are available to the following:

- foreign investment enterprises engaged in production and manufacturing activities with an operating period of 10 years or more;
- foreign investment enterprises engaged in production and manufacturing activities in Special Economic Zones (SEZs), the Pudong Development Zone and Designated Economic and Technical Development Zones;
- export-oriented and technologically advanced joint ventures and foreign enterprises; and
- infrastructure projects in SEZs and in the Pudong Development Zone scheduled to operate 15 years or more.

Capital Gains and Losses

Capital gains and losses are treated the same as other taxable income. However, when a foreign investor disposes of an interest in a foreign investment enterprise, any resulting capital gain is subject to a 20 percent withholding tax even if the gain is realized outside the PRC.

Administration

The taxable year in China is the calendar year, and an annual return is due within five months after the close of the taxable year for all foreign investment enterprises. All outstanding tax liability must be settled at such time. Foreign investment enterprises must also file quarterly provisional returns within 15 days after the end of the quarter, together with payments of provisional tax based on estimated profit for the year or actual profit of the previous tax year.

Dividends

Profits of foreign investment enterprises and foreign enterprises either in the nature of dividends or branch profits are not subject to any withholding tax when remitted outside the PRC.

Foreign Tax Relief

A tax credit is allowed for foreign taxes paid by foreign investment enterprises in other countries, not exceeding the relevant PRC tax payable on such income. Excess foreign credits may be carried forward for a period of 10 years.

DETERMINATION OF TRADING INCOME

General

Taxable income is defined as revenues less deductible expenditures based on accounts prepared in accordance with the accounting system for joint ventures (also applicable to foreign investment enterprises and foreign enterprises by reference). There are no differences between tax and accounting methods for income computation. Included in taxable income are dividends, bonuses, interest, royalties, rental and other income. However, dividends received by foreign investment enterprises from other foreign investment enterprises in the PRC are exempt from tax.

All necessary and reasonable expenses incurred in carrying on a business are deductible for tax purposes. For head office expenses, only actual amounts paid, properly documented and verified by a local certified public accountant are deductible. For interest on loans, only reasonable amounts are deductible.

Nondeductible expenses include interest on equity capital, income tax payments including penalties and surcharges, and business entertainment expenses in excess of 0.3 percent of gross sales or 1 percent of gross income.

Inventories

Inventory valuation is based on historical cost, computed using one of the following three methods: FIFO, moving average or weighted average. The local tax authorities must approve any change in the adopted method. The principle of lower of cost or market value does not apply

Provisions

Foreign investment enterprises operating as financial institutions are allowed to establish bad debt allowances. However, the allowances may not exceed 3 percent of the year-end balance of loans receivable.

With approval from the local tax authorities, unrealized foreign exchange gain or loss can now be recognized or amortized over one to five years.

Tax Depreciation

Depreciation of tangible properties must be computed using the straight-line method. Accelerated depreciation may be used only if permission from the tax authorities has been received. Minimum useful lives for various assets are as follows:

Buildings .... 20 years
Production equipment,
   trains, and ships .... 10 years
Electronic and other transportation
   equipment .... 5 years

Intangible assets, including technical know-how, patents and trademarks, are amortized over the contractual term or over 10 years if a time period has not been specified.

Relief for Losses

Tax losses may be carried forward for up to five years. Carrybacks are not allowed.

Groups of Companies

In general, consolidated returns are not permitted and all companies must file separate tax returns. However, foreign investment enterprises and foreign enterprises may adopt consolidated filing for units operating in different areas of China, but in calculating the tax due these enterprises must apply the relevant tax rate for the location of each operating unit. Losses in one location may offset income in another location.

OTHER SIGNIFICANT TAXES

The table below summarizes other significant taxes.

Nature of Tax	Rate (%)
Consolidated Industrial and Commercial Tax (CICT) on sales or turnover	1.5 to 69
Value-added tax (to replace the CICT after a test period)	6 to 16

MISCELLANEOUS MATTERS

Foreign Exchange Controls

The PRC has a foreign exchange control system. All payments and remittances abroad are subject to government control. The State Administration of Exchange Control implements the provisional regulations for exchange control.

Debt-to-Equity Requirements

For foreign investment enterprises in the PRC, the following debt-to-equity ratios are applicable:

- For investment projects below US$3 million, the capital contribution must equal or exceed 70 percent of the total investment.
- For investment projects of US$3 million to US$10 million, the minimum capital requirement is 50 percent of the total investment but not less than US$2.1 million.
- For investment projects of US$10 million to US$30 million, the minimum capital requirement is 40 percent of the total investment but not less than US$5 million.
- For investment projects in excess of US$30 million, the minimum capital requirement is 33.3 percent of the total investment but not less than US$12 million.

TREATY WITHHOLDING TAX RATES

The rates, effective as of January 1993, reflect the lower of the treaty rate and the rate under domestic tax law.

	Dividends %	Interest %	Royalties %
Australia	15	10	10
Austria	10 (h)	10 (f)	10 (a)
Belgium	10	10	10 (a)
Brazil	15	15	15 (i)
Bulgaria	10	10	10
Canada	10 (b)	10	10
Czechoslovakia (k)	10	10	10
Cyprus	10	10	10
Denmark	10	10	10 (c)
Finland	10	10	10 (c)
France	10	10	10 (a)
Germany	10	10	10
Italy	10	10	10 (c)
Japan	10	10	10
Kuwait	5	5	10
Malaysia	10	10	10(d)
Netherlands	10	10	10 (a)
New Zealand	15	10	10
Norway	15	10	10
Pakistan	10	10	12.5

	Dividends %	Interest %	Royalties %
Poland	10	10	10 (c)
Singapore	12 (e)	10 (f)	10
Spain	10	10	10 (a)
Sweden	10	10	10 (c)
Switzerland	10	10	10 (a)
Thailand	20 (g)	10	15
USSR (l)	5	10	10
United Kingdom	10	10	10 (c)
United States	10	10	10 (c)
Yugoslavia	10	10	10
Nontreaty countries	20 (j)	20	20 (j)

(a) The withholding rate is 10 percent, but for royalties received for the use of or the right to use industrial, commercial, or scientific equipment, if is applied to only 60 percent of the royalties received.

(b) The withholding rate is increased to 15 percent if the recipient is not a company owning at least 10 percent of the voting stock of the company paying the dividends.

(c) The withholding rate is 10 percent, but for royalties received for the rental of industrial, commercial, or scientific equipment, it is applied to only 70 percent of the royalties received.

(d) The withholding rate is increased to 15 percent for royalties received for the use of or the right to use literature and art works, including film and tapes for movies and radio and television broadcasting.

(e) The withholding rate is reduced to 7 percent if the recipient is a company or partnership which holds directly at least 25 percent of the shares of the company paying the dividends.

(f) The withholding rate is reduced to 7 percent if it is received by a bank or financial institution.

(g) The withholding rate is reduced to 15 percent if the recipient holds directly at least 25 percent of the shares of the company paying the dividends.

(h) The withholding rate is reduced to 7 percent if the recipient holds directly at least 25 percent of the voting shares of the company paying the dividend.

(i) The withholding rate apples to only 25 percent of royalties received for the right to use a trademark.

(j) See applicable footnotes in At A Glance.

(k) China will honor the Czechoslovakia treaty with respect to the Czech and Slovak Republics until new treaties are signed.

(l) China is honoring the USSR treaty with respect to the Russian Federation. China is currently negotiating a new treaty with the Commonwealth of Independent States (CIS).

Personal Taxation

AT A GLANCE — MAXIMUM RATES

Income Tax Rate (%)	45*
Capital Gains Tax Rate (%)	45*
Net Worth Tax Rate (%)	0
Estate and Gift Tax Rate (%)	0

*Foreign individuals pay half the rate, but new rates have been proposed. (See Income Tax Rates.)

INCOME TAXES — EMPLOYMENT

Who Is Liable

Individuals who reside in China for one year or more are considered PRC tax residents and are generally subject to individual income tax on worldwide income. However, individuals with a period of residency in the PRC of less than five years are taxed only on income earned in the PRC and foreign income remitted there during the period of residency.

Individuals residing in the PRC for five years or more are subject to PRC individual income tax on worldwide income, regardless of whether the income is remitted to the country. However, if it can be demonstrated that the individual has no intention of permanently residing in the PRC, the one-to-five year residence rule will continue to apply.

Taxable Income

The following table sets out how various types of compensation normally received by an employee are treated under PRC individual income tax law.

Wages and salaries	Taxable
Foreign service/hardship allowance	Taxable
Cost of living and automobile allowances	Taxable
Tax reimbursement	Taxable
Bonuses	Taxable

Housing provided by the employer	Nontaxable
Paid home leave	Nontaxable
Relocation/moving costs	Nontaxable
Paid local transportation	Nontaxable
Meals, laundry and other employee expenses	Taxable if paid in lump-sum as allowances; nontaxable if reimbursed upon presentation of receipt

Income Tax Rates

Income is not accumulated for purposes of calculating monthly tax liabilities.

Income tax for individuals is computed on a monthly basis by applying the following progressive tax rates:

Monthly Income		Rate for Citizens	Rate for Resident Aliens
Exceeding RMB	Not Exceeding RMB	%	%
0	800	0	0
800	1,500	5	2.5
1,500	3,000	10	5
3,000	6,000	20	10
6,000	9,000	30	15
9,000	12,000	40	20
12,000	—	45	22.5

The PRC tax authority has proposed new individual income tax rules, which are subject to finalization. The proposed rules increase tax rates and eliminate the 50 percent rate reduction for resident aliens. The proposed rules apply the following rates to all Chinese and foreign nationals.

Note: This section is courtesy of and © Ernst & Young from their Worldwide Personal Tax Guide, 1993 Edition. This material should not be regarded as offering a complete explanation of the taxation matters referred to. Ernst & Young is a leading international professional services firm with offices in 100 countries, including China. Refer to "Important Addresses" chapter for addresses and phone numbers of Ernst & Young offices in China.

Monthly Income		Rate
Exceeding	**Not Exceeding**	
RMB	RMB	%
0	400	0
400	900	5
900	2,000	10
2,000	20,000	20
20,000	45,000	30
45,000	—	35

Deductible Expenses

An individual is allowed a flat RMB 800 deduction each month.

For US expatriates, the FICA contribution is not deductible.

If the employer is responsible for paying the employee's PRC income tax liabilities, the employee's taxable income is grossed up by the amount of the resulting payment. (The gross-up is actually higher than the tax payment because the tax-on-tax effect computed for purposes of the gross-up uses the regular tax rates, not the reduced rates available to resident aliens.) Any hypothetical tax (not actually a tax but an amount withheld by the employer as full or partial compensation for satisfying the employee's PRC tax liability) withheld by the employer is allowed as a deduction in computing the employee's net taxable income.

Personal Deductions and Allowances

Chinese tax authorities have promulgated new regulations that permit employees with responsibilities both within and outside the PRC to allocate income in proportion to services provided. Thus, if an employee works 50 percent of the time in the PRC, 50 percent of his or her salary will be taxable in China. To qualify, however, an employee must provide supporting documentation. For example, use of dual employment contracts would probably be sufficient provided that the allocation of remuneration between the two is reasonable and acceptable to PRC authorities.

No distinction is made between married and single taxpayers, and no relief by allowance or deduction is provided for dependents.

INCOME TAXES — SELF-EMPLOYMENT/ OTHER INCOME

Who Is Liable

Individuals receiving compensation for personal services performed in the PRC are subject to the Chinese individual income tax.

Taxable Income

Taxable income includes compensation for independent personal services performed in the PRC, bonus payments and income specified to be taxable by the Ministry of Finance.

The following income is tax-exempt:

- prizes and awards for scientific, technological or cultural achievement;
- interest on savings deposits in state banks and credit cooperatives in the PRC;
- welfare benefits, pensions and relief payments;
- severance or retirement pay;
- salaries of diplomatic officials of foreign embassies and consulates in the country;
- tax-free income as stipulated in agreements to which the PRC is a party; and
- other income approved as tax-free by the Ministry of Finance

Income Tax Rates

For 1993, self-employment and passive income are subject to tax at a flat 20 percent rate on gross receipts, subject to the deduction noted in Deductible Expenses.

Deductible Expenses

A deduction of RMB 800 from compensation for personal services, royalties and rental income is allowed for expenses if the amount in a single monthly payment is less than RMB 4,000; 20 percent of the payment is deductible if the amount is RMB 4,000 or more.

No deduction is allowed for interest, dividends or other kinds of income.

DIRECTORS' FEES

Directors' fees, excluding expense reimbursements received by foreign nationals from PRC sources, are considered income from independent personal services.

A company may deduct directors' fees when computing its corporate income tax liabilities.

RELIEF FOR LOSSES

No provisions exist for the carryover of losses.

CAPITAL GAINS AND LOSSES

No special tax rules apply for capital gains. They are considered ordinary income and are taxed according to the general rules.

SOCIAL SECURITY TAXES

No social security taxes are levied in China.

Recent Changes in the Chinese Personal Tax Code

In late 1993 Chinese authorities announced plans for a substantial revision of their tax system to be implemented on January 1, 1994. Details of the changes are not yet available. However, the basic provisions and some of their implications can be outlined. Stephen Lee, senior manager of Ernst & Young's China division, was quoted in the *Wall Street Journal* as saying, based on available preliminary information, that the changes would probably result in little net increase in businesses' overall tax burdens. Interested parties should consult tax specialists in the area for specifics, which may not be settled for some time. In early January 1994 the new tax system had already resulted in such confusion that Chinese authorities were mobilizing officials and an estimated one million "tax tutors" in an attempt to explain the new tax arrangements to local authorities, businesses, and the populace at large.

Personal tax rates for expatriate staff are expected to rise substantially under the new rules. The preexisting effective rate for expatriates topped out at 22.5 percent, while the maximum rate for nationals reached 60 percent above certain income levels. However, this tax on nationals was effectively applied primarily to nationals employed by FIEs that were required to withhold income taxes. The new unified personal tax rate structure is reported to range from a minimum of 5 percent to a maximum of 45 percent, although there are provisions for certain offsetting allowances. These higher personal taxes are of concern to expatriate personal as well as to businesses that gross up or otherwise adjust the income of their expatriate staff or provide other subsidies to compensate them for overseas earnings differentials.

The new tax code also calls for the immediate implementation of a 17 percent value-added tax (VAT) on goods, services, and imported items. This universal tax will replace a preexisting patchwork arrangement of sales taxes. Although authorities argue that the VAT should be relatively neutral for businesses because of offsetting credits, it could result in higher consumer prices, including those paid by expatriate staff. (Refer to the sidebar in "Corporate Taxation" for more information on tax code revisions.)

ADMINISTRATION

The taxation year is the calendar year.

Although the recipient of income is responsible for payment of income tax, it is generally collected through a withholding system under which the payer is the withholding agent. All taxpayers, including those earning PRC-source income but not covered by withholding and employees who are paid outside the PRC, must file monthly income tax returns and pay the relevant tax to the local tax bureau. The return must be filed within seven days after month-end.

Taxpayers with foreign-source income must file an income tax return and pay the tax due within 30 days after the end of the calendar year. Foreign taxes paid on such income are allowed as a tax credit, up to a limit of the relevant PRC individual income tax levied on the same income.

Individuals departing the PRC must pay all taxes within seven days prior to departure.

Late payment of tax is subject to a daily interest charge of 0.5 percent of the taxes overdue. A penalty of up to five times the amount of the unpaid tax may be levied for tax evasion or refusal to pay tax.

NONRESIDENTS

Individuals working in China whose residence does not exceed 90 days during a calendar year are tax-exempt. However, the exemption does not apply to employees of entities registered in China, including Sino-foreign equity joint ventures, cooperative joint ventures, wholly foreign-owned ventures, representative offices of foreign companies, and entities engaged in oil exploration and construction projects in China.

Individuals in the PRC for less than a year but for more than 90 days during a calendar year are considered nonresidents and therefore are subject to PRC individual income tax only for the period of residence. Individuals residing in the PRC for more than 90 days during a calendar year must submit a tax return as soon as possible after their stay has exceeded 90 days.

For nonresidents, the PRC individual income tax is computed by multiplying the normal monthly tax liability calculated under general rules by the ratio of the number of days the individual spent in China to the total number of days in that month. For example, if an individual was in China for 10 days during the month of March, the PRC tax is 10/31 of the normal monthly tax liability.

Fees of directors not normally resident in China are taxable as a lump sum, with tax liability computed by applying the rules outlined for income from independent personal services.

Dividends, interest, royalties and rental income

received by nonresident foreign nationals from PRC sources are normally subject to a 20 percent final withholding tax in accordance with Article 19 of the Unified Income Tax Law. The withholding rate is usually reduced to 10 percent if the recipient is a resident of a country with which China has entered into a double taxation agreement. No tax return is required if the income was subject to final withholding tax.

As noted in Taxable Income (Income Taxes—Employment), interest derived from saving deposits in state banks and credit cooperatives in the PRC is tax-exempt. Dividends paid by a foreign investment enterprise in the PRC are also exempt from withholding tax.

DOUBLE TAX RELIEF/ DOUBLE TAX TREATIES

An individual subject to PRC individual income tax on worldwide income may claim a foreign tax credit on income subject to tax in another country. The credit is limited to the Chinese tax payable on the same income.

As of January, 1993, China had entered into double taxation treaties with the following countries:

Australia	France	Poland
Austria	Germany	Singapore
Belgium	Italy	Spain
Brazil	Japan	Sweden
Bulgaria	Kuwait	Switzerland
Canada	Malaysia	Thailand
Cyprus	Netherlands	USSR*
Czechoslovakia	New Zealand	United Kingdom
Denmark	Norway	United States
Finland	Pakistan	Yugoslavia

China honors the treaty of the former USSR with Russia and is currently negotiating a new treaty with the Commonwealth of Independent States (CIS).

The treaties generally provide that for services as an employee, remuneration derived from employment exercised in China is exempt from PRC individual income tax if:

- the recipient is present in China for a period or periods not exceeding 183 days in the calendar year;
- the remuneration is paid by, or on behalf of, an employer that is not resident in China; and
- the remuneration is not borne by a permanent establishment or a fixed base maintained by the employer in China.

Furthermore, under many of the treaties, income derived from independent professional services or other services of independent character is exempt from PRC individual income tax if:

- the recipient does not have a fixed base regularly available to him or her in China for the purpose of performing the services; and
- he or she is present in China for a period or periods not exceeding 183 days in the calendar year concerned.

Ports & Airports

The late 1980s and early 1990s have seen a major increase in the amount of air and shipping traffic passing through East Asia. Planners saw this coming some years back, and have been scrambling to expand and improve facilities at ports and airports throughout the region; many are currently at or over capacity. Air cargo traffic has been growing faster in Asia than anywhere else in the world, and passenger traffic has increased by leaps and bounds. However, with all the new facilities opening in the near future, there are estimates that by 1997 airport capacity will actually exceed demand. This may mean that airlines and cargo carriers will schedule more frequent service with smaller aircraft, something which is not currently possible, largely because of the small number of slots available at airport terminals and the many major airports operating with only one runway. Long a major center for shipping, Asia is fast becoming the leader in container port traffic. The largest increases in container traffic worldwide have been at the Asian hub ports, and four of the world's five leading countries in container traffic are located on the western side of the Pacific Rim: Japan, Singapore, Hong Kong and Taiwan are ranked two through five, respectively, with the USA at number one. China has lagged in the area of container shipping, but is quickly picking up steam. From 1990 to 1991 alone, container traffic increased by 25 percent, with Shanghai and Tianjin handling most of it.

AIRPORTS

China is in the process of making major upgrades to many of its 98 existing airports, has opened several new ones in the past couple of years and plans to spend a minimum of US$5.25 billion on new airport construction, modernization and air traffic control systems before the year 2000. Particular emphasis is being put on eastern China, where the number of airports is expected jump from 24 to 46 in that time period. Southern Guangdong Province already has two international airports, but will become home

to two more in coming years, giving the area one of the highest concentration of international airports in the world. The two Guangdong airports already in operation, in Guangzhou and Shenzhen, are to be replaced and upgraded, respectively. China's six major airlines, Air China, China Northern, China Southern, China Eastern, China Southwest Airlines, and China Northwest Airlines, have been joined by 29 additional airlines since 1988, for a current total of 35. This number is unlikely to grow anytime soon, since the Civil Aviation Administration of China has suspended approval of any new airlines.

The speed with which China is moving forward with its plans for civil aviation is truly dizzying, but also long overdue. The country's network of airports originated with damaged military airstrips inherited by the Communists in 1949. Only since the 1980s has the Chinese government made serious efforts to bring their facilities up to date, and it is just in time. Airline traffic has been increasing at about 19 percent annually, and passenger numbers are forecast to continue growing at 15 percent a year. In 1992, almost 54 million passengers traveled through China's airports. A few of the airports opened between 1990 and 1992 were in Shenzhen, Xian, Chongqing, Ningbo, Wenzhou, and Jinan City, while some new ones due to open before the end of the decade will be in Shanghai, Guangzhou, Haikou and Tongshi on Hainan Island, Hangzhou, Fuzhou in Fujian Province, Nanjing, and Wuhan.

Chinese airports are administered by:

Civil Aviation Administration of China (CAAC)
155 Dongsi Xi Dajie
Beijing 100710, PRC
Tel: [86] (1) 4012233 Tlx: 22101 CAXT CN

Guangzhou

Baiyun International Airport in Guangzhou is the country's busiest airport, with over nine million passengers in 1992. Despite the opening of a new US$16 million terminal in September, 1991, the airport is past capacity, and is due to be entirely replaced in the near future. The new airport, to be built at a cost of US$697 million, will be situated 28 km (17.5 miles) to the north of the city and is to be completed in 1996 or 1997. The location of Baiyun so close to the city has presented problems for aviation control and flight safety (three of 15 reported aviation accidents in China since the 1980s have been in Guangzhou). The new airport will have two runways and an annual capacity of 35 million passengers and 600,000 metric tons of freight by the year 2010. Other new Guangdong airports at Jieyang and in the coastal Paotai county will also help ease the burden on Guangzhou, along with expansion work going on at the new Shenzhen airport and renovation of Zhuhai.

Baiyun Airport has regular air cargo flights on 17 different carriers, primarily domestic ones. All six major Chinese airlines serve Baiyun as do some smaller domestic lines. Foreign carriers include Garuda Indonesia, Singapore Airlines, Thai Airways, and Vietnam Airlines. For address and telephone information, refer to the Transportation section of "Important Addresses" chapter.

Beijing

Beijing's Capital Airport is the second busiest in China in the number of passengers passing through it each year, a number that is rapidly increasing; there were 8.7 million passengers in 1992, up 37.9 percent from 1991. Work is underway on Terminal 2, a new 120,000 square meter passenger terminal, and should be complete by 1996. Officials are studying the possibility of third terminal, which would potentially be managed by the Lockheed Corporation of Canada. The cost of Terminal 2 is estimated variously between US$300 and US$400 million for the 35-gate, 20 million passenger-capacity building. Plans call for the original 14-gate terminal to be renovated and expanded to 55 gates by 2010.

40 air cargo carriers have scheduled flights into and out of Beijing. China's six major carriers, some smaller domestic lines, and many major international carriers, including Air France, All Nippon Airlines, British Air, Garuda Indonesia, Japan Air Lines, Lufthansa, Northwest, SAS, Singapore, Swissair, and United. For address and telephone information, refer to the Transportation section of "Important Addresses" chapter.

Shanghai

The Shanghai Hongqiao Airport is the number three airport in China, with 6.15 million passengers passing through it in 1992. Shanghai handles 60 percent of the air traffic in East China, and these numbers will continue to increase. A new US$22.3 million passenger terminal opened in 1991, and construction begins in 1994 on a second terminal and runway and a new air traffic control system. In addition, a second airport will be opening in the new Pudong Development Zone soon. Plans call for it to become operational in 1997 and for the project to be completed by 2005, with a new metro link between the city and the airport.

23 regular air cargo carriers currently service Shanghai Hongqiao Airport. Besides the major domestic airlines and several smaller domestic lines, foreign carriers include Air France, Japan Air Lines, Dragonair, Korean Airlines, All Nippon, Northwest, Thai Airways, and United Airlines. For address and telephone information, refer to the Transportation section of "Important Addresses" chapter.

Shenzhen

Shenzhen International Airport, which has only been open since October of 1991, is already the fifth busiest airport in China, and expected to retain that position despite the large amount of airport construction going on throughout the country. Its location 30 km (19 miles) north of Hong Kong and 12 km (7.5 miles) west of the Shenzhen Special Economic Zone makes it particularly important to international trade. In 1992, its first full year of operation, Shenzhen handled 1.67 million passengers, four times the original estimates, and over 100,000 tons of cargo, ten times the original estimates. Current estimates call for the airport to reach a cargo capacity of 120,000 metric tons by 1994, 300,000 metric tons by 1997, and one million tons metric tons by 2000.

To cope with the additional traffic, construction has already started on new passenger and cargo terminals, due to open in 1998, and a second 3,600 meter runway to be finished by 2000. One reason other than its location behind the airport's massive success is its low charges for non-reciprocal foreign services and efficient ground handling. Federal Express and UPS may be considering a move from Hong Kong's Kai Tak to Shenzhen, while Nippon Express plans to set up a base there. One downside to Shenzhen Airport's success and its location is that it has been a cause for friction between Hong Kong and Chinese officials, some of whom have suggested that money earmarked for Hong Kong's new airport be diverted to build up Shenzhen. In addition, Shenzhen, Hong Kong and Macao are all within 180 km (112 miles) of one another. Officials have denied that this is to be a cause for political problems, but it will certainly cause trouble with controlling air space as the number of flights increases.

PORTS

China has 128 large ports along its coastline and inland waterways, of which 15 serve international trade. Of these, Shanghai and Tianjin are the most important to foreign trade. The port of Dalian is the largest oil port in China, and the second largest port overall, although it handles far less foreign trade than Shanghai or Tianjin. Specialized berths for oil, coal, grain and other agricultural products are available and an international airport is nearby.

Over 90 percent of PRC-origin container trade is conducted through Hong Kong, either with Hong Kong bills of lading or transshipment. Hong Kong's port is far superior to any within the PRC, although efforts are being made to upgrade facilities throughout the country. While Guangdong is an important area for trade in China, the ports there have been used less for international trade than those in other cities because of the proximity of Hong Kong. Plans are in process now to build or expand ports in 40 cities, including all the major ones. Construction of deep water berths is being driven not only by the needs of shippers but also shipbuilders, as only Dalian and Shanghai have facilities where ships of over 100,000 deadweight tonnage (dwt) can be built.

China's ports are controlled by:

Ministry of Transportation
10 Fuxing Road
Beijing 100845, PRC
Tel: [86] (1) 3264895, 8643369
Tlx: 22462 COMCT CN

Shanghai

The Port of Shanghai is China's principal port, covering a 3,600 square km (2,250 square miles) water area and a 5 square km (3.1 square miles) land area, extending from the Yangtze River mouth to the Huangpu River and up to the Minhang District. It is also one of the most congested in the world, so that delays of days or even weeks can be expected. There are twelve cargo handling districts, of which half are for general cargo and others are set up to handle containers, bulk grain and ore, timber, and dangerous cargo. The loading and unloading equipment is currently being upgraded, a new coal wharf is under construction, as is the Waigaoqiao Port Area in the Pudong New Development Zone. These projects are scheduled for completion in 1995. Shanghai's wharf is also undergoing renovation with a completion target date of 1994. China is far behind many of its Asian neighbors in handling container cargo, but among Chinese ports, Shanghai is out in front. Shanghai saw a 25 percent increase in the amount of container traffic between 1990 and 1991 alone.

The harbor is administered by:

Shanghai Harbor Bureau
13 Zhongshan East 1 Road
Shanghai, PRC
Tel: [86] (21) 3290660 Fax: [86] (21) 3290202

Facilities available:
Transportation Service—Truck, rail and barge.
Cargo Storage—Covered, 3.76 million square meters. Open, 10 million square meters. Refrigerated, 52,000 square meters.
Special Cranes—Heavy lift capacity is 2500 metric tons. Container, 4 to 40 metric ton capacity.
Air Cargo—Hongqiao International is located 30 km from town, serves a number of foreign destinations and has connections to principal cities in China.
Cargo Handling—Most normal cargo can be handled by existing port equipment. Both liquid and dry bulk container and Ro-Ro equipment are available for specialized handling needs.
Weather—Climate is temperate. Annual rainfall occurs mostly in June through September and reaches 110 cms.
Construction—Plans are underway for port expansion and construction of new berths and port areas, as well as acquisition of additional port equipment.
General note—Vessels can experience delay to one month.

Tianjin

The Port of Tianjin at Xingang is the port which handles shipping needs for Beijing, 180 km (112.5 miles) away. It is generally considered to be the second largest port in China after Shanghai, and handles almost as much foreign freight. Tianjin is also the second major container port, although like Shanghai it is still operating somewhat under its container capacity due to the low quality of the surface transport within China. Several new container berths have been completed in the past three years, while twelve new berths at Dongtudi Wharf were finished in 1991 to handle general cargo as well as timber, minerals, building materials, and containers. Specialized berths for petroleum and chemicals are under construction at Nankai, including one which will accommodate 50,000 metric ton tankers. Ro-Ro equipment is not yet available at Xingang. The port is administered by:

Tianjin Port Affairs Bureau
Banyi Jie
Xingang, PRC

Facilities available:

Transportation Service—Truck, rail and barge.

Cargo Storage—Covered, 189,000 square meters. Open, in excess of 840,000 square meters. Refrigerated, 8,910 square meters.

Special Cranes—Heavy lift capacity is 500 metric ton maximum container.

Air Cargo—Tianjin Airport with connecting flights to other Chinese cities.

Cargo Handling—Most containerized, bulk, and general cargo can all be handled by existing equipment. This port serves the foreign trade requirements of the capital.

Weather—Climate is subtropical, with an average annual temperature of 25°C . Average rainfall is 240 cms.

General Note—A new 142 km expressway from Beijing to this port, designed to ease container transport congestion, opened in 1990.

Business Dictionary

The transliteration system used in this mini-dictionary is known as *pin-yin*, the official Chinese phonetic system used in the People's Republic of China. An older transliteration system know as Wade-Giles is still used in Taiwan. No transliteration system is ideal since there are some sounds which cannot be adequately represented using the Latin alphabet. Only through listening to and imitating the pronunciation of native speakers can a truly accurate reproduction of the actual sounds of the language be achieved.

In the "close-to English" column, multi-syllabic Chinese words have been joined by a hyphen to assist reading and pronunciation.

TONES

Each Chinese syllable contains one of four tones or is unstressed.

1st tone (high level): is spoken high and the voice does not rise or fall.

2nd tone (rising): starts with the voice lower at the entry point, then finishes at the same level as the 1st tone.

3rd tone (falling-rising): starts with the voice lower than the 2nd tone, then dips and rises to a point just lower than the 1st tone.

4th tone (falling): the voice falls from high to low.

Each syllable is pronounced with one of these tones unless it is unstressed. In such cases the tone distinctions are absent and the unstressed syllable is pronounced light and short.

VOWELS

a	like **a** in j**a**r (but without the **r**-sound)
e	like **e** in h**e**r (but without the **r**-sound)
i	1) like **ee** in f**ee**
	2) after **c, s, z, ch, sh, r,** like **i** in h**i**t but sounded at the back of the mouth
o	like **aw** as in p**aw**
u	like **oo** as in m**oo**n
ü	similar to German **ü** or **u** in French l**u**ne
ou	like **ou** in s**ou**l
ian	like **yen**
ui	like **way**

In syllables with compound vowels, the pronunciation starts from one vowel and "flows" into the other(s) e.g., **i, ia, iao.**

CONSONANTS

These are pronounced approximately the same as in English, with the following exceptions:

c	like **ts** in hi**ts**
ch	like **ch** in **ch**urch, but the tip of the tongue is curled back to touch the roof of the mouth
g	always as in **g**ap
h	like **ch** in Scottish lo**ch**
j	like **j** in **j**eep (pronounced as near to the front of the mouth as possible)
q	like **ch** in **ch**eer
r	like **r** in English, but the tongue is curled back to touch the roof of the mouth so that it sounds something like the **s** in plea**s**ure.
s	always like **s** in **s**ap
sh	like **sh** in **sh**ip but with the tongue curled back to touch the roof of the mouth
x	like **sh** in **sh**ip but with the lips spread widely
y	like **y** in **y**ellow
z	like **ds** in bi**ds**
zh	like **j** in **j**eep but with the tip of the tongue curled up to touch the roof of the mouth

The consonants **p, t,** and **k** should be pronounced with a strong puff of breath.

English	Mandarin	Transliteration	Pronunciation

GREETINGS AND POLITE EXPRESSIONS

English	Mandarin	Transliteration	Pronunciation
Hello (morning)	早安	zao3 an1	dzow ahn
(daytime)	您好	nin2 hao3	nin how (rhymes with how)
(evening)	晚安	wan3 an1	wahn ahn
Good-bye	再见	zai4 jian4	dzy jen
Please	请	qing3	ching
Pleased to meet you.	很高兴能认识您	hen3 gao1 xing4 neng2 ren4 shi4 nin2	hun gow-shing nung ren-shi (shi as in ship) nin
Please excuse me.	对不起	dui4 bu qi3	dway boo chee
Excuse me for a moment. (when leaving a meeting)	对不起，请稍等	dui4 bu qi3, qing3 shao1 deng3	dway boo chee, ching show (rhymes with how) dung
Congratulations	祝贺您	zhu4 he4 nin2	jew-her nin
Thank you.	谢谢	xie4 xie	sheh-sheh
Thank you very much.	非常感谢	fei1 chang2 gan3 xie4	fay-chahng gahn-sheh
Thank you for the gift.	谢谢您的礼物	xie4 xie nin2 de li3 wu4	sheh-sheh nin-duh lee-woo
I am sorry. I don't understand Chinese.	对不起，我不懂中文	dui4 bu qi3, wo3 bu4 dong3 zhong1 wen2	dway boo chee, war boo dong jong-wen
Do you speak English?	你会说英语吗？	ni3 hui4 shuo1 ying1 yu3 ma?	nee hway shwaw ying-yu (French u as in lune) mah?
My name is...	我叫...	wo3 jiao4...	war jow...
Is Mr./Ms. ... there? on the telephone)	...先生/女士在吗？	...xian1-sheng/nu3 shi4 zai4 ma?	...shen-shung/nu (French u) -shi dzigh mah?
Can we meet (tomorrow)?	明天见好吗？	ming2 tian1 jian4 hao3 ma?	ming-tyen jen how mah?
Would you like to have dinner together?	我们一起吃晚饭好吗？	wo3 men yi1 qi3 chi1 wan3 fan4 hao3 ma?	warm'n ee-chee chi (as in chip) wahn-fahn how mah?
Yes	好的	hao3 de	how-duh
No	不行	bu4 xing2	boo-shing

DAY/TIME OF DAY

English	Mandarin	Transliteration	Pronunciation
morning	上午	shang4 wu3	shahng-woo
noon	中午	zhong1 wu3	jong-woo
afternoon	下午	xia4 wu3	shah-woo
evening	傍晚	bang4 wan3	bahng-wahn
night	夜晚	ye4 wan3	yeh-wahn
today	今天	jin1 tian1	jin-tyen
yesterday	昨天	zuo2 tian1	dzaw (as in law)-tyen
tomorrow	明天	ming2 tian1	ming-tyen
Monday	星期一	xing1 qi1 yi1	shing-chee ee
Tuesday	星期二	xing1 qi1 er4	shing-chee err

English	Mandarin	Transliteration	Pronunciation
Wednesday	星期三	xing1 qi1 san1	shing-chee sahn
Thursday	星期四	xing1 qi1 si4	shing-chee si (as in sip)
Friday	星期五	xing1 qi1 wu3	shing-chee woo
Saturday	星期六	xing1 qi1 liu4	shing-chee lyoo
Sunday	星期日	xing1 qi1 ri4	shing-chee ri (as in rip)
holiday	假日	jia4 ri4	jyah ri
New Year's Day	新年，元旦	xin1 nian2 , yuan2 dan4	shin nyen, ywahn dahn
time	时间	shi2 jian1	shi-jen

NUMBERS

English	Mandarin	Transliteration	Pronunciation
one	一	yi1	yee
two	二	er4	err
three	三	san1	sahn
four	四	si4	si
five	五	wu3	woo
six	六	liu4	lyoo
seven	七	qi1	chee
eight	八	ba1	bah
nine	九	jiu3	jew
ten	十	shi2	shi (as in ship)
eleven	十一	shi2 yi1	shi-ee
fifteen	十五	shi2 wu3	shi-woo
twenty	二十	er4 shi2	err-shi
twenty-one	二十一	er4 shi2 yi1	err-shi-ee
thirty	三十	san1 shi2	sahn-shi
thirty-one	三十一	san1 shi2 yi1	sahn-shi-ee
fifty	五十	wu3 shi2	woo-shi
one hundred	一百	yi4 bai3	ee-buy
one hundred one	一百零一	yi4 bai3 ling2 yi1	ee buy ling ee
one thousand	一千	yi4 qian1	ee chen
one million	一百万	yi4 bai3 wan4	ee buy wahn
first	第一	di4 yi1	dee-ee
second	第二	di4 er4	dee-err
third	第三	di4 san1	dee-sahn

English	Mandarin	Transliteration	Pronunciation

GETTING AROUND TOWN

English	Mandarin	Transliteration	Pronunciation
Where is...?	...在哪里？	...zai4 na3 li3?	...dzigh nah-lee?
Does this train go to ...?	这辆火车去...吗？	zhe4 liang4 huo3 che1 qu4...ma?	jay lyahng whar-cher chu (French u)...mah?
Please take me to (location)	请送我到...（地点）	qing3 song4 wo3 dao4 ...	ching song war dow (ow as in how)...
Where am I?	这是哪里？	zhe4 shi4 na2 li3?	jay shi nah-lee?
airplane	飞机	fei1 ji1	fay-jee
airport	飞机场	fei1 ji1 chang3	fay-jee chahng
bus (public)	汽车（公共汽车）	qi4 che1(gong1 gong4 qi4 che1）	chee cher (gong-gong chee-cher)
taxi	出租车	chu1 zu1 che1	choo-dzoo cher
train	火车	huo3 che1	whar-cher
train station	火车站	huo3 che1 zhan4	whar-cher jahn
ticket	车票	che1 piao4	cher-pyow (ow as in cow)
one-way (single) ticket	单程车票	dan1 cheng2 che1 piao4	dahn-chung cher-pyow
round trip (return) ticket	双程（往返）车票	shuang1 cheng2 (wang2 fan3) che1 piao4	shwahng-chung(wahng-fahn) cher-pyow

PLACES

English	Mandarin	Transliteration	Pronunciation
airport	飞机场	fei1 ji1 chang3	fay-jee chahng
bank	银行	yin2 hang2	yin-hahng
barber shop	理发店	li3 fa4 dian4	lee-fah-dyen
beauty parlor	美容厅	mei3 rong2 ting1	may-rong ting
business district	商业区	shang1 ye4 qu1	shahng-yeh chu (French u)
chamber of commerce	商会	shang1 hui4	shahng hway
clothes store	服装店	fu2 zhuang1 dian4	foo-jwahng dyen
exhibition	展览	zhan2 lan3	jahn-lahn
factory	工厂	gong1 chang3	gong-chahng
hotel	旅馆	lü2 guan3	lu (French u)-gwahn
hospital	医院	yi1 yuan4	ee-ywahn
market	市场	shi4 chang3	shi-chahng
post office	邮局	you2 ju2	yoe (oe as in Joe)-ju (French u)
restaurant	餐馆	can1 guan3	tsahn-gwahn
rest room/toilet (W.C.)	盥洗室/卫生间	guan4 xi3 shi4/wei4 sheng1 jian1	gwahn-shee-shi, way-shung-jen
sea port	海港	hai2 gang3	high-gahng
train station	火车站	huo3 che1 zhan4	whar-cher jahn

English	Mandarin	Transliteration	Pronunciation
At the bank			
What is the exchange rate?	兑换率是多少？	dui4 huan4 lü4 shi4 duo1 shao3?	dway-hwahn lu (French u) shi daw show (rhymes with how)?
I want to exchange...	我想兑换...	wo2 xiang3 dui4 huan4 ...	war shyahng hwahn...
Australian dollar	澳元	ao4 yuan2	ow (Rhymes with now) ywahn
British pound	英磅	ying1 bang4	ying bahng
Chinese yuan (PRC)	人民币元（中华人民共和国货币）	ren2 min2 bi4 yuan2 (zhong1 hua2 ren2 min2 gong4 he2 guo2 huo4 bi4)	ren-min-bee ywahn (jong hwah ren-min gong- her-gwar hwar-bee)
French franc	法郎	fa4 lang2	fah-lahng
German mark	德国马克	de2 guo2 ma3 ke4	der-gwor mah-ker
Hong Kong dollar	港币	gang3 bi4	gahng-bee
Indonesia rupiah	印度尼西亚卢比	yin4 du4 ni2 xi1 ya4 lu2 bi3	yin-doo-nee-she-ya loo-bee
Japanese yen	日元	ri4 yuan2	ri ywahn
Korean won	韩国圆	han2 guo2 yuan2	hahn-gwar ywahn
Malaysia ringgit	马来西亚林吉特	ma3 lai4 xi1 ya4 lin2 ji2 te4	mah-ly-shee-ya lin-jee-ter
Philippines peso	菲律宾比索	fei1 lü4 bin1 bi3 suo3	fay-lu (French u)-bin bee-saw
Singapore dollar	新加坡元	xin1 jia1 po1 yuan2	shin-jah-paw ywahn
New Taiwan dollar (ROC)	新台币	xin1 tai2 bi4	shin tigh bee
Thailand baht	泰国铢	tai4 guo2 zhu1	tigh-gwaw joo
U.S. dollar	美元	mei3 yuan2	may ywahn
Can you cash a personal check?	可以兑现个人支票吗？	ke2 yi3 dui4 xian4 ge4 ren2 zhi1 piao4 ma?	ker-yee dway-shen ger-ren ji (i as in zip)-pyow mah?
Where should I sign?	我在哪里签字？	wo3 zai4 na2 li3 qian1 zi4?	war dzigh nar-lee chen dzi (i as in zip)?
Traveler check	旅行支票	lü3 xing2 zhi1 piao4	lu (French u)-shing ji-pyow
Bank draft	银行汇票	yin2 hang2 hui1 piao4	yin-hahng hway-pyow
At the hotel			
I have a reservation.	我已经预订了房间	wo2 yi3 jing1 yu4 ding4 le fang2 jian1	war ee-jing yu (French u)-ding-le fahng-jen
Could you give me a single/ double room?	能给我订一个单人/双人房间吗？	neng2 gei3 wo ding4 yi2 ge4 dan1 ren2/shuang1 ren2 fang2 jian1 ma?	nung gay waw ding ee-guh dahn-ren/shwahng-ren fahng-jen mah?
Is there...?	有没有...？	you3 mei2 you3...?	yoe may-yoe...?
air-conditioning	空调	kong1 tiao2	kong-tyow
heating	暖气	nuan3 qi4	nwahn chee
private toilet	专用盥洗室	zhuan1 yong4 guan4 xi3 shi4	jwahn-yong gwahn-shee shi (i as in ship)
hot water	热水	re4 shui3	rer shway
May I have my bill?	请给我帐单	qing3 gei2 wo3 zhang4 dan1	ching gay war jahng-dahn

English	Mandarin	Transliteration	Pronunciation

At the store

English	Mandarin	Transliteration	Pronunciation
Do you sell...?	这里有没有...？	zhe4 li you3 mei2 you3...?	jer-lee yoe may-yoe...?
Do you have anything less expensive?	有便宜些的吗？	you3 pian2 yi xie1 de ma?	yoe pyen-ee sheh-duh mah?
I would like (quantity).	我想要（数量）...	wo2 xiang3 yao4...	war shyahng-yow (rhymes with how)...
I'll take it.	我要这件	wo3 yao4 zhei4 jian4	war yow jay jen
I want this one.	我想要这个	wo2 xiang3 yao4 zhei4 ge4	war shyahng yao jay-guh
When does it open/close?	什么时候开/关门？	shen2 mo shi2 hou4 kai1/ guan1 men2?	shemma shi-hoe ky/gwahn mun?

COUNTRIES

English	Mandarin	Transliteration	Pronunciation
America (USA)	美国	mei3 guo2	may gwaw
Australia	澳大利亚	ao4 da4 li4 ya4	ow-da-lee-ya
China (PRC)	中华人民共和国	zhong1 hua2 ren2 min2 gong4 he2 guo2	jong-hwah ren-min gong her gwaw
France	法国	fa4 guo2	fah-gwaw
Germany	德国	de2 guo2	der-gwaw
Hong Kong	香港	xiang1 gang3	shyahng-gahng
Indonesia	印度尼西亚	yin4 du4 ni2 xi1 ya4	yin-doo-nee-shee-yah
Japan	日本	ri4 ben3	ri-bun
Korea	韩国	han2 guo2	hahn-gwaw
Malaysia	马来西亚	ma3 lai2 xi1 ya4	mah-ly-shee-yah
Philippines	菲律宾	fei1 lü4 bin1	fay-lu (French u)-bin
Singapore	新加坡	xin1 jia1 po1	shin jyah paw
Taiwan (ROC)	台湾	tai2 wan1	tigh wahn
Thailand	泰国	tai4 guo2	tigh gwaw
United Kingdom	英国	ying1 guo2	ying gwaw

EXPRESSIONS IN BUSINESS

1) General business- related terms

English	Mandarin	Transliteration	Pronunciation
accounting	会计	kuai4 ji4	kwyh-jee
additional charge	额外收费	e2 wai4 shou1 fei4	er-wy fay-yong
advertise	登广告	deng1 guang3 gao4	dung gwahng-gow (as in how)
advertisement	广告	guang3 gao4	gwahng-gow (as in how)
bankrupt	破产	po4 chan3	paw-chahn
brand name	商标, 牌子	shang1 biao1, pai2 zi	shahng-byow, pie-dzi
business	生意	sheng1-yi4	shung-ee

English	Mandarin	Transliteration	Pronunciation
buyer	买方	mai3 fang1	my fahng
capital (money)	资金	zi1 jin1	dzi (i as in zip)-jin
cash	现金	xian4 jin1	shyen-jin
charge	记帐	ji4 zhang4	jee-jahng
check	支票	zhi1 piao4	ji-pyow
claim	索赔	suo3 pei2	saw-bay
collect	收帐	shou1 zhang4	show (as in low) jahng
commission	佣金	yong1 jin1	yong jin
company	公司	gong1 si1	gong-si
copyright	版权	ban3 quan2	bahn-chwahn
corporation	股份有限公司	gu3 fen4 you3 xian4 gong1 si	goo-fun yoe-shen gong-si
cost (expense)	费用	fei4 yong4	fay-yong
currency	货币	huo4 bi4	hwaw-bee
customer	客户	ke4 hu4	ker-hoo
D/A (documents against acceptance)	承兑交单	cheng2 dui4 jiao1 dan1	chung-dway jyow-dahn
D/P (documents against payment)	付款交单	fu4 kuan3 jiao1 dan1	foo-kwahn jyow dahn
deferred payment	延期付款	yan2 qi1 fu4 kuan3	yen-chee foo-kwahn
deposit	存款,押金	cun2 kuan3, ya1-jin1	tsoun (ou as in could)-kwahn, yah-jin
design	设计	she4 ji4	sher-jee
discount	折扣	zhe2 kou4	jer-kow (as in low)
distribution	分配	fen1 pei4	fun-pay
dividends	红利	hong2 li4	hong-lee
documents	文件	wen2 jian4	wun-jen
due date	到期日	dao4 qi1 ri4	dow chee ri
exhibit	展览	zhan2 kan3	jahn-lahn
ex works	工厂交货	gong1 chang3 jiao1 huo4	gong-chahng jyow-hwaw
facsimile (fax)	传真	chuan2 zhen1	chwahn-jun
finance	财务，金融	cai2 wu4, jin1 rong2	tsigh-woo, jin-rong
foreign businessman	外商	wai4 shang1	wigh-shahng
foreign capital	外资	wai4 zi1	wigh-dzi
foreign currency	外汇	wai4 hui4	wigh-hway
foreign trade	对外贸易	dui4 wai4 mao4 yi4	dway-wigh mow (as in how)-yee
government	政府	zheng4 fu3	jung-foo

English	Mandarin	Transliteration	Pronunciation
industry	工业	gong1 ye4	gong-yeh
inspection	检查	jian3 cha2	jen-chah
insurance	保险	bao2 xian3	bow (as in cow)-shen
interest	利息	li4 xi1	lee-shee
international	国际的	guo2 ji4 de	gwaw-jee-duh
joint venture	合资	he2 zi1	her-dzi
label	标签	biao1 qian1	byow-chen
letter of credit	信用证	xin4 yong4 zheng4	shin-yong-jung
license	许可证	xu2 ke3 zheng4	shu (French u)-ker jung
loan	贷款	dai4 kuan3	digh-kwahn
model (of a product)	产品模型	chan2 pin3 mo2 xing2	chahn-pin more-shing
monopoly	垄断	long3 duan4	long-dwahn
office	办公室	ban4 gong1 shi4	bahn-gong-shi
patent	专利	zhuan1 li4	jwahn-lee
pay	支付	zhi1 fu4	ji-foo
payment for goods	物品付款	wu4 pin3 fu4 kuan3	woo-pin foo-kwahn
payment by installment	分期付款	fen1 qi1 fu4 kuan3	fun-chee foo-kwahn
permit	许可	xu2 ke3	shu (French u)-ker
principal	本金	ben3 jin1	bun-jin
private (not government)	私营（非政府性）	si1 ying2 (fei1 zheng4 fu3 xing4)	si (as in sip)-ying (fay jung-foo-shing)
product	产品	chan2 pin3	chahn-pin
profit margin	利润幅度	li4 run4 fu2 du4	lee-roun (ou as in could) foo-doo
registration	注册	zhu4 ce4	joo-tser
report	报告	bao4 gao4	bow-gow (both ow as in how)
research and development (R&D)	研究与发展	yan2 jiu1 yu3 fa1 zhan3	yen-jyew yu (French u) fah-jahn
return (on investment)	（投资）收入	(tou2 zi1) shou1 ru4	(toe-dzi)show (as in low)-roo
sample	样品	yang4 pin3	yahng-pin
seller	卖方	mai4 fang1	migh-fahng
settle accounts	结帐	jie2 zhang4	jyeh-jahng
service charge	服务费	fu2 wu4 fei4	foo-woo-fay
sight draft	即期汇票	ji2 qi1 hui4 piao4	jee-chee hway-pyow (as in how)
tax	税	shui4	shway
telephone	电话	dian4 hua4	dyen-hwah
telex	电传	dian4 chuan2	dyen-chwahn
trademark	商标	shang1 biao1	shahng-byow (as in how)

English	Mandarin	Transliteration	Pronunciation

2) Labor

compensation	薪水	xin1 shui3	shin-shway
employee	雇员	gu4 yuan2	goo-ywahn
employer	雇主	gu4 zhu3	goo-joo
fire, dismiss	解雇	jie3 gu4	jyeh-goo
foreign worker	外籍工人	wai4 ji2 gong1 ren2	wigh-jee gong-ren
hire	雇用	gu4 yong4	goo-yong
immigration	移民	yi2 min2	ee-min
interview	面试	mian4 shi4	myen-shi
laborer:	工人	gong1 ren2	gong-ren
skilled	熟练工	shu2 lian4 gong1	shoo-lyen-gong
unskilled	非熟练工	fei1 shu2 lian4 gong1	fay shoo-lyen-gong
labor force	劳动力	lao2 dong4 li4	low (as in how)-dong lee
labor shortage	劳力短缺	lao2 li4 duan3 que1	low-lee dwahn-chweh
labor stoppage	停工	ting2 gong1	ting-gong
labor surplus	人工过剩	ren2 gong1 guo4 sheng4	ren-gong gwaw-shung
minimum wage	最低工资	zui4 di1 gong1 zi1	dzway-dee gong-dzi (i as in zip)
profession/ occupation	职业	zhi2 ye4	ji-yeh
salary	薪水	xin1 shui3	shin-shway
strike	罢工	ba4 gong1	bah-gong
training	培训	pei2 xun4	pay-shune (French u)
union	工会	gong1 hui4	gong-hway
wage	工资	gong1 zi1	gong-dzi (i as in zip)

3) Negotiations (Buying / Selling)

agreement	协议	xie2 yi4	shyeh-ee
arbitrate	仲裁	zhong4 cai2	jong-tsigh
brochure, pamphlet	手册，小册子	shou3 ce4, xiao3 ce4 zi	show (as in low)-tser, shyow (rhymes with how) tser-dzi
buy	买	mai3	migh
confirm	确认	que4 ren4	chweh-ren
contract	合同，契约	he2 tong2, qi4 yue1	her-tong, chee-yweh
cooperate	合作	he2 zuo4	her-dzaw
cost	价值	jia4 zhi2	jah-ji
counteroffer	还价	huan2 jia4	hwahn-jah
countersign	会签	hui4 qian1	hway-chen
deadline	截止日期	jie2 zhi3 ri4 qi1	jyeh-ji ri-chee

English	Mandarin	Transliteration	Pronunciation
demand	要求	yao1 qiu2	yow (as in how)-chyow (as in low)
estimate	估计	gu1 ji4	goo-jee
guarantee	保证	bao3 zheng4	bow (as in how)-jung
label	标签	biao1 qian1	byow (as in how)-chen
license	许可证	xu2 ke3 zheng4	shu (French u)-ker-jung
market	市场	shi4 chang3	shi (i as in ship)-chahng
market price	市场价	shi4 chang3 jia4	shi-chahng jah
minimum quantity	最低量	zui4 di1 liang4	dzway dee lyahng
negotiate	谈判	tan2 pan4	tahn-pahn
negotiate payment	付款谈判	fu4 kuan3 tan2 pan4	foo-kwahn tahn-pahn
order	订单	ding4 dan1	ding-dahn
packaging	包装	bao1 zhuang1	bow (as in how)-jwahng
place an order	发出订单	fa1 chu1 ding4 dan1	fah-choo ding-dahn
price	价格	jia4 ge2	jyah-ger
price list	价格表	jia4 ge2 biao3	jyah-ger-byow (rhymes with how)
product features	产品特点	chan2 pin3 te4 dian3	chahn-pin ter-dyen
product line	产品系列	chan2 pin3 xi4 lie4	chahn-pin shee-lyeh
quality	质量，品质	zhi4 liang4 , pin3 zhi4	ji (short i as in zip)-lyahng, pin-ji
quantity	数量	shu4 liang4	shoo-lyahng
quota	配额	pei4 e2	pay-er
quote (offer)	报价	bao4 jia4	bow (as in how)-jyah
sale	销售	xiao1 shou4	shyow (as in how)-show (as in low)
sales confirmation	销售确认书	xiao1 shou4 que4 ren4 shu1	shyow-show chweh-ren-shoo
sell	销售	xiao1 shou4	shyow-show
sign	签署	qian1 shu3	chen-shoo
signature	签字	qian1 zi4	chen-dzi
specifications	规范	gui1 fan4	gway-fahn
standard (quality)	标准（质量）	biao1 zhun3 (zhi4 liang4)	byow-djoun (ou as in would)ji-lyahng
superior (quality)	优质	you1 zhi4	yow (as in low)-ji
trade	贸易	mao4 yi4	mow (as in how)-ee
unit price	单价	dan1 jia4	dahn-jyah
value	价值	jia4 zhi2	jyah-ji
value added	增值	zeng1 zhi2	dzung-ji
warranty (and services)	保证书（及服务）	bao3 zheng4 shu1 (ji2 fu2 wu4)	bow (as in how)-jung shoo (ji foo-woo)

English	Mandarin	Transliteration	Pronunciation
The price is too high.	价钱太贵	jia4 qian2 tai4 gui4	jyah-chen tigh-gway
We need a faster delivery.	我们需要尽快供货	wo3 men xu1 yao4 jin4 kuai4 gong4 huo4	warm'n shu (French u)-yao jin kwigh gong-hwaw
We need it by...	我们需在...之前收到	wo3 men xu1 zai4 ...zhi1 qian2 shou1 dao4	warm'n shu (French u)-yao dzigh..ji-chen show (as in low)-dow (as in how)
We need a better quality.	我们要比这个质量更好的	wo3 men yao4 bi3 zhe4 ge4 zhi4 liang4 geng4 hao3 de	warm'n yow (as in how) bee jay-guh ji-lyahng gung how (as in cow)-da
We need it to these specifications.	我们要符合这个规范的产品	wo3 men yao4 fu2 he2 zhei4 ge4 gui1 fan4 de chan2 pin3	warm'n yow foo-her jay-guh gway-fahn-da-chahn-pin
I want to pay less.	我想要便宜些的	wo2 xiang3 yao4 pian2 yi2 xie1 de	war shyahng-yao pyen-ee sheh-da
I want the price to include..	我希望这个价钱包括...	wo3 xi1-wang4 zhei4 ge4 jia4 qian2 bao1 kuo4...	war shee-wahng jay-guh jyah-chen bow(as in how)-kaw
Can you guarantee delivery?	您能保证交货时间吗？	nin2 neng2 bao3 zheng4 jiao1 huo4 shi2 jian1 ma?	nin nung bow (as in how)-jung jyow-hwaw shi-jyen mah?

4) Products/ Industries

English	Mandarin	Transliteration	Pronunciation
aluminum	铝	lü3	lu (French u)
automobile	汽车	qi4 che1	chee cher
automotive accessories	汽车零件	qi4 che1 ling2 jian4	chee-cher ling-jyen
biotechnology	生物工艺学	sheng1 wu4 gong1 yi4 xue2	shung-woo gong-ee-shweh
camera	照相机	zhao4 xiang4 ji1	jow (as in how)-shyahng-jee
carpets	地毯	di4 tan3	dee-tahn
cement	水泥	shui3 ni2	shway-nee
ceramics	瓷器	ci2 qi4	tsi-chee
chemicals	化学品	hua4 xue2 pin3	hwah-shweh-pin
clothing:	服装	fu2 zhuang1	foo-jwahng
for women	女装	nu3 zhuang1	nu (French u)-jwahng
for men	男装	nan2 zhuang1	nahn-jwahng
for children	童装	tong2 zhuang1	tong-jwahng
coal	煤	mei2	may
computer	电脑	dian4 nao3	dyen-now (as in how)
computer hardware	电脑硬件	dian4 nao3 ying4 jian4	dyen-now ying-jen
computer software	电脑软件	dian4 nao3 ruan3 jian4	dyen-now rwahn-jen
construction	施工	shi1 gong1	shi-gong
electrical equipment	电器设备	dian4 qi4 she4 bei4	dyen-chee sher-bay
electronics	电子	dian4 zi3	dyen-dzi
engineering	工程	gong1 cheng2	gong-chung
fireworks	鞭炮	bian1 pao4	byen-pow (as in how)

English	Mandarin	Transliteration	Pronunciation
fishery products	渔业产品	yu2 ye4 chan2 pin3	yu (French u)-yeh chahn-pin
food products	食品	shi2 pin3	shi-pin
footwear	鞋类	xie2 lei4	shyeh-lay
forestry products	林业产品	lin2 ye4 chan2 pin3	lin-yeh chahn-pin
fuel	燃料	ran2 liao4	rahn-lyow (as in now)
furniture	家俱	jia1 ju4	jyah-ju (French u)
games	游戏	you2 xi4	yow (as in low)-shee
gas	气体	qi4 ti3	chee-tee
gemstone	宝石	bao3 shi2	bow (as in how)-shi
glass	玻璃	bo1 li2	baw-lee
gold	黄金	huang2-jin1	hwahng-jin
hardware	五金器件	wu3 jin1 qi4 jian4	wu-jin chee-jyen
iron	铁	tie3	tyeh
jewelry	珠宝	zhu1 bao3	joo-bow (as in how)
lighting fixtures	灯具	deng1 ju4	dung-ju(French u)
leather goods	皮革制品	pi2-ge2 zhi4 pin3	pee-ger ji-pin
machinery	机械	ji1 xie4	jee-shyeh
minerals	矿物质	kuang4 wu4 zhi4	kwahng-woo ji
musical instruments	乐器	yue4 qi4	yweh-chee
paper	纸张	zhi3 zhang1	ji-jahng
petroleum	石油	shi2 you2	shi-yow (as in low)
pharmaceuticals	药物	yao4 wu4	yow-woo
plastics	塑料	su4 liao4	soo-lyow (as in how)
pottery	陶器	tao2 qi4	tow (as in how)-chee
rubber	橡胶	xiang4 jiao1	shyahng-jyow (as in how)
silk	丝绸	si1 chou2	si-chow (as in low)
silver	银器	yin2 qi4	yin-chee
spare parts	零配件	ling2 pei4 jian4	ling-pay-jen
sporting goods	体育用品	ti3 yu4 yong4 pin3	tee-yu (French u) yong-pin
steel	钢	gang1	gahng
telecommunication equipment	电讯设备	dian4 xun4 she4 bei4	dyen-shune (rhymes with French lune) sher-bay
television	电视	dian4 shi4	dyen-shi
textiles	纺织品	fang3 zhi1 pin3	fahng-ji-pin
tobacco	烟草	yan1 cao3	yen-tsow (as in how)

English	Mandarin	Transliteration	Pronunciation
tools:	工具	gong1 ju4	gong-ju (French u)
hand (power)	手动	shou3 dong4	show (as in low)-dong
power	电力	dian4 li4	dyen-lee
tourism	旅游	lü3 you2	lu (French u)-yow (rhymes with low)
toys	玩具	wan2 ju4	wahn-ju (French u)
watches/clocks	手表/钟	shou2 biao3/zhong1	show (as in low)-byow (as in how)
wood:	木材	mu4 cai2	moo-tsigh

5) Services

accounting service	会计服务	kuai4 ji4 fu2 wu4	kwigh-jee foo-woo
advertising agency	广告代理商	guang3 gao4 dai4 li3 shang1	gwahng-gow (as in how) digh-lee-shahng
agent	代理人	dai4 li3 ren2	digh-lee-ren
customs broker	报关代理人	bao4 guan1 dai4 li3 ren2	bow (as in how)-gwahn digh-lee-ren
distributor	经销商	jing1 xiao1 shang1	jing-shyow (as in how)-shahng
employment agency	职业介绍所	zhi2-ye4 jie4-shao4-suo3)	ji-yeh jyeh-show(as in how)-saw
exporter	出口商	chu1 kou3 shang1	choo-kow (as in low)-shahng
freight forwarder	货运代理人	huo4 yun4 dai4 li3 ren2	whaw-yune (rhymes with French lune) digh-lee-ren
importer	进口商	jin4 kou3 shang1	jin-kow (as in low)shahng
manufacturer	制造商	zhi4 zao4 shang1	ji-dzow (as in how) shahng
packing service	包装服务	bao1 zhuang1 fu2 wu4	bow (as in how)-jwahng foo-woo
printing company	印刷公司	yin4 shua1 gong1 si1	yin-shwah gong-si
retailer	零售商	ling2 shou4 shang1	ling-show (as in low) shahng
service(s)	服务	fu2 wu4	foo-woo
supplier	供货商	gong4 huo4 shang1	gong hwaw shahng
translation services	翻译服务	fan1 yi4 fu2 wu4	fahn-ee foo-woo
wholesaler	批发商	pi1 fa shang1	pee-fah-shahng

6) Shipping/Transportation:

bill of lading	提单	ti2 dan1	tee-dahn
cost, insurance, freight (CIF)	成本、保险加运费价（到岸价）	cheng2 ben3 , bao2 xian3 jia1 yun4 fei4 jia4 (dao4-an1 jia4)	chung-bun, bow (as in how)-shen jah-yune fay-jah (dow [as in how]-ahn jah)
customs	海关	hai3 guan1	high-gwahn
customs duty	关税	guan1 shui4	gwahn-shway
date of delivery	交货日期	jiao1 huo4 ri4 qi1	jyow (as in how)-hwaw ri-chee
deliver (delivery)	交货	jiao1 huo4	jyow (as in how)-hwaw

English	*Mandarin*	*Transliteration*	*Pronunciation*
export	出口	chu1 kou3	choo kow (as in low)
first class mail	第一类邮件	di4 yi1 lei4 you2 jian4	dee-ee-lay yow (as in low)-jen
free on board (F.O.B.)	船上交货价 （离岸价）	chuan2 shang4 jiao1 huo4 jia4 (li2 an4 jia4)	chwahng-shang jyow-hwaw jah (lee ahn jah)
freight	运费	yun4 fei4	yune (French u) fay
import	进口	jin4 kou3	jin-kow (as in low)
in bulk	散装	san3 zhuang1	sahn-jwahng
mail (post)	邮寄	you2 ji4	yow (as in low)-jee
country of origin	原产地	yuan2 chan3 di4	ywahn chahn dee
packing	包装	bao1 zhuang1	bow (as in how)-jwahng
packing list	装箱单	zhuang1 xiang1 dan1	jwahng shyahng dahn
port	港口	gang2 kou3	gahng-kow (as in low)
ship (to send):	发货	fa1 huo4	fah-hwaw
by air	空运	kong1 yun4	kong yune (French u)
by sea	海运	hai3 yun4	high yune (French u)
by train	火车运输	huo3 che1 yun4 shu1	hwaw-cher yune-shoo
by truck	卡车运输	ka3 che1 yun4 shu1	kah-cher yune shoo

WEIGHTS, MEASURES, AMOUNTS

barrel	桶	tong3	tong
bushel	蒲士尔	pu2 shi4 er3	poo-shi-err
centimeter	厘米，公分	li2 mi3, gong1 fen1	lee-mee, gong-fun
dozen	一打（十二个）	yi1 da2 (shi2 er4 ge4)	ee dah(shi-err-guh)
foot	英尺	ying1 chi3	ying-chi
gallon	加仑	jia1 lun2	jyah-loun (ou as in would)
gram	克	ke4	ker
gross (144 pieces)	罗	luo2	law
gross weight	毛重	mao2 zhong4	mow (as in how)-jong
hectare	公顷	gong1 qing3	gong-ching
hundred (100)	一百	yi4 bai3	ee-bigh
inch	英寸	ying1 cun4	ying-tsoun (ou as in would)
kilogram	公斤	gong1 jin1	gong-jin
kilometer	公里，千米	gong1 li3, qian1 mi3	gong-lee, chen mee
meter	米	mi3	mee
net weight	净重	jing4 zhong4	jing-jong
mile (English)	英里	ying1 li3	ying-lee
liter	升	sheng1	shung

English	Mandarin	Transliteration	Pronunciation
ounce	盎司	ang4 si1	ahng-si
pint	品脱	pin3 tuo1	pin-taw
pound (weight measure avoirdupois)	磅（常衡重量）	bang4 (chang2 heng2 zhong4 liang4)	bahng (chahng hung jong-lyahng)
quart (avoirdupois)	夸脱	kua4 tuo1	kwah-taw
square meter	平方米	ping2 fang1 mi3	ping fahng mee
square yard	平方码	ping2 fang1 ma3	ping fahng mah
size	尺寸	chi3 cun4	chi-tsoun (ou as in would)
ton	吨	dun1	doun (ou as in would)
yard	码	ma3	mah
jin (Chinese pound)	斤	jin1	jin
liang (Chinese ounce)	两	liang3	lyahng
cun (Chinese inch)	寸	cun4	tsoun (ou as in would)
chi (Chinese foot)	尺	chi3	chi (as in chip)

CHINA-SPECIFIC EXPRESSIONS AND TERMS

You are welcome	不客气	bu2 ke4 qi4	boo ker chee
It doesn't matter	没关糸	mei2 guan1 xi4	may gwahn shee
Please do not smoke	请勿吸烟	qing3 wu4 xi1 yan1	ching woo shee yen
Have a nice trip	旅途愉快	lü3 tu2 yu4 kuai4	lu (French u)-too yu (French u) kwigh

COMMON SIGNS

Please do not disturb (sign to put on the door of hotel room)	请勿打扰	qing3 wu4 da2 rao3	ching woo dah-row (as in how)
Enter	入口	ru4 kou3	roo kow (as in low)
Exit	出口	chu1 kou3	choo-kow (as in low)
Men	男厕所（男盥洗室）	nan2 ce4 suo3 (nan2 guan4 xi3 shi4)	nahn tser-saw (nahn gwahn-shee shi)
Women	女厕所（女盥洗室）	nu3 ce4 suo3 (nu3 guan4 xi3 shi4)	nu (French u) tser-saw (nu gwahn shee shi)
No smoking	禁止吸烟	jin4 zhi3 xi1 yan1	jin ji shee yen
Handle with care	小心轻放	xiao3 xin1 qing1 fang4	shyow (as in how) shin ching fahng

Important Addresses

IMPORTANT ADDRESSES
TABLE OF CONTENTS

Government 359
  Government Agencies 359
  Municipal & Provincial Representative
  Offices in Beijing 362
  Overseas Diplomatic Missions
    of the PRC 363
  Diplomatic Missions in the PRC 366
  Foreign Trade Corporations 370
Trade Promotion Organizations 378
  World Trade Centers 378
  General Trade Associations & Local
    Chambers of Commerce in the PRC 379
  Foreign Chambers of Commerce and
  Business Organizations 379
  China Council for Promotion of
    International Trade & China Chamber
    of International Commerce Overseas
    Offices 380
  Industry-Specific Trade Organizations 380
Financial Institutions 383
  Banks 383
    Central Bank 383
    Commercial & Domestic Banks 383
    Foreign Banks 384
  Insurance Companies 385
Services 386
  Accounting Firms 386
  Advertising Agencies 387
  Law Firms 388
  Translators & Interpreters 389
Transportation 389
  Airlines 389
  Transportation & Customs
    Brokerage Firms 391
Publications, Media &
  Information Sources 394
  Directories & Yearbooks 394
  Newspapers 395
  General Business & Trade Periodicals 396
  Industry-Specific Periodicals 398
  Radio & Television 402
  Libraries 402

GOVERNMENT

GOVERNMENT AGENCIES

Beijing Foreign Economic Relations and Trade
Commission
3 Nan Li Shi Road Tou Tiao
Beijing 100045
Tel: (1) 862015, 866511 Fax: (1) 8010353
Tlx: 22476 BJGVT CN

China Council for Promotion of
International Trade (CCPIT)
1 Fu Xing Men Wai Dajie
Beijing 100860
Tel: (1) 8013344, 8013866 Fax: (1) 8011370
Tlx: 22315 CCPIT CN
China Trade Promotion Review
Tel: (1) 4664999

China Council for Promotion of International Trade
(CCPIT), Beijing Sub-Council
4th Fl., Erduan, Zhonglou, Hualong Jie
Nanheyan, Dongcheng Qu
Beijing 100006
Tel: (1) 5125175 Fax: (1) 5125183, 5125165
Liaison Department Tel: (1) 5125176
International Economic Tech. Co.
Tel: (1) 5125179
Patent Agency CCPIT
Tel: (1) 8034086 Fax: (1) 8011207, 8011069

China National Light Industry Council
22-B Fuwai Dajie
Beijing 100833
Tel: (1) 8396338 Fax: (1) 8396351

China National Textile Council
12 Dongchangan Jie
Beijing 100742
Tel: (1) 5129303 Fax: (1) 5136020

China Patent Agency (HK) Ltd.
16th Fl., China Resources Building
25 Harbour Road
Wanchai, Hong Kong
Tel: [852] 8317199 Tlx: 73277 CIREC HX

Civil Aviation Administration of China
155 Dongsi Xi Dajie
Beijing 100710
Tel: (1) 4012233 Tlx: 22101 CAXT CN

Copyright Agency of China
85 Dongsi Nan Dajie
Beijing 100703
Tel: (1) 5127862 Fax: (1) 5127875

Customs General Administration
Building East
6 Jian Guo Men Wei Dajie
Beijing 100730
Tel: (1) 5194114, 5195013 Fax: (1) 5126020, 5194004

Dalian Port Affairs Bureau
1 Gangwam Jie
Dalian, Liaoning

Guangdong Province Foreign Economic
Relations and Trade Commission
305 Dongfeng Road C.
Guangzhou 510030
Tel: (20) 3330860, 3334916, 3343985
Fax: (20) 3344112, 3332347
Tlx: 44388 GDFTC CN

Guangzhou Foreign Economic Relations
and Trade Commission
1 Fu Qian Road
Guangzhou 510032
Tel: (20) 3330360 Fax: (20) 3340362
Tlx: 44526 EECCG CN

Guangzhou Port Affairs Bureau
30 Yanjiang Yi Lu
Guangzhou

Ministry of Aeronautics and Astronautics Industry
67 Jiadaukou Nan Jie, Dongcheng Qu
Beijing
Tel: (1) 8372427 Fax: (1) 8372427

Ministry of Agriculture
11 Nonzhanguan Nanli, Hepinli
Beijing 100026
Tel: (1) 5003366, 5004606 Fax: (1) 5002448
Department of State Farms & Land Reclamation
Tel: (1) 5001285

Ministry of Chemical Industry
Building #16, Blk 7, Hepingli St.
Beijing 100013
Tel: (1) 4217764 Fax: (1) 4217764, 4215982

Ministry of Chemical Industry
Foreign Affairs Dept.
3rd Fl., Second Building, Building 16
Hepingli Qiqu, Dongcheng Qu
Beijing 100013
General Affairs & Liaison Div.
Tel: (1) 4217764 Fax: (1) 4225383/4
Economic Coop. Division Tel: (1) 4216025

Ministry of Civil Affairs
147 Beiheyan Dajie
Beijing 100721
Tel: (1) 5135544

Ministry of Coal Industry
21 Heping Beijie
Beijing 100713
Tel: (1) 4221864 Fax: (1) 4215610

Ministry of Communications
10 Fuxing Lu, Haidian Qu
Beijing 100845
Tel: (1) 3265544 Fax: (1) 3273943
Tlx: 22462

Ministry of Construction
9 San Li He Lu, Haidian Qu
Beijing 100853
Tel: (1) 8394049, 8393833 Fax: (1) 8313669
Tlx: 222302

Ministry of Culture
Jia 83, Donganmen Bei Jie
Beijing 100820
Tel: (1) 4012255

Ministry of Domestic Trade
45 Fuxingmen Neidajie, Xicheng Qu
Beijing 100081
Tel: (1) 6038581 x4433 Fax: (1) 6017809

Ministry of Electronics Industry
27 Wanshou Road
Beijing 100846
Tel: (1) 8282233 Fax: (1) 8221838

Ministry of Finance
3 Nansanxiang, Sanlihe, Xicheng Qu
Beijing 100820
Tel: (1) 868731 Fax: (1) 8013428 Tlx: 222308
Foreign Affairs Bureau
Tel: (1) 8033606 Fax: (1) 8013428

Ministry of Foreign Affairs
225 Chaoyangmennei Dajie, Dongsi
Beijing 100701
Tel: (1) 553831, 5135566, 5555323
Tlx: 210070 FMPRC CN

Ministry of Foreign Trade & Economic Cooperation
(MOFTEC)
2 Dongchangan Jie, Dongcheng Qu
Beijing 100731
Tel: (1) 5198114, 5198322, 5198804 Fax: (1)
5129568, 5198904
Tlx: 22168
American & Oceanian Affairs Dept.
Tel: (1) 5198821 Fax: (1) 5198834
Asian Affairs Dept. Tel: (1) 5198716
European Affairs Dept. Tel: (1) 5198662
Foreign Aid Dept. Tel: (1) 5197558
Foreign Credit Dept. Tel: (1) 5197316
Foreign Economic & Trade Policy Dept.
Tel: (1) 5198529 Fax: (1) 5198912
Foreign Investment Dept. Tel: (1) 5197303
Foreign Trade Dept.
Tel: (1) 5197420, 5198328, 5198504
International Economic Research Institute
Tel: (1) 4211078
International Trade & Economic Affairs Dept.
Tel: (1) 5197973
International Trade Research Institute
Tel: (1) 5129589 Fax: (1) 5128928

Protocol Dept. Tel: (1) 5198203
Science & Technology Dept. Tel: (1) 5196822
Treaty & Law Dept. Tel: (1) 5198723

Ministry of Foreign Trade & Economic
Cooperation, Guangzhou Commissioner
Foreign Trade Center Building
117 Liu Hua Road
Guangzhou 510014
Tel: (20) 6678000 x86011 Fax: (20) 6677040

Ministry of Foreign Trade & Economic
Cooperation, Shanghai Commissioner
1 Yongfu Lu, Xuhui Qu
Shanghai 200031
Tel: (21) 4317212, 4317362 Fax: (21) 4317065

Ministry of Foreign Trade & Economic
Cooperation, Tianjin Commissioner
59 Nanjing Road
Tianjin 300042
Tel: (22) 317060 Fax: (22) 307742

Ministry of Forestry
18 Hepinglidong Jie, Dongchang Qu
Beijing
Tel: (1) 463061 Tlx: 22237

Ministry of Geology and Mineral Resources
64 Funei Dajie
Beijing
Tel: (1) 6018170, 6024522
Fax: (1) 6017791, 6024523 Tlx: 22531

Ministry of Justice
11 Xiaguangli, Sanyuanqiao
Chaoyang Qu
Beijing
Tel: (1) 4081144

Ministry of Labor
12 Hepinglizhong Jie, Dongcheng Qu
Beijing 100708
Tel: (1) 4212454, 4213431 Fax: (1) 4211624

Ministry of Machine-Building Industry
46 San Li He, Xicheng Qu
Beijing 100823
Tel: (1) 3294966 Fax: (1) 8013867

Ministry of Materials and Equipment Supplies
25 Yuetanbei Jie, Xicheng Qu
Beijing 100834
Tel: (1) 8021247, 8391108 Fax: (1) 8391148
Tlx: 200155 WUZIJ CN

Ministry of Metallurgical Industry
46 Dongsixi Dajie
Beijing 100071
Tel: (1) 5133322, 5131921 Fax: (1) 5130074

Ministry of National Defense
25 Huangsi Avenue
Beijing 100011
Tel: (1) 2018356

Ministry of Posts and Telecommunications
13 Xichangan Jie
Beijing 100804
Tel: (1) 6016137, 6020540
Foreign Affairs Dept.
Tel: (1) 6011365 Fax: (1) 6011370 Tlx: 222187

Ministry of Power Industry
137 Fuyou Street
Beijing 100031
Tel: (1) 6054131 Fax: (1) 6011370

Ministry of Public Health
44 Houhaibeiyan, Xicheng Qu
Beijing 100725
Tel: (1) 4033387, 4034433 Fax: (1) 4014338
Tlx: 22193

Ministry of Public Security
14 Dongchangan Jie
Beijing
Tel: (1) 5122831
Foreign Affairs Bureau Tel: (1) 5121176

Ministry of Radio, Film and Television
2 Fu Xing Men Wai Jie
PO Box 4501
Beijing 100866
Tel: (1) 8012176, 6092141 Fax: (1) 8012174
Tlx: 22236

Ministry of Railways
10 Fuxing Lu, Haidian Qu
Beijing 100845
Tel: (1) 8640011 Tlx: 22483

Ministry of Supervision
35 Huayuanbei Lu, Haidian Qu
Beijing 100083
Tel: (1) 2016113, 2016655

Ministry of Transportation
10 Fuxing Road
Beijing 100845
Tel: (1) 3264895, 8643369 Tlx: 22462 COMCT CN

Ministry of Urban and Rural Construction
and Environmental Protection
Baiwanzhuang
Beijing
Tel: (1) 8992211 Tlx: 222302 MURC CN

Ministry of Water Resources
1 Baiguang Lu, Ertiao, Xuanwu Qu
Beijing
Tel: (1) 3273322 Fax: (1) 3260365 Tlx: 22466
Foreign Affairs Dept. Tel: (1) 3260192

Press and Publishing Administration
85 Dongsi South Avenue
Beijing 100703
Tel: (1) 5127806 Fax: (1) 5127875

Register of Shipping of the PRC
40 Donghuangchenggen, Nan Jie
Beijing 100006
Tel: (1) 5136633 Fax: (1) 5130550

Register of Shipping of the PRC, Shanghai Branch
1234 Pudong Dadao
Shanghai 200135
Tel: (21) 8826789 Fax: (21) 8842626

Shanghai Foreign Economic Relations
and Trade Commission
33 Zhongshandongyi Lu
Shanghai 200002
Tel: (21) 3232200 Fax: (21) 3233798 Tlx: 33315

Shanghai Port Affairs Bureau
13 Zhongshan Dong Yi Lu
Shanghai

State Administration of Import and Export
Commodity Inspection
12 Jian Guo Men Wai Dajie
Beijing 100022
Tel: (1) 5003344, 5001830 Fax: (1) 5002387

State Administration for Industry and Commerce
8 Sanlihe Dong Lu, Xicheng Qu
Beijing 100820
Tel: (1) 8031133, 8013300 Fax: (1) 4914783, 8013394

State Administration of Building Materials Industry
Baiwanzhuang
Beijing 100831
Tel: (1) 8311144 Fax: (1) 8311497

State Bureau of Foreign Experts
Friendship Hotel
Dongbei Qu
Beijing 100873
Tel: (1) 8323260 Fax: (1) 8315382

State Bureau of Tax
Zhaolin Quan Jie
Beijing
Tel: (1) 3263366 Fax: (1) 3266836

State Council Office for Special Economic Zones
22 Xianmen Dajie
Beijing 100017
Tel: (1) 3099065

State Council Office of Leading Group
for Foreign Investment
22 Xianmen Dajie
Beijing 100017
Tel: (1) 3099065

State Council Overseas Chinese Affairs Office
1 Beixinqiao Santiao
Beijing 100710
Tel: (1) 4015671 Fax: (1) 4014639

State Economic and Trade Commission
25 Yuetan North St.
Beijing 100834
Tel: (1) 8392227 Fax: (1) 8392222

State Planning Commission
38 Yuetan South St.
Beijing 100824
Tel: (1) 8092107, 8092109, 8092907
Fax: (1) 8092728

State Science and Technology Commission
54 Sanlihe Road
Beijing 100862
Tel: (1) 8012594 Fax: (1) 8012594

MUNICIPAL & PROVINCIAL
REPRESENTATIVE OFFICES IN BEIJING

Anhui Province
17 Beisanhuan Donglu, Chaoyang Qu
Beijing 100029
Tel: (1) 4217647, 4218783 Fax: (1) 4239505

Fujian Province
Madian, Beitaipingzhuang
Beijing 100088
Tel: (1) 2011311 Fax: (1) 2011307

Gansu Province
17 Beisanhuan Donglu, Chaoyang Qu
Beijing 100029
Tel: (1) 4223878 Fax: (1) 4214020

Guangdong Province
17 Beiwalu, Balizhuang, Haidian Qu
Beijing 100037
Tel: (1) 8418506, 8415059 Fax: (1) 8415047

Guangxi Autonomous Region
6 Shuanghuayuan, Dong San Huan Zhong Lu
Beijing 100022
Tel: (1) 7715604 Fax: (1) 7715603

Guizhou Province
Hepingli Xijeibeikou
Beijing 100029
Tel: (1) 4215714 Fax: (1) 4214110

Hainan Province
172 Xizhimen Dajie, Xicheng Qu
Beijing 100035
Tel: (1) 6014173 Fax: (1) 6016816

Hebei Province
1 Zhuiba Hutong, Huanghuamenjie
Dianmen, Dongcheng Qu
Beijing 100009
Tel: (1) 4031116 x262 Fax: (1) 4031302

Heilongjiang Province
5 Fuxingmenwei Dajie
Beijing 100045
Tel: (1) 8033322 Fax: (1) 8033203

Henan Province
117 Guangqumen Neidajie, Chongwen Qu
Beijing 100062
Tel: (1) 5112296, 7015768 x3194
Fax: (1) 7014503

Hubei Province
44A Beishiqiaolu, Haidian Qu
Beijing 100081
Tel: (1) 8314488 x2111 Fax: (1) 8314488

Hunan Province
Madian, Beitaipingzhuang
Beijing 100088
Tel: (1) 2011133 x2717, 2019380
Fax: (1) 2019333

Inner Mongolian Autonomous Region
47 Chongnei Dajie, Chongwen Qu
Beijing 100005
Tel: (1) 5137679 Fax: (1) 5136517

Jiangxi Province
Madain, Beitaipingzhuang
Beijing 100088
Tel: (1) 2029039 Fax: (1) 2011084

Jilin Province
Madain, Beitaipingzhuang
Beijing 100088
Tel: (1) 2011085, 2019321 Fax: (1) 2011084

Liaoning Province
1 Deshengmen Wai Dajie, Liaoning Hotel
Beijing 100088
Tel: (1) 2015588, 2014676

Ningxia Autonomous Region
15 Fensiting Hutong, Annei Dajie
Dongcheng Qu
Beijing 100009
Tel: (1) 4035587

Qinghai Province
Hepingli Xijiebeikou
Beijing 100029
Tel: (1) 4223870 Fax: (1) 4223871

Shandong Province
Madain, Beitaipingzhuang
Beijing 100088
Tel: (1) 2011064 Fax: (1) 2011066

Shanghai
7 Qianzhai Hutong, Beichang Street
Xicheng Qu
Beijing 100031
Tel: (1) 6012852, 6016894 Fax: (1) 3099772

Shanxi Province
16 Jingshan Xijie, Xicheng Qu
Beijing 100009
Tel: (1) 4014674 Fax: (1) 4014654

Shanxi Province
17 Beisanhuan Donglu, Chaoyang Qu
Beijing 100029
Tel: (1) 4214965 Fax: (1) 4211317

Sichuan Province
5 Gongyuan Toutiao, Jianguomen
Beijing 100005
Tel: (1) 5122277 x206, 5122568
Fax: (1) 5122361

Tianjin
5 Building, 12 Qu, Heping Jie
Dongcheng Qu
Beijing 100013
Tel: (1) 4216482

Xinjiang Autonomous Region
7 San Li He Lu, Xicheng Qu
Beijing 100044
Tel: (1) 8318561 Fax: (1) 8354579

Xizang Autonomous Region
149 Gulou Xidajie, Dongcheng Qu
Beijing 100009
Tel: (1) 4018822 Fax: (1) 4019831

Yunnan Province
17 Beisanhuan Donglu, Chaoyang Qu
Beijing 100029
Tel: (1) 4216514 Fax: (1) 4217364

Zhejiang Province
Madian, Beitaipingzhuang
Beijing 100088
Tel: (1) 2032376 Fax: (1) 2011323, 2019436

OVERSEAS DIPLOMATIC MISSIONS OF THE PRC

Algeria
Embassy
34, Blvd. des Martyrs
Algiers, Algeria
Tel: [213] 60-53-62 Tlx: 66193, 53233
Economic Counselor
Tel: [213] 60-31-89

Argentina
Embassy
Avda Crisologo Larralde 5349
1431 Buenos Aires, Argentina
Tel: [54] (1) 543-8862 Tlx: 22871

Australia
Embassy
15 Coronation Dr.
Yarralumla, A.C.T. 2600, Australia
Tel: [61] (62) 273-4780 Fax: [61] (62) 273-4878
Tlx: 62489

Consulate General (Sydney)
539 Elizabeth St., Surry Hills
Sydney, NSW 2010, Australia
Tel: [61] (2) 698-7373, 698-7838 Tlx: 27931 CHISYD

Austria
Embassy
Metternichgasse 4
1030 Vienna, Austria
Tel: [43] (222) 753140/9 Fax: [43] (222) 7136816
Tlx: 135794 CHINB A

Belgium
Embassy
443 avenue de Tervueren
1150 Brussels, Belgium
Tel: [32] (2) 771-3309 Fax: [32] (2) 7723745
Tlx: 23328 AMCHIN B

Brazil
Embassy
SES, Av. das Naçoes, Lote 51
70 443 Brasila, D.F., Brazil
Tel: [55] (61) 2448695 Tlx: 1300

Consulate General (Sao Paulo)
Rua Estados Unidos, 107
Jardim America
CEP 01427 Sao Paulo, S.P., Brazil
Tel: [55] (11) 853-6951, 853-5195
Tlx: 1139911 CGRH BR

Canada
Embassy
511-515 St. Patrick St.
Ottawa, ON K1N 5H3, Canada
Tel: [1] (613) 234-2706, 234-2718
Fax: [1] (613) 230-9497 Tlx: 053-3770

Consulate General (Toronto)
240 St. George St.
Toronto, ON M5R 2P4, Canada
Tel: [1] (416) 324-6455 Tlx: 06-217601

Consulate General (Vancouver)
3380 Granville St.
Vancouver, BC V6H 3K3 Canada
Tel: [1] (604) 736-4021 Tlx: 04-54659

Chile
Embassy
Av. da Pedro de Valdivia 550
1032 Santiago, Chile
Postal address: Casilla 3417, Santiago
Tel: [56] (2) 2239988, 2232465
Tlx: 242190 SICOM CL

Colombia
Embassy
Calle 71, No. 2A-41
Santa Fe de Bogota, D.C., Colombia
Tel: [57] (1) 2118251 Tlx: 45387 CHINACO

Denmark
Embassy
Øregards Alle 25
2900 Hellerup, Copenhagen, Denmark
Tel: [45] 31-62-58-06 Fax: [45] 31-62-54-84
Tlx: 27019

Ecuador
Embassy
Av. Atahualpa No. 349 y Av. Amazonas
Quito, Ecuador
Postal address: Apto Postal 5143, Quito
Tel: [593] (2) 458128 Tlx: 2164 ECHINA ED

Egypt
Embassy
14 Sharia Bahgat Aly, Zamalek
Cairo, Egypt
Tel: [20] (2) 3417691 Tlx: 93180 CHICO UN CAIRO
Economic Councelor Tel: [20] (2) 3412094

Consulate General (Alexandria)
6, Badawi St., Rassaffa, Moharam Bay
Alexandria, Egypt
Tel: [20] (2) 49165953 Tlx: 54544 CHICO UN

Finland
Embassy
Vanha Kelkkamäki 9-11
00570 Helsinki 57, Finland
Tel: [358] (0) 684-8371 Fax: [358] (0) 684-9551

France
Embassy
11 avenue George V
75008 Paris, France
Tel: [33] (1) 47-23-34-45 Tlx: 270114

Germany
Embassy
Kurfürstenallee 12
5300 Bonn 2, Germany
Tel: [49] (228) 361095 Tlx: 885672 VRCHHD

Greece
Embassy
Odos Krinon 2A
Palaio Psychiko, 154
10 Athens, Greece
Postal address: PO Box 65188, Athens
Tel: [30] (1) 6723281 Tlx: 214383

Hungary
Embassy
Benczur utca. 17
1068 Budapest VI, Hungary
Tel: [36] (1) 122-4872 Tlx: 227733 CHIBE H

India
Embassy
50-D, Shanti Path, Chanakyapuri
New Delhi, 110 021, India
Tel: [91] (11) 608944, 600328 Tlx: 3166250 SINO IN

Ireland
Embassy
40 Ailesbury Road
Dublin 4, Ireland
Tel: [353] (1) 269-1707 Tlx: 30626

Italy
Embassy
via Bruxelles 56
00198 Rome, Italy
Tel: [39] (6) 8448186 Tlx: 680159

Consulate General (Milan)
via Carducci 11
20123 Milan, Italy
Tel: [39] (2) 862268, 862968 Tlx: 313065 SCCGC

Jamaica
Embassy
8 Seaview Ave.
Kingston 10, Jamaica, W.I.
Tel: [1] (809) 927-6816, 927-0850
Tlx: 2202 CHINAEMB JA

Japan
Embassy
3-4-33, Moto Azabu, Minato-ku
Tokyo 106, Japan
Tel: [81] (3) 3403-3380 Fax: [81] (3) 3403-3345
Tlx: 28705

Consulate General (Osaka)
Tel: [81] (6) 445-9481, 45-9471
Fax: [81] (6) 445-9476

Consulate General (Fukuoka)
Tel: [81] (93) 713-7532 Tlx: 72 2222 CHICON J

Consulate General (Sapporo)
15, Nishi 23-chome, Minami 13-Jo, Chuo-ku
Sapporo 064, Japan
Tel: [81] (11) 563-5563, 563-1818
Tlx: 934250 CHICOS J

Jordan
Embassy
Shmeisani
Amman, Jordan
Tel: [962] (6) 666139 Tlx: 21770 CHINEM JO

Economic Councelor
Wadi-Sir District, 7th Circle
Amman, Jordan
Tel: [962] (6) 821727, 810243

Kuwait
Embassy
Shamiya Area 2, Street 24, House 1
Safat, Kuwait
Tel: [965] 4840614, 4840617
Tlx: 22688 CHINAEM KT

Economic Councelor
House 12, Street 1, Area 6
Bayan, Kuwait
Postal address: PO Box 23353, Safat
Tel: [965] 5388951 Tlx: 22688 CHINAEM KT

Lebanon
Embassy
72 Nicolas Ibrahim Sursock St.
Ramlet El-Baida
Beirut, Lebanon
Postal address: PO Box 114-5098, Beirut
Tel: [961] (1) 830317 Tlx: CHINCO 21344 LE

Malaysia
229 Jalan Ampang
50450 Kuala Lumpur, Malaysia
Tel: [60] (3) 2428495 Tlx: CHIEMC MA 33675

Mexico
Embassy
Avda. Rio Magdalena 172
Col. Tizapan
01090 Mexico City, D.F., Mexico
Tel: [52] (5) 548-0898 Tlx: 1773907

Morocco
Embassy
2, rue Mekki El Bitaouri Souissi
Rabat, Morocco
Tel: [212] (7) 549-40 Tlx: 32698 COMCHINE
Economic Counselor
Tel: [212] (7) 527-18 Tlx: CHINAMBA 31023M

Netherlands
Embassy
Adriaan Goekooplaan 7
2517 JX The Hague, Netherlands
Tel: [31] (70) 3551515 Fax: [31] (70) 3551651
Tlx: 31699 CHICO NL

New Zealand
Embassy
2-6 Glenmore St.
Wellington, New Zealand
Tel: [64] (4) 472-1382/3 Tlx: CHINEMB NZ 3843

Nigeria
Embassy
19A Taslim Elias Close
Victoria Island
Lagos, Nigeria
Postal address: PO Box 5653, Lagos
Tel: [234] (1) 612404 Tlx: 21541 NCNA CN
Economic Counselor
Tel: [234] (1) 612414

Norway
Embassy
Tuengen alle 2B, Vinderen
0244 Oslo, Norway
Tel: [47] 22-49-38-57 Fax: [47] 22-92-19-78
Tlx: 71919

Pakistan
Embassy
Ramna 4, Diplomatic Enclave
Islamabad Pakistan
Tel: [92] (51) 826667, 821115

Consulate General (Karachi)
207, Aziz Bhatti Shaheed Road
Karachi, Pakistan
Tel: [92] (21) 510425, 514934

Philippines
4896 Pasay Road
Dasmarinas Village, Makati
Metro Manila, Philippines
Postal address:
PO Box 7430 Airmail Exchange Office
Manila International Airport 3120
Tel: [63] (2) 853148

Poland
Embassy
ul. Bonifraterska 1
00-203 Warsaw, Poland
Tel: [48] (22) 313861, 313869
Tlx: 813589 CHINA PL

Portugal
Embassy
Rua de Sao Caetano 2
1200 Lisbon, Portugal
Tel: [351] (1) 3961882 Tlx: 14762

Singapore
Commercial Representative
70-76, Dalvey Road
Singapore 1025
Tel: [65] 7343360, 7343307 Fax: [65] 7338590
Tlx: RS36878 CHICRO

Spain
Embassy
Arturo Soria 113
28027 Madrid, Spain
Tel: [34] (1) 5194242 Tlx: 22808

Sweden
Embassy
Lidovägen 8
115 25 Stockholm, Sweden
Tel: [46] (8) 662-7155 Tlx: 16490

Switzerland
Embassy
Kalcheggweg 10
3006 Berne, Switzerland
Tel: [41] (31) 447333 Fax: [41] (31) 434573

Syria
Embassy
83 Ata Ayoubi St.
Damascus, Syria
Postal address: PO Box 2455, Damascus
Tel: [963] (11) 330845, 333559 Tlx: 412647

Thailand
Embassy
57 Rachadapisake Road
Bangkok 10310, Thailand
Tel: [66] (2) 245-7032/8, 245-7046

All addresses and telephone numbers are in The People's Republic of China unless otherwise noted. The country code for China is [86].

Turkey
Embassy
Gölgeli Sok. 34
Gaziosmanpasa
Ankara, Turkey
Tel: [90] (312) 4361453 Tlx: 46387 CHCM TR

Consulate General (Istanbul)
Mecidiyeroy, Ortaklar Cad. 14
Istanbul, Turkey
Tel: [90] (1) 1666590 Tlx: 26906 CCGT TR

United Arab Emirates
Embassy
Flat No. 1402, Khalifa Khandi Building
Corniche Road
Abu Dhabi, UAE
Postal address: PO Box 8179, Abu Dhabi
Tel: [971] (2) 321677 Tlx: 23829 CHINCO EM
Economic Councelor Tel: [971] (2) 321603

Consulate General (Dubai)
PO Box 9374
Dubai, UAE
Tel: [971] (4) 448032 Tlx: 46268 COMOF EM

United Kingdom
Embassy
56-60 Lancaster Gate
London W2 3NG, UK
Tel: [44] (71) 262-0253, 636-8845 Tlx: 896440
CLEFSL G

Consulate General (Manchester)
Denison House
Denison Road, Victoria Park
Manchester M14 5RX, UK
Tel: [44] (61) 434-0907

United States of America
Embassy
2300 Connecticut Ave., NW
Washington, DC 20008, USA
Tel: [1] (202) 328-2500 Fax: [1] (202) 232-7855
Tlx: 440673 PRCCUI

Consulate General (Chicago)
104 S. Michigan Ave., Suite 1200
Chicago, IL 60603, USA
Tel: [1] (312) 346-0287/8

Consulate General (Houston)
3417 Montrose Blvd.
Houston, TX 77006 USA
Tel: [1] (713) 524-4064, 524-0780 Tlx: 762173

Consulate General (Los Angeles)
501 Shatto Place, Suite 300
Los Angeles, CA 90020, USA
Tel: [1] (213) 380-0587, 380-3104
Fax: [1] (213) 380-1961

Consulate General (New York)
520 12th Ave.
New York, NY 10036, USA
Tel: [1] (212) 868-7752, 330-7427/8 Tlx: 429134

Consulate General (San Francisco)
1450 Laguna St.
San Francisco, CA 94115, USA
Tel: [1] (415) 563-4858, 563-4874 Tlx: 4970121

Uruguay
Embassy
Leyenda Patria 2880 AP
101 Montevideo, Uruguay
Tel: [598] (2) 701456 Tlx: 23328 CHIEMBA UY

Venezuela
Embassy
Quinta "La Majada"
Calle San Pedro Prados Del Este, Apto 80665
Caracas 1080-A, Venezuela
Tel: [58] (2) 978-4424 Tlx: 21734

Zaire
Embassy
73, avenue des Trois "Z"
Kinshasa-Gombe, Zaire
Postal address: B.P. 5745 Kinshasa-Gombe
Tel: [243] (12) 31659 Tlx: 21378 SHIOCOM ZR

Economic Councelor
6, Avenue Bumba
Kinshasa-Binza, Zaire
Tel: [243] (12) 80217

DIPLOMATIC MISSIONS IN THE PRC

Algeria
Embassy
Dong Zhi Men Wai Dajie
7 San Li Tun Lu, Chaoyang Qu
Beijing
Tel: (1) 5321231/2 Tlx: 22437, 22149

Argentina
Embassy
Building 11, 5 San Li Tun Dong Lu
Beijing 100060
Tel: (1) 5322090, 5322281 Tlx: 22269

Australia
Embassy
15 Dong Zhi Men Wai Dajie
Beijing
Tel: (1) 5322331/7 Fax: (1) 5324605 Tlx: 22263

Consulate General (Shanghai)
17 Fuxing Road West
Shanghai 200031
Tel: (21) 4334604 Fax: (21) 4331732 Tlx: 4331732

Austria
Embassy
5 Xiu Shui Nan Jie
Jian Guo Men Wai
Beijing 100600
Tel: (1) 5322061/3 Fax: (1) 5321505 Tlx: 22258

Commercial Councelor
Rm. 2-6-2, Tayuan Office Building
Chaowai
Beijing 100600
Tel: (1) 5321777 Fax: (1) 5321149

Belgium
Embassy
6 San Li Tun Lu
Beijing 100600
Tel: (1) 5321736/8 Fax: (1) 5325097 Tlx: 22260

Brazil
Embassy
27 Guang Hua Lu
Jian Guo Men Wai
Beijing 1000600
Tel: (1) 5322881 Fax: (1) 5322751 Tlx: 22117

Canada
Embassy
10 San Li Tun Lu, Chao Yang Qu
Beijing
Tel: (1) 5323536 Fax: (1) 5324072 Tlx: 22717

Trade Section
Ta Yuan Building
4 South Liang Ma He Road, Apt. 2-4-1
Chao Yang District
Beijing
Tel: (1) 5323031

Consulate General (Shanghai)
Union Building, 4th Fl.
100 Yan An Dong Lu
Shanghai 200002
Tel: (21) 3202822 Fax: (21) 3203623

Chile
Embassy
1 San Li Tun, Dong Si Jie
Beijing
Tel: (1) 5321641 Fax: (1) 5323170 Tlx: 22252

Colombia
Embassy
34 Guang Hua Lu
Beijing
Tel: (1) 5323166 Fax: (1) 5321969 Tlx: 22460

Denmark
Embassy
1 Dong Wu Jie, San Li Tun
Beijing 100060
Tel: (1) 5322431 Fax: (1) 5322439 Tlx: 22255

Ecuador
Embassy
2-41 San Li Tun
Beijing
Tlx: 22710

Egypt
Embassy
2 Ri Tan Dong Lu
Jian Guo Men Wai
Beijing
Tel: (1) 5322541, 5321825 Tlx: 22134
Commercial Section Tel: (1) 5321920

Finland
Embassy
1-10-1 Tayuan Diplomatic Office Building
Liang Ma He Nan Lu
Beijing 100600
Tel: (1) 5321806 Fax: (1) 5321884 Tlx: 22129

France
Embassy
3 Dong San Jie, San Li Tun
Beijing
Tel: (1) 5321331/2, 5014866 Fax: (1) 5014872
Tlx: 22183

Trade Promotion Office
141 Bang Gong Lu, San Li Tun
Beijing
Tel: (1) 522631 Tlx: 22296

Consulate General (Shanghai)
1431 Huai Hai Zhong Lu
Shanghai
Tel: (21) 4723631 Fax: (21) 4725247

Germany
Embassy
5 Dong Zhi Men Wai Dajie, San Li Tun
Beijing 100600
Tel: (1) 5322161/5, 5325556 Fax: (1) 5325336
Tlx: 22259

Trade Promotion Office
3 Dongsi Jie, San Li Tun, Chaoyang Qu
Beijing 100600
Tel: (1) 5325556 Fax: (1) 5325335 Tlx: 210250

Consulate General (Shanghai)
Yong Fun Lu 151/181
Shanghai
Tel: (21) 4336951 Fax: (21) 4714448 Tlx: 33140

Greece
Embassy
19 Guang Hua Lu
Jian Guo Men Wai
Beijing 100600
Tel: (1) 5321317 Tlx: 22267

Hungary
Embassy
10 Dong Zhi Men Wai Dajie
Beijing
Tel: (1) 5321683 Tlx: 22679

India
Embassy
1 Ri Tan Dong Lu
Beijing
Tel: (1) 5321927 Tlx: 22126

Ireland
Embassy
3 Ri Tan Dong Lu, Qui Jia Yuan
Beijing 100600
Tel: (1) 5322691 Fax: (1) 5322280 Tlx: 22425
Commercial Section Tel: (1) 5322888

Israel
Embassy
Rm. 405, 4th Fl., West Wing Office, CWTC
1 Jian Guo Men Wai Dajie
Beijing 100004
Tel: (1) 5050328 Fax: (1) 5050328

Italy
Embassy
2 Dong Er Jie, San Li Tun
Beijing 100600
Tel: (1) 5322131 Fax: (1) 5324676 Tlx: 22414

Consulate General (Shanghai)
127 Wu Yi Lu
Shanghai
Tel: (21) 2524373 Fax: (21) 2511728 Tlx: 33502

All addresses and telephone numbers are in The People's Republic of China unless otherwise noted. The country code for China is [86].

Japan
Embassy
7 Ri Tan Lu, Jian Guo Men Wai
Beijing
Tel: (1) 5322361 Fax: (1) 5324625 Tlx: 22275

Consulate General (Guangzhou)
Garden Tower, Garden Hotel
368 Huanshi Dong Lu
Guangzhou 510064
Tel: (20) 3338999 Fax: (20) 3338972 Tlx: 44333

Consulate General (Shanghai)
1517 Huaihai Road Central
Shanghai
Tel: (21) 4336639 Fax: (21) 4331008 Tlx: 33061

Jordan
Embassy
54 Dong Liu Jie, San Li Tun
Beijing
Tel: (1) 5323906 Tlx: 22651

Kuwait
Embassy
23 Guang Hua Lu
Beijing 100600
Tel: (1) 5322182, 5322216 Fax: (1) 5321607
Tlx: 22127

Lebanon
Embassy
51 Dong Liu Jie, San Li Tun
Beijing
Tel: (1) 5322197, 5322770 Tlx: 22113

Luxembourg
Embassy
21 Nei Wu Bu Jie
Beijing 100600
Tel: (1) 556175 Fax: (1) 5137268 Tlx: 22638

Malaysia
Embassy
13 Dong Zhi Men Wai Dajie, San Li Tun
Beijing
Tel: (1) 5322531/3 Fax: (1) 5325032 Tlx: 22122

Mexico
Embassy
5 Dong Wu Jie, San Li Tun
Beijing 100600
Tel: (1) 5322574, 5322070 Fax: (1) 5323744
Tlx: 22262

Mongolia
Embassy
2 Xiu Shui Bei Jie, Jian Guo Men Wai
Beijing 100600
Tel: (1) 5321203 Tlx: 22262

Morocco
Embassy
16 San Li Tun Lu
Beijing 100600
Tel: (1) 5321796, 5321489 Tlx: 22268

Nepal
Embassy
1 San Li Tun, Xi Liu Jie
Beijing 100600
Tel: (1) 5321795 Fax: (1) 5323251 Tlx: 210408

Netherlands
Embassy
1-15-2 Tayuan Diplomatic Office Building
14 Liang Ma He Nan Lu
Beijing 100600
Tel: (1) 5321131 Fax: (1) 5324689 Tlx: 22277

New Zealand
Embassy
1 Ri Tan, Dong Er Jie, Chaoyang Qu
Beijing 100600
Tel: (1) 5322731 Fax: (1) 5324317 Tlx: 22124

Nigeria
Embassy
2 Dong Wu Jie, San Li Tun
Beijing
Tel: (1) 5321650 Tlx: 22274

Norway
Embassy
1 Dong Yi Jie, San Li Tun
Beijing 100600
Tel: (1) 5322261/2 Fax: (1) 5322392 Tlx: 22266

Pakistan
Embassy
1 Dong Zhi Men Wai Dajie, San Li Tun
Beijing 100600
Tel: (1) 5322504 Fax: (1) 5322715 Tlx: 22673

Peru
Embassy
2-82 San Li Tun
Beijing
Tel: (1) 5324658 Fax: (1) 5322178 Tlx: 22278

Philippines
Embassy
23 Xiu Shui Bei Jie, Jian Guo Men Wai
Beijing
Tel: (1) 5323420 Tlx: 22132

Poland
Embassy
1 Ri Tan Lu, Jian Guo Men Wai
Beijing
Tel: (1) 5321235 Tlx: 210288

Consulate (Guangzhou)
63 Shamian Dajie
Guangzhou 510130
Tel: (20) 8862872

Consulate (Shanghai)
618 Jian Guo Xi Lu
Shanghai 200031
Tel: (21) 4339228

Portugal
Embassy
2-72 San Li Tun
Beijing
Tel: (1) 5323220 Fax: (1) 5324637 Tlx: 22326

Romania
Embassy
Jian Guo Men Wai, Xiushui
Beijing
Tel: (1) 5323255 Tlx: 22250

Russia
Embassy
4 Dong Zhi Men Wai, Bei Zhong Jie
Beijing
Tel: (1) 5321267, 5322181 Tlx: 22247

Singapore
Embassy
1 Xiu Shui Bei Jie
Jian Guo Men Wai
Beijing 100600
Tel: (1) 5323926, 5323143 Fax: (1) 5322215
Tlx: 22578

Spain
Embassy
9 San Li Tun Lu
Beijing 100600
Tel: (1) 5323629, 5321986 Fax: (1) 5323401
Tlx: 22108

Commercial Section
14 Liang Ma He Nan Lu
Beijing 100600
Tel: (1) 5323103 Fax: (1) 5321128

Sweden
Embassy
3 Dong Zhi Men Wai Dajie, San Li Tun
Chaoyang Qu
Beijing 100600
Tel: (1) 5323331 Fax: (1) 5323803, 5325008
Tlx: 22261

Switzerland
Embassy
3 Dong Wu Jie, San Li Tun
Beijing 100600
Tel: (1) 5322736/8 Fax: (1) 5324353 Tlx: 22251

Syria
Embassy
6 Dong Si Jie, San Li Tun
Beijing
Tel: (1) 5321372, 5321347 Tlx: 22138

Thailand
Embassy
40 Guang Hua Lu
Beijing 100600
Tel: (1) 5321903 Fax: (1) 5323986 Tlx: 22145

Turkey
Embassy
9 Dong Wu Jie, San Li Tun
Beijing
Tel: (1) 5322650 Fax: (1) 5323268 Tlx: 210168

United Kingdom
Embassy
11 Guang Hua Lu, Jian Guo Men Wai
Beijing
Tel: (1) 5321961, 5321930 Fax: (1) 5321939, 5321961
Tlx: 22191

Consulate General (Shanghai)
244 Yong Fu Lu
Shanghai
Tel: (21) 4330508 Fax: (21) 4333115, 4330498
Tlx: 33476

United States of America
Embassy
3 Xiu Shui Bei Jie
Jian Guo Men Wai
Beijing 100600
Tel: (1) 5323831 Fax: (1) 5323178, 5323297
Tlx: 22701

Consular Office
2 Xiu Shui Bei Jie
Jian Guo Men Wai
Beijing 100600
Tel: (1) 5323431

Press and Cultural Sections
17 Guang Hua Lu
Jian Guo Men Wai
Beijing
Tel: (1) 5321161 Fax: (1) 5322039

Consulate General (Chengdu)
Jinjiang Hotel, 180 Renmin Nan Lu
Chengdu 610041, Sichuan
Tel: (28) 582222, 583992 Fax: (28) 583520, 583792
Tlx: 60128

Consulate General (Guangzhou)
1 South Shamian Street
Guangzhou, 510016
Tel: (20) 6677842 Fax: (20) 6666409
Tlx: 44439

Consulate General (Shanghai)
1469 Huai Hai Zhong Lu
Shanghai
Tel: (21) 4332492 x1681 Fax: (21) 4331576
Tlx: 33383

Consulate General (Shenyang)
40 Lane 4, Section 5, Sanjing St.
Heping Qu
Shenyang, 110033
Tel: (24) 220035 Fax: (24) 220074, 2820074
Tlx: 80011

Uruguay
Embassy
2-7-2 Tayuan Building
Beijing
Tel: (1) 5324445 Fax: (1) 5324357 Tlx: 211237

Venezuela
Embassy
14 San Li Tun Lu
Beijing
Tel: (1) 5321295 Fax: (1) 5323817 Tlx: 22137

Zaire
Embassy
6 Dong Wu Jie, San Li Tun
Beijing
Tel: (1) 5321360 Tlx: 22273

All addresses and telephone numbers are in The People's Republic of China unless otherwise noted. The country code for China is [86].

FOREIGN TRADE CORPORATIONS

A.B.C. Trading Company [China] (TUHSU)
82 Donganmen Jie
Beijing 100747
Tel: (1) 5124726, 5124375 Fax: (1) 5124726
Tlx: 22894 TUHSU CN

Accessories Import and Export Corporation
[Chinatex]
82 Donganmen Jie
Beijing 100747
Tel: (1) 5124507, 5123048 Fax: (1) 556172
Tlx: 210026 CNTEX CN

Aerotechnology Import and Export Corporation
[China National]
5 Liang Guo Chang, Dongcheng Qu
Beijing 100010
Tel: (1) 4017722 Fax: (1) 4015381 Tlx: 22318

Aerotechnology Import and Export Corporation,
Fujian Company [China National]
Tel: (591) 550663 Fax: (591) 537185

Aerotechnology Import and Export Corporation,
Guangzhou Company [China National]
Tel: (20) 7754973 x8207 Fax: (20) 7765619

Agricultural Machinery Import and Export
Corporation [China National]
Tel: (1) 8012416 Fax: (1) 8012871
Tlx: 22467 AMPRC CN

Agricultural Produce & Native Products [China
National Corporation for Development of]
45 Fuxingmen Nei Street
Beijing 100801
Tel: (1) 651833, 668581 Tlx: 222212 CFSMC CN

Agriculture, Industry, and Commerce [Beijing]
General Corporation of] (BGCAIC)
9 Bei Huan Dong Lu, De Sheng Men Wai
Beijing
Tel: (1) 2014499 x347, x322, x30l
Fax: (1) 2010030 Tlx: 222620 GWTS CN

Animal Breeding Stock Import and Export
Corporation [China National] (CABS)
10 Yangyi Hutong Jia, Dongcheng Qu
Beijing 100005
Tel: (1) 5131107 Fax: (1) 5128694 Tlx: 210101

Arts & Crafts Import and Export Corporation
[China National] (ARTCHINA)
2A Dong San Huan Bei Lu
Beijing 10027
Tel: (1) 4663366 Fax: (1) 4661821

Arts & Crafts Import and Export Corporation
[Shanghai]
16, Zhong Shan Road, E. 1
Shanghai 200002
Tel: (21) 3212100 Fax: (21) 3291871
Tlx: 33053 ARTEX CN

Astronautical Corporation [China]
Department of International Cooperation
8 Fucheng Road
PO Box 848
Beijing 100830
Tel: (1) 8370156 Fax: (1) 8370849

Automobile Import and Export Corporation
[China National]
2 Xinjiekou Waidajie
Beijing 100088
Tel: (1) 6018050 Fax: (1) 6011393

Automotive Industry Corporation [China National]
16 Fuxing Men Wai Dajie
Beijing 100860
Tel: (1) 3262378 Fax: (1) 3263602

Automotive Industry Import and Export
Corporation [China National]
8 Da Tang Fang Hutong, Xisi, Xicheng Qu
Beijing 100034
Tel: (1) 6020782 Fax: (1) 6011393
Tlx: 22092 CAIEC CN

Aviation Industries of China Corporation
67 Jiandaokou Nandajie, Dongcheng Qu
Beijing 100712
Tel: (1) 4013322, 4013645

Aviation Supplies Corporation [China]
155 Xi Dongsi Jie
Beijing
Tel: (1) 4012233 Fax: (1) 4016392 Tlx: 22101

Bearing Joint Export Corporation [China National]
127 West Xuanwumen Street
Beijing 100031
Tel: (1) 6020043 Fax: (1) 3011051
Tlx: 22534 BREXP CN

Beverage and Foodstuffs Import and Export
Company [China]
11th Fl., Jingxin Building
2A Dongsanhuanbei Lu
Beijing 100027
Tel: (1) 4660838 Fax: (1) 4660632
Tlx: 210479 BEFCO CN

Building Materials & Equipment Import and
Export Corporation [China National]
Bai Wan Zhuang, Xijiao
Beijing 100831
Tel: (1) 8992420, 8311144, 8394070 Fax: (1)
8023083, 8329083
Tlx: 222940 CBMIE CN

Carpet Import and Export Corporation [China]
(TUHSU)
82 Donganmen Jie
Beijing 100747
Tel: (1) 5132392, 5124183 Fax: (1) 5124592
Tlx: 22896 TUHSU CN

Ceramics & General Trading Enterprise [China]
Jingxin Building
2A Dongsanhuanbei Lu
Beijing 100027
Tel: (1) 4661648 Fax: (1) 4661651

Cereals, Oils and Foodstuffs Import and Export
Corporation [China National] (CEROILFOOD)
6-11th Fl., Jingxin Building
2A Dongsanhuanbei Lu
Beijing 100027
Tel: (1) 4660854, 4660686 Fax: (1) 4660636
Tlx: 210237, 210239 CEROF CN

Chartering Corp. [China National] (SINOCHART)
21 Xisanhuan Bei Lu
Beijing 100081
Tel: (1) 8415313/4 Fax: (1) 8415312
Tlx: 222508 CHART CN
Agents for SINOTRANS

Chemical Construction Corporation
 [China National]
16-7 Heipingli
Beijing
Tel: (1) 4213697 Fax: (1) 4515982 Tlx: 22492

Chemical Fiber, Wool & Linen Fabrics
Import and Export Corporation [Chinatex]
16 Donghuamen Street
Beijing
Tel: (1) 5124383, 5124758 Fax: (1) 5124746
Tlx: 22468 CNTEX CN

Chemicals Company Ltd. [Sinochem International]
Yulong Hotel
40 Fucheng Road
Beijing 100044
Tel: (1) 8415588 Fax: (1) 8413120
Tlx: 222895 CHEMI CN

Chemicals Import and Export Corporation
[China National] (SINOCHEM)
Erligou, Xijiao
Beijing 100044
Tel: (1) 8316023, 8423225, 8311106
Fax: (1) 8423221 Tlx: 222732 CHEMI CN

Civil Engineering Construction Corporation
[China]
4 Beifengwo, Haidian Qu
Beijing
Tel: (1) 3063392 Fax: (1) 3063864 Tlx: 22471

Coal Import and Export Corporation
[China National] (CNCIEC)
8 Xiaguangli, Chaoyang Qu
Beijing 100016
Tel: (1) 4678866, 4677032 Fax: (1) 4677038, 4664863
Tlx: 211273

Coal Mine Corporation [China National]
21 Bei Jie, Heipingli
Beijing
Tel: (1) 4217766 Tlx: 2102877

Commercial Foreign Trade Corporation
[China National]
45 Fuxingmen Nei St.
Beijing 100801
Tel: (1) 6012807 Fax: (1) 6016024
Tlx: 222814 CCFT CN

Commodities Inspection Corporation
[China National Import and Export]
12 Jian Guo Men Wai Dajie
Beijing 100022
Tel: (1) 5004626, 5003344 Fax: (1) 5004625
Tlx: 210076

Computer Import and Export Company
[Instrimpex]
Erligou, Xijiao
Beijing 100044
Tel: (1) 8311899, 8313388 x10602
Fax: (1) 8315925 Tlx: 22304 CIIEC CN

Computer Import and Export Corporation
[China Great Wall]
48 Baishiqiao Lu, Haidian Qu
Beijing 100081
Tel: (1) 8023107 Fax: (1) 8023558
Tlx: 22383 MEI CN

Computer Software Technology Import and
Export Company [Instrimpex Synopsis]
Erligou, Xijiao
Beijing 100044
Tel: (1) 8317384 Fax: (1) 8315925
Tlx: 22304 MIMET CN

Construction & Energy Machinery Import and
Export Company [China National]
Import Building, Erligou
PO Box 49
Beijing 100044
Tel: (1) 8317733 x4250 Fax: (1) 8021323
Tlx: 22883 CMIEC CN

Consumer Electric & Electronics Import and
Export Corporation [China National]
33 Dongdan Santiao
Beijing
Tel: (1) 5129874/5 Fax: (1) 5123574
Tlx: 210310 LIGHT CN

Cotton Import and Export Corporation [Chinatex]
3rd Fl., 33 Dongdan Santiao
Beijing
Tel: (1) 5124009 Fax: (1) 5124010/2 Tlx: 211278

Culture & Art Articles Import and Export
Corporation [China]
A24 Xiaoshiqiao Lane, Xicheng Qu
Beijing
Tel: (1) 4014613, 5126906 Fax: (1) 4014613

Educational Instrument & Equipment Corporation
[China]
35 Damucang Hutong Xidan
Beijing 100816
Tel: (1) 652305 Tlx: 22014 SEDC CN

Electric Export Corporation [China United]
A16 Da Hongmen Road West, Yong Wai
Beijing 100075
Tel: (1) 7214614, 7214624 Fax: (1) 7214619
Tlx: 22620 CUEC CN

Electric Wire & Cable Export Corporation
[China National]
Langjianyuan Jianguomen Wai
Beijing 100026
Tel: (1) 5021163, 5002998 Fax: (1) 582714
Tlx: 22614 CCC CN

Electronics Corporation [China] (CEC)
27 Wan Shou Lu
Beijing 100846
Tel: (1) 8212233
Fax: (1) 8212801, 8221835, 8213745
Tlx: 22383 MEI CN

Electronics Import and Export Corporation
[China National]
23A Fuxing Lu, POBox 140
Beijing 100036
Tel: (1) 8219532, 8219550 Fax: (1) 8223907, 8212352
Tlx: 222716 CEIEC CN

Equipment Import and Export Corporation
[China Jingan]
43 Xitangzi Lane, Wangfujing Street N.
Beijing 100006
Tel: (1) 4014249 Fax: (1) 5121365
Tlx: 210020 CJIMC CN

Equipment Import and Export Corporation
[Instrimpex]
Erligou, Xijiao
Beijing 10004
Tel: (1) 8327309 Fax: (1) 8315925
Tlx: 22304 CIIEC CN

European-American Import and Export
Corporation [China]
111 Nanheyan Dajie
Beijing
Tel: (1) 5120877/8

Export Bases Development Corporation
[China National]
20 Shatanhou Lu, Dongcheng Qu
Beijing
Tel: (1) 4013639, 4014477 Fax: (1) 4014373
Tlx: 22787

Feather Products Import and Export Corporation
[China] (TUHSU)
82 Donganmen Dajie
Beijing 100747
Tel: (1) 5124741 Fax: (1) 5121626
Tlx: 22897 TUHSU CN

Feeding Stuffs Import and Export Corporation
[China] (TUHSU)
82 Donganmen Dajie
Beijing 100747
Tel: (1) 5125193, 5129116 Fax: (1) 5124736
Tlx: 210203 CHFS CN

Film Equipment Corporation [China National]
25B Xin Wai Street
Beijing 100088
Tel: (1) 2013493 Fax: (1) 2025833
Tlx: 222200 CFEC CN

Flavor & Fragrances Import and Export
Corporation [China] (TUHSU)
82 Donganmen Dajie
Beijing 100747
Tel: (1) 5124319, 5124606 Fax: (1) 5121626
Tlx: 22893 TUHSU CN

Food Industry and Techniques Development
Corporation [China] (CFITDC)
No. 3, Hong Tong Xiang
Dong Zong-bu Hutong, Dongdon
Beijing
Tel: (1) 548710, 5122435

Foreign Trade Corporation [Beijing]
Building 12, Yong An Dong Li, Jian Guo Men Wai
Beijing 100022
Tel: (1) 5001315, 5958210 Fax: (1) 5001668
Tlx: 210064

Foreign Trade Corporation [Shanghai]
27 Zhongshan Dong Yi Lu
Shanghai
Tel: (21) 3217350 Tlx: 33034

Foreign Trade Development (Group) Corporation
[China]
5 Hong Ling Building
Hongling S. Road
Shenzhen 518046
Tel: (755) 243252 Fax: (755) 243254
Tlx: 420326 CTD CN

Foreign Trade General Corporation [China]
Erligou
Beijing 100044
Tel: (1) 8317733

Foreign Trade Leasing Corporation [China]
20 Shatanhou Jie, Dongcheng Qu
Beijing 100009
Tel: (1) 4014477 x223 Fax: (1) 4011062

Foreign Trade Transportation Corporation
[China National] (SINOTRANS)
Import Building
Erligou, Xijiao
Beijing 100044
Tel: (1) 8328709 Fax (1) 8311070 Tlx: 22153

Forest Chemical Products Import and Export
Corporation [China] (TUHSU)
82 Donganmen Dajie
Beijing 100747
Tel: (1) 5124721 Fax: (1) 5124721
Tlx: 22283 TUHSU CN

Fur & Leather Import and Export Corporation
[China] (TUHSU)
Taiwan Hotel, Office Building
Beijing 100006
Tel: (1) 5132362/3 Fax: (1) 5132358
Tlx: 210654 TUHSU CN

Furniture Import and Export Corporation [China]
Jingxin Building
2A Dongsanhuanbei Lu
Beijing 100027
Tel: (1) 4661848 Fax: (1) 4661851

Garments Import and Export Corporation
[Chinatex]
82 Donganmen Dajie
Beijing 100747
Tel: (1) 5124728 Fax: (1) 5124768
Tlx: 22450 CNTEX CN

Garments Import and Export Corporation
[Shanghai]
1040 North Suzhou Road
Shanghai
Tel: (21) 3251000 Fax: (21) 3255148, 3248349
Tlx: 33036, 33056 GAREX CN

Garments Import and Export Corporation
[Zhejiang]
No. 146A Nanshan Road
Hangzhou
Tel: (571) 771424 Fax: (571) 771761
Tlx: 351060, 351061 GMTHZ CN

General Machinery Engineering Corporation
[China National]
2A Taiping Street, Xuanwu Qu
Beijing 100050
Tel: (1) 3017636 Fax: (1) 335720
Tlx: 222233 CMEBJ CN

Geological Technology Development Import and
Export Corporation [China National]
16 Dewai Street, Xicheng
Beijing 100011
Tel: (1) 2020087 Fax: (1) 6011321
Tlx: 22279 CGIEC CN

Gifts Import and Export Corporation [China]
Jingxin Building
2A Dongsanhuanbei Lu
Beijing 100027
Tel: (1) 4661842 Fax: (1) 4661825

Grain and Oil Import Company [China]
9th Fl., Jingxin Building
2A Dongsanhuanbei Lu
Beijing 100027
Tel: (1) 4660645 Fax: (1) 4660678
Tlx: 210315 GRAIN CN

Guangxi Native Produce Import and Export
Corporation [China]
Qixing Road
Nanning, Guangxi Province
Tel: (771) 20828 Fax: (771) 20914
Tlx: 48153 PRONG CN

Industry Corporation [China Great Wall]
21 Huangsi Dajie, Xicheng Qu
Beijing 100011
Tel: (1) 8372729, 8372506/8 Fax: (1) 8373155
Tlx: 22651

Instruments Import and Export Corporation
[China National] (CNIIEC, Instrimpex)
Erligou, Xijiao
PO Box 1818
Beijing 100044
Tel: (1) 8317733, 8312921, 8495191 Fax: (1)
8315925, 8318380 Tlx: 22304 CIIEC CN

Instruments Import and Export Corporation,
Technical Service Company [China National]
B7 Baishiquiao Road, Haidian Qu
Beijing
Tel: (1) 8327397, 8312166 Fax: (1) 8312166
Tlx: 222491 IMSTC CN

International Tendering Company of Technical
Import and Export Corporation
Import Building
Erligou, Xijiao
Beijing 100081
Tel: (1) 8962211, 8323261 Fax: (1) 8316696
Tlx: 22075 CNCIC CN

International Trust Trading Corporation
[Shanghai]
521 Henan Lu, PO Box 002-066
Shanghai 200001
Tel: (21) 3226650 Fax: (21) 3207412 Tlx: 33627

Iron and Steel Complex Corporation (Group)
[Baoshan]
2 Mundangjiang Lu
Shanghai
Tel: (21) 646944 Tlx: 33901

Knitwear Import and Export Corporation [Beijing]
2 Bei Jie, Xiao Huang Zhuang, He Ping L1,
Chao Yang Qu
Beijing
Tel: (1) 4221610 Fax: (1) 4221896
Tlx: 210425, 210426 PKNIT CN

Knitwear Manufactured Goods Import and Export
Corporation [Chinatex]
82 Donganmen Dajie
Beijing 100747
Tel: (1) 5124388, 5124604 Fax: (1) 5124743
Tlx: 210024 CNTEX CN

Light Building Materials Import and Export
Corporation [China]
235 Wangfujing Street
Beijing
Tel: (1) 5126937, 5126917 Fax: (1) 5120594
Tlx: 211182 LIGHT CN

Light Footwear and Headgear Import and Export
Corporation [China]
82 Donganmen Dajie
Beijing 100747
Tel: (1) 5124354 Fax: (1) 5124354
Tlx: 22282 LIGHT CN

Light General Merchandise Import and Export
Corporation [China]
82 Donganmen Dajie
Beijing 100747
Tel: (1) 5126840 Fax: (1) 5123708
Tlx: 210033 LIGHT CN

Light Housewares Import and Export Corporation
[China]
82 Donganmen Dajie
Beijing 100747
Tel: (1) 5124349 Fax: (1) 5124349
Tlx: 210035 LIGHT CN

Light Industrial Products Import and Export
Corporation [China National] (INDUSTRY)
82 Donganmen Dajie
Beijing 100747
Tel: (1) 5123763, 5124184, 5123738 Fax: (1) 5123763
Tlx: 22282 LIGHT CN

Light Industrial Products Import and Export
Corporation [Tianjin]
164 Liao Ning Road
Tianjin
Tlx: 23142 TJLIP CN

Light Industrial Products Import and Export
Technical Service Center [China National]
7 Tiyuguan W. Road, Chongwen Qu
Beijing
Tel: (1) 7016559, 7016560 Tlx: 22282 LIGHT CN

Light Stationery & Sporting Goods Import and
Export Corporation [China]
82 Donganmen Dajie
Beijing 100747
Tel: (1) 5124354 Fax: (1) 5124339
Tlx: 210034 LIGHT CN

Light Suitcases, Bags & Safety Products
Import and Export Corporation [China]
82 Donganmen Dajie
Beijing 100747
Tel: (1) 5123703 Fax: (1) 5123703
Tlx: 210031 LIGHT CN

Livestock & Poultry Associated Company [China]
82 Donganmen Dajie
Beijing 100747
Tel: (1) 5124006 Tlx: 22281 CEROF CN

Machine Tool and Tool Builders' Association
[China] (CMTBA)
26 South Yue Tan Street
Beijing 100825
Tel: (1) 868261 x2668 Fax: (1) 8013472

Machine Tool Corporation [China National]
(CNMTC)
19 Fang Jia Xiaoxiang, An Nei
Beijing 100007
Tel: (1) 4033767, 4011682 Fax: (1) 4015657
Tlx: 210088 CNMTC CN

Machinery & Equipment Import and Export
Corporation [China National] (MACHIMPEX)
16 Fu Xing Men Wai Jie
Beijing 100045
Tel: (1) 3268157, 3268202
Fax: (1) 3261865, 3268203 Tlx: 22186

Machinery & Equipment Import and Export
Corporation [Shanghai]
400 Xikang Road
Shanghai 200040
Tel: (21) 2552540 Fax: (21) 3269616
Tlx: 33028 SCMEC CN

Machinery Import and Export Corporation
[China National] (MACHIMEX)
Erligou, Xijiao, PO Box 49
Beijing 100044
Tel: (1) 8317733 x5160, 8944944, 8494851
Fax: (1) 8314136/7, 8314143
Tlx: 22242, 22328 CMIEC CN

Medical Equipment & Supplies Import and Export
Corporation [China National]
44 Houhai Beiyan
Beijing 100725
Tel: (1) 4012327 Fax: (1) 4012327
Tlx: 22193 MINIH CN

Medicine Corporation [China National]
38A, Beilishi Lu, Xizhimen
Beijing 100810
Tel: (1) 8318311

Medicine and Health Products Import and Export
Corporation [China National] (MEHECO)
L Suite, Huiyuan Apartments
8 Anding Menwai
Beijing 100101
Tel: (1) 4992632/4, 4917482
Fax: (1) 4917462, 4917476

Metallurgical Import and Export Corporation
(CMIEC) [China]
46 Dongsi Xidajie
Beijing 100711
Tel: (1) 5133322 x 1123 Fax: (1) 5133792
Tlx: 22461 MIEC CN

Metals and Minerals Import and Export
Corporation [China National] (MINMETALS)
Building 15, Block 4
Anhuili, Chaoyang Qu
Beijing 100101
Tel: (1) 4916666 Fax: (1) 4917031, 4917652

Metals Products Import and Export Corporation
[China National]
8 Chedaogou, Haidian Qu
Beijing
Tel: (1) 8021201, 8316312 Fax: (1) 8316312
Tlx: 222864 MIMET CN

Minerals Import and Export Corporation [China
National] (Minmetals)
8 Chedaogou, Haidian Qu
Beijing
Tel: (1) 8021275, 8021324 Fax: (1) 8315079
Tlx: 22773 MIMET CN

Minmetals (Minerals Import and Export
Corporation) International Enterprises
Development Company
Erligou, Xijiao
Beijing 100044
Tel: (1) 8315344, 8317733 x4167
Fax: (1) 8315079 Tlx: 22190 MIMET CN

Native Produce and Animal By-Products Import
and Export Corporation [Zhejiang]
102 Feng Qi Road
Hangzhou, Zhejiang
Fax: (1) (571) 552310 Tlx: 35013, 351054 TUHSU CN

Native Produce and Animal By-Products Import
and Export Corporation [China National] (CHINA
TUHSU)
82 Donganmen Dajie
Beijing 100747
Tel: (1) 5124304, 553808, 5124370
Fax: (1) 5121626 Tlx: 22469 TUHSU CN

Native Produce and Animal By-Products Import
and Export Corporation [Shanghai]
23, Zhong Shan Road, E-1
Shanghai
Tel: (21) 3215630 Fax: (21) 3291883
Tlx: 33065 ANIBY CN

New Building Materials Import and Export
Corporation [China National]
2 S. Zizhuyuan Road, Xijiao
Beijing 100044
Tel: (1) 8415577 x210 Fax: (1) 8317608
Tlx: 20038 CNBMC CN

Non-ferrous Metals Import and Export Corporation
[China National] (CNIEC)
12B Fuxing Lu
Beijing 100814
Tel: (1) 8514477 x1207 Fax: (1) 8515368
Tlx: 22086 CNIEC CN

Non-ferrous Metals Industry Corporation
[China National]
9 Xizhang Xiang
Beijing
Tel: (1) 657031 Tlx: 22086

Non-ferrous Metals Trading Company
[Minmetals International]
8 Chedaogou, Haidian Qu
Beijing
Tel: (1) 8021327, 8021278 Fax: (1) 8315079
Tlx: 22773 MIMET CN

North Industries (Group) Corporation [China]
7A, Yuetan Nan Jie
Beijing 100045
Tel: (1) 8013714/6, 8012407
Fax: (1) 867092, 8033236 Tlx: 22339 CNIC CN

Nuclear Energy Industry Corporation (CNEIC)
[China]
21 Nanlishi Lu
Beijing 100045
Tel: (1) 867717 Fax: (1) 8012392
Tlx: 22240 CNEIC CN

Offshore Oil Corporation [China National]
International Liaison Dept.
23rd Fl., Jinxin Building
Jia 2, Dong San Huan Bei Lu,
Chaoyang Qu
Beijing 100027
Tel: (1) 4663697 Fax: (1) 4662994, 4669007

Offshore Oil Corporation [China National]
(CNOOC)
Nansidaokou Lu, Dazhongsi
Beijing 10086
Tel: (1) 2014650 Fax: (1) 2014650 Tlx: 22611

Oil Development Corporation [China National]
Liupukang
Beijing
Tel: (1) 444313 Tlx: 22312

Oriental Trading Corporation [Chinatex]
82 Donganmen Dajie
Beijing 100747
Tel: (1) 5124389, 5124067 Fax: (1) 5124738
Tlx: 4960 Beijing

Overseas Trading Corporation [China National]
17 Fu Cheng Men Bei Street
Beijing 100037
Tel: (1) 8313940 Fax: (1) 8312550
Tlx: 222851 COTCO CN

Packaging Corporation [China National]
31 Dongchangan Street
Beijing 100005
Tel: (1) 5138837 Fax: (1) 5124128
Tlx: 22234 CNPC CN

Packaging Import and Export Corporation
[China National] (CHINAPACK)
28 Donghouxiang, Andingmenwai
Beijing 100731
Tel: (1) 4214058, 4211747 Fax: (1) 4212124
Tlx: 22490 CPACK CN

Packaging Technology Trading Corporation
[China International]
41 Xisongshu Lane, Hepingmen
Xicheng Qu
Beijing 100031
Tel: (1) 6013833 Fax: (1) 6013933

Pearl, Diamond Gems & Jewelry Import and Export
Corporation [China National]
14th Fl., Jingxin Building
2A Dongsanhuanbei Lu
Beijing 100027
Tel: (1) 4661645 Fax: (1) 4661641
Tlx: 22155 CNART CN

Petro-Chemical Corporation [China National]
(SINOPEC)
24 Xiaoguan Jie, Andingmenwai
Beijing 100013
Tel: (1) 4216731, 4216402 Fax: (1) 4216972 Tlx:
22655

Petro-Chemical International Company [China]
Jia 6, Dong Huixin Lu, Chaoyang Qu
Beijing 100092
Tel: (1) 4216402, 4227744 Fax: (1) 4216972
Tlx: 22655 CPCCI CN

Petroleum and Natural Gas Corporation
[China National]
Liu Pu Kang
Beijing 100724
Tel: (1) 2015544 , 2016107 Fax: (1) 4212347, 2018039
Tlx: 22312 CCPRC CN

Petroleum Company Ltd. [Sinochem International]
Yulong Hotel
40 Fucheng Road
Beijing 100044
Tel: (1) 8316020, 8311151 Tlx: 22553 CHEMI CN

Pharmaceutical Foreign Trade Corporation
[China National]
38A, Beilishi Lu, Xizhimenwai
Beijing 100810
Tel: (1) 8316571/2, 8313344 Fax: (1) 8316571
Tlx: 22659 SPAC CN

Plaited Products Import and Export Corporation
[China]
Jingxin Building
2A Dongsanhuanbei Lu
Beijing 100027
Tel: (1) 4661838 Fax: (1) 4661841

Plastics Company Ltd. [Sinochem]
Yulong Hotel
40 Fucheng Road
Beijing 100044
Tel: (1) 8413123 Fax: (1) 8413122
Tlx: 222898 CHEMI CN

Postal and Telecommunications Corporation
[China National]
28 Xin Wai Da Jie, Xicheng Qu
Beijing
Tel: (1) 2021144

Precision Machinery Import and Export
Corporation [China National]
22 Fucheng Lu
Beijing 10036
Tel: (1) 8429113, 8370291 Fax: (1) 8429112

Precious & Rare Minerals Import and Export
Corporation [Minmetals]
Erligou, Xijiao
Beijing 100044
Tel: (1) 8317733 x4167, 8315344
Fax: (1) 8315079 Tlx: 22190 MIMET CN

Processed Food Import and Export Company
[China]
6-11th Fl., Jingxin Building
2A Dongsanhuanbei Lu
Beijing 100027
Tel: (1) 4660641 Tlx: 210478 PROPD CN

Provincial Textiles Import and Export Corporation
[Jilin]
A2, Pu Qing Road
Changchun 130061
Tel: (431) 860916/9 Fax: (431) 860611
Tlx: 83025 JCTIE CN

Publications Import and Export Corporation
[China National]
127 Chaoyangmennei Jie
Beijing 100011
Tel: (1) 440731 Fax: (1) 4015664 Tlx: 22313

Publishing Industry Trading Corporation [China
National]
PO Box 782
504 An Hui Li, An Ding Men Wai
Beijing 100011
Tel: (1) 4215031 Fax: (1) 4214540 Tlx: 210215

Pulp & Paper Corporation [China National]
313 Longhua Jie Zhonglou
Nanheyan Dajie
Beijing 100006
Tel: (1) 5122330/6 Fax: (1) 5125694

Pulp & Paper Import and Export Corporation
[China National]
82 Donganmen Dajie
Beijing 100747
Tel: (1) 5122330/6, 5125131 Fax: (1) 5125694
Tlx: 22048 LIGHT CN

Raw Materials Import and Export Corporation
[Chinatex]
2nd Fl., 33 Dongdan Santiao
Beijing
Tel: (1) 5129866 Fax: (1) 5123389
Tlx: 210025 CNTEX CN

Road and Bridge Corporation [China]
3 Waiguan Jie, An Ding Men Wai
Beijing 100011
Tel: (1) 4213378 Fax: (1) 4217849 Tlx: 22336

Scientific Instruments & Materials Import and
Export Corporation [China National]
75 Dengshikou Street
Beijing
Tel: (1) 550669, 550366, 817665
Tlx: 222451 CSIMC CN

Scientific Instruments Import and Export
Corporation [The Oriental]
52 Sanlihe Road, Xicheng Qu
Beijing
Tel: (1) 8012342 Fax: (1) 8012412
Tlx: 20063 ASCHI CN

Seed Corporation [China National]
31 Min Feng Hu Tong, Xidan
Beijing 100032
Tel: (1) 652592, 651179 Fax: (1) 6012808
Tlx: 22598

Shipbuilding Corporation [China State]
5 Yuetan Jie
Beijing 100861
Tel: (1) 8312561, 8318833 Fax: (1) 8313380
Tlx: 22029 CSSC CN

Shipbuilding Trading Corporation Ltd. [China]
10 Yue Tan Bei Xiao Jie
Beijing 100861
Tel: (1) 8323109, 8312561 Fax: (1) 8313380
Tlx: 22029 CSSC CN

Shougang Corporation
Shijingshan
Beijing
Tel: (1) 8293307 Fax: (1) 8293307 Tlx: 22619

Silk Garments Import and Export Corporation
[China]
105 Beiheyan Street, Dongcheng Qu
Beijing 100006
Tel: (1) 5138198 Fax: (1) 5136839
Tlx: 210596 CSGEC CN

Silk Import and Export Corporation [China
National] (CHINASILK)
105 Beiheyan Street, Dongcheng Qu
Beijing 100006
Tel: (1) 5125125, 5128336, 5123338
Fax: (1) 5126838, 5124746 Tlx: 210594

Silk Materials & Fabrics Import and Export
Corporation [China National]
105 Beiheyan Street, Dongcheng Qu
Beijing 100006
Tel: (1) 5128331 Fax: (1) 5128353
Tlx: 210594 CSMIC CN

Silk Materials Import Corporation [China]
105 Beiheyan Street, Dongcheng Qu
Beijing 100006
Tel: (1) 5125123 Fax: (1) 5136840
Tlx: 210081 CSMIC CN

Spare Parts & Components Company of CNTIC
A2 Hou Niurou Wan, Xidan
Beijing
Tel: (1) 6011018 Fax: (1) 6011018
Tlx: 22244 CNTIC CN

State Construction Engineering Corporation
[China]
Baiwanzhuang, Xicheng Qu
Beijing
Tel: (1) 8992368 Fax: (1) 8314326 Tlx: 22477

State Farms [China Import and Export
Corporations of]
56 Zhuanta Lane, Xisi
Beijing 100810
Tel: (1) 6015101 Fax: (1) 6015102
Tlx: 222911 SFIE CN

Sugar and Sundries Import and Export Company
[China]
9th Fl., Jingxin Building
2A Dongsanhuanbei Lu
Beijing 100027
Tel: (1) 4660681 Fax: (1) 4660642
Tlx: 210058 COFCD CN

Sundries & Flowers Import and Export Corporation
[China] (TUHSU)
82 Donganmen Dajie
Beijing 100747
Tel: (1) 5132381 Fax: (1) 5132380
Tlx: 210653 TUHSU CN

Superfood Import and Export Corporation [China]
(TUHSU)
82 Donganmen Dajie
Beijing 100747
Tel: (1) 5124716 Fax: (1) 5124716
Tlx: 22892 TUHSU CN

Supply & Marketing Cooperative Foreign Trade
Corporation [China]
5 Fu Xing Men Street N.
Beijing 100045
Tel: (1) 868951 x233 Fax: (1) 866329
Tlx: 222926 CN COPCN

Tea Import and Export Corporation [China]
(TUHSU)
82 Donganmen Dajie
Beijing 100747
Tel: (1) 5124192, 5124785 Fax: (1) 5124775
Tlx: 22898 TUHSU CN

Technical Import and Export Corporation
[China National] (CNTIC or TECHIMPORT)
Jiu Ling Building
21 Xi San Huan Bei Lu
Beijing 100081
Tel: (1) 8404802/8, 8404123, 8404000
Fax: (1) 8414877 Tlx: 22244 CNTIC CN
CNTIC Shanghai Tel: (21) 4330405
CNTIC Guangzhou Tel: (20) 3338999 x10009

Textile Machine Technology Import and Export
Corporation [China]
15 Pujiang Road
Pujiang Hotel, Rm. 315
Shanghai 200080
Tel: (21) 3254564 Fax: (21) 3207354

Textile Machinery and Technology Import and
Export Corporation [China National]
75 Chaoyang Mennei Street
Beijing 100010
Tel: (1) 4011870, 4015691 Fax: (1) 4012139
Tlx: 211252 CTMTC CN

Textiles Import and Export Corporation
[China National] (CHINATEX)
82 Donganmen Dajie
Beijing 100747
Tel: (1) 5123844, 5135533 Fax: (1) 5124711
Tlx: 22280 CNTEX CN

Textiles Import and Export Corporation [Guangxi]
33A Tian Tao Road
Nanning, Guangxi 530022
Tel: (771) 27693, 29319, 23315, 23174
Fax: (771) 29023 Tlx: 48106 GXTEX CN

Textiles Import and Export Corporation
[Shenyang]
No. 19, South Sanjing St., Shenhe Qu
Shenyang
Tel: (24) 21993, 28356, 23066, 727478
Fax: (24) 21993 Tlx: 8040-17 TIECS CN

Textiles Import and Export Corporation [Tianjin]
68, Dali Street
Tianjin
Fax: (31) 7843 Tlx: 23151 TJTEX CN

Timber Import and Export Corporation [China]
(TUHSU)
82 Donganmen Dajie
Beijing 100747
Tel: (1) 5124765 Fax: (1) 5124788
Tlx: 222236 TUHSU CN

Tobacco Corporation [China National]
1 Hufang Lu
Beijing
Tel: (1) 3015330 Fax: (1) 652171 Tlx: 222366

Tobacco Import and Export Corporation [China]
A2 Hou Niu Rou Wan Lane
Beijing 100031
Tel: (1) 655492 Fax: (1) 652171
Tlx: 222366 CNTC CN

Trading (Barter) Corporation [China International]
20 Shatanhou Jie, Dongcheng Qu
Beijing 100009
Tel: (1) 4011067 (Exports), 4011071 (Imports)
Fax: (1) 4014373

Trading Co., Ltd. [Minmetals]
5, Building, 8 Compound
Chedaogou, Haidian Qu
Beijing
Tel: (1) 8021306, 8021276 Fax: (1) 8315079
Tlx: 22773 MINMET CN

Transport Machinery Import and Export
Corporation [China National]
Import Building, Erligou
PO Box 49
Beijing 100044
Tel: (1) 8317799 x4400/1/3, 8314128
Fax: (1) 8314136, 8021321 Tlx: 22882

Vehicles Import and Export Corporation
[China National]
42A Baishiqiao, Haidian Qu
Beijing
Tel: (1) 8021235 Fax: (1) 8021259
Tlx: 22877 CVIEC CN

Water and Electric International Corporation
[China]
Block 1 Liupukang
Beijing 100011
Tel: (1) 4015511 Fax: (1) 4014075 Tlx: 22485

Xinshidai Company [China]
92 Dongzhimennei Dajie
Beijing
Tel: (1) 4016625, 4017384
Fax: (1) 4015088, 4032935 Tlx: 22338

Xinxing Corporation Group [China]
17 Xisanhuan, Middle Road
Beijing 10036
Tel: (1) 8016688 Fax: (1) 8014669

Yarns & Fabrics Import and Export Corporation
[Chinatex]
82 Donganmen Dajie
Beijing 100747
Tel: (1) 5124718 Fax: (1) 5124713
Tlx: 210023 CNTEX CN

TRADE PROMOTION ORGANIZATIONS

WORLD TRADE CENTERS

Beijing
China World Trade Center (Beijing), Ltd.
China World Tower
1 Jian Guo Men Wai Dajie
Beijing 100004
Tel: (1) 5052288, 5058340 Fax: (1) 5051002
Tlx: 210087

Beijing
World Trade Center
Rm. 409 4th Fl., 2nd Central Building
Hualong St., Nanheyan
East City District
Beijing 100006
Tel: (1) 5125176/7 Fax: (1) 5125165
Tlx: 210333 BCPIT CN

Chengdu
World Trade Center Club Chengdu
17th Fl., Shudu Building
15 Shudu Road
Chengdu 610016
Tel: (28) 673888, 51715,336693
Fax: (28) 334675 Tlx: 60131 SFTC CN

Chongqing
World Trade Center Club Chongqing
Rm. 3213-3214, Renmin Hotel
No. 175 Renmin Road
Chongquing, Sichuan Province
Tel: (811) 3511456 Fax: (811) 351387
Tlx: 62224 WTCCQ CN

Guangzhou
World Trade Center Club Guanzhou
Rm. 835-837, Garden Tower, Garden Hotel
368 Huanshi Dong Lu
Guanzhou 510064
Tel: (20) 3338999 x7835/6/7 Fax: (20) 3354241
Tlx: 44341 WTCG CN

Haikou
World Trade Center Haikou
Hainan Seg International Plaza Co., Ltd.
Rm. 107-109, Nantian Hotel
Airport Road West
Haikou, Hainan Province
Tel: (898) 797472, 797946, 799227
Fax: (898) 797582 Tlx: 490053 NTHTL CN

Hangzhou
Zhejiang World Trade Center Hangzhou
15 Shuguang Road
Hangzhou
Tel: (571) 753287 Fax: (571) 553447
Tlx: 35037 FETRA CN

Hefei
Hefei World Trade Center Club
8th Fl., Bank of China Hefei Building
155 Chang Jiang Road
Hefei, Anhui Province
Tel: (551) 241482 Fax: (551) 241436, 241409
Tlx: 90204 ATIEC CN

Nanjing
World Trade Center Club Nanjing
Jinling Hotel
2 Hanzhong Road
Nanjing 210005
Tel: (25) 741999, 742888 x4615, 4611
Fax: (25) 643396, 714693 Tlx: 34110 JLHNJ CN

Shanghai
World Trade Center Shanghai
33 Zhong Shan Dong Yi Lu
Shanghai 20002
Tel: (21) 3232348, 3213850 Fax: (21) 3291442
Tlx: 33290 SCPIT CN

Shenyang
Shenyang Sub-Council of CCPIT
44 Wenyi Road, Shenhe Qu
5th Fl., Liaoning Science & Technical Hall
Shenyang, Liaoning Province
Tel: (24) 393733, 390854 Fax: (24) 390854
Tlx: 80 4090 SSJ CN

Shenzhen
World Trade Center Shenzhen
2nd Fl., Area B, International Trade Center Mansion
Renmin South Road
Shenzhen 518014
Tel: (755) 250140/1/2
Fax: (755) 252043, 250140 Tlx: 420296 ITC CN

Tianjin
World Trade Center Tianjin
Tianjin Leader (Group) Corp.
3 Xinyuan, Kumming Road
Heping Qu
Tianjin, 300050
Tel: (22) 314882 Fax: (22) 317471
Tlx: 23254 TJEDC CN

Wuhan
World Trade Center Wuhan
7 Fl., Insurance Company Building
No. 1037, Jie Fang Ave.
Wuhan
Tel: (27) 211202, 211783, 237264
Fax: (27) 211268 Tlx: 40273 CCPIT CN

Xian
World Trade Center Club Xian
CCPIT, Shaanxi Sub-Council
Xinchengnei
Xian 710004
Tel: (29) 791421 Fax: (29) 791461
Tlx: 71249 SXCIC CN

GENERAL TRADE ASSOCIATIONS & LOCAL CHAMBERS OF COMMERCE IN THE PRC

All China Federation of Industry and Commerce
93 Beiheyan Dajie
Beijing 100006
Tel: (1) 5136677 Fax: (1) 5122631, 5131769

All China Federation of Trade Unions
10 Fu Xing Men Wai Dajie
Beijing 100865
Tel: (1) 8012200 Fax: (1) 8012933 Tlx: 222290

Beijing Commission of Technical Cooperation
13 Hufang Lu
Beijing 100052
Tel: (1) 3035931

Beijing Federation of Industry and Commerce
30 Zhushikou Xi Dajie
Xuanwu Qu
Beijing 100050
Tel: (1) 3033236 Fax: (1) 3014194

CCOIC (China Chamber of International Commerce)
1 Fu Xing Men Wai Dajie
Beijing 100860
Tel: (1) 8011156, 8013344 x1304 Fax: (1) 8011370

CCOIC Commercial Chamber of Commerce
45 Fuxingmennei Dajie
Beijing 100801
Tel: (1) 6016043 Tlx: 22547 CCOC CN

CCOIC, Shanghai Chamber of Commerce
14th Fl., New Town Mansion
55 Loushanguan Lu
200335 Shanghai
Tel: (21) 2750700 Fax: (21) 2756364

China International Economic and Trade Arbitration Commission, Shanghai
33 Dongshan Dong Yi Lu
200002 Shanghai
Tel: (21) 3295443 Fax: (21) 3291442

China Society of International Economic Cooperation
28 Donghou Xiang, Andingmenwai
Beijing 100710
Tel: (1) 4216661 Tlx: 22559 COMPT CN

Shanghai Federation of Industry and Commerce
893 Huashan Lu
Shanghai 200031
Tel: (21) 4336914, 4745021 Fax: (21) 4335795

Shanghai Industry Foundation
45 Jiujiang Lu
Shanghai 200002
Tel: (21) 3210264 Fax: (21) 3290385

FOREIGN CHAMBERS OF COMMERCE AND BUSINESS ORGANIZATIONS

American Chamber of Commerce (AMCHAM) of the PRC
Great Wall Sheraton Hotel #301
Beijing 100026
Tel: (1) 5005566 x2271, Fax: (1) 5018273
Guangzhou Tel: (20) 6663388 x1293
Shanghai Tel: (21) 2798056

Hong Kong Trade Development Council, Shanghai Office
Rm. 1004, 10th Fl., Union Building
100 Yan An Dong Lu
Shanghai 200002
Tel: (21) 3264196 Fax: (21) 3287478

All addresses and telephone numbers are in The People's Republic of China unless otherwise noted. The country code for China is [86].

Italian Institute for Foreign Trade, Shanghai
Rm. 404, Hotel Equatorial
65 Yan An Xi Lu
Shanghai 200040
Tel: (1) 2568600 Fax: (1) 2562169

Japan Association for Promotion of International
Trade, Shanghai Office
Rm. 359 New Building, Jinjiang Club
191 Changle Lu
Shanghai 200020
Tel: (1) 4373033

US-China Business Council
Rm. 22-C, CITIC Building
19 Jian Guo Men Wai Dajie
Beijing 100004
Tel: (1) 5051314, 5051302 Fax: (1) 5052201

CHINA COUNCIL FOR PROMOTION OF INTERNATIONAL TRADE & CHINA CHAMBER OF INTERNATIONAL COMMERCE OVERSEAS OFFICES

Australia
Suite 205, 4-8 Waters Road, Neutral Bay
Sydney, NSW 2089, Australia
Tel: [61] (2) 953-0677 Fax: [61] (2) 9530458

Canada
415 Yonge Street, Suite 1102
Toronto, ON M6B 2E7, Canada
Tel: [1] (416) 340-6301 Fax: [1] (416) 340-9539

France
2, place de la Defense CNIT B.P.
Paris, France
Tel: [33] (1) 46.92.25.45/6
Fax: [33] (1) 46.92.25.43

Germany
Schubert Strasse 14
D-6000 Frankfurt/Main 1, Germany
Tel: [49] (69) 740369 Fax: [49] (69) 5484576

Hong Kong
41st Fl., China Resources Building
26 Harbour Road
Wanchai, Hong Kong
Tel: [852] 5727038 Fax: [852] 8380701
Tlx: 68599 CPPRO HX

Italy
viale Premuda, 10
20129 Milano, Italy
Tel: [39] (2) 55018041 Fax: [39] (2) 55018057

Japan
6th Fl., Okashma Building
7-14 Tomizawacho, Chuo-ku
Tokyo, Japan
Tel: [81] (3) 3639-2389 Fax: [81] (3) 3639-2390

Mexico
Calle de Cerrada Monte Tauro no. 140
Colonia Lomas Chapultepec
Mexico D.F. 11000, Mexico
Tel: [52] (5) 5410575 Fax: [52] (5) 5401575
Tlx: 1763515 OCCH ME

United Arab Emirates
PO Box 3911
Abu Dhabi, UAE
Tel: [971] (2) 341643

United Kingdom
20 Market Mews, Mayfair
London W1Y 7HG, UK
Tel: [44] (71) 629-2836 Fax: [44] (71) 408-0677
Tlx: 261164 CCPIT G

United States of America
4301 Connecticut Avenue NW, Suite 139
Washington, DC 20008, USA
Tel: [1] (202) 244-3244 Fax: [1] (202) 244-0478
Tlx: 210626 CCPT UR

INDUSTRY-SPECIFIC TRADE ORGANIZATIONS

Advertising Association for Foreign Economic
Relations and Trade [China National]
7 Liufang Beili, Xiangheyuan
Chaoyang Qu
Beijing 100028
Tel: (1) 4081118 Fax: (1) 4082319

Aeronautics and Astronautics [Chinese Society of]
9 Xiaoguan Dong Jie, Chaoyang Qu
Beijing 100029
Tel: (1) 4912085 Fax: (1) 4914643

Agricultural Economics [Chinese Society of]
30 Baishiqiao Lu, Xijiao
Beijing 100081
Tel: (1) 8314433

Agricultural Machinery [Chinese Society of]
1 Beishatan
Deshengmenwai
Beijing 100083
Tel: (1) 2017131 Fax: (1) 2017326

Agricultural Science Society [Chinese
Association of]
11 Nongzhanguan Lanli
Beijing 100026
Tel: (1) 5003366 Tlx: 22233 MAGR CN

Architectural Society of China
Baiwanzhuang, Xijiao
Beijing 100835
Tel: (1) 8393559 Fax: (1) 8311585

Automation [Chinese Association of]
PO Box 2728
Beijing 100080
Tel: (1) 2544415 Fax: (1) 2545229

Ceramic Society [Chinese]
Baiwanzhuang
Beijing 100831
Tel: (1) 8311144 Fax: (1) 8311497

Chemical Industry and Engineering
Society of China
20 Xueyuan Lu
Beijing 100083
Tel: (1) 2015805 Fax: (1) 2017108

Chemical Society [Chinese]
Zhongguangcun
Beijing 100080
Tel: (1) 2568157 Fax: (1) 2568157

Civil Engineering Society [China]
Baiwanzhuang
Beijing 100835
Tel: (1) 8311313 Fax: (1) 8313669

Coal and Machinery Industry [China
Association for]
21 Bei Jie, Hepingli
Beijing 100713
Tel: (1) 4217766 Fax: (1) 4214010

Coating Industrial Association [China National]
Songjiazhuang, Yongdingmenwai
Beijing 100075
Tel: (1) 7211146 x687 Fax: (1) 7213549

Communication and Transportation
Association [Chinese]
31 Dongchangan Jie
Beijing 100005
Tel: (1) 5125076 Fax: (1) 5125071

Communications [China Institute of]
13 Xichangan Jie
Beijing 100804
Tel: (1) 6018191

Computer Federation [China]
Zhongguancun, Haidian Qu
Beijing 100080
Tel: (1) 2562503 Fax: (1) 2567724

Contractors Association [China International]
28 Donghou Xiang, Andingmenwai
Beijing 100011
Tel: (1) 4212855 Fax: (1) 4213959

Cotton Spinning and Weaving Association
[Shanghai]
Rm. 306, 24 Zhongshan
Dong Yi Lu
Shanghai 200020
Tel: (21) 3214066

Dairy Cattle Association [China]
56 Zhuanta Lane, Xisi
Beijing 100810
Tel: (1) 6018095 Fax: (1) 6024845

Dyeing and Printing Industry Association
[Shanghai]
Rm. 307, 24 Zhongshan
Dong Yi Lu
Shanghai 200020
Tel: (21) 3210938

Electrical Engineering [Chinese Society for]
1 Baiguang Lu, Ertiao
Beijing 100761
Tel: (1) 3273322 Tlx: 22466 MWREP CN

Electrical Material Association [China]
20 Fucheng Lu
Beijing 100036
Tel: (1) 8314685 Fax: (1) 8011242

Enterprise Management Association [China]
17 Zizhuyuan Nan Lu, Haidian Qu
Beijing 100036
Tel: (1) 8416622 Fax: (1) 8414280

Environmental Sciences [Chinese Society of]
115 Xizhimennei Nan Xiao Jie
Beijing 100035
Tel: (1) 6021006 Tlx: 22477 CCEC CN

Finance [China Society of]
Rm. 908-9, Building 7
Erqijuchang Lu Xili
Beijing 100045
Tel: (1) 8317378

Fisheries Association [Chinese]
11 Nongzhanguan Nanli
Beijing 100026
Tel: (1) 5003366 Fax: (1) 5002448

Fisheries [China Society of]
31 Minfeng Lane, Xidan
Beijing 100032
Tel: (1) 6020794 Fax: (1) 6012808

Food Industry Association [China National]
5 Taipingqiao, Dongli
Guanganmenwai
Beijing 100055
Tel: (1) 3062244 Tlx: 222983 CNFIA CN

Forging Industry Association [China]
277 Wangfujing Dajie
Beijing 100740
Tel: (1) 5126679 Fax: (1) 5126675

Highway and Transportation [Chinese Society of]
10 Fuxing Lu
Beijing 100845
Tel: (1) 3265544 Fax: (1) 2014130

Hydraulic Engineering Society [Chinese]
Baiguang Lu Ertiao
Guanganmennei
Beijing 100761
Tel: (1) 3273322 Tlx: 22466 MWREP CN

Information Processing Society of China [Chinese]
PO Box 8718
Beijing 100080
Tel: (1) 2562916 Fax: (1) 2562533

Instrument Society [Shanghai]
225 Longjiang Lu
Shanghai 200082
Tel: (21) 5417350

Law Society [China]
6 Xizhimen, Nan Dajie
Beijing 10035
Tel: (1) 6689719 x5209 Fax: (1) 8317502

Lawyers Association [Beijing]
1 Xishiku Dajie
Xicheng Qu
Beijing 100034
Tel: (1) 6016172 Fax: (1) 6016171

Light Industry of Science and Technology [Chinese Association]
Inside Light Industry Dept.
22B Fuwai Dajie
Beijing
Tel: (1) 2015921

Machinery and Electronics [China Chamber of Commerce for Import and Export of]
127 Xuan Wu Men Wai Dajie
Beijing 100031
Tel: (1) 6015627

Medical Association [Chinese]
42 Dongsi Xidajie
Beijing
Tel: (1) 5133311

Medicines and Health Products Importers and Exporters [China Chamber of Commerce]
12 Jian Guo Men Wai Dajie, 12th Fl.
Beijing 100022
Tel: (1) 5001542, 5003344 Fax: (1) 5001150

Mechanical Engineering Society [Chinese]
Sanlihe
Beijing 100823
Tel: (1) 3295315/6 Fax: (1) 8013867

Medical Society [Chinese]
42 Dongsi Xi Dajie
Beijing 100710
Tel: (1) 5127946 Fax: (1) 5123754

Metals [Chinese Society for]
46 Dongsi Xi Dajie
Beijing 100761
Tel: (1) 5133322 Fax: (1) 5124122

Navigation [China Institute of]
10 Fuxing Lu
Beijing 100845
Tel: (1) 3266227 Tlx: 22462 COMCT CN

Packaging Technology Association [China]
31 Dongchangan Jie
Beijing 100005
Tel: (1) 5124123 Fax: (1) 5124128

Paper Industry [China Technical Association of]
12 Guanghua Lu
Beijing 100020
Tel: (1) 5002880 Tlx: 222717 LIMDI CN

Petroleum Society [Chinese]
Liupukang, Deshengmenwai
Beijing 100724
Tel: (1) 2015544 Tlx: 22312 PCPRC CN

Pharmaceutical Association [Chinese]
38A Beilishi Lu
Beijing 100810
Tel: (1) 8316576

Photographers Association [Chinese]
61 Hongxing Lane
Dongdan
Beijing 100005
Tel: (1) 5138757

Printing Materials Association [Shanghai]
266 Qingyun Lu
Shanghai 2000081
Tel: (21) 6624700 Fax: (21) 6630256

Railway Society [China]
10 Fuxing Lu
Beijing 100844
Tel: (1) 3241681

Rubber Industry Trade Council [Shanghai]
107 Fuzhou Lu
Shanghai 200002
Tel: (21) 3214029

Science and Technology [China Association for]
54 Sanlihe Lu
Beijing 100863
Tel: (1) 8318877 Fax: (1) 8321914

Science and Technology [Shanghai Association for]
47 Nanchang Lu
Shanghai 200020
Tel: (21) 3722040 Fax: (21) 3721566

Scientific and Technological Information [China Society of]
15 Fuxing Lu
Beijing 100036
Tel: (1) 8014024

Solar Energy Society [Chinese]
3 Huayuan Lu, Haidian Qu
Beijing 100083
Tel: (1) 2017009

Sports Federation [All-China]
9 Tiyuguan Lu
Beijing 100763
Tel: (1) 7016669 Fax: (1) 7015858

Textile Engineering Society [China]
Inside Textile Dept. Institute
Yingjiafen, Dongjiao
Beijing 100025
Tel: (1) 5016537 Fax: (1) 5004780

Textiles [China Chamber of Commerce for Import and Export of]
33A Dongdansantiao
Beijing 100005
Tel: (1) 5122029 Tlx: 211143 FANYN CN

Traditional Chinese Medicine and Pharmacy [China Association of]
4A Yiunghua Lu
Hepingli Dong Jie
Beijing 100029
Tel: (1) 4218311/6

Translators' Association of China
24 Baiwanzhuang Lu
Beijing 100037
Tel: (1) 8323576 Fax: (1) 8315599

Urban and Rural Construction Commission [Beijing]
3 Lanlishi Lu, Toutaio
Beijing
Tel: (1) 8013355

FINANCIAL INSTITUTIONS

BANKS

Central Bank

People's Bank of China (Beijing)
32 Chengfang Street
Beijing 100800
Tel: (1) 6016491, 6016722 Fax: (1) 6016724

People's Bank of China (Guangzhou)
421 Yanjiang Dong Lu
Guangzhou 510100
Tel: (20) 7789154, 7771874

People's Bank of China (Shanghai)
23 Zhongshan Dong Yi Ku
Shanghai 200002
Tel: (21) 3217466, 3233898

Commercial & Domestic Banks

Agricultural Bank of China (Beijing)
25 Fuxing Lu
Beijing 100036
Tel: (1) 8413128 Fax: (1) 8416682

Agricultural Bank of China (Guangzhou)
International Business Dept.
Ground Fl., Zhonghua Center
180 Taikang Lu
Guangzhou 510115
Tel: (20) 3327747 Fax: (20) 3350903
Tlx: 44285 ABCGZ CN

Bank of China (Beijing)
410 Fuchengmen Nei Dajie
Beijing 100818
Tel: (1) 6016688 Fax: (1) 6016869
Tlx: 22254 BCHO CN

Bank of China (Guangzhou)
International Financial Building
197-9 Dongfeng Xi Lu
Guangzhou 510180
Tel: (20) 3338080 Fax: (20) 3344066
Tlx: 441042 GZBOC CN

Bank of China (Shanghai)
23 Zhongshan Dong Yi Lu
Shanghai 200002
Tel: (21) 3291979, 3211410 Fax: (21) 3234872
Tlx: 33062 BOCSH CN

Bank of Communications (Beijing)
Beijing Branch
12 Tiantan Dongli Beiqu, Chongwen Qu
Beijing 100061
Tel: (1) 7012255 Fax: (1) 7016524, 7016529
Foreign Trade Dept. Tel: (1) 7016524

Bank of Communications (Guangzhou)
4 Guangwei Lu
Guangzhou 501328
Tel: (20) 3341285 Fax: (20) 3340494

Bank of Communications (Shanghai)
200 Jiangxi Zhong Lu
Shanghai 200002
Tel: (21) 3213400, 3255900
Fax: (21) 3219823, 3206361

China International Trust and Investment
Corporation (CITIC)
Public Affairs Office
Capitol Mansion
6 Xinyuan Nan Lu, Chaoyang Qu
Beijing 100004
Tel: (1) 4660088 Fax: (1) 4661186

China International Trust and Investment
Corporation (CITIC) (Beijing)
19 Jian Guo Men Wai Dajie
Beijing 100004
Tel: (1) 5002255, 5122233
Fax: (1) 5001535, 5004851 Tlx: 22305

China International Trust and Investment
Corporation (CITIC) (Shanghai)
200 Jiangxi Zhong Lu
Shanghai 200002
Tel: (21) 3213400, 3255900
Fax: (21) 3219823, 3206361 Tlx: 33438

China Investment Bank (Beijing)
B-11 Fuxing Lu
Beijing 100859
Tel: (1) 8015900 Fax: (1) 8016088 Tlx: 22537

China Investment Bank (Shanghai)
80 Shaanxi Bei Lu
Shanghai 200041
Tel: (21) 2552817 Fax: (21) 2552681

Industrial and Commercial Bank of China
(Main office)
13 Cuiwei Lu, Haidian Qu
Beijing 100036
Tel: (1) 8217273 Fax: (1) 8217920 Tlx: 22770

Industrial and Commercial Bank of China (Beijing)
Baiyun Lu
Beijing
Tel: (1) 3062299

Industrial and Commercial Bank of China
(Guangzhou)
137 Yanjiang Xi Lu
Guangzhou 510120
Tel: (20) 8862187, 8862699

Industrial and Commercial Bank of China
(Shanghai)
23 Zhongshan Dong Yi Lu
Shanghai
Tel: (21) 3217466, 3291165 Fax: (21) 3213451

People's Construction Bank of China
12C Fuxing Lu
Beijing 100038
Tel: (1) 8014488 Fax: (1) 8015301 Tlx: 222977

Industrial and Commercial Bank of China
(Guangzhou)
Dongfeng Dong Lu
Guangzhou 510100
Tel: (20) 3333556

Industrial and Commercial Bank of China
(Shanghai)
103 Dianchi Lu
Shanghai 200002
Tel: (21) 3232666 Fax: (21) 3291790

Foreign Banks

Banca Commerciale Italiana (Beijing)
Rm. 2, 27th Fl., CITIC Building
19 Jian Guo Men Wai Dajie
Beijing 100004
Tel: (1) 5002255 Fax: (1) 5003930

Banca Commerciale Italiana (Shanghai)
Rm. 10, 14th Fl., Union Building
100 Yan An Dong Lu
Shanghai 200002
Tel: (21) 3200517/8 Fax: (21) 3202350

Banco Di Roma
Rm. 2604, CITIC Building
19 Jian Guo Men Wai Dajie
Beijing 100004
Tel: (1) 5003716 Fax: (1) 5001165

Bank of America NT&SA (Beijing)
Unit 22-23, Level 27, CWTC
1 Jian Guo Men Wai Dajie
Beijing 100004
Tel: (1) 5053508, 5053509 Fax: (1) 5053509
Tlx: 22562 BKAME CN

Bank of America NT&SA (Guangzhou)
Rm. 1325, Dongfang Hotel
Liuhua Lu
Guangzhou 510010
Tel: (20) 6678063, 6669900 x1325
Fax: (20) 6678063 Tlx: 44743 BOAGZ CN

Bank of America NT&SA (Shanghai)
Rm. 104-107A, Union Building
100 Yan An Dong Lu
Shanghai 200002
Tel: (21) 3292828 Fax: (21) 3201297

Bank of Tokyo Ltd. (Beijing)
Rm. 1701-2, China World Tower, CWTC
1 Jian Guo Men Wai Dajie
Beijing 100004
Tel: (1) 5053520 Fax: (1) 5053781

Bank of Tokyo Ltd. (Guangzhou)
Rm. 1206-8, Garden Tower, Garden Hotel
368 Huanshi Dong Lu
Guangzhou 510064
Tel: (20) 3316670, 3338999 x 1206/7
Fax: (20) 3340010 Tlx: 44231 TOHBK CN

Bank of Tokyo Ltd. (Shanghai)
Rm. 1207, Ruijin Building
205 Maoming Nan Lu
Shanghai 200020
Tel: (21) 4374667, 4334036
Fax: (21) 4334175, 4437871

Banque Nationale de Paris
Rm. 3527-31, China World Tower, CWTC
1 Jian Guo Men Wai Dajie
Beijing 100004
Tel: (1) 5053685/7 Fax: (1) 5053688

Banque Nationale de Paris (Guangzhou)
Rm. 2384, Dongfang Hotel
Liuhua Lu
Guangzhou 510010
Tel: (20) 6677042, 6669900 x2384, x2370
Fax: (20) 6677042 Tlx: 44392 BNPRO CN

Banque Nationale de Paris (Shanghai)
Rm. 58142, Jinjiang Foreign Trader's Office Bldg.
59 Maoming Nan Lu
Shanghai 200020
Tel: (21) 4714822, 2582582 Fax: (21) 4713280

Barclays Bank (Beijing)
Rm. 1211, SCITE Tower
22 Jian Guo Men Wai Dajie
Beijing 100004
Tel: (1) 5122288 Fax: (1) 5127889 Tlx: 22589

Barclays Bank (Shanghai)
Suite 530, Shanghai Center, West Podium
1376 Nanjing Xi Lu
Shanghai 200040
Tel: (21) 2798279 Fax: (21) 2798239

Chase Manhattan Bank
Rm. 509, SCITE Tower
22 Jian Guo Men Wai Dajie
Beijing 100004
Tel: (1) 5123457 Fax: (1) 5123693

Citibank, N.A. (Beijing)
18th Fl., Rm. 1, CITIC Building
19 Jian Guo Men Wai Dajie
Beijing 10004
Tel: (1) 5004425 Fax: (2) 5127930
Tlx: 22816 CTBBJ CN

Citibank, N.A. (Shanghai)
5th Fl., Union Building
100 Yan An Dong Lu
Shanghai 200002
Tel: (21) 3289661 Fax: (21) 3731317

Deutsche Bank
Rm. 2620-24, China World Tower, CWTC
1 Jian Guo Men Wai Dajie
Beijing 100004
Tel: (1) 5052305/6 Fax: (1) 5052304

First National Bank of Chicago
CITIC Building, Rm. 1604
19 Jian Guo Men Wai Dajie
Beijing 100004
Tel: (1) 5003281 Fax: (1) 5003166 Tlx: 22433

Hongkong and Shanghai Banking Corporation
(Beijing)
Suite 145-149, Jian Guo Hotel
Jian Guo Men Wai Dajie
Beijing 100020
Tel: (1) 5001074, 5001021 Fax: (1) 5001074
Tlx: 22429

Hongkong and Shanghai Banking Corporation (Guangzhou)
Rm. 1363-1364, China Hotel Office Tower
Liu Hua Lu
Guangzhou
Tel: (20) 6677061, 6663388 Fax: (20) 6677061
Tlx: 44404 HSBC CN

Hongkong and Shanghai Banking Corporation (Shanghai)
185 Yuan Ming Yuan Lu
PO Box 085-151
Shanghai 200002
Tel: (21) 3218383 Fax: (21) 3291659 Tlx: 33058

Hongkong and Shanghai Banking Corporation (Shenzhen)
1st Fl., Century Plaza Hotel
1 Chun Feng Lu
Shenzhen
Tel: (755) 2238016 Fax: (755) 2224045

National Australia Bank
Rm. 1904, CITIC Building
19 Jian Guo Men Wai Dajie
Beijing 100004
Tel: (1) 5002255 Fax: (1) 5003642

Oversea-Chinese Banking Corporation Ltd.
Singapore
120 Jiujiang Lu
Shanghai 200020
Tel: (21) 3233888 Fax: (21) 3290888
Tlx: 33541 OCBCS CN

Overseas Union Bank Ltd. Singapore
Rm. 4126 Yanjing Hotel
19 Fu Xing Men Wai Dajie
Beijing 100086
Tel: (1) 8326130 x4126 Fax: (1) 8326130 x4126

Royal Bank of Canada
Rm. 0618-20, China World Tower, CWTC
1 Jian Guo Men Wai Dajie
Beijing 100004
Tel: (1) 5054205 Fax: (1) 5054206

Standard Chartered Bank (Beijing)
14th Fl., Hong Kong Macau Center
Gongrentiyuchang Lu
Beijing
Tel: (1) 5011578/9 Fax: (1) 5011577

Standard Chartered Bank (Guangzhou)
Rm. 409, China Hotel Office Tower
Liuhua Lu
Guangzhou 510015
Tel: (20) 6677688, 6668833 x2419, x2409
Fax: (20) 6678862 Tlx: 44366 SCBGZ CN

Standard Chartered Bank (Shanghai)
Level 7, Shanghai Center
1376 Nanjin Xi Lu
Shanghai 200040
Tel: (21) 2798823 Fax: (21) 2798002
Tlx: 33271 SMTBK CN

INSURANCE COMPANIES

China Insurance Co. Ltd.
22 Xi Jiao Min Xiang
PO Box 20
Beijing
Tel: (1) 654231 Fax: (1) 6011869 Tlx: 22102

People's Insurance Co. of China (PICC)
410 Fuchengmen Nei Dajie
Beijing
Tel: (1) 6016688 Fax: (1) 6011869 Tlx: 22532

Tai Ping Insurance Co. Ltd.
410 Fuchengmen Nei Dajie
Beijing
Tel: (1) 6016688 Fax: (1) 6011869 Tlx: 22532

China Pacific Insurance Co., Shanghai
431 Fuzhou Lu
Shanghai 200001
Tel: (21) 3260303, 3734746 Fax: (21) 3734746

SERVICES

ACCOUNTING FIRMS

Arthur Andersen & Co.
Direct all mail for China to:
GPO Box 3289
General Post Office
Hong Kong

Arthur Andersen & Co. (Beijing)
Rm. 2525-2529, China World Tower
China World Trade Center
1 Jian Guo Men Wai Avenue
Beijing 100004
Tel: (1) 5053333 Fax: (1) 5051828
Tlx: 210284 ARTHA CN

Arthur Andersen & Co. (Shanghai)
Rm. 2304, Shanghai Int'l Trade Center
2200 Yan An Road West
Shanghai 200335
Tel: (21) 2758811 Fax: (21) 2750408

China Certified Accountants and Financial
Management (CCAFM)
15th Fl., Jungbin Hotel
24 Fuchengmenwai Dajie, Xicheng Qu
Beijing 100037
Tel: (1) 8327655 Fax: (1) 8328713
Tlx: 22852 CCAFM CN

Coopers & Lybrand (Beijing)
Suite 1908, SCITE Tower
22 Jian Guo Men Wai Dajie
Dong Changan Jie
Beijing 100004
Tel: (1) 5129851, 5122288 x1908
Fax: (1) 5129846 Tlx: 222544

Coopers & Lybrand (Guangzhou)
187 Dade Road, 9th Fl.
Guangzhou
Tel: (20) 3324194 Fax: (20) 3338016

Coopers & Lybrand (Shanghai)
1111 Shanghai, Ruijin Building
205 Mao Ming Nan Lu
Shanghai
Tel: (21) 4334552 Fax: (21) 4334651 Tlx: 33273

Deloitte Touche Tohmatsu China
Suite 828, China World Tower, CWTC
1 Jian Guo Men Wai Dajie
Beijing 100004
Tel: (1) 5054604/5 Fax: (1) 5054610
Direct correspondence to:
Wing On Centre, 26th Fl.
111 Connaught Road
Central, Hong Kong
Tel: [852] 5450303 Fax: [852] 5411911

Ernst & Young
Direct all correspondence for China to:
Alfred Y. Shum
Ernst & Young, Hong Kong
15th Fl., Hutchinson House
10 Harcourt Road
Central, Hong Kong
Tel: [852] 8459959 Fax: [852] 8129818

Ernst & Young (Beijing)
Hong Kong Macau Center
10th Fl., Office Building
Dong Si Shi Tiao Li Jiao Quio
Beijing 100027
Tel: (1) 5011520, 5012288 x1050 Fax: (1) 5011519

Ernst & Young (Shanghai)
Suite 531, East Tower, Shanghai Center
1376 Nanjing Xi Lu
Shanghai 200040
Tel: (21) 2798595 Fax: (21) 2798598

Ernst & Young (Shenzhen)
Unit 2B, 8th Fl., Shenzhen Development Center
Renmin Nan Lu
Shenzhen
Tel: (755) 2280788 Fax: (755) 2280077

Guangzhou Certified Public Accountants
322 Huanshi Dong Lu
Guangzhou 510060
Tel: (20) 3340722 Fax: (20) 3342385
Tlx: 44240 GDFDC CN

KMPG Peat Marwick, China (Beijing)
Rm. 2609, Jing Guang Center
Hu Jia Lou, Chaoyang Qu
Beijing 100020
Tel: (1) 5013388 x26081/8 Fax: (1) 5004059
Tlx: 22904 PMMBJ CN

KMPG Peat Marwick, China (Guangzhou)
c/o Guangzhou Certified Public Accountants
322 Huanshi Dong Lu
Guangzhou 510060
Tel: (20) 3340722 Fax: (20) 3342385
Tlx: 44757 PMMGZ CN

KMPG Peat Marwick, China (Shanghai)
Suite 407, American International Center
Shanghai Center
1376 Nanjing Xi Lu
Shanghai 200040
Tel: (21) 2798087 Fax: (21) 2798075

Price Waterhouse
Direct all correspondence for China to:
Price Waterhouse Hong Kong
Prince's Building, 22nd Fl.
Hong Kong
Postal address: GPO Box 690, Hong Kong
Tel: [852] 8262111, 5222111 Fax: [852] 8109888

Price Waterhouse (Beijing)
Suite 2921, China World Tower, CWTC
1 Jian Guo Men Wai Dajie
Beijing 100004
Tel: (1) 5051524/5, 5052288 x2921
Fax: (1) 5051026 Tlx: 210141 PWBJO CN

Price Waterhouse (Shanghai)
Rm. 310, Shanghai Center
1376 Nanjing Xi Lu
Shanghai 200040
Tel: (21) 2798770 Fax: (21) 2798792

Price Waterhouse (Shenzhen)
Rm. 302, Century Plaza Hotel
Jian She Road
Shenzhen
Tel: (755) 2200540

Yangcheng Certified Public Accountants
9th Fl., 187 Dade Lu
Guangzhou, 510120
Tel: (20) 3331225 Fax: (20) 3338016

Yangcheng Certified Public Accountants
Dongfang Hotel Office
Rm. 1243, Dongfang Hotel
Liuha Lu
Guangzhou 510010
Tel: (20) 6669900 x1243

ADVERTISING AGENCIES

Advertising Association for Foreign Economic
Relations and Trade [China National]
7 Liufang Beili, Xiangheyuan
Chaoyang Qu
Beijing 100028
Tel: (1) 4081118 Fax: (1) 4082319

BBDO/CNUAC
23rd Fl., Capital Mansion
6 Xin Yuan Nan Road, Chao Yang Qu
Beijing 100004
Tel: (1) 4663318 Fax: (1) 4662311

Beijing Advertising Corp.
10-11th Fl., Office Building, Universe Building
14 Dongzhimen Nan Dajie
Dongcheng Qu
Beijing 100027
Tel: (1) 5001188 Fax: (1) 5019471
Export Advertising Dept. Tel: (1) 5019479

China International Advertising Corp.
5th Fl., 12 Jian Guo Men Wai Dajie
Beijing 100022
Tel: (1) 5061172 Fax: (1) 5061167

Daiko Advertising Inc.
3007, Jing Guang Center
Hijialou, Chaoyang Qu
Beijing
Tel: (1) 5013008

Dentsu Inc. (Beijing)
Suite 1518, Beijing Fortune Building
5 Dong San Huan Bei-Lu, Chao Yang Qu
Beijing 100004
Tel: (1) 5014141 Fax: (1) 5002851

Dentsu Inc. (Shanghai)
Rm. 605, Garden Hotel Shanghai
58 Mao Ming Nan-Lu
Shanghai 200020
Tel: (21) 4333507 Fax: (21) 4335499

Dentsu, Young & Rubicam (Beijing)
10th Fl., Asia-Pacific Building
8 Ya Bao Lu, Chaoyang Qu
Beijing 100020
Tel: (1) 5125559 Fax: (1) 5125988 Tlx: 716-211209

Dentsu, Young & Rubicam (Shanghai)
Rm. 1206, Shanghai International Trade Center
2200 Yan An Road West
Shanghai 200335
Tel: (21) 2752949 Fax: (21) 2754202
Tlx: 716-30029

Hakuhodo Inc.
Rm. 507, Beijing Fortune Building
5 Dong, Sanhuan Bei-lu, Chaoyang Qu
Beijing
Tel: (1) 5011351 Fax: (1) 5011350
Tlx: 85-210011 (CLH CN)

Interasia Communications
Xuanwu Park, Huaibaishu Jie
Beijing 100053
Tel: (1) 3012159 Fax: (1) 3016159

J. Walter Thompson
Beijing Liaison Office
Ste. 1204, Consultancy & Information Building
B-12 Guanghua Road
Beijing 100020
Tel: (1) 5051570 Fax: (1) 5051573

J. Walter Thompson
Shanghai Liaison Office
Rm. 306-307 Jingan Commercial Office
301 Huashan Road
Shanghai
Tel: (21) 2588414 Fax: (21) 258813

LB (China) Ltd. Guangzhou Representative Office
Gitic Plaza, 15th Fl., Unit B
339 Huanshi Dong Road
Guangzhou
Tel: (20) 3311182/3, 3311163 Fax (20) 3311123

Lintas China
Rm. 2114, Shanghai Intl. Trade Center
2200 Yan An Road West
Shanghai
Tel: (21) 7015299 Fax: (21) 7015129

McCann-Erickson Guanming Ltd.
Rm. 706, SCITE Tower
22 Jian Guo Men Wai Dajie
Beijing 100004
Tel: (1) 5123621 Fax: (1) 5123619

Ogilvy & Mather Marketing Services Ltd.
Rm. 1203, SCITE Tower
22 Jian Guo Men Wai Dajie
Beijing 100004
Tel: (1) 5123665, 5122288 Fax: (1) 5123664

Saatchi & Saatchi Advertising
16-H Vue Hai Center
472 Huanshi Dong Lu
Guangzhou 510075
Tel: (20) 7779688 x1624 Fax: (20) 7785864

Saatchi & Saatchi Advertising
2102 Landmark Tower
8 Dong Sanhuan Bei Lu, Chaoyang Qu
Beijing 100004
Tel: (1) 5066929, 5066931 Fax: (1) 5066932

Shanghai Service Group
Rm. 611, Holiday Inn Center
Huanshi Dong, Chinese Village
28 Guangming Lu
Guangzhou
Tel: [86] (20) 7766999 x611
Fax: [86] (20) 7753126 x611

Shanghai, Ogilvy & Mather Advertising Ltd.
Rm. 707, New Town Mansion
55 Lou Shan Guaw Road
Shanghai
Tel: (21) 2757894 Fax: (21) 2752417

LAW FIRMS

Baker & McKenzie China Consultants (USA)
Ste. 427, China Hotel
Liuhua Lu
Guangzhou 510015
Tel: (20) 6665959, 6666888 x427
Fax: (20) 6665950 Tlx: 44888

Baker & McKenzie China Consultants (USA)
Ste 2609, Union Building
100 Yan An Dong Lu
Shanghai 200002
Tel: (21) 3265522 Fax: (21) 3201769 Tlx: 30146

Baker & McKenzie International Consultants (USA)
Suite 1504-8, China World Tower, CWTC
1 Jian Guo Men Wai Dajie
Beijing 100004
Tel: (1) 5050591/2, 5052288 x1504
Fax: (1) 5052309 Tlx: 22907 ABOGA CN

Beijing Foreign Economic Law Office
Working People's Cultural Palace
Beijing 100006
Tel: (1) 5513167/8 Fax: (1) 5126406

Beijing Lawyers Association
1 Xishiku Dajie
Xicheng Qu
Beijing 100034
Tel: (1) 6016172 Fax: (1) 6016171

Bull, Housser & Tupper
58244 #3 Jin Jiang Office Building
59 Mao Ming Nan Lu
Shanghai 200020
Tel: (21) 4374897 Fax: (21) 4375066 Tlx: 33011

Buxbaum and Choy (USA)
60 Xi Chang An Street
West Cheug Qu
Beijing
Tel: (1) 667007 Fax: (1) 3261232

Buxbaum and Choy (USA)
Ste. 512, China Hotel Office Tower
Liuhua Lu
Guangzhou
Tel: (20) 6663388 x2512 Tlx: 44229 BAOCN

China Global Law Office, Commercial &
Financial Section
Suite 2301, SCITE Tower
22 Jian Guo Men Wai Dajie
Beijing 100004
Tel: (1) 5128810 Fax: (1) 5126607
Tlx: 22222 CGLO CN

China Global Law Office, Maritime Dept.
2 Jinan Xi Jie, Beisanhuan Dong Lu
Chaoyang Qu
Beijing 100028
Tel: (1) 4665666, 4665111 Fax: (1) 4663999

China International Economic and Trade
Arbitration Commission
1 Fu Xing Men Wai St.
Beijing
Tel: (1) 8013344 Fax: (1) 8011369

China Law Society
6 Xizhimen, Nan Dajie
Beijing 10035
Tel: (1) 6689719 x5209 Fax: (1) 8317502

China Legal Consultancy Center
Rm. 409, Television Service Building
20 Wanfujing Dajie
Beijing 100006
Tel: (1) 5135261 Fax: (1) 513259
Tlx: 22505 BOOTH CN

China Legal Consultancy Center, Branch Office
Rm. 141, Building No. 1, Xiyuan Hotel
Erligou, Xijiao
Beijing 100046
Tel: (1) 8313388 Fax: (1) 8314577
Tlx: 22831 XYH CN

Coudert Brothers (USA)
Suite 2708-9, Jingguang Center
Hujialou, Chaoyang Qu
Beijing 100020
Tel: (1) 5012851/2 Fax: (1) 5012856
Tlx: 22291 AMLAW CN

Deacons and Graham & James International
Consultants Ltd., Beijing Rep Office
Suite 1903, CITIC Building
19 Jian Guo Men Wai Dajie
Beijing 100004
Tel: (1) 5002255 x3564/6, x1903
Fax: (1) 5002557 Tlx: 22969 GJPEK CN

Guangdong International Commerce Law Office
3rd Fl., Yuehua Hotel
320 Huanshi Dong Lu
Guangzhou 510060
Tel: (20) 3337899 x325, 3350454
Fax: (20) 3350447 Tlx: 44422 GITIC CN

Guangzhou Foreign Economics Law Office
5th Fl., Dongjian Building
503 Dongfeng Zhong Lu
Guangzhou 510030
Tel: (20) 6677846, 3350207 Fax: (20) 3350001

Guangzhou Notary Public Office
3rd Fl., 87 Cangbian Lu
Guangzhou 510030
Tel: (20) 3331336 Fax: (20) 3350742

Hualian Law Office for Economy and Trade
4 Beixinqiao Santiao
Beijing 100007
Tel: (1) 4013389 Fax: (1) 4011651
Tlx: 211180 HOPO CN

Interjura Consultancy Services Ltd.
Suite 3309, Jing Guang Center
Hujialou, Chaoyang Qu
Beijing 100020
Tel: (1) 5014681, 5013388 Fax: (1) 5014682

Paul, Weiss, Rifkind, Wharton & Garrison (USA)
Rm. 904, SCITE Tower
22 Jian Guo Men Wai Dajie
Beijing 100004
Tel: (1) 5123628 Fax: (1) 5123631 Tlx: 210169

Tianping Law Office
Rm. 409, 4th Fl., Television Service Building
20 Wangfujing Dajie
Beijing 100006
Tel: (1) 5135261, 5127744 Fax: (1) 5135259
Tlx: 22505 BOOTH CN

Shanghai Notary Public Office
13, 691 Lane Pudong Dadao
Shanghai
Tel: (21) 8820768

TRANSLATORS & INTERPRETERS

Beijing Xicheng Library
Foreign Languages Translation Service
4 Xihuamen
Beijing
Tel: (1) 654597

China Scientific and Technical Documents
Translation Co.
15 Fuxing Lu
Beijing 100038
Tel: (1) 8015544 Fax: (1) 8014025
Tlx: 20079 ISTIC CN

Guangzhou Translation Service for Science and
Technology Co.
Rm. 403, 69 Wende Bei Lu
Guangzhou 510030
Tel: (20) 3333767, 3340511 x97
Fax: (20) 3342242

Service Center for Overseas Traders (SCOT)
Jinjiang Hotel
59 Maoming Nan Lu
Shanghai
Tel: (21) 2370115

Shanghai Center
1376 Nanjing Xi Lu
Shanghai 200040
Tel: (21) 2582582

Translator's Association of China
24 Baiwanzhuang Lu
Beijing 100037
Tel: (1) 8323576, 8315599

TRANSPORTATION

AIRLINES

Aeroflot
Hotel Beijing–Toronto
Jian Guo Men Wai Dajie
Beijing 100020
Tel: (1) 5002412
Shanghai Tel: (21) 4711665

Air China
15 Xichangan Jie
Beijing 100031
Tel: (1) 6016667 Fax: (1) 6017587
Guangzhou Tel: (20) 6661803
Shanghai Tel: (21) 2471960

Air France
Rm. 2716, China World Tower, CWTC
1 Jian Guo Men Wai Dajie
Beijing 100004
Tel: (1) 5051818 Fax: (1) 5051435

Air France
Shanghai International Airport
Shanghai 200335
Tel: (21) 2558866 Fax: (21) 2518393

All Nippon
Rm. 1510, China World Tower, CWTC
1 Jian Guo Men Wai Dajie
Beijing 100004
Tel: (1) 5053311 Fax: (1) 5050369

British Airways
Rm. 210, 2nd Fl., SCITE Tower
22 Jian Guo Men Wai Dajie
Beijing 100004
Tel: (1) 5124070/5 Fax: (1) 5124085

CAAC (Civil Aviation Administration of China)
155 Dongsi Xi Dajie
Beijing 100710
Tel: (1) 4012233

CAAC (Civil Aviation Administration of China)
Hongqiao
Shanghai 200335
Tel: (21) 2558899, 2536530

CAAC (Civil Aviation Administration of China)
181 Huanshi Lu
Guangzhou
Tel: (20) 6661803 (International passenger),
6662969 (Domestic passenger), 6662917 (Cargo)

China Eastern
200 Yanan Xi Lu
Shanghai 200040
Tel: (21) 2472255, 2471960 Fax: (21) 2466761
Beijing Tel: (1) 6024070
Guangzhou Tel: (20) 6662969

China Northwest Airlines
Longbai Hotel
Shanghai 200335
Tel: (21) 2558868 x5423/8

China Northwest Airlines
Guangzhou International Financial Building
Guangzhou
Tel: (20) 3321688 x610

China Southern
Baiyun Airport
Guangzhou 510405
Tel: (20) 6661803, 6678901
Shanghai Tel: (21) 552255

China Southwest
Beijing Tel: (1) 5016829
Guangzhou Tel: (20) 6673747

Dragonair Hongkong
Rm. L107, 1st Fl., China World Tower, CWTC
1 Jian Guo Men Wai Dajie
Beijing 100004
Tel: (1) 5054343 Fax: (1) 5054347

Dragonair Hongkong
Rm. 123, North Wing, Jinjiang Hotel
59 Maoming Nan Lu
Shanghai 200020
Tel: (21) 4336435 Fax: (21) 4334814

Ethiopian Airlines
Rm. 0506, China World Tower, CWTC
1 Jian Guo Men Wai Dajie
Beijing 100004
Tel: (1) 5050314/5

Finnair
SCITE Tower
22 Jian Guo Men Wai Dajie
Beijing 100004
Tel: (1) 5127180 Fax: (1) 5127182

Iran Air
Rm. 701, CITIC Building
19 Jian Guo Men Wai Dajie
Beijing 100004
Tel: (1) 5124940

Japan Airlines (JAL)
1st Fl., Changfugong Office Building
26A Jian Guo Men Wai Dajie
Beijing 100022
Tel: (1) 5130888 Fax: (1) 5139865

Japan Airlines (JAL)
Rm. 201, Ruijin Building
205 Maoming Nan Lu
Shanghai 200020
Tel: (21) 4336337, 4333000 Fax: (21) 4338171

Korea Air
Rm. 104-5, Hotel Equatorial
65 Yanan Xi Lu
Shanghai 200040
Tel: (21) 2588450 Fax: (21) 2588748

LOT Polish Airlines
Rm. L102, W. Office, China World Tower, CWTC
1 Jian Guo Men Wai Dajie
Beijing 100004
Tel: (1) 5050136

Lufthansa German Airlines
Beijing Lufthansa Center
50 Liang Ma Qiao Lu, Chaoyang Qu
Beijing 100004
Tel: (1) 4654488 Fax: (1) 4653223
Export Tel: (1) 4562050

Malaysian Airline System
Lot 115A/B, Level 1, West Wing, CWTC
1 Jian Guo Men Wai Dajie
Beijing 100004
Tel: (1) 5052681 Fax: (1) 5052680

Malaysian Airline System
Shop M04-05, Garden Hotel
368 Huanshi Dong Lu
Guangzhou 510064
Tel: (20) 3358828 Fax: (20) 3358898

Northwest Airlines Inc.
Lobby Level, Suite 104, Office Tower
China World Tower, CWTC
1 Jian Guo Men Wai Dajie
Beijing 100004
Tel: (1) 5053505 Fax: (1) 5051855

Northwest Airlines Inc.
Ste. 207, Level 2, E. Podium, Shanghai Center
1376 Nanjing Xi Lu
Shanghai 200040
Tel: (21) 4377387, 2798088 Fax: (21) 2798007

Pakistan International Airlines Corp.
Rm. 106-A, Level-1, World Trade Center
Beijing 100004
Tel: (1) 5051681 Fax: (1) 5052257

Scandinavian Airline System (SAS)
SCITE Tower
22 Jian Guo Men Wai Dajie
Beijing 100004
Tel: (1) 5120575 Fax: (1) 5120577
Beijing Airport Office Tel: (1) 4562053

Shanghai Airlines
North Gate, Hongqiao Airport
Shanghai
Tel: (21) 2550550, 2558558 Fax: (21) 2558107
Beijing Tel: (1) 5011160
Guangzhou Tel: (20) 6668800

Singapore Airlines
Rm. L109, Level 1, China World Tower
Shopping Plaza, CWTC
1 Jian Guo Men Wai Dajie
Beijing 100004
Tel: (1) 5052233 Fax: (1) 5051178

Singapore Airlines
Rm. 208, East Wing, Shanghai Center
1376 Nanjing Xi Lu
Shanghai 200040
Tel: (21) 2798000 Fax: (21) 2798027

Singapore Airlines
Mezzanine Foyer, Garden Hotel
368 Huanshi Dong Lu
Guangzhou 510064
Tel: (20) 3358999 Fax: (20) 3356699

Swissair
Rm. 201, SCITE Tower
22 Jian Guo Men Wai Dajie
Beijing 100004
Tel: (1) 5123555 Fax: (1) 5127481

Thai Airways International Ltd.
Rm. 207-9, SCITE Tower
22 Jian Guo Men Wai Dajie
Beijing 100004
Tel: (1) 5123881/3

United Airlines
Rm. 204, SCITE Tower
22 Jian Guo Men Wai Dajie
Beijing 100004
Tel: (1) 5128888 Fax: (1) 5123456

United Airlines
Shanghai Hilton International Shopping Arcade
250 Huashan Lu
Shanghai 200040
Tel: (21) 2553333, 2558899 x5304

TRANSPORTATION & CUSTOMS BROKERAGE FIRMS

Beijing Air Cargo Transportation Service Center
Inside Chao Yang Gymnasium
Tuan Jie Hu Liu Litun Xi Kou, Chao Yang Qu
Beijing 100026
Tel: (1) 5011015/9 Fax: (1) 5005765
Tlx: 211175 BACT ON

Beijing Friendship Packing and
Transportation Corp.
5 Sanlitun, Xi Liujie, Chaoyang Qu
Beijing 100053
Tel: (1) 5324806, 4652303, 4673893
Fax: (1) 5324304 Tlx: 210349 BFPTC CN

Beijing Large Goods and Materials
Transportation Co.
10 Guangyi Jie, Xuanwu Qu
Beijing 100053
Tel: (1) 338551

Beijing Materials Storage and Transportation Co.
Yangrou Lane, Xisi, Xicheng Qu
Beijing 100034
Tel: (1) 6034143 Fax: (1) 6020728

Burlington Air Express (China)
9 Dongxing Lu, Chaoyang Qu
Beijing
Tel: (1) 4665370 Fax: (1) 4082694
Tlx: 22101 CAXT CN

China Civil Aviation Passenger and Cargo
Sales Corp.
9 Dongxing Jie, Chaoyang Qu
Beijing 100027
Tel: (1) 4665369 (Cargo), 4665360 (Passenger)
Fax: (1) 4082694 Tlx: 22101 CAXT CN

China Interocean Transport Inc.
Rm. 63614, Beijing Friendship Hotel
3 Baishiqiao Lu
Beijing 100873
Tel: (1) 8498888

China National Chartering Corporation
(SINOCHART)
21 Xisanhuan Bei Lu
Beijing 100081
Tel: (1) 8415313/4 Fax: (1) 8415312
Tlx: 222508 CHART CN

China National Foreign Trade Transportation
Corporation (SINOTRANS)
Import Building
Erligou, Xijiao
Beijing 100044
Tel: (1) 8328709 Fax (1) 8311070 Tlx: 22153

China National Foreign Trade Transportation
Corporation (SINOTRANS), Guangzhou Branch
20th Fl., 53 Hua Le Road
Guangzhou 510060
Tel: (20) 7755669, 7758747 Fax: (20) 7755674
Tlx: 44838 GZTRS CN

China National Materials Storage and
Transportation Corporation
25 Yuetan Bei Jie
Beijing 100834
Tel: (1) 8392543, 8392595, 8392579 Fax: (1) 8392535

China Ocean Shipping Agency (Penavico)
6 Dong Chang An Jie
Beijing 100740
Tel: (1) 5134868, 5121188 Fax: (1) 5121924
Tlx: 211208 PENHO CN

China Ocean Shipping Co. (COSCO)
6 Dongchangan Jie
Beijing 100740
Tel: (1) 5121188, 5121702 Fax: (1) 5122408
Tlx: 22264 CPCPK CN

China Railway Foreign Service Corporation,
Beijing Branch
6 Fuxing Lu
Beijing 100038
Tel: (1) 3269601 Tlx: 222734 BRAFE CN

Crown Pacific (China) Ltd., Beijing Office
Rm. 1104, CITIC Building
19 Jian Guo Men Wai Dajie
Beijing 100004
Tel: (1) 5002255 Fax: (1) 5007487

Crown Pacific (China) Ltd., Head Office
Crown Pacific Building
9-11 Yuen On St.
Siu Lek Yuen, Shantin
New Territories, Hong Kong
Tel: [852] 6370186 Tlx: 33898 CPPRC HX

DHL-Sinotrans Ltd., Beijing Head Office
45 Xinyuan Jie, Chaoyang Qu
Beijing 100027
Tel: (1) 4662211 Fax: (1) 4677826

DSR-LINES Rostock, Beijing Rep. Office
Beijing Lufthansa Center
50 Liang Ma Qiao Lu, Chaoyang Qu
Beijing 100004
Tel: (1) 4651030/4 Fax: (1) 4651025
Tlx: 222833 DSRPK CN

EAS Express Aircargo System (China) Ltd.
1st Fl., 12 Nanxiao Jie, Sanyuanli
Zuojiazhuang, Chaoyang Qu
Beijing 100027
Tel: (1) 4677117, 4672902
Fax: (1) 4677866, 4664503 Tlx: 210072 EASY CN

Federal Express, Beijing
c/o Beijing Air Cargo Transportation Service Ctr.
Inside Chao Yang Gymnasium
Tuan Jie Hu Liu Litun Xi Kou, Chao Yan Qu
Beijing 100026
Tel: (1) 5011017, 5014888 Fax: (1) 5011015
Tlx: 211175

Federal Express, Guangzhou
c/o China National Foreign Trade Transportation
Corporation, Guangzhou Branch
20th Fl., 53 Hua Le Road
Guangzhou 510060
Tel: (20) 3805669, 3808747 Fax: (20) 3805674
Tlx: 44838 GZTRS

Federal Express, Shanghai
c/o Qian Tang Company
Shanghai Center, Rm. 460
1376 Nanjing Xi Lu
Shanghai 200040
Tel: (21) 2798040 Fax: (21) 2798042 Tlx: 30155

Federal Express, Shenzhen
c/o China National Foreign Trade Transportation
Corporation, Shenzhen Branch
50 Heping Road
Shenzhen 518001
Tel: (755) 5572346, 5572641 Fax: (755) 5584321
Tlx: 420285 SZFTC CN

Flynt International Forwarders Ltd., Beijing
C-5, Office Building, International Apartment
35 Dongzhimenwai Dajie
Dongcheng Qu
Beijing
Tel: (1) 4677902 Fax: (1) 4677087

Jardine Transport Services (China) Ltd.
Rm. 1314-5, China World Tower, CWTC
1 Jian Guo Men Wai Dajie
Beijing 100004
Tel: (1) 5053183/5/6 Fax: (1) 5053182
Tlx: 210267 JSABJ CN

LEP International, Beijing
Suite 442, Kunlun Hotel
21 Liang Ma Qiao, Chaoyang Qu
Beijing 100004
Tel: (1) 5003388 x441/2 Fax: (1) 6674573

LEP International, China Head Office
Rm. 715, Tower A
Hunghom Commercial Center
39 Matauwai Road
Kowloon, Hong Kong
Tel: [852] 3348787 Fax: [852] 3636414
Tlx: 44053 LEPSP HX

LEP International, Guangzhou
Rm. 1452, China Hotel Office Tower
Liu Hua Lu
Guangzhou 510015
Tel: (20) 6674573 Fax: (20) 6674573

LEP International, Shanghai
Rm. 1418, Ruijin Building
205 Mao Ming Nan Lu
Shanghai 200020
Tel: (21) 4339821, 4374531 Fax: (21) 4339805

Maersk Hong Kong Ltd. Beijing Rep. Office
Rm. 3411, Jin Guang Center
Hujalou, Chaoyang Qu
Beijing 100020
Tel: (1) 5015201/3 Fax: (1) 5015206
Tlx: 222959 MERSK CN

MAT Transport AG, Beijing Office
Rm. 1707, China World Tower, CWTC
1 Jian Guo Men Wai Dajie
Beijing 100004
Tel: (1) 5050911 Fax: (1) 5050910
Tlx: 222459 MATBJ CN

Mitsui-Soko Co. Ltd., Beijing Rep. Office
Rm. 35-19, China World Tower, CWTC
1 Jian Guo Men Wai Dajie
Beijing 100004
Tel: (1) 5051801/3 Fax: (1) 5051802
Tlx: 22744 MWBEJ CN

Natural Ltd. Switzerland, Beijing Office
Suite 442, Kunlun Hotel
21 Liang Ma Qiao, Chaoyang Qu
Beijing 100004
Tel: (1) 5003388 x442 Fax: (1) 5003228 x442

Natural Ltd. Switzerland, Shanghai Office
Rm. 1418, Ruijin Building
205 Mao Ming Nan Lu
Shanghai 200020
Tel: (21) 4339821 Fax: (21) 4339805

Nippon Express Co. Ltd., Beijing Rep. Office
Rm. 502, Beijing Fortune Building
5 Dongsanhuan Bei Lu, Chaoyang Qu
Beijing 100004
Tel: (1) 5010530/1 Fax: (1) 5010533
Tlx: 210511 NEXCO CN

Panalpina World Transport Co., Beijing
Delegation Office
Rm. C618, Beijing Lufthansa Center
50 Liangmaqiao Lu, Chaoyang Qu
Beijing 100016
Tel: (1) 4651027/9 Fax: (1) 4651024
Tlx: 210702 PAPEK CN

Penta Shipping, Beijing Rep. Office
Suite 501, Landmark Building
8 Dongsanhuan Bei Lu, Chaoyang Qu
Beijing 100004
Tel: (1) 5004465 Fax: (1) 5066942

Port of Tianjin Commercial Bonded Warehousing
and Service Co. Ltd., Beijing Branch
Rm. 2417-8 Minzu Hotel
51 Fuxingmennei Dajie
Beijing 100046
Tel: (1) 6014466 x2417/8 Fax: (1) 6017221
Tlx: 22990 MZHTL CN

Rickmers Line, Beijing Rep. Office
Suite C313, Beijing Lufthansa Center
50 Liang Ma Qiao Lu, Chaoyang Qu
Beijing 100004
Tel: (1) 4651618 Fax: (1) 4651619
Tlx: 210711 RLPEK CN

Santa Fe Transport International Ltd., Beijing
East Lake Office Building
35 Dongzhimenwai Main St.
Beijing 100027
Tel: (1) 4677777 Fax: (1) 4678050

Santa Fe Transport International Ltd., Guangzhou
Rm. 504-5, China Hotel Office Tower
Liu Hua Lu
Guangzhou 510015
Tel: (20) 6663388 x2504/5

Santa Fe Transport International Ltd., Shanghai
Xian Xia Lu, Lane No. 137
Shanghai 200051
Tel: (21) 2517701, 2517341 Fax: (21) 2517623

Schenker International Forwarding Organization
AG, Beijing
SCITE Tower, Suite 308
22 Jian Guo Men Wai Dajie
Beijing 100004
Tel: (1) 5126870 Fax: (1) 5126871
Tlx: 210175 SCHE CN

Schenker International Forwarding Organization
AG, Guangzhou
Suite 1300-1, Garden Tower
Huanshi Road East
Guangzhou
Tel: (20) 3338999 x1300/1 Fax: (20) 3344026

Schenker International Forwarding Organization
AG, Shanghai
Rm. 1331-3, 3rd Fl., West Building, Jinjiang Hotel
59 Maoming Road South
Shanghai 200020
Tel: (21) 4336288, 4336388 Fax: (21) 4334010

Shanghai Jinjiang Shipping Corp., Beijing Office
Rm. 5406 Xiyuan Hotel
Erligou, Xijiao
Beijing 100046
Tel: (1) 8313388

Sinotrans Beijing Airfreight Forwarding Co.
Capital Airport
Beijing 100621
Tel: (1) 4668642/7 Fax: (1) 4677887, 4565713
Tlx: 210205, 222931 AIRFT CN

Sinotrans Beijing Co.
Jiu Ling Building
21, Xisanhuan Bei Lu
Beijing 100081
Tel: (1) 8404000 Fax: (1) 8405910, 8415350
Tlx: 22867 TRANS CN

Tai Li Forwarding Beijing
1 Anyuanli, Asian Games Village
Beijing 100029
Tel: (1) 4917666 x2219, 4913602
Fax: (1) 4914386 Tlx: 222432 CMBSC CN

TNT Skypak, Beijing
c/o Sinotrans Ltd.
14 Shu Guang Xi Li, Chao Yang Qu
Beijing 100028
Tel: (1) 4672517, 4677877, 4652227, 4673664
Fax: (1) 4677894 Tlx: 211238 SKYPK CN

TNT Skypak, Guangzhou
c/o Sinotrans Guangdong
Airfreight Department
No. 1131 Guang Yuan Road Central
Guangzhou
Tel: (20) 6680972, 6680957/9
Fax: (20) 6680950, 6680971

TNT Skypak, Shanghai
c/o Sinotrans Ltd., Shanghai Branch
No. 3 Lane, 211 Xin Hua Road
Shanghai 200052
Tel: (21) 2400819, 2521905 Fax: (21) 2400883
Tlx: 33668 ADSHA CN

TNT Skypak, Shenzhen
c/o Sinotrans Airfreight/Courier Dept.
50 Heping Road
Shenzhen, 518001
Tel: (755) 5562240 x220, 5572346
Fax: (755) 5584321 Tlx: 420285 SZFTC CN

United Parcel Service (UPS), Beijing
Sinotrans Ltd.
25 Xibinhe Road
An Dingmen Wai
Beijing
Tel: (1) 4225670 Fax: (1) 4226694

United Parcel Service (UPS), Guangzhou
Sinotrans Ltd., Airfreight Department
1131 Guang Yuan Road Central
Guangzhou
Tel: (20) 6680964 Fax: (20) 6680971
Tlx: 44464 CGTRS CN

United Parcel Service (UPS), Shanghai
Sinotrans Ltd.,
Rm. 0201, Office Building
Hotel Equatorial
65 Yanan Road West
Shanghai
Tel: (21) 2485760 Fax: (21) 2485875

YK Shipping International (Canada) Ltd.
1705-A, Guangming Building
Liang Ma Qiao Road, Chaoyang Qu
Beijing 100016
Tel: (1) 4678822 x1726/7 Fax: (1) 4664740

All addresses and telephone numbers are in The People's Republic of China unless otherwise noted. The country code for China is [86].

PUBLICATIONS, MEDIA & INFORMATION SOURCES

Many Chinese periodicals are distributed through:

China International Book Trading Corp.
PO Box 399
Chegongzhuang Xilu 21
Beijing
Fax: (1) 8412023

In the United States, the following company distributes a large number of Chinese books and periodicals. If you are in the US, it would be advisable to contact them first if you are interested in any of the publications listed in this section.

China Books and Periodicals
2929 24th St.
San Francisco, CA 94110, USA
Tel: [1] (415) 282-2994 Fax: [1] (415) 282-0994

DIRECTORIES & YEARBOOKS

Almanac of China's Foreign Economic
Relations And Trade
(Annual)
The Editorial Board of The Almanac of China's
Foreign Economic Relations and Trade
China Resources Advertising Company
40th Fl., High Block
26 Harbour Road
Wanchai, Hong Kong
Tel: [852] 8318831

Asia Pacific Leather Directory
(Annual)
Asia Pacific Leather Yearbook
(Annual)
Asia Pacific Directories Ltd.
6th Fl., Wah Hen Commercial Center
381 Hennessy Road
Hong Kong
Tel: [852] 8936377 Fax: [852] 8935752

Asian Computer Directory
(Monthly)
Washington Plaza
1st Fl., 230 Wanchai Road
Wanchai, Hong Kong
Tel: [852] 8327123 Fax: [852] 8329208

Asian Printing Directory
(Annual)
Travel & Trade Publishing (Asia)
16th Fl., Capitol Centre
5-19 Jardines Bazaar
Causeway Bay, Hong Kong
Tel: [852] 8903067 Fax: [852] 8952378

Bankers Handbook For Asia
(Annual)
Dataline Asia Pacific Inc.
3rd Fl., Hollywood Center
233 Hollywood Road
Hong Kong
Tel: [852] 8155221 Fax: [852] 8542794

China Coal Industry Yearbook
(Annual)
Economic Information & Agency
342 Hennessy Road, 10th Fl.
Hong Kong
Tel: [852] 5738217 Fax: [852] 8388304
Tlx: 60647 EICC HX

China Commercial Relations Directory
(Semiannual)
American Chamber of Commerce in Hong Kong
1030 Swire House
Hong Kong
Tel: [852] 5260155 Fax: (1) 8101289
Tlx: 83664 AMCC HX

China Directory
(Annual; Chinese and English)
Radiopress, Inc.
R-Building, Shinjuku 5th Fl.
33-8, Wakamatsu-cho, Shinjuku-ku
Tokyo 162
Tel: (3) 5273-2171 Fax: (3) 5273-2180

China Energy Report
(Annual)
American Chamber of Commerce in Hong Kong
1030 Swire House
Hong Kong
Tel: [852] 5260155 Fax: [852] 8101289
Tlx: 83664 AMCC HX

China Importers & Exporters Directory
(Biennial; English and Chinese)
Han Ying Shan Research
PO Box 71006
Wuhan, Hubei Province 430071
Tel: (27) 812804 Fax: (27) 711242

China Phone Book & Business Directory
(Semiannual)
China Phone Book Company
Citicorp Centre, 24th Fl.
18 Whitfield Road
Hong Kong
Tel: [852] 8328300 Fax: [852] 5031526

China Statistical Yearbook
(Annual)
Economic Information & Agency
342 Hennessey Road
Hong Kong

China Telephone Directory
(Chinese)
China Telephone Directory Company
Ministry of Posts and Telecommunications
13 Xichangan Jie
Beijing 100804
Tel: (1) 6016137
Foreign Affairs Dept.
Tel: (1) 6011365 Fax: (1) 6011370 Tlx: 222187

China Telex & Fax Directory
(Annual)
China Phone Book Company
Citicorp Centre, 24th Fl.
18 Whitfield Road
Hong Kong
Tel: [852] 8328300 Fax: [852] 5031526

China's Chemicals and Petrochemicals Directory
(Annual)
China Phone Book Company
Citicorp Centre, 24th Fl.
18 Whitfield Road
Hong Kong
Tel: [852] 8328300 Fax: [852] 5031526

China's Electronics & Electrical Products
(Annual)
China Phone Book Company
Citicorp Centre, 24th Fl.
18 Whitfield Road
Hong Kong
Tel: [852] 8328300 Fax: [852] 5031526

China's Instruments & Meters
(Annual)
China Phone Book Company
Citicorp Centre, 24th Fl.
18 Whitfield Road
Hong Kong
Tel: [852] 8328300 Fax: [852] 5031526

Directory of CCOIC Membership Enterprises
(Annual)
1 Fu Xing Men Wai Dajie
Beijing 100860
Tel: (1) 8011156, 8013344 x1304
Fax: (1) 8011370

Directory of Chinese External Economic
Organizations and Industrial-Commercial
Enterprises
(Irregular)
Economic Information & Agency
342 Hennessy Road, 10th Fl.
Hong Kong
Tel: [852] 5738217 Fax: [852] 8388304
Tlx: 60647 EICC HX

Directory of Chinese Foreign Economic Relations
and Trade Enterprises
(Annual)
China Foreign Economic Relations & Trade
Publishing House
28 Dong Hou Xiang
An Ding Men Wai St.
Beijing 100710

Guide to China's Trade and Investment
Organizations
(Annual)
China Business Forum
1818 N St. NW
Washington, DC 20036
Tel: [1] (202) 429-0340 Fax: [1] (202) 775-2476

Guidebook on Trading with the People's Republic
of China
(Annual)
United Nations Economic and Social Commission
for Asia and the Pacific
United Nations Plaza
New York, NY 10017

International Tax and Duty Free Buyers Index
(Annual)
Pearl & Dean Publishing Ltd.
9th Fl. Chung Nam Building
1 Lockhart Road
Hong Kong
Tel: [852] 8660395 Fax: [852] 2999810

The Official Chinese Customs Guide
General Office of the Customs General
Administration of the PRC
(Annual)
Sino Hong Kong International Co.
Sing Pao Building, 15th Fl.
101 Kings Road
North Point, Hong Kong
Fax: [852] 8070024

Textile Asia Index
(Annual)
Business Press Ltd.
30-32 d'Aguilar Street
Tak Yan Commercial Building, 11th Fl.
GPO 185
Central Hong Kong
Tel: [852] 5247441 Tlx: 60275 TEXIA HX

World Jewelogue
(Annual)
Headway International Publications Co.
907 Great Eagle Center
23 Harbour Road
Hong Kong
Tel: [852] 8275121 Fax: [852] 8277064

NEWSPAPERS

Asian Wall Street Journal
Dow Jones Publishing Co. (Asia)
2nd Fl. AIA Building
1 Stubbs Road
GPO Box 9825
Hong Kong
Tel: [852] 5737121 Fax: [852] 8345291

China Daily
15 Huixin Dongjie, Chaoyang Qu
Beijing
Tel: (1) 4220955 Fax: (1) 4220922

Economic Reporter (Jingji Daobao)
English Supplement
Economic Information & Agency
342 Hennessy Road, 10th Fl.
Hong Kong
Tel: [852] 5738217 Fax: [852] 8388304
Tlx: 60647 EICC HX

Guangzhou Ribao (Guangzhou Daily)
(Chinese)
10 Dongle Lu
Renmin Zhonglu
Guangzhou

International Commerce (Guoji Shangbao She)
(Chinese)
PO Box 6115
Building 14, Part 3, Fangxing Yuan
Fangxhuanglu
Beijing 100061
Tel: (1) 7019921

International Herald Tribune
7th Fl. Malaysia Building
50 Gloucester Road
Wanchai, Hong Kong
Tel: [852] 8610616 Fax: [852] 8613073

International Trade and Economics (Guoiji
Jingmao Xiaoxi)
(Chinese)
China International Book Trading Corp.
PO Box 399
21 Chegongzhuang Xilu
Beijing
Fax: (1) 8412023

Jingji Ribao (Economic Daily)
(Chinese)
27 Wangfujing Dajie
Beijing
Tel: (1) 5125522 Fax: (1) 5125015

Shenzhen Tequ Bao (Shenzhen Special Zone Daily)
(Chinese)
1 Shennan Zhonglu
Shenzhen

GENERAL BUSINESS & TRADE PERIODICALS

Asian Business
(Monthly)
Far East Trade Press Ltd.
2nd Fl., Kai Tak Commercial Building
317 Des Voeux Road
Central, Hong Kong
Tel: [852] 5457200 Fax: [852] 5446979

Asian Finance
(Monthly)
3rd Fl., Hollywood Center
233 Hollywood Road
Hong Kong
Tel: [852] 8155221 Fax: [852] 8504437

Asian Monetary Monitor
(Bimonthly)
GPO Box 12964
Hong Kong
Tel: [852] 8427200

Asiaweek
(Weekly)
Asiaweek Ltd.
199 Des Voeux Road
Central, Hong Kong
Tel: [852] 8155662 Fax: [852] 8155903

Beijing Industrial and Commercial Management
(Beijing Gondshang Xingxheng Guangli)
(Bimonthly; Chinese)
18 Enjizhuang, Haidian Qu
Beijing 100036
Tel: (1) 8311924

Beijing Institute of Finance and Trade Journal
(Beijing Caimao Xueyuan)
(Bimonthly; Chinese)
68 Nanxiange Jie
Guanganmennei
Beijing 100053

Beijing Review
(Weekly)
24 Baiwanzhuang Lu
Beijing 100037
Tel: (1) 8315599 Fax: (1) 8314318 Tlx: 222374

Business China
(Biweekly)
Economist Intelligence Unit
PO Box 154
Dartford, Kent DA1 1QB, UK
Tel: [44] (322) 289194

Business PRC
(Bimonthly)
Enterprise International
1604 Eastern Commercial Centre
393-407 Hennessy Road
Hong Kong
Tel: [852] 5734161 Fax: [852] 8383469

Business Week, Asia Edition
(Weekly)
2405 Dominion Centre
43-59 Queens Road East
Hong Kong
Tel: [852] 3361160 Fax: [852] 5294046

China Banking & Finance
Asia Law and Practice Ltd.
2nd Fl., 29 Hollywood Road
Central, Hong Kong
Tel: [852] 5449918 Fax: [852] 5437617

China Business & Trade
(Semimonthly)
Welt Publishing Co.
1413 K St. NW, Suite 800
Washington, DC 20005
Tel: [1] (202) 3710555

China Business Review
China Business Forum
1818 N St. NW
Washington, DC 20036
Tel: [1] (202) 429-0340 Fax: [1] (202) 775-2476

China Economic News
(Weekly; Chinese)
Economic Information & Agency
342 Hennessy Road, 10th Fl.
Hong Kong
Tel: [852] 5738217 Fax: [852] 8388304
Tlx: 60647 EICC HX

China Market
(Monthly)
Economic Information & Agency
342 Hennessy Road, 10th Fl.
Hong Kong
Tel: [852] 5738217 Fax: [852] 8388304
Tlx: 60647 EICC HX

China News Analysis
(Semimonthly)
China News Analysis
GPO Box 3225
Hong Kong
Tel: [852] 5599620 Fax: [852] 5218814

China Newsletter
(Quarterly)
KMPG Peat Marwick China
8th Fl., Prince's Building
PO Box 50
Central, Hong Kong
Tel: [852] 5226022 Fax: [852] 8452588

China Today
(Monthly)
China Welfare Institute
24 Baiwanzhuang Lu
Beijing 100037
Tel: (1) 8326037 Fax: (1) 8328338

China Trade Report
(Monthly)
Review Publishing Company Ltd.
GPO Box 160
Gloucester Road 181-185
Hong Kong
Tel: [852] 8328338 Fax: [852] 5722439

China Trader Newsletter
(Quarterly)
China Trader Supply
PO Box 630
Milbrook, NY 12545

China's Customs Statistics
(Quarterly)
Economic Information & Agency
342 Hennessy Road, 10th Fl.
Hong Kong
Tel: [852] 5738217 Fax: [852] 8388304
Tlx: 60647 EICC HX

China's Exports
China Chamber of International Commerce
1 Fu Xing Men Wai Jie
Beijing
Tel: (1) 8013344 Fax: (1) 8010201 Tlx: 22315 CCPIT

China's Foreign Trade
(Monthly)
CCPIT
1 Fu Xing Men Wai Dajie
Beijing
Tel: (1) 8013344 Fax: (1) 8011370 Tlx: 22315 CCPIT

The Economist, Asia Edition
(Weekly)
The Economist Newspaper Ltd.
1329 Chater Road
Hong Kong
Tel: [852] 8681425

Far Eastern Economic Review
(Weekly)
Review Publishing Company Ltd.
6-7th Fl., 181-185 Gloucester Road
Hong Kong
Tel: [852] 8328381 Fax: [852] 8345571

International Business
(Monthly)
Ministry of Foreign Economic Relations and Trade
(MOFERT)
2 Dongchangan Jie, Dongcheng Qu
Beijing 100731
Tel: (1) 5198114, 5198322 Fax: (1) 5129568
Tlx: 22168

International Business Monthly (Guoji
Shangbao Yuekan)
(Bimonthly)
Guoji Shangbao She
PO Box 6115
Building 14, Part 3, Fangxing Yuan
Fangxhuanglu
Beijing 100061
Tel: (1) 4212149

International Market (Guoji Shichang)
(Monthly; Chinese)
Shanghai Guoji Jingji Maoyi Yanjiusuo
Shanghai International Economics and Trade
Institute
33 Zhongshan Dongyi Lu
Shanghai 200002
Tel: (21) 3212659

International Trade Journal
(Monthly; Chinese)
University of International Business and
Economics
Yinghua Dongjie Beikou
Andingmenwai
Beijing 100029
Tel: (1) 4225522 Fax: (1) 4212022

International Trade News
(3 per week; Chinese, with English summaries)
International Trade News Supplement
(30 per year; Chinese, with English summaries)
MOFTEC
International Trade Research Institute
Donghouxiang 28
Andingmenwai
Beijing 100710
Tel: (1) 5129589 Fax: (1) 5128928

Newsweek International, Asia Edition
(Weekly)
Newsweek, Inc.
47th Fl., Bank of China Tower
1 Garden Road
Central, Hong Kong
Tel: [852] 8104555

Time, Asia Edition
(Weekly)
Time, Inc.
31st Fl., East Tower, Bond Centre
89 Queensway
Hong Kong
Tel: [852] 8446660 Fax: [852] 5108799

World Executives Digest
(Monthly)
3rd Fl. Garden Square Building
Greenbelt Drive Cor.
Legaspi Makati
Metro Manila, Philippines
Tel: [63] (2) 8179126

Yazhou Zhoukan
(Weekly; Chinese)
13th Fl., South, Somerset House
28 Tong Chong St.
Quarry Bay, Hong Kong
Tel: [852] 5630232 Fax: [852] 5657730

INDUSTRY-SPECIFIC PERIODICALS

Abstracts of Chinese Medicines
(Quarterly)
Chinese University Hong Kong
Chinese Medical Materials Research Center
Shatin, New Territories, Hong Kong

Agricultural Knowledge (Nongye Zhishi)
(Monthly; Chinese)
7 Shimuyuan Dongjie
Jinan, Shandong Province
Tel: (531) 42238

Architecture (Jianzhu)
(Monthly; Chinese)
Jianzhu Zazhishe
Baiwanzhuang
Beijing 100835
Tel: (1) 8992849, 8315217

Asia Computer Weekly
(Bimonthly)
Asian Business Press Pte. Ltd.
100 Beach Road, #26-00 Shaw Towers
Singapore 0718
Tel: [65] 2943366 Fax: [65] 2985534

Asia Labour Monitor
(Bimonthly)
Asia Monitor Resource Center
444-446 Nathan Road, 8th Fl., Flat B
Kowloon, Hong Kong
Tel: [852] 3321346

Asia Pacific Broadcasting & Telecommunications
(Monthly)
Asian Business Press Pte. Ltd.
100 Beach Road
#26-00 Shaw Towers
Singapore 0718
Tel: [65] 2943366 Fax: [65] 2985534

Asia Pacific Food Industry
(Monthly)
Asia Pacific Food Industry Publications
24 Peck Sea St., #03-00 Nehsons Building
Singapore 0207
Tel: [65] 2223422 Fax: [65] 2225587

Asia Pacific Food Industry Business Report
(Monthly)
Asia Pacific Food Industry Publications
24 Peck Sea St., #03-00 Nehsons Building
Singapore 0207
Tel: [65] 2223422 Fax: [65] 2225587

Asia Travel Guide
(Monthly)
Interasia Publications Ltd.
190 Middle Road, #11-01 Fortune Center
Singapore 0718
Tel: [65] 3397622 Fax: [65] 3398521

Asia-Pacific Dental News
(Quarterly)
Adrienne Yo Publishing Ltd.
4th Fl., Vogue Building
67 Wyndham Street
Central, Hong Kong
Tel: [852] 5253133 Fax: [852] 8106512

Asiamac Journal: The Machine-Building and Metal
Working Journal for the Asia Pacific Region
(Quarterly; English, Chinese)
Adsale Publishing Company
21st Fl., Tung Wai Commercial Building
109-111 Gloucester Road
Hong Kong
Tel: [852] 8920511 Fax: [852] 8384119, 8345014
Tlx: 63109 ADSAP HX

Asian Architect And Contractor
(Monthly)
Thompson Press Hong Kong Ltd.
Tai Sang Commercial Building, 19th Fl.
24-34 Hennessy Road
Hong Kong

Asian Aviation
(Monthly)
Asian Aviation Publications
2 Leng Kee Road, #04-01 Thye Hong Centre
Singapore 0315
Tel: [65] 4747088 Fax: [65] 4796668

Asian Computer Monthly
(Monthly)
Computer Publications Ltd.
Washington Plaza, 1st Fl.
230 Wanchai Road
Wanchai, Hong Kong
Tel: [852] 9327123 Fax: [852] 8329208

Asian Defence Journal
(Monthly)
Syed Hussain Publications (Sdn)
61 A&B Jelan Dato, Haji Eusoff
Damai Complex
PO Box 10836
50726 Kuala Lumpur, Malaysia
Tel: [60] (3) 4420852 Fax: [60] (3) 4427840

Asian Electricity
(11 per year)
Reed Business Publishing Ltd.
5001 Beach Road, #06-12 Golden Mile Complex
Singapore 0719
Tel: [65] 2913188 Fax: [65] 2913180

Asian Electronics Engineer
(Monthly)
Trade Media Ltd.
29 Wong Chuck Hang Road
Hong Kong
Tel: [852] 5554777 Fax: [852] 8700816

Asian Hospital
(Quarterly)
Techni-Press Asia Ltd.
PO Box 20494
Hennessy Road
Hong Kong
Tel: [852] 5278682 Fax: [852] 5278399

Asian Hotel & Catering Times
(Bimonthly)
Thompson Press (HK)
19th Fl., Tai Sang Commercial Building
23-34 Hennessy Road
Hong Kong
Tel: [852] 5283351 Fax: [852] 8650825

Asian Manufacturing
Far East Trade Press Ltd.
2nd Fl., Kai Tak Commercial Building
317 Des Voeux Road
Central, Hong Kong
Tel: [852] 5453028 Fax: [852] 5446979

Asian Medical News
(Bimonthly)
MediMedia Pacific Ltd.
Unit 1216, Seaview Estate
2-8 Watson Road
North Point, Hong Kong
Tel: [852] 5700708 Fax: [852] 5705076

Asian Meetings & Incentives
(Monthly)
Travel & Trade Publishing (Asia)
16th Fl., Capitol Centre
5-19 Jardines Bazaar
Causeway Bay, Hong Kong
Tel: [852] 8903067 Fax: [852] 8952378

Asian Oil & Gas
(Monthly)
Intercontinental Marketing Corp.
PO Box 5056
Tokyo 100-31
Fax: [81] (3) 3667-9646

Asian Plastic News
(Quarterly)
Reed Asian Publishing Pte. Ltd.
5001 Beach Road
#06-12 Golden Mile Complex
Singapore 0719
Tel: [65] 2913188 Fax: [65] 2913180

Asian Printing: The Magazine for the Graphic Arts
Industry
(Monthly)
Travel & Trade Publishing (Asia)
16th Fl., Capitol Centre
5-19 Jardines Bazaar
Causeway Bay, Hong Kong
Tel: [852] 8903067 Fax: [852] 8952378

Asian Security & Safety Journal
(Bimonthly)
Elgin Consultants Ltd.
Tungnam Building
Suite 5D, 475 Hennessy Road
Causeway Bay, Hong Kong
Tel: [852] 5724427 Fax: [852] 5725731

Asian Shipping
(Monthly)
Asia Trade Journals Ltd.
7th Fl., Sincere Insurance Building
4 Hennessy Road
Wanchai, Hong Kong
Tel: [852] 5278532 Fax: [852] 5278753

Asian Sources: Computer Products
Asian Sources: Electronic Components
Asian Sources: Gifts & Home Products
Asian Sources: Hardware
Asian Sources: Timepieces
(All publications are monthly)
Asian Sources Media Group
22nd Fl., Vita Tower
29 Wong Chuk Hang Road
Wong Chuk Hang, Hong Kong
Tel: [852] 5554777 Fax: [852] 8730488

Asian Water & Sewage
(Quarterly)
Techni-Press Asia Ltd.
PO Box 20494, Hennessy Road
Hong Kong
Fax: [852] 5278399

Asiatechnology
(Monthly)
Review Publishing Company Ltd.
6-7th Fl., 181-185 Gloucester Road
GPO Box 160
Hong Kong
Tel: [852] 8328381 Fax: [852] 8345571

ATA Journal: Journal for Asia on Textile & Apparel
(Bimonthly)
Adsale Publishing Company
Tung Wai Commercial Building, 21st Fl.
109-111 Gloucester Road
Wanchai, Hong Kong
Tel: [852] 8920511 Fax: [852] 8384119

Beijing Agriculture
(Monthly; Chinese)
Beijing Shi Nongye Ju
19 Bai Sanhuan Dong Lu, Dewai
Beijing 100029
Tel: (1) 2012244

Beijing Real Estate
(Chinese)
Beijing Real Estate Administration
1 Nanwanzi
Nanheyan, Dongcheng Qu
Beijing 100006
Fax: (1) 5124104

Beijing Textile (Beijing Fangzhi)
(Chinese)
Gongcheng Xuehui
2 Shilipu, Chaoyangmennwai
Beijing 100025
Tel: (1) 5004477 Fax: (1) 5004271

Building & Construction News
(Weekly)
Al Hilal Publishing (FE) Ltd.
50 Jalan Sultan, #20-06, Jalan Sultan Centre
Singapore 0719
Tel: [65] 2939233 Fax: [65] 2970862

Business Traveller Asia-Pacific
(Monthly)
Interasia Publications
200 Lockhart Road, 13th Fl.
Wanchai, Hong Kong
Tel: [852] 5749317 Fax: [852] 5726846

Cargo Clan
(Quarterly)
Emphasis (HK) Ltd.
10th Fl., Wilson House
19-27 Wyndham St.
Central, Hong Kong
Tel: [852] 5215392 Fax: [852] 8106738

Cargonews Asia
(Bimonthly)
Far East Trade Press Ltd.
2nd Fl., Kai Tak Commercial Building
317 Des Voeux Road
Central, Hong Kong
Tel: [852] 5453028 Fax: [852] 5446979

Catering & Hotel News, International
(Biweekly)
Al Hilal Publishing (FE) Ltd.
50 Jalan Sultan, #20-26, Jalan Sultan Centre
Singapore 0719
Tel: [852] 2939233 Fax: [852] 2970862

China Agribusiness Report
(Biweekly)
Asia Letter Group
GPO Box 10874
Hong Kong
Tel: [852] 5262950 Fax: [852] 5267131
Tlx: 4X61166 HKNW
US subscriptions: PO Box 92619
Los Angeles CA 90009, USA

China Business Law Guide
CCH Australia
PO Box 230
N. Ryde, NSW 2113, Australia
Tel: [62] (2) 888-2555 Fax: [62] (2) 888-7324

China Computerworld
(Biweekly)
Technology Research Institute
74 Lugu Cun Lu
PO Box 750
Beijing 100039

China Current Laws
(Quarterly)
Longman Group Far East Ltd.
18th Fl., Cornwall House
Tong Chong Street
Quarry Bay, Hong Kong
Tel: [852] 8566335 Fax: [852] 5657440

China Law Quarterly
(Quarterly)
Baker & McKenzie
14th Fl., Hutchinson House
10 Harcourt Road
Hong Kong
Tel: [852] 8461888 Fax: [852] 8450490

China Laws for Foreign Business
CCH Australia Ltd.
PO Box 230
North Ryse, NSW 2113, Australia
Tel: [62] (2) 888-2555 Fax: [62] (2) 8887324

China Packaging (Zhongguo Baozhuang)
(Quarterly; Chinese)
China International Book Trading Corp.
PO Box 399
Chegongzhuang Xilu 21
Beijing
Fax: (1) 8412023

China Pharmaceutical and Medical Instruments
(Chinese)
State Pharmaceutical Administration of China
Export Dept. of CNPIEC
PO Box 88, Chaonei St.
Beijing 100704
Fax: (1) 4015664

China Plastics and Rubber Journal
(Quarterly; Chinese)
Adsale Publishing Co.
PO Box 20032, Hennessy Road
Hong Kong
Tel: [852] 8920511 Fax: [852] 8384119

China Radio and Television (Zhongguo Guangbo Dianshi)
(Monthly; Chinese)
Ministry of Radio, Film and Television
Fu Xing Men Wai Jie 2
PO Box 4501
Beijing 100866
Tel: (1) 8012176, 6092141 Fax: (1) 8012174
Tlx: 22236

China Textile
(Bimonthly)
Adsale Publishing Co.
PO Box 20032, Hennessy Road
Hong Kong
Tel: [852] 8920511 Fax: [852] 8384119

China Tourism
(Monthly)
H.K. China Tourism Press
17th Fl., V. Heun Building
138 Queen's Road Central
Hong Kong
Tel: [852] 5411331 Fax: [852] 8541721
Tlx: 82225 HKCTPHX

China's Advertising (Zhongguo Guanggao Bao)
(Weekly; Chinese)
Editorial Dept., Beijing Exhibition Hall
Xizhimen Wai
Beijing

China-Britain Trade Review
China-Britain Trade Group
Abford House, 5th Fl.
15 Wilton Road
London SW1V 1LT, UK
Tel: [44] (71) 828-5176 Fax: [44] (71) 630-5780

Chinese Science Abstracts
(Monthly)
Science Press
16 Donghuangchenggen Beijie
Beijing 100707
Tel: (1) 4018833 Fax: (1) 4012180
Overseas sales: Pergamon Press
Headington Hill Hall
Oxford OX3 0BW, UK
Tel: [44] (865) 794141

Electronic Business Asia
(Monthly)
Cahners Publishing Company
275 Washington St.
Newton, MA 02158, USA
Tel: [1] (617) 964-3030 Fax: [1] (617) 558-4506

Energy Asia
(Monthly)
Petroleum News Southeast Asia Ltd.
6th Fl., 146 Prince Edward Road W
Kowloon, Hong Kong
Tel: [852] 3805294 Fax: [852] 3970959

Far East Health
(10 per year)
Update-Siebert Publications
Reed Asian Publishing Pte
5001 Beach Road
#06-12 Golden Mile Complex
Singapore 0719
Tel: [65] 2913188 Fax: [65] 2913180

Fashion Accessories
(Monthly)
Asian Sources Media Group
22nd Fl., Vita Tower
29 Wong Chuk Hang Road
Wong Chuk Hang, Hong Kong
Tel: [852] 5554777 Fax: [852] 8730488

International Construction
(Monthly)
Reed Business Publishing Ltd.
Reed Asian Publishing Pte
5001 Beach Road
#06-12 Golden Mile Complex
Singapore 0719
Tel: [65] 2913188 Fax: [65] 2913180

Jewellery News Asia
(Monthly)
Jewellery News Asia Ltd.
Rm. 601-603, Guardian House
32 Oi Kwan Road
Wanchai, Hong Kong
Tel: [852] 8322011 Fax: [852] 8329208

Lloyd's Maritime Asia
(Monthly)
Lloyd's of London Press (FE)
Rm. 1101 Hollywood Centre
233 Hollywood Road
Hong Kong
Tel: [852] 8543222 Fax: [852] 8541538

Media: Asia's Media and Marketing Newspaper
(Biweekly)
Media & Marketing Ltd.
1002 McDonald's Building
46-54 Yee Wo St.
Causeway Bay, Hong Kong
Tel: [852] 5772628 Fax: [852] 5769171

Medicine Digest Asia
(Monthly)
Rm. 1903, Tung Sun Commercial Centre
194-200 Lockhart Road
Wanchai, Hong Kong
Tel: [852] 8939303 Fax: [852] 8912591

Oil & Gas News
(Weekly)
Al Hilal Publishing (FE) Ltd.
50 Jalan Sultan, #20-06, Jalan Sultan Centre
Singapore 0719
Tel: [65] 2939233 Fax: [65] 2970862

Petroleum News, Asia's Energy Journal
(Monthly)
Petroleum News Southeast Asia Ltd.
6th Fl., 146 Prince Edward Road West
Kowloon, Hong Kong
Tel: [852] 3805294 Fax: [852] 3970959

Shipping & Transport News
(Monthly)
Al Hilal Publishing (FE) Ltd.
50 Jalan Sultan, #20-06, Jalan Sultan Centre
Singapore 0719
Tel: [65] 2939233 Fax: [65] 2970862

Telecom Asia
(Bimonthly)
CCI Asia-Pacific (HK)
Suite 905, Guardian House
32 Oi Kwan Road
Wanchai, Hong Kong
Tel: [852] 8332181 Fax: [852] 8345620

Textile Asia: The Asian Textile and Apparel
Monthly
(Monthly)
Business Press Ltd.
11th Fl., California Tower
30-32 d'Aguilar Street
Central, Hong Kong
Tel: [852] 5247467 Fax: [852] 8106966

Travel News Asia
(Bimonthly)
Far East Trade Press Ltd.
2nd Fl. Kai Tak Commercial Building
317 Des Voeux Road
Central, Hong Kong
Tel: [852] 5453028 Fax: [852] 5446979

Travel Trade Gazette Asia
(Weekly)
Asian Business Press Pte. Ltd.
100 Beach Road, #26-00 Shaw Towers
Singapore 0718
Tel: [65] 2943366 Fax: [65] 2985534

What's New in Computing
(Monthly)
Asian Business Press Pte. Ltd.
100 Beach Road, #26-00 Shaw Towers
Singapore 0718
Tel: [65] 2943366 Fax: [65] 2985534

RADIO & TELEVISION

Ministry of Radio, Film, and Television
2 Fu Xing Men Wai Jie
PO Box 4501
Beijing 100866
Tel: (1) 8012176, 6092141 Fax: (1) 8012174
Tlx: 22236

*Controls China Central Television Station, the Central People's
Broadcasting Station (radio) and Radio Beijing (foreign language
radio service).*

LIBRARIES

China Center for Literature Concerning New
Foreign Products
1 Fu Xing Men Wai Dajie
PO Box 1420
Beijing 10027
Tel: (1) 8013344 Tlx: 210214 CEXHNCN

Department of Documentation Service
Institute of Scientific and Technical Information
PO Box 615
Beijing

National Library of China
39 Baishiqiao Road, Haidian Qu
Beijing 100081
Tel: (1) 8315566 Tlx: 222211

All publications are in English unless otherwise noted.

Index

A

ABC. *See* Agricultural Bank of China
accounting
    firms, 40, 386–387
        addresses, 386–387
    regulations
        legal discussion of, 273–274
        standards, 9
ACFIC. *See* All China Federation of Industry and
    Commerce
ACFTU. *See* All China Federation of Trade Unions
actions
    legal discussion of, 247
addresses and telephone numbers, 359–402
advantages to doing business in China, 214
advertising, 178–179, 179–184
    legal discussion of, 249
    rates, 182, 183
    regulation of, 236
advertising agencies, 178–179
    addresses, 387–388
    foreign, 40, 184
advice
    definition of, 326
advising bank
    definition of, 326
aerospace industry. *See* aircraft and avionics
    equipment
affidavits
    legal discussion of, 249
agents, 177
    choosing, 196
    Hong Kong, 211
    legal definition of, 239
    legal discussion of, 254, 278
    tips for helping, 203
Agricultural Bank of China (ABC), 286, 292–293
agriculture
    industry, 34
    sector of economy, 12–13
    trade fairs, 105–106
air travel. *See also* airports
    domestic, 139, 147–148
        airfares, 148
    international, 139
    time to Beijing and Guangzhou, 140

aircraft and avionics equipment
    market for, 37
    trade fairs, 104–105
airlines, 139, 339
    addresses, 390–391
airports, 339–340
    Beijing (Capital), 139, 189, 340
    ground travel to/from, 142–143
    Guangzhou (Baiyun), 139, 191, 339–340
    Hainan Island, 196
    Shanghai (Hongqiao), 139, 190, 340
    Shenzhen, 340
    Tianjin, 189
    upgrading of, 339
    Wenzhou, 201
aliens. *See also* visa regulations
    legal discussion of, 249–250
aliquot
    legal definition of, 239
All China Federation of Industry and Commerce
    (ACFIC), 57–58
All China Federation of Trade Unions (ACFTU),
    12, 228, 233
amendment
    definition of, 326
American International Group, 64
Amoy. *See* Xiamen
Animal and Plant Quarantine Center, 256
APEC. *See* Asia Pacific Economic Cooperation
apparel industry, 31, 89–92
    trade fairs, 133–134
appliance industry, 80–81
arts and crafts industry, 33–34
Asia Pacific Economic Cooperation (APEC), 20
Asia-Europe Continental Bridge, 199
Asian Development Bank, 51
assets
    movement of, 8
assignments
    legal discussion of, 251
associations
    legal discussion of, 251
attachment
    legal definition of, 239
    legal discussion of, 251

attorneys. *See also* law firms
  legal discussion of, 252
  role of, 237
austerity program, 23–24, 55, 289
  easing of, 290
authentication
  legal definition of, 239
automobile industry
  trade fairs, 106–107
automobiles
  for hire, 148
  in use, 27, 174

B

back-to-back letter of credit. *See* letter of credit
bad debt allowances, 332
balancing requirements
  for foreign enterprise, 297
Bank of China (BOC), 51, 65, 142, 186, 286, 287–
    292, 311, 313
  definition of, 208
  hard currency deposits in, 15
  loans to joint ventures, 272
  responsibility for international payments, 309
  upgrading of international operations, 287–292
bank transfers, 310
banking hours, 149
banking industry, 286–296. *See also* financial
    institutions
  for foreign business, 297
  in Shanghai, 296
  international, 287
  reform of, 291
bankruptcy
  legal discussion of, 252
banks
  central, 286–287
    addresses, 383
  commercial and domestic
    addresses, 383–384
  foreign, 15, 286, 294–296
    addresses, 384–385
    in SEZs, 296
  government, 7
  joint venture, 286, 295
  provincial, 294
banqueting, 165–167
barter, 56, 64, 69–70, 216, 299
Beihai
  market profile, 202
Beijing
  Coastal City status, 197
  market profile, 188
Beijing-Tianjin-Tanggu Expressway, 185
beneficiary
  definition of, 326
Berne Convention, 237
beverage industry, 74
bicycle rental, 148–149

bill of exchange, 291
  definition of, 326
  legal definition of, 239
bill of lading
  definition of, 325
  for exported goods, 70
  for imported goods, 66
billboard advertising, 182
bills and notes
  legal discussion of, 254
birth rate, 172
boat travel
  to/from Hong Kong, 139
BOC. *See* Bank of China
body language, 163–164
bond market, 8, 303
bonded warehouses, 63
Boxer Rebellion, 29
brokerage firms
  foreign, 306
budget deficit, 12
building supplies
  market for, 38
Bureau of Weights and Measures, 256
bureaucracy
  streamlining of, 6
bus shelter advertising, 182, 183
bus travel, 148
business associations, foreign. *See also* trade
    associations
  addresses, 379–380
business attire, 138–139
business cards
  exchange of, 147, 161
business centers, 151
business culture, 155–170
business directories
  addresses, 394
business entities and formation, 207–223
  glossary, 208
  laws governing, 236
business hours, 149, 229
business licenses, 68, 218
business negotiations, 168–170
  tactics and tips, 169–170
business organizations
  forms of, 207–218
business registration, 218–222, 254
  application procedure, 219–222
  fees, 218–219, 265
  legal discussion of, 263–265, 264–265
  procedures, 220
  reminders and recommendations for, 222
  selected useful addresses, 222–223
business travel, 137–154
business yearbooks
  addresses, 394–395
buyback trade, 64, 69–70, 216

C

C&F (cost and freight)
   definition of, 326
CAAC. *See* Civil Aviation Administration of China
cable television
   foreign investment in, 39
canned food industry, 74
Canton. *See* Guangzhou
Canton Trade Fair. *See* Chinese Export Commodities Fair
Cantonese dialect, 164
Caohejing High-Technology Park (HTP), 200
capital gains
   taxation of, 331, 336
cash
   personal customs allowances, 141
cash in advance
   terms of, 315
CBC. *See* Communications Bank of China
CCOIC. *See* China Chamber of International Commerce
CCPIT. *See* China Council for the Promotion of International Trade
CCTV. *See* China Central Television
CEITIC. *See* China Everbright International Trust and Investment Corporation
Central China International Group, 186
Central People's Broadcasting Station, 402
certificate of manufacture
   definition of, 325
certificate of origin
   definition of, 325
   for imported goods, 66
CF (cost and freight) terms, 70
chambers of commerce, 251. *See also* China Chamber of International Commerce
   addresses, 379
Changchun, 193
checks, 291
chemical industry, 81–84
   trade fairs, 119–120
child mortality rate, 172
child-care benefits, 228
China Books and Periodicals, 394
China Central Television (CCTV), 180, 402
   advertising, 179
China Chamber of International Commerce (CCOIC)
   overseas office addresses, 380
China Council for the Promotion of International Trade (CCPIT), 57–58, 61, 70, 96, 250
   overseas office addresses, 380
China Everbright International Trust and Investment Corporation (CEITIC), 300
China Insurance Clause, 301
China Insurance Company (CIC), 301
China International Book Trading Corporation, 394
China International Exhibition Center, 96
China International Travel Service (CITS), 137, 138
China International Trust and Investment Corporation (CITIC), 220, 294, 296
   definition of, 208

China Investment Bank (CIB), 293, 301, 307
China National Aviation Industry Corporation (CNAIC), 247
China National Chartering Corporation (SINOCHART), 65
China National Commodity Inspection Bureau, 257
China National Foreign Trade Transportation Corporation (SINOTRANS), 65
China National Import and Export Commodities Inspection Corporation (CNIECIC), 64, 69
China National Petrochemical Corporation (SINOPEC), 39
China National Space Industry Corporation, 247
China National Tourism Office, 137
China Ocean Shipping Company (COSCO), 65
China Travel Service (CTS), 137, 138, 249
China Venturetech Investment Corporation (CVIC), 300
Chinese Export Commodities Fair, 97
Chinese market
   how to approach, 176
Chiu Chow People, 194
Chongqing
   market profile, 193
CIB. *See* China Investment Bank
CIC. *See* China Insurance Company
CICT. *See* Consolidated Industrial and Commercial Tax
CIF (cost, insurance, and freight) terms, 70
   definition of, 326
cigarette smoking, 166. *See also* tobacco consumption
CITIC. *See* China International Trust and Investment Corporation
CITIC Industrial Bank, 300
CITS. *See* China International Travel Service
Civil Aviation Administration of China (CAAC), 139, 147, 339
Civil Code, 235, 236, 254–256
Civil Law, 9, 254–256
civil litigation
   concerning foreign matters, 247–248
climate, 138
Clinton, Bill (US President), 29
clothing
   appropriate for business, 161
CNAIC. *See* China National Aviation Industry Corporation
CNIECIC. *See* China National Import and Export Commodities Inspection Corporation
co-production, 55–56, 299
coal industry, 81
coal production, 13–14
Coastal Cities, 17, 18, 70, 185, 197–203, 283
   Beihai, 202–203
   Dalian, 197–198
   Fuzhou, 202
   Guangzhou, 202
   incentives, 48
   Lianyungang, 199
   map of, 50

Nantong, 199–200
Ningbo, 201
Qingdao, 199
Qinhuangdao, 198
Shanghai, 200–201
taxation rates in, 330, 331
Tianjin, 198
Wenzhou, 201–202
Yantai, 198–199
Zhanjiang, 202
collecting bank
definition of, 327
commercial code
legal discussion of, 256
commercial invoice
definition of, 325
for imported goods, 66
Commission of Foreign Trade and Economic
Cooperation, 186
commodities markets, 308
Communications Bank of China (CBC), 294
Communism, 156
Communist Party, 235
dissension within, 21
founding of, 3–4
growth of, 7
rule by, 4, 155
companies limited by shares
overview, 210
compensation trade, 47, 56, 216
computer industry
trade fairs, 107–108
computer software
market for, 35
computers
market for, 35
Confucianism, 146–147, 157, 227
Consolidated Industrial and Commercial Tax
(CICT), 332
constitution of China, 235
construction equipment
market for, 38
trade fairs, 109–110
consular invoice
definition of, 325
Consular Relations Agreement, 250
consulates. See diplomatic missions
consulting services
foreign, 40
consumer price index (CPI)
(1982-1992), 9
consumer protection standards, 235, 244, 255
legal discussion of, 256–257
contracts
attitudes toward, 170
breach of, 255
legal discussion of, 258, 266–267
cancellation/alteration
legal discussion of, 258–259
construction, etc.
legal discussion of, 262
creditor's rights, 255

formulation of, 258
international
legal discussion of, 256
international sales
legal discussion of, 278
provisions in, 240–242
laws governing, 57, 236
legal discussion of, 237, 257–262
property insurance
legal discussion of, 262
Shenzhen SEZ Foreign Economic Contracts, 259–
260
legal discussion of, 279–280
Contractual Joint Ventures Law, 273
contractual trade arrangements, 219
Control of Entry and Exit of Aliens Law, 249
cooperative trade agreement
approval and licensing, 221
copyright, 237, 255. See also intellectual property
rights
legal discussion of, 263–265
Copyright Law, 236
corporations. See also business organizations
legal discussion of, 264–265
corruption, 7–9, 27, 302
penalties for, 8–9
COSCO. See China Ocean Shipping Company
costs of doing business in China, 214
counterpurchase, 55–56, 64, 69–70, 215, 299
countertrade, 55–56, 64, 69–70, 215–216, 299
courier services, 151
credit availability, 51–52
credit cards, 142, 291, 310
issued by ICBC, 292
issued by PCBC, 293
credit ratings, 58
creditor's rights
legal discussion of, 255
crime, 27, 152–153
CTS. See China Travel Service
Cultural Revolution, 4, 26, 156
impact on legal profession of, 252
culture. See business culture
currency, 141, 309
convertibility of, 55, 291
devaluation of, 16, 299
foreign
shortage of, 312–313
further reading, 313
in circulation, 10
limits on, 153
unavailability of, 12
current issues, 21–30
customs
legal discussion of, 265–266
customs approval
for exports, 69
customs brokerage firms
addresses, 391–393
customs classification, 62
customs clearance, 64–65
of advertising samples, 64
personal, 141, 153

customs duties
   assessment
      appeal of, 63
      exemptions, 63
      normal
         legal discussion of, 266
      on commercial goods, 266
      on passenger baggage
         legal discussion of, 265–266
      reduction in, 57
      with favored nations
         legal discussion of, 266
Customs General Administration, 64, 67, 265
Customs Guide for Passengers Entering and
      Leaving China, 266
customs invoices, 66
Customs Law, 266
Customs Schedule on Imported Goods, 266
customs valuation, 63
CVIS. *See* China Venturetech Investment Corpora-
      tion

D

dairy product industry, 74
Dalian
   market profile, 197–198
damages
   legal discussion of, 266–267
daylight savings time, 140
death rate, 172
debt securities, 307–308
decentralization, 9, 24, 156
demographics, 171–174
Deng Xiaoping, 4, 19, 21, 24, 156
   succession of, 22
departure tax, 153. *See also* customs clearance
development zones
   new and high-technology, 185, 200
dictionary, 343–358
diplomatic and trade relations, 23, 59, 186
   with Great Britain, 59, 161
   with Japan, 161
   with neighbors, 19
   with the former Soviet Union, 4, 186
   with the United States, 4, 27–30, 29–30, 59–60
diplomatic missions, Chinese
   addresses, 363
diplomatic missions, foreign
   addresses, 366
direct mail advertising, 180
disadvantages to doing business in China, 214
discrepancy
   definition of, 327
distrain
   legal definition of, 239
distributors, 177
   choosing, 196
dividends
   taxation of, 332
dock receipt
   definition of, 325

document against acceptance (D/A),
      70, 309, 315, 316
   definition of, 327
document against payment (D/P),
      70, 309, 315, 316
   definition of, 327
documentary collection, 315, 316
   definition of, 327
   procedures, 316
   tips for buyers and suppliers, 317
   types of, 316
documentation
   for exported goods, 70
   for imported goods, 65–66
draft
   definition of, 326
duty-free items
   for personal customs clearance, 141

E

Economic and Technological Development Zones
      (ETDZs), 70, 185, 197, 213
   autonomy of, 42
   Fulaishan, 198
   Fumin, 200
   Guangzhou, 202
   Hongqiao, 200
   map of, 50
   Maqiaozi, 197–198
   Mawei, 202
   Minhang, 200
   Qinhuangdao, 198
   Tianjin (Tanggu), 198
   Wenzhou, 202
   Xiaogang, 201
   Xiashan, 202
   Yantai, 199
   Zhongyuntai, 199
Economic Contract Law, 236, 256, 258, 262
economic zones
   inland, 186
economy, 3–20
   agricultural sector, 225
   cash, 10
   context of, 5–7
   development strategy, 18–19
   development zones, 8
   growth of, 5, 7
   history of, 3–5
   liberalization of, 7
   market reforms, 23–25
   political outlook, 19–20
   private sector, 6–7, 25
   reform of, 285
   sectors of, 12
   size of, 5
   socialist market, 4–5
   state sector of, 5
   structure of, 11
   underground, 7–10, 302

educational system, 174, 225, 227
electric current, 65
electronic components industry, 72
electronics industry, 32–33, 71–74
    consumer, 71–72
    trade fairs, 110–112
embassies. *See* diplomatic missions
emergency information, 153
employees. *See also* labor force
    benefits for, 230–233
    dismissal of, 12
    recruitment of, 230
employment
    conditions for termination of, 229–230
    conditions of, 228–230
    reforms, 12
energy consumption, 174
energy industry
    trade fairs, 112–114
energy production, 18, 19
engineering services
    foreign, 40
Enterprise Bankruptcy Law, 253–254
enterprise income tax, 63
Enterprise Law, 234
environmental law
    legal discussion of, 267–268
environmental protection, 255
    regulation of, 236
    trade fairs, 112–114
Environmental Protection Act, 267
Environmental Protection Law, 236, 247, 257
equities markets, 303
ETDZ Measures of Guangzhou, 246
ETDZs. *See* Economic and Technological Development Zones
etiquette, 146–147, 160–168
    banqueting, 165–167
    cigarette smoking, 166
    conversation, 147, 162
    dining table, 145
    drinking, 166, 166–167
    further reading, 170
    greeting, 147, 161
    of business negotiations, 168
    of giving and receiving gifts, 147, 161–162
    reciprocity, 167
    table manners, 166
evidence accounts, 56, 299
ex dock
    definition of, 326
ex point of origin
    definition of, 326
executions
    legal definition of, 239
    legal discussion of, 268
expenses
    deductible, 336
expenses, business travel
    typical daily, 154

export licenses, 47, 57, 68–69
    definition of, 325
    for individual shipments, 68
    issuance of, 67
    penalties for noncompliance, 69
export marketing
    tips for, 181
export policy, 67–68
    liberalization of, 67
export procedures, 67–70
export quotas, 69
export subsidies, 67
exporters
    leading, 54
exporting
    administrative regulations
        legal discussion of, 269
    methods of settlement, 70
    opportunities, 35
    promotion of, 55
exports
    by commodity, 56
    growth of, 16
    leading, 14, 16, 53–55
    total, 13

F

face (concept), 157–158
FAS (free alongside ship) terms, 70
    definition of, 326
fashion accessory industry, 78–80
fax service, 150
FCPA. *See* Foreign Corrupt Practices Act
FEC. *See* foreign exchange certificates
fen, 141, 309
fertility rate, 172
FIEs. *See* foreign invested enterprises
financial institutions, 285–308
    further reading, 308
financial markets, 302–308
    unofficial and limited, 304–305
financial services industry, 15
    developments and trends, 288
financing. *See also* loans
    domestic, 297–298
finished goods
    as exports, 54
Five-Year Plans, 4, 18
    current (Eighth), 19, 36, 37, 38, 41, 215
floating population, 227
FOA (free on board airport) terms, 70
FOB (free on board) terms, 70
    definition of, 326
food (Chinese), 145–146, 166, 167
food additive industry, 74–75
food industry, 74–77
    trade fairs, 114–115
food processing and packaging machinery
    market for, 36–37
food processing and packaging machinery
    industry, 85

footwear industry, 32, 77–78
  trade fairs, 121–122
force majeure
  legal definition of, 239
  legal discussion of, 256
foreign business activity
  legal discussion of, 269
Foreign Corrupt Practices Act (FCPA), 238
foreign debt, 312–313
Foreign Economic and Trade Arbitration Commission, 247, 250
Foreign Economic Contract Law, 236, 256, 262–263
Foreign Enterprise Income Tax Law, 210, 329
foreign exchange, 141–142, 309–313. *See also* swap centers
  by foreign banks, 294–295
  controls on, 310, 333
  further reading, 313
  limits on, 243
  market, 308
  new regulations, 243
  operations, 311–312
  other sources of, 298
  rates, 312
    at swap centers, 312
    detailed (1981-1993), 313
    year-end (1981-1993), 311
  regulations, 43–44
  shortage of, 15
Foreign Exchange Adjustment Centers. *See* swap centers
foreign exchange certificates (FEC), 310
  abolition of, 291, 297, 310, 312
foreign invested enterprises (FIEs), 43, 287
  attaining FIE status, 210
  number of, 45
  treatment of, 44
foreign investment, 17–18, 43–52
  approval procedures, 220
  by Japan, 17
  by overseas Chinese, 17, 45
  by the United States, 17, 45
  CITIC involvement in, 300
  climate, 43
  debt-to-equity ratios, 333
  in WFOEs, 213
  incentives, 18, 48
  market access, 44
  opportunities, 39
  policy, 46–48
  reforms, 45
  restrictions on, 18, 218
  role in economy of, 17
  selected useful addresses, 52
  sources, 17
Foreign Investment Commission, 273
foreign investors
  leading, 45–46
foreign operations
  financial aspects of, 297–299
foreign owned enterprises, 46. *See also* foreign invested enterprises

foreign parties
  civil relations involving
    legal discussion of, 256
foreign reserves, 312–313
foreign trade, 15–16, 53–60
  balance of, 12, 16, 58
  contract law, 57
  cooperative arrangements, 215
  growth of, 53
  infrastructure, 58
  legal discussion of, 268
  opening of China to, 3, 56–57
  partners, 16–17, 58, 59
  policy, 46–48
  political barriers, 55
  textile agreements
    legal discussion of, 268–269
  total, 13, 15, 53, 53–54
  with Germany, 16, 59
  with Hong Kong, 16, 59
  with Japan, 16, 59
  with Macao, 16
  with Singapore, 59
  with South Korea, 59
  with Taiwan, 16, 45, 59
  with the former Soviet Union, 16, 59
  with the United States, 16, 59, 312
foreign trade corporations (FTCs), 41, 46–47, 56–57, 61, 138, 177
  addresses, 370–378
  definition of, 208
  MOFTEC authorization of, 68
  provincial, 68
forging equipment industry, 85
forward foreign future
  definition, 327
Four Tigers of Guangdong, 204
franchising, 40
fraudulent sales
  legal discussion of, 269
Free Trade Areas (FTAs), 17–18, 51
  map of, 49
Friendship Stores, 142
frozen food industry, 75
FTAs. *See* Free Trade Areas
FTCs. *See* foreign trade corporations (FTCs)
Fujianese dialect, 164
furniture industry
  trade fairs, 115–116
futures markets, 308
Fuzhou
  market profile, 202

G

Gang of Four, 4, 156
General Agreement on Tariffs and Trade (GATT), 18, 20, 57, 296
Geneva Phonograms Convention, 237
geography of China, 3
gold market, 308
Good Manufacturing Practices (GMP) standards, 88
government agencies
    addresses, 359–362
    restructuring of, 247
government structure, 235
gross domestic product (GDP), 5
    growth of, 176
    per capita, 5
gross national product (GNP), 4, 5, 25
    per capita, 173
Guangdong Development Bank, 294
Guangdong Province, 53, 176
Guangzhou
    market profile, 191
Guangzhou ETDZ
    legal discussion of, 283–284
Guangzhou-Kowloon Express Railway, 191
Guangzhou-Shenzhen-Zhuhai Expressway, 194
guanxi, 7. *See also* personal connections
guidebooks on China, 153
Gulangyu Island, 195

H

Haidian High-Technology Zone, 189
Hainan Island
    designation as an SEZ, 185
    market profile, 195–197
Han Chinese, 3, 160, 225
handicraft industry, 78–80
health expenditures, 174
health precautions for travelers, 152–153
health product industry
    trade fairs, 117–118
health regulations, 269
high-technology industries, 14, 38, 205, 300
    foreign investment in, 46
    overview, 14
high-technology products
    market for, 35
high-technology zones. *See* development zones: new and high-technology
historical overview
    of culture, 155–156
    of economy, 3–5
holidays, 12, 149, 232
Hong Kong
    as a destination for flight capital, 8
    Bank of China operations in, 287
    doing Chinese business through, 211
    listing of Chinese shares in, 306
    PRC shipping through, 341

setting up offices in, 176
sovereignty over, 19, 284
travel from, 211
Hong Kong Trade Development Council (HKTDC), 95–96
Hong Kong-Guangzhou-Macao Expressway, 194
hospitals, 153
hotel industry, 40–42
hotels, 143–145
    Beijing, 143–144
    Guangzhou, 144
    Shanghai, 144–145
housewares industry, 80–81
    trade fairs, 115–116
Huangpu River, 190
human resources, 227–228
human rights policies, 19, 28

I

IBIC. *See* Industrial and Commercial Bank of China
ICC. *See* International Chamber of Commerce
ILO. *See* International Labor Organization
immunization requirements, 138
Import and Export Commodity Inspection Bureau, 256
import approval, 62
import licenses, 45, 47, 62
    definition of, 325
    elimination of, 61
import policy and procedures, 61–66
import quotas, 57
import regulations, 61–62
import taxes, 63
importers
    leading, 54
importing
    opportunities, 31
imports, 53–55
    by commodity, 57
    growth of, 16
    leading, 15, 16
    methods of settlement, 65
    of technology, 65
    temporary, 64
    total, 13
income. *See also* wages
    average total, 231
    disposable, 11, 26–27, 175
    per capita, 5
    personal
        distribution of, 173
    rural, 5
    taxable, 332–333, 335, 336
    urban, 5
Income Tax Law, 329
Industrial and Commercial Bank of China (ICBC), 51, 286, 292
Industrial and Commercial Consolidated Tax, 272
industrial and mining products
    provisions of contracts
        legal discussion of, 262

industrial development, 38
industrial materials industry
   trade fairs, 119–120
industrial sector of economy, 13
industrial waste
   legal discussion of, 267
industries
   reviews of, 71–94
industry
   heavy, 13–14
   medium and light, 14
inflation, 10, 23, 24, 175, 288
   (1982-1992), 8
   rate of average annual, 173
infrastructure
   development of, 19
   financial, 24
inspection
   certificates
      definition of, 325
   of exports, 69
   of imports, 64–65
inspection institutes
   foreign, 257
Inspection of Import and Export Commodities
   Laws, 235
instruments
   market for, 36
   trade fairs, 122–126
insurance
   certificates
      for imported goods, 66
   documents
      definition of, 325
   for international business, 301
   health, 231–232
   retirement, 232–233
   unemployment, 232
insurance companies
   addresses, 385, 386–387
   foreign, 301
insurance industry, 301–302
intellectual infrastructure, 185
intellectual property rights, 9–10, 218, 236
   infringement of, 237
   protection of, 44
interest rates, 291, 297
   legal discussion of, 269
International Chamber of Commerce (ICC),
   51, 309, 316, 318, 326, 328
International Labor Organization (ILO), 234
international organizations
   China's membership in, 20
international payments, 309, 315–328
   for imports, 51
   further reading, 328
   glossary, 326
   overview, 315
international reserves, 58
international trade documents
   glossary, 325

inventory valuation, 332
investment banking, 40
investment certificates, 273
investment companies, 301
iron ore industry, 82
irrevocable confirmed credit. *See* letter of credit
irrevocable credit. *See* letter of credit
issuance
   definition of, 327
issuing bank
   definition of, 327

J

jewelry industry, 78–80
   trade fairs, 116–117
Jiang Ze Min, 22
jiao, 141, 309
job assignment system, 225
job training, 226
Joint Venture Law, 46, 236, 256, 257
   legal discussion of, 270–273
joint ventures, 46, 178, 207–212, 270–273
   business registration procedures for, 219
   capital requirements for, 211–212
   contract terms of, 270–271
   cooperative or contractual, 209–211
   equity joint ventures, 208–209
   finding a Chinese partner for, 217
   labor relations in, 234
   liquidation of, 212
   overview, 209
   shareholders, directors, etc. of, 212
Joint Ventures Income Tax Law, 329
judgements
   legal discussion of, 274

K

karaoke, 167–168
Korean War, 4
kuai, 309
Kuomintang (KMT) Party, 3–4

L

labeling
   of imported goods, 65
labor, 10–12, 225–234
   availability, 225–226
   costs, 16. *See also* wages
      update, 232
   disputes
      right to strike, 233–234
labor contract system, 229
labor economy, 225–227
labor force
   children in, 234
   composition of, 10
   distribution by sector, 225

foreign, 226
    legal discussion of, 250
    migration to urban areas, 11, 25
    women in, 159–160, 228
labor insurance, 272
labor regulations
    for joint ventures, 271
    in SEZs, 283
labor relations, 233–234
    in joint ventures
        legal discussion of, 272
    regulation of, 236
labor unions, 12, 233
land use rights in Guangzhou
    new regulations, 246
language, 164
law, 235–284
    administrative
        legal discussion of, 248
    conflicts of
        legal discussion of, 256
    geographical scope of, 236–237
    governing business
        overview, 235–236
    practical application of, 237
law digest, 247–284
law firms, 40, 388–389
    addresses, 388–389
leadership struggles, 21–22
leaves of absence, 229
legal arbitration, 250–251
Legal Counsel Office, 252
legal counselors
    legal discussion of, 252
legal disputes
    resolution of, 44–45, 237
        legal discussion of, 259
        with joint ventures, 273
legal glossary, 239
legal system, 9, 19–20
    basis of, 235
letter of credit (L/C), 309, 315, 318, 327
    amendment of, 319
    application, 322, 323
    back-to-back, 321, 326
    banks permitted to issue, 51
    common problems, 320
    confirmed, 327
    deferred payment, 321, 327
    irrevocable, 327
    irrevocable confirmed credit, 321
    irrevocable credit, 321
    issuance of, 319
    legal obligations of banks toward, 320
    opening, 322
    parties to, 318
    red clause, 321
    revocable, 321, 327
    revolving, 321, 327
    special, 321
    standby, 321, 327
    steps in using, 318

tips for buyers and sellers, 324
    transferable, 321
    types of, 321
    unconfirmed, 321
    utilization of, 320
letter of guarantee (L/G), 51
Li Peng, 21
Lianyungang
    market profile, 199
Liaodong Peninsula OEZ, 205
libraries
    addresses, 402
life expectancy, 172, 225
light box advertising, 182, 183
limited companies
    overview, 210
List of Commodities Subject to Inspection, 256
literacy, 227
Little Dragons, 204
"Little Red Book", 156
living space
    per capita, 5
loans. *See also* financing
    availability of, 51–52
    by foreign banks, 295
    foreign currency, 292, 293
    reform of process, 288
local officials
    power of, 24
locus
    legal definition of, 239
luggage industry, 78–80

M

Macao
    sovereignty over, 19
machinery industry, 32
    industrial, 84–87
    trade fairs, 122–126
magazine advertising, 179, 180
magazines. *See also* periodicals
    English-language, 150
manager's role, 234
Mandarin dialect, 164
manufacturing
    foreign investment in, 39
manufacturing sector of economy, 13–14
mao (unit of currency), 141, 309
Mao Zedong, 4, 155, 156
    death of, 23
Maoism, 147
market surveys, 184–205
marketing, 173–205
marking
    of imported goods, 65
matchmakers, 158
materialism, 25–26
maternity leave, 228
medical equipment
    market for, 36

medical equipment industry, 87–89
 trade fairs, 126–127
Memorandum of Understanding on Intellectual
 Property Rights, 237
metal industry, 33
 trade fairs, 128–129
MFN status. *See* Most Favored Nation status
mianzi. *See* face (concept)
military forces, 19. *See also* Red Guards
mineral resources, 33, 81–84
 legal discussion of, 274
mines
 legal discussion of, 274–275
Ministry of Aeronautics and Astronautics Industry,
 247
Ministry of Coal Industry, 247
Ministry of Commerce, 247
Ministry of Electronics Industry, 247
Ministry of Energy Resources, 247
Ministry of Finance, 293, 313
Ministry of Foreign Affairs, 249
Ministry of Foreign Economic Relations and Trade
 (MOFERT)
 renaming of, 247
Ministry of Foreign Trade and Economic Coopera-
 tion (MOFTEC), 18, 67
 approval of technology-related contracts, 218
 authorization for foreign exchange transactions,
 311
 definition of, 208
 FTCs under, 41
 regulation of foreign trade by, 43, 57, 61–62
Ministry of Health, 256
Ministry of Internal Trade, 247
Ministry of Justice, 252
Ministry of Labor, 228
Ministry of Light Industry, 247
Ministry of Machine-Building and Electronics
 Industry, 247
Ministry of Machine-Building Industry, 247
Ministry of Materials and Equipment, 45, 247
Ministry of Power Industry, 247
Ministry of Public Security, 226
Ministry of Public Security and Foreign Affairs, 249
Ministry of Textile Industry, 247
MOFERT. *See* Ministry of Foreign Economic
 Relations and Trade
MOFTEC. *See* Ministry of Foreign Trade and
 Economic Cooperation
money markets, 307–308
money supply, 10
monopolies
 legal discussion of, 274–275
Most Favored Nation (MFN) status, 27–30, 59
multimedia equipment
 trade fairs, 130
municipal and provincial representatives
 addresses for Beijing offices, 362–363

N

names (Chinese), 164
Nantong
 market profile, 199–200
National Bureau of Standards, 257
National Electronic Trading system, 304, 307
National People's Congress, 235
 approval of free market policies, 25
National Price Bureau, 279
negotiable instrument
 legal definition of, 239
negotiation. *See also* business negotiations
 definition of, 327
neon sign advertising, 182, 183
newspaper advertising, 179, 180
 rates, 182
newspapers
 addresses, 395–396
 circulation, 174
 English-language, 150
 number of dailies, 174
Ningbo
 Beilun Port Industrial Area, 201
 market profile, 201
notaries public
 legal discussion of, 275
 role of, 237
nuclear power and weapons, 29
nutrition, 174

O

OECD. *See* Organization for Economic Cooperation and Development
OEZs. *See* Open Economic Zones
offices
 branch, 213
 liaison, 214
 representative, 177, 213–214
 business registration procedures, 219, 221
 registration of, 236
oil field machinery
 market for, 37
oil industry, 55
 foreign investment in, 39
open account (O/A) terms, 315
 definition of, 327
 use of, 51
Open Cities. *See* Coastal Cities
Open Door policy, 4, 17, 53
Open Economic Zones (OEZs), 185, 203–205
 Liaodong Peninsula, 205
 map of, 49
 Pearl River Delta, 204
 Shandong Peninsula, 204–205
 Southern Fujian Delta, 204
 taxation rates in, 331
 Yangtze River Delta, 203–204
Opinion for Companies Limited by Shares, 210
Opinion for Limited Companies, 210

Opium Wars, 3, 29, 155
Organic Law of People's Courts, 247
Organization for Economic Cooperation and
    Development, 52
Organization of Price Control, 249
Oujiang River, 201
Overseas Economic Cooperation Fund, 51
overseas relationships
    building, 187

P

Pacific War, 29
packaging industry
    trade fairs, 130–132
packing list
    definition, 325
    for imported goods, 66
Paris Convention for the Protection of Industrial
    Property, 276
partnerships, 214–215, 254
    legal discussion of, 275–277
patent disputes
    legal discussion of adjudication, 277
Patent Law, 236, 257, 276
patent rights, 237, 255
    damages for violation of
        legal discussion of, 266–267
    legal discussion of, 276–277
PBOC. See People's Bank of China
PCBC. See People's Construction Bank of China
Pearl River Delta, 191
Pearl River Delta OEZ, 204
Peking. See Beijing
pension funds, 302
People's Bank of China (PBOC), 65, 186, 286, 286–
    287
    reform plans for, 291
People's Construction Bank of China (PCBC),
    286, 293
People's Insurance Company of China (PICC),
    66, 301
People's Liberation Army (PLA), 4
    business investments of, 6–7
periodicals, general business
    addresses, 396–398
periodicals, industry-specific
    addresses, 398–402
personal connections (guanxi)
    value of, 158–159
pesticide registration
    legal discussion of, 267–268
petrochemical industry, 81–82
    foreign investment in, 39
    trade fairs, 132
pharmaceutical industry, 87–89
pharmaceuticals
    market for, 35–36
    trade fairs, 126–127
PICC. See People's Insurance Company of China
pin-yin. See transliteration systems
PLA. See People's Liberation Army

pollutants
    legal discussion of, 267
population, 3, 225
    age structure of, 171
    by age and sex, 172
    density, 3, 171
    growth of, 7, 171
    of principal cities, 172
    rural, 171
    trends (1990-2025), 171
    urban, 171, 225
port tax, 63
ports, 339, 341–342
    Beihai, 203
    Beilun, 201
    Dalian, 197
    Guangzhou, 191
    Lianyungang, 199
    Nantong, 200
    Pudong (Shanghai), 200
    Qingdao, 199
    Qinhuangdao, 198
    Shanghai, 190, 341
    Tianjin, 189, 198, 341–342
    Waigaoqiao (Shanghai), 341
    Wenzhou (Longwan), 201–202
    Xiamen, 195
    Yantai, 198–199
postal service, 150
power of attorney
    legal definition of, 239
    legal discussion of, 277–278
prepared food industry, 75
price controls, 10
price index. See also consumer price index
    by category, 173
price policies, 279
principal
    legal definition of, 239
    legal discussion of, 254, 278
printed circuit board (PCB) machinery industry,
    84–85
printed circuit boards (PCBs)
    market for, 35
printers, 151
printing equipment
    market for, 36
    trade fairs, 130–132
private enterprise
    legal discussion of, 278
    regulation of, 236
pro forma invoice
    for imported goods, 66
processing and assembling agreements, 216–217
Product Quality Law, 244–245
promissory note
    definition of, 326
promoter of corporation, 239
prostitution, 27
public procurement, 178
    approval process, 42
    opportunities, 41
Public Security Bureau, 27

Pudong Development Zone, 17, 48, 185, 200–201, 341
  legal discussion of, 284
  preferential policies in, 200–201
  taxation rates in, 331
purchasing power
  per capita, 175

Q

Qin dynasty, 3
Q'ing dynasty, 3, 5, 155
Qingdao
  market profile, 199
Qinhuangdao
  market profile, 198
quality control
  legal discussion of, 280–281

R

radio
  address, 402
  English-language, 151
  sets in use, 174
radio advertising, 182
Radio Beijing, 402
RCCs. See rural credit cooperatives
real estate
  foreign investment in, 39, 289–290
red clause letter of credit. See letter of credit
Red Guards, 26, 147, 155
reexports, 31
  Hong Kong to China, 55
  Hong Kong to/from China, 59
  of electronics products, 32
religion, 156
remitter
  definition of, 327
remitting bank
  definition of, 327
renminbi (RMB), 141, 309. See also currency
  acceptance in Hong Kong, 309
  convertibility of, 44
repatriation or remittance
  of earnings, 209, 299
    from SEZs, 283
  of profits, 43
restaurant industry, 40–42
restaurants
  Beijing, 145–146
  Guangzhou, 146
  Shanghai, 146
restraint of trade
  legal discussion of, 274–275
retail industry, 12, 175, 178
  foreign investment in, 40
retirement, 232–233
revocable credit. See letter of credit
RMB. See renminbi
Rong Yiren, 300

rubber and plastics industries, 33
rural contracting operations
  registration of, 254
rural credit cooperatives (RCCs), 293

S

SAEC. See State Administration of Exchange Control
SAIC. See State Administration for Industry and Commerce
sale, terms of
  glossary, 326
Sales Convention, 278
savings rate, 175
science and technology institutes, 47
scientific institutes, 61
seals
  legal discussion of, 279–280
Securities Association of China, 303
Securities Trading Automated Quotation system (STAQ), 304, 307
selling in foreign market
  tips for, 192
sequestration
  legal discussion of, 280
service industries
  as sector of economy, 14–15
  foreign
    barriers to, 48
  foreign investment in, 39
service marks
  registration of, 243
SEZ Bankruptcy Law, 252–254
SEZs. See Special Economic Zones
Shandong Peninsula OEZ, 204
Shanghai
  market profile, 190–191, 200–201
Shanghai International Trade Information and Exhibition Company, 96
Shanghai Securities Exchange, 303, 307. See also stock exchanges
Shanghai Television (STV)
  advertising, 179
Shantou
  market profile, 194–195
Share Enterprise Trial Measures, 210
shares. See also stock exchanges
  classes of, 305–306
  foreign listings of Chinese, 306
  listing of, 305
  Red Chip (H), 306
Shekou Industrial District, 193
Shenyang, 193
Shenzhen
  market profile, 193
Shenzhen City Scientific Technology Development Center, 260
Shenzhen SEZ, 193–194
  Foreign Economic Contract Regulations
    legal discussion of, 259–260
  joint ventures in, 211

Shenzhen Stock Exchange, 303. *See also* stock exchanges
Ship Inspection Bureau, 256
shipbuilding industry, 14
    trade fairs, 104–105
shipper's export declaration
    definition, 325
shipping
    restrictions, 65
shipping industry
    foreign investment in, 40
Singapore Trade Development Board, 96
Sino-Japanese War, 4
SINOCHART. *See* China National Chartering Corporation
SINOPEC. *See* China National Petrochemical Corporation
social security trust fund
    plans for, 233
sole proprietorships, 214–215
    registration of, 254
Southern Fujian Delta OEZ, 204
SPC. *See* State Planning Commission
Special Economic Zones (SEZs), 17–18, 193–197
    autonomy of, 159
    definition of, 208
    exporting from, 70
    Guangdong
        business registration in, 265
    Hainan Island, 195–197
    history of, 185
    importing to, 66
    incentives, 48
    legal discussion of, 282–284
    map of, 49
    Shantou, 194–195
    Shenzhen, 193–197
    taxation rates in, 330, 331
    WFOES in, 213
    Xiamen, 195
    Zhuhai, 194
sporting goods industry, 93–94
    trade fairs, 118–119
standards
    legal discussion of, 280–281
standby letter of credit. *See* letter of credit
State Administration for Industry and Commerce (SAIC), 46, 220, 249
    definition of, 208
State Administration of Exchange Control (SAEC), 65, 287, 295, 310, 312
State Administration of Import and Export Commodities, 64, 69
State Council, 235, 244
    reform of, 247
State Economic and Trade Commission, 61, 67, 210
    creation of, 247
state enterprises
    privatization of, 6
    treatment of, 44
State Planning Commission (SPC), 61, 286
State Science and Technology Commission, 88

State Travel Bureau, 250
stationery industry, 80–81
    trade fairs, 116–117
statistics
    legal discussion of, 280–281
statute of frauds, 269
Statute of Limitations, 256
steel industry, 82
stock exchanges, 40, 302, 303–304
    authorization of, 9
    corruption of, 8
    foreign investment in, 210
    market value of, 15
    proxy issues traded on foreign, 306
subway
    Beijing, 148
sugar industry, 75
Sun Yatsen, 3
supplier authorization, 68
Supreme People's Court, 235
Supreme People's Procuratorate, 235
swap centers, 44, 298, 311–312
    importance to foreign exchange, 298
Swedish Arbitration Procedures, 251
switching, 56, 216, 299

T

Tai Ping Insurance Company (TPIC), 301
Tang dynasty, 3
tariffs, 57, 62–63
    reduction of, 61
    without MFN status, 28
tax authorities
    registration with, 222
tax code
    recent changes in, 18, 330–331
        recent changes in, 337
tax credits, 332
tax depreciation, 332
tax relief
    in SEZs, 283
tax residence, 337–338
tax treaties, 333, 338
tax year, 331–332, 337
taxes
    collection of, 331
    corporate, 329–333
        overview, 329
    corporate income, 329
    exemptions on imports, 63
    in special zones, 331
    lowering of business rate, 330
    luxury, 10
    on joint ventures, 208–209, 210
    personal, 335–338
        liability, 335, 336
        overview, 335
    rates
        corporate, 331
        personal, 336
        personal income, 335

taxis, 142–143, 148
technical imports to Xiamen SEZ
 legal discussion of, 261–262
technology
 regulations on acquisition of
  legal discussion of, 263
technology transfer, 217–218
 approval procedures, 219–220
 contract approval application, 221
telecommunications equipment
 market for, 37
telecommunications system
 upgrading of, 18
telegram service, 150
telephone
 dialing codes, 150
 information numbers, 150
 numbers. *See* addresses and telephone
  numbers
 service, 149–150
 sets in use, 18, 174
television
 address of controlling ministry, 402
 English-language, 151
 sets in use, 174
television advertising, 179, 180
 rates, 183
telex service, 150
tertiary industry, 226
textile equipment
 market for, 37
textile industry, 14, 32, 89–92
 trade fairs, 133–134
Tiananmen Square protests, 5, 21, 25
 impact on foreign debt, 312–313
 US reaction to, 27
Tianjin
 market profile, 189–190, 198
time zones, 140
timepiece industry, 32, 78–80
tipping, 142
tobacco consumption, 174
Tobacco Monopoly Regulations, 274
tool industry, 92–93
 trade fairs, 134–135
tortious conduct
 legal discussion of, 255–256
tourism zones, 185
Tourist Complaint Hotline, 150
toy industry, 33, 93–94
 trade fairs, 118–119
TPIC. *See* Tai Ping Insurance Company
Trade Agreement between US and China,
 237, 266, 268
 legal discussion of, 268
trade associations, general
 addresses, 379
trade associations, industry-specific
 addresses, 380–382
trade delegations
 etiquette for, 164–165

trade fairs, 95–136, 177
 Chinese Export Commodities Fair, 97
 tips for attending, 99
trade relations. *See* diplomatic and trade relations
trade secret protection, 237
Trade Union Law, 236
Trademark Law, 236, 243, 257, 281–282
trademark protection, 236, 237, 255. *See also*
  intellectual property rights; service marks
 legal discussion of, 281–282
 recent developments, 243
trading companies, 45. *See also* foreign trade
  corporations
train travel
 domestic, 148
 to/from former Soviet Union, 186
 to/from Hong Kong, 139
translators and interpreters, 152, 165
 addresses, 389
transliteration systems, 343
transportation
 domestic, 147–149
transportation firms. *See also* airlines
 addresses, 391–394
transportation system
 upgrading of, 18–19
travel. *See* air travel; boat travel; bus
  travel; business travel; train travel
travel advisories and restrictions, 146
traveler's checks, 310
treasury bills, 307–308
trust and investment corporations, 296–300
turnkey contract
 legal definition of, 239

U

UCP. *See* Uniform Customs and Practices
unconfirmed credit. *See* letter of credit
unemployment, 6, 11, 24, 226–227
 comparative, 226
 in rural areas, 227
Uniform Customs and Practices (UCP), 51, 309,
 318
Uniform Rules for Collections (URC), 316
Union Law, 233
United Nations
 China's membership in, 20
 recognition of China by, 4
United Nations Convention on Contracts for
 International Sale of Goods, 236, 278
United Nations Convention on the Recognition and
 Enforcement of Foreign Arbitral Awards, 251
United States. *See* diplomatic and trade relations:
  with the United States; Foreign Corrupt
  Practices Act; foreign investment: by the
  United States; foreign trade: with the United
  States; Trade Agreement between the US and
  China
Universal Copyright Convention, 237
Urban Credit Cooperatives (UCCs), 292
URC. *See* Uniform Rules for Collections

V

vacation benefits, 12, 229, 232
validity
    definition of, 327
value-added tax (VAT), 10, 18, 175, 332
    implementation of, 330
visa regulations, 137–138, 249–250. *See also*
        aliens: legal discussion of
    for SEZs, 283
vocational training, 228
void ab initio
    legal definition of, 239

W

Wade-Giles. *See* transliteration systems
wages, 11–12, 26, 230–233
    average, 231
    average monthly
        at foreign invested enterprises, 231
        at joint venture companies, 230
    average weekly
        by industry, 230
        by occupation, 230
        comparative, 229
    minimum, 231
    monthly manufacturing, 173
Wenzhou
    market profile, 201
Western influence, 155, 161
Westerners
    how viewed in China, 160–161
WFOEs. *See* wholly foreign-owned enterprises
Wholly Foreign-Owned Enterprise Law, 236
wholly foreign-owned enterprises (WFOEs), 212–
        213
    business registration procedures, 219
    labor relations in, 234
women
    in business, 160, 165. *See also* labor force:
        women in
Women's Protection Law, 228
work attitudes, 228
work environment, 159–160
work units, 159, 225
worker congresses, 233
workweek, 12, 229
World Bank, 51, 301, 312
World Connect telephone service, 150
World Intellectual Property Organization, 276
world trade centers
    addresses, 378–379
Wuhan
    market profile, 193

X

Xia dynasty, 3
Xiamen
    market profile, 195
Xiamen SEZ
    regulations on technical imports to
        legal discussion of, 261–262
Xiamen-Zhangzhou-Quanzhou Open Economic
        Triangular Zone, 204

Y

Yangpu Development Zone, 17, 48–51
Yangtze River Delta, 190
Yangtze River Delta OEZ, 203
Yantai
    market profile, 198
youth in China, 25–26
yuan, 141, 309
Yunnan Province
    growth of economy, 185

Z

Zhanjiang
    market profile, 202
Zhao Ziyang, 21
Zhu Rongji, 22, 45, 287, 289, 290, 310
Zhuhai
    market profile, 194
Zhujiang Delta. *See* Pearl River Delta